THE LITERATURES OF THE WORLD
IN ENGLISH TRANSLATION

THE LITERATURES OF THE WORLD
IN ENGLISH TRANSLATION

A Bibliography

VOLUME I

THE GREEK AND LATIN LITERATURES
Edited by George B. Parks and Ruth Z. Temple

VOLUME II

THE SLAVIC LITERATURES
Compiled by Richard C. Lewanski
assisted by Lucia G. Lewanski and Maya Deriugin

VOLUME III

THE ROMANCE LITERATURES
Edited by George B. Parks and Ruth Z. Temple

VOLUME IV

THE CELTIC, GERMANIC,
AND OTHER LITERATURES OF EUROPE

VOLUME V

THE LITERATURES OF ASIA AND AFRICA

The Literatures of the World in English Translation

A Bibliography

Editors

GEORGE B. PARKS
and RUTH Z. TEMPLE

Volume I

THE GREEK AND LATIN LITERATURES

FREDERICK UNGAR PUBLISHING CO.
NEW YORK

Copyright © 1968 by
Frederick Ungar Publishing Co., Inc.

Printed in the United States of America

Library of Congress Catalog Card Number 68-31454

Dedicated to the Memory of

ARTHUR EDWARD CHRISTY
1899–1946

the only begetter

CONTRIBUTORS TO VOLUME I

PROCOPE S. COSTAS   BYZANTINE
                                              MODERN GREEK

    Associate Professor of Classics and Comparative Literature
    Brooklyn College of the City University of New York

CHARLES R. DAHLBERG   MEDIEVAL LATIN (Background)
    Associate Professor of English
    Queens College of the City University of New York

ANNA E. DOUGHERTY   BIBLIOGRAPHIES OF TRANSLATIONS
    Assistant Chief
    National Institutes of Health Library, Washington, D.C.

†DWIGHT L. DURLING   GREEK
    Late Professor of English
    Queens College of the City University of New York

RICHARD W. EMERY   MEDIEVAL LATIN
    Professor of History
    Queens College of the City University of New York

LILLIAN FEDER   GREEK
    Professor of English
    Queens College of the City University of New York

KONRAD GRIES   GREEK AND ROMAN
                                                       GREEK
                                                       LATIN

    Professor of Classical and Oriental Languages
    Queens College of the City University of New York

MURIEL J. HUGHES   COLLECTIONS OF TRANSLATIONS
    Professor of English
    University of Vermont

CHARLTON G. LAIRD   HISTORY AND THEORY OF TRANSLATION
                       COLLECTIVE HISTORIES OF LITERATURE
    Professor of English
    University of Nevada

WILLIAM V. PAPPAS   MODERN GREEK
    Consultant, Near- and Middle-Eastern Affairs

GEORGE B. PARKS   GREEK CHRISTIAN
                                                  LATIN CHRISTIAN
                                                      NEO-LATIN
    Professor Emeritus of English
    Queens College of the City University of New York

RUTH Z. TEMPLE   BIBLIOGRAPHIES OF TRANSLATIONS
                                     COLLECTIONS OF TRANSLATIONS
    Professor of English
    Brooklyn College of the City University of New York

CONTENTS

ix

PREFACE

These volumes aim to list for the first time the English translations of all works of foreign literatures (as defined later). The series was begun some twenty-five years ago as one section of the extensive bibliographical Guide to Comparative and World Literature which was conceived and planned by the late Arthur E. Christy, then of Columbia University, later of the University of Illinois. The preparation of the Guide was undertaken for the National Council of Teachers of English by its Committee on Comparative Literature, in collaboration with the American Library Association and with the added sponsorship of the Association of American Colleges; it was aided at first by a small grant from the Rockefeller Foundation.

Under the direction of Professor Christy as the general editor of the Guide, and, after his early death in 1946, of Professor Charlton G. Laird of the University of Nevada, the translations section of the Guide was compiled by the present editors in turn from the contributions of numerous scholars, all of us unpaid volunteers. It was completed by 1955, but for various reasons—one of which was the proportions it had assumed—the sponsoring societies were not able to undertake publication. At that time Professor Laird ceased his editorial connection with the translation section, remaining editor of the Guide proper.

When a publisher was found for the translations bibliography, now grown from a section of a volume into a series of volumes, the National Council of Teachers of English, acting through its executive secretary Professor James R. Squire, graciously released the work for publication. We have now greatly expanded it and brought it down to date. We list publications down to and including the year 1965.

As this volume was about to go to press, we discovered that the New York Public Library was publishing a bibliography of English translations from the Slavic languages, edited by Mr. Richard C. Lewanski. To avoid duplication of material, an arrangement has been made to incorporate the Slavic volume as the second in our series. The principles of inclusion, as well as the editorial style, of the Slavic volume differ in some respects from those adopted for the series. Each system is explained in its appropriate volume. The volumes to follow are: III, the Romance literatures; IV, the Celtic, Germanic, and other European literatures; V, the literatures of Asia and Africa.

As in the making of any scholarly book, the special knowledge and the time of literally innumerable friends and colleagues, fellow committee members, and librarians have been laid under contribution, and to all these, collaborators and editors convey their gratitude. We owe a particular debt to

Professor Laird, who, as general editor of the overall project, was for more than ten years actively involved with our copy and correspondence; indeed the original version of our bibliography was prepared for the printer under his direction.

Professor Christy made up the original roster of contributors, and, though many have died or withdrawn, many have stayed the course. Contributors and consultants at earlier stages of our book will be gratefully named in the appropriate volumes.

To bring our volumes down to date, we have found much help in some new current bibliographies: notably the *Index Translationum* published annually by UNESCO for the years since 1948; the annual *British National Bibliography*, from 1950, which classifies new books according to the Dewey decimal system; and the *Yearbook of Comparative and General Literature,* which has since 1960 listed translations published in the United States. For the Greek and Latin literatures, we have drawn help from two useful bibliographies: Finley M. K. Foster, *English Translations from the Greek* (1918), which does not, however, include Christian literature; and Clarissa P. Farrar and Austin P. Evans, *English Translations from Medieval Sources* (1946), which includes works written between A.D. 300 and 1500, adding also earlier Christian writings. The latter is a model bibliography for comprehensiveness and accuracy, and has set us a high standard.

Finally we pay our grateful tribute to the many libraries in which this work has been compiled by many persons, and to the librarians who have made our work in them possible.

GEORGE B. PARKS
RUTH Z. TEMPLE

ACKNOWLEDGMENTS

For this Volume I, Greek and Latin, we note gratefully the early collaboration for the ancient literatures of Professors Allen R. Benham (now deceased) and William M. Read of the University of Washington; for ancient Greek and Byzantine, of the late Professor Dwight L. Durling of Queens College, whose contribution, though revised, is still the basis of the ancient Greek section; for modern Greek, Miss Sophie A. Vrahnos and Mrs. Marion Moore Coleman, both of New York City. Consultants who have aided us in Volume I include Professor B. Q. Morgan of Stanford University and Mr. William Moellering; Professors Ursula Schoenheim and James E. Tobin of Queens College; the Rev. Professor Walter J. Ong, S.J., of St. Louis University; Professor C. D. O'Malley of the University of California Medical School (Los Angeles); and Mr. Tomas Spiers and Mrs. Virgina Branston of the Swedenborg Foundation (New York), together with Mr. E. Boyd Asplundh of the Swedenborg Scientific Association. We give them our thanks, assuring them also that the editors are solely responsible for whatever faults may appear in the book.

For the material in later volumes, we have been much indebted to many persons, to whom we shall give our thanks in due course. We must especially note here our former contributors to the bibliography of Slavic literatures, whose work is now replaced by that edited by Mr. Lewanski in our Volume II. We note our special gratitude to Professor Arthur P. Coleman, now President Emeritus of Alliance College. On the original request of Professor Christy, he energetically obtained contributions for our section then called The Literatures of Eastern Europe. In his office of secretary of the American Association of Teachers of Slavonic and East European Languages (AATSEEL), he enlisted the collaboration of scholars whose contribution to our earlier version covered sixteen literatures from Albanian to Yugoslav. Since most of these were Slavic, we thank these scholars: for Bulgarian and for Byelo-Russian, Marion Moore Coleman (Mrs. Arthur P. Coleman); for Czech, Mrs. Zdenka Munzer, of the United Nations Libraries; for Polish, the Reverend Francis Bolek and thirteen collaborators, including Professor Sigmund Sluszka, now of Nassau Community College; for Russian, Professor Dimitri von Mohrenschildt of Dartmouth College and (for Soviet literature) Mrs. Katherine Strelsky, then of Vassar College; for Slovak, the Reverend Cyril J. Potocek; for Ukrainian, Professor Clarence A. Manning of Columbia University; for Yugoslav (Croat, Serbian, Slovene), the late Professor Nikander Strelsky of Vassar College, with additions by Mr. A. J. Klancar. To all of them, all thanks.

THE PLAN OF THE BOOK

By literature we mean both imaginative literature (*belles lettres*), together with its history and criticism, and the literature of thought: the greater works of history, philosophy, theology, law, science. We perforce exclude specialized works of science or learning, technical books and textbooks, collections of documents; and we must also omit children's books, and books of journalistic interest or of light entertainment. Literature, broadly defined, is our subject.

It is our aim to list all translations of reasonable length, even early ones, which, since they are now recorded and located in the English *Short-Title Catalogues* (for 1475 to 1700), are usually available on microfilm. For a few frequently retranslated authors, such as Dante, we abridge our list to include the more important and the more recent translations, making cross-reference to other special bibliographies.

We divide the literature of each language into the conventional chronological periods, and within these list the authors alphabetically (including dates of birth and death); an index at the end of each volume gives in alphabetical order the names of all translated authors listed in the volume. The books of each author are listed alphabetically by title of the English translation, except that for prolific authors collected works precede, followed by selected works, and then by separate titles. If the title of the translation differs notably in meaning from the original title of a work, it is followed in parentheses by the original title (or by a literal translation of it). Successive translations of a given work are listed chronologically. We note whether a translation is in verse or in prose. An asterisk beside a translation designates one of particular merit and sometimes an annotation calls attention to some special feature or excellence of a translation.

It may be supposed that a bibliography of translations will be consulted by readers not themselves specialists in the literature translated, and for them we provide preliminary sections listing books in English, or in French or German or sometimes other languages, useful for the study of that literature: first, general background—the history, geography, art of the country where the language is written; then bibliography—of literature, of literature in English translation, of literary scholarship; then histories and studies of the literature; finally, collections of literature in English translation. Thus the volumes will serve as a bibliographic introduction to foreign literatures as well as a guide to those literatures in English translation.

Each volume is prefaced by an annotated bibliography of general literature: collective bibliographies of literature in translation, collective histories of literature, collections of translations from more than one literature, and, further, books on the history and theory of translation. We do not duplicate the work of two other comprehensive bibliographies: the *Bibliography of Comparative Literature* (1950) of Fernand Baldensperger and Werner P. Friederich, with its supplements in the *Yearbook of General and Comparative Literature*; and the forthcoming *Guide to Comparative Literature*, edited by Charlton G. Laird.

We note one unanticipated result of our plans. By listing early as well as recent translations, we have collected some of the material for a history of the fashions in translation and the tastes of translators and, presumably, their readers. Who were the favorite Latin poets of the eighteenth century, to judge by those most often translated? Who were the favorite translators of a given writer in the eighteenth, nineteenth, and twentieth centuries respectively? On the other hand, which foreign writers were translated in a given era, and which were not translated? The translators who were favored by one generation, say the Andrew Lang who was an accepted Victorian interpreter of Homer, have yielded to translators of different flavor and emphasis; has taste now reverted to an expansive Chapman or a sophisticated Pope, or has it turned the clock forward to the "colloquial prose" of Rouse? Which works of an author have been translated, and which not? The facts are here assembled, awaiting the historian who will account for them.

ABBREVIATIONS

GENERAL

abr.	abridged
Amer.	American, America
assn	association
bibliog.	bibliography, bibliographical
bk	book
c.	century (with an ordinal numeral); *circa* (with a date)
comp.	compiled
cont.	continued, continuation
ed.	editor, edited by
edn	edition
enl.	enlarged
et al.	and others
et seq.	and following
facs.	facsimile
lib. or Lib.	library
fl.	flourished (with a date, fixing an author's lifetime)
intro.	introduction (by)
ms., mss.	manuscript, manuscripts
n.d.	no date (given)
n.p.	no place (given)
no., nr.	number
n.s.	new series
p.	page, pages
Pr.	press
pr.	printed
pr. pr.	privately printed
pref.	preface by
pt.	part
pub.	published, publisher, publication
q.v., qq.v.	see the indicated item or items
repr.	reprinted: used for a new impression, a new issue, a new edition
retr.	re-translated
rev.	revised (by)
sec.	section

ser. or Ser.	series
s.v.	*sub verbo*: look under the word or name
tr.	translated by, translation, translator
Univ.	University
v.	volume, volumes

Note: An asterisk preceding a translation indicates that the translation is recommended.

PUBLICATIONS, SERIES, SOCIETIES

BCL	Bohn's Classical Library (London, Bohn, later Bell, 1847–1913)
Bull.	Bulletin
CBEL	Cambridge Bibliography of English Literature (Cambridge Univ. Pr., 1940, and N.Y., Macmillan, 1941, 4 v. V. 1, 600–1660; v. 2, 1660–1800; v. 3, 1800–1900; v. 4, Index. Supplement, v. 5, 1957. Bibliographies of translations into English, v. 1, p. 799–822 [1500–1660]; v. 2, p. 757–814 [1660–1800])
CURC	Columbia University Records of Civilization (English translations of important medieval books)
EETS	Early English Text Society (London, 1864—). Two series of editions: OS, Ordinary Series (eds. of mss.); ES, Extra Series (eds. of books). Recent volumes are numbered in one series.
EL	Everyman's Library (London, Dent, and N.Y., Dutton, 1906—)
Great Books	Great Books of the Western World (Chicago, Encyclopaedia Britannica, 1952, 54 v.)
LCL	Loeb Classical Library (London, Heinemann, and N.Y., Putnam, later Cambridge, Mass., Harvard Univ. Pr., 1912—. Eds. of Greek and Latin classics in parallel texts)
ML	Modern Library (N.Y., now published by Random House, 1925—)
MLA	Modern Language Association (of America)
NCTE	National Council of Teachers of English
New Amer. Lib.	New American Library (N.Y., 1946—, paperback)
Penguin	Penguin Books (Harmondsworth, England, and Baltimore, Md., 1935—, paperback)

PMLA	Publications of the Modern Language Association (New York, 1884—)
Proc.	Proceedings
S. C. M. Pr.	Student Christian Movement Press (London, 1929—)
S. P. C. K.	Society for Promoting Christian Knowledge (London, 1698—)
Trans.	Transactions
WC	World's Classics (London and N.Y., Oxford University Press, 1901—)

THE LITERATURES OF THE WORLD
IN ENGLISH TRANSLATION

Volume I

GENERAL REFERENCE

HISTORY AND THEORY OF TRANSLATION

CHARLTON G. LAIRD

AMOS, FLORA ROSS. Early Theories of Translation. (Columbia Univ. diss.) N.Y., Columbia Univ. Pr., 1920. 184 p.

Traces theories of translation as formulated by English writers through Pope, with emphasis on the 16th century. For the latter, see also W. Schwarz, *Modern Language Review*, v. 40 (1945), pp. 289–99; and Paul Herbert Larwill, *La Théorie de la traduction au début de la renaissance* (*d'après les traductions imprimées en France entre 1427 et 1527*), ([Munich diss.] Munich, C. Wolf, 1934, 64 p.), especially the bibliography. For other developments, see Samuel K. Workman, *Fifteenth Century Translation as an Influence on English Prose* (Princeton, N.J., Princeton Univ. Pr., 1940, 210 p.); Eric Jacobsen, *Translation: A Traditional Craft* (Copenhagen, Gyldendal, 1958, 219 p.), with special reference to Marlowe, including bibliography; William Frost, *Dryden and the Art of Translation* (Yale Studies in English 128, New Haven, Conn., Yale Univ. Pr., 1955, 100 p.), with bibliographical footnotes; John W. Draper, "The Theory of Translation in the 18th Century," *Neophilologus*, v. 6 (1921), p. 241–54, with extensive bibliography.

ARROWSMITH, WILLIAM, and SHATTUCK, ROGER, eds. The Craft and Context of Translation: A Symposium. Austin, Univ. of Texas Pr. for Humanities Research Center, 1961. 206 p.

The first ten essays are lectures given at a University of Texas symposium on translation, November 1959.

BABEL. INTERNATIONAL JOURNAL OF TRANSLATION. Fédération internationale des traducteurs, Paris. V. 1—, 1955—.

Quarterly issues may be irregular. Articles in various languages on latest developments in translation as well as on the history of the translation of specific authors; reports of congresses and of the translation work of UNESCO; book reviews; annotated international bibliography of translation, including articles. See also *Translation Monthly*, Chicago, Ill., v. 1–4, 1955–58 (no more published); and, for articles on and reviews of translations, and (since 1960) an annual bibliography of English translations published in the United States, *The Yearbook of Comparative and General Literature*,1952—. Useful information is to be found in William W. Bower, *International Manual of Linguists and Translators* (N.Y., Scarecrow Pr., 1959, 451 p.), and *First Supplement* (ibid., 1961, 450 p.).

BATES, E[RNEST] S[TUART]. Modern Translation. London, Oxford Univ. Pr., 1936. 162 p.

Theory and practice, with problems illustrated by citations of translations into English from European languages, mostly in verse. See also the same author's *Intertraffic: Studies in Translation* (London, Cape, 1943, 179 p.), a survey of translations of poetry done in Italy and the Far and Near East; it has appendices with examples.

BAYERISCHE AKADEMIE DER SCHÖNEN KÜNSTE, MUNICH. Die Kunst der Übersetzung. Munich, Oldenbourg, 1963. 205 p. (Gestalt und Gedanke, 8).

BEEDE, GRACE LUCILE. Vergil and Aratus: A Study in the Art of Translation. (Univ. of Chicago diss.) Chicago, Univ. of Chicago Pr., 1936. 90 p.

A study of the *Georgics* translated from the Greek of Aratus, revealing Virgil's techniques and devices for creating poetic effects.

BELLOC, HILAIRE. On Translation. (Taylorian Lecture, 1931). Oxford, Clarendon Pr., 1931. 44 p.

Still a useful essay.

BLIGNIÈRES, AUGUSTE LE BARBIER DE. Essai sur Amyot et les traducteurs français au XVIᵉ siècle. Paris, Durand, 1851. 464 p.

Amyot's translations of the classics studied beside later French versions of the same works.

* BROWER, REUBEN A., ed. On Translation. (Harvard Studies in Comparative Literature, 23). Cambridge, Mass., Harvard Univ. Pr., 1959. xi, 297 p.

Contributions from eighteen distinguished scholars and translators, divided into: I. Translators and Translating; II. Approaches to the Problem; III. Critical Bibliography of Works on Translation. The last, chronological from 46 B.C. to 1958, by Bayard Quincy Morgan, mainly follows the Western cultural tradition, and is especially strong for recent years. Parts I and II deal with translations into English from the Bible, from Greek, Latin, French, German, and Russian, and with period differences in taste.

CARY, EDMOND. La Traduction dans le monde moderne. Geneva, Librairie de l'Université, 1956. 196 p.

Systematic treatment of the whole subject, including translation of all kinds of material and use of machines.

CARY, EDMOND, and JUMPELT, RUDOLF WALTER, eds. Quality in Translation: Proceedings of the Third Congress of the FIT (International Federation of Translators), Bad Godesberg, 1959. Oxford, Pergamon Pr., and N.Y., Macmillan, 1963. xxiii, 544 p.

One section on literary, one on scientific and technical translation. Many contributions, mostly short, by many hands, on theory and practice.

CATFORD, J[OHN] C[UNNISON]. A Linguistic Theory of Translation: An Essay in Applied Linguistics. (Language and Learning, 8) London, Oxford Univ. Pr., 1965. viii, 103 p.

COHEN, J[OHN] M[ICHAEL]. English Translators and Translations. (Bibliographical Series of Supplements to British Book News). London, pub. for British Council by Longmans, Green, 1962. 56 p., ill.

Excellent historical intro.; selected list of "best" translations of authors from Aeschylus to Proust.

COWAN, G[EORGE] H[AMILTON]. Latin Translation, Principle to Practice. London, Macmillan, 1964, and N.Y., St. Martin's Pr., 1965. viii, 184 p.

ETKIND, EFIM GRIGOR'EVICH. Poezia i perevod (Poetry and Translation). Moscow, Soviet Writers, 1963. 428 p.

FÉDÉRATION INTERNATIONALE DES TRADUCTEURS. Rome, Associazione italiana dei traduttori ed interpreti, 1956—.

Transactions of Premier Congrès mondial de la traduction; subsequent reports irregular.

* FEDOROV, ANDREI VENEDIKTOVICH. Vvedenie v teoriju perevoda; lingvisticheskie problemy. (Introduction to the Theory of Translation; Linguistic Problems). 2d ed. Moscow, Literature Publishing House, 1958. 370 p.

Historical sketch of Russian views on problems of translation, both linguistic and artistic, by the chief Russian specialist in translation. See also the report of a meeting (June 1961) at Leningrad University: *Teoriia i kritika perevoda* (Theory and Criticism of Translation), ed. B. A. Larin (Leningrad, Pubns. of Leningrad Univ., 1962, 166 p.). For other east European studies of translation, see *O sztuce tłumaczenia* (On the Art of Translation), ed. Michal Rusinek (Breslau, Ossolínskich Publishing House, 1955, 559p.), containing 24 essays by various authors with English summaries at pp. 534–49; and Olgierd Weytasiewicz, *Wstep do teorii tłumaczenia* (History of the Theory of Translation) (Breslau, Ossolínskich Publishing House, 1957, 135 p.), also with English summaries; Jiří Levý, *Ceské theorie překladu* (Czech Theories of Translation: Literature, Music, Science) (Prague, State Publishing House, 1957, 946 p.), a history of Czech translation since the 16th century, with essays by translators and critics, and detailed international bibliography. See also this author's *Uměni překladu* (Art of Translation) (Prague, The Czech Writer, 1963, 283 p.).

FRÄNZEL, WALTER FRIEDRICH ARTUR. Geschichte des Übersetzens im 18. Jahrhundert. In Beiträge zur Kultur- und Universalgeschichte, ed. Karl Kamprecht, Heft 25. Leipzig, H. Voigtländer, 1914. viii, 233 p.

GESCHICHTE DER TEXTÜBERLIEFERUNG DER ANTIKEN UND MITTELALTERLICHEN LITERATUR. Mit einem Vorwort von Martin Bodmer. Zürich, Atlantis, [1961–64]. 2 v. ill.

V. 1 by Herbert Hunger et al., ed. M. Meier; v. 2 by Karl Langosch et al., ed. G. Ineichen et al.

GÜTTINGER, FRITZ. Zielsprache: Theorie und Technik des Übersetzens. Zürich, Manesse, 1963. 263 p.

HAGGARD, J[EAN] VILLASANA, assisted by MALCOLM DALLAS MCLEAN. Handbook for Translators of Spanish Historical Documents. Austin, Univ. of Texas, 1941. vii, 198 p.

A guide to procedure, with practical helps in special terms and paleographical practice; extensive bibliography. For scientific material in Spanish, see Justo Garate, *Cultura biologica y arte de traducir* (Buenos Aires, Ekin., 1943, 284 p.). For esthetic and linguistic problems involving Spanish, see Aron Benvenuto Terracini, *Conflictos de lenguas y de cultura* (Buenos Aires, Ediciones Imán, 1951, 229 p.); Olaf Blixen, *La Traducción literaria y sus problemas* (Montevideo, Universidad de la Repúlica, Facultad de Humanidades y Ciencias, 1954, 72 p.); Ronald M[axwell] Macandrew, *Translation from Spanish* (London, Black, 1936, xxii, 239 p.). Rodolfo Lenz, *El Arte de la traducción* (Santiago, Chile, 1914), important but very rare.

HECK, PHILIP. Übersetzungsprobleme im frühen Mittelalter. Tübingen, J. C. B. Mohr, 1931. 303 p.

KNOX, R[ONALD] A[RBUTHNOT]. On English Translation. (Romanes Lecture, Oxford University, 1957) Oxford, Clarendon Pr., 1957. 26 p.

LARBAUD, VALÉRY. Sous l'invocation de Saint Jérôme. Paris, Gallimard, 1946. 341 p.

Thorough discussion, including literary, cultural, philological, and technical questions; richly illustrated with a wide range of citations.

* MATTHIESSEN, F[RANCIS] O. Translation, An Elizabethan Art. Cambridge, Mass., Harvard Univ. Pr., 1931. viii, 232 p. Repr. N.Y., Octagon Books, 1965.

The general qualities of the Elizabethan translator as revealed in the work
of Hoby, North, Florio, and Holland; closely documented, with bibliographical notes.

MOUNIN, GEORGES. Les Problèmes théoriques de la traduction. Paris,
    Gallimard, 1963. 296 p.

Historical and theoretical. Author calls it with justice a "défense et illustration de l'art de traduire". See also, a classic, the author's *Les Belles infidèles*
(Paris, Cahiers du Sud, 1955, 159 p.), and *La Machine à traduire, histoire
des problèmes linguistiques* ([2d thesis, Paris 1963] The Hague, Mouton,
1964, 209 p., charts).

NIDA, EUGENE ALBERT. Toward a Science of Translating, with Special
    Reference to Principles and Procedures Involved in Bible Translating.
    Leiden, Brill, 1964. x, 331 p.

OETTINGER, ANTHONY G. Automatic Language Translation: Lexical
    and Technical Aspects, with Particular Attention to Russian. (Har-
    vard Monographs in Applied Science, 8). Cambridge, Mass., Harvard
    Univ. Pr., 1960. 380 p.

Perhaps the best general work now available; Joshua Whatmough in the
foreword calls it "quite a remarkable baby." Bibliography. For a simpler
treament, see Emile Delavenay, *An Introduction to Machine Translation,*
tr. Katharine M. Delavenay and the author from the French (pub. 1959)
(N.Y., Praeger, and London, Thames and Hudson, 1960, 144 p.). For
a more technical treatment, see *Linguistic and Engineering Studies in the
Automatic Translation of Scientific Russian into English,* Technical Report,
Phase 2 (Seattle, Univ. of Washington Pr., 1960, 492 p.), detailed bibliog-
raphy by Irwin Reifler, p. 35–65; see also *National Symposium on
Machine Translation, Univ. of California, Los Angeles, 1960*: *Proceed-
ings,* ed. H. P. Edmundson (Englewood Cliffs, N.J., 1961, xvii, 525 p.);
and *Proceedings of the 1961 International Conference on Machine
Translation of Languages and Applied Language Analysis* (London, H. M.
Stationery Office, 1962, 2 v.). A very recent study is I[saak] I[osifovich]
Revzin and V. Iu. Rozentsveig, *Osnovy ohshchego i machinnogo perevoda*
(Fundamentals of General and Machine Translation) (Moscow, Vysshaia
Shkola, 1964, 242 p.). Books on this phase of translation are subject to

early obsolescence, and bibliographies are now available. See Emile and Katharine Delavenay, *Bibliographie de la traduction automatique* (with English tr.), ('s-Gravenhage, Mouton, 1960, 69 p.); *Literature on Information Retrieval and Machine Translation*, ed. Charles F. Balz and Richard H. Stanwood (White Plains, N.Y., International Business Machines Corporation, 1962, 117 p.); Josephine L. Walkowitz, *A Bibliography of Foreign Developments in Machine Translation and Information Processing* (Washington, D.C., U.S. Government Printing Office, 1963, ii, 191 p.).

P. E. N. (World Association of Writers). Translation and Translations: A Round Table Discussion in Rome, Nov. 1–4, 1961. Reported by Ladislas Gare et al. London, International P. E. N., n.d. 179 p.

General discussion of translation of various kinds; specific and practical discussion of problems and status of translators.

* POSTGATE, J[OHN] P[ERCIVAL]. Translation and Translations: Theory and Practice. London, Bell, 1922. xii, 206 p.

Intensive study of problems in translating Greek and Latin verse into English. For the handling of classical hexameters and for general theory, see Matthew Arnold, *On Translating Homer* (1861–62), ed. with intro. and notes by W. H. D. Rouse (London, Murray, 1905, 200 p.).

RICHARDS, I[VOR] A[RMSTRONG]. Mencius on the Mind: Experiments in Multiple Definition. London, Kegan Paul, 1932. 131, 44 p.

Chapters 1 and 4 study puzzling linguistic situations of interest outside English-Chinese translation. See also Richards' "Toward a Theory of Translating," in *Studies in Chinese Thought,* ed. A[rthur] F[rederick] Wright et al. (Amer. Anthropological Assn Memoir no. 75, Chicago, 1953, p. 247–61).

RITCHIE, R[OBERT] L[INDSAY] GRAEME. Translation from French. Cambridge University Pr., 1918. xii, 258 p.

* SAVORY, THEODORE HORACE. The Art of Translation. London, Cape, 1957. 159 p. Repr. Philadelphia, Dufour, 1960.

Bayard Quincy Morgan has called this "the best book on the subject in English."

STOERIG, HANS JOACHIM. Das Problem des Übersetzens. Stuttgart, Goverts, 1963. xxviii, 488 p.

STUDIES IN COMMUNICATION 2: Aspects of Translation. (The Communications Research Center, University College, London) London, Secker and Warburg, 1958. viii, 145 p.

Includes: Leonard Foster, "Translation: An Introduction"; L. W. Tancock, "Some Problems of Style in Translations from the French"; D. J. Furley, "Translation from Greek Philosophy"; A. D. Booth, "The History and Recent Progress of Machine Translation"; C. Rabin, "The Linguistics of Translation."

TEELE, ROY EARL. Through a Glass Darkly: A Study of English Translations of Chinese Poetry. (Columbia Univ. diss.) Ann Arbor, Mich., n. pub., 1949. xi, 173 p.

TYTLER, ALEXANDER [FRASER], [Lord Woodhouselee]. Essay on the Principles of Translation. London, 1791. 3d ed. rev., enl. 1813; repr. EL, 1907, xiv, 239 p.

Still a standard work; largely directed to Greek and Latin, but includes discussion of various genres, languages, and individual works.

WEIJNEN, ANTONIUS ANGELUS. De Kunst van het Vertalen. Tilburg, W. Bergmans, 1946. 2d ed., 1947, 144 p.

Scholarly consideration of diverse special cases.

WIDMER, WALTER. Fug und Unfug des Übersetzens. Cologne, Küpenheuer und Witsch, 1959. 167 p.

COLLECTIVE BIBLIOGRAPHIES OF TRANSLATION INTO ENGLISH†

ANNA E. DOUGHERTY AND RUTH Z. TEMPLE

AMERICAN SCANDINAVIAN FOUNDATION. A List of Books by Scandinavians and about Scandinavia. 4th ed. rev. N.Y., ASF, 1946. 37 p.

Includes selected bibliography of Scandinavian literature in translation; alphabetical by author.

BAKER, ERNEST A[LBERT], and PACKMAN, JAMES. A Guide to the Best Fiction, English and American, Including Translations from Foreign Languages. [1903]. New enl. ed. N.Y., Macmillan, and London, Routledge, 1932. viii, 634 p.

Lists selected trs. from various languages, by country and by period, with descriptive and analytical annotations of some. Selected critical bibliography for some items.

BLOCK, ANDREW. The English Novel, 1740–1850: A Catalogue Including Prose Romances, Short Stories, and Translations of Foreign Fiction. Intro. John Crow and Ernest A. Baker. [1939] 2d ed. rev. London, Dawson's, 1961. xv, 349 p.

Gives all data from title page; alphabetical by author, including foreign authors. Index of titles.

CAMBRIDGE BIBLIOGRAPHY OF ENGLISH LITERATURE. Ed. F. W. Bateson, Cambridge Univ. Pr., and N.Y., Macmillan, 1941. 4 v. Supplement, v. 5, 1957.

In v. 1, for the period 1500–1660, and v. 2, for the period 1660–1800, is a section, Translations into English (v. 1, p. 799–822; v. 2, p. 757–814).

† This list includes only bibliographies which, because they include translations from more than one language, are included in no language section or in more than one section.

Each v. has also a section, Literary Relations with the Continent, which lists many trs. (v. 1, p. 325–345; v. 2, p. 31–71), and v. 2 includes a section of Translations of Foreign Literary Criticism (p. 27–30). Each v. includes also a section, under Prose Fiction, of Translations into English (v. 1, p. 732–36; v. 2, p. 532–35, 540–43, 551–53).

CLASSICS OF THE WESTERN WORLD. Ed. Alan Willard Brown et al. [1st ed. 1927, ed. J. Bartlett Brebner] 3d ed. rev. Chicago, American Library Association, 1943. 145 p.

Recommended and supplementary readings in major authors. Trs. listed in order of availability and excellence, or, in some cases, by names of translators alphabetically. From the Bible and Homer to Proust. Critical works on authors and texts.

* EMENEAU, M[URRAY] B[ARNSON], comp. A Union List of Printed Indic Texts and Translations in American Libraries. Amer. Oriental Ser. 7. New Haven, Conn., Amer. Oriental Soc., 1935, 540 p.

Includes all books in Sanskrit, Pali, Prakit, and Apabhramsa, and most of the books in the older stages of the vernacular.

EMRYS, SIR WILLAM, ed. The Reader's Guide: A Guide and Companion for the General Reader. Penguin, 1960. 351 p.

I, Introduction includes, p. 97–107, a note on the practice of English translation of the classics from the beginning, by E. V. Rieu (ed. of Penguin Classics from their beginning in 1945, and tr. of *Odyssey* and *Iliad*); II, A Guide to the Reading List (comment on the various translations); III, A Reading List (British publications, including Penguin, of English tr. of classics) by genre.

* FARRAR, CLARISSA P., and EVANS, AUSTIN P. Bibliography of English Translations from Medieval Sources. Records of Civilization, 39. N.Y., Columbia Univ. Pr., 1946. xiii, 534 p.

Comprehensive listing of works to 1500 in English translation. Alphabetical by author.

THE FICTION CATALOG: THE STANDARD CATALOG SERIES. [1908] 7th ed. N.Y., Wilson, 1961 and supplements. 650 p.

Under author translated, a selection of trs. with first as well as later editions listed and excerpts from reviews. Only the most read authors included and, of course, only fiction, but so far useful, and kept up to date.

GRIMM, MINERVA E[THEL], comp. Translations of Foreign Novels: A Selected List. Boston, Boston Book Co., 1917. 84 p.

Of very limited usefulness because so selective (e.g., 1 from Flemish, 1 from Greek), but full bibliographical information is provided.

HARRIS, WILLIAM J[AMES]. The First Printed Translations into English of the Great Foreign Classics: A Supplement to Text-Books of English Literature. N.Y., Dutton, and London, Routledge, 1909. vii, 209 p.

Alphabetical by author, from the beginning. Only translator's name and date of translation given. Index of titles.

HOPPER, VINCENT F[OSTER], and GREBANIER, BERNARD D.M. Bibliography of European Literature. N.Y., Barron's Educational Series, 1954. xiii, 158 p.

A list of standard translations of European classics from the beginning, with a selected list of standard studies of the works and authors.

* INDEX TRANSLATIONUM: RÉPERTOIRE INTERNATIONAL DES TRADUCTIONS. No. 1–31 (July, 1932–Jan. 1940). Paris, Société des nations, Institut international de coöpération intellectuelle; New Series 1— (1948—). Paris, UNESCO, 1949—.

All languages covered. Quarterly, 1932–40; annual, 1948—. Suspended Feb. 1940–47. Indispensable.

THE READER'S ADVISER: An Annotated Guide to the Best in Print in Literature, . . . Translations, . . . Ed. Hester R. Hoffmann. [1921 and through 8th ed. as Bookman's Manual] 10th ed. rev. enl. N.Y., Bowker, 1964. xxii, 1292 p.

Annotated bibliography by subject. Includes Classical drama; modern drama; Greek and Roman classics in translation; French: authors, history, and criticism, recent collections; Germanic, Russian; other foreign literatures: Africa to Yugoslavia; books on translation, bibliography, collections, translations. Selective lists but strong on recent paperback editions.

* SMITH, F. SEYMOUR. The Classics in Translation. London and N.Y., Scribner, 1930. 307 p.

Annotated guide to preferred translations, mostly modern, of many Greek and Latin works. Alphabetical by author.

SOLBERG, THORVALD. Bibliography of Scandinavia: A Catalogue of the Important Books in the English Language Relating to the Scandinavian Countries. In Frederick Winkel Horn, History of the Literature of the Scandinavian North. Chicago, Griggs, 1884, p. 413–500.

Includes English translations, alphabetically by author and translator.

TATUM, GEORGE MARVIN. Translations from European Literature Published in One Hundred and Eight American Little Magazines 1909–1959. Chapel Hill, North Carolina, 1960 (Univ. of Kentucky Pr. microcards). 397 1.

THE YEARBOOK OF COMPARATIVE AND GENERAL LITERATURE. 1952— (1952–1960, Chapel Hill, Univ. of North Carolina Pr.; 1960—, Bloomington, Univ. of Indiana Pr.)

From 1960 this annual has carried a list of English translations for the year published in the U.S.

COLLECTIVE HISTORIES OF LITERATURE†

CHARLTON G. LAIRD

ALGEMENE LITERATUR GESCHIEDENIS: Geschiedenis van de be-
langrijkste Figuren en Stromingen in de Wereldliteratur. Ed. F. de
Backer and others. Utrecht, W. De Haan, 1943–55. 5 v. plus register.

Strong in Mediterranean and Western European cultures; no east Asian.
Selective bibliographies.

AUERBACH, ERICH. Introduction to Romance Languages and Literature:
Latin, French, Spanish, Provençal, Italian. [Original German ed.,
1949]. Tr. Guy Daniels from French. N.Y., Capricorn Books, 1961.
291 p. paper.

From the Roman colonization to Proust. Necessarily brief; writers considered are relatively few, but treatment of them is critical, and the idea
of Romance Literature is pursued throughout. Excellent brief bibliography
of linguistics and literature, including periodicals.

CASSELL'S ENCYCLOPEDIA OF LITERATURE. London, Cassell,
1953, and N.Y., Funk and Wagnalls (as Cassell's Encyclopedia of
World Literature), 1954. 2 v.

Largely biographical.

CHADWICK, H[ECTOR] MUNRO, and KERSHAW, N[ORA]. The Growth
of Literature. Cambridge Univ. Pr., 1934–40. 3 v.

V. 1: The Ancient Literatures of Europe; v. 2: Russian Oral Literature,
Yugoslav Oral Poetry, Early Indian Literature, Early Hebrew Literature;
v. 3: The Oral Literature of the Tatars, The Oral Literature of Polynesia
and a Note on the Oral Literature of the Sea Dyaks of North Borneo, Notes

† Many so-called histories of world literature merely reduce and combine histories of various
particular literatures. As such books are obviously inferior to histories of the several literatures,
there is no point in listing them. This list is selective, and notes samples of the various kinds
of books useful for a general view of literature, including studies of a movement or period in
several literatures, but excluding theory of comparative literature.

on the Oral Literature of Some African Peoples. Pt. 4, A General Survey, examines various types of literature in their rise and development (e.g., heroic, theological, gnomic, and descriptive); connections of written with oral literature; problems of authorship.

* COHEN, J[OHN] M[ICHAEL]. A History of Western Literature. Penguin, 1956. Repr. rev. London, Cassell, 1961, 381 p.

From the 12th century to the present, excluding English and American and writings in Latin. A history of western literature as a "single expanding tradition." Highly selective; emphasizing ideas, not facts, and also international relationships.

———— Poetry of this Age: 1908–65. [1960] London, Hutchinson Univ. Lib., 1966. 256 p. cloth and paper.

Considers connections in theme and technique between poetry of various languages. Includes, besides English and American, Alberti, Aleixandre, Campana, Eluard, George, Guillén, Jiménez, Lorca, Machado, Mayakovsky, Montale, Molinari, Neruda, Pasternak, Paz, Quasimodo, Rilke, Valéry.

THE COLUMBIA DICTIONARY OF MODERN EUROPEAN LITERATURE. Ed. Horatio Smith. N.Y., Columbia Univ. Pr., 1947. 899 p.

Survey articles and biographies, with bibliography, by a number of specialists. Thirty-one European literatures from 1870.

COMMISSION INTERNATIONALE D'HISTOIRE LITTÉRAIRE MODERNE. Répertoire chronologique des littératures modernes. Directed by Paul Van Tieghem. Paris, Droz, 1935. 145 p. (issued in parts, 1935–37).

A chronological list, giving for each year from 1455 to 1900 the principal literary works of that year in European, English, and American literatures. Less detailed but more nearly comprehensive is Adolf Spemann, *Vergleichende Zeittafel der Weltliteratur von Mittelalter bis Neuzeit (1150–1939)* (Stuttgart, Engelehornverlag, 1951, 160 p.).

THE CONCISE ENCYCLOPEDIA OF MODERN WORLD LITERATURE. Ed. Geoffrey Grigson. London, Hutchinson, 1963. 512 p. ill.

Biographical and critical (indeed often dogmatic) articles, with photographs of authors. Articles not signed, though contributors are listed. Limited in scope (160 authors).

* DIZIONARIO LETTERARIO BOMPIANI DEGLI AUTORI DI TUTTI I TEMPI E DI TUTTE LE LETTERATURE. Milan, Bompiani, 1951–57. 9 v. ill.

Highly factual and relatively comprehensive, treating all periods and literatures, including the Oriental, and thus, in spite of some Romanic and religious bias, perhaps the most satisfactory of the world literary dictionaries. V. 9 contains a comparative table and elaborate indexes, with titles in the original languages. Lavish illustrations.

ENCICLOPEDIA DELLO SPECTACOLO. Ed. Salvio D'Amico and others. Rome, Casa Editrice Le Maschere, 1954–62. 9 v.

Encyclopedic treatment of spectacle, including drama and modern mass media. Western emphasis, but with some attention to Slavic and Oriental drama. Sumptuously illustrated.

ENCYCLOPEDIA OF LITERATURE. Ed. Joseph T. Shipley. N.Y., Philosophical Library, 1946. 2 v.

Brief articles varying in quality on numerous literatures, from Accadian to Yugoslav.

* ENCYCLOPEDIA OF POETRY AND POETICS. Ed. Alex Preminger et al. Princeton, N.J., Princeton Univ. Pr., 1965. 906 p.

Standard, relatively long, scholarly and philosophical articles, many signed, and some with bibliographies. Treats periods, genres, and schools, but neither individual authors nor works.

* ENCYCLOPEDIA OF WORLD LITERATURE IN THE 20TH CENTURY. Ed. Wolfgang Bernard Fleischmann. N.Y., Ungar, 1965—. v. 1—.

Revision of Herder's *Lexikon der Weltliteratur im 20. Jahrhundert*. Promised in three volumes, to include surveys of all national literatures, treatments of representative authors, genres, and movements, and "comprehensive record of English translations."

EPPELSHEIMER, HANNS W. Handbuch der Weltliteratur, von den An-
fängen bis zur Gegenwart. [1947–50]. 3d ed. rev., Frankfurt-am-
Main, Klostermann, 1960. xiv, 808 p.

Really a bibliography. Studies of men and movements, arranged by literature and by period; two or three sentences on each author. The first ed.
includes the literatures of Asia, the later has European only, including
English, and North American.

FORD, FORD MADOX. The March of Literature from Confucius' Day to
Our Own. N.Y., Dial Pr., 1938, and London, Allen and Unwin, 1939.
vii, 878 p.

Emphasis on Europe, and, within that, on England. By a writer, not a
scholar. Lacks scholarly apparatus, though it has index of names and titles,
and makes no attempt to surmount personal preferences. Nevertheless, it
is readable, and includes many quotations (in translation).

* FRIEDERICH, WERNER P., and MALONE, DAVID HENRY. Outline
of Comparative Literature from Dante Alighieri to Eugene O'Neill.
Chapel Hill, University of North Carolina Pr., 1954. 451 p.

Excellent within its area and purpose, to trace the "flow of forms and
ideas across national borders and the dissemination of cultural values."
Arranged by conventional periods and by countries within periods. Brief
mention of many works; some broad observations.

* GUÉRARD, ALBERT. Preface to World Literature. N.Y., Holt, 1940.
xv, 536 p.

For students. An excellent introduction to the principles and practice of
literary study, with wide-ranging examples. Appendix: bibliography and
list of world masterpieces; a critic's glossary.

HALLAM, HENRY. Introduction to the Literature of Europe in the Fifteenth, Sixteenth, and Seventeenth Centuries. [1842]. 4th ed. rev.
N.Y., Armstrong, 1887. 4 v. in 2.

A serious attempt to write world history of literature. The preface (1842)
traces the development of writing on world literature, mentioning the most
important books.

HANDBUCH DER LITERATURWISSENSCHAFT. Ed. Oskar Walzel. Berlin (later Potsdam), Akademische Verlagsgesellschaft Athenaion, 1923–36. 23 v. ill.

V. 1. Bernard Fehr. Englische Literatur (19th–20th c.). 1923. 524 p.

V. 2. Hanns Heiss et al. Romanische Literaturen (19th–20th c.). 1925–36 (3 parts). 834, 273, 158 p.

V. 3. Andreas Heusler. Altgermanische Dichtung. 1923. 200 p.

V. 4. Oskar Walzel. Gehalt und Gestalt im Kunstwerk des Dichters. 1923. 408 p.

V. 5. Erich Bethe. Griechische Dichtung. 1924. 382 p.

V. 6. Victor Klemperer. Romanische Literaturen von der Renaissance bis zur französischen Revolution. 1924. 419 p.

V. 7. Helmuth von Glasenapp. Literaturen Indiens. 1929. 340 p.

V. 8. Alfred Kappelmacher and Moriz Schuster. Literatur der Römer. 1934. 485 p. (to Charlemagne).

V. 9. Richard Wilhelm. Chinesische Literatur. 1926. 200 p.

V. 10. Wilhelm Gundert. Japanische Literatur. 1929. 136 p.

V. 11. Hans Hecht and L. L. Schücking. Englische Literatur des Mittelalters. 1927. 191 p.

V. 12. Günther Müller. Deutsche Dichtung von der Renaissance zum Ausgang des Barock. 1927. 262 p.

V. 13. Max Pieper. Ägyptische Literatur. 1927. 102p.

V. 14. Bruno Meissner. Babylonisch-Assyrische Literatur. 1927. 103 p.

V. 15. Wolfgang Keller and Bernard Fehr. Englische Literatur von der Renaissance zur Aufklärung. 1928. 283 p.

V. 16. Walther Fischer. Literatur der Vereinigten Staaten. 1929. 133 p.

V. 17. P. N. Sakulin. Russische Literatur. 1927. 259 p. Julius Klein. Polnische Literatur. 1929. 114 p.

V. 18. Arne Novak. Tschechische Literatur. 1930. 114 p. Gerhard Geseman. Serbo-Kroatische Literatur. 1931. 47 p.

V. 19. Oskar Walzel. Deutsche Dichtung von Gottsched bis zur Gegenwart. 1927–30 (2 parts). 369, 395 p.

V. 20. Leonardo Olschki. Romanische Literaturen des Mittelalters. 1928.
260 p.

V. 21. Johann Hempel. Alt-Hebräische Literatur. 1930. 203 p.

V. 22. Hilmer Borelius. Nordische Literaturen. 1931. 170 p.

V. 23. Julius Schwietering. Deutsche Dichtung des Mittelalters. 1932.
311 p.

In spite of its title, more a series of histories of literature (left uncompleted)
than a handbook, treating some bodies of writing by area or tradition
(e.g., Romance, Hellenic, Scandinavian), some by language or nation (e.g.,
England, Germany). Especially valuable for areas often neglected
(e.g., eastern and southeastern Europe, Babylonian-Assyrian), but modern
Asiatic, African, and Latin American literatures not yet reached. Germanic
bias; excellent illustrations.

* HISTOIRE DES LITTÉRATURES. Directed by Raymond Queneau.
Encyclopédie de la Pléiade. Paris, Gallimard, 1955–58. 3 v. maps.

As the title indicates, this is a collection of histories of literature. It is,
however, extremely thorough and up-to-date, and thus warrants inclusion.
Sections are by specialists. The preface to each volume, by Raymond
Queneau, discusses principles of organization. Each article includes bibliography; each volume has an index of names (with dates and brief identifi-
cation) and a glossary of literary genres. V. 1: Ancient, Eastern, and Oral
Literatures; v. 2: Western Literatures except French; v. 3: French Literature, including the literatures of areas of strong French influence or colonization. Also chronological tables of world literary events divided into
Orient, Occident, and France; table of literary movements; alphabetical
table of literatures.

HOPPER, VINCENT F., and GREBANIER, BERNARD D. M. Essentials
of European Literature. Brooklyn, N.Y., Barron's Educational Series,
1952. 2 v.

A guide to great books. Brief historical introduction to periods and movements of European literatures; description and appraisal of selected major
authors, analysis of selected great books. V. 1: from the early Christian
writers through the 18th c.; v. 2: the 19th c.

KROEBER, A[RTHUR] L. Configurations of Culture Growth. Berkeley and Los Angeles, Univ. of California Pr., 1944. 882 p.

Literature studied broadly in the context of society: see especially p. 409–623. Includes areas often neglected.

MOULTON, RICHARD G[REEN]. World Literature and Its Place in General Culture. N.Y., Macmillan, 1911. ix, 502 p.

Useful introduction, though only a survey. Argues for the unity of literature as a concept. Emphasis on certain great authors, books, and genres.

PRAMPOLINI, GIACOMO. Storia universale della Letteratura. Turin, U.T.E.T., 1933–38. 3 v. in 5 (v. 3 has 3 pts., each a v.).

Competent and well-balanced, factual and historical, with emphasis on continuity, though each literature is treated separately. Literature is correlated with art, philosophy, history. A good book to read. From the earliest written Chinese to the present. Alphabetical index of authors and works in each volume. Bibliography for each section includes list of trs. of literary works into the various European languages.

✓ THE READER'S COMPANION TO WORLD LITERATURE. Ed. Lillian Herlands Hornstein. General ed. Calvin S. Brown. N.Y., Dryden Pr., 1956. 493 p.

Like the Oxford "Companions," this has dictionary listing of great and minor authors, titles, literary forms.

DER ROMANFÜHRER. Ed. Wilhelm Olbrich. Stuttgart, Hiersmann, 1950–56. 6 v.

Standard guide to the novel; comprehensive and capable. Includes bibliographies, summaries, some criticism.

SCOTT-JAMES, R[OLFE] A. The Making of Literature: Some Principles of Criticism Examined in the Light of Ancient and Modern Theory. 2d ed. N.Y., Holt, 1930. 396 p.

Central problems of the art of literature in western Europe from the Greeks to the moderns (e.g., Croce and Pirandello), "as they have presented themselves to men experienced in the arts."

VAN TIEGHEM, PAUL. Outline of the Literary History of Europe since the Renaissance. Tr. Aimee Leffingwell McKenzie [1925]. N.Y., Century, 1930. xvi, 361 p.

By genre rather than by country. Facts, dates, continuity, to about 1900. See also this author's *Précis d'histoire littéraire de l'Europe depuis la Renaissance* (Paris, Alcan, 1925, vii, 352 p.); his massive and classic work, *Le Préromantisme: études d'histoire littéraire européenne* (Paris, Rieder, 1921, 1930, 1945, 3 v.) and (v. 4) *Le Sentiment de la nature dans le préromantisme* (Paris, Nizet, 1960, 275 p.); also *Le Romantisme dans la littérature européenne* (Paris, Michel, 1948, xxv, 560 p.).

THE WORLD THROUGH LITERATURE. Ed. Charlton Grant Laird. N.Y., Appleton-Century-Crofts, 1951. xx, 506 p. NCTE Monograph no. 18.

A symposium to which various specialists have contributed chapters on: Primitive Literature, Chinese, Japanese, Indian, Near Eastern, Arabic, Hebrew, Greek and Latin, Italian, French, Spanish, Portuguese, German, Scandinavian, Slavic, Latin American Literatures.

YEARBOOK OF COMPARATIVE AND GENERAL LITERATURE, 1952—. Chapel Hill, N.C., 1952–60; Bloomington, Ind., 1961—.

Articles on general literature; short reviews of works on world literature; annual bibliography since 1960 of trs. published in the United States; annual bibliography: "Literary Currents"; "Literary and Semi-literary Genres and Forms," which brings up to date Fernand Baldensperger and Werner P. Friederich, *Bibliography of Comparative Literature* (Chapel Hill, N.C., Univ. of North Carolina Studies in Comparative Literature, 1950, xxiv, 701 p.).

See also *Books Abroad, An International Literary Quarterly* (Norman, Okla., Univ. of Oklahoma, 1927), for surveys of various literatures (including since 1961 Asian, African, and Slavic) for recent years; for short reviews of important books in all languages; for annual lists of the outstanding books of the year by country (annual index with—not in—winter issue).

See also *Helicon: Revue internationale des problèmes généraux de la littérature,* directed by Janós Hankiss (Amsterdam, Éds. académiques Panthéon, 1938–43, v. 1–5, no more pub.), for articles in five European languages.

COLLECTIONS OF TRANSLATIONS FROM SEVERAL LANGUAGES†

MURIEL J. HUGHES AND RUTH Z. TEMPLE

ADVENTURES IN WORLD LITERATURE. Ed. R[ewey] B[elle] Inglis and M. K. Stewart. [1936] N.Y., Harcourt, Brace, 1946. xix, 1268 p. ill.

Pt. 1, European literature; pt. 2, Greek and Roman classic literature; pt. 3, Oriental literature. Biography of authors.

AN ANTHOLOGY OF WORLD LITERATURE. Ed. Philo M[elvin] Buck, Jr. and Hazel Stewart Alberson. [1934] Rev. ed. N.Y., Macmillan, 1940. xiii, 1146 p.

European literature from Homer through the 19th c.; Oriental literature from India, Egypt, Arabia, Persia, and Palestine.

* AN ANTHOLOGY OF WORLD POETRY. Ed. Mark Van Doren. [1928] Rev. enl. N.Y., Halcyon, 1939. lxii, 1467 p.

World poetry, including Oriental, from 35 B.C. to the present day; notable among one-volume anthologies for its critical discrimination in selections

---

† Collections of translations from one language only will appear in the appropriate language section. Included in this section are various kinds of collections, for the general reader and the small library as well as for the student, but only those which have some merit and, with a very few exceptions, only those published in the twentieth century.

and translations, the latter by, for example, Chaucer, Herrick, Pope, Swinburne, Rossetti, Symons, Dowson. Index of translators.

AN ANTHOLOGY OF WORLD PROSE. Ed. Carl Van Doren. [1935] N.Y., Halcyon, 1939. vii–xxvi, 1582 p.

Contains material not available in other common anthologies, notably for the Orient. Translators such as Dryden, Shelley, Carlyle.

THE BEST OF THE WORLD'S CLASSICS, RESTRICTED TO PROSE. Ed. Henry Cabot Lodge; assoc. ed. F[rancis] W. Halsey. N.Y. and London, Funk and Wagnalls, 1909. 10 v.

Six of the small v. devoted to English and American literature; the other four include Greece, Rome, and Continental Europe: very short selections.

THE BOOK OF ORIENTAL LITERATURE. Ed. Iḳbāl 'Alī Shāh. N.Y., Garden City Pub., 1938, and London, Low, Marston, 1937 (as The Coronation Book of Oriental Literature). xii, 404 p.

Arranged by countries: Afghanistan to Turkey.

CENTURY READINGS IN ANCIENT CLASSICAL AND MODERN EUROPEAN LITERATURE. Ed. John W[illiam] Cunliffe and Grant Showerman. N.Y., Century, 1925. 2 v. in 1. xx, 614; v, 543 p.

Wide range of important authors represented by whole works or long selections in "classic" translations (e.g., Chaucer's of Boethius's *Consolation*, Pope's *Iliad*, 1683 tr. of *Praise of Folly*). Explanatory notes. V. 2 is published separately as *Century Readings in European Literature, From the Medieval Period through Croce,* ed. John W. Cunliffe (N.Y., Century, 1925, xi, 542). The modern works, more briefly excerpted, extend from Romance and Saga to 19th c. French (especially), Russian and, for Italian, Croce.

* CHIEF CONTEMPORARY DRAMATISTS. Ed. Thomas H[erbert] Dickinson. Boston and N.Y., Houghton Mifflin, 1915, 1921, 1930. 1st series, ix, 676; 2nd series, vi, 734; 3d series, ix, 698 p.

Series 1, 8 Continental plays; 2, 9 Continental; 3, 15 Continental. Reading lists, notes on authors, plays, and productions.

THE CHIEF EUROPEAN DRAMATISTS. Ed. Brander Matthews. Boston and N.Y., Houghton Mifflin, 1916. xi, 786 p.

Twenty-one plays, 500 B.C. to A.D. 1879. Standard translations. Biography, notes, bibliography.

COLUMBIA UNIVERSITY COURSE IN LITERATURE. Ed. John W[illiam] Cunliffe et al. N.Y., Columbia Univ. Pr., 1928–29, and London, J. A. Richards, 1945. 18 v.

Each pt. edited by a specialist. A representative selection of the literature of different epochs, languages, and civilizations, chronologically arranged, designed for use in Columbia College. V. 1, the East; 2, Greece; 3, Rome; 4, medieval Europe including Middle English; 5, Italy; 6, France through the Revolution; 7, Modern France; 8, the small nations; 9, Germany; 10, Scandinavian and Slavonic; remaining v. English and Amer.

CONFUCIUS TO CUMMINGS: AN ANTHOLOGY OF POETRY. Ed. Ezra Pound and Marcella Spann. [1926] N.Y., New Directions, 1964. xxii, 353 p. (also paper).

Brief selections, usually one per poet. Well over half English and Amer. but some Provençal, Italian, medieval and Renaissance French.

CONTINENTAL PLAYS. Ed. Thomas H. Dickinson. Boston and N.Y., Houghton Mifflin, 1935. 2 v.

Types of contemporary drama. Bibliography.

THE COPELAND TRANSLATIONS. Chosen, arranged, with intro., by Charles Townsend Copeland. N.Y. and London, Scribner, 1934. xxiii, 1080 p.

Mainly in prose, from French, German (slight), Italian, Russian, Irish. Some unusual not to say idiosyncratic selections; some popular writers.

DRAMA OF THE EAST AND WEST: A CRITICAL ANTHOLOGY OF PLAYS, with Special Sections on Oriental and Philippine Drama. Ed. Jean Edades and Carolyn Fosdick. Manila, Bookman, 1956. vii, 658 p.

Plays from India, China, Japan; 5 one-act Philippine plays. The standard Western plays from Euripides to Chekov. Collection interesting only for the Philippine plays. Notes on history of drama.

THE DRAMA: ITS HISTORY, LITERATURE, AND INFLUENCE IN CIVILIZATION. Ed. Alfred Bates et al. London, [Athenian Soc.] Stuart and Stanley, and N.Y., Smart and Stanley, 1903. 20 v. ill.

For the general reader. Translators not named. Largely discussion, with excerpts for illustration from plays standard to ephemeral. Addenda, 1904, v. 21–22: "Classic Curiosities of Dramatic Literature."

EUROPEAN THEORIES OF THE DRAMA. Ed. Barrett H. Clark. [1918] Rev. Henry Popkin. N.Y., Crown Pub., 1965. xiv, 628 p.

Subtitle: "An Anthology of Dramatic Theory and Criticism from Aristotle to the Present Day, in a Series of Selected Texts . . . Including Commentary, Biography and Bibliography."

FROM THE MODERN REPERTOIRE. Ed. Eric R[ussell] Bentley. Denver, Univ. of Colorado Pr., 1949. 1st series, xiv, 406 p.

Rather unusual selections, including Musset, Büchner, Becque, Schnitzler, Sternheim, Brecht, Lorca, Cocteau.

———— 2nd series, ibid., 1952. 511 p.

Inter alia: Grabbe, Ostrovsky, Mirbeau, Wedekind, Obey, Giraudoux, Brecht.

———— 3d series, Bloomington, Indiana Univ. Pr., 1956. 527 p.

Inter alia: Büchner, Musset, Zola, Schnitzler, Romains, Brecht, Cocteau, Anouilh.

THE GENIUS OF THE ORIENTAL THEATRE. Ed. George Lincoln Anderson. N.Y., New Amer. Lib., 1966. 416 p. (Mentor).

Includes bibliography.

THE GOLDEN TREASURY OF INDIAN LITERATURE. Ed. Iḳbāl 'Alī Shāh. London, Low, Marston, 1938, 294 p.

Poetry and prose from "most Indian languages" (Preface). No translators named, no critical apparatus. Mostly short poems.

* GREAT BOOKS OF THE WESTERN WORLD. Ed. Robert Maynard Hutchins; assoc. ed. Mortimer Adler. Chicago, Encyclopaedia Britannica, 1952. 54 v.

V. 1, the great conversations, the substance of a liberal education; 2, 3, the great ideas: a synopticon of great books of the western world; each of remaining v. devoted to one or two authors, usually with complete books, chronologically from Homer to 20th c., including English and Amer., and documents in the history of thought (e.g., 38, Montesquieu and Rousseau; 46, Hegel; 50, Marx; 53, William James).

GREAT SHORT BIOGRAPHIES OF ANCIENT TIMES, THE MIDDLE AGES AND THE RENAISSANCE: A Collection of Short Biographies, Literary Portraits, and Memoirs. Chosen by Barrett H[arper] Clark. N.Y., Boni, 1935. xi, 615.

Chronological arrangement, excluding Oriental; strong in English and Amer. Completed by *Great Short Biographies of Modern Times: The Seventeenth, Eighteenth, and Nineteenth Centuries,* ed. Clark, N.Y., Boni, 1934, xii, 615–1406. The two parts originally pub. together 1928 as *Great Short Biographies of the World.*

GREAT SHORT STORIES OF ALL NATIONS. Ed. Maxim Lieber and Blanche Colton Williams. N.Y., Brentano's, 1932. xii, 1121 p.

One hundred sixty stories of all periods and nations.

GREAT SHORT STORIES OF THE WORLD. Ed. Barrett H. Clark and Maxim Lieber. N.Y., McBride, 1926. xv, 1072 p.

Stories from 28 countries or regions, for the general reader; introduction and bibliographical comments for each section.

* THE HARVARD CLASSICS. Ed. Charles W[illiams] Eliot. N.Y., Collier, 1909–10. 50 v.

The classics of Western literature (East represented only by *The Thousand and One Nights* in Lane's translation, rev. Stanley Lane-Poole) in volumes by genre, with short critical and biographical introductions. V. 12, Plutarch's *Lives* (9), tr. "called Dryden's," rev. Arthur Hugh Clough; 14, *Don Quixote*, tr. Thomas Shelton; 17, Aesop, Grimm, Anderson; 33, voyages and travels; 35, Froissart's *Chronicles*, tr. Lord Berners; 49, epic and saga. Completed by *Lectures on the Harvard Classics*, ed. William Allan Neilson (N.Y., Collier, 1914, 400 p.).

HEATH READINGS IN THE LITERATURE OF EUROPE. Ed. Tom Peete Cross and Clark H. Slover. [1927] Boston and N.Y., Heath, 1933. xv, 1194 p.

". . . characteristic examples of the major streams of ancient, medieval and modern European literature" together with readings to illustrate "the literary, philosophical and critical backgrounds of the English-speaking peoples." (Preface) By period and genre, from the *Iliad* to Keller and Sudermann; European except for the Book of Job and Ecclesiastes and some psalms. Many genres and authors, some unusual; translations standard. Scholarly notes on each selection.

THE HERITAGE OF EUROPEAN LITERATURE. Ed. Edward H[owell] Weatherly et al. Boston, Ginn, 1948–49. 2 v.

Fairly liberal selections from major works. V. 1, Greece, Rome, the Middle Ages, the Renaissance; v. 2, the Age of Reason, the 19th c., Russian literature before the Soviet Era, 20th c. including Soviet literature. Modern portion less satisfactory: merely chapters from novels, etc. Chronological chart, index of authors and titles, critical introductions.

LIBRARY OF THE WORLD'S BEST LITERATURE. See WARNER LIBRARY.

THE LIMITS OF ART. POETRY AND PROSE CHOSEN BY ANCIENT AND MODERN CRITICS. Ed. Huntington Cairns. N.Y., Pantheon Books, 1948. xliv, 1473 p. Bollingen Series, 12.

Parallel texts; critic's estimate of each. Brief passages, chosen by named critics as greatest, from authors Homer to Joyce. Standard translations used.

* LITERARY CRITICISM: PLATO TO DRYDEN. Ed. Allan H. Gilbert. N.Y., Amer. Book, 1940. ix, 704 p.

The best available collection of criticism. Notes.

* LITERARY CRITICISM: POPE TO CROCE. Ed. Gay Wilson Allen
    and Harry H. Clark. N.Y., Amer. Book, 1941. 659 p.

See above comment. Modern selections somewhat too brief.

LITERATURE OF WESTERN CIVILIZATION. Sel. and ed. Louis G[lenn]
    Locke, John Pendy Kirby, and M. E. Porter. N. Y., Ronald Pr., 1952.
    2 v. ill.

Not useful by reason of shortness of selections and inferiority of translations.

* A LITTLE TREASURY OF WORLD POETRY. Ed. Hubert Creekmore.
    N.Y., Scribner, 1952. 904 p.

From the great poets of other languages, 2600 B.C. to A.D. 1950. By lan-
guage and then by poets chronologically. Indexes of authors, titles, trans-
lators, languages. Standard translations, many 20th c. and some by editor.
Egyptian, Babylonian, Sanskrit (liberal selection), Hebrew, Yiddish,
Persian, Arabian, Arakanese, Chinese, Japanese. European includes:
Anglo-Saxon, Gaelic, Welsh, Old Norse, Icelandic, Provençal, Latin
American, besides the modern Continental.

LYRICS OF THE MIDDLE AGES. Ed. Hubert Creekmore. N.Y., Grove,
    1959. 278 p.

167 poems translated from 14 languages including Scandinavian but not
those of eastern Europe.

MASTERPIECES OF THE ORIENT. Ed. George L. Anderson. N.Y.,
    Norton, 1961. xiii, 396 p. paper.

For students. Complete or long selections of fiction, poetry, drama, essays,
philosophical and religious documents. Near East, China, India, Japan.

MASTERWORKS OF WORLD LITERATURE. Ed. Edwin M[allard]
    Everett, Calvin S. Brown, and John C. Wade. [1947] N.Y., Dryden,
    1955. 2 v.

V. 1, Homer to Cervantes; 2, Shakespeare to Mann. European only,
except for Bible; English amply represented. More extensive selections
from fewer works than in most anthologies, though in v. 2 one poem each

for many authors. "Method of abridgement varies" but attempt made to convey unity of work.

* MEDIEVAL LITERATURE IN TRANSLATION. Ed. Charles W[illiam] Jones. [1950] N.Y., and London, Longmans, Green, 1957. xx, 1004 p. Maps.

Tries to represent all genres, so short selections, but wide range of literatures and good choice of material.

MEDIEVAL NARRATIVE: A BOOK OF TRANSLATIONS. See Schlauch.

MODERN CONTINENTAL DRAMAS. Ed. Harlan Hatcher. N.Y., Harcourt, Brace, 1941. viii, 747 p.

Late 19th c. to present. Biography and bibliography. Whole plays.

MODERN CONTINENTAL PLAYS. Ed. S[amuel] Marion Tucker. N.Y., and London, Harper, 1929. xi, 836 p.

Late 19th, early 20th c. Standard plays. See also *Twenty-Five Modern Plays* ([ed. S. Marion Tucker, 1931], 3d ed. rev. Alan S. Downer, N.Y., Harper, 1953, xx, 1008 p.) Most of the Continental plays from above; some English and Amer. added.

* MODERN EUROPEAN POETRY. Ed. Willis Barnstone et al. N.Y., Bantam, xxiii, 605 p. paper.

Short introduction to each language section: German, French, Greek, Italian, Russian, Spanish. Wide selection, translators various.

THE MODERN THEATRE. PLAYS. Ed. Eric Russell Bentley. Garden City, N.Y., Doubleday ,1955— (also Anchor) 6 v. to date.

From late 19th c. Modern translations, many by editor. Each v. has an assortment of Continental plays except v. 4, American.

MODERN STORIES FROM MANY LANDS. Ed. Clarence R[aymond] Decker and Charles Angoff. N.Y., Maryland Books, 1963. 316 p.

24 stories from 13 countries, incl. Indonesia, Philippines, Turkey.

NICHOLSON, R[EYNOLD] A[LLEYNE] [translator]. Translations of Eastern Poetry and Prose. Cambridge Univ. Pr., 1922. xi, 200 p.

About 50 authors, 6th to 15th c. A.D., chronologically by authors. Translations prose into prose, verse into verse. Brief notes on authors. Selections deal with history, morals, religion, culture and character.

OUR HERITAGE OF WORLD LITERATURE. Ed. Stith Thompson and John Gassner. [1938] Rev. ed. N.Y., Dryden, 1942. 2 v.

Little Eastern, many selections short, undistinguished translations, many genres. Aeschylus through Ibsen and Chekhov.

ONE THOUSAND AND ONE POEMS OF MANKIND: MEMORABLE SHORT POEMS FROM THE WORLD'S CHIEF LITERATURES. Comp. Henry Willis Wells. N.Y., McKay, 1953. 448 p.

Chronological under theme. All periods; "classic" translations. Good representation of Chinese, Japanese, Sanskirt. English and Amer. included.

THE ORIENTAL CARAVAN: A REVELATION OF THE SOUL AND MIND OF ASIA. Ed. Iḳbāl 'Alī Shāh. N.Y., Kendall, and London, Archer, 1933. 331 p.

Many genres, translators, and countries. Selections from the great religious works.

PAINTER, WILLIAM. The Palace of Pleasure [1566]. Ed. Joseph Jacobs. London, Joseph Jacobs, 1890. 3 v.

Elizabethan versions of classical, French and Italian novellas. Authors include Boccaccio, Bandello, Cinthio, Straparola, Queen Margaret of Navarre.

THE POEM ITSELF: 45 MODERN FOREIGN POETS IN A NEW PRESENTATION. Ed. Stanley Burnshaw. N.Y., Holt, 1960. Repr. Cleveland, World (Meridian), 1962. 377 p.

Original poem, literal translation and analysis by a critic. Over 150 poems in French, Spanish, German, Italian, and Portuguese.

POEMS OF PLACES. Ed. Henry W[adsworth] Longfellow. Boston, Osgood, 1876–79. 31 v.

By country. Most of the poems by famous poets.

POETIC DRAMA: AN ANTHOLOGY OF PLAYS IN VERSE FROM THE ANCIENT GREEK TO THE MODERN AMERICAN. Ed. Alfred Kreymborg. N.Y., Modern Age Books, 1941. vii, 855 p.

Translations of varying excellence. Aeschylus to *The Chalk Circle*.

THE POETRY OF THE ORIENT: AN ANTHOLOGY OF THE CLASSIC SECULAR POETRY OF THE MAJOR EASTERN NATIONS. Ed. Eunice Tietjens. N.Y. and London, Knopf, 1928. xxv, 328, xli p.

Various translators, mostly well known. Arabia, China, India, Japan, Persia.

THE POETS AND POETRY OF EUROPE. Ed. Henry W[adsworth] Longfellow. [1845] Rev. enl. Boston, Houghton, 1896. xxi, 921 p.

Selections from 10 languages, not including Celtic, Slavonic, or Romaic. Translations by Longfellow and others. Biographical notices mostly by C. C. Felton.

POUND, EZRA. *See* The Translations of Ezra Pound.

PRIEST, HAROLD M[ARTIN] [translator]. Renaissance and Baroque Lyrics: An Anthology of Translations. Evanston, Ill., Northwestern Univ. Pr., 1962. lxiv, 288 p.

* PROSE AND POETRY OF THE CONTINENTAL RENAISSANCE IN TRANSLATION. Ed. Harold Hooper Blanchard. [1949] 2nd ed. N.Y. and London, Longmans, Green, 1955, Repr. 1959. xix, 1084 p.

Excellent for quality and range of selections and choice of translation. Introduction to each author, including bibliography of his works and translations of them, standard biographical and critical works on him. Lyric poetry (e.g., Ronsard, Petrarch), *The Praise of Folly* (entire) tr. John Wilson 1668 (rev. Mrs. P. S. Allen), Ariosto, 13 cantos, *inter alia*.

THE SACRED BOOKS OF THE EAST. Ed. F[riedrich] Max Müller. [1879–1910] Oxford, Oxford Univ. Pr., 1926—. 50 v. Repr. N.Y., Dover, 1963—. (v. 1, 15, 21, 34–36, 38–40, 16 to date).

Indispensable. V. 50 General Index. Translators all Oriental scholars. For individual v. see under Arabic, Chinese, Indic, Persian, etc.

THE SACRED BOOKS OF THE EAST, with Critical and Biographical Sketches by Epiphanius Wilson. [1900] Rev. ed. N.Y., Willey, 1945. 480 p.

Vedic hymns, *Zend-Avesta* (sel), The *Dhamnapada*, The *Upanishads*, The *Koran* (sel.), Life of Buddha by Bodhisatuva A.D. 420.

THE SACRED BOOKS AND EARLY LITERATURE OF THE EAST. Dir. Charles F. Horne, N.Y. and London, Parke, Austin and Lipscomb, 1917. 14 v.

With historical surveys of the chief writings of each nation. Bibliography. V. 1, Babylonia and Assyria; 2, Egypt; 3, Ancient Hebrew; 4, Medieval Hebrew; 5, Ancient Arabia; 6, Medieval Arabia, Moorish and Turkish; 7, Ancient Persia; 8, Medieval Persia; 9, India and Brahminism; 10, India and Buddhism; 11, Ancient China; 12, Medieval China; 13, Japan; 14, the great rejected books of the Biblica Apocrypha.

* SCHLAUCH MARGARET. Medieval Narrative, A Book of Translations. N.Y., Prentice-Hall, 1928. viii, 456 p.

Teacher's and scholar's selection; all translations by Schlauch. Icelandic saga, chansons de geste, Tristan legend, legends of Holy Grail, Nibelung cycle, Tale of Troy, Legend of Alexander the Great, pious tales and miracle stories, Saints' lives, fabliaux; introduction to each.

TELLERS OF TALES. Sel. and with intro. by W. Somerset Maugham. N.Y., Doubleday, Doran, 1939. xxxix, 1526 p.

100 short stories from U.S., England, France, Russia, Germany. Good selection including some authors not usually collected (e.g., Villiers de l'Isle Adam). Standard translations.

* TRANSLATIONS OF CHRISTIAN LITERATURE. General eds. W. J. Sparrow Simpson and W. K. L. Clarke. London, SPCK, and N.Y., Macmillan 1898–1940.

For the several series and many volumes of this indispensable work, see Christian Literature under Greek and Roman Literature.

THE TRANSLATIONS OF EZRA POUND. N.Y., New Directions, and London, Faber and Faber, 1933. 4o8 p.

Introduction by Hugh Kenner. Poets: Arclamon, Catullus, Cavalcanti, Arnaut Daniel, du Bellay, Charles d'Orléans, Leopardi, Rémy de Gourmont, Jules Laforgue, and Noh plays.

A TREASURY OF ASIAN LITERATURE. Ed. John D. Yohannen. [1956] N.Y., New Amer. Lib. (Mentor), 1961. 432 p.

Mostly short selections. Introduction and commentaries. Prose, poetry, drama, scriptures.

A TREASURY OF MODERN ASIA STORIES. Ed. William Clifford and Daniel L. Milton. N.Y., New Amer. Lib. (Mentor), 1961. 237 p.

* A TREASURY OF THE THEATRE. Ed. John Gassner. Rev. enl. N.Y., Simon and Schuster, 1963. 3 v.

V. 1, Aeschylus to Turgenev; 2, Modern European from Ibsen to Sartre; 3, Modern British and Amer. A standard text since its appearance in 1935, ed. Burns Mantle and Gassner (2 v.). Rev. and adapted for colleges 1940 by Philo M. Buck, Gassner, and H. S. Alberson (2 v.) with apparatus; rev. by Gassner, 1951 (3 v.).

A TREASURY OF THE WORLD'S GREAT LETTERS, FROM ANCIENT DAYS TO OUR OWN TIME. Ed. M. Lincoln Schuster. N.Y., Simon and Schuster, 1940. xlvii, 563 p.

From Greece to Thomas Mann on Hitler. Interesting selection precisely documented.

TUDOR TRANSLATIONS. Ed. W. E. Henley. London, Nutt, 1892–1909. 44 v.

———— Second Series. Ed. Charles Whibley. London, Constable, and N.Y., Knopf, 1924—27. 12 v. Both series repr. N.Y., AMS Pr., 1967.

Re-eds. of classic trs. made in the Tudor century from Greek (Heliodorus, Herodotus, Plutarch); Latin (Apuleius, Sallust, Seneca, Suetonius); French (Commines, Froissart, Montaigne); Italian (Bandello, Boccaccio, Castiglione, Guazzo, Machiavelli); Spanish (Alemán, Cervantes). A sampling of Tudor trs. was given in *Tudor Translations: An Anthology*, ed. Arthur F. Clements (Oxford, Blackwell and N.Y., Salloch, 1940. xv, 214 p.), with intro. on major translators, biographical notes on minor.

THE TWENTY BEST EUROPEAN PLAYS ON THE AMERICAN STAGE. Ed. John Gassner. [1957] N.Y., Crown 1960. 733 p.

Modern. Including Anouilh, S. Ansky, Benavente, Capek, Chekhov, R. Fauchois, Giraudoux (4), Heijermans, Albert Husson, Molnar, Obey, Pirandello, Sartre, Tolstoy, Turgenev, Werfel.

TYPES OF WORLD LITERATURE. Ed. Percy Hazen Houston and Robert Metcalf Smith. N.Y., Odyssey, 1930. xviii, 1200 p.

Masterpieces excerpted for students of comparative literature. Many genres (history, philosophy, letters, satire, biography, politics). From *Iliad* (tr. Edward, Earl of Derby) to Croce. Arranged by genre.

TYPES OF WORLD TRAGEDY. Ed. Robert Metcalf Smith, N.Y., Prentice-Hall, 1928. viii, 667 p.

Oedipus, Medea, Phaedra, Othello, The Cenci, Ghosts, The Weavers, The Lower Depths.

THE WARNER LIBRARY OF THE WORLD'S BEST LITERATURE, ANCIENT AND MODERN. Ed. Charles Dudley Warner et al. N.Y., International Soc., 1896–98. 30 v.

Several editions in varying number of v. to 1928–29, ed. John W. Cunliffe and Ashley Thorndike. "The selections are made for household and general reading." Very short selections but wide variety of literatures. Each v. a pot-pourri, since listing is alphabetical by author.

WARNKE, FRANK J. European Metaphysical Poetry. New Haven, Yale
     Univ. Pr., 1961. xi, 317 p.

Anthology in parallel texts of late 16th and 17th c. poetry, French, German,
Dutch, Spanish, Italian, all translated by Warnke. Long, important historical
and critical introduction.

WESTERN WORLD LITERATURE. Ed. Harry Wolcott Robbins and
     William Harold Coleman. N.Y., Macmillan, 1938. xix, 1422 p. Maps.

A teaching book, with apparatus. Wide range but generally short selections;
mostly old translations (e.g., *Misanthrope*, 1739). Emphasis on English
literature.

THE WISDOM OF THE EAST SERIES. Original eds., L. Cranmer-Byng
     and S. A. Kapadia, later L. Cranmer-Byng and Alan W. Watts. Lon-
     don, Orient Pr. (for first item), then John Murray, 1904— (in
     progress). Some 125 v. to 1962, the v. not numbered.

Trs. of Oriental books or selections, or discussions, from Egyptian to
Japanese.

WORLD DRAMA. Ed. Barrett H[arper] Clark. [1933] N.Y., Appleton,
     1956. 2 v. V. 2 also N.Y., Dover, 1956.

V. 1, Ancient Greece, Rome, India, China, Japan, Medieval Europe. V. 2,
Italy, Spain, France, Germany, Denmark, Russia, Norway.

A WORLD OF GREAT STORIES. Ed. Hiram Haydn and John Cournos.
     N.Y., Crown, 1947. x, 950 p.

Aim was "to choose at least one first-rate story from every country in the
world with any appreciable literature." (Preface) All 20th c. Almost one-
third of book English and Amer. Oriental included, also Latin American.

* THE WORLD IN LITERATURE. Ed. George K. Anderson and Robert
     Warnock. [1950–51] Rev. ed. Chicago, Scott, Foresman, 1967. 2 or
     4 v. ill.

One-v. ed. 1959 omits English and Amer. Literary classics and other
writings chosen judiciously to illuminate the history of thought. Long

introductory sections on movements, works, etc.; author biographies. Selections are whole units. V. 1, The Ancient Foundations (China, India, Hebrew Bible, *Iliad, Odyssey* [both in Rouse tr.], Aeschylus, Sophocles, Euripides, etc., Rome). V. 2, Centuries of Transition (from *Koran, Arabian Nights,* Omar, Hafiz, etc.). V. 3, Tradition and Revolt, The Literature of the Age of Reason and of the Romantic Era. V. 4, Science and Uncertainty (1850—, including Schopenhauer, Rilke, Sartre, Kafka, Gide, Mann etc.). An epitome of world literature.

WORLD LITERATURE. Ed. E[than] A[llen] Cross. N.Y., Amer. Book, 1935. xv, 1396.

Chronological arrangement. Sketch of literature of each country with short (except for modern plays) illustrative selections, Egypt through 20th c. Europe. Contemporary translations used where possible (e.g., Smollett's *Gil Blas*).

WORLD LITERATURE: AN ANTHOLOGY OF HUMAN EXPERIENCE. Ed. Arthur E. Christy and Henry W. Wells. N.Y., Amer. Books, 1947. xxiii, 1118 p.

By themes, as subtitle indicates (e.g., travel, the unfolding universe, the critical intellect) and chronological under these. Selections mostly very short. Wide range of nations. Author biographies. A teaching book (questions included) to illustrate the unity of human experience. Less useful as introduction to world literature.

* WORLD MASTERPIECES. General ed. Maynard Mack. [1956] Rev. N.Y., Norton, 1965. 2 v. (*The Continental Edition of World Masterpieces,* pub. 1962 in one v. excluded English and Amer.)

This is now (1966) enlarged to 2 v. but does not include revisions as in 1965 *World Masterpieces*, of which v. 1 is The Literature of Western Culture through the Renaissance; v. 2, The Literature of Western Culture since the Renaissance. Good introductions; modern translations (e.g., Louis MacNeice of *Agamemnon*, Yeats of Sophocles' *Oedipus*, Rex Warner of *Medea*). Policy is to use whole works wherever possible. For variety, wise selection and length of selections a superior anthology,—of European not world, literature.

THE WORLD'S BEST ESSAYS FROM CONFUCIUS TO MENCKEN. Ed.
F[rancis] H[enry] Pritchard. [1929] N.Y., Halcyon, 1939. 6,1012 p.

229 essays from English and foreign literature.

THE WORLD' BEST HUMOR, BEING A TRUE CHRONICLE FROM
PREHISTORIC AGES TO THE TWENTIETH CENTURY. Ed.
Carolyn Wells, N.Y., Boni. 1933. x, 782 p.

Chronological outline of humor with illustrations, from Ancient Egypt
to Wilde and Bret Harte. Index.

THE WORLD'S BEST ORATIONS, FROM THE EARLIEST PERIOD
TO THE PRESENT TIME. Ed. David J. Brewer. St. Louis, Mo.,
Kaiser, 1900. 10 v.

Alphabetical. A great deal of English and Amer. but all interesting selections, with indication of source, translator etc.

THE WORLD'S BEST POEMS. Ed. Mark Van Doren and Garibaldi M.
Lapolla. [1929] Cleveland, Ohio, and N.Y., World, 1946. xv,
xxi–xlv, 672 p.

750 poems from 19 languages including Gaelic, Old Norse, Sanskrit.

* THE WORLD'S GREAT CLASSICS. Ed. Julian Hawthorne. N.Y., Colo-
nial Pr., and London, M. Walter Dunne, 1899–1902. 61 v.

Inclusive: Babylonian, Assyrian, Armenian, Egyptian, Hebrew, Moorish,
Malaysian, Turkish, Persian, Arabian, Indian, Chinese, Japanese (v. 57
is Sacred Books of the East) as well as European from Greek to de Tocque-
ville and Taine (*History of English Literature*, v. 24–26). Also memoirs,
orations, decisive battles, essays, ideal commonwealths, Froissart's *Chronicles*, Montesquieu, Voltaire's *History of Charles XII*, Kant, Hegel, Dante,
Tasso.

WRITERS OF THE WESTERN WORLD. Ed. Cyril B. Judge. U.S. Naval
Academy Ed., ed. [Clarence] Addison Hibbard. [1942] Boston and
N.Y., Houghton Mifflin, 1946. xxii, 1261 p.

GREEK AND ROMAN LITERATURE

Konrad Gries

BACKGROUND

General Reference

ATLAS OF THE CLASSICAL WORLD. Ed. A. A. M. van der Heyden and
H. H. Scullard. London and N.Y., Nelson, 1959. 221 p. Repr. as
Shorter Atlas of the Classical World, ibid., 1962. 238 p.

A picture book (475 plates, 73 maps in the original ed.) dealing systematically with the political, social, and cultural history of the classical pagan
world; abundant and detailed explanatory text.

THE CAMBRIDGE ANCIENT HISTORY. Ed. J. B. Bury, et al. Cambridge
Univ. Pr., and N.Y., Macmillan, 1924–39. 12 v. with 5 additional v.
of plates.

V.1 and 2 are in process of revision, the revised chapters being issued in
separate fascicles as they become available. The first of them ("Troy" by
C. W. Blegen) was published in 1961.

CROON, J. H. The Encyclopedia of the Classical World. Tr. J. Muller-Van
Santen from the Dutch (Amsterdam, Elsevier, 1962), with emenda-
tions by Claire Jones. Englewood Cliffs, N.J., Prentice-Hall, 1965.
Cloth and paper. viii, 239 p.

EVERYMAN'S CLASSICAL DICTIONARY 800 B.C.–A.D. 337. Rev. by
John Warrington. EL, 1952. Repr. 1961, xxxvii, 537 p.

A compact volume for rapid consultation. Originally ed. Sir William
Smith as *A Smaller Classical Dictionary,* London, 1852 et seq.; after many
re-eds., rev. E. H. Blakeney, EL, 1910 et seq., with same title.

HARPER'S DICTIONARY OF CLASSICAL LITERATURE AND ANTI-
QUITIES. Ed. Harry Thurston Peck. N.Y., Harper, and London,
Osgood, 1897. Many re-eds. to latest repr. N.Y., Cooper Square
Publishers, 1963, xv, 1701 p., 1500 ill.

THE OXFORD CLASSICAL DICTIONARY. Ed. M[ax] Cary, et al. Oxford, Clarendon Pr., and N.Y., Oxford Univ. Pr., 1949. xx, 971 p.

Similar in design to *Paulys Real-Encyclopädie* (see next item), but more limited in scope, this is the standard reference work in English.

PAULYS REAL-ENCYCLOPÄDIE DER CLASSISCHEN ALTERTUMS-WISSENSCHAFT. Stuttgart, J. B. Metzler, 1899—.

This monumental German work, begun by August Friedrich von Pauly and continued successively by W. Kroll, K. Mittelhaus, K. Ziegler, and W. John, is the standard reference work on all matters pertaining to classical antiquity (including persons and places), with articles contributed by specialists from many countries, arranged alphabetically and supplied with bibliographies. The volumes have been issued in two series: v. 1–24 (as of 1964), Aal-Quosenus, and v. 1A–9A,1 (1961), Ra-Vulca. In addition, there are nine supplementary volumes, the latest dated 1962.

SARTON, GEORGE. Introduction to the History of Science. V. 1, From Homer to Omar Khayyam. Washington D.C., Carnegie Institution, 1927.

This monumental work, which in its five volumes reaches the year 1400, is among other things a bibliography of the history of learning, including science, in the Orient as well as in Europe. It is especially valuable for its capsule accounts of the lives and writings of individual authors.

SEYFFERT, OSKAR. A Dictionary of Classical Antiquities: Mythology, Religion, Literature, Art. Tr. from the German (original, 1882), rev. and ed. Henry Nettleton and J. E. Sandys. London, Sonnenschein, and N.Y., Macmillan 1891. Many re-eds., latest repr. (of 3d ed., 1899), N.Y., Meridian Books, 1956, 716 p. paper.

HISTORY

THE CAMBRIDGE ANCIENT HISTORY. See above, General Reference.

GRANT, MICHAEL. The Birth of Western Civilization: Greece and Rome. N.Y. and London, McGraw-Hill, 1964. 360 p., 727 ill.

ROSTOVTZEFF, M[IKHAIL] I[VANOVICH]. A History of the Ancient World. Tr. J. D. Duff from the Russian. Oxford, Clarendon Pr., and N.Y., Oxford Univ. Pr., 1926–27. 2 v. Re-ed. 1930–33.

V. 1, The Orient and Greece (418 p.); v. 2, Rome (404 p.). Part of v. 1 as *Greece* (see Greek below); v. 2 repr. as *Rome* (see Roman, below). See also in the same respective places his *Social and Economic History of the Hellenic World*, and *of the Roman Empire*.

STARR, CHESTER G. A History of the Ancient World. N.Y., Oxford Univ. Pr., 1965. xvii, 742 p., 52 ill.

MYTHOLOGY

AKEN, A. R. A. Van. The Encyclopedia of Classical Mythology. Tr. D. R. Welsh from the Dutch (Amsterdam, Elsevier, 1961). Englewood Cliffs, N.J., Prentice-Hall, 1965. iv, 155 p., cloth and paper.

GRANT, MICHAEL. Myths of the Greeks and Romans. London, Weidenfeld, and N.Y., World, 1962. xxiii, 487 p. Repr. N.Y., New American Library, 1964. 432 p. paper.

LAROUSSE ENCYCLOPEDIA OF MYTHOLOGY. Tr. Richard Aldington and Delano Ames from the French (Paris, Larousse, 1935, ed. Felix Guirand). London, Batchworth Pr., and N.Y., Prometheus Pr. (distributed by Putnam), 1959. xii, 500 p., 842 ill. *1960 intro Robert graves*

ROSE, H. J. A Handbook of Greek Mythology including its Extension to Rome. London, Methuen, 1928, and N.Y., Dutton, 1929. Re-ed. to 8th ed., 1958, repr. 1964, ix, 363 p.

CULTURAL ASPECTS AND INFLUENCES

BUNBURY, E. H. A History of Ancient Geography Among the Greeks and Romans. London, Murray, 1879. 2 v. Re-ed., 1883; N.Y., Dover, 1959.

BURGH, W. G. de. The Legacy of Greece and Rome. London, Macdonald and Evans, 1912. xi, 192 p. Re-ed. as The Legacy of the Ancient World, London and N.Y., Macmillan, 1924, xvi, 462 p. Repr. N.Y., 1926; rev. ed., London, Macdonald and Evans, 1947, xx, 548 p.; repr. Penguin, 1961, xvi, 608 p.

COCHRANE, CHARLES NORRIS. Christianity and Classical Culture: A Study of Thought and Action from Augustus to Augustine. Oxford, Clarendon Pr., 1940. xi, 523 p. Repr. London and N.Y., Oxford Univ. Pr., 1944; 1957, paper.

HICKS, R. D. Stoic and Epicurean. N.Y., Scribner, and London, Longmans, 1910. xix, 412 p. Repr., N.Y., Russell, 1962.

KERENYI, KAROLY. The Religion of the Greeks and Romans. Tr. Christopher Holme from German (original, 1940, re-ed. 1952). London, Thames and Hudson, and N.Y., Dutton, 1962. 303 p., 124 ill.

LAROUSSE ENCYCLOPEDIA OF PREHISTORIC AND ANCIENT ART. Tr. Michael Heron, Corinne Lambert, and Wendela Schurmann from the French (ed. René Huyghe, Paris, Larousse, 1957). London, Hamlyn, and N.Y., Prometheus Pr. (distributed by Putnam), 1962. 414 p., 761 ill.

MARROU, H. I. A History of Education in Antiquity. Tr. George Lamb from the French (Paris, 1948, et seq.). London and N.Y., Sheed and Ward, 1956. xviii, 466 p. Repr. N.Y., New Amer. Library, 1964, 600 p. paper.

MULLER, HERBERT J. Freedom in the Ancient World. N.Y., Harper, 1961, and London, Secker, 1962. ix, 360 p. Repr. N.Y., Bantam, 1964.

NEUGEBAUER, OTTO. The Exact Sciences in Antiquity. Princeton, N.J., Princeton Univ. Pr., and London, Oxford Univ. Pr., 1952. xvi, 191 p. Re-ed. Providence, R.I., Brown Univ. Pr., 1957, xi, 240 p.; repr. N.Y., Harper, 1962, paper.

OUR DEBT TO GREECE AND ROME. Ed. George D. Hadzsits and David M. Robinson. Boston, Mass., Marshall Jones, 1922–24, N.Y., Longmans, 1925–35, and London, Harrap, 1922–28. 44 v. Repr., N.Y., Cooper Square Publishers, 1963.

This series of volumes by leading classical scholars discusses important cultural topics and the work of important writers. The volumes dealing with Greece and Rome together are listed here; those dealing with Greece and Rome separately, and with individual authors, are listed in appropriate places below.

V. 3. Ancient Beliefs in the Immortality of the Soul, by Clifford H. Moore. 1931. xi, 188 p.

V. 4. Ancient Education and its Meaning for Us, by John F. Dobson. 1932. v, 205 p.

V. 5. Ancient Writing and its Influence, by B. L. Ullman. 1932. vii, 234 p.

V. 7. Architecture, by Alfred M. Brooks. 1924. xix, 189 p.

V. 13. Engineering, by Alexander P. Gest. 1930. xv, 221 p.

V. 15. Greek and Roman Folklore, by William R. Halliday. 1927. xi, 154 p.

V. 23. Language and Philology, by Roland G. Kent. 1924. vii, 174 p.

V. 24. Love of Nature among the Greeks and Romans, by H. R. Fairclough. 1930. ix, 270 p.

V. 28. Mathematics, by David Eugene Smith. 1923. x, 175 p.

V. 30. Mythology, by Jane E. Harrison. 1924. xx, 155 p.

V. 35. Psychology Ancient and Modern, by George S. Brett. 1928. ix, 164 p.

V. 40. Stage Antiquities, by James T. Allen. 1927. xii, 206 p.

V. 41. Stoicism and its Influence, by Robert M. Wenley. 1924. xi, 194 p. Repr. 1927.

V. 44. Warfare by Land and Sea, by Eugene S. McCartney. 1923. xix, 206 p. Repr. 1931.

REYMOND, ARNOLD. History of the Sciences in Greco-Roman Antiquity. Tr. Ruth Gheury de Bray from the French (Paris, Blanchard, 1924). London, Methuen, and N.Y., Dutton, 1927. x, 245 p. Repr. N.Y., Biblio and Tannen, 1963.

ROBERTSON, D. S. A Handbook of Greek and Roman Architecture. Cambridge Univ. Pr., 1929. xxiv, 406 p., and 159 ill. Repr. 1943, and N.Y., Macmillan, 1944.

SELTMAN, CHARLES. Women in Antiquity. London, Thames and Hudson, 1956, and N.Y., St. Martin's Pr., 1957. 224 p., 45 ill. Repr. London, Pan Books, 1956; N.Y., Collier Books, 1962, paper.

TATON, RENÉ, ed. Ancient and Medieval Science from the Beginnings to 1450. Tr. A. J. Pomerans from the French (Paris, Presses Universitaires, 1957). N.Y., Basic Books, 1963, and London, Thames and Hudson, 1964. xx, 552 p., 104 ill.

V. 1. of *A History of Science* to 1800 (2 v.).

THOMSON, J. OLIVER. History of Ancient Geography. London, Cambridge Univ. Pr., 1948, and N.Y., the same, 1949. x, 427 p., 68 ill. Repr. N.Y., Biblio and Tannen, 1965.

TOZER, H. F. A History of Ancient Geography. Cambridge Univ. Pr., 1897. xvii, 387 p. Re-ed. with notes by M. Cary, 1935. Repr. N.Y., Biblio and Tannen, 1964.

URE, P. N. The Origin of Tyranny. Cambridge Univ. Pr., and N.Y., Macmillan, 1922. xi, 347 p., 46 ill. Repr. N.Y., Russell, 1962.

BIBLIOGRAPHY

BRUEGGEMANN, LUDWIG WILHELM. A View of the English Editions, Translations and Illustrations of Ancient Greek and Latin Authors. Stettin, I. S. Leich, 1797–1801. xvi, 838, 150 p. (1 v. plus supplement). Repr. N.Y., Burt Franklin, 1964, 2 v.

FARRAR, CLARISSA P., and EVANS, AUSTIN P. Bibliography of English Translations from Medieval Sources. N.Y. and London, Columbia Univ. Pr., 1946. xiv, 534 p.

This painstaking work includes translations from Latin and Greek literature written between 300 and 1500 A.D. and from Greek Christian literature from the first century A.D.

MCGUIRE, MARTIN R. P. Introduction to Classical Scholarship: A Syllabus and Bibliographical Guide. Washington, D.C., Catholic University Pr., 1958. xvii, 204 p., paper, with separately paged (1–86) bibliography.

NAIRN, J. A. Classical Hand-list. Oxford, Blackwell, 1931. Re-ed. to 3d ed., 1953. viii, 164 p.

A comprehensive list of books relating to the classics and to classical antiquity.

SMITH, F. SEYMOUR. The Classics in Translation. London and N.Y., Scribner, 1930. 307 p.

An annotated guide to the best trs. (in the author's judgement) of some Greek and Latin authors, including medieval and Renaissance Latin. More authoritative lists of English trs. in certain periods are: Henrietta R. Palmer, *A List of English Editions and Translations of the Classics Printed Before 1641* (London, Bibliographical Society, 1911. xxxii, 119 p.); and in the *Cambridge Bibliography of English Literature* (Cambridge Univ. Pr., and N.Y., Macmillan, 1941, 4 v.), v. 1 (1500 to 1660), p. 799–809, and v. 2 (1660–1800), p. 758–768. Studies of the earlier trs. are: Carey H. Conley, *The First English Translators of the Classics* (New Haven, Conn., Yale Univ. Pr., and London, Oxford Univ. Pr., 1927. 158 p.); and Henry B. Lathrop, *Translations from the Classics into English from Caxton to Chapman*, 1477–1620 (Univ. of Wisconsin Studies in Language and Literature 34, 1934, 350 p.).

CURRENT BIBLIOGRAPHIES
(in chronological order of the years covered)

JAHRESBERICHT ÜBER DIE FORTSCHRITTE DER KLASSISCHEN ALTERTUMSWISSENSCHAFT. Berlin, Calvary, 1875–1898; Leipzig. Reisland, 1899–1943.

This annual annotated bibliography, popularly known from its first editor as Bursian, is the fullest and most complete.

THE YEAR'S WORK IN CLASSICAL STUDIES. Ed. for the Classical Association by various scholars. London, Murray, 1907–50.

This series covers material through 1947.

L'ANNÉE PHILOLOGIQUE: bibliographie critique et analytique de l'antiquité gréco-latine. Paris, Les belles lettres, 1928—.

The only complete current bibliographical survey. Founded by J. Marouzeau, it has been ed. by Juliette Ernst since v. 33 (for 1962, pub. 1964). Two supplementary surveys form a "bibliographie récapitulative". *Bibliographie de l'antiquité classique (1896–1914)*, ed. Scarlat Lambrino, v. 1 Paris, ibid., 1951, xvi, 761 p.), dealing with "auteurs et textes", with a planned v. 2 to deal with "matières et disciplines". This work is designed to lead up to *Dix années de bibliographie critique et analytique de l'antiquité gréco-latine pour la période 1914–1924*, ed. J. Marouzeau (Paris,, *ibid.,* 1927–28, 2 v.; 1 repr. rev. 1957).

New books on the classics and on classical antiquity are listed in the monthly *The Classical World* (N.Y., Fordham Univ., 1957—).

LITERARY STUDIES

General

ATKINS, J. W. H. Literary Criticism in Antiquity: A Sketch of its Development. Cambridge Univ. Pr., and N.Y., Macmillan, 1934, 2 v. Repr. Gloucester, Mass., Peter Smith, 1961. (v. 1, Greek; v. 2, Graeco-Roman).

BIEBER, MARGARETE. The History of the Greek and Roman Theater. Princeton, N.J., Princeton Univ., Pr., 1939. 2d rev. ed., *ibid.,* 1961, 343 p.

FEDER, LILLIAN. Crowell's Handbook of Classical Literature. N.Y., Crowell, and London, Barker (as The Handbook of Classical Literature), 1964. 450 p.

GOODSPEED, EDGAR J. A History of Early Christian Literature (to c. A.D. 300). Chicago, Univ. of Chicago, Pr., 1942. xiii, 324 p. Repr. 1966.

GRUBE, G. M. A. The Greek and Roman Critics. London, Methuen, 1965. 372 p.

HARSH, PHILIP WHALEY. A Handbook of Classical Drama. Stanford, Calif., Stanford Univ. Pr., and London, Oxford Univ. Pr., 1944. xii, 526 p. Repr. 1948.

LABRIOLLE, PIERRE DE. The History and Literature of Christianity: from Tertullian to Boethius. Tr. Herbert Wilson from French. [Paris, les belles lettres, 1920] 2d ed. rev. enl. London, Kegan Paul, and N.Y., Knopf, 1925, xxiii, 555 p.

THE OXFORD COMPANION TO CLASSICAL LITERATURE. Ed. Sir Paul Harvey. Oxford, Clarendon Pr., and N.Y., Oxford Univ. Pr., 1937. xi, 468 p. Repr. rev., 1940, 1951.

A dictionary guide to authors, dates, events, characters in literature and mythology, etc., with maps and plates. It does not include Christian Literature.

QUASTEN, JOHANNES. Patrology. Westminster, Md., and Utrecht/Antwerp, Spectrum Pub., 1950—. 3 v. (v. 4 to come).

V. 1, Beginnings of Patristic Literature; v. 2, The Ante-Nicene Literature after Irenaeus; v. 3, The Golden Age of Greek Patristic Literature from the Council of Nicaea to the Council of Chalcedon (A.D. 451).

ROOY, C. A. van. Studies in Classical Satire and Related Literary Theory. Leiden, Brill, 1965. xiii, 229 p.

ROSE, H. J. Outlines of Classical Literature for Students of English. London, Methuen, 1959. Repr. Cleveland and N.Y., World (Meridian Books), 1961, paper. xiv, 303 p. (omitting the last four words of the title).

TUSCULUM-LEXIKON GRIECHISCHER UND LATEINISCHER AUTOREN des Altertums und des Mittelalters. Ed. Wolfgang Buchwald, Armin Hohlweg, and Otto Prinz. Munich, Heimeran, 1963. xvi, 544 p.

This work grew out of Eduard von Stemplinger, *Griechischer-lateinischer Literatur-führer* (1934. 234 p.); it was published under its present title in 1948, ed. Wilhelm Schöne and Hans Ruppert (281 p.). A valuable compact dictionary of authors and their works.

Literary Influences on Later Literatures

BOLGAR, R. R. The Classical Heritage and its Beneficiaries from the Carolingian Age to the End of the Renaissance. London and N.Y., Cambridge Univ. Pr., 1954. Repr. N.Y., Harper, 1964, paper. viii, 591 p.

HIGHET, GILBERT. The Classical Tradition: Greek and Roman Influences on Western Literature. Oxford, Clarendon Pr., and N.Y., Oxford Univ. Pr., 1949. xxxviii, 763 p. Repr. N.Y., 1957, paper.

SANDYS, (SIR) JOHN EDWIN. A History of Classical Scholarship. Cambridge Univ. Pr., 1903–1908. 3 v. Re-eds. to 3d ed., 1935, repr. N.Y., Hafner, 1958. 3 v.

V. 1, To the end of the Middle Ages; v. 2, To the end of the Eighteenth Century (except for 18th c. Germany); v. 3, The Eighteenth Century in Germany, the Nineteenth Century in Europe and the United States.

TAYLOR, HENRY OSBORN. The Classical Heritage of the Middle Ages. N.Y., Columbia Univ. Pr., 1901. Re-eds. to 4th ed., rev., N.Y., Ungar, 1961, xv, 416 p., cloth and paper.

COLLECTIONS

BOHN'S CLASSICAL LIBRARY (BCL). London, Bohn (later Bell), 1848–1913. 116 v.

Now largely superseded by later trs.

CLASSICAL LITERARY CRITICISM. Tr. T. S. Dorsch. Penguin, 1965. 157 p.

Aristotle, Horace, Longinus.

GREEK AND ROMAN CLASSICS IN TRANSLATION. Ed. Charles T. Murphy, Kevin Guinagh, and Whitney J. Oates. N.Y., Longmans, 1947. lvi, 1052 p.

GREEK AND ROMAN PHILOSOPHY AFTER ARISTOTLE. Ed. Jason L. Saunders. N.Y., Free Press, and London, Collier-Macmillan, 1966. xi, 371 p.

Selections to Tertullian, various trs.

* THE LOEB CLASSICAL LIBRARY (LCL). London, Heinemann, and N.Y., Putnam (later Cambridge, Mass., Harvard Univ. Pr.), 1912—.

Described as A Comprehensive and Uniform Series of Classical Greek and Latin Texts with Parallel English Translations, this series is notable for the standards of scholarship maintained in both the texts and the trs. Each volume is equipped with introduction, brief critical apparatus, and compact exegetical notes. 425 volumes have been published by 1965; individual volumes are noted below (as LCL) under the individual classical author.

MASTERS OF ANCIENT COMEDY. Tr. Lionel Casson. N.Y., Macmillan, 1960. xi, 424 p.

Selected plays: Aristophanes, *Acharnians*; Menander: *Grouch, Woman of Samos, Arbitration,* and *She Who Was Shorn;* Plautus: *Haunted House,*

Rope; Terence: *Phormio, Brothers.* Notable as the only volume containing all the plays of Menander in tr.

PRIVATE LETTERS PAGAN AND CHRISTIAN. Ed. and tr. Dorothy Brooke. London, Benn, 1929, and N.Y., Dutton, 1930. 207 p.

An anthology of Greek and Roman private letters from 500 B.C. to A.D. 500.

THE STOIC AND EPICUREAN PHILOSOPHERS: The Complete Extant Writings of Epicurus, Epictetus, Lucretius, Marcus Aurelius. Ed. Whitney J. Oates. N.Y., Random House, 1940. xxvi, 627 p.

Trs.: C. Bailey, F. S. Matheson, H. A. J. Munro, G. Long.

CHRISTIAN LITERATURE

GEORGE B. PARKS

ANCIENT CHRISTIAN WRITERS: The Works of the Fathers in Translation. Ed. Johannes Quasten and Joseph C. Plumpe. Westminster, Md., Newman Pr., and London, Longmans, 1946— (34 v. to date).

Apostolic Fathers (1, 6); Arnobius (7, 8); Athanasius (10); Athenagoras (23); Augustine (2, 3, 5, 9, 12, 15, 22, 29, 30); Barnabas (6); Chrysostom (31); Clement of Rome (1); Cyprian (25); the *Didache* (6); Diognetus (6); Gregory the Great (11); Gregory of Nyssa (18); Ignatius (1); Irenaeus (16); Jerome (22); Maximus Confessor (21); Methodius (27); Origen (19, 26); Palladius (34); Papias (6); Patrick (17); Polycarp (6); Pomerius (4); Prosper of Aquitaine (14, 32); Rufinus Tyrannius (20); Tertullian (13, 24, 28).

ANTE-NICENE CHRISTIAN LIBRARY: Translations of the Writings of the Fathers down to A.D. 325. Ed. Alexander Roberts and James Donaldson. Edinburgh, Clark, 1868–72. 24 v.; v. 25 (ed. Allen Menzies), 1896. Repr. as The Ante-Nicene Fathers, ed. A. Cleveland Coxe, Buffalo, N.Y., Christian Literature Pub. Co., 1885–97, 10 v.; repr. N.Y., Scribner, 1899–1900, 10 v.; repr. ibid., 1917–25. 10 v.;

repr. ibid., 1926. 10 v.; repr. Grand Rapids, Mich., Eerdmans, 1951. 10 v.

(Arabic numerals indicate the volume in the first ed., hereafter called Ante-Nicene Library; and Roman numerals the volume in the later eds., called Ante-Nicene Fathers. For contents by volumes, see Library of Congress Catalogue.) *Apocrypha of the New Testament* (16, 25; VIII, IX); Apostolic Fathers (1; I, VII, IX); Arnobius (19; VI); Athenagoras (2; II) Clement of Alexandria (4, 12, 22, 24; II); Clement of Rome (1, 17; I, VIII, IX); Commodianus (18; IV); Cyprian (8, 13; V); Dionysius of Alexandria (20; VI); Hippolytus (6, 9; V); Irenaeus (5, 9; I); Julius Africanus (9; VI); Justin Martyr (2; I); Lactantius (21, 22; VII); Methodius (14; VI); Minucius Felix (13; IV); Novatian (13; V); Origen (10, 23, 25; IV, IX); Peter of Alexandria (14; VI); Tatian (3, 25; II, IX); Tertullian (7, 11, 15, 18; III, IV); Theophilus (3; II).

APOCRYPHA OF THE NEW TESTAMENT. See Greek Christian Literature, below.

THE APOSTOLIC FATHERS. See Greek Christian Literature, below.

THE BIBLE. See Hebrew Literature, in v. V.

THE EARLY CHRISTIAN FATHERS: A Selection . . . from St. Clement of Rome (to St. Athanasius). Tr. Henry Bettenson. London and N.Y., Oxford Univ. Pr., 1956. vii, 424 p.

THE FATHERS OF THE CHURCH: A New Translation. Ed. Roy J. Deferrari et al. Washington, D.C., Catholic Univ. Pr., 1946— (in progress).

The first volumes were published in New York, under the successive imprints of Cima Publishing Co., and Fathers of the Church, Inc. The series has reached v. 57; 100 are projected. The authors so far published and the volumes in which they appear are as follows: Ambrose (22, 26, 42, 44); Apostolic Fathers (1); Athanasius (15); Augustine (2, 4, 5, 8, 11, 12, 14, 16, 18, 21, 24, 27, 30, 32, 35, 38, 45, 56); Barnabas (1); Basil (9, 13, 28, 46); Caesarius of Arles (31, 47); Chrysostom (33, 41); Clement of Alexandria (23); Clement of Rome (1); Cyprian (36, 51); the *Didache*

(1); Diognetus (1); Early Christian Biographies (15); Ennodius (15); Eugippius (55); Eusebius (19, 29); Gregory the Great (39); Gregory Nazianzen (22); Hermas (1); Hilary (25); Ignatius (1); Jerome (15, 48, 53, 57); John of Damascus (37); Justin Martyr (6); Lactantius (49, 54); Leo (34); Minucius Felix (10); Niceta (7); Orosius (50); Papias (1); Paulinus (7); Peter Chrysologus (17); Polycarp (1); Pontius (15); Possidius (15); Prosper (7, 32); Prudentius (43, 52); Rufinus (20); Salvian (3); Sulpicius Severus (7); Tertullian (10, 40); Valerian (17); Vincent of Lérins (7).

THE FATHERS OF THE PRIMITIVE CHURCH. Ed. and tr. Herbert Musurillo, S. J. N.Y., New Amer. Library, and London, New English Library, 1966. 272 p.

Clement of Rome to Athanasius and the first Council of Nicaea.

FATHERS OF THE THIRD CENTURY. Tr. S. D. F. Salmond. Ante-Nicene Library, v. 20, 1871. Repr. Ante-Nicene Fathers, v. VI, 1886. vii, 572 p.

Writings of Anatolius, Arnobius, Dionysius the Great, Gregory Thaumaturgus, Julius Africanus, Methodius, and minor writers.

LIBRARY OF CHRISTIAN CLASSICS (to A.D. 1600). Tr. various hands, ed. Cyril C. Richardson and Edward R. Hardy. Philadelphia, Westminster Pr., and London, Student Christian Movement Pr., 1953–61. 26 v.

1. Early Christian Fathers (Apostolic Fathers, Athenagoras, Irenaeus). 2. Alexandrian Christianity: Select Trs. of Clement and Origen. 3. Christology of the Later Fathers (Athanasius, Gregory of Nazianza, Gregory of Nyssa. Documents from the Councils). 4. Cyril of Jerusalem and Nemesius of Emesa. 5. Early Latin Theology (Tertullian, Cyprian, Ambrose, Jerome: Selections). 6. Augustine, Earlier Writings. 7. Augustine: *The Confessions, The Enchiridion*. 8. Augustine, Later Works. 9. Early Medieval Theology (Vincent de Lérins to Guibert of Nogent, 5th to 12th c.). 10. A Scholastic Miscellany, Anselm to Ockham. 11. Aquinas on Nature and Grace. 12. Western Asceticism (Sayings of the Fathers, Cassian, Rule of S. Benedict). 13. Late Medieval Mysticism (St. Bernard to Nicholas of Cusa). 14. Advocates of Reform from Wycliffe to Erasmus. 15. Luther,

Lectures on Romans. 16. Luther, Early Theological Works. 17. Luther and Erasmus on Free Will. 18. Luther, Letters of Spiritual Counsel. 19. Melanchthon and Bucer. 20, 21. Calvin, *Institutes*. 22. Calvin, Theological Treatises. 23. Calvin, Commentaries and Letters. 24. Zwingli and Bullinger. 25. Spiritual and Anabaptist Writers. 26. The English Reformers.

A LIBRARY OF THE FATHERS of the Holy Catholic Church Anterior to the Division of the East and West. Ed. E. B. Pusey. Tr. by Members of the English Church. Oxford, Parker, 1838–85. 48 v.

Ambrose (47); Athanasius (8, 13, 19, 38, 45); Augustine (1, 16, 20, 22, 24, 25, 26, 29, 30, 32, 37, 39); Chrysostom (4, 5, 6, 7, 9, 11, 12, 14, 15, 27, 28, 33, 34, 35, 36, 44); Cyprian (3, 17); Cyril of Alexandria (43, 46, 48); Cyril of Jerusalem (2); Ephraem the Syrian (41); Gregory (18, 21, 23, 31); Irenaeus (42); Justin Martyr (40); Pacian (7); Tertullian (10)

LOEB CLASSICAL LIBRARY (LCL).

Has published so far trs of Greek: Apostolic Fathers, Basil (Letters), Clement of Alexandria, Eusebius, John of Damascus; and of Latin: Augustine (*City of God*, *Confessions*, Letters), Jerome (Letters), Lactantius, Minucius Felix, Prudentius, Sidonius, Tertullian (*Apology, De spectaculis*).

NEW TESTAMENT. See The Bible, Hebrew Literature, in v. V.

A SELECT LIBRARY of the Nicene and Post-Nicene Fathers of the Christian Church. Tr. various hands, ed. Philip Schaff et al. N.Y., Christian Literature, 1886–90. 14 v. Repr. N.Y., Scribner, 1890–1908. 14 v.; repr. Grand Rapids, Mich., Eerdmans, 1956, 14 v. (Referred to below as Nicene Fathers.)

V. 1–8: Augustine (repr. rev. of the Marcus Dods tr., see below, Augustine).

V. 9–14. John Chrysostom (repr. rev. from Library of the Fathers).

————— Second Series. Ed. Philip Schaff and Henry Wace. Edinburgh, Clark, and N.Y., Christian Literature, 1890–1903. 14 v. Repr. Grand Rapids, Mich., Eerdmans, 1952–56, 14 v.

Ambrose (10), Athanasius (4), Basil (8), Cassian (11), Cyril of Jerusalem (7), Eusebius (1), Gennadius (3), Gregory the Great (12, 13),

Gregory Nazianzen (7), Gregory of Nyssa (5), Hilary of Poitiers (9), Jerome (3, 6), John of Damascus (9), Leo (12), Rufinus (3), Seven Ecumenical Councils, Canons and Decrees (14), Socrates (2), Sozomenus (2), Sulpicius Severus (11), Theodoret (3), Vincent of Lérins (11); Syriac authors: Aphranat (13), Ephraim Syrus (13).

TRANSLATIONS OF CHRISTIAN LITERATURE. London, S.P.C.K, and N.Y., Macmillan, 1898–1940.

Series 1: Greek Texts. Basil, Chrysostom, Clement of Alexandria, Clement of Rome, the *Didache*, Dionysius of Alexandria, Dionysius the Areopagite, Gregory of Nyssa, Gregory Thaumaturgus, Hermas, Hippolytus, Ignatius, Irenaeus, Justin Martyr, St. Macarius, Macarius Magnes, Origen, Palladius, Photius, Polycarp.

Series 2: Latin Texts. Augustine, Bernard, Cyprian, Ebbo, Epistle of the Gallican Churches, Minucius Felix, Novatian, Tertullian.

Series 3: Liturgical Texts. Ambrose, Anon. on the Sacraments, Anaphora of the Ethiopic Liturgy, Consecration Prayers, Coptic Offices, St. Silvia of Aquitaine (Aetheria).

Series 4: Oriental Texts. *Didascalia* (Ethiopic), Irenaeus (from an Armenian version).

Series 5: Lives of the Celtic Saints. St. Bernard, *Life of St. Malachy*; *Lives* of St. Ciaran (Latin and Irish); St. Patrick, *Life and Writings*; Rhygfarch, *Life of St. David*; Walahfrid Strabo, *Life of St. Gall*.

A TREASURY OF EARLY CHRISTIANITY. Ed. Anne Fremantle. N.Y., Viking, 1953. xiv, 625 p.

Selections, 1st c. to Bede: reprs. of various trs.

THE WRITINGS OF THE EARLY CHRISTIANS OF THE SECOND CENTURY. Tr. J. A. Giles. London, J. R. Smith, 1857. xvi, 270 p.

Selections from Athenagoras, Hegesippus, Theophilus, Tatian, etc.

GREEK LITERATURE

Konrad Gries and †Dwight L. Durling;
revised by Lillian Feder

BACKGROUND

A COMPANION TO GREEK STUDIES. Ed. Leonard Whibley. Cambridge Univ. Pr., 1905. Re-eds. to 4th ed. rev., 1931; repr. New York and London, Hafner, 1963, xxxviii, 790 p.

HISTORY

BARR, STRINGFELLOW. The Will of Zeus: A History of Greece from the Origins of Hellenic Culture to the Death of Alexander. Philadelphia, Pa., Lippincott, 1961, and London, Weidenfeld, 1962. xv, 496 p. Repr. N.Y., Dell, 1965, paper.

BLEGEN, CARL. Troy and the Trojans. N.Y., Praeger, and London, Thames and Hudson, 1963. 240 p.

BOARDMAN, JOHN. The Greeks Overseas. Penguin Books, 1964. 288 p., 99 ill., paper.

BOTSFORD, G. W., and SIHLER, E. G., eds. Hellenic Civilization. With Contributions from William L. Westermann, Charles J. Ogden, and others. N.Y., Columbia Univ. Pr., 1915. xiii, 719 p. Repr. N.Y., Octagon Books, 1965.

BOWRA, C. M., and The Editors of Time-Life Books. Classical Greece. N.Y., Time, Inc., 1965. 192 p., ill.

BURN, A[ndrew] R. Alexander the Great and the Hellenistic World. London, English Universities Press, 1947, and N.Y., Macmillan, 1948. xlii, 297 p. Re-ed. rev. N.Y., Collier Books, 1962, 221 p., paper.

——— Pericles and Athens. London, Hodder, 1948. xxv, 253 p. Repr. N.Y., Collier Books, 1962, paper.

BURY, J. B. A History of Greece to the Death of Alexander the Great. London, Macmillan, 1902. 2 v. Re-ed. to 3d ed., rev. Russell Meiggs, London and N.Y., Macmillan, 1951, xxv, 925 p., ill.

THE CAMBRIDGE ANCIENT HISTORY. See Greek and Roman, Background, above.

ELIOT, ALEXANDER, and the Editors of *Life*. Greece. N.Y., Time, Inc., 1963. 160 p., 111 ill.

FINLEY, M. I. The Ancient Greeks: An Introduction to their Life and Thought. London, Chatto, 1963, and N.Y., Viking, 1964. xiv, 178 p., 20 ill. Repr. N.Y., 1964, paper.

FLACELIÈRE, ROBERT. Daily Life in Greece at the Time of Pericles. Tr. Peter Green from the French (Paris, Hachette, 1959). London, Weidenfeld, and N.Y., Macmillan, 1965. xvi, 310 p., 39 ill.

FORSDYKE, (SIR EDGAR) JOHN. Greece before Homer. V. 1. Ancient Chronology and Mythology. London, Parrish, 1956, and N.Y., Norton, 1957. 176 p. Repr. N.Y., Norton, 1964.

GLOTZ, GUSTAVE, Aegean Civilization. Tr. M. R. Dobie and E. M. Riley from the French (Paris, 1923). London, Kegan Paul, and N.Y., Knopf, 1925. xvi, 422 p.

———— Ancient Greece at Work: An Economic History of Greece from the Homeric Period to the Roman Conquest. Tr. M. R. Dobie from the French (Paris, 1920). London, Kegan Paul, and N.Y., Knopf, 1926. xii, 402 p. Repr. N.Y., Barnes and Noble, 1965.

———— The Greek City and its Institutions. Tr. N. Mallinson from the French (Paris, 1928). London, Routledge, and N.Y., Knopf, 1929. xx, 416 p.

HAYWOOD, RICHARD MANSFIELD. Ancient Greece and the Near East. N.Y., McKay, and London, Vision Pr., 1964. xiii, 626 p.

THE HORIZON BOOK OF ANCIENT GREECE. Ed. William Harlan Hale and the Editors of Horizon Magazine. N.Y., American Heritage (distributed by Doubleday), 1965. 415 p., ill.

KITTO, H. D. F. The Greeks. Penguin, 1951. 256 p. Repr. Chicago, Aldine Pr., 1964.

LLOYD-JONES, HUGH, ed. The Greeks. London, Watts, 1962, and Cleveland, Ohio, World, 1963. 262 p. Repr. as The Greek World, Penguin, 1965. 264 p., 16 ill.

PALMER, LEONARD R. Mycenaeans and Minoans: Aegean Prehistory in the Light of the Linear B Tablets. London, Faber, 1961, and N.Y., Knopf, 1962. 264 p. Re-ed. London, Faber, 1965, 368 p.

PAYNE, ROBERT. Ancient Greece: The Triumph of a Culture. N.Y., Norton, 1964. 449 p., ill.

ROSTOVTZEFF, M. I. Greece. Tr. J. D. Duff from the Russian, ed. Elias J. Bickerman. London and N.Y., Oxford Univ. Pr., 1963. xx, 331 p. ill., paper; and Gloucester, Mass., Peter Smith, 1964, cloth.

Repr. rev. pertinent parts of v. 1 of *A History of the Ancient World*: see Greek and Roman, above.

———— The Social and Economic History of the Hellenistic World. Oxford, Clarendon Pr., and N.Y., Oxford Univ. Pr., 1941. 3 v., xxiv, viii, 1779 p., 112 ill.

STARR, CHESTER G. The Origins of Greek Civilization, 1100–650 B.C. N.Y., Knopf, 1961, and London, Cape, 1962. xviii, 385, ix p., 24 ill.

STOBART, J. C. The Glory That Was Greece: A Survey of Hellenistic Culture and Civilization. London, Sidgwick, 1911. xxiv, 289 p. Repr. 1915, 1933; rev., N.Y., Grove Pr., 1962, paper; rev. N.Y., Hawthorn Books, 1964.

TARN, SIR WILLIAM W. Hellenistic Civilization. London, Edward Arnold, and N.Y., Longmans, 1927. viii, 312 p. Re-ed. 1930; rev. 1952, xi, 372 p.

ZIMMERN, SIR ALFRED. The Greek Commonwealth: Politics and Economics in Fifth-Century Athens. Oxford, Clarendon Pr., 1911. 454 p. Re-ed. 1915, 1922, 1924, 1931; N.Y., ML, 1956; N.Y., and London, Oxford Univ. Pr., 1961, paper. 471 p.

GREEK THOUGHT

BONNARD, ANDRÉ. Greek Civilization. Tr. A. Lytton Sells (v. 1 and 2) and R. C. Knight (v. 3) from the French [Lausanne, 1954–57–59]. London, Allen and Unwin, and N.Y., Macmillan, 1957–61. 3 v.

V. 1, From the *Iliad* to the Parthenon, 1957, 199 p. V. 2, From the *Antigone* to Socrates, 1959, 248 p. V. 3, From Euripides to Alexandria, 1961, 288 p.

BOWRA, C. M. The Greek Experience. London, Weidenfeld, 1957, and Cleveland and N.Y., World, 1959. Repr. N.Y., New American Library, 1959. 223 p., paper.

BRUMBAUGH, ROBERT S. The Philosophers of Greece. N.Y., Crowell, 1964. xi, 276 p., 15 ill.

BURNET, JOHN. Early Greek Philosophy. London, Black, 1892. vi, 378 p. Re-eds. to 4th ed., 1930 (also N.Y., Macmillan); repr. N.Y., World, 1964, paper.

———— Greek Philosophy: Part I. Thales to Plato. London and N.Y., Macmillan, 1914. x, 360 p. Re-ed. 1920, 1928, and London, Macmillan, and N.Y., St. Martin's Press, 1961, paper.

CLAGETT, MARSHALL. Greek Science in Antiquity. N.Y., and London, Abelard-Schuman, 1956. 217 p. Re-ed. N.Y., Collier Books, 1963, paper. 256 p., 39 ill.

FARRINGTON, BENJAMIN. Greek Science: Its Meaning for Us. Penguin, 1953. 320 p. Repr. 1961.

Originally published in two parts: 1, Thales to Aristotle, 1944, repr. 1949; 2, Theophrastus to Galen, 1949.

GREENE, WILLIAM CHASE. Moira: Fate, Good and Evil and Greek Thought. Cambridge, Mass., Harvard Univ. Pr., and London, Oxford Univ. Pr., 1963. Repr. N.Y., Harper, 1963, paper. vii, 450 p.

GULICK, CHARLES B. Modern Traits in Old Greek Life. Our Debt to Greece and Rome. 1927. vii, 159 p.

GUTHRIE, W. K. C. The Greek Philosophers: From Thales to Aristotle. London, Methuen, and N.Y., Philosophical Library, 1950. Repr. N.Y., Harper, 1960. vii, 168 p. paper.

———— The Greeks and their Gods. London, Methuen, and Boston, Mass., Beacon Pr., 1950. Repr. rev. Boston, 1955, xiv, 388 p., paper.

HARRISON, JANE ELLEN. Epilegomena to the Study of Greek Religion. London, Cambridge Univ. Pr., and N.Y., Macmillan, 1921. 40 p. Repr. with Themis, 1962, see below.

———— Prolegomena to the Study of Greek Religion. Cambridge Univ. Pr., 1903. xxii, 680 p. Re-ed. 1908; 1922; N.Y., Meridian, 1955; London, Merlin Pr., 1961.

———— Themis: A Study of the Social Origins of Greek Religion. With an Excursus on the Ritual Forms Preserved in Greek Tragedy, by Gilbert Murray, and A Chapter on the Origin of the Olympic Games, by F. M. Cornford. Cambridge, Eng., Univ. Pr., 1912. xxxii, 559 p. Repr. Cleveland and N.Y., World, 1962; repr. with Epilegomena (see above), New Hyde Park, N.Y., Univ. Books, 1962. lvi, 600 p.

HYDE, WALTER W. Greek Religion and Its Survivals. Our Debt to Greece and Rome. 1923. ix, 230 p.

JAEGER, WERNER. Paideia: The Ideal of Greek Culture. Tr. Gilbert Highet from the German [2d ed., 1936–44–47]. Oxford, Blackwell, and N.Y., Oxford Univ. Pr., 1939–44. 3 v. Repr. 1945; repr. 1965, paper.

V. 1, Archaic Greece; The Mind of Athens; v. 2, In Search of the Divine Centre; v. 3, The . . . Age of Plato.

THE LEGACY OF GREECE. Ed. R. W. Livingstone. Oxford, Clarendon Pr., and N. Y., Oxford Univ. Pr., 1921. xii, 424 p., ill.

MYLONAS, GEORGE E. Eleusis and the Eleusinian Mysteries, Princeton, N.J., Princeton Univ., Pr., 1961. xx, 346 p.

NILSSON, MARTIN P. A History of Greek Religion. Tr. F. J. Fielden from the Swedish. Oxford, Clarendon Pr., and N.Y., Oxford Univ. Pr., 1925. Re-ed. 1949. iv, 316 p.

———— Greek Popular Religion. N.Y., Columbia Univ. Pr., and London, Oxford Univ. Pr., 1940. Repr., as Greek Folk Religion, N.Y., Harper. and London, Hamilton, 1961, paper. xviii, 166 p., 38 ill.

———— The Mycenaean Origin of Greek Mythology. Berkeley, Calif., Univ. of California Pr., and London, Cambridge Univ. Pr., 1932. vi, 258 p. Repr. N.Y., Norton, 1963, paper.

OTTO, WALTER F. Dionysus: Myth and Cult. Tr. Robert B. Palmer from the German (Frankfurt, 1960 [3d ed.]). Bloomington, Indiana Univ. Pr., 1965. xxi, 243 p.

———— The Homeric Gods: The Spiritual Significance of Greek Religion. Tr. Moses Hadas from the German (Bonn, Cohen, 1929). N.Y., Pantheon, 1954, and London, Thames and Hudson, 1955. viii, 310 p. Repr. Boston, Mass., Beacon Pr., 1964, paper.

ROSE, H. J. Ancient Greek Religion. London, Hutchinson, 1948, and N.Y., Longmans, 1950. 160 p.

SANTILLANA, GIORGIO DE. The Origins of Scientific Thought from Anaximander to Proclus, 600 B.C. to A.D. 500. (V. 1 of The History of Scientific Thought) Chicago, Univ. of Chicago, Pr., and London, Weidenfeld, 1962. 320 p. Repr. N.Y., New American Library, 1961.

SNELL, BRUNO. The Discovery of the Mind: The Greek Origins of European Thought. Tr. T. G. Rosenmeyer from the German. Oxford, Blackwell, and Cambridge, Mass., Harvard Univ. Pr., 1953. Repr. N.Y., Harper, 1960. xii, 325 p., paper.

TAYLOR, HENRY O. Greek Biology and Greek Medicine. Our Debt to Greece and Rome, 1922. xv, 159 p.

ART AND ARCHEOLOGY

ALSOP, JOSEPH. From the Silent Earth: A Report on the Greek Bronze Age. New York and London, Harper, 1964. xix, 296 p., 102 ill.

ARIAS, P. E. (text and notes), and HIRMER, MAX (photographs). A History of 1000 Years of Greek Vase Painting. Tr. rev. B. Shefton from the German (Munich, 1960). London, Thames and Hudson, and N.Y., Abrams, (1963) 410 p., 335 ill.

BARRON, JOHN. Greek Sculpture. London, Studio Vista, and N.Y., Dutton, 1965. 160 p., ill., paper.

BERVE, HELMUT, and GRUBEN, GOTTFRIED. Greek Temples, Theatres and Shrines. Photographs by Max Hirmer. Tr. Richard Waterhouse from the German (Munich, 1961). London, Thames and Hudson, and N.Y., Abrams, 1963. 508 p., 372 ill.

BIEBER, MARGARETE. The Sculpture of the Hellenistic Age. N.Y., Columbia Univ. Pr., and London, Oxford Univ. Pr., 1955. 232 p. Re-ed. rev. N.Y., 1961, xi, 259 p., 818 ill.

BOARDMAN, JOHN. Greek Art. London, Thames and Hudson, and N.Y., Praeger, 1964. 286 p., 251 ill., cloth and paper.

CASSON, STANLEY. The Technique of Early Greek Sculpture. Oxford, Clarendon Pr., and N.Y., Oxford Univ. Pr., 1933. xiii, 246 p.

CHARBONNEAUX, JEAN. Greek Bronzes. Tr. Katherine Watson from the French (Paris, 1958). London, Elek, and N.Y., Viking, 1962. 164 p., 53 ill.

DINSMOOR, WILLIAM B. The Architecture of Ancient Greece. London, Batsford, and N.Y., Scribner, 1927. x, 241 p., 65 pl. Re-ed., 1950. xxiv, 424 p., 260 ill.

Published as v. 1 of a re-ed. rev. of William J. Anderson and R. P. Spiers, *The Architecture of Greece and Rome* (London Batsford, 1900, xvii, 300 p., 179 ill.; rev. 1907, xxi, 359, p., 255 ill.)

FAIRBANKS, ARTHUR. Greek Art, The Basis of Later European Art. Our Debt to Greece and Rome. 1933. x, 136 p.

GARDNER, ERNEST ARTHUR. A Handbook of Greek Sculpture. London, Macmillan, 1905. xxii, 591 p. Re-ed., London and N.Y., Macmillan, 1915. xxxii, 605 p.; re-ed. 1920, 1924.

✓ HUTCHINSON, R. W. Prehistoric Crete. Penguin, 1962. 373 p., 105 ill.

LULLIES, REINHARD (text and notes) and HIRMER, MAX (photographs). Greek Sculpture. Tr. Michael Bullock from the German (Munich, 1956). London, Thames and Hudson, and N.Y., Abrams, 1957. 88 p., 264 ill. Re-ed. rev., 1960. 115 p., 323 ill.

✓ MACKENDRICK, PAUL. The Greek Stones Speak: The Story of Archeology in Greek Lands. N.Y., St. Martin's Pr., 1962, and London, Methuen, 1963. xviii, 470 p., 176 ill.

MARINATOS, SPYRIDON (text), and HIRMER, MAX (photographs). Crete and Mycenae. Tr. John Boardman from the Greek (Athens, 1959). London, Thames and Hudson, and N.Y., Abrams, 1960. 190 p., 421 ill.

MATZ, FRIEDRICH. The Art of Crete and Early Greece: The Prelude to Greek Art. Tr. Ann E. Keep from the German (Baden-Baden, 1962). N. Y., Crown, 1962, and London, Methuen, 1963 (as Crete and Early Greece). 259 p., 128 ill.

PENDLEBURY, J. D. S. The Archaeology of Crete: An Introduction. London, Methuen, 1939. xxxii, 400 p., 120 ill. Repr. N.Y., Biblio and Tannen, 1963; N.Y., Norton, 1965, paper.

RICHTER, GISELA M. A. The Sculpture and Sculptors of the Greeks. (Metropolitan Museum of Art). New Haven, Conn., Yale Univ. Pr., 1929. xxix, 242 p., ill. Re-ed. 1930. xxxiv, 613 p.; re-ed., 1950, and London, Oxford, Univ. Pr.

SCRANTON, ROBERT L. Greek Architecture. N.Y., Braziller, and London, Prentice-Hall, 1962. 128 p., 111 ill.

SCULLY, VINCENT. The Earth, the Temple, and the Gods: Greek Sacred Architecture. New Haven and London, Yale Univ. Pr., 1962. xxvi, 257 p., 424 ill.

SELTMAN, CHARLES. Approach to Greek Art. London, Studio Pubs., 1948. xi, 132 p., 111 ill. Re-ed. EL, 1960. 256 p., 204 ill.

TAYLOUR, LORD WILLIAM. The Mycenaeans. London, Thames and Hudson, and N.Y., Praeger, 1964. 243 p., 137 ill.

VERMEULE, EMILY. Greece in the Bronze Age. Chicago, Ill., and London, Univ. of Chicago Pr., 1964. xx, 406 p., 100 ill.

BIBLIOGRAPHY

In addition to the entries in Greek and Roman Bibliography, above, the following:

FOSTER, FINLEY M. K. English Translations from the Greek. N.Y., Columbia Univ. Pr., 1918. xxix, 146 p.

Does not include Christian literature.

LITERARY STUDIES

ARNOTT, PETER D. An Introduction to the Greek Theatre. London, Macmillan, and N.Y., St. Martin's Pr., 1959. Re-ed. Bloomington, Indiana Univ. Pr., 1963, xvi, 240 p.

BARDY, GUSTAVE. The Greek Literature of the Early Christian Church. Tr. Mother Mary Reginald from the French (Paris, 1928). London, Sands, 1929. vii, 191 p.

BOWRA, C. M. Ancient Greek Literature. London, Butterworth, and N.Y., Oxford Univ. Pr., 1933. Repr. Oxford Univ. Pr., 1949; ibid., 1960. 265 p., paper.

———— Early Greek Elegists. Cambridge, Mass., Harvard Univ. Pr., 1935, and London, Oxford Univ. Pr., 1938. 208 p. Repr. N.Y., Barnes and Noble, 1960.

———— Greek Lyric Poetry from Alcman to Simonides. Oxford, Clarendon Pr., and N.Y., Oxford Univ. Pr., 1936. viii, 490 p. Re-ed. 1961. viii, 444 p.

BURN, ANDREW R. The Lyric Age of Greece. London, Edward Arnold, and N.Y., St. Martin's Pr., 1960. xvi, 422 p.

CAMPBELL, JAMES M. The Greek Fathers. Our Debt to Greece and Rome. 1929. ix, 167 p.

FLACELIÈRE, ROBERT. A Literary History of Greece. Tr. Douglas Garman from the French (Paris, Fayard, 1962). London, Elek, and Chicago, Ill., Aldine Pr., 1964. x, 395 p., 16 ill.

FLICKINGER, ROY C. The Greek Theater and Its Drama. Chicago, Ill., Univ. of Chicago Pr., 1918. xxi, 358 p. 4 re-eds. to 1960, xxviii, 384 p., 89 ill.

HADAS, MOSES. History of Greek Literature. N.Y., Columbia Univ. Pr., and London, Oxford Univ. Pr., 1950. vi, 327 p. Re-ed. 1962.

HAVELOCK, ERIC ALFRED. Preface to Plato. (History of the Greek Mind, v. 1) Cambridge, Mass., Harvard Univ. Pr., 1963. xiv, 328 p.

JEBB, R. C. The Attic Orators from Antiphon to Isaeos. Cambridge, 1876. 2 v. Re-ed. London, Macmillan, 1893; repr. N.Y., Russell, 1962.

KITTO, H. D. F. Greek Tragedy: A Literary Study. London, Methuen, 1939. x, 410 p. Repr. rev., *ibid.*, and N.Y., Doubleday, 1954, paper; re-ed., London, Methuen, and N.Y., Barnes and Noble, 1961.

LATTIMORE, RICHMOND. The Poetry of Greek Tragedy. Baltimore, Md., Johns Hopkins Univ. Pr., and London, Oxford Univ. Pr., 1958. 158 p. Repr., N.Y., Harper, 1966, paper.

LEGRAND, PHILIPPE E. The New Greek Comedy. Tr. James Loeb from the French (Lyons, 1910). London, Heinemann, and N.Y., Putnam, 1917. xix, 547 p.

LESKY, ALBIN. Greek Tragedy. Tr. H. A. Frankfort from the German (Stuttgart and Leipzig, 1938; re-ed. 1958, 1964). London, Benn, and N.Y., Barnes and Noble, 1965. xiii, 229 p.

———— A History of Greek Literature. Tr. James Willis and Cornelius de Heer from the German (Bern, 1957–59, re-ed., 1963). London, Methuen, and N.Y., Crowell, 1966. xviii, 921 p.

LEVER, KATHERINE. The Art of Greek Comedy. London, Methuen, 1956, and N.Y., Hillary House, 1957. xi, 212 p.

MURRAY, GILBERT. A History of Ancient Greek Literature. London, Heinemann, and N.Y., Appleton, 1897. xvii, 420 p. Many reprs. to N.Y., Ungar, 1966.

NORWOOD, GILBERT. Greek Comedy. London, Methuen, 1931, and Boston, Luce, 1930. vii, 413 p. Re-ed., N.Y., Hill and Wang, 1963, paper, and London, Methuen, 1964.

———— Greek Tragedy. London, Methuen, and Boston, Luce, 1920. vii, 394 p. Re-eds. to 4th ed., London, 1948, repr. 1957, repr. N.Y., Hill and Wang, 1960.

PICKARD-CAMBRIDGE, A. W. Dithyramb, Tragedy and Comedy. Oxford, Clarendon Pr., and N.Y., Oxford Univ. Pr., 1927. xvi, 435 p. Re-ed. rev. T. B. L. Webster, *ibid.*, 1962, xii, 334 p., 22 ill.

ROBERTS, W. RHYS. Greek Rhetoric and Literary Criticism. Our Debt to Greece and Rome. 1928. vii, 164 p.

ROSE, H. J. A Handbook of Greek Literature from Homer to the Age of Lucian. London, Methuen, 1934. ix, 454 p. Re-ed. to 4th ed., 1950, re-ed. EL, 1960.

TRENKNER, SOPHIE. The Greek Novella in the Classical Period. Cambridge and N.Y., Cambridge Univ. Pr., 1958. xvi, 191 p.

WEBSTER, T. B. L. Hellenistic Poetry and Art. London, Methuen, 1964, and N.Y., Barnes and Noble, 1965. xx, 321 p.

WRIGHT, F. A. A History of Later Greek Literature, from the Death of Alexander in 323 B.C. to the Death of Justinian in 565 B.C. London, Routledge, 1923. 415 p. Re-ed. 1932, 1951.

COLLECTIONS

NOTE: *See also* Greek and Roman Literature, Collections, above.

ANCILLA TO THE PRE-SOCRATIC PHILOSOPHERS. Tr. Kathleen Freeman. Oxford, Blackwell, and Cambridge, Mass., Harvard Univ. Pr., 1948. xii, 162 p.

A complete tr. of Diels, *Fragmente der Vorsokratiker*.

AN ANTHOLOGY OF GREEK DRAMA. Ed. C. A. Robinson, verse trs. by various hands. N.Y., Rinehart, 1949. 269 p.

Includes trs. by R. C. Trevelyan, A. S. Way, C. T. Murphy.

THE ATHENIAN DRAMA . . . with Commentaries. London, George Allen, and N.Y., Longmans, 1900–1902. 3 v.

V. 1. Aeschylus (*Oresteia*). Tr. verse George C. W. Warr.

V. 2. Sophocles (*Oedipus Tyrannus, Oedipus Coloneus, Antigone*). Tr. verse John S. Phillimore.

V. 3. Euripides (*Hippolytus*) and Aristophanes (*Frogs*). Tr. verse Gilbert Murray.

CLASSICS IN TRANSLATION. V. 1, Greek Literature. Ed. Paul MacKendrick and Herbert M. Howe. Madison, Univ. of Wisconsin Pr., 1952. xiv, 426 p.

THE COMPLETE GREEK COMEDY. Ed. William Arrowsmith, tr. various hands. Ann Arbor, Univ. of Michigan Pr., 1961— (in progress, 5 plays of Aristophanes published separately to 1964).

THE COMPLETE GREEK DRAMA. Ed. Whitney J. Oates and Eugene O'Neill, Jr., prose and verse tr. various hands. N.Y., Random House, 1938. 2 v.

Includes trs. of Aeschylus by Morshead, Potter, More; of Sophocles by Trevelyan, Franklin, Jebb; of Euripides by Aldington, E. P. Coleridge, Murray, Potter, and Stawell; of Aristophanes by Murray, and the anonymous Athenian Society version; of Menander by Post.

THE COMPLETE GREEK TRAGEDIES. Ed. David Grene and Richmond Lattimore; tr. various hands. Univ. of Chicago Pr., 1953–59. 9 v. Repr. *ibid*. and Cambridge Univ. Pr., 1959, 4 v., and ML, 1961. 4 v. Selected plays repr. as Greek Tragedies, Chicago, 1960, 3 v.

For trs. of individual plays, see Library of Congress Catalogue.

ELEGY AND IAMBUS: The Remains of all the Greek Elegiac and Iambic Poets from Callinus to Crates, excepting the Choliambic Writers, with the Anacreontea. Ed. and tr. John Maxwell Edmonds. LCL, 1931. 2 v.

Prose trs. except of *Anacreontea*.

FIFTEEN GREEK PLAYS. Tr. Gilbert Murray, Robert Whitelaw, and Benjamin Bickley Rogers; ed. with intro. Lane Cooper. N.Y., Oxford Univ. Pr., 1943. xxii, 794 p.

Rev. and enl. ed. of *Ten Greek Plays* (1929). Includes passages tr. by Lane Cooper from Aristotle's *Poetics*.

FOUR GREEK PLAYS. Ed. Dudley Fitts, tr. by him et al. N.Y., Harcourt, 1960. 310 p.

Aeschylus, *Agamemnon*, tr. Louis MacNeice; Aristophanes, *The Birds*, tr. Dudley Fitts; Euripides, *Alcestis*, and Sophocles, *Oedipus,* tr. Dudley Fitts and Robert Fitzgerald.

FOUR GREEK PLAYS. Tr. and adapted Kenneth McLeish. London, Longmans, 1964. xviii, 205 p.

Sophocles, *Oedipus*, *Antigone*; Aristophanes, *Acharnians*, *Peace*.

GREAT BOOKS OF THE WESTERN WORLD. Chicago, Encyclopaedia Britannica, 1952. 54 v.

The works tr. from the Greek (usually the complete works) are: v. 4, Homer; 5, Four Dramatists; 6, Herodotus, Thucydides; 7, Plato; 8, 9, Aristotle; 10, Hippocrates, Galen; 11, Euclid, Archimedes, Apollonius of Perga, Nicomachus of Gerasa; 12, Epictetus, Marcus Aurelius; 14, Plutarch; 16, Ptolemy, 17, Plotinus. For the trs., see individual authors, below.

THE GREEK ANTHOLOGY. Tr. prose, chiefly by G. Burges, with verse tr. by others. BCL, 1848.

* Tr. prose W. R. Paton. LCL, 1916–18. 5 v.

This collection of short Greek poems by 320 authors from the 7th century B.C. was made in the 12th c. A.D. by Constantinos Cephalas. It is also known as the Palatine Anthology, since the single ms. is in the Palatine Library, Heidelberg.

Selections†

Ed. Graham R. Tomson (pseud.) as Selections from the Greek Anthology, trs. various. London, Scott, and N.Y., Cape, 1889. xl, 227 p.

Trs. include Garnett, Lang, Smith, Symonds.

* Tr. verse J.W. Mackail as Select Epigrams. London and N.Y., Longmans, 1890. 403 p. (parallel texts). Repr. rev. 1906, 1913; abridged, Mount Vernon, N.Y., Peter Pauper Pr., 1940, 127 p.

† See also, below, Greek Literary Papyri, LCL; Lyra Graeca; Oxford Book of Greek Verse.

Ed. G. B. Grundy, various trs., as Ancient Gems in Modern Settings. Oxford, Blackwell, and London and N.Y., Oxford Univ. Pr., 1913. lxii, 392 p.

Tr. verse Humbert Wolfe as Others Abide. London, Benn, 1927, and Garden City, N.Y., Doubleday, 1928. 118 p.

> An attempt at close tr. of a wide range of poems.

Tr. Shane Leslie. London, Benn, and N.Y., Appleton, 1929. 234 p.

Tr. verse F. L. Lucas as The Golden Cockerel Greek Anthology. London, Golden Cockerel Pr., 1937. 81 p. Enl. as A Greek Garland, London, and N.Y., Oxford Univ. Pr., 1939, 105 p.; repr. 1949.

Tr. Dudley Fitts as One Hundred Poems from the Greek Anthology in English Paraphrase. Norfolk, Conn., New Directions, 1938. 111 p. Repr. 1936. A sequel is more successful: More Poems from . . . *Ibid.*, 1941. 31 p.

Tr. Kenneth Rexroth. Ann Arbor, Univ. of Michigan Pr., 1962. 111 p.

Other trs. of selections: Robert Bland, 1813; Lord Neaves, 1874; W. H. D. Rouse, 1900; A. J. Butler, 1922; Walter Leaf, 1922; Richard Aldington, 1930; Robert A. Furness, 1931; A. S. Way (books v–vii), 1939; Forrest Reid, 1943. Cf. F A. Wright, *The Poets of the Greek Anthology* (London, Routledge, and N.Y., Dutton, 1924, 259 p.), and *The Girdle of Aphrodite* (*ibid.*, 1923, xxxvii, 315 p.), the latter illustrated by a number of trs.

GREEK ECCLESIASTICAL HISTORIANS of the First Six Centuries of the Christian Era. Tr. C. F. Crusé et al. London, Bagster, 1844–47. 6 v.

THE GREEK HISTORIANS: The Complete and Unabridged Historical Works. Ed. Francis R. B. Godolphin. N.Y., Random House, 1942. 2 v.

Includes Rawlinson's Herodotus, Jowett's Thucydides, Dakyns' Xenophon, Chinnock's Arrian.

GREEK LITERARY PAPYRI. Ed. and tr. D. L. Page. LCL, 1942, v. 1. 2 v. projected.

Important papyrus fragments of tragedy, comedy, mime, lyric, elegy, iambic verse, and hexameters are included.

GREEK LITERATURE IN TRANSLATION. Ed. George Howe and Gustave Adolphus Harrer. N.Y., Harper, 1924. Repr. rev. Preston Herschel Epps, 1948, 903 p.

An inclusive survey with trs. by many hands.

GREEK LITERATURE IN TRANSLATION. Ed. Whitney J. Oates and C. T. Murphy. N.Y., Longmans, 1914. 1072 p.

An inclusive survey with trs. by many hands.

GREEK LYRIC POETRY. Tr. verse Willis Barnstone. N.Y., Bantam, 1962. x, 194 p.

GREEK LYRICS. Tr. verse Richmond Lattimore. Chicago, Ill., Univ. of Chicago Pr., 1961. 81 p.

GREEK MATHEMATICAL WORKS. Ed. and tr. Ivor Thomas. LCL, 1939–41. 2 v.

GREEK ORATIONS: Lysias, Isocrates, Demosthenes, Aeschines, Hyperides. Ed. W. Robert Connor. Ann Arbor, Univ. of Michigan Pr., 1966. vii, 224 p.

GREEK PLAYS IN MODERN TRANSLATION. Ed. Dudley Fitts. N.Y., Dial Pr., 1947. 596 p.

Aeschylus, *Agamemnon*, tr. Richmond Lattimore; *Eumenides*, tr. George Thomson; *Prometheus Bound*, tr. Edith Hamilton. Sophocles, *Antigone*, tr. Dudley Fitts and Robert Fitzgerald; *Electra,* tr. Francis Fergusson; *Oedipus*, tr. W. B. Yeats; *Oedipus at Colonus*, tr. Dudley Fitts and Robert Fitzgerald. Euripides, *Alcestis*, tr. Fitts and Fitzgerald; *Hippolytus*, tr. David Grene; *Medea,* tr. Frederic Prokosch; *Trojan Women,* tr. Richmond Lattimore.

GREEK SONGS IN THE MANNER OF ANACREON. Tr. Richard Aldington. Poets' Translation Series, 2d set, no. 1. London, Egoist, 1919. 34 p.

HERODES, CERCIDAS, AND THE GREEK CHOLIAMBIC POETS (except Callimachus and Babinus). Ed. and tr. A. D. Knox. LCL, 1929. xxvi, 364 p.

LIBRARY OF GREEK THOUGHT. London, Dent, and N.Y., Dutton, 1923–34. 8 v. (translated selections).

Greek Astronomy. Tr. Sir T. L. Heath. 1932. lvii, 192 p.

Greek Economics. Ed. M. L. W. Laistner 1923. xiii, 204 p.

Greek Ethical Thought from Homer to the Stoics. Ed. Hilda Diana Oakley. 1925. xlii, 226 p.

Greek Geography. Ed. and tr. E. H. Warmington. 1934. xlvii, 269 p.

Greek Historical Thought from Homer to the Age of Heraclius. Ed. and tr. A. J. Toynbee and (two pieces) Gilbert Murray. 1924. xxxiv, 256 p. Repr. N.Y., Mentor Books, 1952.

Greek Medicine: Being Extracts Illustrative of Medical Writers from Hippocrates to Galen. Ed. and tr. A. J. Brock. 1929. 256 p.

Greek Religious Thought from Homer to the Age of Alexander. Ed. F. M. Cornford. 1923. xxxv, 252 p.

Later Greek Religion. Ed. Edwyn Robert Bevan. 1927. xl, 234 p.

LUCAS, F. L. Greek Poetry for Everyman. London, Dent, and N.Y., Macmillan, 1951. 414 p. Repr. as Greek Poetry, EL, 1966, xxxviii, 250 p.

Selections expertly tr. into verse by Lucas from Homer to 6th c. A.D. with useful notes. Wide range of material. Intended for nonclassical students.

LYRA GRAECA, Being the Remains of All the Greek Lyric Poets from Eumelus to Timotheus excepting Pindar. Ed. and tr. prose John Maxwell Edmonds. LCL, 1922–27. 3 v.

MINOR ATTIC ORATORS. Ed. and tr., v. 1, Kenneth John Maidment (Antiphon, Andocides); v. 2, tr. John Ormiston Burtt (Lycurgus, Dinarchus, Demades, Hyperides). LCL, 1941, 1954.

THE OXFORD BOOK OF GREEK VERSE IN TRANSLATION. Ed. T. F. Higham and C. M. Bowra, tr. various hands. Oxford, Clarendon Pr., and N.Y., Oxford Univ. Pr., 1938. cxii, 781 p.

124 translators, versions of various degrees of merit. An abridged version, *From the Greek*, pub. 1943, viii, 246 p.

OXYRHYNCHUS PAPYRI. Ed. and tr. B. P. Grenfell et al. London, Egypt Exploration Society, 1891–1941. 18 v.

Includes fragments of extant authors, new classical fragments, Homeric fragments, documents, etc.

SELECT PAPYRI. Tr. A. S. Hunt and C. C. Edgar. LCL, 1932–34. 4 v.

SELECTIONS FROM EARLY GREEK PHILOSOPHY. Ed. Milton Charles Nahm. 3d ed. N.Y., Crofts, 1947. 268 p.

SELECTIONS FROM HELLENISTIC PHILOSOPHY. Ed. Gordon Haddon Clark. N.Y., Crofts, 1940. 267 p.

SELECTIONS ILLUSTRATING THE HISTORY OF GREEK MATHE-MATICS. Ed. and tr. Ivor Thomas. LCL, 1939–41. 2 v.

A SOURCE BOOK IN GREEK SCIENCE. Ed. Morris Raphael Cohen and Israel E. Drabkin, N.Y., McGraw-Hill, 1948. 579 p.

TEN GREEK PLAYS IN CONTEMPORARY TRANSLATIONS. Ed. with intro. L. R. Lind. Boston Houghton Mifflin, 1957. xxviii, 419 p. paper.

Aeschylus: *Agamemnon*, tr. Louis MacNeice; *Prometheus Bound*, tr. Rex Warner; *Suppliants*, tr. L. R. Lind. Aristophanes: *Lysistrata*, tr. Charles T. Murphy. Euripides: *Andromache*, tr. L. R. Lind; *Bacchae*, tr. Henry Birkhead. Sophocles: *Alcestis*, tr. Richard Aldington; *Antigone*, tr. Shaemas O'Sheel; *Oedipus Rex*, tr. Albert Cook; *Philoctetes*, tr. Kathleen Freeman.

THREE GREEK PLAYS FOR THE THEATRE. Tr. verse Peter D. Arnott. Bloomington, Indinana Univ. Pr., 1964. 220 p.

Euripides, *Medea, Cyclops*; Aristophanes, *The Frogs*.

THREE GREEK ROMANCES. Tr. Moses Hadas. N.Y., Doubleday, 1953. 189 p.

Longus, *Daphnis and Chloe*; Xenophon, *An Ephesian Tale*; Dio Chrysostom, *The Hunters of Euboea*.

TRANSLATIONS OF CHRISTIAN LITERATURE. Series 1, Greek Texts. Ed. Philip Schaff and Henry Wace, tr. C. L. Feltoe et al. London, SPCK, 1918–40. 15 v.

INDIVIDUAL AUTHORS

EARLY AND CLASSICAL PERIODS: 1000 TO 323 B.C.

AENEAS TACTICUS (fl. c. 350 B.C.) On the Defence of Fortified Positions. Tr. Illinois Greek Club. LCL, 1923 et seq. (with Asclepiodotus and Onosander). x, 531 p.

AESCHINES (389–314 B.C.). The Speeches. Tr. Charles Darwin Adams. LCL, 1919. xxiii, 527 p.

AESCHYLUS (525-546 B.C.). The Tragedies. Tr. Robert Potter. Norwich, 1777. xxviii, 602 p. Many reprs. elsewhere to 1888.

Tr verse J. S. Blackie as The Lyrical Dramas. London, Parker, 1850. 2 v. Reprs. include EL, 1906 et seq.

Called "spirited" by Carlyle.

Tr. verse Edward H. Plumptre. London, Strahan, 1869. 2 v. Repr. 1869, 1873, 1882, 1901, 1914.

Called successful in the use of the original metres.

* Tr. verse E. D. Morshead in separate volumes: The Suppliant Maidens, etc. (4 plays). London, Simpkin and Marshall, 1881. 216 p. Repr. 1890

(Golden Treasury), 1901, 1908, 1921.—The House of Arteus (3 plays). *Ibid.,* 1881. xxvii, 187 p. Repr. 1889, 1890 (Golden Treasury), 1901 (Harvard Classics, v. 9).

Tr. verse Lewis Campbell as The Seven Plays. London, Kegan Paul, 1890. xvii, 349 p. Repr. rev. WC, 1906 et seq.

* Tr. verse Arthur S. Way. London and N.Y., Macmillan, 1906–8. 3 v.

Tr. prose Walter Headlam and C. E. S. Headlam. BCL, 1909, xvii, 319 p. Called "dignified."

* Tr. rhymed verse Gilbert Murray, published singly: Agamemnon, 1920; Libation-Bearers, 1923; Furies, 1925; Suppliant Women, 1930; prometheus Bound, 1931; Seven Against Thebes, 1935; Persians, 1939; all, London, Allen and Unwin, and N.Y., Oxford Univ. Pr., [1952]. 266 p.

* Tr. prose Herbert Weir Smyth. LCL, 1922-26. 2 v.

Tr. verse G. M. Cookson in two separate v.: Four Plays of Aeschylus. Oxford, Blackwell, 1922. 212 p.; The Oresteia. London, Chapman and Hall, 1924. 160 p. Repr. Great Books, v. 5, 1952.

* Tr. verse Philip Vellacott in two separate v.: The Oresteian Trilogy. Penguin, 1956. 201 p.; Prometheus Bound, etc. *Ibid.,* 1961. 159 p.

See also *The Complete Greek Drama,* in Collections, above.

Other trs. of the seven plays: anon., Oxford, 1882; anon., 1842; T. A. Buckley, BCL, 1849, reprs. to 1888; T. A. Paley, Cambridge, 1864, repr. 1871; R. S. Copleston, London and Philadelphia, 1871, repr. 1897; Anna Swanwick, London, Bell, 1873, reprs. to 1890; anon., 1906-08.

Selected Plays

———— The Oresteia Trilogy and Prometheus Bound. Tr. Michael Townsend. San Francisco, Calif., Chandler, 1966. xiii, 125 p.

* ———— The Oresteia. Tr. verse R. C. Trevelyan. Cambridge, Bowes and Bowes, 1920. 163 p.

Tr. verse J. T. Sheppard (with Greek text for performance). *Ibid.,* 1939. 169 p.

Ed. with verse tr. George Thomson. Cambridge Univ. Pr., 1938. 2 v.

* Tr. verse Richmond Lattimore. Univ. of Chicago Pr., 1953. vii, 169 p.

* Tr. verse Paul Roche. N.Y., New Amer. Lib., 1963. 252 p.

* Tr. verse Peter D. Arnott. Crofts Classics. N.Y., Appleton-Century, 1964. 2 v.

Four earlier trs. are recorded by Foster, *English Translations from the Greek*, in Bibliography, above, including that in *The Athenian Drama*, in Collections, above.

Individual Plays

——————— The Agamemnon. Tr. verse Edward Fitzgerald. London, Quaritch, 1876. Repr. in Collected Works, 1887; repr. Woodstock, Vt., Elm Tree, 1906, 71 p.

Tr. verse Robert Browning. London, Smith Elder, 1877. 148 p. Repr. in collected eds. of Browning.

Tr. prose A. W. Verrall. London and N.Y., Macmillan, 1904. lxii, 252 p.

* Tr. verse John Conington. Oxford, Clarendon Pr., 1907. xlvii, 74 p.

Tr. T. G. Tucker. Melbourne, Univ. Pr., and London, Oxford Univ. Pr., 1935. 63 p.

* Tr. verse Louis MacNeice. London, Faber, 1936, and N.Y., Harcourt, 1937. 71 p. (See also *Four Greek Plays*, *Ten Greek Plays*, in Collections, above).

Tr. verse Archibald Y. Campbell. Liverpool, Univ. Pr., and London, Hodder and Stoughton, 1940. xxi, 95 p.

Foster lists 25 other trs. of *Agamemnon*.

——————— The Eumenides. Tr. prose A. W. Verrall. Cambridge Univ. Pr., 1885. 85 p.

Four earlier trs. are listed by Foster.

——————— The Persians. Tr. T. G. Tucker. Melbourne and London, Melbourne Univ. Pr., 1935. 43 p.

Foster records 8 earlier trs.

——————— Prometheus Bound. Tr. verse Elizabeth Barrett Browning. London, Valpy, 1833. xxiv, 163 p. Repr. in collected eds. of her poems.

* Tr. prose and verse Paul Elmer More. N.Y., Houghton Mifflin, 1899. 110 p.

Tr. verse Robert Whitelaw, notes by J. Churton Collins. Oxford, Clarendon Pr., 1907. xlviii, 53 p. Repr. in *Fifteen Greek Plays,* see Collections, above.

Ed. and tr. verse George Thomson. Cambridge, Univ. Pr., 1932. 183 p. (parallel texts).

Tr. T. G. Tucker. Melbourne, Univ. Pr., and London, Oxford Univ. Pr., 1935. 49 p.

* Tr. R. C. Trevelyan. Cambridge, Univ. Pr., 1939. 47 p.

* Tr. prose David Grene, in his *Three Greek Tragedies,* 1942, see Collections, above.

Tr. verse Rex Warner. London, Bodley Head, 1947. 54 p. Repr. in *Ten Greek Plays,* see Collections, above.

Tr. verse Warren B. Anderson. N.Y., Bobbs-Merrill, 1963. xxiii, 70 p.

* Tr. verse Paul Roche. N.Y., New Amer. Lib., 1964. 128 p.

Foster lists 23 other trs.

——————— The Seven Against Thebes. Foster lists 9 trs.

——————— The Suppliant Women. Tr. L. R. Lind as The Suppliants, in *Ten Greek Plays,* see Collections, above.

Foster lists 3 other trs.

For Aeschylus, see John Huston Finley, Jr., *Pindar and Aeschylus* (Cambridge, Mass., Harvard Univ. Pr., 1955, vii, 307 p.); Gilbert Murray, *Aeschylus, the Creator of Tragedy* (Oxford, Clarendon Pr., and N.Y., Oxford Univ. Pr., 1940, xii, 242 p.; repr. 1962, paper); Friedrich Solmsen, *Hesiod and Aeschylus* (Ithaca, N. Y., Cornell Univ. Pr., and London, Oxford Univ. Pr., 1949, ix, 230 p.); J. T. Sheppard, *Aeschylus and Sophocles, Their Work and Influence* (Our Debt to Greece and Rome, 1927, vii, 204 p.); Herbert Weir Smyth, *Aeschylean Tragedy* (Berkeley, Univ. of California Pr., 1924, vii, 234 p.); George D. Thomson, *Aeschylus and Athens* (London, Lawrence and Wishart, 1941, xii, 476 p., re-ed. *ibid.* and N.Y., International Publishers, 1950).

AESOP (fl. 570 B.C.). Fables of Aesop. Tr. William Caxton. Westminster, Caxton, 1484. Repr. London, Nutt, 1898; San Francisco, Calif., Grabhorn, 1930. 167 p.

Tr. John Ogilby as Fables, Paraphrased in Verse. London, 1651. Repr. 1672.

Tr. Sir Roger L'Estrange in Fables of Aesop and Other Eminent Mythologists. London, 1669. 480 p. Repr. Waltham St. Lawrence, Golden
Cockerel Pr., 1926. 94 p.

Tr. John Locke (into English and Latin). London, 1703. Repr. 1723.

Tr. V. S. Vernon Jones, with intro. G. K. Chesterton. London, Heinemann,
and N.Y., Doubleday, 1912. xxix, 223 p.

Tr. S. A. Handford. Penguin, 1954. xxi, 228 p.

Tr. Denison B. Hull. Univ. of Chicago Pr., 1960. 141 p.

Tr. Lloyd W. Daly as Aesop Without Morals: The Famous Fables, and a
Life of Aesop. N.Y., and London, Yoseloff, 1961. 317 p.

The fables ascribed to Aesop (though, as we know them, actually the
version by Valerius Babrius, 2d c. A.D.) are known to have been tr. into
English, often from the Latin, by 21 translators before 1800: including
notably Samuel Croxall, whose version, published 1722, was repr. at least
10 times. A useful selection from Caxton, L'Estrange, and other translators
was pub. as *Aesop's Fables: An Anthology of the Fabulists of All Countries*
(EL, 1913, xxiv, 231 p., et seq.)

ALCAEUS (fl. 600 B.C.). The Songs. Literal and verse trs., with the Greek
text, by J. S. Easby-Smith. Washington, D.C., Lowdermilk, 1901.
xiii, 146 p.

Also in *Greek Anthology, Lyra Graeca*, and *Oxford Book of Greek Verse in
Translation*, in Collections, above.

ALCMAN (fl. 650 B.C.). Poems. Tr. Olga Marx and Ernst Morwitz, in Poems
of Alcman, Sappho, and Ibycus. N.Y., Knopf, 1945. 32, 50 p.

See also *Lyra Graeca, Oxford Book of Greek Verse in Translation*, in
Collections, above.

ANACREON (6th c. B.C.) and the Anacreontea. Tr. verse Thomas Stanley,
in Anacreon, Bion, and Moschus. London, 1651. 260 p. Repr. ed.
Sir Egerton Brydges, 1815; repr. (Anacreon only) ed. A. H. Bullen,
1893; repr. 1906; repr. Oxford, 1962, as The Poems and Translations.

Preferred for accuracy to the Moore trs., see below.

Tr. verse Abraham Cowley as Odes, in Poems of A. Cowley. Oxford, 1683. Repr. London, Nonesuch Pr., 1923; also in eds. of Cowley.

Tr. verse Thomas Moore. London, Stockdale, 1800. 251 p. Repr. in collected eds. of Moore's poems.

Tr. verse J. P. Davidson as The Anacreontea and Principal Remains of Anacreon. London, Dent, and N.Y., Dutton, 1915. 212 p.

Tr. verse Philip M. Pope. London, Bowes, and Philadelphia, Saifer, 1935. viii, 48 p.

Tr. also John Addison and others, 1735; Francis Fawkes, 1760. Trs. in *Elegy and Iambus* (LCL); *Greek Lyric Poetry*; *Oxford Book of Greek Verse in Translation*; see Collections, above.

ARCHILOCHUS (7th c. B.C.). The Fragments of Archilochus. Tr. Guy Davenport. Berkeley, Univ. of California Pr., 1964. xxi, 104 p.

ARISTOPHANES (480–385 B.C.). The Eleven Comedies. Tr. anon. Athens, Athenian Society, 1898. xxvii, 238 p. (parallel texts). Repr. London, Athenian Society, 1912, 2 v. Repr. N.Y., Liveright, 1928; Rarity Pr., 1931; Tudor, 1934.

Ten of the plays in this tr. were repr. in *Complete Greek Drama*; see Collections, above.

* Tr. verse Benjamin Bickley Rogers as The Comedies. London, Bell, 1906– 16. 11 parts (parallel texts). Repr. LCL, 1924, 3 v., and 1950–55, 3 v. Repr. Bell, 1930, 11 parts. Repr. Great Books, v. 5, 1952.

The Rogers trs. of individual plays began to appear in 1867. Three plays in this tr. (*The Clouds, The Birds, The Frogs*) were repr. in *Fifteen Greek Plays*, see Collections, above; *The Frogs* repr. in Harvard Classics, v. 9.

Other trs. of the complete plays by C. A. Wheelwright (verse), Oxford, 1837, 2 v.; William James Hickie, London, Bohn, 1848–53, 2 v.; reprs. to 1901–02; W. Lucas Collins, 1872; Arthur S. Way (verse), London, Macmillan, 1927, and N.Y., Macmillan, 1982. xxiv, 328 p.

Selected Plays

————— The Plays. EL, 1909 et seq. 2 v. V. 1, Acharnians, Knights, Birds, Peace, tr. J. Hookham Frere; v. 2, Frogs, tr. the same; Trial of Euripides or Thesmophoriazusae, tr. W. J. Hickie; Clouds, tr. Thomas Mitchell; Wasps, tr. Richard Cumberland.

Actually Cumberland tr. *Clouds*, and Mitchell tr. *Wasps*: see next entry but one.

———————— Eight Comedies. Tr. rhyming verse Leonard Hampson Rudd. London, 1867.

———————— The Comedies (four). Tr. Thomas Mitchell and Richard Cumberland. London, 1812. 2 v. Repr. 1820–22.

Acharnians, Knights, Wasps, tr. Mitchell; and Cumberland's tr. of *Clouds*, (published in his *The Observer*, v. 6, 1798). The last two plays were repr. EL, see above.

———————— (Four Plays). Tr. verse John Hookham Frere. In Works. London, 1872, v. 2. Repr. *ibid.*, 1874, v. 3; repr. WC, 1907 et seq.; repr. EL, 1909 et seq., see above (adding Peace).

The Frere trs. began in 1839.

*———————— Four Comedies. Tr. verse Dudley Fitts. N.Y., Harcourt, 1962. 341 p .(Lysistrata, Frogs, Birds, Ladies' Day).

*———————— The Frogs and Other Plays. Tr. prose and verse David Barrett. Penguin, 1964. 224 p. (with The Poet and the Women, and The Wasps).

———————— The Birds and The Frogs. Tr. Marshall MacGregor. London. Arnold, 1927. vii, 134 p.

———————— Two Plays: Peace and Lysistrata. Tr. Doros Alastos. London, Zeno, 1953. 144 p.

Individual Plays

Foster's *English Translations from the Greek* lists 56 trs. of individual plays before 1917. Among these and later ones may be listed the following. (Stage versions [Greek-English] of many of the plays as performed at Oxford and Cambridge 1892–1938 are not listed, nor are literal trs. for schools. For them, see British Museum Catalogue.)

*———————— The Acharnians. Tr. verse Douglass Parker. Ann Arbor, Univ. of Mich. Pr., 1961. 112 p.

———————— The Birds. Tr. Henry F. Cary. London, 1824. xxxvi, 179 p.

Tr. verse Gilbert Murray. London, Allen and Unwin, 1950. 183 p.

* Tr. verse William Arrowsmith. Ann Arbor, Univ. of Mich. Pr., 1961. 127 p.

——————— The Clouds .Tr. Thomas Stanley (before 1678). London, 1708.

Tr. Richard Cumberland. London, 1798 (in his The Observer, v. 6). Repr. in The Comedies (with trs. by Thomas Mitchell), 1812; 1822; in EL, v. 2, 1909 (ascribed to Mitchell).

* Tr. William Arrowsmith. Ann Arbor, Univ. of Mich. Pr., 1962, 133 p.

Also tr. Lewis Theobald, 1715; James White, 1759.

——————— The Frogs. Tr. Charles Dunster. London, 1780.

Tr. verse Gilbert Murray, in The Athenian Drama, v. 3, 1902. Repr. London, George Allen, 1908, 136 p., repr. in Greek Literature in Translation, see Collections, above.

* Tr. verse Richmond Lattimore. Ann Arbor, Univ. of Mich. Pr., 1962. 100 p.

* Tr. verse Peter D. Arnott, in Three Greek Plays, 1964; see Collections, above.

——————— Lysistrata. Tr. in paraphrase Laurence Housman. London Woman's Pr., 1911. 77 p.

* Tr. Jack Lindsay. London, 1926. xii, 51 p.

Tr. Gilbert Seldes. N.Y., Farrar and Rinehart, 1930. xiii, 146 p.

Tr. C. T. Murphy, in Greek Literature in Translation, 1944. Repr. in Ten Greek Plays. See Collections, above.

* Tr. verse Dudley Fitts. N. Y., Harcourt, 1954, and London, Faber, 1955. 132 p.

Tr. Donald Sutherland. San Francisco, Chandler, 1961. xv, 47 p.

* Tr. verse Douglass Parker. Ann Arbor, Univ. of Mich. Pr., 1963. 98 p.

Tr. Robert Henning Webb. Charlottesville, Univ. Pr. of Virginia, 1963. 160 p.

——————— Plutus. Tr. Thomas Randolph. London, 1651. 47 p.

Tr. Henry Fielding and William Young. London, 1742.

Tr. Sir William Rann Kennedy. London, Murray, 1912. xxi, 66 p.

Also tr. H. B. B., 1659; Lewis Theobald, 1715.

*———— The Wasps. Tr. verse Douglass Parker. Ann Arbor, Univ. of Mich. Pr., 1962. 130 p.

*———— Women in Parliament (*Ecclesiazusae*). Tr. Jack Lindsay. London, Fanfrolico Pr., 1929. xiv, 59 p.

* Tr. Dudley Fitts as Ladies' Day. N.Y., 1959. Repr. in his Four Comedies (by Aristophanes), 1962. See above, Selected Plays.

For Aristophanes, see Victor Ehrenberg, *The People of Aristophanes: A Sociology of Old Attic Comedy* (Oxford, Blackwell, and N.Y., Salloch, 1943, xii, 320 p.; re-ed., Oxford, *ibid.*, and Cambridge, Mass., Harvard Univ. Pr., 1951, xx, 417 p.; re-ed., N.Y., Schocken Books, 1962, xii, 385 p., 19 pl., paper); Louis E. Lord, *Aristophanes, His Plays and His Influence* (Our Debt to Greece and Rome, 1925, xi, 183 p.); Gilbert Murray, *Aristophanes: A Study* (Oxford, Clarendon Pr., and N.Y., Oxford Univ. Pr., 1933, xi, 268 p.; repr. N.Y., Russell, 1964); Cedric H. Whitman, *Aristophanes and the Comic Hero* (Cambridge, Mass., Harvard Univ. Pr., 1964, xiii, 333 p.).

ARISTOTLE (384–322 B.C.). The Works. Tr. Thomas Taylor. London, the Translator, 1812. 9 v.

The trs. were also published separately: *The Metaphysics,* 1801, 1 v, 467 p.; *The History of Animals, . . . and . . . Treatise on Physiognomy,* 1809, xxi, 437 p.; *The Parts, and Progressive Motion, of Animals, . . . Problems on Indivisible Lines,* 1810, vii, 607 p.; *The Great, and Eudemian, Ethics, the Politics, and Economics,* 1811, viii, 535 p.; *The Rhetoric, Poetic,* and *Nicomachean Ethics,* 1818.

Tr. various hands (of certain works). BCL, 1850–62.

(These are listed in the same order as in the next entry: as logic, science, philosophy.) *The Organon* (the treatises on logic), tr. Octavus Freire Owen, 1853 et seq., 2 v. *The History of Animals,* tr. Richard Cresswell, 1862. *Metaphysics,* tr. John McMahon, 1857, et seq. *Nicomachean Ethics,* tr. R. W. Browne, 1850, et seq. *Politics,* with the *Economics,* tr. Edward Walford, 1853, et seq. *Poetic,* with the *Rhetoric,* tr. Theodore Buckley, 1850, et seq.

Ed. Sir W. David Ross and J. A. Smith as The Oxford Aristotle, tr. various hands (24 translators). Oxford, Clarendon Pr., 1908–52.

12 v. parallel texts. The pages of text are numbered consecutively through the 12 v., the other pages are unnumbered.

Part repr. as *The Student's Oxford Aristotle* (London and N.Y., Oxford Univ. Pr., 1942, 6 v.): the works included are given complete, and are marked in the table below with *. Part repr. in *Great Books*, v. 8, 9 (1952): the works marked † below. Those works retr. in LCL (the next item following) are marked °.

V. 1, 1928. * † Categories. Interpretation, tr. E. M. Edgehill. * † Prior Analytics, tr. A. J. Jenkinson. * † Posterior Analytics, tr. G. R. G. Mure. ° † Topics. *De sophisticis elenchis,* tr. W. A. Pickard-Cambridge.

V. 2, 1930. * † ° Physics, tr. R. F. Hardie and R. K. Gaye. * † ° Heaven, tr. J. L. Stocks. * † ° Generation and Corruption, tr. H. H. Joachim.

V. 3, 1931. † ° *Meterologica,* tr. E. M. Webster. ° World, tr. E. S. Forster. * † ° Soul, tr. J. A. Smith. * † *Parva Naturalia,* tr. J. I. Beare and G. R. T. Ross.

V. 4 1910. † History of Animals, tr. D. W. Thomson.

V. 5, 1912. † ° Of Parts of Animals, tr. William Ogle (a repr.). † ° Of Movement and Incession of Animals, tr. A. S. Farquharson. † ° Of Generation of Animals, tr. A. Platt.

V. 6, 1913. *Opuscula*: ° Colors, Audible, Physiognomies, tr. T. Loveday and E. S. Forster. Plants, tr. E. S. Forster. Marvellous Auscultations, tr. L. D. Dowdell. Mechanics, tr. E S. Forster. Of Indivisible Lines, tr. H. H. Joachim. Of Sites and Names of Winds, tr. E. S. Forster. Of Melissos, Xenophon, Gorgias, tr. T. Loveday and E. S. Forster.

V. 7, 1927. ° *Problemata,* tr. E. S. Forster.

V. 8, 1908. * † ° Metaphysics, tr. W. D. Ross.

V. 9, 1925. * † ° Nichomachaean Ethics, tr. W. D. Ross. ° *Magna Moralia,* tr. S. Stock. ° Eudemian Ethics. Virtues and Vices, tr. J. Solomon.

V. 10. 1921. * † ° Politics, tr. Benjamin Jowett (a repr.). ° Economics, tr. E. S. Forster. † ° Republic of the Athenians, tr. Sir F. G. Kenyon (a repr.).

V. 11, 1924. † ° Rhetoric, tr. W. Rhys Roberts. ° Rhetoric to Alexander, tr. E. S. Forster. * † ° Poetics, tr. Ingram Bywater (a repr.).

V. 12, 1952. Select Fragments. Bibliography.

Other reprs.: A Selection from the Oxford Aristotle, ed. W. D. Ross (Modern Student's Library, N.Y., Scribner, 1927, xxxii, 359 p., repr. 1938); The Basic Works of Aristotle, ed. Richard McKeon (N.Y., Random House, 1941, xxxix, 1487 p., part repr. as Introduction to Aristotle [ML, 1947, xxix, 667 p.])

Tr. various hands. LCL, 1926— (in progress. V. not numbered, 19 published to 1960. They are here listed in the order of the Oxford edition, above: all parallel texts.)
Posterior Analytics, tr. Hugh Tredennick. Topics, tr. E. S. Forster, 1960. On Sophistical Refutations, tr. E. S. Forster (with On Coming to Be [*De generatione*] and On Cosmos), 1955. Physics, tr. P. H. Wicksteed and F. M. Cornford, 1929–34, 2 v. On the Heavens, tr. W. K. C. Guthrie, 1939. On Coming to Be, tr. E. S. Forster (with Sophistical Refutations and On Cosmos), 1955. Meteorologica, tr. H. D. P. Lee, 1952. On the Cosmos, tr. D. J. Furley (with Sophistical Refutations and *De generatione*), 1955. On the Soul, *Parva Naturalia,* tr. W. S. Hett, 1935. Of Parts of Animals, Of Movement and Progression, tr. E. S. Forster, 1937. Of Generation of Animals, tr. A. L. Peck, 1943. Of Colours (etc., 9 treatises), tr. W. S. Hett, 1936. *Problemata* (i–xxi), tr. W. S. Hett, 1936. *Problemata* (xxii–xxxviii), tr. idem (with Rhetoric to Alexander), 1937. Metaphysics, tr. Hugh Tredennick, 1933–35, 2 v. (v. 2 adding *Oeconomica and Magna Moralia*). Nicomachean Ethics, tr. H. Rackham, 1926. *Magna Moralia,* tr. G. C. Armstrong (with Metaphysics, v. 2). Eudemian Ethics, On Virtues and Vices, tr. H. Rackham, 1935 (with The Athenian Constitution). Politics, tr. H. Rackham, 1932. Economics, tr. G. C. Armstrong, 1935 (with Metaphysics, v. 2, and Magna Moralia). The Athenian Constitution, tr. H. Rackman, 1935 (with Eudemian Ethics, Virtues and Vices). Rhetoric, tr. J. H. Freese, 1926. Rhetoric to Alexander, tr. H. Rackham, 1937 (with Problemata, 2). Poetics, tr. W. Hamilton Fyfe, 1927 (with "Longinus" on the Sublime, tr. the same, and Demetrius on Style, tr. W. Rhys Roberts).

Selected Works

————— Aristotle: from Natural Science, Psychology, the Nicomachaean Ethics. Tr. Philip Wheelwright. Garden City, N.Y., Doubleday, 1935. xlii, 244 p. Repr. 1951, enl. xlviii, 336 p.

From seven works: Physics, Metaphysics, zoological treatises, Soul, Ethics, Politics, Poetics.

————— The Philosophy of Aristotle. Ed. Renford Bambrough, tr. A. E. Wardman and J. L. Creed. N.Y., New Amer. Lib., 1963. 432 p.

Selections from Metaphysics, Categories, On Interpretation, Posterior Analytics, Physics, Psychology, Ethics, Politics, Poetics.

Individual Works (if separately published)

————— On the Athenian Constitution. Tr. Sir F. G. Kenyon. London, Bell, and N.Y., Macmillan, 1891. xliii, 126 p. Repr. Oxford Aristotle, v. 10, 1921, etc.

Tr. Thomas I. Dymes. London, Seeley, 1891. x, 147 p.

Tr. Edward Poste. London, Macmillan, 1891. x, 101 p.

Tr. H. Rackham (with The Eudemian Ethics, etc.). LCL, 1935. vii, 505 p.

Tr. Kurt von Fritz and Ernst Kapp (with related texts). N.Y., Hafner, 1950. 245 p.

Tr. John Warrington (with the Politics). EL, 1959. xvi, 319 p.

————— On Fallacies, or the *Sophistici Elenchi*. Tr. Edward Poste. London, Macmillan, 1866. viii, 252 p. See also Oxford Aristotle, and LCL.

————— The Metaphysics. Tr. Thomas Taylor. London, The Translator, 1801. iv, 467 p. Repr. in The Works, above.

Tr. John H. McMahon. BCL, 1857.

Tr. W. D. Ross, in Oxford Aristotle, v. 8, 1908, etc.

Tr. Hugh Tredennick, LCL, 1935, 2 v.

Tr. Richard Hope. N.Y., Columbia Univ. Pr., 1952, and London, Oxford Univ. Pr., 1953. 394 p. Repr. Ann Arbor, Univ. of Mich. Pr., 1960.

Tr. John Warrington, with intro. Sir David Ross. EL, 1956. xxviii, 388 p.

————— The Nicomachaean Ethics. Tr. John Gillies (with the Politics). London, 1797. 2 v. Reprs. to 1893.

Tr. D. P. Chase. Oxford, 1847. viii, 397 p. Repr. rev. 1861, 1877, 1890, 1906, 1910, EL 1911 et seq. to 1950.

Tr. R. W. Browne, BCL, 1850.

Tr. W. D. Ross, in Oxford Aristotle, v. 9, 1908, etc.

Tr. H. Rackman. LCL, 1926. xxvi, 649 p.

Tr. J. A. K. Thomson. Penguin Books, 1955. 319 p.

Tr. Martin Ostwald. N.Y., Bobbs-Merrill, 1962. xxviii, 316 p.

Tr. John Warrington. EL, 1963. xviii, 253 p.

Other trs.: anon., Oxford, 1819; Robert Williams, 1869, repr. 1876, 1877; J. A. Giles, 1870; Walter M. Hatch, 1879; F. H. Peters, 1886; J. E. C. Welldon, 1892, repr. 1912, 1920.

———— On the Parts of Animals. Tr. William Ogle. London, Kegan Paul, 1882. xxxv, 263 p. Repr. in Oxford Aristotle, v. 5, 1912, etc.

Tr. E. S. Forster. LCL, 1937 (with Movement of Animals, etc.). v, 555 p.

———— The Physics. Tr. Philip H. Wicksteed and F. M. Cornford. LCL, 1929. 2 v.

Tr. R. Hardie and R. K. Gaye (with Heaven, The Generation of Animals), in Oxford Aristotle, v. 2, 1930.

Tr. Richard Hope. Lincoln, Univ. of Nebraska Pr., 1961. xiii, 241 p.

———— The Poetics. Tr. T. A. Buckley (with the Rhetoric). BCL, 1850.

* Tr. S. H. Butcher as Aristotle's Theory of Poetry and Fine Art. London and N.Y., Macmillan, 1895. 384 p. Repr. 1895, 1896, 2d ed. 1898, 3d ed., 1902, 4th ed. N.Y., Dover, 1951 (with intro. John Gassner), lxxvi, 421 p. (parallel texts). Repr. with a supplement On Music [from the Politics, VIII, vii] tr. Milton C. Nahm, N.Y., Liberal Arts Pr., 1948, xvii, 51 p. Repr. ed. Francis Fergusson, N.Y., Hill and Wang, 1961, 118 p. Repr. (with the Politics), N.Y., Limited Edns Club, 1964.

* Tr. Ingram Bywater as Aristotle on the Art of Poetry. Oxford, Clarendon Pr., 1909. Repr. 1920, 95 p.; in Oxford Aristotle, v. 11, 1924, etc.; in Modern Reader's series, ed. Charles S. Baldwin (with Longinus), N.Y., Macmillan, 1930; repr. rev. W. Hamilton Fyfe, Oxford, 1940.

Tr. D. S. Margoliouth (with Latin tr. of Arabic version). London, Hodder and Stoughton, 1911. 336 p. (Greek, Latin, English).

* Tr. Lane Cooper in an Amplified Version. Boston, Ginn, 1913. xxix, 101 p. Repr. rev. as Aristotle on the Art of Poetry, Ithaca, N.Y., Cornell Univ. Pr., 1947, xxix, 100 p.; repr. 1962, paper.

* Tr. W. Rhys Roberts (with Longinus and Demetrius). LCL, 1927. xx, 500 p.

Tr. Leonard James Potts as Aristotle on the Art of Fiction. Cambridge, Univ. Pr., 1953. 94 p.

Tr. G. M. A. Grube as On Poetry and Style. N.Y., Liberal Arts Pr., 1958. xxxii, 110 p.

Other trs.: anon. from French, 1705, reprs. to 1714; anon., 1775; Henry James Pye, 1775, repr. 1778, 1788, 1792; Thomas Twining, Oxford, 1789, repr. 1812, 1851, 1889, EL 1934; E. S. Bouchier, Oxford, 1907.

————— The Politics. Tr. William Ellis as A Treatise on Government. London, 1776. Repr. 1778, 1888, EL 1912, xviii, 264 p.

Tr. John Gillies (with the Ethics). London, 1797. 2 v. Reprs. to 1893.

Tr. Edward Walford (with the Economics). BCL, 1853.

Tr. Benjamin Jowett. Oxford, Clarendon Pr., 1885. 2 v. Repr. in Oxford Aristotle, v. 10, 1921, etc.; repr. (with the Poetics), N.Y., Limited Edns Club, 1964.

Tr. J. E. C. Welldon. London and N.Y., Macmillan, 1883. Repr. 1888, 1893, 1932, xcvi, 412 p.

Tr. Sir Ernest Barker. Oxford, Clarendon Pr., 1946. Repr. London and N.Y., Oxford Univ. Pr., 1958, lxxvi, 411 p.

Tr. T. A. Sinclair. Penguin Books, 1962. 320 p.

Other tr.: J. D., 1598 (from the French).

————— The Posterior Analytics. Tr. Edward Poste as The Logic of Science. Oxford, Macpherson, 1850. xvi, 143 p.

Tr. G. R. G. Mure, in Oxford Aristotle, v. 1, 1928, etc.

Tr. Hugh Tredennick (with Topica), in LCL, 1960. v, 754 p.

————— The Prior and Posterior Analytics. Tr. John Warrington. EL, 1964. xx, 266 p.

————— The Rhetoric. Tr. T. A. Buckley (with the Poetics). BCL, 1850.

Tr. J. E. C. Welldon. London and N.Y., Macmillan, 1886. xlvii, 306 p.

* Tr. Sir Richard Jebb. Cambridge Univ. Pr., and N.Y., Macmillan, 1909. xxviii, 207 p.

Tr. W. Rhys Roberts, in Oxford Aristotle, v. 11, 1924, etc. (with Rhetoric to Alexander).

* Ed. and tr. John Henry Freese. LCL, 1926. xlvii, 491 p.

* Tr. Lane Cooper as An Expanded Translation. N.Y., and London, Appleton, 1932. xlviii, 259 p. Repr. 1960.

Other trs. H. C., 1686, repr. 1693, 1816; D. M. Crimmin, 1812; John Gillies, 1823;—Parsons, 1836; anon., Oxford, 1847; E. M. Cope, 1867.

——————— The Soul (*De Anima*). Ed. and tr. Edwin Wallace. Cambridge Univ. Pr., and N.Y., Macmillan, 1882. cxxviii, 327 p. (parallel texts).

Tr. William A. Hammond as The Psychology. London, Swan Sonnenschein, and N.Y., Macmillan, 1902. lxxxvii, 339 p.

Ed. and tr. R. D. Hicks. Cambridge Univ. Pr., 1907, and N.Y., Macmillan, 1908. lxxxiii, 626 p.

Tr. J. A. Smith in Oxford Aristotle, v. 3, 1931, etc.

Ed. and tr. W. S. Hett. LCL, 1935. xii, 518 p. Repr. 1957.

For Aristotle, see Donald James Allan, *The Philosophy of Aristotle* (London, Oxford Univ. Pr., 1952; re-ed., N.Y., the same, 1963, 220 p.); Harold F. Cherniss, *Aristotle's Criticism of Plato and the Academy* (Baltimore, Md., Johns Hopkins Pr., 1944; repr. N.Y., Russell, 1962, xxvii, 610 p.); Lane Cooper, *The Poetics of Aristotle* (Our Debt to Greece and Rome, 1923, x, 157 p.); Werner Jaeger, *Aristotle: Fundamentals of the History of his Development*, tr. Richard Robinson from the German [1923] (Oxford, Clarendon Pr., 1934, 410 p.; re-ed., 1948, 475 p.; repr. London and N.Y., Oxford Univ. Pr., 1962, paper); John Herman Randall, Jr., *Aristotle* (N.Y., Columbia Univ. Pr., and London, Oxford Univ. Pr., 1960, xv, 309 p.; repr. 1962, paper); W. D. Ross [now Sir David], *Aristotle* (London, Methuen, 1923, vii, 300 p.; re-eds. to 5th ed. 1949; repr., *ibid.* and N.Y., Barnes and Noble, 1964, paper); John L. Stocks, *Aristotelianism* (Our Debt to Greece and Rome, 1925, vii, 165 p.); Henry B. Veatch, *Rational Man: A Modern Interpretation of Aristotelian Ethics* (Bloomington, Indiana Univ. Pr., 1962, 226 p., also 1964, paper).

ARISTOXENUS of Tarentum (fl. 318 B.C.). The Harmonics. Ed. and tr. H. S. Macran. London and N.Y., Oxford Univ Pr., 1902. 303 p.

ASCLEPIODOTUS (c. 100 B.C.). The Tactics. Tr. Illinois Greek Club (with Aeneas Tacticus, Onosander). LCL, 1923 et seq. x, 531 p.

BACCHYLIDES (505–450 B.C.). (The Poems). Tr. prose Edward Poste. London, Macmillan, 1898. vi, 39 p.

* Tr. prose Sir Richard Jebb as The Poems and Fragments. Cambridge Univ. Pr., and N.Y., Macmillan, 1905. xvii, 524 p. (parallel texts).

* Tr. verse Arthur S. Way as The Odes. London, Macmillan, 1929. vii, 63 p.

* Tr. verse Robert Fagles as The Complete Poems, with foreword by Sir Maurice Bowra. New Haven, Yale Univ. Pr., 1961. 123 p.

CHION OF HERACLEA (4th c. B.C.). Letters. See below, Graeco-Roman Period, for these letters, once ascribed to a friend of Plato.

DEMOCRITUS (or Democrates, c. 460–c. 370 B.C.). The Golden Sentences. Tr. William Bridgman, in Translations from the Greek. London. Bridgman, 1804. 135 p.

DEMOSTHENES (383–322 B.C.). The Orations, Erotic Essay (LX, LXI), Exordia, and Letters. Tr. J. H. and C. A. Vince, et al. LCL, 1926–49. 9 v.

————The Orations. Tr. Charles Rann Kennedy. BCL, 1852. 5 v. Repr. N.Y., Appleton, 1900–1903. Part repr. (*De Corona,* Philippic and Olynthian orations) EL, 1911, 292 p.

Selected orations tr. Philip Francis, 1752–58, 2 v.; Thomas Leland, 1756–78, 3 v., many reprs. to N.Y., Lamb, 1908; W. J. Brodribb, 1877; A. W. Pickard-Cambridge, EL, 1906, and Oxford Univ. Pr., 1912, 2 v. For trs. of one or several orations beginning 1570, see Foster, *English Translations from the Greek*, and British Museum Catalogue.

For Demosthenes, see Charles D. Adams, *Demosthenes and his Influence* (Our Debt to Greece and Rome, 1927, v, 184 p.); Werner Jaeger, *Demosthenes: The Origin and Growth of his Policy* (Berkeley, Univ. of California Pr., and Cambridge Univ. Pr., 1938, x, 273 p.; repr. N.Y., Octagon Books, 1963).

EMPEDOCLES (494–434 B.C.). Fragments. Tr. verse William Ellery Leonard. Chicago, Open Court, 1908. 92 p.

EURIPIDES (480–406 B.C.). The Tragedies. Tr. Robert Potter. London, 1781–83. 2 v. Repr. 1807, 1808, 1814, 1832, 1835, 1850–52, 1887.

Tr. Michael Wodhull as The Nineteen Tragedies. London, 1782. 4 v. Partial reprs. to 1894.

Tr. T. A. Buckley. BCL, 1850. 2 v.

Tr. W. B. Donne. London and Philadelphia, 1872.

* Tr. prose Edward P. Coleridge. BCL, 1891. 2 v. Repr. Great Books, 1952, v. 5; repr. (12 plays) in Complete Greek Drama, Collections above.

* Tr. verse A. S. Way. London, Macmillan, 1894–98. 5 v. Rev. repr. LCL, 1912–13, 4 v.

> Excellent trs.

Tr. verse Percy Bysshe Shelley et al. EL, 1906 et seq. 2 v.

> The trs. generally by Potter and Wodhull, with Shelley's *Cyclops*.

Tr. prose Moses Hadas and J. M. McLean. N.Y., Dial, 1936. 499 p.

Selected Plays

*———— (Eight plays). Tr. rhyming verse Gilbert Murray. Newtown, Gregynog, 1931. 2 v. Repr. as Collected Plays, London, George Allen, 1955, 752 p.

Excellent trs. of *Alcestis, Bacchae, Electra, Hippolytus, Iphigenia in Tauris, Medea, Rhesus, Trojan Women*. The trs. were published separately from 1902 to 1920 (London, Allen and Unwin, and N.Y., Oxford Univ. Pr., or Longmans); two plays (*Bacchae, Hippolytus*) repr. Harvard Classics, v. 9, and two more repr. in *Ten Greek Plays*, and in *Fifteen Greek Plays*. The same tr. added the *Ion* in 1954.

*———— (Eleven plays). Tr. verse Philip Vellacott. Penguin, 1953–61–63. 3 v. 1953: Alcestis, Hippolytus, Iphigenia in Tauris, 165 p.; 1961: Bacchae, Helen, Ion, Women of Troy, 234 p.; 1963: Electra, Hecuba, Heracles, Medea, 205 p.

———— Four Dramas. Tr. verse Hugh Meredith. London, Allen and Unwin, 1937. 253 p. (Andromache, Hecuba, Heracles, Orestes.)

*———— Three Great Plays. Tr. verse Rex Warner. N.Y., New American Library, 1958, and London, Muller, 1959. 192 p. (Helen, Hippolytus, Medea.)

Individual Plays

* ———Alcestis. Freely adapted in verse by Robert Browning in Balaustion's Adventure. London, Smith Elder, 1871. 170 p. Repr. in collected eds. of Browning.

> Excellent tr.

Tr. verse and prose Richard Aldington. London, Chatto and Windus, 1930, 72 p. Repr. in Ten Greek Plays, see Collections, above.

Tr. free verse Dudley Fitts and Robert Fitzgerald. N.Y., Harcourt, 1933. 91 p. Repr. in Greek Plays in Modern Translation, and in Four Greek Plays; see Collections, above.

Tr. prose D. W. Lucas. London, Cohen and West, 1951, and N.Y., Russell F. Moore, 1952. 52 p.

Foster, *English Translations from the Greek,* records 26 separate trs. of the *Alcestis.*

——————— Andromache. Tr. L. R. Lind in Ten Greek Plays, see Collections, above. (Foster records 3 separate trs.)

——————— Bacchae. Tr. verse Henry Hart Milman (with the Agamemnon of Aeschylus). London, Murray, 1865. 328 p.

> Good tr.

Tr. prose D. W. Lucas. Cambridge, England, Bowes, 1930. 96 p.

Tr. Henry Birkhead, in Ten Greek Plays, see Collections, above.

Foster, *English Translations from the Greek,* notes 11 separate trs.

——————— Cyclops. Tr. verse Percy Bysshe Shelley. (in all collected eds. of Shelley, and in Euripides' Plays, EL)

> Excellent tr.

Tr. and adapted freely in verse J. T. Sheppard. Cambridge Univ. Pr., and N.Y., Macmillan, 1923. 27 p.

Tr. verse Roger L. Green, in Two Satyr Plays (with the *Ichneutai* of Sophocles). Penguin, 1957. 94 p.

* Tr. verse Peter D. Arnott, in Three Greek Plays (with the Medea, and The Frogs of Aristophanes). Bloomington, Indiana Univ. Pr., 1964.

————— Electra. Tr. Moses Hadas. Indianapolis, Ind., Bobbs-Merrill, 1964. viii, 42 p., paper.

————— Hecuba.

Foster, *English Translations from the Greek,* notes 15 trs.

* ————— Helen. Tr. J. T. Sheppard Cambridge Univ. Pr., 1925. 49 p.

————— Heracleidae.

Foster, *English Translations from the Greek,* notes 5 trs.

*————— Hercules Furens. Tr. verse Robert Browning, in Aristophanes' Apology. London, Smith Elder, 1875. 366 p. Repr. in collected eds. of Browning.

Foster records 4 other trs.

————— Hippolytus. Tr. verse Gilbert Murray, in The Athenian Drama, v. 3; see Collections, above.

Tr. David Grene, in his Three Greek Tragedies (with Agamemnon and Oedipus). Chicago, Univ. of Chicago Pr., 1942. Repr. in The Complete Greek Tragedies; see Collections, above.

Tr. Rex Warner. London, Bodley Head, 1949. 72 p.

Tr. Donald Sutherland, in Hippolytus in Drama and Myth. Lincoln, Univ. of Nebraska Pr., 1960. 123 p.

Tr. Kenneth Cavander. San Francisco, Chandler, 1962. 44 p.

Foster notes 15 separate trs.

————— Ion. Tr. verse H[ilda] D[oolittle]. London, Chatto, and Boston, Houghton-Mifflin, 1937. 132 p.

Tr. verse D. W. Lucas, N.Y., Moore, and London, Cohen and West, 1950. 90 p.

Foster notes 4 other trs.

————— Iphigenia in Aulis. Tr. Jane Lady Lumley (1555). Ed. from ms. Harold Child. London, Malone Society, 1909. xi p., 35 leaves.

Tr. verse F. M. Stawell. London, Bell, 1929. 128 p. Repr. in The Complete Greek Drama; see Collections, above.

Foster notes 6 other trs.

——————— Iphigenia in Tauris. Tr. verse Witter Bynner. N.Y., Kennerley, 1915. 87 p.

Foster notes 8 trs.

——————— Medea. Tr. verse John Jay Chapman, in his Two Greek Plays. Boston, Houghton Mifflin, 1928. 118 p.

Tr. prose and verse Countee Cullen, in The Medea and Some Poems. N.Y., Harper, 1935, p. 1–64.

* Tr. R. C. Trevelyan. Cambridge, Univ. Pr., 1939. 57 p.

* Tr. unrhymed verse Rex Warner. London, Lane, 1944. 64 p.

* Tr. verse Frederic Prokosch, in Greek Plays in Modern Translation, 1947, see Collections, above.

Tr. verse D. W. Lucas. N.Y., Russell F. Moore, and London, Cohen and West, 1950. 77 p.

* Tr. verse Peter D. Arnott, in Three Greek Plays, 1964; see Collections, above.

Tr. Michael Townsend. San Francisco, Chandler, 1966. xxxi, 31 p., paper.

Foster records 16 separate trs.

——————— Orestes. (Foster notes 3 separate trs.)

——————— Phoenissae. (Foster notes 4 separate trs.)

*——————— The Trojan Women. Tr. verse Edith Hamilton, in Three Greek Plays (with Agamemnon and Prometheus Unbound). N.Y., Norton, 1937. 239 p.

* Tr. verse Richmond Lattimore, in Greek Plays in Modern Translation, 1947, see Collections, above.

Tr. Neil Curry. Old Woking, England, Gresham Pr., 1964, Re-ed. London, Methuen, 1966, 64 p.

Foster notes 3 other trs.

For Euripides, see Paul Decharme, *Euripides and the Spirit of his Dramas*, tr. James Loeb from the French (Paris, 1893: N.Y., and London, Macmillan, 1906; re-ed., 1909, xxiii, 392 p.); G. M. A. Grube, *The Drama of Euripides* (London, Methuen, 1941, viii, 456 p.; repr. N.Y., Barnes and Noble, 1961); F. L. Lucas, *Euripides and his Influence* (Our Debt to Greece and Rome, 1924, xv, 188 p.); Gilbert Murray, *Euripides and his*

Age (London, Oxford Univ. Pr., 1913, 256 p.; re-ed. rev., *ibid.*, and N.Y., Oxford Univ. Pr., 1946, 170 p.; repr. 1965, paper); Gilbert Norwood, *Essays on Euripidean Drama* (Berkeley, etc., Univ. of California Pr., and London, Oxford Univ. Pr., 1954, 197 p.).

HERACLITUS of Ephesus (fl. 513 B.C.). Fragments of the Work on Nature. Tr. G. T. W. Patrick. Baltimore, Md., Murray, 1889. x, 131 p.

* Tr. W. H. S. Jones as On the Universe. In Hippocrates, v. 4, p. 449–509. LCL. 1931.

* Ed. and tr. G. S. Kirk as The Cosmic Fragments. London, Cambridge Univ. Pr., 1954. xv, 423 p. Repr. 1962.

* Tr. Philip Wheelwright. Princeton, N.J., Princeton Univ. Pr., 1959, and London, Oxford Univ. Pr., 1960 viii, 181 p.

HERODOTUS (c. 484–425 B.C.). The History. Tr. Henry F. Cary. BCL, 1843. Reprs. to 1899.

Tr. George Rawlinson, et al. London, Murray, 1858–60. 4 v. Repr. 1862, 1880, N.Y., 1889, 1897, 1909, 1928, 1935, 1936; EL 1910, et seq., 2 v. Repr. in The Greek Historians, Collections above; repr. Great Books, 1952, v. 6; repr. N.Y., Washington Square Pr., 1963, xxxviii, 369 p.

   Called the classic tr.

Tr. G. C. Macaulay. London and N.Y., Macmillan, 1890. 2 v. Repr. 1904.

* Tr. A. D. Godley. LCL, 1920–24. 4 v.

   Has been called the best tr.

Tr. J. Enoch Powell. Oxford, Clarendon Pr., 1949. 2 v.

* Tr. Aubrey de Selincourt. Penguin, 1954. 599 p. (The first Penguin tr. 1941 was abridged, 155 p.)

Tr. Harry Carter. N.Y., Heritage Pr., 1958. 2 v. Repr. WC, 1962, 557 p.

Other trs.: part (books 1, 2) tr. Barnabe Rich, 1584, repr. Tudor Trs., 1924; Isaac Littlebury, 1709, repr. 1729, 1737, 1818; William Beloe, 1791, et seq. to 1876; anon., Oxford, 1824; T. E. Laurent, Oxford 1827, repr. 1837, 1846; Isaac Taylor, 1829; G. S. Swayne, 1870; anon., 1885; G. Woodrouffe Harris, 1906–07; George Robinson, 1910.

For Herodotus, see Aubrey de Selincourt. *The World of Herodotus* (London, Secker, and Boston, Little Brown, 1962, 392 p.).

HESIOD (fl. c. 700 B.C.). Works. Tr. prose John Banks, verse J. H. Frere. In Works of Hesiod, Callimachus, and Theognis. BCL, 1856. xxi, 434 p. Repr. 1873.

Tr. prose A. W. Mair as Poems and Fragments. Oxford, Clarendon Pr., 1908. xlvii, 174 p.

* Tr. prose H. G. Evelyn-White. In Hesiod, The Homeric Hymns, and Homerica. LCL, 1914, p. 2–283.

* Tr. verse Arthur S. Way as Hesiod. London, Macmillan, 1934. 68 p.

Other trs. Thomas Cooke, 1728, repr. 1728, 1740, 1743, and in Chalmers' English Poets 20, 1810; C. A. Elton, 1815, repr. 1832, 1856, 1894.

*——— The Works and Days, Theogony, Shield of Herakles. Tr. verse Richmond Lattimore. Ann Arbor, Univ. of Mich. Pr., and London, Mayflower, 1959. 241 p.

*——— Theogony. Tr. prose Norman O. Brown. N.Y., Liberal Arts Pr., 1953. 87 p.

*——— Works and Days. Tr. verse George Chapman as The Georgicks. London, 1618. 39 p. Repr. in eds. of Chapman's poems.

Tr. Samuel Butler. London, Cape, 1923. 27 p.

For Hesiod, see Friedrich Solmsen, *Hesiod and Aeschylus* (Ithaca, N.Y., Cornell Univ. Pr., and London, Oxford Univ. Pr., 1949, ix, 230 p.)

HIPPOCRATES (460–357 B.C.). The Genuine Works. Tr. Francis Adams. London, Sydenham Society, 1849. 2 v. Repr. N.Y., 1886; Baltimore, Md., 1938, and London, Bailliere, 1939; Great Books, 1952, v. 10.

Tr. W. H. S. Jones and E. T. Withington. LCL, 1923–31. 4 v.

——— Aphorisms. Tr. anon. London, 1665.

Tr. Sir Conrad Joachim Sprengell (with the Sentences of Celsus). London, 1708. Re-ed. 1735, 435 p.

——— The Medical Works. Tr. John Chadwick and W. R. Mann. Oxford, Blackwell, and Springfield, Ill., C. C. Thomas, 1950. vii, 301 p.

——— The Theory and Practice of Medicine. Intro. Emerson C. Kelly. N.Y., Philosophical Library, 1964. x, 374 p.

HOMER (9th or 8th c. B.C.). The Iliad and the Odyssey. Tr. verse George Chapman as The Whole Works of Homer. London, 1616. Repr. 1857, 4 v.; Temple Classics, 1898, 4 v.; Oxford, Shakespeare Head, 1930–31, 5 v.; N.Y., Pantheon, 1956, 2 v.

The reprs. include the pseudo-Homerica (*Hymns, Battle of Frogs and Mice*), tr. by Chapman 1624 as *The Crowne of All Homers Workes*.

The double dates in the following entries indicate separate publications of Iliad and Odyssey.

Tr. John Ogilby. London, 1660 (Iliads), 1665 (Odysses). Repr. 1669, 2 v.

Tr. Thomas Hobbes. London, 1675, 1676. Repr. combined 1677, 1683, 1685, 1686.

* Tr. couplets Alexander Pope. London, 1715, 1726. 11 v. Repr. numerous, esp. BCL, 1876, et seq.; 1931 (Nonesuch Pr.); (Iliad only) ed. R. A. Brower and W. H. Bond, N.Y., Macmillan, and London, Collier-Macmillan, 1965, 574 p.

Tr. verse William Cowper. London, 1791, 2 v. Many reprs. in eds. of Cowper's poems, and EL, 1916 et seq.

Tr. prose T. A. Buckley. London, 1851. 2 v.

Tr. verse (Spenserian stanza) Philip Stanhope Worsley. Edinburgh, Blackwood, 1861 (2 v.), 1865–68 (2 v.) V. 2 of the Iliad (1868) tr. John Conington.

Tr. verse William Cullen Bryant. Boston, Houghton, 1870–71. 4 v. Repr. 1881 et seq.

Tr. prose Andrew Lang, Walter Leaf, and Ernest Myers (Iliad), and Andrew Lang and S. H. Butcher (Odyssey). London, Macmillan, 1883, (506 p.) 1879 (427 p.). Repr., esp. Harvard Classics, v. 22 (Odyssey), ML, 1929.

Tr. verse Arthur S. Way. London, Low, 1886–88, 2 v. Repr. 1904, 1910.

Tr. prose Samuel Butler. London and N.Y., Longmans, 1898 (2 v. in 1), 1900 (326 p.). Repr. London, Cape, 1920; repr. "corrected", 1921, 1923; repr. Great Books, 1952, v. 4; repr. (Iliad only) N.Y., Washington Sq. Pr., 1964, xxiv, 389 p.

* Tr. prose A. T. Murray. LCL, 1919 (2 v.), 1920–28 (2 v.)

Tr. verse Sir William Marris. London, Oxford Univ. Pr., 1934 (565 p.), 1925 (438 p.)

Tr. "colloquial" prose W. H. D. Rouse as The Story of Odysseus and The Story of Achilles. London, Nelson, 1937 (329 p.), 1938 (504 p.). Repr. N.Y., Mentor Books, 1949, 1950.

* Tr. verse Ennis Rees. N.Y., Random House and ML, 1963 (xiv, 529 p.), 1960 (xviii, 416 p.)

Foster records also trs. of both epics by W. L. Collins, 1869–70, repr. 1872–76; M. Barnard, 1876.

————— Iliad. At least 30 separate published trs. of the Iliad may be counted, beginning with John Ozell et al., translating into prose from the French 1712, 5 v. et seq. Some of the more interesting ones follow.

Tr. prose James Macpherson. London, 1773. 2 v.

Tr. blank verse Edward Earl of Derby. London, Murray, 1864. Repr. 1865, 1867, 1870, 1872–76, 1876, 1880, 1907, EL, 1910 et seq.

Tr. prose E. H. Blakeney. London, Bell, 1905–13. 12 parts. Repr. 1910–13, 2 v.

* Tr. prose Alston Hurd Chase and William G. Perry, Jr. Boston, Little, Brown, 1950. 489 p.

Tr. shortened I. A. Richards as The Wrath of Achilles. N.Y., Norton, 1950. 208 p.

Tr. prose E. V. Rieu. Penguin, 1950. 469 p.

* Tr. verse Richmond Lattimore. Chicago, Univ. of Chicago Pr., and London, Routledge, 1951. 527 p. Repr. 1962.

Tr. S. O. Andrew and M. J. Oakley. EL, 1955. xiv, 370 p.

Tr. Robert Graves as The Anger of Achilles. Garden City, N.Y., Doubleday, 1959, and London, Cassell, 1960. xxxiv, 357 p. Repr. London, New English Library, 1962.

————— Odyssey. At least 19 separate published versions of the Odyssey may be counted, of which the more interesting follow.

Tr. verse William Morris. London, Reeves and Turner, 1887. 2 v. Repr. London and N.Y., Longmans, 1896.

* Tr. rhythmic prose George Herbert Palmer. Boston, Houghton Mifflin, 1891. 387 p. Repr. rev. 1921.

Tr. verse J. W. Mackail. London, Murray, 1903–10. 3 v. Repr. rev. Oxford, Clarendon Pr., 1932, 513 p.

* Tr. prose T. E. Shaw (pseud. of T. E. Lawrence). London, Walker, and N.Y., Oxford Univ. Pr., 1932. 327 p. Repr. London and N.Y., 1935; N.Y., 1940, 442 p.; WC, 1955, xvi, 442 p.; N.Y., 1956, paper.

Tr. S. O. Andrew. EL, 1948. x, 309 p.

* Tr. verse Robert Fitzgerald. Garden City, N.Y., Doubleday, 1961, and London, Heinemann, 1962. 475 p. Repr. London, Panther, 1965, 429 p. paper.

Tr. Gregory H. Palmer. N.Y., Bantam, 1962. 306 p.

Tr. Preston H. Epps. (unabridged school ed.) 306 p. N.Y., Macmillan, and London, Collier-Macmillan, 1965. xviii, 398 p.

Pseudo-Homerica

*——— Batrachomyomachia Or the Battaile of Frogs and Mise. Tr. verse George Chapman, in The Crowne of all Homers Workes. London, [1624?]. 207 p. Repr. 1818, 1858, 1887, Oxford 1930–31 (in The Whole Works), N.Y., 1956 (in Chapman's Homer).

Tr. verse Thomas Parnell. London, 1717. 30 p. Repr. corrected by Pope in Pope's Odyssey, 1726, v. 5. Many reprs. in eds. of Pope.

Tr. verse William Cowper in The Iliad and Odyssey, 1791, q.v.

* Tr. prose H. G. Evelyn-White, in Hesiod, the Homeric Hymns and Homerica. LCL, 1914.

Other trs. William Fowldes, 1603; Samuel Parker, 1700; Samuel Wesley, 1726; H. Price, 1736; H. Morgan Brown, 1891; Jane Barlow, 1894.

——— Homeric Hymns (7th c. B.C.) Tr. George Chapman as Al the Hymnes of Homer, with Batrachomyomachia, see above.

* Tr. verse Percy B. Shelley as Seven Homeric Hymns. London, 1824. Repr. 1839, London, Halcyon, 1929, also in eds. of Shelley.

Called admirable.

Tr. prose Andrew Lang. London, Allen, and N.Y., Longmans, 1899. 255 p.

Tr. H. G. Evelyn-White, in Hesiod, the Homeric Hymns, and Homerica. LCL, 1915.

* Tr. verse Arthur S. Way. London, Macmillan, 1934. 84 p.

Other trs.: W. M. Call, 1842; John Edgar, Edinburgh, 1891.

For Homer, see C. M. Bowra, *Tradition and Design in the Iliad* (Oxford, Clarendon Pr., and N.Y., Oxford Univ. Pr., 1930, ix, 278 p.); Rhys Carpenter, *Folk Tale, Fiction and Saga in the Homeric Epics* (Berkeley, etc., Univ. of California Pr., and London, Cambridge Univ. Pr., 1946, vii, 198 p.; repr. 1958, paper); *A Companion to Homer*, ed. Alan J. B. Wace and Frank H. Stubbings (London and N.Y., Macmillan, 1962, xxix, 595 p., 109 ill.); *Essays on the Odyssey: Selected Modern Criticism,* ed. Charles H. Taylor, Jr. (Bloomington, Indiana Univ. Pr., 1963, x, 136 p. paper and cloth); G. S. Kirk, *The Songs of Homer* (Cambridge, England, and N.Y., Cambridge Univ. Pr., 1962, 423 p.; re-ed. abridged as *Homer and the Epic: A Shortened Version of "The Songs of Homer", ibid.,* 1965, x, 243 p., paper); Gilbert Murray, *The Rise of the Greek Epic* (Oxford, Clarendon Pr., 1907; re-ed. to 4th ed., 1934; repr. London and N.Y., Oxford Univ. Pr., 1960, xxvii, 356 p. paper); John L. Myres, *Homer and his Critics*, ed. Dorothea Gray (London, Routledge, and Fair Lawn, N.J., Essential Books, 1958, xii, 302 p.); Denys L. Page, *History and the Homeric Iliad* (Berkeley, etc., Univ. of California Pr., 1959, and London, Oxford Univ. Pr., 1960, vii, 350 p.; repr. 1963, paper); Denys L. Page, *The Homeric Odyssey* (Oxford, Clarendon Pr., and N.Y., Oxford Univ. Pr., 1955, vii, 186 p.); John A. Scott, *Homer and his Influence* (Our Debt to Greece and Rome, 1925, vii, 169 p.); John A. Scott, *The Unity of Homer* (Berkeley, Univ. of California Pr., 1921, 275 p.; repr. N.Y., Biblio and Tannen, 1965): Thomas Day Seymour, *Life in the Homeric Age* (N.Y., Macmillan, 1907, xvi, 704 p.; re-ed. 1914; repr. N.Y., Biblio and Tannen, 1963); Cedric H. Whitman, *Homer and the Heroic Tradition* (Cambridge, Mass., Harvard Univ. Pr., and London, Oxford Univ. Pr., 1958, vii 365 p.; repr. N.Y., Norton, 1965, paper).

IBYCUS (fl. 550 B.C.). Poems. Tr. Olga Marx and Ernst Morwitz. In Alcman, Sappho, and Ibycus, see Alcman, above.

ISAEUS (fl. c. 400 B.C.). The Speeches. Tr. Edward S. Forster. LCL, 1927. 486 p.

ISOCRATES (436–338 B.C.). The Orations and Epistles. Tr. Joshua Dinsdale and William Young. London, 1752.

Tr. John H. Freese. London, Bell, 1894. 2 v.

Tr. George Norlin and LaRue Van Hook. LCL, 1928–48. 3 v.

Trs. of individual orations begin with *The Doctrinal of Princes,* tr. Sir Thomas Elyot, 1534. See British Museum Catalogue, and Foster's *English Translations from the Greek.*

"ORPHEUS" (poems of various times ascribed to a pre-Homeric Orpheus). Mystical Institutions, or Hymns of Orpheus. Tr. verse Thomas Taylor. London, the Translator, 1787. 227 p. Repr. 1792, 1824, 1896.

PARMENIDES (fl. c. 500 B.C.). Tr. F. M. Cornford, in Parmenides' Way of Truth and Plato's Parmenides. London, Kegan Paul, 1939. xvii, 251 p.

See Kathleen Freeman, *Ancilla to the Pre-Socratic Philosophers*, in Collections, above.

PINDAR (522–?448 B.C.). Pindaric Odes. Tr. verse Abraham Cowley, in his Poems. London, Moseley, 1656. 5 pts. Repr. in collected eds. of Cowley's poems.

Rather paraphrases than trs.

Tr. verse Henry Francis Cary. London, Moxon, 1833. 214 p.

Tr. verse Abraham Moore, with prose tr. by D. W. Turner. BCL, 1852. xxvii, 434 p.

Tr. prose Sir J. E. Sandys. LCL, 1915. xlv, 635 p. Repr. 1962.

* Tr. A. S. Way. London, Macmillan, 1922. 160 p.

Ed. and tr. Lewis R. Farnell. London, Macmillan, 1930–32. 3 v. (parallel texts).

Tr. verse Alexander F. Murison. London and N.Y., Longmans, 1923. xi, 288 p.

Ed. and tr. verse C. J. Billson as The Odes of Victory. Oxford, Blackwell, 1928–30. 2 v. (parallel texts)

* Tr. verse Richmond Lattimore. Chicago, Univ. of Chicago Pr., 1947. 169 p. Repr. 1959.

Foster records 15 trs. before 1915, and also 14 partial trs.

For Pindar, see C. M. Bowra, *Pindar* (Oxford, Clarendon Pr., 1964, and N.Y., Oxford Univ. Pr., 1965, xvii, 446 p.); John Huston Finley, Jr.,

Pindar and Aeschylus (Cambridge, Mass., Harvard Univ. Pr., 1955, vii, 307 p.); Gilbert Norwood, *Pindar* (Berkeley, etc., Univ. of California Pr., and London, Cambridge Univ. Pr., 1945, xi, 302 p.).

PLATO (429–347 B.C.). The Works. Tr. Floyer Sydenham (1759–80) and Thomas Taylor. London, Taylor, 1804. 5 v. Repr. 1892.

Tr. Henry Francis Cary, H. Davis, and G. Burges. BCL, 1848–52. 6 v. Repr. Boston and Philadelphia, 1872–76; London, 1880–85; N.Y., 1888; London and New York, 1891–97; London, 1900.

    The tr. of the *Phaedo* repr. in EL Plato, 1911.

Tr. William Whewell as The Platonic Dialogues for English Readers. Cambridge and London, Macmillan, 1859–61. 3 v. Repr. London and N.Y,. 1892.

* Tr. Benjamin Jowett as The Dialogues. Oxford, Clarendon Pr., 1868. 4 v. Repr. 1871, N.Y., 1872, Oxford 1875, Oxford 1892, 5 v.; Oxford and N.Y., 1914, London 1931, N.Y. 1936; N.Y., Random House, 1937, 2 v.; Oxford, 1953, 1964.

Selections (*Apology, Phaedo, Crito*), Harvard Classics, v. 2. Selections, ed. Irwin Edman, ML 1930, xlviii, 577 p. Selections, ed. Scott Buchanan, Portable Library, N.Y., Viking, 1948, 696 p. Selections (four dialogues) repr. as *The Trial and Death of Socrates*, N.Y., Heritage Pr., 1963, xi, 274 p.

Ed. and tr. H. N. Fowler et al. LCL, 1914–35. 15 v.

* Tr. Lane Cooper et al. as The Collected Dialogues, ed. Edith Hamilton and Huntington Cairns. N.Y., Pantheon, 1961. xxv, 1743 p.

The first comprehensive tr. into English was *The Works of Plato Abridged*, tr. various hands from the French, London, 1701, 2 v.: numerous reprs. to 1839. Two American versions by unidentified trs. were *Plato's Works,* Boston 1848–52, 6 v., repr. 1888; and *The Divine and Moral Works of Plato*, N.Y., 1858–60, repr. Boston 1872–76.

Selected Works

———— Five Dialogues Bearing on Poetic Inspiration. Tr. Percy Bysshe Shelley et al. EL, 1910 et seq. xxi, 277 p.

Includes the *Ion* and *Symposium,* tr. by Shelley, and repr. in collected ed. of his works; *Meno,* tr. F. Sydenham, 1769; *Phaedo,* tr. Henry F. Cary, 1848; *Phaedrus,* tr. Josiah Wright, 1888.

——————Four Dialogues, Including the Apology of Socrates. Tr. John Stuart Mill, ed. Ruth Borchardt. London, Watts, 1946, and N.Y., Universal Distributors, 1947. 194 p.

—————— Gorgias, Phaedrus. Tr. R. Hackforth. London and N.Y., Cambridge Univ. Pr., 1952. vii, 172 p.

—————— Great Dialogues. Tr. W. H. D. Rouse. N.Y., New Amer. Lib., and London, Muller, 1956. 525 p.

—————— Parmenides, Theaetetos, Sophist, Statesman. Tr. John Warrington. EL, 1961. xii, 294 p.

—————— Phaedrus, Ion, Gorgias, and Symposium, with Passages from the Republic and Laws. Tr. Lane Cooper. N.Y. and London, Oxford Univ. Pr., 1938. lviii, 436 p.

—————— Philebus and Epinomis. Tr. A. E. Taylor, ed. R. Klibansky. LCL, 1952.

—————— Plato's Theory of Knowledge: The Theaetetus and the Sophist. Tr. F. M. Cornford. London, Kegan Paul, and N.Y., Harcourt, 1935. 336 p.

—————— Socratic Dialogues. Euthyphro, Apology, Crito, Phaedo, Gorgias. Tr. W. D. Woodhead. Edinburgh, Nelson, 1953. xxxii, 308 p.

—————— Socratic Discourses by Plato and Xenophon. Trs. various. EL, 1910, et seq. xxiii, 364 p.

Apology of Xenophon, tr. Sarah Fielding 1788; *Symposium,* tr. James Wellwood; *Lysis,* tr. Josiah Wright 1888; *Euthyphro,* tr. F. M. Stawell 1908; Xenophon's *Memorabilia,* tr. J. S. Watson 1854.

—————— Timaeus and Critias. Tr. A. E. Taylor. London, Methuen, 1929. 136 p.

—————— The Trial and Death of Socrates: Euthyphro, Apology, Crito, Phaedo. Tr. F. J. Church. London, Macmillan, 1880. xlviii, 190 p.

Tr. Lane Cooper. Ithaca, N.Y., Cornell Univ. Pr., 1941. 200 p.

Tr. John Warrington. EL, 1963, xv, 174 p.

Individual Works

———————— Gorgias. Tr. W. Hamilton. Penguin, 1960. 149 p.

———————— The Laws. Tr. A. E. Taylor. EL, 1934. lxviii, 380 p. Repr. 1960.

———————— Parmenides. Tr. F. M. Cornford, with Parmenides' Way of Truth. See Parmenides, above.

Tr. A. E. Taylor. Oxford, Clarendon Pr., 1934. 161 p.

———————— Phaedo. Tr. Lewis Theobald as Plato's Dialogue on the Immortality of the Soul. London, 1713. 72 p.

Tr. Patrick Duncan. London, Oxford Univ. Pr., 1928. 175 p.

———————— [Philebus]. Tr. R. Hackforth as Plato's Examination of Pleasure. Cambridge Univ. Pr., and N.Y., Macmillan, 1945. 143 p.

———————— The Republic. Tr. A. D. Lindsay. EL, 1935. xlix, 406 p.

Tr. F. M. Cornford. Oxford, Clarendon Pr., 1941. xxvii, 356 p. Repr. 1942.

Tr. I. A. Richards (in simplified English). N.Y., Norton, 1942. 218 p.

Tr. H. D. P. Lee. Penguin, 1955. 405 p.

Tr. Hary Spens. Glasgow 1763, repr. EL 1906 et seq. (xv, 348 p.).

The Jowett tr. repr. ML 1941. For other trs. of the dialogue, see Fosters's *English Translations from the Greek*.

———————— The Symposium or Supper. Tr. Francis Birrell and Shane Leslie. London, Nonesuch Pr., 1924. 106 p, Repr. *ibid.*, 1925, 130 p.

Tr. Michael Joyce. London, Dent, 1935. 111 p.

Tr. William Hamilton. Penguin, 1951. 121 p.

See also tr. by P. B. Shelley, in *Five Dialogues*, above.

———————— Timaeus. Tr. F. M. Cornford, in Plato's Cosmology: The Timaeus. London, Methuen, 1929. 136 p.

Tr. John Warrington. EL, 1966. xv, 138 p.

Spurious and Doubtful Works

———————— The Axiochus: On Death and Immortality. Tr. E. H. Blakeney. London, Muller, 1937. 47 p.

Cf. the tr. by Edmund Spenser, London, 1592, repr. ed. F. M. Padelford (Baltimore, Johns Hopkins Pr., 1934, 29 p.); and the tr. from the French version of Philippe de Mornay, 1592, repr. in his *Six Excellent Treatises of Life and Death*, 1607.

———————— The Epinomis. Tr. John Harward. Cambridge, Univ. Pr., 1932. 146 p.

———————— Thirteen Epistles. Tr. L. A. Post. Oxford, Clarendon Pr., 1925. 167 p.

Tr. John Harward as The Platonic Epistles. Cambridge, Univ. Pr., 1932. 243 p.

Tr. Glenn R. Morrow as Plato's Epistles. N.Y., Bobbs-Merrill, 1962. 282 p.

For Plato, see Robert S. Brumbaugh, *Plato for the Modern Age* (N.Y., Crowell-Collier, 1962, 256 p.; repr. N.Y., Collier Books, and London, Collier-Macmillan, 1964); I. M. Crombie, *An Examination of Plato's Doctrines*: v. 1, *Plato on Man and Society*; v. 2, *Plato on Knowledge and Reality* (London, Routledge, and N.Y., Humanities Press, 1962–63); I. M. Crombie, *Plato: The Midwife's Apprentice* (London, Routledge, 1964, and N.Y., Barnes & Noble, 1965, ix, 195 p.); R. C. Cross and A. D. Woozley, *Plato's Republic: A Philosophical Commentary* (London, Macmillan, 1965, and N.Y., St. Martin's Pr., 1964, xv, 295 p.); James K. Feibleman, *Religious Platonism: The Influence of Religion on Plato and the Influence of Plato on Religion* (London, Allen & Unwin, and N.Y., Macmillan, 1959, 236 p.; repr. N.Y., Barnes & Noble, 1962); Paul Friedländer, *Plato*, tr. Hans Meyerhoff from the German [1928–30, 3 v.], v. 1, *An Introduction*, v. 2, *The Dialogues: First Period*, v. 3 to come (London, Routledge, 1958–65, and N.Y., Pantheon, 1958–64; v. 1 repr., N.Y., etc., Harper, 1964, paper); G. M. A. Grube, *Plato's Thought* (London, Methuen, 1935, xvii, 320 p.; repr. Boston, Mass., Beacon Pr., 1958, paper); Paul Elmer More, *Platonism* (Princeton, N.J., Univ. Pr., 1917, xi, 307 p.; re-ed. to 3d ed., 1931); Sir David Ross, *Plato's Theory of Ideas* (Oxford, Clarendon Pr., and N.Y., Oxford Univ. Pr., 1951, viii, 250 p.; repr. 1953); J. A. Stewart, *Plato's Doctrine of Ideas* (Oxford, Clarendon Pr., and N.Y., Oxford Univ. Pr., 1909, vii, 206 p.; repr. N.Y., Russell, 1964); A. E. Taylor, *Plato, the Man and his Work* (London, Methuen, and N.Y., Dial Pr., 1927, xi, 522 p.; re-ed. to 6th ed., 1952; repr. N.Y., Meridian Pr., 1956); A. E. Taylor, *Platonism and its Influence* (Our Debt to Greece and Rome, 1924, ix, 153 p.).

PRODICUS (fl. 400 B.C.). The Choice of Heracles. Tr. K. S. Guthrie. Yonkers, N.Y., Platonist, 1925. 45 p.

PYTHAGORAS (582–500 B.C.). No extant writings.

See *Pythagoras Source-Book and Library*, tr. Kenneth Sylvan Guthrie (Alpine, N.J., Platonist, 1920, 177, 190 p.); and *The Life of Pythagoras with his Symbols* and *Golden Verses, with the Life of Hierocles and his Commentaries upon the Verses*, tr. Nicholas Rowe (London, Tonson, 1707, xxxiv, 389 p.).

SAPPHO (7th c. B.C.). Tr. verse Dante Gabriel Rossetti as Sapphic Fragments, in his Poems. London, 1870. Repr. in eds. of his poems.

* Tr. various hands and ed. H. T. Wharton as Sappho: Selected Renderings and a Literal Translation. London, Marshall, 1885. Repr. London, Lane, 1895; N.Y., Brentano, 1920, 177 p.

   Includes versions by Merivale, Palgrave, Symonds; commended.

Tr. Bliss Carman as Sappho: One Hundred Lyrics. Boston, Page, 1904. xx, 130 p. Repr. King's Classics, London, Chatto, 1907.

* Tr. verse A. S. Way. London, Macmillan, 1920. 36 p.

Tr. verse various hands, ed. E. M. Cox. London, Williams and Norgate, and N.Y., Scribner, 1925. 154 p.

Tr. prose and verse Marion Mills Miller and D. M. Robinson. Lexington, Ky., Maxwelton, 1925. 435 p.

Tr. rhymed verse C. R. Haines as Poems and Fragments. Broadway Trs. London, Routledge, and N.Y., Dutton, 1926. 255 p. (parallel texts and biography).

Tr. verse J. M. Edmonds as Sappho Revocata. London, Davies, 1928. 85, 81 p. (parallel texts).

* Tr. verse P. Maurice Hill. London, Staples Pr., and N.Y., Philosophical Library, 1953. xxii, 73 p.

* Tr. verse Mary Barnard. Berkeley, Univ. of California Pr., and London, Cambridge Univ. Pr., 1958. 114 p.

* Tr. verse Willis Barnstone. Garden City, Doubleday (Anchor Books), 1965. xiii, 207 p.

Other trs.: John Addison, 1735; Francis Fawkes, 1760, repr. Chalmers' English Poets 20, 1810; C. A. Elton, 1832; J. S. Easby-Smith, 1891; Percy Osborn, 1909; Edward Storer, 1916.

Many trs. in anthologies: Sir Edwin Arnold, *The Poets and Poetry of Greece* (London, Cassell, 1869, 226 p.); C. M. Bowra, *Greek Lyric Poetry*, (Oxford, 1936, repr. 1961) good prose trs.; David M. Robinson, *Sappho and Her Influence* (Our Debt to Greece and Rome, 1924, xii, 272 p.), with versions by the author, by Edmonds (in excellent prose), Fairclough, E. A. Robinson, etc.; *Lyra Graeca,* v. 1; *Oxford Book of Greek Verse in Translation;* J. A. Symonds, *Studies in the Greek Poets* (London, 1873–76, et seq., 2 v.

SOLON (fl. 638 B.C.). Poems. Tr. Kathleen Freeman, in Work and Life of Solon. Cardiff, Univ. of Wales Pr. Board, and London, Oxford Univ. Pr., 1926. 236 p.

Tr. prose Ivan M. Linforth, in Solon the Athenian. Berkeley, Univ. of California Pr., 1919, p. 130–245. (parallel texts).

SOPHOCLES (496–406 B.C.). The Tragedies. Tr. verse E. H. Plumptre. London, Strahan, 1865. 2 v. Repr. 1866, 1867, 1872, 1882, Boston, 1884, 1902, 1908. Two plays (Oedipus, Antigone) repr. Harvard Classics, v. 9.

Tr. verse Lewis Campbell. London, Kegan Paul, 1883. xxvii, 404 p. Repr. rev. 1896; WC, 1906 et seq.

Tr. verse Sir George Young. London, Bell, 1888. xxviii, 558 p. Repr., EL, 1906 et seq.

* Ed. and tr. prose Sir Richard Jebb as Plays and Fragments. Cambridge, Univ. Pr., and N.Y., Macmillan, 1883–1902. 7 v. (parallel texts) Repr. 1904, 1912 (tr. only), 1917 (tr. only), et seq.; repr. Great Books, 1952, v. 5.

> Excellent tr. Five plays of this tr. (the *Oedipus* trilogy, *Trachiniae, and Electra*) repr. in *Complete Greek Drama,* see Collections, above.

* Tr. verse A. S. Way. London and N.Y., Macmillan, 1909–14. 2 v.

† Tr. verse Francis Storr. LCL, 1912–13. 2 v.

See also *The Complete Greek Tragedies,* v. 2, Collections, above.

Other trs. of the seven plays: George Adams, 1729, repr. 1818; Thomas Francklin, 1759 et seq. to 1894; Robert Potter, 1788 et seq. to 1813; anon. prose, 1822; anon. prose, 1823 et seq. to 1888; T. Dale, 1824;

T. A. Buckley, BCL 1849 et seq.; anon. prose, N.Y. 1866; G. V. Dorsey, Piqua, Ohio, 1880; Robert Whitelaw, 1883, repr. 1897, 1906, 1907; J. S. Phillimore, 1902 (in The Athenian Drama, see Collections, above).

Selected Plays

*————— The Ajax and Electra. Tr. prose E. D. A. Morshead. London, Methuen, 1895. 137 p.

*————— Electra and Other Plays (Ajax, Women of Trachis, Philoctetes). Tr. verse Ernest Fairchild Watling. Penguin, 1953. 217 p.

Tr. Theodore H. Banks as Four Plays. London and N.Y., Oxford Univ. Pr., 1966. 192 p., also paper.

*————— Oedipus the King and Antigone. Tr. verse Peter Arnott. Crofts Classics. N.Y., Appleton, 1960. xi, 107 p.

————— (Oedipus Tyrannus, Oedipus at Colonus, Antigone). Tr. E. F. Watling as The Theban Plays. Penguin, 1947. 185 p.

* Tr. verse Theodore H. Banks as Three Theban Plays. N.Y. and London, Oxford Univ. Pr., 1956. xvi, 144 p.

* Tr. verse Paul Roche as The Oedipus Plays. N.Y., New Amer. Lib., 1958. 223 p.

*————— Three Tragedies (Antigone, Oedipus the King, Electra). Tr. verse H. D. F. Kitto. London and N.Y., Oxford, 1962. vii, 159 p.

Individual Plays

————— The Ajax. Tr. verse R. C. Trevelyan. London, Allen and Unwin, 1919. 57 p.

*————— The Antigone. Tr. verse George Herbert Palmer. Boston, Mass. Houghton Mifflin, 1899. 100 p. (commended)

Tr. John Jay Chapman. Boston, Houghton Mifflin, 1930. 70 p.

Tr. verse Dudley Fitts and Robert Fitzgerald. N.Y., Harcourt, 1939. 97 p. Repr. in Greek Plays in Modern Translation, see Collections, above.

Tr. verse R. C. Trevelyan. Liverpool, Univ. Pr., and London, Hodder and Stoughton, 1924. 61 p. Repr. with the Greek text arranged for performance at Cambridge: Cambridge, Bowes, 1939, viii, 87 p.

* Tr. rhymed verse Gilbert Murray. London, Allen and Unwin, and N.Y., Oxford Univ. Pr., 1941. 95 p.

Tr. verse F. Kinchin Smith. N.Y., Oxford Univ. Pr., 1951. 68 p.

Tr. Shaemas O'Sheel, in Ten Greek Plays, see Collections, above.

————— Electra. Tr. J. T. Sheppard. Cambridge, Bowes, 1927. 157 p.

Tr. verse Francis Fergusson. N.Y., Scott, 1938. 74 p. Repr. Norfolk, Conn. New Directions, 1936; and in Greek Plays in Modern Translation, see Collections, above.

Other trs.: Christopher Wase, 1649; Lewis Theobald, 1714; and many more.

————— Ichneutai. Tr. verse Roger L. Green, in Two Satyr Plays (with Euripides' Cyclops). Penguin, 1957. 94 p.

————— Oedipus at Colonus. Tr. Robert Fitzgerald. N.Y., Harcourt, 1941. 156 p. Repr. in Greek Plays in Modern Translation.

Tr. rhymed verse Gilbert Murray. London, Allen and Unwin, and N.Y., Oxford Univ. Pr., 1941. 131 p.

Tr. verse R. C. Trevelyan. Cambridge Univ. Pr., 1946. 75 p.

*————— Oedipus Rex. Tr. verse E. D. A. Morshead as Oedipus the King. London, Macmillan, 1885. 123 p. (commended)

Tr. rhymed verse Gilbert Murray. London, Allen, and N.Y., Oxford Univ. Pr., 1911. 92 p. Repr. in Fifteen Greek Plays, see Collections, above.

Tr. verse J. T. Sheppard. Cambridge Univ. Pr., and N.Y., Macmillan, 1920. lxxix, 179 p. (parallel texts)

Tr. verse W. B. Yeats as King Oedipus, A Version for the Modern Stage. London and N.Y., Macmillan, 1928. 61 p. Repr. in Greek Plays in Modern Translation, see Collections, above.

Tr. prose David Grene, in Three Greek Tragedies. Chicago, Univ. of Chicago Pr., 1942. 228 p. Repr. in Complete Greek Tragedies, see Collections, above.

Tr. verse Dudley Fitts and Robert Fitzgerald. N.Y., Harcourt, 1949. 109 p. Repr. in Four Greek Plays, see Collections, above.

Tr. Albert Cook, in Ten Greek Plays, see Collections, above.

Tr. Frank K. Wilson as Oedipus Tyrannus. Bath, Brodie, 1966. 44 p.

Other trs.: Lewis Theobald, 1715; George Somers Clarke, 1790, etc. See Foster, *English Translations from the Greek,* and LC Catalogue.

——————— Philoctetes. Tr. Kathleen Freeman, in Ten Greek Plays, see Collections, above.

Tr. Robert Torrance (with the next play). Boston, Mass., Houghton Mifflin, 1966. 91 p.

*——————— The Trachinian Women. Tr. rhymed verse Gilbert Murray as The Wife of Heracles. London, Allen, and N.Y., Oxford Univ. Pr., 1948. 89 p. (commended)

Tr. Ezra Pound as Women of Trachis. London, Spearman, 1956, and N.Y., New Directions, 1957. xxiii, 66 p.

Tr. Robert Torrance as The Women of Trachis (with Philoctetes). Boston, Houghton Mifflin, 1966. 91 p.

For Sophocles, see C. M. Bowra, *Sophoclean Tragedy* (Oxford, Clarendon Pr., and N.Y., Oxford Univ. Pr., 1944, vi, 384 p.; repr. London and N.Y., 1965, paper); Gordon MacDonald Kirkwood, *A Study of Sophoclean Drama* (Ithaca, N. Y., Cornell Univ. Pr., and London, Oxford Univ. Pr., 1958, xiii, 304 p.); H. D. F. Kitto, *Sophocles, Dramatist & Philosopher* (London and N.Y., Oxford Univ. Pr., 1958, 64 p.); Bernard M. W. Knox, *The Heroic Temper: Studies in Sophoclean Tragedy* (Berkeley, etc., Univ. of California Pr., 1964, ix, 210 p.); J. T. Sheppard, *Aeschylus and Sophocles* (Our Debt to Greece and Rome, 1927, vii, 204 p.); Cedric H. Whitman, *Sophocles, A Study in Heroic Heroism* (Cambridge, Mass., Harvard Univ. Pr., and London, Oxford Univ. Pr., 1951, 292 p.); Arthur J. A. Waldock, *Sophocles the Dramatist* (Cambridge, Eng., and N.Y., Cambridge Univ. Pr., 1951, ix, 234 p.).

THEOGNIS (fl. 550 B.C.). Elegies. Tr. prose James Banks, verse J. H. Frere, in Works of Hesiod, Callimachus, and Theognis. BCL, 1856.

Also tr. (with Hesiod) James Davies, 1873; and in Elegy and Iambus; in Oxford Book of Greek Verse. See Collections, above.

THUCYDIDES (b. 471 B.C.). Eight Books of the Peloponnesian Warre. Tr. Thomas Hobbes. London, 1629. Repr. 1634; repr. ed. W. Molesworth and W. B. Whittaker, 1845; repr. ed. David Grene, Ann Arbor, Univ. of Michigan Pr., 1959, and London, Mayflower Pr., 1960, 2 v.

Tr. Henry Dale. London, Bohn, 1848–49. Repr. BCL, 1868; N.Y., Harper, 1855, 1860, et seq.

Tr. Richard Crawley. London, Longmans, 1874. xxxiii, 630 p. Repr. 1876; Temple Classics, 1903; EL, 1910 et seq.; N.Y., ML, 1934; ed. Sir R. W. Livingstone, WC 1943, repr. London and N.Y., Oxford Univ. Pr., 1960, xxxii, 399 p.; repr. Great Books, 1952, v. 6.

Tr. Benjamin Jowett. Oxford, Clarendon Pr., 1881. 2 v. Repr. Boston, 1881, 1883; repr. rev. Oxford, 1900; N.Y., 1900, 1909; London, Ashdene Pr., 1930; N.Y., Bantam, 1960; N.Y., Washington Square Pr., 1963, xxxvii, 370 p.; in The Greek Historians, see Collections, above.

Tr. C. F. Smith. LCL, 1919–23. 4 v.

* Tr. Rex Warner. Penguin, 1954. 553 p. Repr. London, Cassell, 1962.

Other trs.: Thomas Nicolls from the French, 1550; anon. 1607; William Smith, 1753, many reprs. to 1898; S. T. Bloomfield, 1829; W. L. Collins, 1878.

For Thucydides, see Sir Frank E. Adcock, *Thucydides and his History* (Cambridge and N.Y., Cambridge Univ. Pr., 1963, viii, 146 p.; Charles Norris Cochrane, *Thucydides and the Science of History* (London and N.Y., Oxford Univ. Pr., 1929, vii, 180 p.; repr. N.Y., Russell, 1965); John H. Finley, Jr., *Thucydides* (Cambridge, Mass., Harvard Univ. Pr., 1942, vii, 344 p.; repr. 1947; repr. Ann Arbor, Univ. of Michigan Pr., 1963, paper); Jacqueline de Romilly, *Thucydides and Athenian Imperialism*, tr. Philip Thody from the French [1947] (N.Y., Barnes & Noble, 1963, and Oxford, Blackwell, 1964, 400 p.).

TYRTAEUS (7th c. B.C.). The Elegies. Tr. verse William Cleaver. London, Payne, 1761. xxiv, 36 p. (parallel texts).

Tr. verse Richard Polwhele in Theocritus' Idyllia. London, 1792. Repr. 1811, 1813, 1822.

———— The War Songs. Tr. Richard Polwhele, in Idylls of Theocritus, Bion, Moschus, and the War Songs of Tyrtaeus. BCL, 1853, p. 337–43.

Tr. J. W. Bailey as The Martial Fragments. London, 1862.

See *The War-Elegies Imitated* by H. J. Pye. London, Cadell, 1795. 48 p. See also *Elegy and Iambus; Oxford Book of Greek Verse in Translation,* in Collections, above.

XENOPHON (434-354 B.C.). The Whole Works. Tr. Ashley Cooper et al. London, Jones, 1832. 733 p. Repr. Philadelphia, 1845, N.Y., 1855.

Tr. Henry G. Dakyns. London and N.Y., Macmillan, 1890–97. 4 v. Repr. N.Y., 1910. The *Cyropaedia* repr. EL, 1914, 305 p.; the historical works repr. in The Greek Historians, see Collections, above.

Tr. Walter Miller et al. LCL, 1914–20. 7 v.

———— The Minor Works. Tr. Sarah Fielding et al. London, Walker, 1873. vii, 467 p.

Tr. J. S. Watson. London, 1854. 3 v. Repr. 1857, 1872–76, 1887.

Individual Works

———— The Anabasis: or Expedition of Cyrus, with the Memorabilia of Socrates. Literally tr. J. S. Watson. BCL, 1854. vii, 518 p. Many reprs. esp. Temple Classics, 1904; N.Y., Tr. Pub. Co., 1920.

* Tr. W. H. D. Rouse as The March Up Country. London, Nelson, 1948. Repr. N.Y., New Amer. Lib., 1959, 192 p.; repr. Ann Arbor, Univ. of Michigan Pr., 1964, 205 p. paper.

* Tr. Rex Warner as The Persian Expedition. Penguin, 1949. 309 p.

Other trs.: John Bingham, 1623; Edward Spelman, 1742, repr. 1749, 1776, 1806, 1811, 1812, 1813, 1830, 1849, 1875; William Smith, 1770; anon., N.Y., 1820–52; N.Y., 1855–58, repr. 1887, 1896.

———— Cyropaedia: The Institution and Life of Cyrus. Tr. Philemon Holland. London, 1632. Repr. Newton, Gregynog, 1936, 321 p.

Other trs.: William Barker, 1560–67; Francis Digby and John Norris, 1685; Maurice Ashley, 1770, et seq. to 1841; J. S. Watson and Henry Dale (with the Hellenica), BCL, 1880; Roscoe Mongan, 1880–81.

———— (Hellenica). Tr. John Newman as History of the Affairs of Greece. London, 1685. vii, 413 p.

Tr. William Smith .London, 1770. Repr. 1812, 1816.

Tr. Henry Dale and J. S. Watson, in BCL, 1880 (with the Cyropaedia). xvi, 579 p.

Tr. Rex Warner as History of my Times. Penguin, 1966. 363.

———— Hiero. Tr. Leo Strauss as On Tyranny. Chicago, Free Pr., 1948. xiii, 121 p.

————— Memorabilia of Socrates. Tr. J. S. Watson, with The Anabasis, above. Repr. in Socratic Discourses, by Plato and Xenophon, EL, 1910, et seq.

Other trs.: Edward Bysshe, 1712, repr. 1758, 1889, 1901, 1904; Sarah Fielding, 1762 et seq.; George B. Wheeler, 1862; Edward Levien, N.Y., 1872.

————— (Oeconomicus) Tr. Richard Bradley as The Science of Good Husbandry. London, Gorbet, 1727. 131 p.

Tr. Alexander Wedderburn and W. G. Collingwood, intro. John Ruskin. London, Ellis and White, 1876. xlvi, 141 p.

Other trs.: Gentian Hervet, 1532, many reprs. to 1577; William J. Hickie, 1879; B. J. Hayes, 1888.

HELLENISTIC ERA: 323–30 B.C., AND GRAECO ROMAN ERA: TO A.D. 330

PAGAN LITERATURE

ACHILLES TATIUS (end of 2d c. A.D.). The Loves of Clitophon and Leucippe. Tr. William Burton. London, 1597. Repr. ed. by Stephen Gaselee and H. F. B. Brett-Smith, Oxford, Blackwell, 1923. xxxi, 152 p.

Tr. Anthony Hodges. Oxford, 1638. 255 p.

Tr. Rowland Smith. London, Bell, 1882. Repr. in The Greek Romances of Heliodorus, Longus, and Achilles Tatius, BCL, 1901.

Tr. Stephen Gaselee. LCL, 1917. 461 p.

AELIAN, CLAUDIUS, of Praeneste (A.D. c. 170–235). The Letters. Tr. A. R. Benner and F. H. Forbes. In Alciphron, Aelian, and Philostratus. LCL, 1949. 587 p.

————— On Animals. Tr. A. F. Scholfield. LCL, 1959. 3 v.

————— A Registre of Histories, conteining Martiall Exploites. Tr. Abraham Fleming, London, 1576.

Tr. Thomas Stanley. London, 1665. Repr. 1670, 1677.

AELIANUS TACTICUS (fl. A.D. 106). The Tactiks of Aelian. Tr. John Bingham. London, 1616. Repr. 1616–29; 1631.

ALCIPHRON (fl. A.D. 180). Letters from the Country and the Town of Fishermen, Farmers, Parasites, and Courtesans. Tr. F. A. Wright. Broadway Trs. London, Routledge, and N.Y., Dutton, 1923. 221 p.

Also tr. T. Monro and W. Beloe as Alciphrons Epistles, 1791.

ANTONINUS, MARCUS AURELIUS (A.D. 121–180). Meditations Concerning Himself. Tr. Meric Casaubon. London, 1634, 27, 210, 46 p. Repr. 1635, 1664, 1673, 1692, 1694, 1702, 1898; ed. W. H. D. Rouse, Temple Classics, 1900; EL, 1906, et seq., 205 p.; N.Y., Heritage, 1956, xv, 230 p.

Tr. Jeremy Collier as His Conversation with Himself. London, Sare, 1701. 2 pts. Repr. 1708, 1726, 1887, 1891, 1905; rev. W. Reeve, with The Apology of Tertullian, 1889, repr. 1894.

Tr. Robert Foulis? as The Meditations. Glasgow, 1742. 308 p. Repr. 1749, 1752, 1764; rev. G. W. Chrystal, Edinburgh 1902, repr. 1904.

Tr. James Thomson as The Commentaries. London, 1747. viii, 234 p. Repr. Glasgow 1749, 1752, 1764, 1766.

Tr. R. Graves as The Meditations. London, Robinson, 1792. 377 p. Repr. 1811, 1826, 1905.

Tr. Henry McCormac (with Epictetus). London, Longmans, 1844. 126 p.

Tr. George Long as Thoughts. London, Bell, 1862. lxxviii, 224 p. Repr. BCL, 1869; Boston, 1876, 1890, 1900, 1901, 1903, 1905, 1906, 1908, 1909, 1910, 1912, 1923, 1926; repr. in Harvard Classics, v. 2, and in Stoic and Epicurean Philosophers (see Greek and Roman Collections, above); repr. Great Books, 1952, v. 12; repr. N.Y., Washington Square Pr., 1964, xv, 128 p.

Tr. Gerald H. Rendall as Marcus Aurelius Antoninus to Himself. London and N.Y., Macmillan, 1898. cxlvi, 195 p. Repr. Golden Treasury, 1901.

Tr. John Jackson as The Meditations. WC, 1906. xx, 135 p.

Tr. C. R. Haines as Communings with Himself. LCL, 1916. xxxii, 414 p.

Ed. and tr. A. S. L. Farquharson. Oxford, Univ Pr., 1944. 2 v.

Tr. G. M. A. Grube. N.Y., Bobbs-Merrill, 1963. xxvii, 143 p.

Tr. Maxwell Staniforth. Penguin, 1964. 187 p.

ANYTE OF TEGEA (3d c. B.C.). The Poems. Tr. Richard Aldington. London, The Egoist, 1915. 6 p. Repr. with Poems of Sappho, 1919; repr. in Medallions of Clay, N.Y., Knopf, 1921; repr. as Medallions from Anyte of Tegea, etc., London, Chatto, 1930.

APOLLODORUS OF ATHENS (fl. 140 B.C.). The Library. Tr. Sir James G. Frazer. LCL, 1921. 2 v.

The Poems are tr. in *Lyra Graeca,* see Collections, above.

APOLLONIUS OF PERGA (c. 200 B.C.). On Conic Sections. Tr. R. Catesby Taliaferro. Annapolis, Md., St. John's College Classics, 1939, v. 1 (mimeographed). Repr. Great Books, 1952, v. 11.

APOLLONIUS RHODIUS (295–215 B.C.). The Argonautica. Tr. prose Edward Philip Coleridge. London, Bell, 1889. xxviii, 209 p. Repr. N.Y., Heritage Pr., 1960.

* Tr. A. S. Way as The Tale of the Argonauts. Temple Classics. London, Dent, and N.Y., Dutton, 1901. 208 p.

* Tr. prose R. C. Seaton. LCL, 1912. 432 p.

* Tr. prose E. V. Rieu as The Voyage of the Argo: The Argonautica. Penguin, 1959. 207 p.

Other trs.: verse E. B. Greene, 1780; Francis Fawkes, 1780, repr. in Chalmers' English Poets 20, 1810; W. Preston, Dublin, 1803, repr. London, 1811, 1813.

APOLLONIUS OF TYANA. (4 B.C.–A.D. 130). Epistles. Tr. F. C. Conybeare, in Philostratus, The Life of Apollonius of Tyana, the Epistles of Apollonius, and the Treatise of Eusebius. LCL, 1926, v. 2, p. 408–81.

APPIAN OF ALEXANDRIA (fl. A.D. 130). Appian's Roman History. Tr. Horace White. London, Macmillan, 1899. 2 v. Repr. LCL, 1912–13, 4 v.

Other trs.: William Barker?, 1578; John Davies, 1678, repr. 1679, 1692, 1703.

ARATUS (fl. 270 B.C.). Aratus, Callimachus, and Lycophron. Tr. G. R. and A. W. Mair. LCL, 1921, p. 359–473

For four partial trs., see British Museum Catalogue.

ARCHIMEDES (287–212 B.C.). Works. Ed. with intro. Sir T. L. Heath. Cambridge, Univ. Pr., and N.Y., Macmillan, 1897. clxxxvi, 326 p. Supplement, 1912, 51 p. Repr. Great Books, 1952, v. 11.

———— Geometrical Solutions Derived from Mechanics. A Treatise Recently Discovered. Tr. J. L. Heiberg, intro. David Eugene Smith. Chicago, Open Court, 1909. 28 p.

ARISTARCHUS OF SAMOS (fl. 280 B.C.). Aristarchus of Samos, the Ancient Copernicus, with Aristarchus' Treatise on the Sizes and Distances of the Sun and Moon. Tr. Sir T. L. Heath. Oxford, Clarendon Pr., 1913. 425 p.

ARISTIDES, AELIUS (2d c. A.D.). To Rome. Tr. Saul Levin. Glencoe, Ill., Free Pr., 1950. 31 p.

ARRIAN (b. A.D. 90). Arrian. Tr. E. I. Robinson. LCL, 1929–33. 2 v.

———— The Anabasis of Alexander. Tr. E. J. Chinnock. London, Hodder and Stoughton, 1884. xiii, 443 p. Repr. with his tr. of Arrian's Indica, BCL, 1893, xx, 452 p.; repr. in The Greek Historians, v. 2.

Tr. Aubrey de Sélincourt as The Life of Alexander the Great. Penguin, 1958. 256 p.

Other trs.: Mr Rooke, 1729, 2 v. repr. 1862; William Vincent, 1797, repr. 1809; William Falconer, Oxford 1805; J. W. McCrindle, with The Periplus of the Eritrean Sea, 1879.

———— Arrian on Coursing: The Cynegeticus. Tr. William Dansey. London, Bohn, 1831. 314 p.

Tr. Denison B. Hull as Cynegeticus, or The Book of the Chase. Chicago, Pr. pr., 1958. 46 p.

——————— The Lamp of Epictetus: Arrian's Lectures on Epictetus to Young Men. Paraphrased by Edward Jacomb. London, Methuen, 1938. 320 p.

——————— Voyage Round the Euxine Sea. Tr. Thomas Falconer. Oxford, Cooke, 1805. 212 p.

ASCLEPIADES BITHYNIUS (1st c. B.C.). Asclepiades, his Life and Writings. Tr. Robert M. Green of Antonio Cocchio's Life of Asclepiades and Christian Gottlieb Gumpert's Fragments of Asclepiades. New Haven, E. Licht, 1955. ix, 167 p.

ATHENAEUS (fl. A.D. 230). The Deipnosophists: or The Banquet of the Learned. Tr. C. B. Gulick. LCL, 1927–34. 7 v.

Also tr. H. Younge, 1854, 3 v.

AURELIUS ANTONINUS, MARCUS. See Antoninus, above.

BABRIUS (1st c. A.D.). The Fables. Tr. verse James Davies. London, Lockwood, 1860. xxxii, 231 p.

Ed. and tr. Ben Edwin Perry (with the Fables of Phaedrus). LCL, 1965. cii, 634 p.

BION OF SMYRNA (fl. 180 B.C.). The Idylls of Bion and Moschus. Tr. Thomas Stanley (with Anacreon). London, 1651. Repr. 1683, 1815.

Tr. John M. Edmonds, in The Greek Bucolic Poets, LCL, 1912. xxviii, 527 p.

Tr. Arthur S. Way (with Theocritus). Cambridge Univ. Pr., 1913. viii, 156 p.

Tr. H. H. Chamberlin, in Last Flowers: A Translation of Moschus and Bion. Cambridge, Mass., Harvard Univ. Pr., 1937. 81 p.

Tr. prose A. S. F. Gow, in Theocritus, Moschus, Bion. London and N.Y., Cambridge Univ. Pr., 1953. 156 p.

Other trs.: Thomas Cooke 1724, with Moschus; Francis Fawkes, 1760, with Anacreon, repr. 1789, and in Chalmers' English Poets 20, 1810, and with Hesiod, 1832; Richard Polwhele, 1792, with Theocritus, repr. 1810, 1811, 1822; M. J. Chapman, 1836, in The Greek Pastoral Poets, repr. 1853 BCL with prose tr. James Banks; Andrew Lang, 1880, with Theocritus etc,. repr. 1889, 1922; J. H. Hallard, 1924, with Theocritus.

CALLIMACHUS (310–240 B.C.). The Works. Tr. verse H. W. Tytler, London, Davison, 1793. viii, 268 p. Repr. in The Works of Hesiod, BCL, 1856.

Tr. A. W. Mair, in Callimachus and Alciphron. LCL, 1921. viii, 643 p.

———— Aetia, Iambi, Lyric Poems, Hecale, minor poems, fragments. Tr. prose C. A. Trypanis. LCL, 1958. xvi, 317 p.

———— Epigrams. Ed. and tr. Gerald Mackworth Young. London, Oxford Univ. Pr., 1934. xv, 142 p.

———— The Hymns. Tr. verse William Dodd. London, 1755. 212 p.

Tr. prose James Banks, with the Epigrams, and verse trs. of Elton, Tytler, Frere. BCL, 1856.

Tr. verse Arthur S. Way as Hymns of Callimachus, with the Hymn of Kleanthes. London, Macmillan, 1934. 36 p.

Tr. Robert Allason Furness as Four Hymns and the Epigrams. London, Cape, 1931. xiv, 123 p.

———— Hymn V, tr. K. J. McKay as The Poet at Play: Kallimachos, "The Bath of Pallas." Leiden, Brill, 1962. x, 139 p.

———— Hymn VI. Tr. J. K. McKay, as Erysichthon: A Callimachean Comedy. Leiden, Brill, 1962. x, 202 p.

See also *Oxford Book of Greek Verse in Translation,* in Collections, above.

CALLISTHENES (Pseudo, c. A.D. 200). The Life of Alexander of Macedon. Tr. Elizabeth H. Haight. N.Y., Longmans, 1955. xiii, 159 p.

This Alexander-legend was the main source of the Alexander romances of the Middle Ages, by way of the Latin epitomes (of Julius Valerius, c. A.D. 300; and of the Archpresbyter Leo, c. A.D. 950, q.v. under Medieval Latin). It existed also in Ethiopic and in Syriac, and the versions in those languages have been ed. and tr. into English: see Farrar and Evans, nos. 133 and 132 respectively.

CALLISTRATUS SOPHISTA (3d c. B.C.). Descriptions. Tr. Arthur Fairbanks, in Philostratus and Callistratus. LCL, 1931. xxxii, 429 p.

CEBES (2d c. A.D.). The Tablet of Cebes, or the Embleme of Humane Life. Tr. John Davies from the French of Boileau, with Epictetus. London, Martyn, 1670. 170 p. Repr. separately as The Emblem of Human Life, Glasgow, 1901.

Tr. Jeremy Collier as The Mythological Picture, with Marcus Aurelius. London, 1701, et seq.

Tr. Robert Thomson Clark as The Tablet of Kebes, in The Characters of Theophrastus, The Mimes of Herondas, The Tablet of Kebes. London, Routledge, and N.Y., Dutton, 1909. xxxi, 159 p.

Other trs.: Sir Francis Poyntz, c. 1530; John Healey, with Epictetus and Theophrastus, 1610, repr. 1616, 1636; anon., 1676; Robert Warren, Cambridge, 1699; verse Thomas Scott, 1754; Samuel Boyse, 3d ed., Glasgow, 1750; anon. 2d ed., Cambridge, 1777; Hugh E. Seebohm, 1906.

CERCIDAS (fl. 220 B.C.). Poems. Ed. and tr. verse Alfred D. Knox, in Herodes, Cercidas, and the Greek Choliambic Poets. LCL, 1929. xxiv, 364 p.

CHION OF HERACLEA: A Novel in Letters (1st c. A.D.) Ed. and tr. Ingemar Dürring. Goteborg, Acta Universitatis, 1951. 123 p.

CLEANTHES THE STOIC (331–232 B.C.). Hymn to Zeus. Tr. T. W. Rolleston, in Greek Literature in Translation (Oates-Murphy), see Collections, above.

Ed. and tr. E. H. Blakeney as The Hymn of Cleanthes. London, SPCK, 1921. 16 p.

*DEMETRIUS OF PHALERON (345–307 B.C.). Demetrius on Style (supposititious work). Tr. W. Rhys Roberts. Cambridge, Univ. Pr., and N.Y., Macmillan, 1902. 388 p. Repr. with Aristotle and Longinus, LCL, 1927, p. 255–487.

Tr. T. A. Moxon, in Aristotles's Poetics, etc. EL, 1934, p. 197–268.

* Tr. G. M. A. Grube as A Greek Critic, Demetrius on Style. Toronto, Univ. of Toronto Pr., 1961. ix, 171 p.

DIO CASSIUS (b. A.D. 155). Dio's Roman History. Tr. Ernest Cary. LCL, 1914–27. 9 v.

For Dio Cassius, see Fergus Millar, *A Study of Cassius Dio* (Oxford, Clarendon Pr., and N.Y., Oxford Univ. Pr., 1964, xiv, 239 p.).

DIO CHRYSOSTOM (1st c. A.D.). Speeches. Tr. J. W. Cohoon and M. L. Crosby. LCL, 1938–51. 5 v.

DIODORUS OF SICILY (c. 50 B.C.–A.D.). The History. Tr. John Skelton (c. 1500 from the Latin of Poggio). Ed. F. M. Salter and H. L. R. Edwards. EETS 233, 239: 1956–57. 2 v.

Tr. Thomas Cogan. London, 1653.

Tr. G. Booth as The Historical Library. London, 1700. 797 p. Repr. 1814.

Ed. and tr. C. H. Oldfather, Russel Geer, and C. L. Sherman. LCL, 1933–51. 12 v.

DIOGENES LAERTIUS (2d c. A.D.). The Lives and Opinions of Eminent Philosophers. Tr. C. D. Yonge. BCL, 1853. viii, 488 p.

Tr. R. D. Hicks. LCL, 1925. 2 v.

Also tr. several hands, London, 1688, 589 p., repr. 1696, 2 v.

DIONYSIUS OF ALEXANDRIA (or Periegetes, fl. c. 120 A.D.). The Surveye of the World, or Situation of the Earth. Tr. prose Thomas Twine. London, 1572. 90 p.

DIONYSIUS OF HALICARNASSUS (fl. 29 B.C.). The Literary Treatises. Tr. Stanley Frederick Bonner. Cambridge Univ. Pr., 1939. 108 p.

————— On Literary Composition. Ed. and tr. William Rhys Roberts. London, Macmillan, 1910. xiii, 358 p.

————— Roman Antiquities. Tr. Edward Spelman. London, 1758. 4 v. Repr. rev. Ernest Cary. LCL, 1937–45. 5 v.

————— The Three Literary Letters. Tr. William Rhys Roberts. Cambridge Univ. Pr., and N.Y., Macmillan, 1901. xi, 232 p.

See also Longinus *On the Sublime*, now generally ascribed to Dionysius.

EPICTETUS (c. A.D. 55–c. 138). All the Works. Tr. Elizabth Carter. London, 1758. xli, 505 p. Repr. 1759, 1807, Boston 1865 (rev. T. W. Higginson); 1890; Boston, 1897; Temple Classics, ed. W. H. D. Rouse, 1899; EL, 1910, as Moral Discourses, Enchiridion, and Fragments, xxviii, 356 p., repr. 1955.

Tr. George Long, as The Discourses, with the Encheiridion and Fragments. BCL, 1877. xliii, 452 p. Repr. 1888, 1890, 1892, 1895, 1897, 1902, 1903; repr. Great Books, 1952, v. 12.

Tr. P. E. Matheson as The Discourses and the Manual. Oxford, Clarendon Pr., 1916. 2 v.

Tr. W. A. Oldfather as The Discourses as Reported by Arrian, the Manual, and Fragments. LCL, 1926–28. 2 v.

Part trs.: The Manual, by James Sanford (from the French), 1567; John Healey, 1610, with Cebes, repr. 1616, 1636; Ellis Waller, verse paraphrase, 1692, repr. 1697, 1702, 1708, 1716, 1724, 1737; J. W., verse, with Cebes, 1707. The Discourses, etc., tr. John Davies, 1670; George Stanhope, with Simplicius, 1964, repr. 1700, 1721, 1741, 1750; anon. M. D., 1702, repr. 1703; H. McCormac, with Marcus Aurelius, 1844; Hon. T. Talbot, 1881; T. W. Rolleston, 1888, repr. 1891; Hastings Crossley (as The Golden Sayings, with the Hymn of Cleanthes), 1903, repr. Harvard Classics, v. 2.

EPICURUS (342–270 B.C.). The Extant Remains. Tr. Cyril Bailey. Oxford, Clarendon Pr., 1926. 432 p. Repr. in Stoic and Epicurean Philosophers, in Greek and Roman Collections, above.

Tr. George K. Strodach as The Philosophy of Epicurus: Letters, Doctrines, and Parallel Passages from Lucretius. Evanston, Ill., Northwestern Univ. Pr., 1963. x, 262 p.

————— Letters, Principal Doctrines, and Vatican Sayings. Tr. Russel M. Geer. Indianapolis, Ind., Bobbs-Merrill, 1964. xii, 98 p. paper.

Earlier trs.: John Digby, as Epicurus's Moralls, 1655, repr. 1670, 1712; W. Charleton, 1656, repr. 1926.

ERINNA (4th c. B.C.). Poems. Tr. Marion Mills Miller, in Songs of Sappho, 1925, q.v.

See also *Greek Literary Papyri,* in Collections, above.

EUCLID (fl. 300 B.C.). The Thirteen Books of Euclid's Elements. Tr. Sir T. L. Heath. Cambridge, Univ. Pr., 1908. 3 v. Repr. *ibid.,* and N.Y., Macmillan, 1926, 3 v.; repr. Great Books, 1952, v. 11; repr. rev. N.Y., Dover, 1956.

Ed. and tr. Ivor Thomas, in Greek Mathematical Works. LCL, v. 1, 1939.

At least eight earlier trs., from Henry Billingsley, 1570, plus countless part trs. The Robert Simson tr. of books 1–6 and 10–12 (Glasgow, 1756) was rev. repr. EL, 1933, xviii, 398 p., repr. 1955.

GALEN (A.D. 130–200). Certaine Workes of Galen (*Methodus medendi,* Office of a Chirurgion, epitome of Naturall Faculties). Tr. Thomas Gale. London, 1586.

———— On Anatomical Procedures. Tr. Charles Singer. London and N.Y., Oxford Univ. Pr., 1956. 288 p.

Tr. W. L. H. Duckworth (On Anatomical Procedures, the Later Books). London and N.Y., Cambridge Univ. Pr., 1962. 278 p.

———— The Art of Physick. Tr. N. Culpeper. London, 1652.

Tr. P. English as Method of Physick. Edinburgh, 1656.

———— A Translation of Galen's Hygiene. Tr. Robert Montraville Green. Springfield, Ill., C. C. Thomas, 1951, and Oxford, Blackwell, 1952. xxiv, 227 p.

———— Institutio Logica. Tr. J. S. Kieffer. Baltimore, Md., Johns Hopkins Pr., 1964. 150 p.

———— On Medical Experience. Tr. R. Walzer from the Arabic version, rev. H. A. R. Gibb. London, Oxford Univ. Pr., 1944. 164 p.

———— On the Natural Faculties. Ed. and tr. Arthur John Brook. LCL, 1916. 339 p. Repr. (English only) Great Books, 1952, v. 10.

———— On the Passions and Errors of the Soul. Tr. Paul W. Harkins. Columbus, Ohio State Univ. Pr., 1963. 136 p.

HELIODORUS (3d c. A.D.). An Aethiopian Historie. Tr. Thomas Under-downe from Latin. London, 1569? Repr. 1587, 1606, 1622; Tudor Trs. 1895; rev. F. A. Wright, 1923; ed. George Saintsbury, 1924.

Tr. Nahum Tate et al. London, 1685. Repr. 1687.

Tr. anon. as The Adventures of Theagenes and Chericlia. London, 1717.

* Tr. Moses Hadas as An Ethiopian Romance. Ann Arbor, Univ. of Mich. Pr., 1957. x, 277 p.

Tr. Sir Walter Lamb. EL, 1961. xxvi, 278 p.

HEPHAESTION (fl. A.D. 170). The Enkheiridion: Concerning Metres and Poems. Tr. T. F. Barham. Cambridge, Parker, 1843. 229 p.

HERODIAN (fl. A.D. 200). History of Twenty Roman Caesars and Emperors (of his Time). Tr. James Maxwell. London, 1629. 2 pt. Repr. 1635, 434 p.

Tr. Edward C. Echols as History of the Roman Empire from the Death of Marcus Aurelius to the Accession of Gordian III. Berkeley, Univ. of California Pr., and London, Cambridge Univ. Pr., 1961. 220 p.

Other trs.: Nicholas Smyth from Latin, 1550?; verse C. B. Stapylton, 1652; anon., Oxford, 1698; J. Hart, 1749.

HERONDAS (or Herodas, 3d c. B.C.). The Mimiambs. Tr. verse Hugo Sharpley as A Realist of the Aegean. London, Nutt, 1906. x, 57 p.

Tr. R. Thomson Clark, with Theophrastus, 1909 (q.v.).

Tr. M. S. Buck. N.Y., pr. pr., 1921. 119 p.

Ed. and tr. A. D. Knox as The Mimes and Fragments, notes by Walter Headlam. Cambridge Univ. Pr., 1922. lxiv, 465 p. Repr. in LCL (with Cercidas and the Greek Choliambic Poets), 1929.

Tr. verse Jack Lindsay as The Mimiambs. London, Franfrolico Pr., and N.Y., McKee, 1929. ill.

J. A. Symonds' *Studies of the Greek Poets* includes trs. of 6 works of Herondas. See also Cebes, above.

JOSEPHUS, FLAVIUS (A.D. 37–98). The Famous and Memorable Workes. Tr. Thomas Lodge from French. London, 1602, Repr. 1609, 1620, 1632, 1640, 1655, 1676, 1683, 1693.

Tr. Sir Roger L'Estrange, 1702. Repr. 1709, 1725, 1733, 1776, 1773.

Tr., William Whiston as The Genuine Works. London, 1737. Repr. Dublin, 1741, 5 v.; London, 1755, 4 v. Repr. Edinburgh, 1793; Dublin, 1796; London, 1806; N.Y., 1808–09; London, 1812; Edinburgh, 1815; N.Y., 1815; N.Y., 1823–24; London, 1825; Edinburgh, 1840; London, 1841, 1850?; Edinburgh, 1864; London, 1865, 1867; N.Y., 1873; London, 1875, 1878, 1878–79, 1884, 1889–90, 1890, 1893, 1896; Grand Rapids, Mich., Kregel, 1960, xxi, 770 p.

Ed. and tr. H. St. J. Thackeray and Ralph Marcus. LCL, 1926–43. 7 v.

————— The Jewish War. Tr. G. A. Williamson, Penguin, 1959. 411 p.

Other trs. of one or both of Josephus' histories: John Court, 1733, repr. 1754, 1770; E. Thompson and W. C. Price, 1777–78, 2 v.; Edward Kimpton, 1785 (723 p.), repr. 1790, 1800; Charles Clarke, 1785, repr. 1794, 1803; T. Bradshaw, 1792.

For Josephus, see G. A. Williamson, *The World of Josephus* (London, Secker, 1964, and Boston, Mass., Little Brown, 1965, 318 p.).

LEONIDAS OF TARENTUM (fl. 294–281 B.C.). Poems. Ed. and tr. verse Edwyn Bevan. Oxford, Clarendon Pr., 1931. xlviii, 119 p.

LONGINUS (3d c. A.D.). On the Sublime. Tr. William Smith. London, 1739. Repr. 1740, 1742, 1743, 1751, 1752, 1756, 1757, 1770; Dublin 1777, 1800, 1819.

* Tr. William Rhys Roberts. Cambridge, Univ. Pr., and N.Y., Macmillan, 1899. x, 288 p. Repr. 1907.

* Tr. W. H. Fyfe, in Demetrius on Style, etc. LCL, 1927.

Tr. Frank Granger. London, Nott, 1935. 114 p.

Tr. T. G. Tucker as On Elevation of Style. Melbourne, Univ. Pr., and London, Oxford Univ. Pr., 1935. 64 p.

* Tr. G. M. A. Grube as On Great Writing. N.Y., Liberal Arts Pr., 1957. 66 p.

Earlier trs.: John Hall, 1652; John Pulteney, from the French of Boileau, 1680; anon., Oxford, 1698; Mr Welsted, 1712; anon., 1821; anon., 1830?; W. T. Spurdens, 1838; T. R. R. Stebbing, Oxford 1867; H. A. Giles, 1870; H. L. Havell, 1890; A. O. Prickard, 1906.

The treatise is now generally attributed to an earlier writer, perhaps Dionysius of Halicarnassus, q. v.

LONGUS (2d to 4th c. A.D.). Daphnis and Chloe. Tr. Angell Daye from French. London, 1587. Repr. 1890, 1905.

Tr. George Thornley. London, 1657. Rev. and enlarged J. M. Edmonds, LCL, 1916, xxiii, 423 p. Repr. London, Lesley, 1948, 196 p.; N.Y., Pantheon, 1949, 183 p. ill. Maillol.

Tr. Rowland Smith, in The Greek Romances of Heliodorus, Longus, and Achilles Tatius. BCL, 1901. xxxii, 511 p.

Tr. adapted George Moore from the French. London, Heinemann, and N.Y., Putnam, 1924. 163 p. Repr. N.Y., Duschnes, 1954.

* Tr. Jack Lindsay. London, Daimon Pr., 1948. 114 p.

* Tr. Paul Turner. Penguin, 1956. 124 p.

Other trs.: C. P. LeGrice, 1804; anon. from French, 1896; ed. and tr. W. D. Lowe, 1908; Moses Hadas, in Three Greek Romances, 1953, see Collections, above.

LUCIAN (fl. A.D. 150). Lucian's Works. Tr. Ferrand Spence. London, 1684. 5 v.

Tr. John Carr as Lucian's Dialogues. London, 1774. 5 v.

Tr. Thomas Francklin. London, 1780. 2 v. Repr. 1781, 1887.

Tr. Howard Williams. London, 1888. Repr. 1904.

* Tr. H. W. and F. G. Fowler. Oxford, Clarendon Pr., 1905. 4 v.

    Excellent tr.

* Ed. and tr. A. M. Harmon, K. Kilburn, and M. D. Macleod. LCL, 1913–59. 8 v.

    Commended.

* Tr. Paul Turner as Satirical Sketches. Penguin, 1961. 320 p.

Many trs. of individual dialogues from Sir Thomas Elyot, c. 1530, and of selected dialogues, including the following.

* ———— Certain Select Dialogues, with his True History. Tr. Francis Hickes. Oxford, 1634. 196 p. Repr. 1663, 1664, 1894, 1902; London, Chapman, 1925; Ann Arbor, Mich., Edwards, 1938.

Commended.

* Tr. Lionel Casson as Selected Satires. Chicago, Aldine, 1962. 382 p.

For Lucian, see Francis G. Allinson, *Lucian, Satirist and Artist* (Our Debt to Greece and Rome, 1926, ix, 204 p.).

LYCOPHRON (fl. 250 B.C.). The Alexandra. Ed. and tr. verse G. W. Mooney. London, Bell, 1921. xvii, 178 p. (parallel texts)

Also tr. Viscount Royston, verse, 1806; C. A. Elton (with Hesiod), 1832; A. W. Mair (with Aratus and Callimachus), LCL, 1921.

LYSIAS (4th c. B.C.). Orations. Tr. W. R. M. Lamb. LCL, 1930. xxvi, 706 p.

Also tr. John Gillies (with Isocrates), 1778.

MANETHO (283–248 B.C.). (Fragments of Egyptian History). Ed. and tr. W. G. Waddell (with Ptolemy's *Tetrabiblos*). LCL, 1940. xxxii, 256 p.

Also ed. and tr. I. P. Cory, 1828.

MAXIMUS OF TYRE (fl. A.D. 130). Dissertations. Tr. Thomas Taylor. London, Whittingham, 1804. 2 v.

MELEAGER OF GADARA (1st c. A.D.). Fifty Poems. Tr. Walter Headlam. London and N.Y., Macmillan, 1890. 103 p.

* Tr. verse Richard Aldington, in Medallions (with Anyte, Anacreontea, etc.). London, Chatto and Windus, 1930. 116 p.

Commended.

* Tr. verse Humbert Wolfe as Homage to Meleager. N.Y., Fountain, 1930. 129 p.

Commended.

Also tr. in *Oxford Book of Greek Verse in Translation,* see Collections, above.

MENANDER (342–291 B.C.). The Principal Fragments. Ed. and tr. verse Francis G. Allinson. LCL, 1921. xxxi, 539.

———— The Lately Discovered Fragments. Ed. and tr. Unus Multorum (J. S. Pomeroy, Viscount Haberton). Oxford, Parker, 1909. 135 p. (The Litigants. The Lady with the Shorn Locks. The Woman of Samos. The Hero.)

———— Three Plays. Tr. L. A. Post. Broadway Trs. London, Routledge, and N.Y., Dutton, 1929. vii, 128 p.

*———— Two Plays. The Rape of the Locks. The Arbitration. The Fragments; tr. verse Gilbert Murray, and the Gaps Conjecturally Filled. London, Allen and Unwin, and N.Y., Oxford Univ. Pr., 1945. 239 p.

The trs. were first published separately, London, 1942, 1945.

*———— Dyskolos, or The Man Who Didn't Like People. Tr. prose W. G. Arnott. London, Athlone Pr., 1960. viii, 45 p.

Tr. prose Philip Vellacott as The Bad-Tempered Man or The Misanthrope. London and N.Y., Oxford Univ. Pr., 1960. xxxi, 50 p.

———— The Samia (The Augmented Text). Tr. verse J. M. Edmonds. Cambridge, Deighton Bell, 1951. 41 p.

MOSCHUS (fl. 150 B.C.). Fragments of Moschus. Tr. Percy Bysshe Shelley. London, 1824. Repr. in collected eds. of Shelley's Poems.

For other trs. of Moschus, see also Anacreon, Bion, and Theocritus.

*NICANDER OF COLOPHON (2d c. B.C.). The Poems and Poetical Fragments. Ed. and tr. prose A. S. F. Gow and A. F. Scholfield. London and N.Y., Cambridge Univ. Pr., 1953. 247 p. (parallel texts)

NICOMACHUS OF GERASA (A.D. 2d c.). Introduction to Arithmetic. Tr. Martin L. D'Ooge. Univ. of Michigan, Humanistic Ser. N.Y., Macmillan, 1926. ix, 318 p. Repr. Great Books, 1952, v. 11.

ONOSANDER (fl. c. A.D. 59). Of the Generall Captaine and of his Office (*Strategicus*). Tr. Peter Whytehorne from the Italian version. London, 1563. 136 leaves.

Tr. by Illinois Greek Club as The General (with Aeneas Tacticus, Asclepiodotus). LCL, 1923 et seq. x, 531 p.

OPPIAN OF ANAZARBA (fl. c. A.D. 180). On Fishing (*Halieutica*). Ed.
and tr. prose A. W. Mair, in Colluthus, Tryphiodorus, Oppian.
LCL, 1928. xxx, 635 p.

OPPIAN OF APAMEA (fl. c. A.D. 206). On Hunting (*Cynegetica*). Included
with the preceding item.

PARTHENIUS OF NICAEA (fl. 50 B.C.). The Love Romances and Other
Fragments. Tr. Stephen Gaselee. In Longus, Daphnis and Chloe.
LCL, 1916, q.v.

PAUSANIAS (fl. A.D. 150). The Description of Greece. Tr. Thomas Taylor.
London, 1794. 3 v. Repr. 1824.

Tr. A. R. Shilleto. London and N.Y., 1886. 2 v.

* Tr. Sir James Frazer. London and N.Y., Macmillan, 1896. 6 v.

Excellent tr. and annotation.

Ed. and tr. W. H. S. Jones and H. A. Ormerod. LCL, 1918–35. 5 v.

PHILO OF ALEXANDRIA (Philo Judaeus, fl. A.D. 49). The Works. Tr. C.
D. Yonge. BCL, 1854–55. 4 v.

Ed. and tr. F. H. Colson, G. H. Whitaker, Ralph Marcus. LCL, 1929–53.
11 v.

————— The Biblical Antiquities. Tr. from Latin by M. R. James. London,
SPCK, 1917. 280 p.

————— On the Contemplative Life. Tr. Frank W. Tilden. Bloomington,
Indiana Univ. Pr., 1922. 37 p.

PHILODEMUS (1st c. B.C.). The Rhetorica. Tr. H. M. Hubbell. Transactions of Connecticut Academy of Arts and Sciences 23 (1920),
p. 243–382.

Abridged paraphrase.

——————— On Methods of Inference: A Study in Ancient Empiricism. Ed. and tr. Philip Howard DeLacy and Estelle Allen DeLacy. Philadelphia, American Philosophical Association, 1941. ix, 200 p.

PHILOSTRATUS, FLAVIUS (b. A.D. 182). The Life of Apollonius of Tyana, The Epistles of Apollonius, and The Treatise of Eusebius. Ed. and tr. F. C. Conybeare. LCL, 1921–26. 2 v.

——————— The Letters. Tr. A. R. Benner, in Alciphron, Aelian, and Philostratus. LCL, 1949. 587 p.

——————— The Life of Apollonius, tr. J. S. Phillimore as In Honour of Apollonius. Oxford, Clarendon Pr., 1912. 2 v.

Tr. Charles P. Eells. Stanford, University, 1923. 263 p.

Earlier trs.: C. Blount, 1680; E. Berwick, 1809.

——————— The Lives of the Sophists. Ed. and tr. Wilmer Cave Wright, in Philostratus and Eunapius: The Lives of the Sophists. LCL, 1922, p. 2–313.

PHILOSTRATUS LEMNIUS, The Elder and the Younger (3d c. A.D.). *Imagines.* Ed. and tr. Arthur Fairbanks, in Philostratus and Callistratus. LCL, 1931. xxxii, 429 p.

PLOTINUS (A.D. 203–282). The Enneads. Tr. Kenneth Sylvan Guthrie as The Complete Works, with Biography by Porphyry, Eunapius, and Suidas, and Commentary by Porphyry. London, Bell, and Grantwood, N.J., Comparative Literature, 1918. 4 v.

Tr. Stephen McKenna as Plotinus, with Porphyry's Life . . . Forming a Conspectus of the Plotinian System. London, P. L. Warner, 1917–30. 5 v., published separately with separate titles, the last three also published London and Boston, Medici Society, 1924–1926–1930. Repr. rev. S. B. Page in Great Books, 1952, v. 17; repr. as The Enneads, London, Faber, and N.Y., Pantheon Books, 1957. 686 p.

Selections: *The Essence of Plotinus. Extracts,* ed. Grace H. Turnbull, N.Y., Oxford, 1934, xx, 303 p.; *The Philosophy of Plotinus: Representative Books from the Enneads,* tr. Joseph Katz, N.Y., Appleton, and London, Noble, 1950, xxxii, 158 p.; *The Essential Plotinus: Representative Treatises from the Enneads,* ed. Elmer O'Brien, N.Y., New American Library, 1964, 224 p.

Earlier tr.: *Selected Works*, tr. Thomas Taylor, separately published 1787, 1794, combined 1817, 600 p., repr. London, Bohn, 1895.

PLUTARCH (A.D. 46–120). The Greek Questions. Tr. with commentary W. R. Halliday. Oxford, Clarendon Pr., 1928. 233 p.

*———— The Lives of the Noble Grecians and Romanes. Tr. Sir Thomas North from French of Jacques Amyot. London, 1579. Repr. 1595, 1603, 1610–12, 1631, 1657, 1676; repr. ed. W. W. Skeat as Shakespeare's Plutarch, Oxford, 1875; repr. Tudor Trs., 1895–96, 6 v.; repr. Temple Classics, 1898–99, 10 v.; repr. ed. C. F. T. Brooke, Oxford, 1909, 2 v., repr. Oxford, Blackwell, 1928, 8 v.; repr. Nonesuch Pr., 1929–30, 5 v.; repr. N.Y., Heritage Pr., 1954, 1975 p.

* Tr. various hands, introductory matter by John Dryden. London, 1683–86, 5 v. Repr. 1702–11, 1716, 1727, 1749, 1758, 1763. Repr. rev. Arthur Hugh Clough, Boston, Little, Brown, 1859, 5 v. Repr. 1864, 1876, 1902, Harvard Classics, v. 12 (eight lives); EL, 1910 et seq., 3 v.; ML, 1932, xxiv, 1309 p.; Great Books, 1952, v. 14. Abridged as Everybody's Plutarch. N.Y., Dodd, Mead, 1962, ix, 780 p.

* Tr. and ed. Bernadotte Perrin. LCL, 1914–26. 11 v.

Also tr. J. & W. Langhorne, 1770, reprs. to 1884; Francis Wrangham, 1813, reprs. to 1832.

*———— The Moralia. Tr. Philemon Holland as The Philosophie, Commonly Called the Morals (and Romane Questions). London, 1603. Repr. 1657, 1888, 1892, part (as Plutarch's Moralia), ed. E. H. Blakeney, EL, 1912 et seq., 432 p.

Ed. and tr. Frank Cole Babbitt and others. LCL, 1927–65. 12 v. (of 15).

Also tr. several hands, 1684, 5 v., repr. 1694–95, 1704, 1718; with intro. R. W. Emerson, London, 1870. Tr. C. W. King and A. R. Shilleto, BCL, 1882–88, 2 v., repr. 1908. Part trs. include *Selected Essays*, tr. (v. 1) R. G. Tucker and (v. 2) A. O. Prickard, Oxford, Clarendon, 1913–18. Single essays: *Quyete of Mind*, tr. Thomas Wyat 1528, facs. ed. C. R. Baskervill, Harvard Univ. Pr., 1931; *The governaunce of good helthe*, 1530?, retr. John Hales, 1543; *Howe one may take profete of his enmyes*, tr. Sir Thomas Elyot, 1533?, repr. 1550; *The Education or Bringing Up of Children*, tr. the same, 1535; *De Curiositate*, tr. Queen Elizabeth, pr. EETS 113, 1899; *On Music*, tr. J. H. Bromby, 1822; *On the Delay of*

Divine Justice, tr. A. P. Peabody, Boston, 1885; *On the Right Use of Greek Literature*, tr. F. M. Padelford in *Essays on the Study and Uses of Poetry by Plutarch and Basil the Great*, N.Y., Holt, 1902, 136 p.

——————— The Roman Questions. Tr. Philemon Holland in The Morals, 1603, above. Repr. London, Nutt, 1892, xxxviii, 170 p., repr. 1904.

Tr. with commentary H. J. Rose. Oxford, Clarendon Pr., 1924. 219 p.

*POLYBIUS (205–123 B.C.). The Histories. Tr. Evelyn S. Shuckburgh. London and N.Y., Macmillan, 1889. 2 v. Repr. Bloomington, Indiana Univ. Pr., 1962, 2 v.

* Ed. and tr. W. R. Paton. LCL, 1922–27. 6 v.

Earlier trs.: Christopher Watson, 1568, repr. 1647; Edward Grimeston, 1633, repr. 1634; Sir Henry Shearn, with preface John Dryden, 1693, repr. 1698; James Hampton, 1756, repr. 1772, 1809, 1811, 1812, 1823.

PORPHYRY (b. A.D. 233). Select Works. Tr. Thomas Taylor. London, Rodd, 1823. 271 p.

——————— Introduction to the Organon, or Logical Treatises of Aristotle. Tr. O. F. Owen, in The Organon. BCL, 1853. 2 v. Repr. 1893–95.

——————— Life of Plotinus. Tr. Stephen McKenna, in his tr. of Plotinus, v. 1. London, Warner, 1917, see above. Repr. 1957.

POSEIDIPPUS (3d c. B.C.). Poems. In Askleipiades, Windflowers, and the Poems of Poseidippus. Tr. Edward Storer. London, Egoist, 1920. 26 p.

Also in *The Greek Anthology*, tr. Shane Leslie, London, Benn, and N.Y., Appleton, 1929, 234 p.

PTOLEMY (Claudius Ptolomaeus, fl. A.D. 160). The Almagest. Tr. R. Catesby Tagliaferro and Charles G. Wallis (with Copernicus and Kepler). Great Books, v. 16, 1952, xiv, 1085 p.

——————— The Geography. Tr. Edward Luther Stevenson (with maps from a 1460 A.D. Ms.). New York, Public Library, 1932. xvi, 167 p.

——————— Tetrabiblos, or Quadripartite of the Influence of the Stars from the Greek Paraphrase of Proclus, Containing Extracts from the Almagest of Ptolemy and the Whole of his Centiloquy. Tr. J. M. Ashmand.

London, Davis and Dickson, 1822. xxviii, 240 p. Repr. London, W. Foulsham, 1917.

Tr. F. E. Robbins. LCL. 1940. xxiv, 466 p.

SECUNDUS, LIFE OF. Ed. and tr. Ben Edwin Perry as Secundus the Silent Philosopher: The Greek Life of Secundus, with trs. of Greek and Oriental texts and versions. Ithaca, N.Y., Cornell Univ. Pr., for Amer. Philological Assn, 1964. xiv, 160, 7, 11, 74, 96 p.

Relating to Secundus of Athens, Sophist (A.D. 1st c.?).

SEXTUS EMPIRICUS (fl. A.D. 190). The Works. Ed. and tr. R. G. Bury. LCL, 1939–49. 4 v.

————— (Selections) Tr. Sanford G. Etheridge as Scepticism, Man, and God: Selections from the Major Writings. Middletown, Conn., Wesleyan Univ. Pr., 1964. xi, 236 p.

STRABO (60 B.C.–A.D. 24). The Geography. Tr. W. Falconer and H. C. Hamilton. BCL, 1854–57. 3 v

Ed. and tr. Horace L. Jones. LCL, 1917–32. 8 v.

————— On the Troad. Tr. Walter Leaf. Cambridge Univ. Pr., 1923. xlviii, 352 p.

Also tr. in *Greek Geography,* see Collections, above.

THEOCRITUS (fl. 280 B.C.). The Idylls. Tr. James Banks (with Bion, Moschus, and Tyrtaeus). BCL, 1848. Repr. 1853, 1872, 1881, 1913.

* Tr. verse C. S. Calverley. Cambridge and London, Deighton Bell, 1869. xvi, 182 p. Repr. rev. London, Bell, 1883, 184 p.; repr. 1896, Boston, 1906; repr. (with Eclogues of Virgil) London, Bell, 1908, xxxvii, 230 p., repr. 1913 et seq.

Commended.

* Tr. verse James Henry Hallard. London, Longmans, 1894. xvi, 146 p. Repr. 1901, 1913, rev, (with Bion and Moschus), Broadway Trs., London, Routledge, and N.Y., Dutton, 1924.

Commended.

Tr. verse and prose J. M. Edmonds, in The Greek Bucolic Poets. LCL, 1912. xxviii, 527 p. (parallel texts)

* Tr. verse R. C. Trevelyan. London, Casanova Society, 1925. xv, 105 p. Repr. London, Cambridge Univ. Pr., and N.Y., Macmillan, 1947. 110 p.

Tr. verse Marion Mills Miller in The Greek Idyls. Lexington, Ky., Maxwelton Pr., 1926. xx, 338 p.

Tr. verse Jack Lindsay as The Complete Poems. London, Fanfrolico Pr., 1929. xxiv, 162 p.

* Tr. verse Henry Harmon Chamberlin as Late Spring: A Translation of Theocritus. Cambridge, Mass., Harvard Univ. Pr., 1936. xvi, 237 p.

* Ed. and tr. prose A. S. F. Gow. London and N.Y., Cambridge Univ. Pr., 1952. 2 v. Re-ed. (English only, with Bion and Moschus) *ibid.*, 1953, xxvii, 156 p.

* Tr. verse W. Douglas P. Hill as The Idylls. Oxford, Blackwell, and N.Y., Macmillan, 1959. 120 p.

Tr. verse Barriss Mills. Lafayette, Ind., Purdue Univ. Studies, 1963. 113 p.

Earlier trs.: Francis Fawkes as *The Idylliums,* Oxford 1684, repr. 1713, 1721; Thomas Creech, London 1767, repr. Chalmer's *English Poets* 20, 1810; Richard Polwhele (with Bion and Tyrtaeus), London 1786, 2 v., repr. 1792, 1810, 1811, 1813, 1822; Herbert Kynaston as *Idylls and Epigrams* (parallel texts), Oxford 1869, repr. 1892.

———— Selections. Tr. verse Leigh Hunt as Five Idylls and Some Passages. London, 1818. Repr. in his Poetical Works, London and N.Y., Oxford, 1923.

* Tr. verse M. J. Chapman in The Greek Pastoral Poets. London, Fraser, 1836. vii, 419 p. Repr. 1848, 1865.

Commended.

Tr. prose Andrew Lang in Theocritus, Bion and Moschus. London, Macmillan, 1880. xxxvii, 200 p. Repr. London, Golden Treasury, 1889; Boston, Medici Society, 1922.

Tr. verse Arthur S. Way in Theocritus, Bion, and Moschus. Cambridge, Univ. Pr., 1913. 158 p.

Other trs.: John Dryden, 1684, 1685.

THEOPHRASTUS (d. 278 B.C.). The Characters. Tr. John Healey (with Epictetus and Cebes). London, Blount, 1616. 2 pt. Repr. 1636; Temple Classics, 1899.

   Tr. Eustace Budgell. London, 1713. Repr. 1714, 1715, 1718, 1743, 1751.

* Tr. Sir R. C. Jebb. London and N.Y., Macmillan, 1870. 328 p. Repr. ed. J. E. Sandys, *ibid.*, 1902, 229 p.

   Commended.

   Ed. and tr. J. M. Edmonds. LCL, 1929. 32, 132 p.

   Other trs.: Henry Gally, 1725; W. Rayner, Norwich 1797; Isaac Taylor, 1866; C. E. Bennett and W. A. Hammond, New York 1902; Robert Thomson Clark (with Herondas and Cebes), 1909.

————— Enquiry into Plants, and Minor Works. Tr. Sir F. A. Hort. LCL, 1916. 2 v.

————— The Metaphysics. Tr. W. D. Ross and F. H. Forbes. Oxford, Clarendon Pr., 1929. xxxii, 87 p.

XENOPHON OF EPHESUS (A.D. 2d or 3d c.). Ephesian History, or The Love Adventures of Abracoman and Anthia. Tr. John Rocke. London, 1727.

GREEK CHRISTIAN LITERATURE: TO A.D. 300†

George B. Parks

APOCRYPHA OF THE NEW TESTAMENT. (Seven gospels, etc.) Tr. Jeremiah Jones in A New and Full Method of Settling the Canonical Authority of the New Testament, v. 2. London, 1726. Repr. Oxford, 1798; Oxford, 1827; repr. without acknowledgement in The Apocryphal New Testament, London, Hone, 1820, xii, 251 p.; many reprs. of this so-called Hone's Collection, to 1926.

   Tr. B. Harris Cowper as The Apocryphal Gospels and Other Documents (from Greek, Latin, Syriac, etc.). London, Williams and Norgate, 1867. cx, 456 p. Reprs. to 6th ed., 1897.

† Note: For collections, see above, p. 54ff.

Tr. Alexander Walker as Apocryphal Gospels, Acts, and Revelations, in Ante-Nicene Library, v. 16, 1870. xxiv, 547 p. Repr. Ante-Nicene Fathers, v. VIII, 1886. More recently discovered apocrypha were tr. by various hands, Ante-Nicene Library, additional volume, 1896; repr. Ante-Nicene Fathers, v. IX, 1896.

Tr. Montague Rhodes James as The Apocryphal New Testament. Oxford, Clarendon Pr., 1924. xxxxi, 584 p. Repr. 1926.

Other collections tr. from Coptic, Ethiopic, Syriac, q.v. See the long list of trs. in Farrar and Evans, nos. 287–322, p. 14, above.

APOCRYPHA OF THE OLD TESTAMENT. See Hebrew Literature, v. V.

THE APOSTOLIC FATHERS (1st c. A.D.). The Genuine Epistles of the Apostolic Fathers, St. Barnabas, St. Ignatius, St. Clement, St. Polycarp, the Shepherd of Hermas, and the Martyrdoms of St. Ignatius and St. Polycarp. Tr. William Wake. London, 1693. 196, 547 p. Repr. rev. 1710, 1719, 1810, 1817, 1834, 1840, 1846, 1850, 1893; part repr. (minus Barnabas and the Shepherd) as A Translation of the Epistles, etc., ed. Temple Chevalier, Cambridge, 1833; repr., N.Y., 1834; Cambridge, 1851; also repr. (adding the Didache and the Epistle to Diognetus) ed. Edward Burton: London, Griffith Farran, 1888–89, 2 v., repr. Edinburgh, 1909.

Tr. Alexander Robert, James Donaldson, and Frederick Crombie, as The Writings of the Apostolic Fathers, in Ante-Nicene Library, 1, 1870, repr. Ante-Nicene Fathers, I, also 2,7,9: 1885–86, 1896.

> Adds Epistle to Diognetus, fragments of Papias, the supposed Second Epistle of Clement.

Ed. and tr. Kirsopp Lake. LCL, 1912–13. 2 v.

> Does not include the *Martyrdom of Ignatius.*

Tr. James A. Kleist in Ancient Christian Writers, v. 1, 1946 (Clement and Ignatius); v. 6, 1948 (the rest), repr. 1957.

Tr. Francis X. Glimm et al., in Fathers of the Church, v. 1, 1946. xii, 401 p.

Tr. Edgar J. Goodspeed as The Apostolic Fathers: An American Translation. N.Y., Harper, 1950. xi, 321 p.

> Barnabas, Clement of Rome, the *Didache* (Teaching of the Twelve Apostles), Diognetus, Ignatius, Papias, Polycarp, Quadratus, *Shepherd* of Hermas.

Tr. Cyril C. Richardson et al., in Library of Christian Classics, v. 1, 1953. 397 p.

Other trs. Charles H. Hoole, London, 1872; J. B. Lightfoot, separate trs. 1869 to 1889, completed J. R. Harmer, 1891, repr. 1907, 1912, 1926. See Farrar and Evans, nos. 332, 334, p. 14, above.

ATHENAGORAS (late 2d c. A.D.). The Apologeticks . . . I, For the Christian Religion, II, For the Truth of the Resurrection. Tr. David Humphreys. London, 1714. 307 p.

Tr. J. A. Giles in The Writings of the Early Christians of the Second Century. London, 1857. p. 1–77.

Tr. B. P. Pratten in Ante-Nicene Library, v. 2, 1870, p. 371–456. Repr. Ante-Nicene Fathers, v. II, 1885.

Tr. Joseph H. Crehan, in Ancient Christian Writers, v. 23, 1956. 193 p. (The Embassy of the Christians, The Resurrection of the Dead)

Other tr.: The Resurrection of the Dead, tr. Richard Porder, 1573.

BARNABAS, EPISTLE OF. For trs. in collections, see Apostolic Fathers, above. Separate trs.:

————— The Epistle of Barnabas, from the Sinaitic Manuscript of the Bible. Tr. Samuel Sharpe. London and Edinburgh, Williams and Norgate, 1880. xxvi, 63 p.

Tr. anon. as An English Translation of the Epistle. London, S.P.C.K., 1923. iv, 32 p.

THE BIBLE. See Hebrew Literature, v. V.

CLEMENT OF ALEXANDRIA (A.D. c. 150–c. 212). (Treatises). Tr. William Wilson, in Ante-Nicene Library, v. 4, 12, 22, 24: 1868–72. Repr. together in Ante-Nicene Fathers, v. II, 1885.

Tr. G. W. Butterworth (The Exhortation to the Greeks, The Rich Man's Salvation, and a Fragment of an Address to the Newly Baptized). LCL, 1919. xv, 408 p. Repr. 1953.

————— Christ the Educator. Tr. Simon P. Wood. Fathers of the Church, 23, 1954. xxiii, 309 p.

Other trs. of individual treatises or selections are noted, from A.D. 1711, in Farrar and Evans, nos. 992-997, p. 14, above.

CLEMENT OF ROME, St. (Pope Clement I, 1st c.). The Epistles.

See *Apostolic Fathers*, above, for trs. in collections. Of the two epistles only incomplete versions were known before 1875, but trs. of these go back to 1647. Separate eds. of the complete versions (in addition to those in collections):

Ed. and tr. J. B. Lightfoot, London, Macmillan, 1877 (as appendix to his previous ed., 1869). Many reprs., see Farrar and Evans, no. 344, p. 14, above.

———————— The Epistle. Tr. John A. F. Gregg. London, S.P.C.K., 1899. vi, 80 p.

Tr. W. K. Lowther Clarke as The First Epistle. London, S.P.C.K., 1937. 144 p.

———————— The So-Called Second Epistle to the Corinthians. Tr. anon. London, S.P.C.K., and N.Y., Macmillan, 1922. 22 p.

Now thought to have been written by an anon. of the 2d c. Other pseudo-Clementine writings:

———————— The Clementine Homilies. Tr. Thomas Smith, et al., in Ante-Nicene Library, v. 17, 1870. 340 p. Repr. Ante-Nicene Fathers, v. VIII, 1886.

———————— The Recognitions. Tr. William Whiston, in Primitive Christianity Reviv'd. London, 1712. vol. V.

Tr. Thomas Smith from the Latin, in Ante-Nicene Library, v. 3, 1868, p. 135–471. Repr. Ante-Nicene Fathers, v. VIII, 1886.

The two works make up a legend of St. Peter. *The Recognitions* survives only in a Latin version by Rufinus.

THE DIDACHE (Teachings of the Twelve Apostles, earlier 2d c. A.D., an informative work on the early organization of the churches). For the twelve separate trs. (1884–1903) since the discovery and first pub. in 1833, see Farrar and Evans, *English Translations from Medieval Sources,* nos. 3580–91, in Collections, above. In collections, trs. in Apostolic Fathers; Ante-Nicene Fathers, v. VIII; Library of Christian Classics, v. 1; LCL, v. 1; Ancient Christian Writers, v. 6; Fathers of the Church, v. 1.

DIOGNETUS, EPISTLE TO (2d c. A.D.). For two separate trs., both in 1908, see Farrar and Evans, *English Translations from Medieval Sources,* nos. 1463, 1464, in Collections, above. Trs. in Apostolic Fathers; Ante-Nicene Fathers, v. I; LCL, v. II, and the rest.

DIONYSIUS, ST., Bishop of Alexandria, called the Great (d. A.D. 265). The Extant Fragments. Tr. S. D. F. Salmond, in Ante-Nicene Library, v. 20, 1871, p. 161–266. Repr. Ante-Nicene Fathers, v. VI, 1886.

Tr. Charles L. Feltoe as Letters and Treatises. London, S.P.C.K., and N.Y., Macmillan, 1920. viii, 110 p.

GREGORY THE MIRACLE-WORKER (Thaumaturgus), St., Bishop of Neocaesarea (A.D. c. 213–270). The Writings. Tr. S. D. F. Salmond, in Ante-Nicene Library, v. 20, 1871, p. 1–160. Repr. Ante-Nicene Fathers, v. VI, 1886.

HERMAS (2d c. A.D.). The Shepherd. Tr. in all collections of the Apostolic Fathers. Separate trs.:

Tr. Charles H. Hoole. London, Rivingtons, 1870. xxxi, 184 p.

Tr. C. Taylor. London, S.P.C.K., and N.Y., E. and J. B. Young, 1903–06. 2 v.

HIPPOLYTUS OF ROME, ST. (fl. A.D. 225). The Refutation of All Heresies. Tr. J. H. MacMahon, . . . with Fragments from his Commentaries on Various Books of Scripture, tr. S. D. F. Salmond. Ante-Nicene Library, v. 6, 1870. 508 p. Repr. Ante-Nicene Fathers, v. V, 1886.

The remaining fragments and supposititious works are tr. *ibid.,* v. 9, 1871, and repr. *ibid.,* v. V, 1886.

———— The Apostolic Tradition. Tr. Burton Scott Easton. Cambridge, Univ. Pr., and N.Y., Macmillan, 1934. 122 p.

Tr. Gregory Dix. London, S.P.C.K., and N.Y., Macmillan, 1937. lxxxi, 90 p.

———— Philosophumena, or The Refutation of All Heresies. Tr. F. Legge. London, S.P.C.K., and N.Y., Macmillan, 1921. 2 v.

IGNATIUS, ST., Bishop of Antioch (d. c. A.D. 117). Epistles. Tr. in all collections of Apostolic Fathers. Syriac as well as Greek versions of the letters make for complex texts. See the following.

————— The Antient Syriac Versions of the Epistles of St. Ignatius. Tr. William Cureton. London and Berlin, 1845. Repr. rev. with Syriac text in Corpus Ignatianum. A Complete Collection of the Ignatian Epistles, London, Rivington, 1849, xvii, lxxxvii, 365 p. Repr. tr. only, Glasgow, 1887.

————— The Epistles. Tr. (from Greek) J. H. Srawley. London, S.P.C.K., and N.Y., Macmillan, 1900. 132 p. Repr. 1913, 1919.

IRENAEUS, ST. Bishop of Lyon (from A.D. 178). The Writings. Tr. Alexander Roberts and W. H. Rambaut. Ante-Nicene Library, v. 5, 9: 1869, 1871. Repr. Ante-Nicene Fathers, v. I, 1885.

The Five Books Against Heresies, and fragments.

Tr. John Keble, in Library of Fathers, 42, 1872. viii, 594 p.

————— The Proof of the Apostolic Preaching. Tr. Joseph P. Smith. Ancient Christian Writers, v. 16, 1952. 233 p.

For trs. of Armenian version of The Proof of the Apostolic Preaching, see Farrar and Evans, *English Translations from Medieval Sources,* nos. 2149, 2150, in Collections, above.

JUSTIN MARTYR, ST. (d. c. A.D. 165). The Works Now Extant. Tr. G. J. Davie. Library of Fathers, v. 40, 1861. xxii, 284 p.

Tr. various hands as The Writings (including the supposititious), in Ante-Nicene Library, v. 2, 1870, p. 1–370. Repr. Ante-Nicene Fathers, v. I, 1885.

Tr. T. B. Falls, in Fathers of the Church, v. 6, 1949. 486 p.

For trs. of individual treatises (beginning in 1709), see Farrar and Evans, *English Translations from Medieval Sources,* nos, 2325–2330, in Collections, above.

MARTYRS. Some Authentic Acts of the Early Martyrs. Tr. E. C. E. Owen. Oxford, Clarendon Pr., 1927. 183 p. Repr. London, S.P.C.K., 1933.

METHODIUS, ST. Bishop of Olympus (d. A.D. 311). The Writings. Tr. William R. Clark, in Ante-Nicene Library, v. 14, 1869, p. 1–230. Repr. Ante-Nicene Fathers, v. VI, 1886. p. 309–355.

Notably the *Symposium.*

———— The Symposium: A Treatise on Chastity. Tr. Herbert Musurillo. Ancient Christian Writers, v. 27, 1958. 249 p.

THE NEW TESTAMENT. See the Bible, in Hebrew Literature, v. V.

ORIGEN (Origenes Adimantius, A.D. c. 185–54). The Writings. Tr. Frederick Crombie and W. H. Cairns. Ante-Nicene Library, v. 10, 23, 25: 1869, 1872, 1896. Repr. Ante-Nicene Fathers, v. IV, IX: 1886, 1896.

The important writings tr. are, in v. 10, the *De principiis;* in v. 10, 23, the *Contra Celsum;* in 25, the *Commentaries on Matthew* and *John.*

———— Selections from the Commentaries and Homilies. Tr. R. B. Tollinton. London, S.P.C.K., and N.Y., Macmillan, 1929. lviii, 272 p.

———— On First Principles. Tr. G. W. Butterworth. London, S.P.C.K., 1936. xliii, 342 p.

———— Treatise on Prayer. Tr. Eric George Jay. London, S.P.C.K., 1954. x, 237 p.

———— On Prayer, Exhortation to Martyrdom, Dialogue with Heracleides. Tr. J. E. L. Oulton and Henry Chadwick, in Library of Christian Classics, v. 2, 1954, p. 180–455.

———— On Prayer, Exhortation to Martyrdom. Tr. John J. O'Meara. Ancient Christian Writers, v. 19, 1954. 253 p.

———— The Song of Songs: Commentary and Homilies. Tr. R. P. Lawson. Ancient Christian Writers, v. 26, 1957. 385 p.

PAPIAS OF HIERAPOLIS in Phrygia (A.D. c. 60–135). Exposition of the Lord's Oracles (fragments preserved in Eusebius' Ecclesiastical History). Tr. in these eds. of the Apostolic Fathers: Ante-Nicene Library, v. 1, 1870; Ante-Nicene Fathers, v. I, 1885; J. B. Lightfoot tr. rev. J. R. Harmer, 1891, et seq.; Ancient Christian Writers, v. 6,

1948; Fathers of the Church, v. 1, 1946; An American Translation, 1950.

PETER, ST. Bishop of Alexandria (d. A.D. 311). The Writings. Tr. James B. H. Hawkins, in Ante-Nicene Library, v. 14, 1869, p. 269–322. Repr. in Ante-Nicene Fathers, v. VI, 1886.

POLYCARP, ST. Bishop of Smyrna (A.D. c. 69–c. 155). The Epistle to the Philippians, and the Martyrdom of Polycarp (ascribed to Marcion), have been tr. in virtually all eds. of the Apostolic Fathers, beginning with the Wake tr. A separate tr.:

Tr. Bloomfield Jackson. London, S.P.C.K., and N.Y., E. and J. B. Young, 1898. 78 p.

TATIAN (fl. A.D. 160). The Address to the Greeks. Tr. J. A. Giles, in The Writings of the Early Christians of the Second Century. London, 1857.

Tr. J. E. Ryland, in Ante-Nicene Library, v. 3, 1868, p. 1–48. Repr. in Ante-Nicene Fathers, v. II, 1888.

———— The Diatessaron of Tatian. Tr. Hope W. Hogg, in Ante-Nicene Library, v. 25, 1896, p. 33–138. Repr. in Ante-Nicene Fathers, v. IX, 1896.

An abridgement was tr. Samuel Hemphill, London and Dublin, 1888. A tr. from the Arabic version was made by J. Hamlyn Hill, Edinburgh, 1894, as *The Earliest Life of Christ Ever Compiled from the Four Gospels.*

THEOPHILOS, Bishop of Antioch (later 2d c. A.D.). The Three Books to Autolycus. Tr. J. A. Giles, in The Writings of the Early Christians of the Second Century. London, 1857.

Tr. W. B. Flower. London, 1860.

Tr. Marcus Dods, in Ante-Nicene Library, v. 3, 1868, p. 49–133. Repr. Ante-Nicene Fathers, v. II, 1885.

Also tr. Joseph Betty (with Tertullian's Prescription Against Heretics), Oxford, 1722.

BYZANTINE LITERATURE
A.D. 300 TO 1453

PROCOPE S. COSTAS

BACKGROUND

BAYNES, NORMAN H. The Byzantine Empire. Home University Library, no. 118. London, Oxford Univ. Pr., 1925. 256 p. Reprs. to 6th ed., 1949. (The bibliog., p. 243–55, was revised for the 1943 ed.)

BECKWITH, JOHN. The Art of Constantinople: An Introduction to Byzantine Art, 330–453. Greenwich, Conn., Phaidon Pr., 1961. 184 p.

BRÉHIER, LOUIS. Le Monde byzantin. Paris, Albin Michel, 1947–50. 3 v.

BYRON, ROBERT. The Byzantine Achievement: An Historical Perspective. A.D. 330–1453. London, Routledge, 1929. 345 p. maps, ill., bibliog.

BYZANTIUM: An Introduction to East Roman Civilization. Ed. Norman H. Baynes and H. St. L. B. Moss. Oxford, Clarendon Pr., 1948. xxxi, 436 p. Repr., *ibid.*, and N.Y., Oxford Univ. Pr., 1961, paper.

Contains articles on various aspects of Byzantine civilization and an excellent bibliographical appendix. This is the best all-round introduction to Byzantine civilization.

THE CAMBRIDGE MEDIEVAL HISTORY. Vol. IV: The Eastern Roman Empire (717–1453). Cambridge Univ. Pr., 1923. Repr. rev. 2d ed. by Joan M. Hussey, 1964, in 2 parts: 1. Byzantium and Its Neighbours; 2. Government, Church, and Civilization. (Plates, maps, bibliog.)

DIEHL, CHARLES. Byzantium: Greatness and Decline. Tr. Naomi Walford from the French. New Brunswick, N.J., Rutgers Univ. Pr., 1957. xviii, 366 p.

The value of this work is considerably enhanced by the detailed bibliography provided by Peter Charanis, p. 30–57.

———— Manuel d'art byzantin. 2d ed. Paris, Picard, 1925. 2 v.

HUNGER, HERBERT, ed. Byzantinische Geisteswelt, von Konstantin dem grossen bis zum Fall Konstantinopels. Baden-Baden, Holle-Verlag, 1958. 335 p.

Contains a full list of German translations of Byzantine authors, p. 303–11.

HUSSEY, JOAN M. The Byzantine World. London, Hutchinson's Universal Library, and N.Y., Rinehart, 1957. 191 p. Repr. N.Y., Harper (Torch Books), 1961. (select bibliog. p. 181–86)

OSTROGORSKY, GEORGE. History of the Byzantine State. Tr. Joan Hussey from the German. New Brunswick, N.J., Rutgers Univ. Pr., 1957. xxv, 548 p.

A scholarly introduction to Byzantine history, rich in original comments, and provided with an extensive biblography and excellent maps.

RICE, D. TALBOT. Byzantine Art. Oxford, Clarendon Pr., 1935. xiii, 255 p. Repr. rev., Pelican Books, 1954; repr. rev., 1962. 272 p.

RUNCIMAN, SIR STEVEN. Byzantine Civilization. London, Edward Arnold, 1933. 320 p. Repr. London, Methuen, and N.Y., Meridian, 1961, paper.

TATAKIS, BASILE. La Philosophie byzantine. In E. Bréhier, Histoire de la philosophie. Fascicule supplémentaire, no. 2. Paris, Presses universitaires, 1949. viii, 323 p.

VASILIEV, A. A. History of the Byzantine Empire, 324–1453. Madison, Univ. of Wisconsin Pr., 1928. 2 v. Repr., *ibid.*, 2 v., and Oxford, Blackwell, 1952, xi, 846 p.

Exhaustive bibliography.

WELLESZ, EGON. A History of Byzantine Music and Hymnology. Oxford, Clarendon Pr., 1949. Repr. rev. and enl., *ibid.*, 1961, xiv, 461 p.

BIBLIOGRAPHY

BLACKWELL'S BYZANTINE HAND LIST. Oxford, Blackwell, 1938.
67 p.

A catalogue of Byzantine authors and books on Byzantine literature, history, religion, art, archeology, etc.

DIX ANNÉES D'ÈTUDES BYZANTINES. Bibliographie internationale, 1939–1948. Paris, Ecole des Hautes Etudes, 1949.

Compiled under the auspices of UNESCO.

DOLGER, FRANZ, and SCHNEIDER, A. M. Byzanz. Bern, Francke, 1952. 328 p.

For the literature between 1938 and 1950.

See also Byron, Byzantium, Diehl, Hunger, Ostrogorsky, and Vasiliev, above, and the bibliographical sections in Marouzeau, *L'Année philologique*, Paris, 1924—, and in the periodicals *Byzantinische Zeitschrift, Byzantion, Revue des études byzantines.*

LITERARY STUDIES

BAXTER, J. H. "Byzantine Literature," in Chambers' Encyclopedia (1955), 6: 569–75.

COTTAS, VENETIA. Le Théâtre à Byzance. Paris, Guenther, 1931. xix, 290 p.

Cf. the review by G. La Piana in *Speculum*, 11 (1936), 171–211.

COURCELLE, PIERRE. Les Lettres grecques en occident de Macrobe à Cassiodore. Bibliothèque des écoles françaises d'Athènes et de Rome, 1st. ser., fasc. 159. Paris, Boccard, 1943. 440 p.

DIETERICH, K. "Byzantine Literature," in Catholic Encyclopedia (1908), 3: 113–24.

————— Geschichte der byzantinischen und neugriechischen Literatur. Leipzig, Amelung, 1902. x, 242 p. Repr. 1909.

"GREEK LITERATURE, MEDIEVAL," in Cassell's Encyclopedia of Literature (1953), 1: 266–69.

HIGGINS, M. J. "Byzantine Literature," in Encyclopedia of Literature (N.Y., 1946), 1: 109–17.

KNÖS, B. L'histoire de la littérature néo-grecque (to 1821). Acta Univ. Uppsala. Stockholm, Almqvist and Wiksell, 1962. 690 p.

Byzantine literature, p. 39–157.

KRUMBACHER, KARL. Geschichte der byzantinischen Literatur (527–1453). 2d ed., Munich, Beck, 1897. xx, 1193 p. In Handbuch der klassischen Altertumswissenschaft, ed. Iwan von Müller, v. 9, pt. 1.

Still the indispensable work.

————— and Dölger, F. "Byzantine Literature," in Encyclopaedia Britannica (1964), 10: 875–80.

MAVROGORDATO, JOHN, and MARSHALL, F. H. "Byzantine Literature," in Byzantium (1948, see above), p. 221–51.

MIRAMBEL, A. In Histoire des littératures (Encyclopédie de la Pléiade). Paris, 1953, 1: 697–750.

Good bibliography.

TRYPANIS, C. A., ed. Medieval and Modern Greek Poetry: An Anthology. Oxford, Clarendon Pr., 1951. lxiii, 285 p.

Review of Byzantine literature, p. ix–xl.

WRIGHT, F. A. A History of Later Greek Literature (to A.D. 565). London, Routledge, 1932. xi, 415 p.

COLLECTIONS

CANTARELLA, RAFFAELE. Poeti byzantini. Milan, Vita e pensiero, 1948. 2 v.

V. 1 contains texts; v. 2, an intro., trs. into Italian, and commentary.

ELLISSEN, A., ed. Analekten der mittel- und neugriechischen Literatur. Leipzig, 1855–62. 5 v.

Eds., with trs. into German, of a number of substantial texts. V. 1 (1855), The *Christos paschon,* religious drama (here assigned to Gregory of Nazianzus q.v., though now known to have been written in the 11th to 12th c.). V. 2 (1856), *The Chronicle of the Morea,* q.v.; and *The Prince of Morea,* historical novel by the Modern Greek historian, Alexander Rhisos Rhangavis. V. 3 (1857), *The Lament for Constantinople.* V. 4 (1860), *Byzantine Paralipomena, The Descents into Hell of Timarion and Mazarian*; and G. Gemistius Plethon, *Memorials of the Events of the Peloponnesus.* V. 5 (1862), *Belthandros and Chrysantza,* q.v.

RECUEIL DE CHANSONS POPULAIRES GRECQUES. Ed. and tr. Emile Legrand. Paris, Maisonneuve, 1874. xliii, 376 p. (parallel texts).

RECUEIL DE CONTES POPULAIRES GRECS. Tr. Emile Legrand. Paris, Leroux, 1881. xix, 274 p.

SOCIAL AND POLITICAL THOUGHT IN BYZANTIUM from Justinian I to the Last Palaeologus. Tr. Ernest Barker. London, Oxford Univ. Pr., 1957. xvi, 239 p.

Passages from Byzantine writers and documents.

SOYTER, GUSTAV, ed. Byzantinische Dichtung. Texte und Forschungen zur byzantinische-neugriechischen Philologie, nr. 28. Athens, 1938. 211 p.

Trs. into German of selected passages of Byzantine poets from the 4th to the 15th c.

INDIVIDUAL AUTHORS

NON-CHRISTIAN AND SECULAR: A.D. 300 TO 900

AGAPETUS (6th c.). The Preceptes teaching a prynce of noble Estate his duetie. Tr. Thomas Paynell from the Latin. London, Berthelet, 1530?

Tr. J. Whit. London, Serll, 1564.

AGATHIAS (536–582). Histoire de l'empereur Justinien., Tr. L. Cousin, in Histoire de Constantinople. Paris, 1672, v. 2.

———— Epigrams. Tr. W. R. Paton, in The Greek Anthology, LCL, passim in the 5 v.

Selected epigrams also tr. in Dudley Fitts, *Poems from the Greek Anthology*, and *One Hundred Poems from the Palatine Anthology* (N.Y., New Directions, 1938); and in F. A. Wright, *The Poets of the Greek Anthology* (London, Routledge, and N.Y., Dutton, 1924).

ARISTAENETUS (5th c.). Letters of Love and Gallantry. Tr. anon. prose (books i, ii). London, Lintot, 1715. 120 p.

Part (book i) tr. verse Richard B. Sheridan and N. B. Halhed. London, Wilkie, 1771. xvi, 174 p. Repr. 1773. Repr. in Erotica, ed. W. K. Kelly, London, Bohn, 1854, repr. 1880, 1883.

Other part tr. Thomas Brown, prose and verse (19 letters), London, 1707, reprs. to 1760.

BYZANTINE LAW (or Roman Law of the Later Empire). See the many trs. of manuals of Byzantine law by E. H. Freshfield, Cambridge Univ. Pr., 1907 to 1938.

COLUTHUS (6th c.). The Rape of Helen. Tr. verse Sir Edward Sherburne, in Salmacis with Other Poems and Translations. London, 1651. Repr. in The Tragedies of Seneca Translated, 1701; repr. in Chalmers' English Poets, v. 6, 1810.

Tr. anon. London, Roberts, 1731. viii, 34 p.

Tr. Henry Meen in The Argonautics of Apollonius Rhodius, tr. Francis
Fawkes and Henry Meen. London, 1780. Repr. in Chalmers' English
Poets, v. 20, 1810.

Tr. William Beloe. London, Egerton, 1786. vii, 59 p.

Ed. and tr. A. W. Mair. LCL, 1928 (with Oppian and Tryphiodorus).

DAMASCIUS (fl. c. 500). Lectures on the Philebus [of Plato] Wrongly
Attributed to Olympiodorus. Ed. and tr. L. G. Westerink. Amsterdam,
North Holland Pub. Co., 1959. xxii, 149 p.

———— Life of Isidoros. Ed. and tr. German by Rudolf Asmus. Leipzig,
1911. xvi, 224 p.

———— The Theogonies. Tr. in Isaac P. Cory, Ancient Fragments of the
Phoenician, Chaldaean, . . . and Other Writings. London, William
Pickering, 1832 p. 310–21 (parallel texts). Tr. rev. enl. E. Richmond
Hodges, London, Reeves and Turner, 1876.

EUNAPIUS (c. 345–420). The Lives of the Sophists. Tr. anon. from Latin
as The Lyves of Philosophers and Oratours. London, 1579. 43
leaves.

Tr. Edward Smith as A Continuation of Diogenes Laertius, in The Lives
. . . of the . . . Ancient Philosophers, by Diogenes Laertius (several
translators). London, 1688, v. 2, 299–460. Repr. 1696.

Tr. anon. London, 1702.

Tr. W. C. Wright, in Philostratus and Eunapius. LCL, 1922.

GEOPONICA (6th–7th c.). Agricultural Pursuits. Tr. Thomas Owen.
London, 1805–06. 2 v.

Compiled by Bassus in 6th or 7th c.; rev. anon. in 10th c.

HIEROCLES OF ALEXANDRIA (5th c.). Hierocles upon the Golden
Verses of Pythagoras. Tr. John Hall. London, 1657. 177 p.

Tr. John Norris. London, 1682. 166 p. Repr. Glasgow, Foulis, 1756.

Tr. anon. from the French in The Life of Pythagoras, with his Symbols
and Golden Verses, together with the Life of Hierocles and his Commentaries upon the Verses. London, Tonson, 1707. xxxiv, 389 p.

Repr. Glasgow, Urie, 1756; London, Theosophical Pub. Society, 1906.

Tr. Dr. Warren. Norwich, 1797. iv, 110 p.

HIEROCLES THE GRAMMARIAN (6th c.). Select Jests of Hierocles. Tr. C. C. Bubb. Cleveland, Ohio, 1916. Repr. in The Jests of Hierocles and Philagrius, Cleveland, Ohio, Rowfant Club, 1920, 110 p.

IAMBLICHUS (c. 250–325). Exhortation to the Study of Philosophy, Fragments of Iamblichus, etc. (The Protrepticus) Tr. Thomas M. Johnson. Osceola, Mo., Press of The Republican, 1907. vi, 138 p.

———— Iamblichus on the Mysteries of the Egyptians, Chaldeans, and Assyrians. Tr. Thomas Taylor. Chiswick, 1821. xxiv, 365 p. Repr. London, Dobell, 1895.

Tr. Alexander Wilder as Theurgia, or The Egyptian Mysteries. N.Y., Metaphysical Pub. Co., 1911. 283 p. Repr. 1915.

Published earlier in periodicals: *The Platonist*, 1881–87; *The Metaphysical Magazine*, 1909–11.

———— Life of Pythagoras, or Pythagoric Life, etc. Tr. Thomas Taylor. London, Valpy, 1818. xiii, 252 p. Repr. London, Watkins, 1926.

JULIAN THE APOSTATE, Emperor (Flavius Claudius Julianus, emperor A.D. 361–363). The Works. Ed. and tr. W. C. Wright. LCL, 1913–23. 3 v.

———— Select Works of the Emperor Julian and Some Pieces of the Sophist Libanius. (orations and epistles) Tr. John Duncombe. London, Cadell, 1784. 2 v.

———— Theosophical Works. In Julian the Emperor, Containing Gregory Nazianzen's Two Invectives and Libanius' Monody, tr. Charles W. King. BCL, 1888. xiv, 288 p.

———— The Arguments of the Emperor Julian Against the Christians. Tr. Thomas Taylor. London, 1809. xi, 98 p. Repr. as Three Letters on the Christians, in The Arguments of Celsus, Porphyry, and the Emperor Julian Against the Christians, London, Rodd, 1830, xiv, 116 p. Repr. separately, London, Williams and Norgate, 1873.

———— The Orations, One to the Sovereign Sun, and the Other to the Mother of the Gods. Tr. Thomas Taylor. London, 1793. lxviii, 204 p.

———— Public Letters. Tr. E. J. Chinnock, in A Few Notes on Julian. London, Nutt, 1901. 82 p.

LIBANIUS (314–393). A Monody (on Julian). Tr. Charles W. King, in Julian the Emperor, BCL, 1888 (see preceding author).

———— A Monody on Nicomedia. A Monody on the Daphnaean Temple of Apollo. Tr. John Duncombe, in Select Works of Julian, 1784, v. 2 (see preceding author).

———— Oration . . . in Defense of the Temples of the Heathen. Tr. Nathaniel Lardner, in Ancient Jewish and Heathen Testimonies. London, 1767, v. 4. Repr. with tr. Thomas Taylor, Arguments of Celsus . . . and . . . Julian Against the Christians, 1830 (see preceding author).

———— Oration 5, Artemis. Tr. Glanville Downey, in A History of Antioch in Syria. Princeton, N.J., Princeton Univ. Pr., 1961, p. 681–88.

———— Oration 10, on the Plethron. Ibid., p. 688–94.

———— Oration 11. Tr. Glanville Downey, in Proceedings of American Philosophical Society, 103 (1959), 652–86.

———— On the Silence of Socrates. Tr. Michael Crosby and W. W. Calder, III, in Greek, Roman, and Byzantine Studies, 3 (1960), 186–96.

———— (Sixteen Letters to Julian). Tr. John Duncombe, in Select Works of the Emperor Julian, 1784, v. 1 (see preceding author).

———— The Speech Concerning the Prisoners. Tr. Roger A. Pack, in Studies in Libanius and Antiochene Society under Theodosius. Menasha, Wis., Banta, 1935, p. 83–92.

MARCIANUS OF HERACLEA (5th c.). Periplus of the Outer Sea, East and West, and of the Great Islands Therein. Tr. Wilfrid H. Schoff. Philadelphia, Commercial Museum, 1927. 56 p.

MARINUS (5th c.). Life of Proclus. Tr. Thomas Taylor, in The Philosophical and Mathematical Commentaries of Proclus. London, 1788–89. 2 v. Repr. 1792.

Tr. K. S. Guthrie from the French, in his Proclus, Life, Hymns, and Works. North Yonkers, N.Y., Platonist Pr., 1925. 7 parts.

Tr. L. J. Rosán, in The Philosophy of Proclus. N.Y., Cosmos, 1949, p. 13–35.

MENANDER PROTECTOR (6th c.). The Tyrian Annals (Fragments). Tr. Isaac P. Cory, in The Ancient Fragments, etc. London, 1828. p. 89–93. (parallel texts). Repr. 1876, p. 196–200.

METRODORUS (5th–6th c.). "Metrodorus' Arithmetical Epigrams." Ed. and tr. W. R. Paton, in The Greek Anthology, LCL, 1918. v. 5, p. 85–105.

MUSAEUS (6th c.). Hero and Leander. Tr. George Chapman, as The Divine Poem of Musaeus. London, 1616. Repr. in Homer's Batrachomyomachia, etc., ed. Richard Hooper, London, 1858; repr. 1888. Repr. separately, Philadelphia, 1902; Shaftesbury, High House Pr., 1936, 28 p.

> This tr. is not the same as the Marlowe-Chapman adaptation with the same title (pub. 1598).

Tr. Sir Robert Stapleton. Oxford, 1645. Repr. rev. London, 1647.

Tr. Lewis Theobald, in The Grove. London, 1721.

Tr. Francis Fawkes, in The Works of Anacreon, Sappho, Bion, Moschus, and Musaeus. London, Newberry, 1760. Repr. 1789 et seq., notably in Chalmers' English Poets, v. 20, 1810, and separately, 1832.

Tr. Sir Edwin Arnold. London, 1873.

Tr. Elizabeth H. Haight, in Poet-Lore, 20 (1909), 449–56.

Tr. E. E. Sikes. London, Methuen, 1920. 27 p.

Tr. verse Arthur S. Way, with The Homeric Hymns. London, Macmillan, 1934. 84 p.

Ed. and tr. E. H. Blakeney. Oxford, Blackwell, 1935. 52 p.

Tr. F. L. Lucas. London, Golden Cockerel Pr., 1949. 47 p.

Other trs.: Thomas Hoy, 1692; Laurence Eusden, 1709; A. S. Catcott (paraphrase), 1715; James Sterling, 1728; Robert Luck, 1736; George Bally, 1747; John Slade, 1753; James Graeme, 1773; Edward

B. Greene, 1773; anon., 1774; Edward Taylor, 1783; G. C. Bedford, 1797; Francis Adam, 1821.

NONNUS OF PANOPOLIS (5th c.). Dionysiaca. Ed. and tr. W. H. D. Rouse. LCL, 1940. 3 v.

"ORPHEUS" (4th c.). Orpheus on Gems (The Lithica, a poem). Tr. C. W. King, in The Natural History of Precious Stones and Gems. London, 1865, p. 375–96.

PALLADAS OF ΛLEXANDRIA (5th c.). Select Epigrams. Tr. Dudley Fitts, in One Hundred Poems from the Greek Anthology. N.Y., New Directions, 1938.

PAULUS AEGINETA (7th c.). The Seven Books [on medicine]. Tr. Francis Adams. London, Sydenham Society, 1844–47. 3 v.

PAULUS SILENTIARIUS (fl. 540). Description of the Church of Sancta Sophia. Tr. W. R. Lethaby and Harold Swainson, in The Church of Sancta Sophia Constantinople. London, 1894, p. 35–65.

———— Poems. Tr. verse (Italian) Alessandro Veniero, in Studi sulla letteratura bizantina del VI. secolo. Catania, 1916.

Tr. verse Dudley Fitts as Select Epigrams, in Poems from the Greek Anthology, and One Hundred Poems from the Palatine Anthology. N.Y., New Directions, 1938.

PHYSIOLOGUS (The Naturalist, 4th–5th c.). Tr. Francis J. Carmody. San Francisco, Calif., The Book of California, 1953. 38 leaves.

Tr. James Carlill from a German tr. of the Greek (by Emil Peters, Munich 1921). In the Epic of the Beast (with Reynard the Fox). Broadway Trs. London, Routledge, and N.Y., Dutton, 1924, p. 185–250.

This tr. includes 67 descriptions of animals, with some plants and jewels, adding to the 62 descriptions in the German tr. (and 48 in the earliest Greek ed.)

Trs. from the Latin versions:

Tr. anon. into Old English (3 verse fragments). Ed. and tr. Albert S. Cook into modern English prose, and tr. Joseph H. Pitman into modern

English verse. New Haven, Yale Univ. Pr., 1921. v, 25 p. (parallel Old English and modern English texts)

Tr. anon. Middle English verse (13th c.) as A Bestiary (13 descriptions). Ed. and tr. Richard Morris in EETS OS 49, 1872, p. 1–25 (Middle English text), p. 201–9 (Latin text of Theobaldus).

12 of the descriptions are tr. from the verse *Liber Fisiologus* by the supposed Abbott Thetbald (11th c.), as here ed.; the 13th is from Alexander Neckam's *De naturis rerum* (c. 1200).

Tr. Alan Wood Rendell from the 1492 ed. of Theobaldus. London, Bumpus, 1928. xxvii, 34, 99 p. parallel texts

Tr. T. H. White from a 13th c. version as The Book of Beasts. London, Cape, and N.Y., Putnam, 1954. 296 p.

> The original Latin of this version is ed. M. R. James, Roxburghe Club, 1928.

For Old French versions of the *Physiologus* (as *Bestiaire*), see French Literature, medieval, v. III.

PISIDES, GEORGIUS (6th c.). Poemi. V. 1. Panegirici epici. Ed. and tr. (Italian) Agostino Pertusi. Studia Patristica e Byzantina, 7. Ettal, 1960. 322 p.

PRISCUS OF PANIUM (5th c.). (Account of an embassy to the court of Attila). Tr. freely in J. B. Bury, History of the Later Roman Empire (1889), in latest ed., 1958, v. 1, p. 279–88.

———— (Excerpts of reports of diplomatic missions), in Byzantinische Diplomaten und östliche Barbaren . . . Abschnitte des Priskos und Menander Protektor. Tr. (German) Ernst Doblhofer. Byzantinische geschichtsschreiber, no. 4, Graz, Verlag Styria, 1955. 223 p.

———— Fragments inédits relatifs au siège de Noviadunum et à la prise de Naisson. Tr. C. Wescher. Paris, 1868.

PROCLUS, LYCIUS (A.D. 410–485). Proclus's Life, Hymns and Works. Ed. Kenneth Sylvan Guthrie. North Yonkers, N.Y., Platonist Pr., 1925. 7 parts, typescript.

Trs. of 8 works, as indicated below under separate titles.

Hymns

————— Hymns, Greek and English. Tr. verse Thomas Taylor. London, 1793.

> Six of the seven hymns. This tr. was included by Taylor in his tr. of Sallust in the same year: see Sallustius, below.

Tr. K. S. Guthrie from the French, in Life, Hymns and Works, above.

Mathematical Writings

————— The Commentaries on the Timaeus of Plato. Tr. Thomas Taylor. London, the translator, 1820. 2 v.

————— The Descripcion of the Sphere or Frame of the Worlde (*De sphaera*). Tr. Wyllyam Salysburye. London, 1550?

————— The Philosophical and Mathematical Commentaries on the First Book of Euclid's Elements. Tr. Thomas Taylor. London, 1792. 2 v.

> Includes also trs. of *Elements of Theology,* and of Marinus' *Life of Proclus,* for which see below.

Tr. adapted by W. B. Frankland, together with his tr. of The first Book of Euclid's Elements. Cambridge Univ. Pr., 1905. xvi, 139 p.

————— Ptolemy's Tetrabiblos or Quadropartite. Tr. James Wilson from the Greek Paraphrase of Proclus. London, Hughes, 1820. xxv, 224 p.

Tr. J.M. Ashmand. London, Davis and Dickson, 1822. xxvii, 240 p.

————— Treatise on Motion. Tr. K. S. Guthrie from the French, in Life, Hymns and Works, above.

Part tr. Thomas Taylor as Select Theorems on the Perpetuity of Time, from the Second Book of Proclus on Motion (with other trs.). London, 1831, p. 85–96.

Philosophical Writings

————— The Chaldaic Philosophy. Tr. Thomas M. Johnson, in Iamblichus' Exhortation to Philosopy. Osceola, Missouri, Press of The Republican, 1907. vi, 138 p. Repr. in Guthrie, above.

————— The Elements of Theology. Tr. Thomas Taylor, in Commentaries on Euclid, 1792, q.v. above. Repr. 1816 in The Six Books on Plato, see below.

Tr. Thomas M. Johnson as Metaphysical Elements. Osceola, Missouri, Press of The Republican, 1909. xvi, 201 p.

Tr. A. C. Ionides, as "Divine Arithmetic." London and N.Y., Lane, 1917. 130 p.

Ed. and tr. E. R. Dodds. Oxford, Clarendon Pr., 1933. xvi, 348 p. Repr. 1963, xlvi, 340 p.

———— (Notes on Treatises of Plotinus). Tr. Thomas Taylor. London, 1834.

———— On Providence and Fate. Tr. Thomas Taylor, in the following item. Repr. K. S. Guthrie, above.

———— The Six Books of Proclus on the Theology of Plato. Tr. Thomas Taylor (with Elements of Theology, and three treatises, see below). London, the author, 1816.

———— Two Treatises of Proclus on the Ten Doubts Concerning Providence and . . . On the Nature of Evil. Tr. Thomas Taylor. London, Pickering, 1833. vii, 175 p. Repr. K. S. Guthrie. above.

Portions of these works had been tr. in The Six Books of Proclus, above.

Other Works

———— Fragments of the Lost Writings. Tr. Thomas Taylor. London, the author, 1825. xi, 113 p.

———— Marinus' Life of Proclus. Tr. Thomas Taylor, in The Commentaries on Euclid, above.

Tr. K. S. Guthrie from the French, in Life Hymns and Works, above.

PROCOPIUS (490–575). (The Complete Works). Ed. and tr. H. B. Dewing. LCL, 1914–40. 7 v.

V. 1–5, History of the Wars of the Emperor Justinian; v. 6, Secret History (*Anecdota*); v. 7, Buildings.

———— History of the Warres. Tr. Sir Henry Holcroft. London, 1653. 68, 55, 156 p.

———— The Secret History. Tr. anon. London, 1674. 162 p.

Tr. anon. London, Athenian Society, 1895. xxvii, 247 p.

Tr. Richard Atwater. Chicago, Covici, 1927. 286 p. Repr. Ann Arbor, Univ. Michigan Pr., 1961, xvi, 150 p.

QUINTUS OF SMYRNA (4th c.). The Fall of Troy. Ed. and tr. verse Arthur S. Way. LCL, 1913. 627 p.

———— Select Translations. Tr. Alexander Dyce. Oxford, Baxter, 1821. v, 123 p.

SALLUSTIUS THE PLATONIST (4th c.). On the Gods and the World. Tr. Thomas Taylor (with the Pythagoric Sentences of Demophilus . . . and Five Hymns of Proclus). London, 1793. xvi, 169 p.

Tr. Gilbert Murray, in Four Stages of Greek Religion. Oxford, Univ. Pr., 1912. Repr. in enlarged Five Stages of Greek Religion, 1925 et seq., esp. in Anchor Books, 1951, p. 191–212.

Ed. and tr. Arthur Darby Nock as Concerning the Gods and the Universe. Cambridge Univ. Pr., 1926. ccxiii, 48 p.

SIMPLICIUS (6th c.). Commentary on Epictetus. Tr. George Stanhope, in Epictetus his Morals with Simplicius his Comment. London, 1694. 552 p. Reprs. to 1750.

STEPHANUS OF ALEXANDRIA (7th or 8th c.). The Alchemical Works. Tr. F. Sherwood Taylor, in Ambix, 1 (1937), 116–33; 2 (1938), 39–49 (parallel texts)

STOBAEUS, JOANNES (5th c.). Pythagoric Sentences. Tr. Thomas Taylor, in Iamblichus' Life of Pythagoras. London, 1818.

THEOPHANES THE CONFESSOR (c. 752–818). (Selections from the World History relating to the 8th c. 717–811). Bilderstreit und Arabersturm in Byzanz. Tr. Leopold Breyer into German. Byzantinische Geschichtsschreiber, no. 6. Graz, Verlag Styria, 1957. 244 p.

THEOPHRASTUS, ALCHEMIST (8th c.). "The Poem of the Philosopher Theophrastus upon the Secret Art." Tr. verse C. A. Browne, in Scientific Monthly, 11 (1920), 193–214.

TRYPHIODORUS (fl. 470). The Destruction of Troy, Being the Sequel of the Iliad. Tr. James Merrick. Oxford, 1739. lxxxviii, 151 p.

Tr. A. W. Mair, in Oppian, Colluthus, and Tryphiodorus. LCL, 1928.

ZOSIMUS (5th c.). The New History of Count Zosimus. Tr. anon. London, 1684. 416 p. Repr. London, 1814, 241 p.

Tr. W. A. Craigie as The Narrative of Zosimus Concerning the Life of the Blessed. In Ante-Nicene Fathers, v. IX, p. 220–24.

Cf. French tr. M. Cousin, in *L'Histoire romaine écrite par Xiphilin, par Zonare, et par Zosime*. Paris, 1686. 2 v.

CHRISTIAN WRITERS: A.D. 300 TO 900

GEORGE B. PARKS

AKÁTHISTOS HYMNOS (A.D. 626). The Acáthist Hymn of the Holy Orthodox Eastern Church. Tr. verse G. R. Woodward, ed. W. J. Birbeck and G. R. Woodward. London, Longmans, 1917. viii, 62 p.

Tr. John Christopher and Anita Bartle as Akáthistos Hymn (part 1). London, Northern Printing Co., 1922. 7 p. Repr. rev. 1922, 11 p.

Tr. Rev. Vincent McNabb as Ode in Honour of the . . . Virgin Mary. Ditchling, Sussex, Pepler and Sewell, 1934. Repr. rev. London, Humphries, 1935; rev. Oxford, Blackfriars, 1948, 40 p.

Cf. "The 'Akathistos': A Study in Byzantine Hymnography," by Egon Wellesz: *Dumbarton Oaks Papers*, v. 9–10 (1955–56), 141–74, which translates several passages.

ASTERIUS (4th–5th c.). Ancient Sermons for Modern Times. Tr. Galusha Anderson and Edgar J. Goodspeed. N.Y. and Boston, Pilgrim Pr., 1904. 157 p.

ATHANASIUS, ST., Patriarch of Alexandria (269–373). (Collected Works). Tr. various hands in Library of the Fathers, v. 8, 13, 19, 38, 45: 1842–81, as follows.

V. 8, 1844, and 19, 1844. Select Treatises in Controversy with the Arians. Tr. J. H. Newman. See below for separate reprs.

V. 13, 1843. Historical Tracts. Tr. Miles Atkinson.

V. 38, 1854. The Festal Epistles. Tr. Henry Burgess.

V. 45, 1881. Later Treatises. Tr. William Bright.

Repr. rev. as Select Writings and Letters of Athanasius, ed. Archibald Robertson. Nicene Fathers, ser. 2, v. 4, 1892. xci, 606 p. (18 Select Writings, adding to the previous collection the Oration against the Gentiles and the Incarnation of the Word of God, tr. Archibald Robertson [see below]; the De sententia Dionysii; 19 Personal Epistles added to the Festal Epistles to a total of 64; and the Life of St. Anthony, tr. H. Ellershaw.)

———— Four Orations Against the Arians, and Oration Against the Gentiles. Tr. Samuel Parker. Oxford and London, 1713. 2 v.

Tr. J. H. Newman (Against the Arians), in Library of the Fathers, v. 8, 19, above. Repr. Nicene Fathers, above. Repr., omitting the fourth oration, London, Pickering, 1881, 2 v., et seq. to 1903.

Tr. W. C. L. as The Orations Against the Arians. London, Griffith, Farran, [1888?]. 299 p.

———— On the Incarnation of the Word of God. Tr. Archibald Robertson. London, Nutt, 1885. viii, 88 p. Repr. 1891; repr. Nicene Fathers, above; repr. Library of Christian Classics, v. 3, 1954, p. 55–110.

Tr. T. Herbert Bindley. London, Religious Tract Society, 1887. 139 p. Repr. 1903.

Tr. by a Religious of C. S. M. V. London, Bles, and N.Y., Macmillan, 1944. 65 p. Repr. London, Mowbray, 1953, 120 p.

———— Life of St. Anthony. Tr. Edward Stephens. London, 1697. 96 p.

Tr. H. Ellershaw, in Nicene Fathers, 1892, above.

Tr. J. B. McLaughlin. London, Burns Oates, and N.Y., Benziger, 1924. x, 122 p.

Tr. Sister Mary Emily Keenan, in Fathers of the Church, v. 15, 1952, p. 133–216.

———— On the Psalms. Tr. prefixed to Thomas Sternhold and John Hopkins, The Whole Booke of Psalmes. London, 1562, et seq. to 1664.

BASIL, ST., THE GREAT, Archbishop of Caesarea (329–379). The Ascetic Works. Tr. W. K. L. Clarke. London, S.P.C.K., and N.Y., Macmillan, 1925. 362 p.

Tr. Sister M. Monica Wagner. Fathers of the Church, v. 9, 1950. 537 p.

———— Exegetic Homilies. Tr. Agnes Clare Way. Fathers of the Church, v. 46, 1963. 378 p.

———— The Letters. Ed. and tr. Roy J. Deferrari. LCL, 1926–34. 4 v.

Tr. Agnes Clare Way. Fathers of the Church, v. 13, 28; 1951, 1955. (nos. 1–185 in v. 13; 186–308 in v. 28).

———— The Treatise on the Holy Spirit, the Nine Homilies on the Hexameron, and the Letters. Tr. Blomfield Jackson, in Nicene Fathers, ser. 2, v. 8, 1895. lxxvii, 363 p.

Cf. a French tr. of the *Homilies* by Stanislas Giet (Paris, Editions du Cerf, 1950, 539 p.).

Individual Works

———— Address to Young Men on the Right Use of Greek Literature. Tr. F. M. Padelford, in Essays on the Study and Use of Poetry by Plutarch and Basil the Great. N.Y., Holt, 1902, p. 97–120.

The Address was also tr. in the LCL edition of the Letters.

———— (Four homilies), in The Fathers Not Papists: or, Six Discourses by the Most Eloquent Fathers of the Church. Tr. Hugh Stuart Boyd. London, Bagster, 1834. xlviii, 446 p.

———— On the Holy Spirit. Tr. George Lewis. London, Religious Tracts Society, 1888. 176 p.

———— Scripture Ethics (*Moralia*). Ed. and tr. John M. Maguire. London, Bagster, 1871. 49 p.

———— Sixty-sixe Admonitory Chapters . . . to his Sonne Leo. Tr. James Scudamore. Paris, 1638. 122 p.

An Old English version of the *Admonition to his Spiritual Son* was tr. into modern English by Henry W. Norman, together with an *Old English Hexameron*: London, J. R. Smith, and Oxford, Macpherson, 1848, x, 55 p.; repr. London, 1849.

CHRYSOSTOM, ST. JOHN, Patriarch of Constantinople (d. 407). (Collected Works). Tr. many hands in Library of the Fathers, v. 4, 5, 6, 7, 9, 11, 12, 14, 15, 27, 28, 33, 34, 35, 36, 44 (16 volumes): 1838–85.

Virtually all the writings are sermons on the books of the New Testament: see the list of contents of each volume in Farrar and Evans, no. 941, see p. 14. V. 9 is, however, Homilies on the Statues, or To the People of Antioch. V. 6, 7, 14 were later repr., and all were repr. in the next entry.

Repr. rev. and rearranged in Nicene Fathers, v. 9–14, 1889–90, the contents as follows.

V. 9. Homilies on the Statues, with additional treatises and Homilies tr. W. R. W. Stephens, T. P. Brandram, and R. Blackburn (mostly listed separately below).

V. 10. Homilies on the Gospel of St. Matthew (repr. of Library of the Fathers, 34, tr. Sir George Prevost).

V. 11. Homilies on the Acts of the Apostles and the Epistle to the Romans (repr. of Library of the Fathers, 35, tr. J. Walker, J. Sheppard, and H. Browne; and of *ibid.*, 7, tr. J. B. Morris)

V. 12. Homilies on the Epistles of Paul to the Corinthians (repr. of Library of the Fathers, 4, 5, 27, tr. H. K. Cornish, John Medley, and John Ashworth).

V. 13. Homilies on the Epistles of Paul to the Galatians, etc. (repr. of Library of the Fathers, 6, 12, 14, tr. W. J. Copeland, James Tweed, W. C. Cotton, and John Ashworth).

V. 14. Homilies on the Gospel of St. John and on the Epistle to the Hebrews (repr. of Library of the Fathers, 28, 36, and 44, tr. G. T. Stupart, and Thomas Keble and John Barrow)

———— Address on Vainglory and the Right for Parents to Bring Up their Children. Tr. M. L. W. Laistner, in Christianity and Pagan Culture in the Later Roman Empire. Ithaca, N.Y., Cornell Univ. Pr., 1951, p. 85–122.

———— Admonition, wherein hee Recalls Theodorus the Fallen, or Generally an Exhortation for Desperate Sinners (*Ad Theodorum lapsum*). Tr. Viscount Grandison, Prisoner in the Tower. London, 1654. 126 p.

Cf. two earlier trs.: anon., 1553; by Robert Wolcomb, 1609.; and the tr. in Nicene Fathers, v. 9, above.

———————— Baptismal Instructions. Tr. Paul W. Harkins. Ancient Christian Writers, 31, 1963. 375 p.

Also tr. in Nicene Fathers, 9, above.

———————— A Companion for the Sincere Penitent. Tr. anon. London, 1728. xxxii, 174 p.

———————— The Divine Liturgies of our Fathers Among the Saints, John Chrysostom and Basil the Great. Ed. and tr. J. N. W. B. Robertson. London, Nutt, 1894. vii, 519 p. (parallel texts)

The Liturgy appears generally in collections of liturgies.

———————— The Golden Book of St. John Chrysostom Concerning the Education of Children. Tr. John Evelyn. London, 1659. 90 p. Repr. in Miscellaneous Writings of John Evelyn, 1825; repr. in Literary Remains of John Evelyn, 1834.

Homilies

———————— Commentary on St. John the Apostle and Evangelist: Homilies 1–47; Homilies 48–88. Tr. Sister Thomas Aquinas Goggin. Fathers of the Church, v. 33, 41, 1957–59.

———————— An Exposition upon the Epistle . . . to the Ephesians. Tr. anon. London, 1581. 341 p.

———————— A Godly Exhortation Made unto the People of Antioch. Tr. Robert Rouse. London, 1597. (Also tr. in Library of the Fathers, v. 9, and Nicene Fathers, v. 9.)

———————— A Homilie . . . upon that Saying of St. Paul, Brethren, I wold not have you ignorant, what is becom of those that slepe. Tr. Christopher Chaloner. London, 1544.

———————— Oration on Eutropius. Tr. Hugh Stuart Boyd, in The Fathers Not Papists: or, Six Discourses by the Most Eloquent Fathers . . . London, Bagster, 1834. xlviii, 446 p.

Also tr. in Nicene Fathers, 9, above.

———————— In Praise of St. Paul. Tr. Thomas Halton. Boston, St. Paul Eds. 1963. 123 p.

———————— Sermon on Alms. Tr. Margaret M. Sherwood. N.Y., New York School of Philantropy, 1917. 24 p.

———————— A Sermon on Christmas Day. Tr. William Scott. London, 1774, et seq. to 1778.

The same translator also published in 1775 trs. of individual sermons on Good Friday, Easter, Ascension, Whit Sunday, and Trinity Sunday, each one preached on a New Testament text.

———————— A Sermon . . . on Patience. Tr. Thomas Sampson. London, 1550.

———————— A Sermon . . . wherein . . . he Proveth that No Man is Hurted but of Hym Selfe. Tr. Thomas Lupset. London, 1541. Repr. 1542.

Also tr. in Nicene Fathers, 9, above.

———————— Two Orations of Prayeng to God. Tr. anon. in The Diuisyon of the Places of the Laws and of the Gospell . . . by Petrum Arotopoeum. London, 1548.

Other Writings

———————— Four Discourses . . . Chiefly on the Parable of the Rich Man and Lazarus. Tr. F. Allen. London, Longmans, 1869. viii, 110 p.

———————— Meditations . . . on the Study of the Word of God. Tr. Robert King. 2d ed. Dublin, G. Herbert, 1853. 108 p.

———————— Six Books Concerning the Priesthood. Tr. H. Hollier. London, 1728. 208 p.

Tr. T. Allen Moxon. London, S.P.C.K., and N.Y., Gorham, 1907. 271 p.

Tr. Patrick Boyle. Dublin, Gill, 1910. xxiii, 131 p. Repr. Westminster, Md., Newman Pr., 1943, xxxiv, 145 p.

Tr. W. A. Jurgens. N.Y., Macmillan, 1955. xxv, 133 p.

Tr. Graham Neville. London, S.P.C.K., 1964. 160 p.

Also tr. J. Bunce, London, 1759; Henry M. Mason, Philadelphia, 1826; F. W. Hohler, Cambridge, 1837; E. G. Marsh, London, 1844; B. H. Cowper, London, 1866; and W. R. W. Stephens, in Nicene Fathers, v. 9, 1889.

———————— A Treatise Concerning the Restitucion of a Synner. London, 1553.

COSMAS INDICOPLEUSTES (6th c.). The Christian Topography. Tr. J. W. McCrindle. Hakluyt Society Publications, 98, 1897. xii, xxviii, 398 p. Repr. N.Y., Burt Franklin, 1964.

CYRIL, ST., Patriarch of Alexandria (fl. 412–444). Commentary on the Gospel According to St. John. Tr. (v. 1) P. E. Pusey, and (v. 2) Thomas Randell. Library of the Fathers, v. 43, 48: 1874, 1885.

———— Five Tomes Against Nestorius, Scholia on the Incarnation, Christ is One, Fragments. Tr. P. E. Pusey. Library of the Fathers, v. 46, 1881. cv, 406 p.

———— The Three Epistles [two to Nestorius, one to John of Antioch]. Tr. P. E. Pusey. Oxford, Parker, 1872. v, 75 p. (parallel texts)

Tr. Charles A. Heurtley, in On Faith and the Creed. Oxford, Parker, 1886. vi, 237 p.

Ed. and tr. T. Herbert Bindley in The Oecumenical Documents of the Faith. London, Methuen, 1899. xii, 311 p. Repr. 1906.

An Armenian version of the *Scholia on the Incarnation* was ed. and tr. F. C. Conybeare (London, Text and Translation Society, 1907, 189 p.); and a Syriac version of *The Commentary upon the Gospel of St. Luke* was tr. R. Payne Smith (Oxford, Univ. Pr., 1859, 2 v.).

CYRIL, ST., Bishop of Jerusalem (348–?386). The Catechetical Lectures. Tr. R. W. Church. Library of the Fathers, v. 2, 1838. xxxviii, 312 p. Repr. rev. by Edward H. Gifford, in Nicene Fathers, ser. 2, v. 7, 1894.

Eighteen lectures to candidates for baptism; five to the newly baptized on the subject of the mysteries.

———— The Five Lectures on the Mysteries and Other Sacramental Treatises. Tr. anon. Ed. H. De Romestin. Oxford, Parker, 1887. vi, 137 p.

Tr. Reginald M. Wooley as Instructions on the Mysteries. London, Faith Pr., and Milwaukee, Wis., Morehouse, 1930. v, 27 p.

Tr. R. W. Church as Lectures on the Christian Sacraments: The Procatechesis and the Five Mystogogical Catecheses. London, S.P.C.K., 1951. xli, 83 p. (repr. from the first entry, above)

———— (The fourth lecture). Tr. C. A. Heurtley as On the Ten Doctrines of the Faith, in On Faith and the Creed. Oxford, 1886. vi, 237 p.

—————— (The tenth lecture). Tr. as The Creator Seen in the Creation, in H. C. Fish, History and Repository of Pulpit Eloquence. N.Y., 1857, v. 1. Repr. in The Great Sermons of the Great Preachers, London, 1858.

—————— (The fifteenth lecture). Tr. anon. as The Second Advent. London, Elliott Stock, 1886. vi, 29 p.

—————— Selections from the Catechetical Lectures. Tr. William Telfer (with A Letter to Constantius), in Library of Chrstian Classics, v. 4, 1955, p. 64–199.

The Fifth Mystagogical Catechism was tr. in Thomas Brett, *Collection of the Principal Liturgies, London,* 1720.

DIONYSIUS THE AREOPAGITE (fl. c. 500). The Works. Tr. John Parker. London and Oxford, Parker, 1897–99. 2 v.

V. 1. The Divine Names, Mystic Theology, letters, liturgy.

V. 2. The Heavenly Hierarchy, The Ecclesiastical Hierarchy.

The works in v. 2 were published earlier as *The Celestial and Ecclesiastical Hierarchy* (London, Skeffington, 1894, 99 p.)

—————— The Celestial Hierarchies. Tr. by the editors of the Shrine of Wisdom. London, 1935. 55 p. Repr. with The Mystical Theology (Brook, Surrey, Shrine of Wisdom, 1949, 76 p.)

—————— On the Divine Names and Mystical Theology. Tr. C. E. Rolt. London, S.P.C.K., and N.Y., Macmillan, 1920. viii, 223 p.

—————— The Ecclesiastical Hierarchy. Tr. Thomas L. Campbell. Washington, D.C., Catholic Univ. of America, 1955. 48 p.

—————— The Mystical Divinity. Tr. John Everard, in Some Gospel Treasures Opened. London, 1653, p. 767–79.

Tr. A. B. Sharpe as The Mystical Theology (with letters to Gaius and Dorotheus, 1, 2, 5), in Mysticism: Its True Nature and Value. London, Sands & Co., 1910. xi, 233 p. Repr. St. Louis, Mo., Herder, 1910, xliii, 261 p.

Tr. anon. Shrine of Wisdom Manual 6. London, 1923. 15 p.

An early 14th c. anon. tr. from the Latin as Deonise Hid Diuinite was ed. Phyllis Hodgson, EETS, v. 231, 1955, p. 1–10.

EUSEBIUS PAMPHILI, Bishop of Caesarea (260–340). (History of the Church). Tr. Meredith Hanmer as Auncient Ecclesiastical Histories . . . by . . . Eusebius, Socrates, and Evagrius. London, 1576–77. 2 parts. Repr. 1585, 1607, 1619, 1636–37 (with the Life of Constantine, see below), 1650.

Tr. Thomas Shorting (also with Socrates and Evagrius, and the Life of Constantine). Cambridge, 1683. 700 p. Repr. 1692, 1709. (These three histories abridged, tr. Samuel Parker. London, 1720. 3 v.)

Tr. I. Boyle. N.Y., T. N. Stanford, 1856.

Tr. Christian Frederick Crusé. Philadelphia and N.Y., 1833 (2d ed.). Repr. London, 1838; 1847; N.Y. 1856; London, Bohn, 1858; London, Bell and Daldy, 1865, xl, 430 p.; London, 1867, 1876, 1897, 1917: repr. Grand Rapids, Mich., Baker, 1955, xxxiii, 480, 59 p.

Tr. A. C. McGiffert (with Life of Constantine, from 1845 tr., see below). Nicene Fathers, ser. 2, v. 1, 1890. x, 632 p.

Ed. and tr. Kirsopp Lake. LCL, 1926, v. 1 (books 1–5). V. 2, 1932, repr. from next entry.

Tr. H. J. Lawlor and J. E. L. Oulton (with The Martyrs of Palestine). London, S.P.C.K., and N.Y., Macmillan, 1927–28 2 v. Repr. part with preceding entry, 1932; repr. 1954.

Tr. Roy J. Deferrari. Fathers of the Church, v. 19, 29, 1953–55.

Tr. G. A. Williamson. Penguin, 1965. 429 p.

———— Life of Constantine. Tr. Wye Saltonstall, in Meredith Hanmer tr. of the History, 1637.

Tr. Thomas Shorting, in his tr. of the History, 1683 et seq., see above.

Tr. anon. London, Bagster, 1845. xx, 380 p. Repr. rev. E. C. Richardson, in Nicene Fathers, ser. 2, v. 1, 1890, with the History.

———— The Martyrs of Palestine. Tr. H. J. Lawlor (with the History), 1927–28, see above.

A Syriac version was ed. and tr. William Cureton (London, Williams and Norgate, 1861, xi, 86, 54 p.).

———— Preparation for the Gospel. Ed. and tr. E. H. Gifford. Oxford, Univ. Pr., 1903. 4 v. in 5 (parallel texts). Also pub. separately, 1903.

The first book was tr. R. Cumberland, London, 1720.

———— The Proof of the Gospel (*Demonstratio evangelica*). Tr. W. J. Ferrar. London, S.P.C.K., and N.Y., Macmillan, 1920. 2 v.

———— On the Theophania or Divine Manifestation of our Lord and Saviour. Tr. Samuel Lee from a Syriac version. Cambridge, Univ. Pr., 1843. clix, 344 p.

———— The Treatise of Eusebius (against Hierocles). Ed. and tr. F. C. Conybeare, in Philostratus, The Life of Apollonius of Tyana. LCL, 1912. v. 2, p. 483–605.

EVAGRIUS SCHOLASTICUS (6th c.) (History of the Church, 431–594). Tr. Meredith Hanmer, with Eusebius, etc., 1576–77, see above.

Tr. Thomas Shorting, with Eusebius, etc., 1683, see above.

Tr. anon. (? Edward Walford). London, Bagster, 1846. xvi, 318 p. Repr. (with Theodoret), London, Bohn, 1854.

GREGORY, ST., OF NAZIANZUS (4th c.). Epigrams and Spirituall Sentences. Tr. Thomas Drant. London, 1568.

Ed. and tr. W. R. Paton as The Epigrams, in The Greek Anthology. LCL, 1917. v. 2, p. 399–505.

The epigrams make up book 8 of the Palatine Anthology. Selected poems were tr. Hugh Stuart Boyd in *Select Poems of Synesius and Gregory Nazianzen*, London, 1814, p. 10–62. Elizabeth Barrett Browning tr. "Soul and Body: A Poem," in *The Athenaeum*, 1842.

———— Funeral Orations. Tr. L. P. McCauley, in Fathers of the Church, 22, 1953, p. 3–156.

———— A Panegyric upon the Maccabees. Tr. Jeremy Collier. London, 1716. 108 p.

———— Select Orations and Select Letters. Tr. Charles G. Browne and J. E. Swallow. Nicene Fathers, ser. 2, v. 7, 1894, p. 185–498.

———— The Theological Orations, Letters on the Apollinarian Controversy. Tr. Charles G. Browne and James E. Swallow, in Library of Christian Classics, v. 3, 1954, p. 111–232.

For the *Christos paschon* once assigned to him, see this title, below (11th c.).

GREGORY, ST., Bishop of Nyssa (4th c.). Select Writings and Letters. Tr. William Moore and Henry A. Wilson. Nicene Fathers, ser. 2, v. 5, 1893. ix, 567 p.

——————— An Answer to Ablabius: An Address on Religious Instruction. Tr. Cyril C. Richardson. Library of Christian Classics, v. 3, 1954, p. 256–325.

——————— The Catechetical Oration. Tr. J. H. Srawley. London, S.P.C.K., 1917. v, 123 p.

——————— Encomium . . . on his Brother, Saint Basil. Ed. and tr. Sister James Aloysius Stein. Washington, D.C., Catholic Univ. of America, 1928. xcvi, 166 p.

——————— From Glory to Glory. Texts from the Mystical Writings. Tr. Herbert Musurillo. N.Y., Scribner, 1961. xiv, 298 p.

——————— The Goal of the True Ascetic Life According to God. Tr. James J. Artzer. Washington, D.C., Catholic Univ. of America, 1956. (typescript)

——————— The Life of Gregory Thaumaturgus. Tr. H. G. Evelyn White from a Coptic version. in The Monasteries of the Wadi 'n Natrûn. N.Y., Metropolitan Museum, 1926. v. 1.

——————— The Life of St. Macrina. Tr. W. K. L. Clarke. London, S.P.C.K. 1916. 79 p

——————— The Lord's Prayer. The Beatitudes. Tr. Hilda C. Graef. Ancient Christian Writers, v. 18, 1954. 210 p.

JOANNES CLIMACUS, ST. (6th c.). The Holy Ladder of Perfection. Tr. Father Robert. London, Richardson and Son, 1858. xii, 473 p.

Tr. Archimandrite Lazarus Moore as The Ladder of Divine Ascent. London, Faber, and N.Y., Harper, 1959. 270 p.

JOHN OF DAMASCUS, ST. (d. c. 754). Barlaam and Joasaph. Tr. Henry Parson as The History of the Five Wise Philosophers. London, 1672. Repr. 1711, 1725?, 1732, and 1895 in The Story of Barlaam and Ioasaph, ed. K. S. Macdonald (Calcutta, Thacker, Spink, 1895).

Ed. and tr. G. R. Woodward and H. Mattingly. LCL, 1914. xx, 640 p.

An abridgement of the legend included in the medieval *Golden Legend* was printed in Caxton's tr., and repr. in the Macdonald ed. and in a separate ed. by Joseph Jacobs (London, Nutt, 1896, cxxxii, 56 p.).

————— Exposition of the Orthodox Faith. Tr. S. D. F. Salmond. Nicene Fathers, ser. 2, v. 9, 1899. viii, 106 p.

————— On Holy Images. Tr. Mary H. Allies. London, Baker, and Philadelphia, McVey, 1898. ix, 216 p.

————— Writings. (The Fount of Knowledge; Philosophical Chapters; On Heresies; The Orthodox Faith). Tr. Frederic H. Chase, Jr. Fathers of the Church, v. 37, 1958. 426 p.

LITURGIES. A Collection of the Principal Liturgies Used by the Christian Church in the Celebration of the Holy Eucharist. Tr. various hands. London, 1720. xvi, 160 p. Repr. 1838.

Liturgies of St. James, St. Mark, St. Chrysostom, St. Clement, St. Basil, and others from other languages. For numerous other liturgies translated from the Greek, see Farrar and Evans, no. 2467 following, and 2538 to 2563, p. 14, above.

MACARIUS MAGNES (4th–5th c.). The Apocriticus. Tr. T. W. Crafer. London, S.P.C.K., and N.Y., Macmillan, 1919. 169 p.

MACARIUS THE ELDER, ST., of Egypt (4th c.). Institutes of Christian Perfection [*The Opuscula*, or Sayings]. Tr. Granville Penn. London, Murray, 1816. xlvi, 230 p. Repr. 1828.

————— Primitive Morality: or, The Spiritual Homilies. Tr. Thomas Haywood. London, 1721. 482 p.

Tr. A. J. Mason as Fifty Spiritual Homilies. London, S.P.C.K., and N.Y., Macmillan, 1921. li, 316 p.

MARCUS DIACONUS (4th–5th c.). The Life of Porphyry, Bishop of Gaza. Tr. G. F. Hill. Oxford, Clarendon Pr., 1913. xliii, 190 p.

MAXIMUS, ST., Confessor (580–622). The Ascetic Life: The Four Centuries of Charity. Tr. Polycarp Sherwood. Ancient Christian Writers, v. 21, 1955. viii, 284 p.

NEMESIUS OF EMESA (4th c.). The Nature of Man. Tr. George Wither. London, 1636. 661 p.

Tr. W. Telfer, in Library of Christian Classics, v. 4, 1955, p. 201–466.

PALLADIUS, Bishop of Helenopolis (c. 365–425). The Dialogue Concerning the Life of Chrysostom. Tr. Herbert Moore. London, S.P.C.K., and N.Y., Macmillan, 1921. xxv, 213 p.

———— The Lausiac History. Tr. W. K. Lowther Clarke. *Ibid.*, 1918. xiv, 188 p.

Tr. Robert T. Meyer. Ancient Christian Writers, v. 34, 1965. vii, 265 p.

A Syriac version was tr. in *The Book of Paradise*, tr. E. A. Wallis Budge, London, 1904, et seq.: see Farrar and Evans, no. 3779, p. 14, above.

PHILOSTORGIUS (4th c.). The Ecclesiastical History as Epitomized by Photius. Tr. Edward Walford (with The Ecclesiastical History of Sozomen). London, Bohn, 1855, p. 425–528.

PHOTIUS, Patriarch of Constantinople (9th c.). The Ecclesiastical History of Philostorgius Epitomized by Photius. See Philostorgius, above.

———— The Homilies. Tr. Cyril A. Mango. Dumbarton Oaks Studies. Cambridge, Mass., Harvard Univ. Pr., 1958. xii, 327 p.

———— The Library. Tr. J. H. Freese. London, S.P.C.K., and N.Y., Macmillan, 1920. v. 1 only, xiv, 243 p.

Cf. an ed. and tr. into French by René Henry (Paris, Les Belles Lettres, 1959–62, 3 v.).

SOCRATES SCHOLASTICUS (c. 379–440). Ecclesiastical History. Tr. Meredith Hanmer (with Eusebius and Evagrius) in Ancient Ecclesiastical Histories, 1576–77: see Eusebius, above.

Tr. Thomas Shorting (with Eusebius and Evagrius), 1683: see Eusebius, above.

Tr. anon. (William Walford?) as A History of the Church from the Accession of Constantine to the 38th Year of Theodosius. London, Bagster, 1844. xxiv, 556 p. Repr. 1851; 1853 (Bohn's Ecclesiastical Library); repr. rev. A. C. Zenos, in Nicene Fathers, ser. 2, v. 2. 1890, p. 1–178.

SOLOMON, THE TESTAMENT OF (4th c.?). Tr. J. J. Conybeare. Jewish
Quarterly Review, v. 11, 1899, p. 1–45.

For later development of the Solomon legend, see Latin Literature, early
Medieval.

SOZOMEN HERMIAS (5th c.). The Ecclesiastical History . . . from A.D.
324 to A.D. 440. Tr. W. Walford. London, Bagster, 1846. xvi, 448 p.
Repr. London, Bohn, 1855, xvi, 536 p. Repr. rev. Chester D. Har-
tranft, Nicene Fathers, ser. 2, v. 2, 1890.

SYNESIUS OF CYRENE, Bishop of Ptolemais (4th–5th c.). The Essays and
Hymns. including the Address to the Emperor Arcadius and the
Political Speeches. Tr. Augustine Fitzgerald. London, Oxford Univ.
Pr., 1930. 2 v.

——————— On Dreams. Tr. Isaac Myer. Philadelphia, 1888. 36 p.

Ed. and tr. (paraphrase) A. C. Ionides. London and Aylesbury, 1929.
120 p.

——————— The Letters. Tr. Augustine Fitzgerald. London, Oxford Univ. Pr.,
1926. 272˙ p.

——————— In Praise of Baldness. Tr. Abraham Fleming as A Paradoxe . . .
Proving that Baldness is much better than Bushie Hair. London,
1579. Repr. 1597.

——————— The Ten Hymns. Tr. verse Alan Stevenson. London, pr. pr., 1865.

Parts of four hymns were tr. Hugh Stuart Boyd in Select Poems of Synesius
and Gregory Nazianzen (London, 1814); and by A. W. Chatfield in Songs
and Hymns of the Earliest Christian Poets (verse tr., London, Rivingtons,
1876). See also a tr. by Elizabeth Barrett Browning in The Athenaeum
(1842), repr. in her Collected Poems.

——————— Treatise on Providence. Extracts tr. Thomas Taylor in Select
Works of Plotinus. London, 1817, p. 508–59.

THEODORE OF MOPSUESTIA (4th–5th c.). Commentary on the Lord's
Prayer and on the Sacraments of Baptism and the Eucharist. Tr.
Alphonse Mingana. Woodbrooke Studies, 5. Cambridge, Heffer, 1953.
xxv, 265 p.

———————— Commentary on the Nicene Creed. Tr. the same. *Ibid.*, 1932. vii, 240 p.

———————— "A Hitherto Unpublished Prologue to the Acts of the Apostles." Ed. and tr. Ernst von Dobschütz, in American Journal of Theology, 2 (1898), 353–87. (probably written by Theodore)

THEODORET, Bishop of Cyprus (c. 393–458). The Ecclesiastical History, Dialogues, and Letters. Tr. Blomfield Jackson, in Nicene Fathers, ser. 2, v. 3, 1892, p. 1–348.

———————— The Ecclesiastical History. Tr. G. E. St. Omer, 1612.

Tr. anon. London, Bagster, 1843. xxiv, 360 p. Repr. London, Bohn 1854, xiv, 480 p.

———————— A Treatise of Laws (The *Therapeutica*). Ed. and tr. Thomas Comber. Cambridge, J. Archdean, 1776. vii, 85 p.

LATER BYZANTINE: A.D. 900 TO 1453

Procope S. Costas

BELTHANDROS AND CHRYSANTZA (13th c.). Tr. (German) A. Ellissen, in Analekten der mittel- und neugriechischen Literatur. Leipzig, 1862, v. 5, p. 169–77.

Tr. (German) Ernst Nischer as Belthandros und Chrysantza: Ein byzantinischer Minnesang. In Jahrbuch der österreichischen byzantinischen Gesellschaft, 8 (1959–60), 87–122.

CABASILAS, NICOLAS (14th c.). "Anti-Zealot" Discourse. Text and Summary by Ihor Ševčenko. Dumbarton Oaks Papers, 11 (1957), 79–171.

———————— A Commentary on the Divine Liturgy. Tr. J. J. Hussey and P. A. McNulty. London, S.P.C.K., 1960. xi, 120 p.

CABASILAS, NILUS, Metropolitan of Thessalonica (13th–14th c.). A briefe Treatise conteynynge a playne declaration of the Popes Usurped Primacye. Tr. Thomas Gressop. London, Sutton, 1560.

CALECAS, EMMANUEL (d. 1410). *Correspondance.* Résumé in French by R. J. Loenertz. Studi e Testi, 150. Vatican City, Vatican Library, 1950. xii, 350 p.

CALLIMACHUS AND CHRYSORRHOE (12th–13th c.). *Le Roman de Callimaque et de Chrysorrhoé.* Tr. (French) M. Prichard. Paris, Les Belles Lettres, 1956. xi, 118 p.

CANANUS, LASCARIS (15th c.). *Die Nordlandreise* (c. 1438). Tr. (German) Franz Grabler. Byzantinische Geschichtsschreiber, 2. Graz, Verlag Styria, 1954, p. 103–5.

CECAUMENOS (11th c.). (Handbook of Strategy, or *Strategikon.*) Tr. Hans-Georg Beck into German as *Vademecum des Byzantinischen Aristokraten.* Byzantinische Geschichtsschreiber, 5. Graz, Verlag Styria, 1956. 164 p.

CHALCONDYLAS, LEONICUS (c. 1423–c. 1490). (Selections from the History.) Tr. Franz Grabler into German, in Europa im XV. Jahrhundert von Byzantinern gesehen. Byzantinische Geschichtsschreiber, 2. Graz, Verlag Styria, 1954, p. 16–97.

CHONIATES, NICETAS (d. 1213). (The Chronicle History, from 1118 to 1206.) Tr. Franz Grabler into German. Byzantinische Geschichtsschreiber, v. 7, 8, 9. Granz, Verlag Styria, 1958. 3 v.

The volumes have individual titles: v. 7. *Die Krone der Komnenen.* v. 8. *Abenteurer auf dem Kaiserthron.* v. 9. *Die Kreuzfahrer Erobern Konstantinopel.* V. 9 adds a work by Nicolaus Mesarites, q.v. below.

CHRISTOS PASCHON (The Passion of Christ, anon. drama, 11th–12th c.) Tr. into German verse in A. Ellissen, ed., Analekten: see Collections, above.

CHRONICLE OF MONEMVASIA (10th 11th c.). Tr. (a few passages) Peter Charanis, in Dumbarton Oaks Papers, 3 (1950), 139–66.

Ed. and part tr. P. Lemerle into French, in Revue des études byzantines, 21 (1963), 5–49.

CHRONICLE OF MOREA (14th c.). Tr. Harold E. Lurier as Crusaders as Conquerors. N.Y., Columbia Univ. Pr., 1964. 346 p.

CHRYSOLORAS, MANUEL (c. 1350–1415). (Two Letters.) Tr. Günther Stökl into German, in Europa im XV. Jahrhundert von Byzantinern gesehen. Byzantinische Geschichtsschreiber, 2. Graz, Verlag Styria, 1954, p. 111–45.

COMNENA, ANNA (11th–12th c.). The Alexiad, Being the History of the Reign of her Father Alexius I, Emperor of the Romans 1081–1118 A.D. Tr. Elizabeth E. S. Dawes. London, Kegan Paul, 1928. 439 p.

CONSTANTINE PORPHYROGENITUS (10th c.). *De Administrando Imperio*. Tr. R. J. H. Jenkins (with Greek text, ed. G. Moravcsik). Budapest, 1949–62.

———— *Le livre des cérémonies*. Ed. and tr. A. Vogt into French. Paris, Les Belles Lettres, 1935–40. 2 v.

CRITOBOULOS, MICHAEL (15th c.). History of Mehmed the Conqueror. Tr. Charles T. Riggs. Princeton, N.J., Princeton Univ. Pr., and London, Oxford Univ. Pr., 1955. ix, 222 p.

CYPRUS PASSION. Tr. A. C. Mahr. Notre Dame, Ind., Notre Dame Univ. Pr., 1947. xvi, 225 p. (parallel texts)

DIGENIS AKRITAS (10th–11th c.). Tr. Salvatore Impellizeri into Italian as *Il Digenis Akritas: L'Epopea di Bisanzio*. Florence, G. C. Sansoni, 1940. 191 p.

Ed. and tr. John Mavrogordato. Oxford, Clarendon Pr., and N.Y., Oxford Univ. Pr., 1956. lxxxiv, 273 p.

EUSTATHIUS (12th c.). Labor and Reward: A Sermon on Psalm xlix, 8, 9. Tr. anon. in The Great Sermons of the Great Preachers, London, 1858.

———— *Die Normanen in Thessalonika. Die Eroberung durch die Normanen* (1185 A.D.) in der Augenzeugenschilderung des Bischofs

Eustathios. Tr. Herbert Hunger into German. Byzantinische Geschichtsschreiber, 3. Graz, Verlag Styria, 1955. 163 p.

Tr. V. Rotolo into Italian. Palermo, 1961. lxiv, 192 p.

EUSTATHIUS MACREMBOLITES (12th c.). Ismene and Ismenias. Tr. anon. from the French version by L. H. LeMoine. London, 1788. xi, 200 p.

GEMISTUS, GEORGIUS (PLETHO) (c. 1355–1451). *Pléthon: Traité des lois ou recueil des fragments . . . de cet ouvrage.* Tr. into French A. Pellissier. Paris, Firmin-Didot, 1858. 472 p.

An important author, very little of whose work has been translated into a modern language.

GREGORAS, NICEPHORUS (13th–14th c.). *Correspondance.* Ed. and tr. R. Guilland into French. Paris, Les Belles Lettres, 1927. xxii, 392 p.

LEO DIACONUS (10th c.). The History (A.D. 959–976). Tr. Franz Loretto into German as *Nikephoras Phokas . . . und Johannes Tzimiskes: Die Zeit von 959 bis 976 . . . .* Byzantinische Geschichtsschreiber, 10. Graz, Verlag Styria, 1961. 193 p.

MACHAIRAS, LEONTIOS (15th c.). Recital Concerning the Sweet Land Cyprus entitled "Chronicle." Ed. and tr. R. M. Dawkins. Oxford, Clarendon Pr., 1932. 2 v. (Covers the years 1359–1432.)

MESARITES, NICOLAUS (12th–13th c.). Description of the Church of the Holy Apostles at Constantinople. Tr. Glanville Downey. Transactions of American Philosophical Society, 43 (1957), 855–924.

———— (The Palace Revolution of John Comnenos 1201). Tr. Franz Grabler into German, in Byzantinische Geschichtschreiber, 9, p. 271–316. Graz, Verlag Styria, 1958.

PALAMAS, GREGORY (14th c.). *Défense des saints hésychastes.* Ed. and tr. Jean Meyendorff into French. Louvain, Catholic University, 1959. 768 p.

Cf. Jean Meyendorff, *A Study of Gregory Palamas,* tr. George Lawrence from French, London, Faith Pr., 1964, 245 p.

PLETHO: see GEMISTUS.

HO POULOLOGOS (The Ornithologist: 14th c. satirical poem). Ed. and tr. Stamatia Krawczynski into German. Berlin, Akademie-Verlag, 1960. xx, 166 p.

PSELLUS, MICHAEL, Constantinus (c. 1020–110). The Chronographia. Tr. E. R. A. Sewter. London, Routledge, and New Haven, Conn., Yale Univ. Pr., 1953. viii, 320 p.

———— [Concerning the Ideas of which Plato Speaks] (title in Greek). Tr. J. M. Hussey, in Church and Learning in the Byzantine Empire. London, Oxford Univ. Pr., 1937, p. 226–29.

———— Dialogue on the Operation of Daemons. Tr. Marcus Collisson. Sydney, J. Tegg, 1843. 52 p.

SPHRANTZES, GEORGIUS (1401–1478). *Die letzten Tage von Konstantinopel* (from the Greater Chronicle). Tr. Endré von Ivanka into German. Byzantinische Geschichtsschreiber, 1. Graz, Verlag Styria, 1954. 101 p.

STILBES, CONSTANTINUS (12th–13th c.). *Les griefs contre l'église latine au sujet de dogmes.* Ed. and tr. J. Darrouzès into French, in Revue des études byzantines, 21 (1963), 50–100.

SYMEON, THE NEW THEOLOGIAN (11th c.). *Chapitres théologiques, gnostiques et pratiques.* Ed. and tr. J. Darrouzès into French. Sources chretiennes, 51. Paris, 1957.

THEODORE OF GAZA (c. 1400–1476). *De Fato.* Ed. and tr. J. W. Taylor. Univ. of Toronto Studies. Toronto, 1925. 29 p. (parellel texts)

XIPHILINUS (11th c.). *Histoire romaine.* Tr. M. Cousin into French (with Zonaras and Zosimus). Paris, 1686. 2 v.

A tr. into Greek of the lost books of history of Dio Cassius.

ZONARAS (12th c.). *Histoire romaine.* Tr. M. Cousin into French (with Xiphilinus and Zosimus). Paris, 1686. 2 v.

MODERN GREEK LITERATURE
FROM A.D. 1453

Procope S. Costas and William V. Pappas

BACKGROUND

FINLAY, GEORGE. A History of Greece, from the Conquest by the Romans to the Present Time. Ed. H. F. Tozer. Rev. ed. Oxford, Clarendon Pr., 1877. 7 v.

Especially v. 6 and 7. Finlay published v. 1 of his *History in* 1844.

FORSTER, EDWARD S. A Short History of Modern Greece (1821–1956). 3rd ed., rev. and enl. by Douglas Dakin. London, Methuen, 1958. xi, 268 p.

HEURTLEY, W. A. et al. A Short History of Greece . . . to 1964. Cambridge, and N.Y., Cambridge Univ. Pr., 1965. viii, 202 p.

A survey from antiquity.

LAWSON, JOHN C. Modern Greek Folklore and Ancient Greek Religion: A Study in Survivals. Cambridge Univ. Pr., 1910. Repr. N.Y., University Bks., 1965. xxii, 620 p.

Old, but still useful.

MAVROGORDATO, JOHN. Modern Greece: A Chronicle and a Survey, 1800–1931. London and N.Y., Macmillan, 1931. xi, 251 p.

MILLER, WILLIAM. Greece. London, Benn, 1928. 351 p.

NOEL-BAKER, FRANCIS. The Land and People of Greece. 2nd ed. London, Black, 1960. viii, 88 p.

PAPARRAGOPOULOS, KONSTANTINOS (1815–91). *Histoire de la civilisation hellénique*. Paris. Hachette, 1878. 470 p.

The "father" of modern Greek historiography.

PERSPECTIVE OF GREECE. An Atlantic Monthly Supplement. Ed. Kimon Friar and Donald Freelander. N.Y., Intercultural Pubns., and London, H. Hamilton, 1955. 74 p.

From the *Atlantic Monthly* (1955).

RANGAVÉS, ALEXANDROS RIZOS (1810–92). Greece: Her Progress and Present Position. Tr. from the French by Charles K. Tuckerman. N.Y., Putnam, 1867. 102 p.

ROUX, JEANNE AND GEORGES. Greece. Tr. from the French by Lionel and Miram Kochan. London, Kaye, 1958. 253 p., new and rev. ed., 1965. Les Beaux Pays Series.

SANDERS, IRWIN T. Rainbow in the Rock: The People of Rural Greece. Cambridge, Mass., Harvard Univ. Pr., 1962. xvi, 363 p.

An excellent sociological survey.

STAVRIANOS, L. S. The Balkans since 1453. N.Y., Rinehart, 1958, xxii, 970 p.

The best historical survey currently available. Excellent bibliographies.

LITERARY STUDIES

ANTONIADIS, SOPHIE. *La Place de la liturgie dans la tradition des lettres grecques*. Leiden, Netherlands, A. W. Sijthoff, 1939.

AVATANGHELOS, HENRIETTE. "Modern Literary Forms and Currents in Greece." Books Abroad, 28 (1954), 160–65.

BOURCHIER, J. D. et al. "Modern Greek Literature," in Encyclopaedia Britannica (1928).

COSTAS, PROCOPE S. An Outline of the History of the Greek Language with Particular Emphasis on the Koine and the Subsequent Periods. Chicago, Ill., 1936. xxxvi, 143 p.

KNÖS, B. *L'Histoire de la littérature néo-grecque. La période jusqu'à* 1821. Uppsala, Almqvist and Wiksell, 1962. 690 p.

Excellent.

MANNING, CLARENCE A. "Greek Literature, Modern," in Encyclopedia of Literature. N.Y., 1946. v. 1, p. 379–384.

MAVROGORDATO, J. N. "Greek Literature, Modern," in Chambers' Encyclopedia, Oxford, 1955. v. 6, p. 575–6.

MIRAMBEL, ANDRÉ. "General Characteristics of Modern Greek Literature," in Athene, v. 4, no. 5 (1943), p. 42 ff.

———— "Modern Greek Theater," in Athene, v. 4, no. 8 (1943), p. 47 ff.

———— *La littérature grecque moderne*. Paris, Presses Universitaires, 1953. 117 p.

———— *"Littérature néo-hellénique,"* in *Histoire des littératures,* v. 2 of *Encyclopédie de la Pléiade.* Paris, 1956. p. 840–83.

   Good bibliography.

PHOUTRIDES, ARISTIDES E. "The Literary Impulse of Modern Greece," in Poet Lore, v. 24 (1915), p. 56–67.

RANGAVÉS, ALEXANDROS RIZOS (1809–92). *Histoire littéraire de la Grèce moderne.* Paris, Lévy, 1877. 2 v.

RIZOS NEROULOS, IACOBUS (1778–1850). *Cours de littérature grecque moderne donné á Genève.* 2nd ed., rev. Genève, Cherbuliez, 1828. xxiv, 204 p.

TRYPANIS, C. A. "Greek Literature, Modern," in Encyclopaedia Britannica, v. 10 (1964), p. 800–84.

VALSA, M. *Le Théâtre grec moderne de 1453 à 1900.* Berlin, Akademie-Verlag, 1960. 384 p.

VRAHNOS, SOPHIE A. "Greek Literature" [from 1870], in Columbia Dictionary of Modern European Literature. N.Y., Columbia Univ. Pr., 1947. p. 345–46.

COLLECTIONS

ANTIGONE LEBT. *Neugriechische Erzählungen*. Ed. Melpo Axioti and Hadzis Dim. Berlin, 1960. 584 p.

Introduction by the editors on modern Greek literature with special reference to prose. Tr. by other hands of prose pieces from 37 authors.

BAGGALLY, JOHN WORTLEY. The Klephtic Ballads in relation to Greek history (1715–1821). Oxford, Blackwell, 1936. xiv, 109 p.

CHANSONS POPULAIRES GRECQUES *des XVe et XVIe Siècles, publiées et traduites*. Paris, Les Belles Lettres, 1931. 151 p.

DAWKINS, R. M. Modern Greek in Asia Minor. A Study of the Dialect of Silli Cappadocia and Pharasa, with grammar, texts, translations and glossary. With a chapter on the subject matter of folk tales, by W. R. Halliday. Cambridge Univ. Pr., 1916. p. xiv, 695.

EMBIRICOS, ALEXANDRE. *La Renaissance crétoise aux XVIème et XVIIème siècles*. v. 1, *La Littérature*. (Collection de l'Institut d'Etudes Byzantines et Néo-helléniques) Paris, Les Belles Lettres, 1960. 300 p.

FORTY-FIVE STORIES FROM THE DODECANESE. Ed. and tr. from MSS. R. M. Dawkins. Cambridge Univ. Pr., 1950. xi, 559 p. (parallel texts)

"GREEK DEMOTIC SONGS." Tr. Michalaros and others in Athene, v. 4, no. 8 (1943). p. 12–17.

GREEK FOLK-SONGS from the Ottoman Provinces of Northern Hellas. Literal and metrical tr. Lucy M. J. Garnett. Classified, rev. and ed. . . ., John Stuart Stuart-Glennie. London, Stock, 1885. Repr. rev. and enl., London, Ward and Downey, 1888. 290 p.

GREEK LAYS, IDYLLS, AND LEGENDS. Tr. Elizabeth Meyhew Edmonds. London, Trübner, 1886. 264 p.

HADJICOSTA, ISMERE. Cyprus and Its Life. Morals and Customs of Cyprus, Folk Songs, etc. Tr. D. A. Percival. London, 1943 [for 1949]. 48 p. (English text), ix p., plates, 93 p. (Greek text)

MODERN GREEK FOLKTALES. Ed. and tr. R. M. Dawkins. Oxford, Clarendon Pr., and N.Y., Oxford Univ. Pr., 1953. xxxviii, 491 p.

MODERN GREEK LITERARY GEMS from the Works of Pheraios (and others). Tr. George C. Pappageotes et al. N.Y., Cortina, 1962. 64 p.

MODERN GREEK POEMS. Selected and rendered into English by T. Stephanides and George C. Katsimbalis. London, 1926.

Poems from the Old School of Athens.

MODERN GREEK POETRY. Tr. and ed. Rae Dalven. N.Y., Gaer Associates, 1949. 32 p.

MODERN GREEK STORIES. Tr. Demetra Vaka (Brown) and Aristides Phoutrides. N.Y., Duffield, 1920. 270 p.

MORE GREEK FOLKTALES. Ed. and tr. R. M. Dawkins. Oxford, Clarendon Pr., and N.Y., Oxford Univ. Pr., 1955. viii, 178 p.

NEW FOLKLORE RESEARCHES. Greek Folk Poetry. Annotated tr. from the Whole Cycle of Romaic Folkprose, L. M. J. Garnett. Ed. J. S. Stuart-Glennie. Guildford, Billing and Sons, 1896. 2 v.

POÉSIE DE LA GRÈCE MODERNE. Tr. Samuel Baud-Bovy. Lausanne, Éditions La Concorde, 1946. 191 p.

Translations of poems by Kalvos, Solomos and Palamas.

A PROVERB FOR IT. 1510 Greek Sayings comp. and ed. B. T. Marketos. Tr. Ann Arpajoglou, intro. Clarence A. Manning. N.Y., New World Pub., 1945. 191 p.

ROUSSEL, LOUIS. *Kargheuz, ou un théâtre d'ombres à Athènes.* Athènes, Imprimérie de A. Raftanis, 1921. 2 v.

Text and tr. of one play with French résumé of twenty-eight plays.

SHERRARD, PHILIP. The Marble Threshing Floor. Study in Modern Greek
Poetry. N.Y., Essential Bks., 1955, and London, Valentine, Mitchell,
1956. 258 p.

SIAPKARAS-PITSILLIDÈS, THEMIS. *Le Pétarquisme en Chypre. Poèmes
d'amour en dialecte chypriote d'après un ms. du XVIᵉ siècle.* Athènes,
L'Institut Français d'Athènes, 1952. viii, 446 p.

A critical edition with 156 poems in French tr.

SIX POETS OF MODERN GREECE. Ed. and tr. Edmund Keeley and Philip
Sherrard. London, Thames and Hudson, 1960. 192 p., and N.Y.,
Knopf, 1961. xi, 186 p.

Poems of Cavafy, Sikelianos, Seferis, Antoniou, Elytis and Gatsos.

SONGS OF MODERN GREECE. Ed. and tr. G. F. Abbott. Cambridge Univ.
Pr., 1900. ix, 307 p.

Translates some folk songs.

THREE CRETAN PLAYS: The Sacrifice of Abraham, Erophile, and
Gyparis. Tr. Frederick Henry Marshall. Intro. John Mavrogordato.
London, Oxford Univ. Pr., 1929. 338 p.

Includes the Cretan pastoral poem "The Fair Shepherdess." These Cretan
works mark the beginning of modern Greek literature.

WACE, A. J. B. Greece Untrodden: A Selection of Greek Folk-tales. Athens,
pr. pr., 1964. 116 p.

WAR SONGS OF THE GREEKS, and Other Poems. Tr. David Ross
Fotheringham. Cambridge, England, Deighton Bell, 1907. 87 p.

INDIVIDUAL AUTHORS

ANTHIAS, TEFCROS (pseud. of Andreas Paulou). Human Epic: Epico-
Lyric Poem. Tr. A. Raysson. London, Flame Publications, 1949.
30 p.

———— The Song of Earth. Tr. Philip L. Nicolaides. London, Union Pub., 1952. 70 p.

———— A Trip to the Sun (Children's Play in three acts). Tr. Rae Dalven. London, Flame Publications, 1954. 61 p.

AXIOTI, MELPO (1906-   ) *XXe Siècle*. Tr. into French J. Darlet. Paris, La bibliothèque française, 1949. 175 p.

BASILEIADES, SPYRIDON N. (1845–1874) *Galatée*. (Parallel texts, French and Greek.) Intro. and notes le Baron d'Estournelles de Constant. (Bibl. orient. elzév, 18.) Paris, 1878. xlix, 211 p.

BIKELAS, DEMETRIOS (1835–1908). Loukis Laras: Reminiscences of a Chiote Merchant during the War of Independence. Tr. J. Gennadios. London, Macmillan, 1881. xxiv, 273 p.

———— *Nouvelles grecques*. Tr. into French by Marquis de Queux de Saint-Hilaire. Paris, Maison Didot, 1897. viii, 287 p.

———— The Pappas Narkissos. See Karkavitsas, below.

———— Seven Essays on Christian Greece. Tr. John, Marquess of Bute. Paisley and London, Gardner, 1890. 298 p. (Repr. from Scottish Review.)

———— Tales from the Aegean. Tr. Leonard E. Opdycke, intro. Henry A. Huntington. Chicago, McClurg, 1894. 258 p. Translated from the French version of the Marquis de Queux de Saint-Hilaire.

CAPETANAKIS, DEMETRIOS (1912–1944). Demetrios Capetanakis: a Greek Poet in England. Ed. John Lehmann. London, J. Lehmann, 1947, and N.Y., Devin-Adair, 1949, as The Shores of Darkness: Poems and Essays. 183 p.

CAVAFY, CONSTANTINE P. (1868–1933). The Poems. Tr. John Mavrogordato, intro. Rex Warner. London, Hogarth Press, 1951, and N.Y., Grove Press, 1952. 199 p.

———— The Complete Poems. Tr. Rae Dalven, intro. W. H. Auden. London Hogarth Pr., and N.Y., Harcourt, Brace, 1961. xxii, 234 p.

CHORTATZES, GEORGIOS (16th c.). Erophile, a Tragedy, in Three Cretan Plays: see Collections, above.

CHOUMNOS, GEORGIOS (15th c.). Old Testament Legends from a Greek Poem on Genesis and Exodus. Ed. and tr. F. H. Marshall. Cambridge Univ. Pr., 1925. xxxii, 116 p.

Approximately one quarter of the poem is translated.

DROSINES, GEORGIOS (1859–1951). Amaryllis. Tr. anon. N.Y., Cassell, 1891. 154 p.

———— The Herb of Love. Tr. Elizabeth M. Edmonds. N.Y., Tait, and London, Unwin, 1892. 223 p.

A mediocre tr. of a fanciful idyll.

———— Stories from Fairyland (with A. Kourtides, The Cup of Tears). Tr. Mrs. Edmonds. (Children's Library, v. 3.) London, Unwin, 1892. x, 153 p. 3rd ed., 1903.

EFTALIOTIS, ARGYRIS (1849–1924). *Le Chant de la Vie, sonnets*. Tr. into French M. Valsa. Paris, Librairie de France, 1929. 47 p.

———— Tales from the Isles of Greece, being Sketches of Modern Greek Peasant Life. Tr. W. H. D. Rouse. London, Dent, 1897. 231 p. Repr. as Modern Tales of the Greek Islands. London, Nelson, 1942.

ELIYIA, JOSEPH (1901–1931). Poems. Tr. Rae Dalven. N.Y., Anatolia Pr., 1944. 205 p. (parallel texts)

ELYTIS, ODYSSEUS (1911–   ). *Poèmes*. Tr. into French Robert Levesque. Athènes, Hestia, 1945. 106 p.

———— "Anniversary." Tr. Demetrius Capetanakis, in The Shores of Darkness. N.Y., Devin-Adair, 1949. p. 179–180.

GYPARIS. See Three Cretan Plays, in Collections, above.

KALVOS, ANDREAS (1792–1969). *La Lyre patriotique de la Grèce, odes*. Tr. into French Stanislas Julien. Paris, Librairie de Peytieux, 1824. xii, 94 p.

———— *Odes nouvelles . . . suivies d'un choix de poésies de Chrestopoulo*. Tr. into French Pauthier de Censay. Paris, 1826. xii, 251 p. (parallel texts)

KARKAVITSAS, ANDREAS (1866–1922). The Outcast, and the *Pappas Narkissos* (by D. Bikelas). Tr. and adapted F. B. Harrison. London, Christian Knowledge Society, 1895. 78 p.

KAZANTZAKIS, NIKOS (1882–1957). The Fratricides. Tr. Athene Gianakas Dallas. N.Y., Simon and Schuster, 1964. 254 p.

————— Freedom or Death. Tr. Jonathan Griffin. N.Y., Simon and Schuster, 1956. viii, 432 p. Also, as Freedom and Death, Oxford, Cassirer, and London, Faber, 1956. 472 p. Repr. N.Y., 1961; London, 1966.

————— The Greek Passion. Tr. Jonathan Griffin. N.Y., Simon and Schuster, 1953. 432 p. Repr., as Christ Recrucified, Oxford, Cassirer, and London, Faber, 1954. 470 p. Repr. (paper) N.Y., Simon and Schuster, 1959, 472 p., and Oxford, Cassirer, 1961.

————— Japan, China. Tr. George C. Pappageotes, with an epilogue by Helen Kazantzakis. N.Y., Simon and Schuster, 1963, and Oxford, Cassirer, and London, Faber, 1964 (as Travels in China and Japan). 382 p.

————— Journey to the Morea. Tr. F. A. Reed. N.Y., Simon and Schuster, 1965. 190 p.

————— The Last Temptation of Christ. Tr. P. A. Bien. N.Y., Simon and Schuster, 1960, 506 p., and Oxford, Cassirer, 1961, 519 p.

————— The Odyssey: A Modern Sequel. Tr. English verse by Kimon Friar. N.Y., Simon and Schuster, 1958, and London, Secker and Warburg, 1959. xxxviii, 826 p. Cf. P. Prevelakis, below.

————— Report to Greco—An Autobiography. Tr. Peter A. Bien. N.Y., Simon and Schuster, 1965. 512 p.

————— The Rock Garden: Passages from The Saviors of God. Tr. Richard Howard and Kimon Friar from the French. N.Y., Simon and Schuster, 1963. 251 p.

————— Saint Francis. Tr. P. A. Bien. N.Y., Simon and Schuster, 1962. 379 p. and, as God's Pauper: Saint Francis of Assisi, Oxford, Cassirer, 1962. 390 p. Repr. (paper) N.Y., 1964.

————— The Saviors of God: Spiritual Exercises. Tr. Kimon Friar. N.Y., Simon and Schuster, 1960. 143 p.

————— Spain. Tr. Amy Mims. N.Y., Simon and Schuster, 1963. 254 p.

———— Toda Raba. Tr. Amy Mims. N.Y., Simon and Schuster, 1964. 220 p.

———— Zorba the Greek. Tr. Carl Wildman. London, J. Lehmann, 1952. 319 p., and N.Y., Simon and Schuster, 1953. 311 p. Repr. (paper) N.Y., Simon and Schuster, and Oxford, Cassirer, 1959; London Faber, 1961.

KORAËS, ADAMANTIOS I. (1748–1833). Koray's Letters Written from Paris, 1788–92. Tr. and ed. P. Ralli. London, pr. pr., 1898. viii, 108 p.

KORNAROS, VINTZENTZOS (17th c.). *Erotokritos* Tr. John Mavrogordato, intro. Stephen Gaselee. London and N.Y., Oxford Univ. Pr., 1929. vii, 61 p.

For a contemporary adaptation, see Apollonios Phocaeus, below.

KOUTSOCHERAS, Iòannes Panagiotou. The March of the Lilies. Tr. Philip Sherrard. London, Hutchinson, 1966. 50 p.

LELY, NICHOLAS (1887–1959). *Epinikion*: Victorial Poems. A Collection in Greek and Some Translations by Joseph Auslander. N.Y., Anatolia Pr., 1944. 121 p.

MAVILIS, LORENZO (1860–1912). *12 Sonetti. A cura di Bruno Lavagnini con due scritti di Alberto Savino e Aldo Spallici.* Milano, 1960. 64 p.

MOSCHOS, DEMETRIOS (16th c.). *Neaira.* Greek text ed. A. Mustoxydis with German tr. and notes by A. Elissen. Hanover, Karl Rumpler, 1859. 115 p.

MYRIVILIS, STRATIS (1892–   ). *De Profundis* (Life in the Tomb). Tr. (French) A. Protopazzi and Louis Carle Bonnard. Paris, Flammarion, 1933. 295 p.

———— The Mermaid Madonna. Tr. Abbott Rick. London, Hutchinson, and N.Y., Crowell, 1959. 310 p.

———— The Schoolmistress with the Golden Eyes. Tr. Philip Sherrard. London, Hutchinson, 1964. 288 p.

NAKOS, LILIKA (1903–   ). *L'Enfer des Gosses*. Tr. (French) J. Schidin. Lausanne, Éditions Spes, 1946. 132 p.

PALAMAS, KOSTES (1859–1943). *Choix de poésies*. Tr. (French verse) Pierre Baudry. Paris, Les Belles Lettres, 1930. 70 p.

——————— *Oeuvres choisies*. Tr. (French) Eugène Clément. Paris, Chiberre, 1922. 2 v.

——————— *Pages choisies*. Tr. (French) André Chédel. La Chaux-de-Fonds, Éditions de Nouveaux Cahiers, 1942. xiv, 98 p.

——————— Poems. Tr. T. P. Stephanides and G. C. Katsimbalis. London, Hazell, 1925. 143 p.

Individual Works

——————— Byron. Tr. A. Michalopoulos. Repr. in Verses Mild and Harsh, Kostes Palamas, ed. K. T. Argoe. Chicago, Neo-Hellenic Pub., 1928. p. 72–74.

The remainder of this v. contains mostly Greek texts.

——————— *La Flûte du Roi*. Tr. (French) Eugène Clément. Paris, Stock, 1934. 221 p.

——————— The Grave. Tr. D. A. Michalaros. Chicago, 1930.

——————— Life Immovable. Pt. 1. Tr. Aristides Phoutrides. Cambridge, Mass., Harvard Univ. Pr., 1919. ix, 237 p. Pt. 2, part tr. Aristides Phoutrides as A Hundred Voices and Other Poems. *Ibid.*, 1921. vi, 227 p.

The same translator published selections, as *Life Immovable,* in Athene, v. 4, no. 5 (1943), 19–68.

——————— A Man's Death. Tr. A. E. Phoutrides, with foreword D. C. Hesseling. Athens, Hestia, 1934. 59 p.

Originally tr. in Modern Greek Stories: see Collections, above.

——————— Royal Blossoms: or Trisevyene. Tr. Aristides Phoutrides. New Haven, Yale Univ. Pr., 1923. 163 p. (a play in four acts)

——————— The Twelve Words of the Gypsy. Tr. Frederick Will. Lincoln, Univ. of Nebraska Pr., 1964. xxi, 205 p.

Cf. R. J. H. Jenkins, *Palamas: An Inaugural Lecture Delivered at King's College, London* (London, 1927, 28 p.), which contains some trs. Also Palamas Memorial Issue of *Athene* (v. 4, no. 5, 1943), which includes trs. with texts of his poems.—The Palamas issue of *Nea Hestia* (v. 34, Christmas 1943) contains a biblography of trs. of his works into other languages (p. 463–471).

PALAMAS, LEANDRO (1891–1958). A Study of the Palm-Tree of Kostes Palamas. Tr. Th. P. Stephanides and George C. Katsimbalis. Athens, Hestia, 1931. 27 p.

PAPADIAMANTIS, ALEXANDROS (1851–1911). *Skiathos, île grecque: nouvelles.* Tr. (French) Octave Marlier. Paris, Les Belles Lettres, 1934. 320 p.

PAPASTAMOU, OLGA. Ancestral Dynamo. Tr. D. Carion, Cali Orfanidi, Ascreo, Gaston-Henri Aufrère. Athens, 1959. 43 p.

——————— The Apotheosis of the Mind. Tr. Daniel Carion, André Hammel, Ascreo, Cali Orfanidi, Gaston-Henri Aufrère. Athens, 1959. 45 p.

——————— Awakened Daffodil. Tr. Gaston-Henri Aufrère, André Hammel. Paris, Office Français d'Informations Culturelles, n.d. 21 p.

——————— Beauty of Life. Tr. Gaston-Henri Aufrère, André Hammel. Alexandria, Egypt. 1960. 21 p.

——————— Deep Flames. Tr. Henri Boissin. Athens, 1957. 43 p.

——————— Far Beyond Countries. Tr. Gaston-Henri Aufrère, André Hammel, Henri Boissin. Athens, 1958. 45 p.

——————— Process of People. Tr. Gaston-Henri Aufrère, André Hammel, Ascreo. Athens, 1961. 43 p.

——————— Shady Eyelids. Tr. Gaston Henri Aufrère, André Hammel, Henri Boissin. Athens, 1958. 45 p.

——————— Sun's Tale. Tr. André Hammel, Henri Boissin. Athens, 1958. 45 p.

PAPPAS, ANGELOS (pseud. of Evangelos Pappazissis, 1883–   ). In the Path of the Beast. Tr. Stavroula Will. Cleveland, pr. pr., 1952. 238 p.

PHOCAEUS, APOLLONIOS (pseud. of Stephen Gargilis). The Path of the Great. An Adaptation of the Epic Poem *Erotokritos*. Boston, Athena, 1945. 480 p.

Adapted from the Cretan 16th-century poem of Vintzentzos Kornaros, above.

PREVELAKIS, PANDELIS (1909–   ). *Chronique d'une cité. L'arbre, la première liberté, la cité*. Tr. (French) Jacques de Lacarrière. Paris, Gallimard, 1961. 110 p.

A novel.

————— Nikos Kazantzakis and his Odyssey: a study of the poet and the poem. Tr. Philip Sherrard. N.Y., Simon and Schuster, 1961. 192 p.

————— The Sun of Death. Tr. Abbott Rick, preface Henry Miller. N.Y., Simon and Schuster, 1964. 255 p.

Tr. Philip Sherrard. London, Murray, 1965. 206 p.

RHEGAS PHERRHAIOS (1751–1798). See A. Dascalakis, *Les oeuvres de Rhigas Velestinlis*. Paris, diss., 1937. 127 p.

RHOIDES, EMMANUEL D. (1836–1904). Pope Joan, the Female Pope: An Historical Study. Tr. with pref. C. H. Collette. London, Redway, 1886. 102 p.

Tr. T. D. Kriton as *Papissa Joanna*. Athens, 1931. 179 p.

Tr. Lawrence Durrell as Pope Joan, a romantic biography. London, Verschoyle, 1954. 164 p. Repr. rev., London, Deutsch, 1960, and N.Y., Dutton, 1961, 164 p.; repr. London, World, 1962, 157 p.; repr. London, Mayflower, 1965, paper.

RODOCANACHI, CONSTANTINE P. (1880–   ). No Innocent Abroad. Tr. Patrick Leigh Fermor. London, Heinemann, 1937. 299 p., and, as Forever Ulysses, N.Y., Viking, 1938, 315 p.

THE SACRIFICE OF ABRAHAM. Tr. in Three Cretan Plays. See Collections, above.

SEFERIS, GEORGE (pseud. of Georgios Sepheriades, 1900–). *Poèmes.* Tr. (French) Robert Levesque. (Collection de L'Institut Français d'Athènes). Athènes, Ikaros, 1945. 203 p. (parallel texts)

———— The King of Asine, and other Poems. Tr. Bernard Spencer, Nanos Valaoritis, and Lawrence Durrell. London, Lehmann, 1948. 82 p.

———— Poems. Tr. Rex Warner. London, Bodley Head, 1960, and Boston, Atlantic, Little, Brown, 1961. 127 p.

SIKELIANOS, ANGELO (1884–1951). *Poèmes.* Tr. (French) R. Levesque. Paris, Egloff, 1947. 237 p.

———— Akritan Songs (1941–42). Tr. Paul Nord. N.Y., Spap, 1944. 31 p.

———— The Delphic Word; The Dedication. Tr. Alma Reed. N.Y., Harold Vinal, 1928. 53 p.

Poem written for the Delphic Festival in 1927.

———— The Dithyramb of the Rose. Tr. Frances Sikelianos. [Pittsfield, Massachusetts], 1939. 16 p.

Tr. Eva Sikelianou, as "Excerpts from the *Dithyramb of the Rose*" in Athene, v. 4, no. 8 (1943), p. 31 ff.

———— *Serment sur le styx, cinq poèmes.* Tr. (French) Octave Merlier. Aurillac, Poirier-Bottreau, 1944.

———— The Song of Kalypso. Tr. D. Michalaros, in Athene, v. 4, no. 8 (1943), p. 53–54.

SKIPES, SOTERIS (1881–1951). *Anthologie, 1899–1918.* Tr. (French) Philéas Lebesgue et André Castagnon. Paris, Figuière, 1919. 265 p.

———— Patterns from a Grecian Loom. Tr. from the French by John Harwood Bacon. London, Unwin, 1928. 141 p.

SOLOMOS DIONYSIOS (1798–1857). The Greek National Anthem. Rendered into English by Rudyard Kipling. Garden City, N.Y., Doubleday Page, 1918.

———— *Poèmes.* Tr. (French) Robert Levesque. (Collection de L'Institut Français d'Athènes). Athènes, Ikaros, 1945.

See Romilly Jenkins, *Dionysios Solomos* (Cambridge Univ. Pr., 1940, 225 p.), a biographical study which includes some tr.

SPYROPOULOS, N. J. (1893–1958). Bellerophon. Tr. Clarence A. Manning. N.Y., Bookman Associates, 1935. 71 p.

THEODOROU, NELLY. Pastorale. Tr. Abbott Rick. N.Y., Crowell, 1961, and London, Redman, 1962. 180 p.

THEOTOKAS, GEORGE (1905–   ). Argo. A Novel. Tr. E. Margaret Brooke and Ares Tsatsopolous. London, Methuen, 1951. viii, 357 p.

————— *Le Démon*. Tr. (French) Marie Colombos. Paris, Stock, 1946. 175 p.

THEOTOKIS, KOSTAS (1872–1923). *Le Condamné*. Tr. (French) Léon Krajewski. Paris, Calmann-Lévy, 1929. xxxvi, 217 p.

————— *L'honneur et l'argent*. Tr. (French) Léon Krajewski, in Les Oeuvres libres, Paris, no. 139 (January 1933), p. 63–139.

TRIKOUPIS, SPYRIDON (1788–1873). Translation of the Funeral Oration of the late Lord Byron. London, W. Davy, 1836. 15 p. Reprinted in Cornelius C. Felton, Selections from Modern Greek Writers in Prose and Poetry. Cambridge, Mass., 1856.

TRIVOLIS, IAKOVOS (16th Century). *Histoire de Tagiapiera, surcomité Vénitien; poëme grec en vers trochaïques rimés*. Tr. (French) with intro. and notes by Émile Legrand. (parallel texts), Paris, Maisonneuve, 1875. 63 p.

————— *Iakovos Trivolis Poiemata*. Tr. (German) and ed. Johannes Irmscher. (Berliner byzantinische Arbeiten) Berlin, Akademie-Verlag, 1956. 121 p.

VALAORITES, ARISTOTELIS (1824–1879). *Poèmes patriotiques*. Tr. (French) J. Blanchard. Paris, Leroux, 1883. 2 v.

VARNALIS, COSTAS (1884–   ). The True Apology of Socrates. A Satire. Tr. Stephen Yaloussis. London, Zeno, 1955. 79 p.

VASSILIKOS, VASSILIS (1933–   ). The Plant, The Well, The Angel. A Trilogy. Tr. Edmund and Mary Keeley. N.Y., Knopf, 1964. 272 p.

VENEZIS, ILIAS (pseud. of Ilias Mellos) (1904–   ). Aeolia. Tr. E. D. Scott-Kilvert. London, W. Campion, 1949. x, 259 p., and Denver, Colorado, Univ. of Denver Press, 1951. 269 p.

———— Beyond the Aegean. Tr. E. D. Scott-Kilvert. N.Y., Vanguard Pr., 1956. 260 p.

———— La Grande pitié (Register Number 31328), Tr. (French) Hélène et Henri Boissin. Paris, Éditions du Pavois, 1945. 287 p.

VLACHOS, ANGE (1915–   ). Their Most Serene Majesties. Tr. Kay Cicellis. London, Bodley Head, 1963, and N.Y., Vanguard Pr., 1964. 318 p.

Historical novel on 12th-century Byzantium.

XENOPOULOS, GREGORIOS (1867–1951). La Mauvaise voie. Tr. (French) E. Clément. Athènes, 1924.

———— Red Rock: from Ecstasy to Tragedy. Tr. William D. Spanos. N.Y., Pageant Pr., 1955. 202 p.

———— Il segreto della Contessa Valeri. (Play) Tr. (Italian) Nicola Catone. Bari, Scuola Grafica Salesiana, 1960. 82 p.

———— The Stepmother. A Tale of Modern Athens. Tr. Elizabeth M. Edmonds. London, John Lane, 1897. 143 p.

A sentimental novella.

XENOS, STEPHANOS THEODOROS (1821–1894). Andronike, the Heroine of the Greek Revolution. Tr. Edward Grosvenor. Boston, Roberts Brothers, 1897. xii, 527 p. Repr. Boston, Little Brown, 1899.

Excellent tr. of the historical novel.

———— The Devil in Turkey, or Scenes in Constantinople. Tr. Henry Corpe. London, E. Wilson, 1851. 3 v.

———— East and West: A Diplomatic History of the Annexation of the Ionian Islands to Greece. London, Trübner, 1865. 303 p.

ZALOCOSTAS, CHRISTOS. Rupel. Tr. anon. Athens, 1945. 90 p.

LATIN LITERATURE
TO A.D. 450

Konrad Gries

BACKGROUND

A COMPANION TO LATIN STUDIES. Ed. (Sir) John Edwin Sandys. Cambridge, England, Univ. Pr., 1910. Re-eds. and reprs. to 3d ed., 1935, repr. N.Y. and London, Hafner, 1963, xxxv, 891 p.

ABBOTT, FRANK FROST. The Common People of Ancient Rome: Studies of Roman Life and Literature. N.Y., Scribner, and London, Routledge, 1911. xii, 290 p. Repr. N.Y., Biblio and Tannen, 1965.

———————— Roman Politics. (Our Debt to Greece and Rome) 1923. vi, 177 p.

ARNOLD, E. VERNON. Roman Stoicism, Being Lectures on the History of Stoic Philosophy with Special Reference to its Development within the Roman Empire. Cambridge Univ. Pr., 1911. ix, 468 p. Repr. N.Y., Humanities Pr., 1958.

ASHBY, THOMAS. The Architecture of Rome. London, Batsford, and N.Y., Scribner, 1927. xiii, 202, 94 p.

Also listed as v. 2 of a re-ed. of William J. Anderson and R. P. Spiers, *The Architecture of Greece and Rome*, London, Batsford, 1900, xvii, 300 p., 179 ill.; re-ed. 1907, xxi, 359 p., 255 ill.

BALSDON, J. P. V. D. Roman Women: Their History and Habits. London, Bodley Head, 1962, and N.Y., Day, 1963. 351 p., 16 ill.

———————— The Romans. London, Watts, 1965. xiv, 288.

BLOCH, RAYMOND. The Etruscans. Tr. Stuart Hood from the French [Paris, 1954], rev. London, Thames and Hudson, and N.Y., Praeger, 1958. 260 p., 117 ill.

———————— The Origins of Rome. Tr. Margaret Shenfield from the French [Paris, 1959]. London, Thames and Hudson, and N.Y., Praeger, 1960. 212 p., 77 ill.

BOAK, ARTHUR E. R. A History of Rome to 565 A.D. London and N.Y., Macmillan, 1921. Re-eds. to 5th ed., rev. William G. Sinnigen, 1965, xv, 576 p.

BROWN, FRANK E. Roman Architecture. N.Y., Braziller, and London, Prentice-Hall, 1962. 127 p., over 100 ill.

CARCOPINO, JÉRÔME. Daily Life in Ancient Rome: The People and the City at the Height of Empire. Tr. E. O. Lorimer from the French [1939], ed. Henry T. Rowell. New Haven, Yale Univ. Pr., and London, Routledge, 1941. xv, 342 p. Repr. 1960, paper.

CARY, M[ax]. A History of Rome Down to the Reign of Constantine. London, Macmillan, 1935. Re-ed. 1954, xvi, 835 p.

DILL, (Sir) SAMUEL. Roman Society from Nero to Marcus Aurelius. London and N.Y., Macmillan, 1904. xxii, 639 p. Repr. N.Y., Meridian Books, and London, Mayflower, 1957, paper.

———— Roman Society in the Last Century of the Western Empire. London and N.Y., Macmillan, 1898. xx, 382 p. Re-ed. 1899, xxviii, 459 p.; repr. N.Y., Meridian Books, 1958, and London, Mayflower, 1959, paper.

DUDLEY, DONALD R. The Civilization of Rome. London, Muller, and N.Y., New American Library, 1960. 256 p., 16 p. of ill.

ETRUSCAN CULTURE: Land and People: Archeological Research and Studies Conducted in San Giovenale and its Environs by Members of the Swedish Institute in Rome. Ed. Axel Boethius, et al. Tr. Nils G. Sahlin from the Swedish. Malmö, Sweden, Allhem Publishing House, 1962, and N.Y., Columbia Univ. Pr., 1963. xv, 478 p., 592 ill., 22 maps.

FRIEDLÄNDER, LUDWIG. Roman Life and Manners under the Early Empire. Tr. Leonard A. Magnus, J. H. Freese, and A. B. Gough from the German of the 7th ed. [1901, original 1862–71]. London, Routledge, and N.Y., Dutton, 1908–13. 4 v. Repr. N.Y., Barnes and Noble, 1965, 4 v.

GRANT, MICHAEL. The World of Rome. Cleveland, Ohio, and N.Y., World, and London, Weidenfeld, 1960. Repr. N.Y., New American Library, 1961, 349 p., paper.

GRIMAL, PIERRE. The Civilization of Rome. Tr. W. S. Maguiness from the French [Paris, 1960]. London, Allen and Unwin, and N.Y., Simon and Schuster, 1963. 531 p., 229 ill.

HADAS, MOSES, and The Editors of Time-Life Books. Imperial Rome. N.Y., Time, Inc., 1965. 190 p.

HANFMANN, GEORGE M. A. Roman Art: A Modern Survey of the Art of Imperial Rome. Greenwich, Conn., N.Y., Graphic Society, and London, Cory Adams, 1964. 224 p., 197 ill.

JONES, A. H. M. The Later Roman Empire, 284–602: A Social, Economic, and Adminstrative Survey. Norman, Okla., University of Oklahoma Pr., and Oxford, Blackwell, 1964. 2 v. (4 v. in Oxford ed.), 1517 p.

KÄHLER, HEINZ. The Art of Rome and her Empire. Tr. J. R. Foster from the German [Munich, 1958–60, 2 v.]. N.Y., Crown, and London, Methuen (as Rome and her Empire), 1963. 263 p., 125 ill.

LAING, GORDON J. Survivals of Roman Religion. (Our Debt to Greece and Rome) 1931. xiii, 257 p.

LANCIANI, RODOLFO. Ancient and Modern Rome. (Our Debt to Greece and Rome) 1925. xix, 165 p. Repr. 1931, xiii, 257 p.

THE LEGACY OF ROME. Ed. Cyril Bailey. Oxford, Clarendon Pr., and N.Y., Oxford Univ. Pr., 1923. xiii, 512 p.

McDANIEL, WALTON B. Roman Private Life and its Survivals. (Our Debt to Greece and Rome) 1924. xii, 203 p.

MacKENDRICK, PAUL. The Mute Stones Speak: The Story of Archeology in Italy. N.Y., St. Martin's Pr., 1960, and London, Methuen, 1963. xiii, 369 p., over 175 ill.

MATTINGLY, HAROLD. Roman Imperial Civilization. London, Edward Arnold, and N.Y., St. Martin's Pr., 1957. 312 p. Re-ed. Garden City, N.Y., Doubleday, 1959, xxii, 374 p.

NASH, ERNEST. Pictorial Dictionary of Ancient Rome. (Pubns. of the Deutsches Archaeologisches Institut, Rome) London, Zwemmer, 1961–63, and N.Y., Praeger, 1961–62. 2 v., 695 ill.

PAOLI, UGO ENRICO. Rome: Its People, Life, and Customs. Tr. R. D. Macnaghten from the Italian (Florence, LeMonnier, 1940). N.Y., McKay, 1963, and London, Longmans, 1964. xv, 336 p., 104 ill.

RICHARDSON, EMELINE. The Etruscans: Their Art and Civilization. Chicago and London, Univ. of Chicago Pr., 1964. xvii, 285 p., 52 ill.

ROSE, H. J. Ancient Roman Religion. London, Hutchinson, 1948, and N.Y., Longmans, 1950. 164 p.

ROSTOVTZEFF, M. I. Rome. Tr. J. D. Duff from the Russian, ed. Elias J. Bickerman. London and N.Y., Oxford Univ. Pr., 1960. xii, 347 p., paper, ill.

A re-ed., with addenda, of the author's *A History of the Ancient World,* v. II, 1930: see Greek and Roman, Background, above.

———— The Social and Economic History of the Roman Empire. Oxford, Clarendon Pr., and N.Y., Oxford Univ. Pr., 1926. xxv, 695 p., 60 ill. Re-ed. rev. P. M. Fraser. London and N.Y., Oxford Univ. Pr., 1958, 2 v.

ROWELL, HENRY THOMPSON. Rome in the Augustan Age. Norman, Univ. of Oklahoma Pr., 1962. xv, 242 p.

STAHL, WILLIAM H. Roman Science: Origins, Development, and Influence to the Later Middle Ages. Madison, Univ. of Wisconsin Pr., 1962. x, 308 p,

STARR, CHESTER G. Civilization and the Caesars: The Intellectual Revolution in the Roman Empire. Ithaca, N.Y., Cornell Univ. Pr., 1954, and London, Oxford Univ. Pr., 1955. Repr. N.Y., Norton, 1965, xiv, 413 p., paper.

STENICO, ARTURO. Roman and Etruscan Painting. Tr. Angus Malcolm from the Italian. London, Weidenfeld, and N.Y., Viking, 1963. vi, 41 p., 176 ill.

STOBART, J. C. The Grandeur that Was Rome. London, Sidgwick, 1912, and Philadelphia, Lippincott, 1913. xxviii, 351 p. Re-ed. 1922, 1934; repr. London, Sedgwick, 1961, and Englewood Cliffs, N.J., Hawthorn Books, 1962.

STRONG, EUGENIE. Art in Ancient Rome. N.Y., Scribner, 1928, and London, Heinemann, 1929. 2 v.

SYME, (SIR) RONALD. The Roman Revolution. Oxford, Clarendon Pr., and Oxford Univ. Pr., 1939. xi, 568 p. Re-ed., Oxford, 1951; London and N.Y., Oxford Univ. Pr., 1960.

VACANO, OTTO-WILHELM von. The Etruscans in the Ancient World. Tr. Sheila Ann Ogilvie from the German (Stuttgart, 1955). London, Edward Arnold, and N.Y., St. Martin's Pr., 1960. xii, 195 p., 54 ill. Repr. Bloomington, Indiana Univ. Pr., 1965, paper.

WELLS, JOSEPH. A Short History of Rome to the Death of Augustus. London, Methuen, 1896. Re-ed. to 21st ed., 1928; repr. N.Y., Barnes and Noble, 1963, xiii, 353 p.

———— and R. H. Barrow. A Short History of the Roman Empire to the Death of Marcus Aurelius. London, Methuen, 1931. viii, 399 p. Re-eds. to 5th ed., 1950; repr. N.Y., Barnes and Noble, [1964]

WHEELER, SIR MORTIMER. Roman Art and Architecture. London, Thames and Hudson, and N.Y., Praeger, 1964. 250 p., 250 ill., cloth and paper.

LITERARY STUDIES

BARDY, GUSTAVE. The Christian Latin Literature of the First Six Centuries. Tr. Mother Mary Reginald from the French [Paris, 1929]. London, Sands, and St. Louis, Mo., Herder, 1930. viii, 222 p.

BEARE, W. The Roman Stage: A Short History of Latin Drama in the Time of the Republic. Cambridge, Mass., Harvard Univ. Pr., and London, Methuen, 1950. Repr. 3d. ed., N.Y., Barnes and Noble, 1965, xiv, 397 p., 16 ill.

CLARKE, M. L. Rhetoric at Rome: A Historical Survey. London, Cohen and West, 1953. Repr. N.Y., Barnes and Noble, 1963, vii, 203 p.

CRITICAL ESSAYS ON ROMAN LITERATURE: ELEGY AND LYRIC. Ed. J. P. Sullivan. Cambridge, Mass., Harvard Univ. Pr., and London, Routledge, 1962. 226 p.

CRITICAL ESSAYS ON ROMAN LITERATURE: SATIRE. Ed. J. P. Sullivan. London, Routledge, and N.Y., Humanities Pr., 1963. viii, 182 p.

DOREY, T. A., and DUDLEY, DONALD R., eds. Roman Drama (Studies in Latin Literature and its Influence, 3). N.Y., Basic Books, and London, Routledge, 1965. x, 229 p.

DUCKWORTH, GEORGE E. The Nature of Roman Comedy: A Study in Popular Entertainment. Princeton, N.J., Univ. Pr., and London. Oxford Univ. Pr., 1952. xv, 501 p.

DUFF, J. WIGHT. A Literary History of Rome from the Origins to the Close of the Golden Age. London, Unwin, 1909. xvi, 395 p. Re-ed. to 3d ed., ed. A. M. Duff, London, Benn, and N.Y., Barnes and Noble, 1960, xvi, 543 p.; repr. 1963, paper.

———— A Literary History of Rome in the Silver Age: From Tiberius to Hadrian. London, Unwin, and N.Y., Scribner, 1927. xiv, 647 p. Repr. 1930; re-ed. 2d ed. A. M. Duff, London, Benn, and N.Y., Barnes and Noble, 1960, xvi, 599 p.; repr. 1964, also paper.

——————— Roman Satire: Its Outlook on Social Life. Berkeley, Univ. of California Pr., 1936, and London, Cambridge Univ. Pr., 1937. Repr. Hamden, Conn., Archon Books, 1964. ix, 205 p.

FRANK, TENNEY. Life and Literature in the Roman Republic. Berkeley, Univ. of California Pr., and Cambridge, Univ. Pr., 1930. vi, 256 p. Repr. 1965, paper.

GRANT, MICHAEL. Roman Literature. Cambridge Univ. Pr., 1954. viii, 297 p. Repr., Penguin, 1958, 1964.

GWYNN, AUBREY, S. J. Roman Education from Cicero to Quintilian. Oxford, Clarendon Pr., 1926. 260 p. Repr. N.Y., Russell, 1964.

HADAS, MOSES. History of Latin Literature. N.Y., Columbia Univ. Pr., and London, Oxford Univ., Pr., 1952. viii, 474 p. Re-ed. 1964.

HIGHET, GILBERT. Poets in a Landscape. N.Y., Knopf, 1957. xiii, 267 p.

   Catullus, Vergil, Propertius, Horace, Tibullus, Ovid, Juvenal.

LABRIOLLE, PIERRE de. History and Literature of Christianity from Tertullian to Boethius. Tr. Herbert Wilson from the French [1920]. London, Kegan Paul, 1924, and N.Y., Knopf, 1925. xxiii, 555 p.

LAISTNER, M. L. W. The Greater Roman Historians. Berkeley, Univ. of California Pr., 1947, and London, Cambridge Univ. Pr., 1948. viii, 196 p. Repr. 1963, paper.

LOCKWOOD, DEAN P., ed. A Survey of Classical Roman Literature. N.Y., Prentice-Hall, 1934. 2 v. Re-ed., Chicago, Ill., Univ. of Chicago Pr., 1962, 2 v.

LUCK, GEORG. The Latin Love Elegy. London, Methuen, and N.Y., Barnes and Noble, 1960. 182 p.

MACKAIL, J. W. Latin Literature. London, Murray, and N.Y., Scribner, 1895 et seq. viii, 289 p. Repr. N.Y., Ungar, 1966.

MENDELL, CLARENCE W. Latin Poetry: The New Poets and the Augustans. New Haven, Conn., and London, Yale Univ. Pr., 1965. ix, 258 p.

QUINN, KENNETH. Latin Explorations: Critical Studies in Roman Literature. London, Routledge, 1963, and N.Y., Humanities Pr., 1964. xii, 282 p.

ROSE, H. J. A Handbook of Latin Literature from the Earliest Times to the Death of St. Augustine. London, Methuen, 1936, and N.Y., Dutton, 1937. xi, 557 p. Repr. London, 1949, 1954; repr. EL, 1960, paper.

SELLAR, W. Y. The Roman Poets of the Augustan Age: Horace and the Elegiac Poets. Oxford, Clarendon Pr., 1892. xlv, 362 p. Re-ed. 1899; N.Y., Biblio and Tannen, 1965.

———— The Roman Poets of the Republic. Edinburgh, 1893. Re-ed. rev., Oxford, Clarendon Pr., 1881; re-ed., 1889, 3d ed., repr. N.Y., Biblio and Tannen, 1965, xix, 474 p.

COLLECTIONS

NOTE. *See also* Collections *in* Greek and Roman Literature, *above, pp. 53–54, and for collections of* Christian Literature, *see above, pp. 54–58.*

CLASSICS IN TRANSLATION. V. II: Latin Literature. Ed. Paul MacKendrick and Herbert M. Howe. Madison, Univ. of Wisconsin Pr., 1952. xii, 436 p.

THE COMPLETE ROMAN DRAMA. Ed. George E. Duckworth, various trs. (including the editor). N.Y., Random House, 1942. 2 v. Part re-ed. as Roman Comedies, ML, 1963, xx, 396 p. (7 plays).

LATIN LITERATURE IN TRANSLATION. Ed. Kevin Guinagh and Alfred P. Dorjahn. N.Y., and London, Longmans, 1942. 2d ed., 1952, xix. 822 p.

LATIN POETRY IN VERSE TRANSLATION from the Beginnings to the Renaissance. Ed. L. R. Lind. Boston, Houghton Mifflin, 1957, paper. xxxix, 438 p.

THE LATIN POETS: The Poems of Catullus, Lucretius, Virgil, Horace, Propertius, Ovid, Seneca, Lucan, Juvenal, Martial and Others in a Variety of English Translations. Ed. Francis R. B. Godolphin. N.Y., Random House, 1949. 609 p.

MINOR LATIN POETS, with English Translations. Ed. and tr. J. W. and A. M. Duff. LCL, 1934. 838 p. (parallel texts)

Aetna, Avianus, Calpurnius Siculus, *Elegiae in Maecenatem*, Florus, Grattius, Hadrian, Nemesianus, *Phoenix*, Publilius Syrus, Rutilius Namatianus, etc.

THE PENGUIN BOOK OF LATIN VERSE. Tr. prose Frederick Brittain. Penguin, 1962. lxvi, 381 p.

Not more than a fourth of this anthology is devoted to classical Latin, the latest author represented being Allen B. Ramsay (d. 1955). The Latin text is accompanied by a plain prose tr.

THE PORTABLE ROMAN READER. Ed. Basil Davenport. N.Y., Viking, 1951. 667 p.

REMAINS OF OLD LATIN. Ed. and tr. E. H. Warmington. LCL, 1935–40. 4 v. (parallel texts)

V. 1, Ennius, Caecilius; v. 2, Livius Andronicus, Naevius, Pacuvius, Accius; v. 3, Lucilius, Twelve Tables; v. 4, Archaic Inscriptions.

ROMAN DRAMA. Ed. Samuel Lieberman. N.Y., Bantam, 1964. 384 p.

Tr. Samuel Lieberman: Plautus, *The Menaechmi Twins; Prisoners of War; The Rope;* Terence, *The Brothers; Phormio; The Woman of Andros.*

Tr. Frank Justus Miller: Seneca, *Hippolytus, or Phaedra; Oedipus; Medea.*

ROMAN LITERATURE IN TRANSLATION. Sel. and ed. George Howe and G. A. Harrer. N.Y., Harper, 1924. xiv, 630 p. Re-ed. rev. Albert Suskin, 1959. xvi 649 p.

ROMAN READINGS. Ed. Michael Grant. Penguin, 1958. 464 p.

INDIVIDUAL AUTHORS†

REPUBLICAN ERA: TO 30 B.C.

CAESAR, C. JULIUS (100–44 B.C.). The Commentaries (on the Civil War and on the War in Gaul). Tr. William Duncan. London, Tonson, 1753. civ, 335 p. Many reprs. to N.Y., 1858.

Tr. W. A. McDevitt. BCL, 1851, et seq. Repr. EL, 1915, et seq.

Tr. F. P. Long as The Commentaries on the Civil War. Oxford, Clarendon Pr., 1906. xxviii, 228 p.; and The Gallic War. *Ibid.*, 1911. viii, 278 p.

Tr. A. G. Peskett (The Civil Wars) and H. J. Edwards (The Gallic War). LCL, 1914, x, 369 p.; 1917, xxii, 620 p.

Tr. Somerset de Chair. London, Golden Cockerel Pr., 1951. 312 p.

Tr. John Warrington as War Commentaries. EL, 1953, 320 p. Part repr. as The Gallic Wars, N.Y., Limited Edns Club, 1954.

Tr. Rex Warner. N.Y., New American Library, and London, Muller, 1960. 335 p.

Earlier trs.: Clement Edmondes, 1609 et seq.; Martin Bladen, 1705 et seq.

———— The Gallic War. Tr. Arthur Golding as Martiall Exploytes in the Realm of Gallia. London, 1565. 272 leaves.

This has been called "our earliest and best version" (F. Seymour Smith).

Tr. T. Rice Holmes. London, Macmillan, 1908. xx, 297 p.

† The editions of the Loeb Classical Library are ordinarily recommended.

Tr. S. A. Handford as The Conquest of Gaul. Penguin, 1951. 283 p.

Tr. Moses Hadas as The Gallic War and Other Writings. ML, 1957. xix, 363 p. Repr. 1964.

> *The Other Writings* are 3 books of *The Civil War,* and *The Alexandrian* etc. *Wars* ascribed to Caesar (see below).

Tr. Joseph Pearl. Great Neck, N.Y., Barron, 1962. xv, 296 p.

Other trs.: Roscoe Mongan, Dublin, 1850; J. B. Owgan and C. W. Bateman, Dublin, 1882.

———— (*De bello Alexandrino, De bello Africano, De bello Hispaniensi*: spuriously attributed to Caesar). Tr. A. G. Way. LCL, 1955. xiv, 426 p.

For Caesar, see F. E. Adcock, *Caesar as Man of Letters* (Cambridge and N.Y., Cambridge Univ. Pr., 1956, x, 115 p.); J. F. C. Fuller, *Julius Caesar: Man, Soldier, and Tyrant* (London, Eyre and Spottiswoode, and New Brunswick, N.J., Rutgers Univ. Pr., 1965, 336 p.).

CATO, M. PORCIUS (Cato the Censor, 234–149 B.C.). On Agriculture.

Tr. Fairfax Harrison as Roman Farm Management (with Varro, On Agriculture). N.Y., Macmillan, 1913. xii, 365 p.

Tr. Ernest Brehaut as Cato the Censor on Farming. CURC. N.Y., Columbia Univ. Pr., 1933. xlv, 156 p.

Tr. William Davis Hooper (with Varro, On Agriculture), rev. Harrison Boyd Ash. LCL, 1934. xxv, 542 p.

CATULLUS, C. VALERIUS (c. 85–c. 55 B.C.). The Poems. Tr. prose F. W. Cornish. Cambridge, Univ. Pr., 1904. Repr. (with Tibullus and the *Pervigilium Veneris*) LCL, 1912. xi, 375 p. Repr. 1964.

* Tr. verse Frederick A. Wright. London, Routledge, and N.Y., Dutton, 1926. viii, 249 p.

> Includes previous good trs. of many poems.

Tr. verse Horace Gregory. N.Y., Covici, 1931. Repr. N.Y., Grove Pr., 1956. xxiv, 184 p.

Tr. verse Arthur S. Way (with Tibullus). London, Macmillan, 1936. 123 p.

Tr. verse Frank O. Copley. Ann Arbor, Univ. of Michigan Pr., 1957. xv, 141 p.

Tr. verse Roy A. Swanson as *Odi et Amo*. N.Y., Liberal Arts Pr., 1959. xix, 128 p.

Tr. J. H. A. Tremenheere as The Lesbia. N.Y., Philosophical Library, 1962. 173 p.

Tr. Peter Whigham. Penguin, 1966. 246 p.

Other trs.: Thomas Tooly (with Joannes Secundus), 1719; John Nott, 1795; *George Lamb, 1821; W. K. Kelly, BCL, 1854; James Cranstoun, Edinburgh, 1867; Robinson Ellis, 1871; Sir Theodore Martin, 1875 (2d ed.); Sir Richard F. Burton and Leonard C. Smithers, 1894 (not recommended); Sir William Marris, 1924; Hugh MacNaughten, 1925; F. C. W. Hiley, 1929; Jack Lindsay, 1929. And see *Eleanor S. Duckett, *Catullus in English Poetry* (Northampton, Mass., Smith College Classical Studies 6, 1925, 199 p.) for many poems in tr.

For Catullus, see Tenney Frank, *Catullus and Horace: Two Poets in their Environment* (N.Y., Holt, and Oxford, Blackwell, 1928, 291 p.; repr. N.Y., Russell, 1965); K. P. Harrington, *Catullus and His Influence* (Our Debt to Greece and Rome, 1923, xi, 245 p.); E. A. Havelock, *The Lyric Genius of Catullus* (Oxford, Blackwell, 1939, xii, 198 p.); Kenneth Quinn, *The Catullan Revolution* (Cambridge, England and N.Y., Cambridge Univ. Pr., 1960, x, 119 p.); Arthur Leslie Wheeler, *Catullus and the Traditions of Ancient Poetry* (Berkeley, Univ. of California Pr., 1934, ix, 291 p.; repr. 1964, paper).

CICERO, M. TULLIUS (106–43 B.C.). There is no complete tr. of his numerous writings. BCL reached 13 v., 1850–1900; LCL has reached 27 v., 1912–58. See under separate titles below.

———— Basic Works. Ed. Moses Hadas. ML, 1951. 448 p.

Selections reprinting trs. by various hands (On Moral Duties, bk 1; Tusculan Disputations, bk 1; Old Age; Scipio's Dream; The Character of the Orator, bk 1; 4 Orations; Letters).

———— Select Letters, Offices (or Duties: part), On Friendship, On Old Age. Reprs. of trs. William Melmoth, Thomas Cockman (see below under separate titles). EL, 1910. x, 333 p.

———————— (Selections). Brutus. On the Nature of the Gods. On Divination. On Duties. Tr. Hubert M. Poteat. Chicago, Univ. Pr., 1950. v, 660 p.

———————— Selected Works. Tr. Michael Grant. Penguin, 1960. 272 p.

Two orations, two essays (part), 23 letters.

Essays and Treatises on Philosophy and Politics

———————— The Treatises: On the Nature of the Gods, on Divination, on Fate, on the Republic, on the Laws, and on Standing for the Consulship. Tr. chiefly by C. D. Yonge. BCL, 1853. Repr. 1872, 510 p.

———————— The Academic Questions [*Academica*], Treatise *De finibus* [The Supreme Good], and Tusculan Disputations. Tr. C. D. Yonge. BCL, 1835. xxxii, 474 p. Repr. 1872.

———————— The Academic Questions, The Nature of the Gods. Tr. Harris Rackham. LCL, 1933. xx, 663 p.

Also tr. William Guthrie, 1744.

———————— Divination. Tr. W. A. Falconer (with Old Age, Friendship). LCL, 1923. vii, 567 p.

Also tr. in The Treatises, BCL, above.

———————— Duties (*De officiis*). Tr. Sir Roger L'Estrange as The Offices. London, 1680. Many reprs., especially Temple Classics, 1900, 195 p.

Tr. William Miller. LCL, 1913. xvi, 423 p.

Other trs.: Robert Whittington, 1534; Nicholas Grimald, 1553, 10 reprs. to 1610; Thomas Cockman, 1699 et seq. part repr. EL, 1910; William Guthrie, 1755; Cyrus R. Edmonds, BCL, 1850.

———————— Friendship. Tr. W. A. Falconer (see Divination). For other trs., see Old Age, below.

———————— The Nature of the Gods. Tr. Harris Rackham (see The Academic Questions).

Also tr. anon., 1683; Thomas Francklin, 1741; C. D. Yonge, in Treatises, BCL, above; Francis Brooks, 1896.

———————— Old Age. Tr. W. A. Falconer (see Divination).

Tr. Herbert N. Couch as Cicero on the Art of Growing Old. Providence, R.I., Brown Univ. Pr., 1959. xv, 112 p.

The two essays *Old Age* and *Friendship* were tr. John Tiptoft, Earl of Worcester, c. 1460, and published by Caxton in 1481, 120 leaves. Later trs.: Thomas Newton, 1577; Samuel Parker, 1704; J. D., 1744; William Guthrie, 1755; William Melmoth, 1773–77 et seq., repr. EL, see above; BCL, 1889. *Friendship* was tr. separately, anon., 1691; Robert Hicks, 1713.*Old Age* was tr. separately Robert Whittington, 1535; William Austin, 1648; anon., 1716; William Massey, 1753.

————— The Political Works: Treatise on the Republic, and Treatise on the Laws. Tr. F. Barham. London, Spettigue, 1841–42. 2 v.

Tr. Clinton W. Keyes. LCL, 1929. v, 535 p.

Also tr. C. D. Yonge, *Treatises*, BCL, above.

The *De republica* was tr. George H. Sabine and S. B. Smith as *On the Commonwealth*: Columbus, Ohio State Univ. Pr., 1929; repr. N.Y., Liberal Arts Pr., 1960, 276 p.

————— The Supreme Good and the Supreme Evil (*De finibus bonorum et malorum*). Tr. Harris Rackham. LCL, 1914. xxix, 511 p.

Also tr. C. D. Yonge in The Academic Questions, BCL, above; Samuel Parker, 1702; William Guthrie (with The Academics), 1744.

————— Tusculan Disputations. Tr. J. E. King. LCL, 1927. xxxvii, 577 p.

See also tr. C. D. Yonge in The Academic Questions, BCL, above; John Dolman, 1561; Christopher Wase, 1671; anon., 1715; anon., 1758.

Essays on Rhetoric

————— Brutus. Orator. Tr. G . L. Hendrickson and H. M. Hubbell. LCL, 1939. v, 537 p.

Also tr. Edward Jones, 1776.

————— On the Orator, On Fate, Paradoxes of the Stoics, Divisions of the Speech (*Partitiones oratoriae*). Tr. E. W. Sutton and Harris Rackham. LCL, 1942. 2 v.

On the Orator was tr. William Guthrie, 1742.

————— Rhetoric (*De inventione*), The Best Kind of Speaker, Topics.

Tr. H. M. Hubbell. LCL, 1949. xviii, 466 p.

————— [Rhetoric for Herennius] (*Rhetorica ad Herennium*), spuriously ascribed to Cicero. Tr. Harry Caplan. LCL, 1954. lviii, 433 p.

Letters

———————— The Whole Extant Correspondence. Tr. Evelyn S. Shuckburgh.
BCL, 1899–1900. 4 v. Part repr. (36 letters) Harvard Classics, v. 9.

———————— The Familiar Epistles (*ad Familiares*). Tr. Joseph Webbe. London, 1620. 919 p.

Tr. William Melmoth as Letters to Several of His Friends. London, Dodsley,
1753–78. 3 v. Many reprs., esp. in part, EL, 1910.

Tr.W. Glynn Williams as Letters to his Friends. LCL, 1927–29. 3 v.

———————— Letters to Atticus. Tr. William Guthrie. London, 1752. 2 v.

Tr. E. O. Winstedt. LCL, 1912–18. 3 v.

Orations

———————— The Orations. Tr. William Guthrie. London, 1741–43, et seq.
3 v. Repr., ed. F. W. Norris: London, Scott, and N.Y., Simmons,
1900.

Tr. various hands as The Speeches. LCL, 1923–58. 10 v.

Many trs. have been made of the 58 speeches, singly or in groups.

For Cicero, see F. R. Cowell, *Cicero and the Roman Republic* (N.Y., Pitman, 1948, xii, 306 p.; repr. Penguin Books, 1962, xvii, 398 p.); T. A.
Dorey, ed., *Cicero* (London, Routledge, and N.Y., Basic Books, 1965,
xiii, 218 p.); Torsten Petersson, *Cicero: A Biography* (Berkeley, Univ. of
California Pr., 1920, x, 699 p.; repr. N.Y., Biblio and Tannen, 1963);
John C. Rolfe, *Cicero and his Influence* (Our Debt to Greece and Rome:
1923, vii, 178 p.); Robert N. Wilkin, *Eternal Lawyer:A Legal Biography
of Cicero* (London and N.Y., Macmillan, 1947, xvi, 264 p.).

HIRTIUS, AULUS (d. 43 B.C.). See Caesar, the work ascribed to Hirtius
being a supplement to Caesar's Commentaries.

LUCRETIUS CARUS, T. (c. 95–c. 55 B.C.), On the Nature of Things.

* Tr. prose H. A. J. Munro. Cambridge, Deighton, 1864. 2 v. Many reprs.
to London, Bell, 1920–28, 3 v.; repr. in Stoic and Epicurean Philosophers, see Collections, Greek and Roman, above; repr. Great Books,
12 (1952), p. 1–97; repr. N.Y., Washington Square Books, 1965,
xii, 191 p.

Tr. verse William Ellery Leonard. EL, 1916, 316 p. Repr. 1921, 1957.

Tr. prose W. H. D. Rouse. LCL, 1924. xxi, 537 p.

Tr. verse W. Hannaford Brown. New Brunswick, N.J., Rutgers Univ. Pr., 1950. xxi, 262 p.

Tr. prose Ronald Latham. Penguin, 1951. 256 p.

Tr. verse Alban Dewes Winspear. N.Y., Harbor Pr., and London, Calder, 1956. xx, 299 p.

Tr. L. L. Johnson in the original metre. London, Centaur Pr., 1963. 242 p.

Tr. verse James H. Mantinband. N.Y., Ungar, 1965. xxiv, 215 p.

Other trs.: Thomas Creech, 1682; John Dryden, parts, 1692; anon., 1743; Thomas Busby, 1813, 2 v.; Cyril Bailey, prose, Oxford, 1910, repr. 1947 with Latin; Sir Robert Allinson, verse, 1919, repr. 1925; Thomas Jackson, prose, 1929.

For Lucretius, see George D. Hadzsits, *Lucretius and His Influence* (Our Debt to Greece and Rome: 1935, viii, 372 p.); *Lucretius*, ed. D. R. Dudley (London, Routledge, and N.Y., Basic Books, 1965, ix, 166 p.); John Masson, *Lucretius, Epicurean and Poet* (London, Murray, and N.Y. Dutton, 1907, xxxi, 453 p.); George Santayana, *Three Philosophical Poets: Lucretius, Dante, Goethe* (Cambridge, Mass., Harvard Univ. Pr., and London, Oxford Univ. Pr., 1910, 215 p.; repr. Garden City, N.Y., Double-day, 1953, paper); E. E. Sikes, *Lucretius, Poet and Philosopher* (Cambridge Univ. Pr., and N.Y., Macmillan, 1936, 186 p.).

NEPOS, CORNELIUS (c. 110–c. 30 B.C.). The Works. Tr. J. S. Watson (with Justin and Eutropius). BCL, 1853. 551 p.

Tr. J. C. Rolfe (with Florus). LCL, 1929. xvi, 743 p.

PLAUTUS, T. MACC[I]US (c. 250–184 B.C.). The Comedies. Tr. verse Bonnell Thornton and Richard Warner. London, T. Becket, 1769–74. 5 v.

Tr. H. T. Riley. BCL, 1852. 2 v. Reprs. to 1913.

Tr. prose Paul Nixon. LCL, 1916–38. 5 v.

———— (Five) Comedies. Tr. E. H. Sugden in the original metres. London, Sonnenschein, and N.Y., Macmillan, 1863. 315 p. (Amphitryon, Comedy of Asses, Pot of Gold, The Two Bacchides, Captives)

———— Five Plays. Tr. verse Sir Robert Allison. London, Humphreys, 1914. xxiii, 317 p. (Pot of Gold, Captives, Twin Brothers, Tempest, Amphitryon)

———— The Pot of Gold, and Other Plays. Tr. E. F. Watling. Penguin, 1965. 268 p. (The Pot of Gold, The Prisoners, The Brothers Menaechmus, The Swaggering Soldier, Pseudolus).

———— The Rope and Other Plays. Tr. E. F. Watling. Penguin, 1964. 284 p. (The Rope, The Haunted House, Treasure, Amphitryon).

———— Six Plays. Tr. Lionel Casson. Garden City, N.Y., Doubleday, 1963. xxi, 415 p. (Amphitryon, The Twins [*Menaechmi*], Pot of Gold, The Cottage, The Trickster, The Rope)

———— (Three) Comedies. Tr. Laurence Echard. London, 1694. Repr. 1716. (Amphitryon, Epidicus, The Rope).

———— Three Comedies. Tr. verse C. W. Parry. Pembroke Dock (Wales), Grammar School, 1954. 181 p. (Three-Coin Day, Prisoners, The Rope)

———— (Three Comedies). Tr. Samuel Lieberman in Roman Drama. N.Y., Bantam, 1964. (The Twins, Captives, The Rope).

———— Three Plays. Tr. verse Frederick A. Wright and H. Lionel Rogers. Broadway Trs. London, Routledge, and N.Y., Dutton, 1925. 330 p. (Slip-Knot [*Rudens*], Crock of Gold, Trickster)

Individual Plays

———— The Haunted House (*Mostellaria*). Tr. Frank O. Copley. N.Y., Liberal Arts Pr., 1956. vi, 64 p.

———— The Rope (*Rudens*). Tr. Frank O. Copley. *Ibid.*, 1956. vii, 76 p.

———— The Twins (*Menaechmi*). Tr. William Warner. London, 1595. Repr. ed. W. H. D. Rouse (Shakespeare Classics), London, Chatto, 1912, xiv, 122 p.; repr. Carbondale, Ill., 1961.

Ed. and tr. Joseph H. Drake. Boston, Allyn and Bacon, 1890. viii, 129 p. Repr. N.Y. and London, Macmillan, 1916.

Tr. Benjamin Bickley Rogers, in Aristophanes, Comedies, v. 6. London, Bell, 1907. p. 169–209.

Tr. Barrett H. Clark. N.Y., French, 1915. 36 p.

Tr. Frank O. Copley. N.Y., Liberal Arts Pr., 1949. Repr. 1956. vi, 64 p.

Tr. Smith Palmer Bovie. San Francisco, Chandler, 1962. xi, 64 p.

For Plautus, see Gilbert Norwood, *Plautus and Terence* (Our Debt to Greece and Rome, 1923, vii, 212 p.).

SALLUST (C. Sallustius Crispus, 86–35 B.C.). The Conspiracy of Catiline and the War of Jugurtha. Tr. Thomas Heywood. London, 1608. Repr. ed. Charles Whibley (Tudor Translations), London, Constable, and N.Y., Knopf, 1924, xxxvi, 245 p.

Tr. J. C. Rolfe. LCL, 1921. xxvi, 536 p.

Tr. S. A. Handford. Penguin, 1963. 240 p.

Tr. Ian Scott-Kilvert. London, New English Library, 1963. xi, 163 p.

Other trs.: 1687, 1709, 1734, 1744, 1746, 1751, 1772; J. S. Watson, BCL, 1861 et seq.; A. W. Pollard, 1882 .

For Sallust, see D. C. Earl, *The Political Thought of Sallust* (Cambridge and N.Y., Cambridge Univ. Pr., 1961, xi, 132 p.); Sir Ronald Syme, *Sallust* (Berkeley, etc., Univ. of California Pr., 1964, vii, 381 p.).

TERENCE (P. Terentius Afer. c. 190–159 B.C.). Six Comedies. Tr. Robert Bernard as Terence in English. Cambridge, 1598. 455 p. 5 reprs. to 1641.

Tr. Laurence Echard et al. London, 1694. 6 reprs. to 1741; repr. with intro. Robert Graves, Garden City, N.Y., Doubleday (Anchor Books), and Chicago, Aldine Pub., 1962, and London, Cassell, 1963. xii, 335 p.

Tr. verse George Colman. London, 1765, et seq. xlvii, 619 p.

Tr. prose H. T. Riley. BCL, 1883. vii, 535 p.

Tr. prose John Sargeaunt. LCL, 1912. 2 v.

Tr. verse William Ritchie. London, Bell, 1927. xi, 363 p.

Tr. verse F. Perry. London, Oxford Univ. Pr., 1929. vii, 366 p.

Tr. prose Frank O. Copley. N.Y., Liberal Arts Pr., 1949-63.
(Published seriatim: Woman of Andros, 1949; Phormio, 1958; The Brothers, 1962; The Mother-in-Law, 1962; The Eunuch, 1963; The Self-Tormentor, 1963)

Tr. Betty Radice as The Brothers and Other Plays (The Eunuch, The Mother-in-Law). Penguin, 1965. 190 p.

See also Collections, above: *Complete Roman Drama*; and *Roman Drama* (The Brothers, Phormio, Woman of Andros). Other complete trs.: Charles Hoole, 1667; Thomas Cooke, 1734; Samuel Patrick, 1745 et seq.; Thomas Gordon, 1752. A number of trs. of individual plays began with an anon. *Woman of Andros*, 1520?

For Terence, see Gilbert Norwood, *The Art of Terence* (Oxford, Blackwell, 1925, 156 p.; repr. N.Y., Russell, 1965); also *Plautus and Terence* (Our Debt to Greece and Rome, 1923, vii, 212 p.).

VARRO, M. TERENTIUS (116–27 B.C.). On Farming (*De re rustica*). Tr. Lloyd Storr-Best. BCL, 1912. xxxi, 375 p.

Tr. Fairfax Harrison, with Cato, 1913 (q.v. above).

Tr. William Davis Hooper, rev. Harrison Boyd Ash, with Cato. LCL, 1934 (q.v. above).

———— On the Latin Language. Ed. and tr. Roland G. Kent. LCL, 1938. 2 v.

LITERATURE OF THE EMPIRE: PAGAN
30 B.C. TO A.D. 450

THE AETNA (A.D. 1st c.). Ed. and tr. prose Robinson Ellis. Oxford, Clarendon Pr. 1901. cii, 258 p.

See also in Collections, above: Minor Latin Poets, p. 358–419.

AMMIANUS MARCELLINUS (A.D. c. 330–c. 395). The Roman History. Tr. Philemon Holland. London, 1609. 432, (71) p.

Tr. C. D. Yonge. BCL, 1848 et seq. vii, 646 p.

Tr. J. C. Rolfe. LCL, 1935–39. 3 v.

APICIUS (A.D. 3d c.?). The Roman Cookery Book: A Critical Translation. Tr. Barbara Flower and Elizabeth Rosenbaum. Toronto, Clarke Irwin, 1958. 14 p. (parallel texts)

Also tr. as *Apicius Redivivus* by William Kitchiner, London, 1817.

APULEIUS, L. (fl. c. A.D. 155). The Metamorphosis . . . and Philosophical Works. Tr. Thomas Taylor. London, Triphook, 1822. xxiv, 400 p.

Tr. anon. as The Works. BCL, 1853. 533 p. Repr. to 1911.

————— The Apologia and Florida. Tr. H. E. Butler. Oxford, Clarendon Pr., 1909. 239 p.

————— The Golden Ass. Tr. William Adlington. London, 1566. 126 leaves. Many reprs., esp.: Tudor Trs., 1893; rev. Stephen Gaselee, LCL, 1915, xxiv, 608 p.; ML, 1928; Chiltern Library, with intro. Louis MacNeice, London, Lehmann, 1946, 239 p.; N.Y., Collier Books, 1962, 286 p.

Tr. Sir George Head. London, Longmans, 1851. xxiii, 411 p.

Tr. Francis D. Byrne. London, Imperial Pr., 1905. xlix, 588 p.

Tr. H. E. Butler as The Metamorphoses, or Golden Ass. Oxford, Clarendon Pr., 1910. 2 v.

Tr. Jack Lindsay. N.Y., Limited Editions Club, 1932. xiii, 392 p. Repr. Bloomington, Indiana Univ. Pr., 1962, 255 p.

Tr. Robert Graves as The Transformation of Lucius, Otherwise Known as the Golden Ass. Penguin, 1950, 298 p. Repr. N.Y., Farrar, Straus, 1951; N.Y., Pocket Books, 1952; London, Folio Society, 1960.

For Apuleius, see Elizabeth H. Haight, *Apuleius and His Influence* (Our Debt to Greece and Rome, 1927, xi, 190 p.).

AUGUSTUS (Imperator Caesar Augustus Divi Filius, 63 B.C.–A.D. 14). The Deeds of Augustus (*Res gestae divi Augusti*). Tr. E. S. Shuckburgh in his Augustus. London, Unwin, 1908. p. 239-301.

Tr. Frederick W. Shipley (with Velleius Paterculus). LCL, 1924. xx, 406 p.

For the *Historia Augusta* (lives of the emperors) see History of the Emperors. *The Monumentum Ancyranum* (the Ankara Memorial) was ed. and tr. E. G. Hardy. (Oxford, Clarendon Pr., 1923, 166 p.)

AURELIUS VICTOR, SEX. (fl. c. A.D. 350). Brief Imperial Lives (*Caesares*). Tr. Edward C. Echols. Exeter, N.H., pr. pr., 1962. x, 68 p.

AUSONIUS, D. MAGNUS (A.D. c. 310–c. 390). The Writings. Tr. prose H. G. Evelyn-White. LCL, 1919-21. 2 v.

———— The Moselle. Tr. verse F. S. Flint. London, Ballantyne (The Egoist), 1915. 22 p.

Ed. and tr. verse E. H. Blakeney. London, Eyre and Spottiswoode. 1933. xxii, 74 p.

———— Poems. Tr. Jack Lindsay. London, Fanfrolico Pr., 1930. n. pag.

AVIANUS, FLAVIUS (fl. c. A.D. 400). The Fables. Tr. Roger L'Estrange in Fables of Aesop and Other Eminent Mythologists. London, 1692, Many reprs., esp. London, J. Gray, 1879.

See also in Collections, above: Minor Latin Poets, p. 680–749.

CALPURNIUS SICULUS, T. (fl. c. A.D. 60). The Eclogues. Tr. verse E. J. L. Scott. London, Bell, 1890. 143 p. (parallel texts)

See also in Collections, above: Minor Latin Poets, p. 218–85.

CATO MAGNUS, or Distichs of Cato (A.D. 3d c.). Tr. Benet Burgh (12th c.) with Parvus Cato. Westminster, Caxton, c. 1477. 36 leaves. Repr. 1478?, 1481?, 1558, 1906 (Cambridge Univ. Pr.).

Tr. William Caxton. *Ibid.,* 1483.

Tr. Wayland Johnson Chase. Madison, Univ. of Wisconsin Pr., 1922. 43 p. (parallel texts)

Tr. J. W. Duff, in Minor Latin Poets, LCL, p. 592–639.

Many translations of this schoolbook were made down to the 18th C., one of them published by Benjamin Franklin, 1735.

CELSUS, A. CORNELIUS (fl. c. A.D. 30). *De Medicina.* Tr. W. G. Spencer. LCL, 1935–38. 3 v.

Earlier trs. James Greive, 1756; J. W. Underwood, 1830; Alexander Lee, 1831–36 (parallel texts).

CLAUDIAN (Claudius Claudianus, fl. c. A.D. 400). Works. Tr. verse A. Hawkins. London, 1817. 2 v.

Tr. prose Maurice Platnauer. LCL, 1922. 2 v.

——————— His Elegant History of Rufinus. Tr. verse Jabez Hughes, in Miscellanies in Verse and Prose. London, 1737. Repr. 1741 as Two Books against Rufinus, p. 155–203.

——————— The Rape of Proserpine. Tr. Verse Leonard Digges. London, 1617. Repr. Liverpool, Univ. Pr., 1959, xiii, 81 p.

Tr. verse R. Martin Pope. (Temple Classics) London, Dent, 1934. 97 p.

Other trs.: Jabez Hughes, 1714; Richard Polwhele, 1792; Jacob G. Strutt, 1814; Henry E. J. Howard, 1854.

COLUMELLA, L. JUNIUS MODERATUS (fl. c. A.D. 50). On Agriculture (*De re rustica*). Tr. Harrison B. Ash, Edward S. Forster, and E. H. Heffner. LCL, 1949–55. 3 v.

Also tr. anon. 1745.

CURTIUS RUFUS, Q. (fl. c. A.D. 40). History of Alexander the Great.

Tr. J. C. Rolfe. LCL, 1946. 2 v.

Also tr. John Brande, 1553; R. Codrington, 1661; John Digby, 1714, rev. William Young, 1747; H. J. C. Wright, Cambridge 1882.

DICTYS OF CRETE (Latin version, 4th c. A.D.). Chronicle of the Trojan War. Tr. R. M. Frazer, Jr. in The Trojan War: The Chronicles of Dictys of Crete and Dares the Phrygian. Bloomington, Indiana Univ. Pr., 1966. 185 p.

DONATUS, AELIUS (fl. c. A.D. 360). Beginning Grammar (*Ars minor*). Ed. and tr. Wayland J. Chase. Madison, Univ. of Wisconsin Pr., 1926. 55 p.

ELEGIES FOR MAECENAS (*Elegiae in Maecenatem*, c. 8 B.C.).

Tr. Mary Cecilia Miller. Philadelphia, University of Pennsylvania dissertation, 1941. 176 p. (parallel texts).

See also in Collections, above: Minor Latin Poets, p. 120–139.

EUTROPIUS (fl. c. A.D. 370). Compendious History of Rome (*Breviarium ab urbe condita*). Tr. John Clarke. York, 1722. Many reprs. to 1793.

Tr. J. S. Watson as An Abridgement of Roman History, in Justin, Nepos, and Eutropius. BCL, 1853. 16, 551 p. Repr. 1876, 1910.

Also tr. Nicholas Haward, 1564; Mr. Thomas, 1760.

FLORUS, ANNIUS (fl. c. A.D. 140). Epitome of Roman History. Tr. J. S. Watson, in Sallust, Florus, and Velleius Paterculus. BCL, 1852, p. 287–424. Repr. 1861, 1884, N.Y., Harper, 1859.

Tr. Edward S. Forster (with Nepos). LCL, 1929. xvi, 743 p.

Also tr. Philemon Holland (with Livy), 1600; Edmund Bolton, 1618 et seq.; Meric Casaubon, 1659; John Davies, 1669 et seq.; ed. and tr. John Clarke, 1727.

———— Poems. See in Collections, above: Minor Latin Poets, p. 426–35.

FRONTINUS, SEX. JULIUS (d. c. A.D. 100). Stratagems and Aqueducts. Tr. C. E. Bennett and M. B. McElwain. LCL, 1925. xl, 483 p.

———— The Stratagems. Tr. Sir Richard Moryson. London, 1539.

Also tr. R. Scott, 1816.

———— The Water Supply of Rome (*De aquis*). Tr. Clemens Herschel. Boston, Estes, 1899. Repr. London, Longmans, 1913. Repr. rev. in LCL, above.

FRONTO, M. CORNELIUS (fl. c. A.D. 140). Correspondence. Tr. C. R. Haines. LCL, 1919–1920. 2v.

GAIUS (fl. c. A.D. 160). The Institutes. Ed. and tr. J. T. Abdy and B. Walker as The Commentaries (with Ulpian). Cambridge Univ. Pr., 1870. Repr. 1874, 1876, 1885. xxvi, 501 p.

Ed. and tr. F. de Zulueta. Oxford, Clarendon Pr., 1946–53. 2 v.

Also tr. F. Tomkins and W. G. Lemon, 1869; D. Nasmith, 1890; J. Ashton Cross, 1903.

GELLIUS, A. (Aulus Gellius, fl. c. A.D. 170). The Attic Nights.

Tr. William Beloe, London, Johnson, 1795. 3 v.

Ed. and tr. J. C. Rolfe. LCL, 1927–28. 3 v.

GRATTIUS (1st c. A.D.) The Chase (*Cynegetica*). See Minor Latin Poets, LCL, p. 150–205.

HISTORY OF THE EMPERORS (*Historia Augusta,* c. A.D. 325). Tr. David Magie as The Scriptores Historiae Augustae. LCL, 1921–32. 3 v.

The lives of the emperors from Hadrian through 284 A.D. by Aelius Spartianus, Julius Capitolinus, Vulcacius Gallicanus, Trebellius Pollio, Flavius Vopiscus.

HORACE (Q. Horatius Flaccus, 65–8 B.C.). Collected Works.

Tr. verse Philip Francis. London, A. Miller, 1743–46. 4 v. (parallel texts). 8 reprs. to 1807; 6 reprs. thereafter (English only) to 1831, including one in Chalmers' English Poets 19, 1810; repr. 1902 (Universal Library, ed. W. H. D. Rouse), 2 v.

Tr. prose Christopher Smart. London, Newberry, 1756. 2 v. 5 reprs. to 1827, repr. BCL, 1850 et seq.; repr. (part) EL, 1911.

Tr. verse Christopher Smart. London, 1767. 4 v.

Trs. various hands in prose and verse. EL, 1911 et seq.

> *Art of Poetry,* tr. verse Earl of Roscommon (1680); *Odes, Epodes, and Secular Hymn,* tr. verse John Marshall (1907); *Satires and Epistles,* tr. prose Christopher Smart (1756).

Ed. and tr. in separate v.: The Odes and Epodes, tr. prose C. E. Bennett, LCL, 1914, 430 p.—Satires, Epistles, and Ars Poetica, tr. prose H. R. Fairclough, LCL, 1926, xxx, 508 p.

Tr. various earlier hands, ed. Caspar J. Kramer, Jr. ML, 1936. 412 p.

Tr. Lord Dunsany (repr. of Odes, 1947) and Michael Oakley. EL, 1961. xiii, 304 p.

Many other trs. of the complete works: Leonard Welsted, prose, 1726; David Watson, prose, 1741–42, and Samuel Patrick, prose, 1743; Philip Francis, verse, 1746 et seq.; John Stirling, prose, 1751–53; William Duncombe et al, verse, 1757–59; William Boscawen, verse, 1793–97; 8 trs. in 19th century, especially *Sir Theodore Martin, verse, 1881; *John Conington, verse, 1863–70, reprs. to 1922; and Alexander Falconer Murison, verse, 1931.

Individual Works

———————— Art of Poetry. Tr. verse Ben Jonson, in Workes, 1640, and in subsequent eds.; also repr. in next item.

Tr. prose E. H. Blakeney. London, Scholartis Pr., 1928. 135 p. (parallel texts, adding the Jonson tr.) Repr. ML, see above.

———————— Epodes. Tr. verse A. S. Way. London, Macmillan, 1898. 78 p.

*———————— Odes. Various verse trs. ed. H. E. Butler. London, Bell, 1929, and Boston, Houghton, 1932. 302 p. (parallel texts)

Tr. verse Edward Marsh. London, Macmillan, 1941. xiv, 182 p.

Tr. verse James Michie. N.Y., Orion Pr., 1963. xvi, 376 p. (parallel texts) Repr. London, Hart-Davis, 1964, 296 p.

Numerous other trs., including W. E. Gladstone, 1894; Arthur S. Way, 1876, repr. 1936; going back to Sir Thomas Hawkins, 1621.

———————— Odes and Epodes. Tr. verse Joseph P. Clancy. Chicago, Univ. Pr., 1960. v, 257 p.

Numerous other trs., from Henry Rider, verse, 1638, including Lord Lytton, 1887, and EL and LCL trs. above.

*———————— Satires. Tr. verse as Horace Talks: A Translation, by H. H. Chamberlin. Norwood, Mass., Plimpton Pr., 1940. 180 p.

Numerous other trs.

———————— Satires and Epistles. Tr. verse Smith Palmer Bovie. Chicago, Univ. of Chicago Pr., 1959. vii, 318 p.

Numerous trs., from Thomas Drant, 1567; Thomas Creech, 1684, etc., to EL, LCL. See British Museum Catalogue, v. 106, cols. 831–971, for the almost countless trs.

For Horace, see C. C. Brink, *Horace on Poetry: Prolegomena to the Literary Epistles* (Cambridge, England, and N.Y., Cambridge Univ. Pr., 1963, xi, 300 p.); Steele Commager, *The Odes of Horace: A Critical Study* (New Haven, Conn., and London, Yale Univ. Pr., 1962, xv, 365 p.); John F. D'Alton, *Horace and his Age: A Study in Historical Background* (London and N.Y., Longmans, 1917, xii, 296 p.; repr. N.Y., Russell, 1962); Eduard Fraenkel, *Horace* (Oxford, Clarendon Pr., and N.Y., Oxford Univ. Pr., 1957, xiv, 464 p.); Tenney Frank, *Catullus and Horace: Two Poets in their*

Environment (N.Y., Holt, and Oxford, Blackwell, 1928, 291 p.; repr. N.Y., Russell, 1965); Jacques Perret, *Horace*, tr. Bertha Humez from the French [1960] (N.Y., New York Univ. Pr., 1964, ix, 212 p., paper and cloth); Grant Showerman, *Horace and his Influence* (Our Debt to Greece and Rome, 1922, xvii, 176 p.); L. P. Wilkinson, *Horace and his Lyric Poetry* (Cambridge, England, and N.Y., Cambridge Univ. Pr., 1945, ix, 185 p.; repr. 1951).

HYGINUS (2d c. A.D.) The Myths. Tr. Mary Grant. Lawrence, Univ. of Kansas Pr., and Nottingham, Hall, 1960. 244 p.

JUSTIN (M. Junianus Justinus, before A.D. 400). Epitome of the History of Pompeius Trogus. Tr. J. S. Watson (with Nepos and Eutropius). BCL, 1853. 551 p. Repr. 1876, 1882, 1910.

Earlier trs.: Arthur Golding, 1564; G. Wilkinson, 1606; R. Codrington, 1654.

JUVENAL (D. Junius Juvenalis, c. A.D. 60–c. A.D. 130). Satires. Tr. verse William Gifford. London, 1802. Repr. BCL (with Persius) 1852; rev. John Warrington, intro. H. J. Rose, EL, 1954, xvii, 230 p.

Tr. prose G. G. Ramsay (with Persius). LCL, 1918. lxxxii, 415 p.

Tr. verse Rolfe Humphries. Bloomington, Indiana Univ. Pr., and London, M. Paterson, 1958. 186 p.

Tr. verse Hubert Creekmore. N.Y., New Amer. Lib., 1963. 288 p.

Tr. Jerome Mazzaro. Ann Arbor, Univ. Michigan Pr., 1965. 235 p.

Other trs.: John Dryden, 1693 et seq. (satires 1, 3, 6, 10, 16); Thomas Sheridan (prose), 1739; John Stirling (prose), 1760; Edward Owen, 1785; Martin Madan, 1789; H. A. Strong and A. Leeper, 1882, repr. 1912; S. G. Owen, 1903.

For Juvenal, see Gilbert Highet, *Juvenal the Satirist* (London and N.Y., Oxford Univ. Pr., 1954, xviii, 373 p.; repr. 1961, paper).

LIVY (Titus Livius, 59 B.C.–A.D. 17). History of Rome. Tr. Philemon Holland. London, Islip, 1600. 1403 p. Repr. 1659.

Tr. D. Spillan and C. R. Edmonds, BCL, 1849–50. 4 v. Repr. 1870–77; N.Y., 1880–81.

Tr. W. M. Roberts. EL, 1912–24. 6 v.

Tr. B. O. Foster, F. G. Moore, Evan T. Sage, A. G. Schlesinger. LCL, 1919–59. 14 v.

Tr. (parts) Aubrey de Sélincourt as The Early History of Rome (books 1–5). Penguin, 1960. 388 p.; and as The War with Hannibal (books 21–30). Penguin, 1965. 688 p.

Other trs.: J. Hayes et al., 1744–45; George Baker, 1797; (selections) Moses Hadas and J. P. Poe, ML, 1962, 399 p.

For Livy, see Patrick G. Walsh, *Livy: His Historical Aims and Methods* (Cambridge and N.Y., Cambridge Univ. Pr., 1961, xii, 302 p.)

*LUCAN (M. Annaeus Lucanus, A.D. 39–65). The Pharsalia. Tr. verse Nicholas Rowe. London, Tonson, 1713. Many reprs., esp. Chalmers' English Poets, v. 20, 1810.

* Tr. verse Sir Edward Ridley. London, Longmans, 1896. 335 p. Repr. London, Humphreys, 1925, 2 v. (parallel texts).

Tr. prose J. D. Duff. LCL, 1928. xlv, 637 p.

Tr. verse Robert Graves. Penguin, 1956. 239 p. Repr. London, Cassell, 1961.

First tr.: Sir Arthur Gorges [1614?].

"LYGDAMUS" (b. 43 B.C.). See Tibullus, the poems of "Lygdamus" forming part of the *Corpus Tibullianum*

MACROBIUS, AMBROSIUS THEODOSIUS (fl. c. A.D. 400). Commentary on the Dream of Scipio. Tr. William Harris Stahl. N.Y., Columbia Univ. Pr., 1952. xi, 278 p.

MANILIUS, M. (fl. c. A.D. 20). The Five Books of Manilius: Containing a System of the Ancient Astronomy and Astrology. Tr. verse Thomas Creech. London, Tonson, 1697. 68, 134, 88 p.

*MARTIAL (M. Valerius Martialis, c. A.D. 40–104). The Epigrams. Tr. both prose and verse various hands. BCL, 1860. 600 p. Repr. 1877.

Ed. and tr. prose Walter C. A. Ker. LCL, 1919–20. 2 v. Repr. 1925, 1930, 1943.

* Tr. A. L. Francis and H. F. Tatum as Martial's Epigrams: Translations and Imitations. Cambridge Univ. Pr., 1924. 245 p.

* Tr. verse J. A. Pott and F. A. Wright as Twelve Books of Epigrams. Broadway Trs. London, Dent, and N.Y., Dutton, 1924. 401 p.

Tr. verse Rolfe Humphries as Selected Epigrams. Bloomington, Indiana Univ. Pr., 1963. 127 p.

Also tr. James Elphinstone, 1782.

For Martial, see Paul Nixon, *Martial and the Modern Epigram* (Our Debt to Greece and Rome, 1927, vii, 208 p.).

MELA, POMPONIUS (later 1st c. A.D.). The Cosmographer, concerninge the Situation of the world. Tr. Arthur Golding. London, 1585. Repr. 1590 (with Solinus Polyhistor).

NEMESIANUS (later 3d c. A.D.). Four Eclogues, The Chase. In Minor Latin Poets, LCL, p. 456–615.

OVID (P. Ovidius Naso, 43 B.C.–A.D. 18). Trs. of the complete poems do not appear as collected works, but are in BCL and LCL:

Tr. prose Henry T. Riley (Heroides, Amours, Arts of Love, Remedy of Love, and Minor Works). BCL, 1852. Repr. 1879, 1892; *Fasti, Tristia*, Pontic Epistles, *Ibis*, and *Halieuticon*. BCL, 1859. Repr. 1879, 1893 (does not include Metamorphoses).

Ed. and tr. prose various hands. LCL, 1914–31. 5 v. See under separate titles, below.

————— Selected Works. Tr. various hands, ed. J. C. and M. J. Thornton. EL, 1934. xv, 432 p.

Love Poems

————— The Mirror of Venus: Love Poems and Stories from Ovid's *Amores, Medicamina faciei femineae, Ars amatoria, Remedia amoris, Heroidae, Fasti, Metamorphoses*. Tr. F. A. Wright. Broadway Trs. London, Routledge, and N.Y., Dutton, 1925. vii, 300 p.

————— Love Poems of Ovid: *Amores*, Art of Love, Cures for Love. Selections, tr. Horace Gregory. N.Y., New Amer. Lib., 1964. xxiii, 126 p.

————— *Amores*. Tr. Christopher Marlowe as The Elegies. Middelburg, c. 1597. Repr. in eds. of Marlowe's Poems, esp. ed. C. F. Tucker Brooke, Oxford, Clarendon Pr., 1910; and ed. separately, L. C. Martin, London, Etchells and Macdonald, 1925, 102 p., repr. (with Art of Love) N.Y., Liveright, 1931, x, 318 p. The Elegies repr. from the Brooke ed., Swinford, Fantasy Pr., 1954, 115 p.

Tr. prose Henry T. Riley as The Amours, in BCL, 1852, above.

Ed. and tr. prose Grant Showerman (with *Heroides*). LCL, 1914. 523 p.

————— The Art of Love (*Ars amatoria*). Tr. verse F. A. Wright as The Lover's Handbook: A Complete Translation. London, Dent, and N.Y., Dutton, 1923. 305 p.

Tr. J. Lewis May. London, Lane, 1925. Repr. London. Elek, 1959, xxxii, 224 p.

Tr. Prose J. H. Mozley (with *Remedium Amoris, De medicamine faciei* [Cosmetics], *Nux* [Walnut-tree], Invective against Ibis, *Halieuticon* [Fishes], Consolation to Livia). LCL, 1929. xiv, 381 p.

Tr. verse E. Phillips Barker as The Lover's Manual. Oxford, Blackwell, 1931. 158 p.

Tr. Charles D. Young (with the *Amores* in the Marlowe tr.). N.Y., Liveright, 1931. x, 318 p.

Tr. E. Powys Mathers. Waltham St. Lawrence, Golden Cockerel Pr., 1932. 81 p.

Tr. verse B. F. Moore as The Art of Love. London, Blackie, 1935. 169 p. Repr. London, Folio Soc., 1965, 127 p.

Tr. verse Rolfe Humphries. Bloomington, Indiana Univ. Pr., 1957, and London, Calder, 1958. 206 p.

Other trs.: Thomas Heywood, 1612 et seq.; Francis Wolferston, 1661; John Dryden et al. (with Remedy of Love), 1709 et seq.; BCL, see above; Ronald Seth, 1953.

————— Letters of Mythical Heroines (*Heroides*). Tr. prose Grant Showerman (with *Amores*). LCL, 1914. 523 p.

Other trs.: George Turbervile as Heroycall Epistles, 1567 et seq., ed. F. S. Boas, 1928; Wye Saltonstall, 1636; John Sherburne, 1679; John Dryden et al., 1680 et seq.; Joseph Davidson, 1748; Stephen Barrett, 1759; James Ewen, 1787; W. W. Fitzthomas, 1807; BCL, 1852; John Jump, 1857; C. A. Kincaid, 1937.

———— Remedy of Love. Tr. BCL, 1852; LCL, 1929.

Other trs.: L. F., 1600; John Carpenter, 1636.

Major Poems

———— Calendar of Festivals (*Fasti*). Tr. prose James G. Frazer. London, Macmillan, 1929. 5 v. Repr. LCL, 1931, xxxii, 460 p.

Other trs.: John Gower, 1640; William Massey, 1757; Isaac Butt, 1833; BCL, 1859; J. B. Rose, 1866.

———— Metamorphoses. Tr. verse Arthur Golding. London, 1567. Many reprs., esp. as Shakespeare's Ovid, ed. W. H. D. Rouse: London, Moring, 1904, 321 p., repr. facs. London, Centaur Pr., and Carbondale, Southern Illinois Univ. Pr. 1961, vi, 321 p.; repr. ed. John Frederick Nims, N.Y., Macmillan, and London, Collier-Macmillan, 1965, xxxiv, 461 p.

Tr. verse Sir Samuel Garth, Dryden, Congreve, Addison, Pope, Gay, etc. London, 1717. Many reprs., to Chalmers' English Poets 20, 1810; repr. N.Y., Heritage Pr., 1961, lii, 519 p.

Tr. prose F. J. Miller. LCL, 1916. 2 v.

Tr. verse A. E. Watts, with Picasso ill. Berkeley, Univ. of Calif. Pr., and London, Cambridge Univ. Pr., 1954. xvi, 397 p.

Tr. verse Rolfe Humphries. Bloomington, Indiana Univ. Pr., 1955, and London, Calder, 1957. xiv, 401 p.

Tr. verse Mary M. Innes. Penguin, 1955. 393 p.

Tr. verse Horace Gregory. N.Y., Viking, 1958. xxix, 461 p. Repr. N.Y., New American Library, 1960, xxviii, 448 p.

Other trs.: George Sandys, 1626 et seq.; George Sewell, 1717; John Clarke, 1735; Joseph Davidson, 1748; Nathan Bailey, 1797; J. J. Howard, 1807; J. B. Rose, 1866; H. King, 1871.

Poems of Exile

———— Complaints (*Tristia*). Tr. prose Arthur L. Wheeler (with Letters from Pontus). LCL, 1924. xliv, 510 p.

Other trs.: Wye Saltonstall, 1633, repr. 1637; Zachary Catlin, 1639; T. P., 1713, repr. 1726; John Stirling, 1728, repr. 1736, 1752; BCL, 1859.

———— Invective against Ibis. Tr. prose J. H. Mozley (with Remedy of Love, etc.) LCL, 1929, above.

Other trs.: Thomas Underdown, 1569, repr. 1577; John Jones, 1658; BCL, 1859.

———— Letters from Pontus. Tr. prose Arthur L. Wheeler (with *Tristia*). LCL, 1924, above.

Other trs.: Wye Saltonstall, 1639, repr. 1640; BCL, 1859.

For minor poems, see BCL and LCL, above.

For Ovid, see Hermann Fränkel, *Ovid: A Poet Between Two Worlds* (Berkeley, etc., Univ. of California Pr., 1945, viii, 282 p.); Brooks Otis, *Ovid as an Epic Poet* (Cambridge, Eng., Univ. Pr., 1966, xiv, 411 p.); E. K. Rand, *Ovid and his Influence* (Our Debt to Greece and Rome, 1925, xii, 184 p.); L. P. Wilkinson, *Ovid Recalled* (Cambridge, England, and N.Y., Cambridge Univ. Pr., 1955, xviii, 484 p.; re-ed. abridged as *Ovid Surveyed: An Abridgement for the General Reader, ibid.*, 1962, xii, 236 p.).

PALLADIUS, Rutilius Taurus Aemilianus (A.D. 4th c.). Palladius on hosbondrie (*Opus agriculturae*). Tr. verse anon. (c. A.D. 1420). Ed. Barton Lodge and S. J. H. Herrtage. EETS OS, v. 52, 72: 1873, 1879. xxxvi, 387 p. Re-ed. Mark Liddell, Berlin, Eberling, 1896, viii, 289 p.

Tr. T. Owen. London, J. White, 1807. (16,) 349 p.

PANEGYRICUS MESSALLAE (Praise of Messalla, c. 30 B.C.). See Tibullus, this poem forming part of the *Corpus Tibullianum*.

PERSIUS FLACCUS, A. (A.D. 34–62). The Satires. Tr. verse John Dryden (with some of Juvenal). London, 1693. Many reprs., esp. in Chalmer's English Poets v. 19, 1810, and in eds. of Dryden's Poems.

Tr. verse William Gifford (with Juvenal). London, 1817. Repr. BCL, 1852 et seq.; repr. rev. John Warrington, EL, 1954, 230 p.

Tr. prose G. G. Ramsay (with Juvenal). LCL, 1918. lxxxii, 415 p.

Tr. verse W. S. Merwin. Bloomington, Indiana Univ. Pr., 1961. 119 p.

Other trs. Barten Holyday, 1616 et seq.; Henry Eelbeck, 1719; Thomas Sheridan, 1728; John Senhouse, 1730; et al.; John Conington, prose, rev ed. 1893; Samuel Hemphill, 1901.

PERVIGILIUM VENERIS (The Vigil of Venus, A.D., date uncertain). Tr. verse Sir Cecil Clementi. Oxford, Blackwell, 1911. xv, 52 p. Repr. 1928, 166 p.; 1936, xi, 269 p. (parallel texts)

Tr. prose J. W. Mackail (with Catullus, Tibullus). LCL, 1912. xi, 375 p.

Tr. verse Sir Arthur Quiller-Couch. London, Methuen, 1912. 146 p.

Tr. verse Joseph Auslander as The Vigil of Venus. N.Y., Cheshire House, 1931. 31 p. (parallel texts)

Tr. verse F. L. Lucas. London, Golden Cockerel Pr., 1939. Repr. in Aphrodite, Cambridge Univ. Pr., 1948, 53 p. (parallel texts)

Tr. verse Allen Tate. Cummington, Mass., Cummington Pr., 1943. 28 p. (parallel texts)

Tr. verse Lewis Gielgud. London, Muller, 1952. 50 p.

PETRONIUS, C. (d. A.D. 66). The Civil Wars (*Bellum civile*). Tr. verse Sir Richard Fanshawe. London, 1655. Repr. J. D. M. Ford in his preface to Fanshawe's tr. of the Lusiad, Cambridge, Mass., Harvard Univ. Pr., 1940.

Ed. and tr. verse Florence T. Baldwin. London, Frowde, 1911.

———— Satyricon. Tr. William Burnaby. London, 1694. Repr. ML, 1929. xxii, 238 p. Repr. N.Y., Limited Edns Club, 1964, 246 p.

* Tr. Michael Heseltine (with Seneca's *Apocolocyntosis*). LCL, 1913. xxii, 418 p. Repr. 1916, 1922, 1925, rev. 1930.

Tr. Jack Lindsay as The Satyricon and Poems. London, 1927. Repr. London, Elek, 1960, 223 p.

Tr. Paul Dinnage. London, Spearman, 1953. xiii, 162 p. Repr. London, H. Hamilton, 1963.

Tr. William Arrowsmith. Ann Arbor, Univ. of Michigan Pr., and London, Mayflower, 1959. xxiii, 218 p. Repr. N.Y., New Amer. Lib., and London, Muller, 1960, 192 p., and Ann Arbor, 1962, paper.

Tr. John Sullivan as The Satyricon, and the Fragments. Penguin, 1965. 204 p.

Other trs.: John Addison, 1736; W. K. Kelly, BCL, 1854; W. C. Firebaugh, N.Y., 1922, repr. 1927; J. M. Mitchell, Broadway Trs., 1923.

For Petronius, see Gilbert Bagnani, *Arbiter of Elegance: A Study of the Life and Works of Caius Petronius* (Toronto and London, Oxford Univ. Pr., 1954, xi, 91 p. paper).

PHAEDRUS (fl. c. A.D. 20). Fables. Tr. prose H. T. Riley (with Terence). BCL, 1853. Repr. 1883.

   Ed. and tr. Ben Edwin Perry (with the Fables of Babrius). LCL, 1965. cii, 634 p.

PLINY THE ELDER (C. Plinius Secundus, A.D. c. 24–79). The Natural History. Tr. Philemon Holland as The Historie of the World, Commonly Called the Naturall Historie. London, 1601. Repr. 1634. Selections from this tr. repr. Carbondale, Southern Illinois Univ. Pr., 1962, and N.Y., McGraw-Hill, 1964, 496 p.—A Selection, ed. J. Newsome, repr. Oxford Univ. Pr., 1964, xxviii, 341 p.

   Tr. John Bostock and H. T. Riley. BCL, 1885. 6 v.

   Tr. Harris Rackham, W. H. S. Jones, and D. E. Eichholz. LCL, 1938–64. 11 v.

PLINY THE YOUNGER (C. Plinius Caecilius Secundus, A.D. c. 61–c. 114). The Letters. Tr. William Melmoth. London, Dodsley, 1748. 2 v. Many reprs., esp. BCL; rev. F. C. T. Bosanquet, Harvard Classics, v. 9; rev. W. M. L. Hutchinson, LCL, 1915, 2 v.

   Tr. Betty Radice. Penguin, 1963. 319 p.

   Other trs.: John Boyle, Earl of Orrery, 1751; J. D. Lewis, 1879; J. B. Firth, 1910–16.

POMPEIUS TROGUS (fl. c. 25 B.C.). See Justin, author of The Abridgement of the History.

PROPERTIUS, SEXTUS (c. 50–c. 15 B.C.). Elegies. Tr. prose H. E. Butler. LCL, 1912. xvi, 362 p.

   Tr. verse Seymour G. Tremenheere. London, Simpkin Marshall, 1931. 539 p. (parallel texts)

   Tr. verse A. E. Watts. London, Centaur Pr., 1961. 171 p.

   Tr. verse Constance Carrier. Bloomington, Indiana Univ. Pr., 1963. 224 p.

Other trs.: P. J. F. Gantillon, ed. W. K. Kelley, BCL, 1854; J. S. Phillimore, Oxford 1906.

PUBLILIUS SYRUS (1st c. A.D.). Maxims (*Sententiae*). See Minor Latin Poets, LCL, p. 14–111.

QUINTILIAN (M. Fabius Quintilianus, A.D. c. 30–c. 96). *Institutio Oratoria*. Tr. H. E. Butler. LCL, 1921–22. 4 v.

Other trs. John Warr 1686 (as The Declamations); William Guthrie, 1756 (as Institutes of Eloquence), repr. 1805; J. Patsall, 1774; J. S. Watson (as Institutes of Oratory), BCL, 1856, 2 v.

RES GESTAE DIVI AUGUSTI. See Augustus.

RUTILIUS CLAUDIUS NAMATIANUS (fl. A.D. c. 415). The Home-Coming (*De reditu suo*). Tr. verse G. F. Savage-Armstrong, ed. C. H. Keene. London, Bell, 1907. 237 p.

See also Minor Latin Poets, LCL, p. 764–829.

SENECA, L. ANNAEUS (Seneca Philosophus, c. 2 B.C.–A.D. 65). Workes . . . Both Morall and Naturall. Tr. Thomas Lodge. London, Stansby, 1614. 917 p.

———— The Stoic Philosophy of Seneca: Essays and Letters. Tr. Moses Hadas. Garden City, N.Y., Doubleday, 1958. viii, 261 p.

———— *Apocolocyntosis* (The Pumpkinification of Claudius) Tr. W. H. D. Rouse (with Petronius). LCL, 1913. xxii, 420 p. Repr. 1916, 1922, 1925, rev. 1930.

———— Letters to Lucilius. Tr. R. M. Gummere. LCL, 1917–25. 3 v.

Tr. E. Phillips Barker, Oxford, Clarendon Pr., 1932. 2 v. Repr. 1951.

———— Moral Essays. Tr. J. W. Basore. LCL, 1928–35. 3 v.

———— On Benefits. Repr. from the Thomas Lodge tr., above, ed. W. H. D. Rouse, Temple Classics, 1899, 328 p.

Other trs. Arthur Golding, 1578; A. Stewart, BCL, 1859.

———— Physical Science in the Time of Nero (*Quaestiones Naturales*). Tr. John Clarke. London and N.Y., Macmillan, 1910. liv, 368 p.

——————— Tragedies. Tr. verse various hands as Seneca His Tenne Tragedies, ed. Thomas Newton. London, 1581. 217 p. Repr. Tudor Trs., with intro. T. S. Eliot, London, Constable, and N.Y., Knopf, 1927, 2 v.; repr. Bloomington, Indiana Univ. Pr., 1966, 544 p.

Tr. prose William Bradshaw. London, Swan Sonnenschein, 1902. x, 723 p.

Tr. verse Ella I. Harris. London and N.Y., Oxford Univ. Pr., 1904. 466 p.

Tr. prose Frank J. Miller. Chicago Univ. Pr., 1907. 534 p. Repr. LCL, 1917, 2 v.

——————— Four Tragedies and Octavia. Tr. E. F. Watling. Penguin, 1966. 319 p.

See also in Collections, above: *The Complete Roman Drama,* and *Roman Drama* (three plays); also trs. by Moses Hadas of *Medea, Oedipus, Thyestes,* printed separately N.Y., Liberal Arts Pr., 1955, 1956, 1957.

For Seneca, see Richard M. Gummere, *Seneca, the Philosopher* (Our Debt to Greece and Rome, 1922, xvi, 150 p.); Clarence Mendell, *Our Seneca* (New Haven, Conn., Yale Univ. Pr., and London, Oxford Univ. Pr., 1941, viii, 285 p.).

SENECA, L. ANNAEUS (Seneca Rhetor, c. 55 B.C.–c. A.D. 40). *Suasoriae.* Ed. and tr. W. A. Edward. Cambridge, Univ. Pr., and N.Y., Macmillan, 1928. xlvi, 160 p.

SILIUS ITALICUS, Ti. Catius Asconius (d. c. A.D. 100). The Second Punic War. Tr. verse Thomas Ross. London, 1661. 507 p.

Tr. prose J. D. Duff. LCL, 1934. 2 v.

Also tr. H. W. Tytler, 1828.

SOLINUS, C. JULIUS (called Polyhistor, A.D. 3d c.) The excellent and pleasant worke . . . (*De memorabilibus mundi*). Tr. Arthur Golding. London, 1587. Repr. 1590 (with Pomponius Mela).

STATIUS, P. PAPINIUS (fl. c. A.D. 90). The Poems. Ed. and tr. prose J. H. Mozley. LCL, 1928. 2 v. (The *Silvae, Thebaid,* and *Achilleid*)

——————— *Achilleis.* Tr. verse Sir Richard Howard, in Poems. London, 1660.

——————— *Silvae* (Miscellany). Tr. prose D. A. Slater. Oxford, Clarendon Pr., 1908. 214 p.

———— *Thebaid*. Tr. verse William L. Lewis. Oxford, Clarendon Pr., 1767. 2 v. Repr. 1773; in Chalmers' English Poets, v. 20, 1810.

SUETONIUS TRANQUILLUS, C. (fl. c. A.D. 120). The Works. Tr. J. C. Rolfe. LCL, 1914. 2 v. (Lives of the Caesars, and Lives of Illustrious Men)

———— History of the Twelve Caesars. Tr. Philemon Holland. London, 1606. Repr. 1672, 1717, 1732, 1796; 1899 (Tudor Trs., ed. Charles Whibley, 2 v.); 1923 (London, Routledge, and N.Y., Dutton, Broadway Trs., ed. J. H. Freese, 488 p.); 1965 (rev., intro. Moses Hadas, N.Y., Heritage Pr., xviii, 483 p.).

Tr. Robert Graves as Lives of the Twelve Caesars. Penguin, 1957. 315 p. Repr. London, Cassell, 1962; London, Folio Soc., 1964.

Also tr. several hands, 1672, repr. 1677, 1698, 1704; Jabez Hughes, 1717; John Clarke, 1732, repr. 1739, 1761 (parallel texts); Alexander Thomson, 1796.

———— Lives of the Grammarians. Tr. Alexander Thomson. London, 1796. Repr. rev. Thomas Forester. BCL, 1855. 557 p.

SULPICIA (fl. c. 25 B.C.). Poems. Tr. verse James Grainger. London, 1760. Repr. Chalmers' English Poets, v. 20, 1810.

See also Tibullus, Sulpicia's poems forming part of the *Corpus Tibullianum*.

SYMPHOSIUS, C. FIRMIANUS (A.D. 4th or 5th c.). The Hundred Riddles. Tr. verse Elizabeth Hickman du Bois. Woodstock, Vt., Elm Tree Pr., 1912. 88 p. (parallel texts)

Tr. Raymond Theodore Ohl as The Enigmas. Philadelphia, Pa., Univ. of Pennsylvania dissertation, 1928. 137 p.

TACITUS, CORNELIUS (fl. c. A.D. 100). Complete Works. Tr. Arthur Murphy. London, Robinson, 1793. 4 v. Many reprs., esp. as Historical Works, EL, 1908 et seq., 2 v.

Tr. A. J. Church and W. J. Brodribb. London, 1864–77. Repr. 1891–94; repr. (ed. Moses Hadas) ML, 1942, 773 p.; repr. Great Books, v. 15 (1952), v, 313 p.

Tr. various hands LCL, 1914–37. 5 v. (See separate titles, below).

Also tr. Thomas Gordon 1728–31 et seq.; BCL, 1854, many reprs.

——————— *Agricola*. Tr. W. Hamilton Fyfe (with Dialogue on Orators, and *Germania*). Oxford, Clarendon Pr., 1908. 143 p.

Tr. Maurice Hutton (with Dialogue on Orators, and *Germania*). LCL, 1914. v, 371 p.

Tr. H. Mattingly (with *Germania*) as Britain and Germany. Penguin, 1948. 174 p.

——————— Annals. Tr. Sir G. G. Ramsay. London, Murray, 1904–9. 2 v.

Tr. J. Jackson (with Histories). LCL, 1925–37, v. 2–4.

Tr. Michael Grant as Annals of Imperial Rome. Penguin, 1956. Repr. rev. 1959; repr. London, Cassell, and N.Y., Barnes and Noble, 1963, 443 p.

Tr. D. R. Dudley. N.Y., New Amer. Lib., and London, New English Lib., 1966. 432 p.

——————— Histories. Tr. Sir G. G. Ramsay. London, Murray, and N.Y., Dutton, 1915. lxxv, 463 p.

Tr. C. H. Moore (with Annals). LCL, 1925. v. 1–2.

Tr. Kenneth Wellesley. Penguin, 1964. 316 p.

Also tr. Sir Henry Savile and Richard Greneway, 1591–98; John Dryden et al., 1698, repr. 1716.

For Tacitus, see Clarence W. Mendell, *Tacitus: The Man and his Work* (New Haven, Yale Univ. Pr., and London, Oxford Univ. Pr., 1957, viii, 397 p.); Sir Ronald Syme, *Tacitus* (Oxford, Clarendon Pr., and N.Y., Oxford Univ. Pr., 1958, 2 v.).

THEODOSIUS II (A.D. 401–450). The Theodosian Code and Novels and the Sirmondian Constitutions. Tr. Clyde Pharr with Theresa S. Davidson and Mary Brown Pharr. Princeton, N.J., Princeton Univ. Pr., and London, Oxford Univ. Pr., 1952. xxvi, 643 p.

TIBULLUS, ALBIUS (c. 55–19 B.C.). Elegies. Tr. verse James Grainger. London, 1759. 2 v. Repr. in Chalmers' English Poets v. 20, 1810; repr. in the next item.

Tr. prose W. K. Kelly (with Catullus, and with preceding verse tr.) as Erotica. BCL, 1854. 400 p. Repr. 1880.

Tr. verse Theodore C. Williams. Boston, Badger, 1905. 118 p.

Tr. prose J. P. Postgate (with Catullus and *Pervigilium Veneris*). LCL, 1912. xi, 375 p.

Tr. verse A. S. Way as Catullus and Tibullus. London, Macmillan, 1936. 123 p.

ULPIAN (Domitianus Ulpianus, fl. c. A.D. 200). Rules. Tr. J. T. Abdy and B. Walker (with the Commentaries of Gaius). Cambridge Univ. Pr. 1870. Repr. 3d ed. 1885, xxvi, 501 p. (parallel texts)

VALERIUS FLACCUS Setinus Balbus, C. (d. c. A.D. 90) *Argonautica.* Tr. prose J. H. Mozley. LCL, 1934. xxi, 458 p.

VALERIUS MAXIMUS (fl. c. A.D. 30). *Facta ac Dicta Memorabilia.* Tr. Samuel Speed as A View of the Religion, Laws, and Dispositions of the Romans. London, 1678. 478 p.

VEGETIUS RENATUS, FLAVIUS (fl. c. A.D. 400). *De re militari.* Tr. anon. in verse paraphrase as Knyghthode and Bataile (15th c.). Ed. from Ms. R. Dyboski and Z. M. Arend. EETS OS 201, 1935. lxxvi, 205 p.

Tr. William Caxton as . . . the book of fayttes of armes and of chyualrye from the French paraphrase by Christine de Pisan. Westminster, Caxton, 1489. 144 leaves.

Tr. John Sadler as The Foure books [out of five] . . . of Martiall policye. London, 1572. 66 leaves.

Tr. Lieutenant John Clarke as Military Institutions of the Romans. London, 1767. xxxi, 211 p. Part repr. (3 books), ed. Brig. Gen. Thomas R. Phillips, U.S.A., Harrisburg, Pa., Military Service Pub. Co., 1944, 114 p.

VELLEIUS PATERCULUS (fl. c. A.D. 20). Compendium of Roman History. Tr. Frederick W. Shipley (with *Res gestae Divi Augusti*). LCL, 1924. xx, 431 p.

Tr. J. S. Watson (with Sallust and Florus). BCL, 1861. See also Florus.

VERGIL (P. Vergilius Maro, 70–19 B.C.). Poetical Works. Tr. verse John Dryden. London, 1697. Many reprs. in eds. of Dryden's Poems, also in Chalmers' English Poets, v. 19, 1810; WC, 1903 et seq.; Harvard

Classics (Aeneid only), v. 13; London and N.Y., Oxford Univ. Pr., 1961, xvi, 487 p.

Tr. prose J. Lonsdale and Sidney Lee. Globe Ed. London, Macmillan, 1871.

Tr. prose J. W. Mackail (Aeneid) London, 1885; (Eclogues and Georgics) London, 1889. Both repr. ML, 1934 xxvi, 352 p., repr. 1951.

Tr. verse James Rhoades as The Poems of Virgil. London, Longmans, 1906. Repr. WC, 1921; repr. Great Books, v. 13, 1952, vii, 379 p.

Tr. prose H. R. Fairclough. LCL, 1916–18. 2 v. Repr. rev. 1934–35.

Tr. verse C. Day Lewis (Georgics) London, Cape, 1940; (Aeneid) London, Hogarth Pr., 1952; (Eclogues) London, Cape, 1963. All repr. London, Oxford Univ. Pr., 1966, ix, 529 p. paper.

———— Minor Poems . . . comprising the *Culex, Dirae, Lydia, Moretum, Copa, Priapeia,* and *Catalepton.* Tr. verse Joseph J. Mooney. Birmingham, Cornish, 1916. Repr. 1920, 121 p. (parallel texts).

———— Aeneid. Tr. verse Gavin Douglas (c. 1513). London, 1553. Repr. Edinburgh, 1710; Bannatyne Club, 1839; ed. David F. C. Coldwell, Scottish Text Society, 1957–64, 3 v.

14 trs. are recorded before 1800, the most notable being Dryden's, above; later trs. include C. S. Calverley (verse), 1867, repr. 1962; John Conington (verse), 1870, (prose) 1872; William Morris (London, Longmans, 1876), repr. 1900, and in The Works of William Morris, v. 10; Harlan H. Ballard (verse), Boston 1902, repr. 1908, 1911, 1930 (333 p.); C. J. Billson (verse), Oxford 1906, repr. 1924; E. Fairfax Taylor (verse: Spenserian stanza), EL, 1907; T. C. Williams (verse), Boston 1908, repr. Harvard Univ. Pr., 1915; J. Jackson (prose), Oxford 1910. Recent trs. follow.

Tr. verse Arthur S. Way. London, Macmillan, 1916–30. 4 v.

Tr. verse Rolfe Humphries. N.Y., Scribner, 1951. xii, 381 p.

Tr. verse C. Day Lewis. London, Hogarth Pr., and N.Y., Oxford Univ. Pr. 1952. 288 p. Repr. Garden City, N.Y., Doubleday, 1953, 320 p.; London, New English Library, 1962; (with the other poems) 1966, see above.

Tr. prose W. F. Jackson Knight. Penguin, 1956. 366 p. Repr. 1958.

Tr. verse Patric Dickinson. N.Y., New Amer. Library, 1961. 319 p.

Tr. verse L. R. Lind. Bloomington, Indiana Univ. Pr., 1963. xxv, 301 p.

Tr. T. H. Delabere. N.Y., Bantam, 1963. 346 p.

Tr. James H. Mantinband. N.Y., Ungar, 1964. ix, 309 p.

————— Eclogues. Tr. verse C. S. Calverley. London, 1868. Repr. (with Theocritus) 1908, 1926; repr. N.Y., Limited Edns Club, 1960, xxvii, 96 p.

Tr. prose E. V. Rieu as The Pastoral Poems. Penguin, 1949. 151 p. Repr. 1954.

Tr. Geoffrey Johnson. Lawrence, Univ. of Kansas Pr., and Nottingham, Hall, 1960. 61 p.

Tr. C. Day Lewis. London, Cape, 1963. 46 p. Repr. (with Georgics), 1964, q.v.; repr. (with the other poems), 1966, q.v. above.

15 trs. are recorded to 1800, the first being by Abraham Fleming, 1575.

————— Eclogues and Georgics. Tr. verse T. F. Royds. EL, 1907. 181 p. Repr. rev. Oxford, Blackwell, 1922.

Tr. hexameters A. F. Murison. London, Longmans, 1932. 129 p.

Tr. verse R. C. Trevelyan. Cambridge Univ. Pr., 1944. 118 p.

Tr. verse C. Day Lewis (published separately, 1940, 1963 et seq.). Garden City, N.Y., Doubleday, 1964. 233 p.

The first tr. was Abraham Fleming, 1575–1589.

————— Georgics. Tr. hexameters C. W. Brodribb. London, Benn, 1928, and N.Y., Appleton, 1929. 86 p.

Tr. verse C. Day Lewis. London, Cape, 1940. Repr. N.Y., Oxford Univ. Pr., 1947, 95 p.; repr. (with Eclogues), 1964, and (with the other poems) 1966, see above.

Tr. verse L. A. S. Jermyn as The Singing Farmer. Oxford, Blackwell, 1947. 133 p.

Tr. verse Smith Palmer Bovie. Chicago, Univ. of Chicago Pr., and London, Cambridge Univ. Pr., 1956. xxx, 111 p. Repr. Chicago, 1966, paper.

10 trs. are recorded to 1800, beginning with Abraham Fleming, 1589.

For Virgil, see C. M. Bowra, From Virgil to Milton (Virgil, Camões, Tasso, Milton: London, Macmillan, 1945, and N.Y., St. Martin's Pr., 1946, vii,

246 p.; repr. 1962, paper); George E. Duckworth, *Structural Patterns and Proportions in Vergil's Aeneid: A Study in Mathematical Composition* (Ann Arbor, Univ. of Michigan Pr., 1962, x, 268 p.); Tenney Frank, *Vergil: A Biography* (N.Y., Holt, and Oxford, Blackwell, 1922, vii, 200 p.; repr. N.Y., Russell, 1965); W. F. Jackson Knight, *Roman Vergil* (London, Faber, and N.Y., Transatlantic Arts, 1946, viii, 348 p.); F. J. H. Letters, *Virgil* (Sydney, N.S.W., Angus & Robertson, 1943, 119 p.; re-ed. London and N.Y., Sheed & Ward, 1946, 168 p.); J. W. Mackail, *Virgil and His Meaning to the World of Today* (Our Debt to Greece and Rome, 1923, x, 159 p.); Brooks Otis, *Virgil: A Study in Civilized Poetry* (Oxford, Clarendon Pr., and N.Y., Oxford Univ. Pr., 1963, xiii, 436 p.); Viktor Pöschl, *The Art of Vergil: Image and Symbol in the Aeneid*, tr. Gerda Seligson from the German [Wiesbaden and Innsbruck, 1950] (Ann Arbor, Univ. of Michigan Pr., 1962, 216 p.); Michael C. J. Putnam, *The Poetry of the Aeneid: Four Studies in Imaginative Unity and Design* (Cambridge, Mass., Harvard Univ. Pr., and London, Oxford Univ. Pr., 1965, xvii, 238 p.); W. Y. Sellar, *The Roman Poets of the Augustan Age: Virgil* (Oxford, Clarendon Pr., 1877; re-ed. 1883; 1897; repr. N.Y., Biblio and Tannen, 1965, xx, 423 p.).

VITRUVIUS POLLIO (fl. c. 25 B.C.). On Architecture. Tr. Morris H. Morgan. Cambridge, Mass., Harvard Univ. Pr., 1914. Repr. N.Y., Dover, 1960, xiii, 331 p.

Tr. Frank Granger. LCL, 1931–34. 2 v.

LATIN LITERATURE, CHRISTIAN: TO A.D. 450

George B. Parks

COLLECTIONS

NOTE. *Many of the works listed under* Individual Authors and Works, *below, are published in series. For full information on these, see* Collections, Christian Literature, *under* Greek and Roman Literature, *above, p. 54 to p. 58. An additional title is*:

FATHERS OF THE CHURCH, Tertullian, Cyprian, Arnobius, Lactantius, Ambrose, Jerome, Augustine: A Selection from the Writings of the

Latin Fathers. Tr. F. A. Wright. London, Routledge, 1928, and N.Y., Dutton, 1929. vii, 351 p.

AETHERIA (fl. A.D. c. 400). The Pilgrimage of St. Silvia of Aquitaine to the Holy Places (c. A.D. 385). Tr. with intro. John Bernard. Palestine Pilgrims' Text Society 1, 1896. 150 p.

Tr. M. L. McClure and C. L. Feltoe as The Pilgrimage of Etheria. Trs. of Christian Literature, ser. 3. London, S. P. C. K., and N.Y., Macmillian, 1919. xlviii, 103 p.

The work, first discovered in 1884, was then ascribed to St. Silvia, later to Abbess Aetheria, most recently to Egeria.

AMBROSE, ST. (Ambrosius, Bishop of Milan, A.D. c. 340–397). Some of the Principal Works. Tr. H. De Romestin et al. Nicene Fathers, ser. 2, v. 10, 1896. xxii, 497 p.

————— The Letters. Tr. Henry Walford. Library of the Fathers, v. 47, 1881. xvi, 521 p.

Ed. and tr. Sister Mary Melchior Beyenka. Fathers of the Church, v. 26, 1954. xviii, 515 p.

————— Theological and Dogmatic Works. Tr. Roy J. Deferrari. Fathers of the Church, v. 44, 1963. xxiii, 515 p.

————— Thirteen Homilies on St. John 14. Ed. and tr. H. F. Stewart. Cambridge Univ. Pr., 1900., 140 p. Repr. 1902.

————— A Treatise . . . Touching the benefit and happinesses of death (*De bono mortis*). Tr. anon. from French in Philippe de Mornay, Six Excellent Treatises of Life and Death. London, 1607.

————— Christian Offices Crystall Glasse . . . Conviction of Symmachus the Gentile. Tr. Richard Humfrey. London, 1637. 3 pts.

————— Of Consolation for Valentinian. Ed. and tr. Thomas A. Kelly. Washington, D.C., Catholic Univ. of Amer. Pr., 1940. xxi, 324 p.

————— On the Death of Theodosius. Ed. and tr. Sister Mary Dolorosa Mannix. Washington, D.C., Catholic Univ. of Amer. Pr., 1925. 166 p.

————— Explanation of the Creed. Ed. and tr. R. H. Connelly, rev. J. H. Srawley. London and N.Y., Cambridge Univ. Pr., 1952. 39 p.

————— On Gluttony and Fasting. Ed. and tr. Sister Mary Joseph Aloysius Buck. Washington, D.C., Catholic Univ. of Amer. Pr., 1929. 233 p. (parallel texts)

————— Funeral Orations (with St. Gregory Nazianzen). Tr. Martin R. P. McGuire, et al., in Fathers of the Church, v. 22, 1953.

————— Hexameron, Paradise, and Cain and Abel. Tr. John J. Savage. Fathers of the Church, v. 42, 1961. xi, 449 p.

————— On Holy Virginity. Tr. A. J. Christie. Oxford, Parker, 1843. xxxvi, 64 p.

Tr. anon. as The Nun's Ideals. Dublin, Scepter Pr., 1963, and Chicago, Scepter Pr., 1963 as Given to Love. 126 p.

————— On the Mysteries. Tr. H. De Romestin, in St. Cyril on the Mysteries. Oxford, Parker, 1887, p. 52–103.

Tr. T. Thompson, ed. J. H. Srawley. Translations of Christian Literature, ser. 3, 1919. p. 45–143. Repr. 1950.

————— On Naboth. Ed. and tr. Martin R. P. McGuire. Washington, D.C. Catholic Univ. of Amer. Pr., 1927. 294 p. (parallel texts)

————— On Tobias. Ed. and tr. Lois Miles Zucker. Washington, D.C. Catholic Univ. of Amer. Pr., 1933. 210 p. (parallel texts)

————— Of the Vocation and Calling of All Nations. Tr. Henry Becher. London, 1561.

Tr. P. de Letter. Ancient Christian Writers, v. 14, 1952. 234 p.

ARNOBIUS of Sicca (fl. A.D. c. 300). The Seven Books *Adversus gentes*. Tr. Hamilton Bryce and Hugh Campbell. Ante-Nicene Christian Library, v. 19 (1871). xix, 386 p. Repr. Ante-Nicene Fathers, v. VI (1886), p. 403–543.

Tr. George E. McCracken in Ancient Christian Writers, v. 7–8 (1949).

Selections in F. A. Wright, *Fathers of the Church*, see Christian Latin Literature, Collections, above.

AUGUSTINE, ST. (Aurelius Augustinus, Bishop of Hippo, A.D. 354–430).

Five collective translations of the works of St. Augustine have been made into English, none including all his numerous works, and many translations and retranslations have been made of individual works. We list first the contents of the large collections, then the smaller collections, then the individual treatises combined in an index of all the items translated.

Large Collections

I. Tr. various hands, ed. E. B. Pusey, in 12 v. of the Library of the Fathers, Oxford 1838–57, as follows:

V. 1 (1838). The Confessions, tr. William Watts (1631), rev. E. B. Pusey.

V. 16, 20 (1844, 1845). Sermons on Selected Lessons of the New Testament, tr. R. G. Macmullen. Repr. Nicene Fathers, v. 6.

V. 22 (1847). Seventeen Short Treatises, tr. C. L. Cornish and H. Browne. (The *Enchiridion*, or Faith, Hope, and Charity—The Catechizing of the Uninstructed—On Faith and the Creed—Concerning the Faith in Things Not Seen—On the Profit of Believing—On the Creed: A Sermon to Catechumens—On Faith and Works—On the Christian Conflict—Of Continence—Of the Good of Marriage—Of Holy Virginity—On the Good of Widowhood—On Lying—Against Lying—Of the Work of Monks—On Patience—On Care to be Had for the Dead. The first six repr. in Nicene Fathers (see below), v. 3 as Doctrinal Treatises; the last 9 repr. ibid., as Moral Treatises.

V. 24, 25, 30, 32, 37, 39 (1847–57). Expositions on the Book of Psalms, tr. J. E. Tweed, et al. Repr. Nicene Fathers, v. 8.

V. 26, 29 (1848-49). Homilies on the Gospel of St. John and on his First Epistle, tr. H. Browne. Repr. Nicene Fathers, v. 7.

II. Tr. various hands, ed. Marcus Dods, as The Works of Aurelius Augustine. Edinburgh, Clark, 1872–76. 15 v. Repr. Edinburgh 1934. Most of this tr. repr. in Nicene Fathers, the entry following.

V. 1, 2. The City of God, tr. Marcus Dods.

V. 3. Writings in Connection with the Donatist Controversy, tr. J. R. King. (On Baptism, Against the Donatists—Answer to the Letters of Petilian—On Correction of the Donatists).

V. 4, 12, 15. The Anti-Pelagian Works. Tr. Peter Holmes and (the last four treatises) Robert E. Wallis.

V. 4. On Merits and the Forgiveness of Sins—On the Spirit and the Letter—On Nature and Grace—On the Perfection of Man's Righteousness—On the Proceedings [*gestis*] of Pelagius.

V. 12. On the Grace of Christ and Original Sin—On Marriage and Concupiscence—On the Soul and its Origin.
V. 15. Against Two Letters of the Pelagians on Grace and Free Will—On Rebuke [*correptione*] and Grace—On the Predestination of the Saints—On the Gift of Perseverance.

V. 5. Writings in Connection with the Manichaean Heresy, tr. Richard Stothert. (Of the Morals [*moribus*] of the Catholic Church—On the Morals of the Manichaeans—Against the Epistle of Manicheaus—Reply to Faustus the Manichaean).

V. 6, 13. The Letters, tr. J. G. Cunningham (168 in all, i.e., nos. 1–92 in v. 6; in v. 13, 76 selected further letters of the total 272).

V. 7. On the Trinity, tr. Arthur W. Haddan.

V. 8.   The Sermon on the Mount Expounded, tr. William Findlay. The Harmony of the Evangelist, tr. S. D. F. Salmond.

V. 9. On Christian Doctrine, The *Enchiridion,* tr. F. J. Shaw. On Catechizing, On Faith and the Creed, tr. S. D. F. Salmond. (The last three are retrs. of items in the Pusey ed., v. 16.)

V. 10, 11. Lectures or Tractates on the Gospel According to St. John, tr. John Gibb and James Innes.

V. 14. The Confessions, tr. J. G. Pilkington.

III. Tr. various hands, ed. Philip Schaff, in A Select Library of the Nicene and Post-Nicene Fathers (here called Nicene Fathers), v. 1–8, 1886–90.

Almost entirely a repr. rearranged and rev. of the Dods ed., together with nine v. of the Pusey ed.

V. 1. The Confessions. Letters. (repr. of Dods, v. 6, 13, 14)

V. 2. The City of God. Christian Doctrine. (repr. of Dods, v. 1, 2, part of 9)

V. 3. On the Trinity. Doctrinal Treatises. Moral Treatises. (repr. of Dods, v. 7, Pusey v. 22)

V. 4. Writings Against the Manichaeans and Donatists (repr. of Dods, v. 3, 5, adding three treatises on the first controversy, tr. Albert B. Newman: On Two Souls, Against the Manichaeans. Acts or Disputation Against Fortunatus the Manichaean. Concerning the Nature of Good. Against the Manichaeans)

V. 5. Anti-Pelagian Writings. (repr. of Dods, v. 4, 12, 15)

V. 6. Sermon on the Mount Expounded. The Harmony of the Evangelists (repr. of Dods, v. 8). Sermons on Selected Lessons of the New Testament (repr. from Pusey ed., v. 16, 20).

V. 7. Homilies on the Gospel of St. John and the First Epistle of John (repr. from Pusey ed., v. 26, 29). The Soliloquies (an added item, tr. C. C. Starbuck).

V. 8. Expositions on the Book of Psalms (repr. of Pusey ed., v. 24, 25, 30, 32, 37, 39).

IV. Tr. various hands in Ancient Christian Writers, 1946–61: see individual entries for details.

V. 2 (1946). The First Catechetical Instruction, tr. Joseph P. Christopher.

V. 3 (1947). Faith, Hope, and Charity, tr. Louis A. Anand.

V. 5 (1948). The Lord's Sermon on the Mount, tr. John J. Jepson.

V. 9 (1950). The Greatness of the Soul, The Teacher, tr. Joseph M. Colleran.

V. 12 (1950). The Case Against the Academics, tr. John J. O'Meara.

V. 15. (1952). Sermons for Christmas and Epiphany, tr. Thomas C. Lawler.

V. 22. (1955). The Problem of Free Choice (On Free Will), tr. Mark Pontifex.

V. 29, 30 (1960–61). Expositions on the Psalms, tr. Scholastica Hebgin and Felicitas Corrigan.

V. Tr. various hands in Fathers of the Church:

V. 2 (1948. The Happy Life. Answer to Skeptics. Divine Providence and Evil (On Order), Soliloquies. Tr. various hands.

V. 4 (1948). On Immortality of the Soul. The Magnitude of the Soul. On Music. The Advantage of Believing. Faith in Things Unseen. Tr. various hands.

V. 5 (1948). Commentary on the Lord's Sermon on the Mount, tr. Denis J. Kavanagh.

V. 8 (1947). On Christian Instruction. On Admonition and Grace. On Christian Combat. On Faith, Hope, and Charity. Tr. various hands.

V. 11, 14, 24 (1950–54). The City of God, tr. Gerald G. Walsh, et al.

V. 12, 18, 20, 30, 32. (1951–56). The Letters, tr. Sister Wilfrid Parsons.

V. 16 (1952). Treatises on Various Subjects (The Christian Life. On Lying. Against Lying. On Continence. On Patience. The Excellence of Widowhood. The Work of Monks. The Usefulness of Fasting. The Eight Questions of Dulcitius), tr. Sister Mary Sarah Muldowney.

V. 21 (1953). The Confessions, tr. Vernon J. Bourke.

V. 27 (1954). Treatises on Marriage and Other Subjects (On the Good Marriage. On Adulterous Marriage. On Holy Virginity. On Faith and Works. On the Creed: To Catechumens. On Faith and the Creed. On the Care to be Taken for the Dead. In Answer to the Jews. The Divination of Demons). Tr. various hands.

V. 35 (1957). Against Julian, tr. Matthew A. Schumacher.

V. 38 (1959). Sermons on the Liturgical Seasons, tr. Sister Mary Sarah Muldowney.

V. 45 (1963). On the Trinity, tr. Stephen McKenna.

Other Collections

———— The Basic Writings. Trs. repr. principally from the Nicene Fathers, ed. Whitney J. Oates. N.Y., Random House, 1948. 2 v.

V. 1. Confessions (bks 1, 2, 4, 6, 8, 9, 12, 15). Twelve Treatises (mostly doctrinal: Soliloquies. On Immortality. On the Morals of the Catholic Church. On the Teacher. The Profit of Believing. The Nature of Good. The Spirit and the Letter. Nature and Grace. The Grace of Christ and Original Sin. The Enchiridion. On Grace and Free Will. The Pre-destination of the Saints).

V. 2. The City of God (bks. 1, 8, 11–22, parts of bks. 2, 4, 6, 7, 9, 10). On the Trinity.

———— The Letters. Tr. J. G. Cunningham, in Dods ed., v. 6, 13: 1876. Repr. Nicene Fathers, v. 1, 1886. (168 out of 272)

Selected and tr. Mary H. Allies. London, Burns and Oates, 1890. vii, 342 p. (49 letters)

Ed. and tr. J. H. Baxter. LCL, 1930. liii, 534 p. (62 letters)

Tr. Sister Wilfrid Parsons, in Fathers of the Church, v. 12, 18, 20, 30, 32: 1951–56.

———— Selected works in The Library of Christian Classics, v. 6, 7, 8: 1953–55.

V. 6 (1953). The Earlier Writings. Tr. John H. S. Burleigh. 413 p. (Soliloquies. The Teacher. Free Will. True Religion. The Usefulness of Belief. The Nature of the Good. Faith and the Creed. To Simplicius on Various Questions, bk. 1.)

V. 7. (1955). The Confessions, The *Enchiridion,* tr. Albert C. Outler. 423 p.

V. 8 (1955). The Later Works. Tr. John Burnaby. 359 p. (On the Trinity. On the Spirit and the Letter. Ten Homilies on St. John's Epistle I.)

————— Political Writings. Ed. Henry Paolucci, with intro. Dino Bigongiari. Chicago, Regnery, 1962. 358 p.

————— St. Augustine, in Great Books, 18, 1952. x, 697 p. (On Christian Doctrine. The City of God. The Confessions, all repr. from the Dods ed., v. 1, 2, 9, 14.)

Sermons

————— Commentary on the Lord's Sermon on the Mount, with Seventeen Related Sermons. Tr. Denis J. Kavanagh. Fathers of the Church, v. 5, 1948. vi, 382 p.

————— Homilies on the Gospel of St. John and on his First Epistle. Tr. H. Browne, in Library of Fathers (Pusey ed.), v. 26, 29: 1848–49. Repr. in Nicene Fathers, v. 7, 1888.

Part tr. (Ten Homilies, abridged John Burnaby in Library of Christian Classics, v. 8, 1955, p. 259–349.)

————— Nine Sermons on the Psalms. Tr. Edmund Hill. London, Longmans, 1958, and N.Y., Kenedy, 1959, 177 p.

————— Selected Easter Sermons (30). Tr. Philip T. Weller. St. Louis and London, Herder, 1959. 336 p.

————— Sermons for Christmas and Epiphany (from *Sermones ad populum*). Tr. Thomas C. Lawler. Ancient Christian Writers, v. 15, 1952. 249 p.

————— Sermons on the Liturgical Seasons. Tr. Sister Mary Sarah Muldowney. Fathers of the Church, v. 38, 1959. xxii, 481 p.

————— Sermons on Selected Lessons of the New Testament. Tr. R. G. McMullen. Library of the Fathers, v. 16, 20: 1844, 1845. Repr. in Nicene Fathers, v. 6, 1888.

Treatises

———— The Anti-Pelagian Writings. Tr. Peter Holmes and Robert E. Wallis. Dods ed., v, 4, 12, 15. Repr. Nicene Fathers, v. 5, 1887.

———— Lectures and Tractates on the Gospel of John. Tr. John Gibb and James Innes. Dods ed., v. 10–11. (124 lectures)

———— Seventeen Short Treatises. Tr. C. L. Cornish and H. Browne. Library of the Fathers, v. 22, 1847. Most repr. as Doctrinal and Moral Treatises, in Nicene Fathers, v. 3, 1886: see Collection I, above, for contents.

———— Treatises of Marriage and Other Subjects. Tr. Charles T. Wilcox, Charles T. Huegelmeyer, John McQuade, Sister Marie Liguori, Robert P. Russell, John A. Lacy, Ruth W. Brown. Fathers of the Church, v. 27, 1955. 456 p.

———— Treatises on Various Subjects. Tr. Sister Mary Sarah Muldowney, H. B. Jaffee, Sister Mary Francis McDonald, Sister Luanne Meagher, Sister M. Clement Eagan, Mary E. Deferrari. Fathers of the Church, v. 10, 1952. viii, 479 p.

———— Writings on the Donatist Controversy. Tr. J. R. King. Dods ed., v. 3. Repr. Nicene Fathers, v. 4.

———— Writings on the Manichaean Heresy. Tr. Richard Stothert. Dods ed., v. 5. Repr. Nicene Fathers, v. 4.

Particular Works

———— Acts or Disputation against Fortunatus the Manichaean. Tr. Albert B. Newman, in Nicene Fathers, v. 4, 1887.

———— On Admonition and Grace. Tr. Robert E. Wallis, in Dods ed., Works, v. 15, 1873. Repr. Nicene Fathers, v. 5, 1887.

Tr. J. C. Murray, in Fathers of the Church, v. 2, 1947.

———— On Adulterous Marriages. Tr. Charles T. Huegelmeyer, in Fathers of the Church, v. 27, 1954.

———— The Advantage of Believing. Tr. C. L. Cornish, in Library of the Fathers, v. 22, 1847. Repr. as The Profit of Believing, in Nicene Fathers, v. 3, 1887. Repr. H. De Romestin, in On Instructing the Unlearned, etc., 1885. Repr. in Basic Works, v. 1, 1948.

Tr. Sister Luanne Meagher, in Fathers of the Church, v. 4, 1948.

———— Against the Academics. Ed. and tr. Denis J. Kavanagh as Answer to Skeptics. N.Y., Cosmopolitan Science and Arts Service, 1943. xxv, 269 p. (parallel texts) Repr. (English only) in Fathers of the Church, v. 5, 1948.

Tr. John J. O'Meara as Against the Academicians. Ancient Christian Writers, v. 12, 1950. vi, 213 p.

Tr. Mary Patrick Garvey. Milwaukee, Marquette Univ. Pr., 1957. 85 p.

———— Against the Epistle of Manichaeus. Tr. Richard Stothert, in Dods ed., v. 5, 1873. Repr. Nicene Fathers, v. 4, 1887.

———— Against Julian. Tr. Matthew A. Schumacher in Fathers of the Church, v. 35, 1957. xx, 407 p.

———— Against Lying. Tr. H. Browne, in Library of the Fathers, v. 22, 1847. Repr. in Nicene Fathers, v. 3, 1887.

Tr. Harold B. Jaffe, in Fathers of the Church, v. 16, 1952.

———— Against Two Letters of the Pelagians on Grace and Free Will. Tr. Robert E. Wallis, in Dods ed., v. 15, 1876. Repr. in Nicene Fathers, v. 5, 1887. Repr. in Basic Writings, v. 1, 1948.

———— In Answer to the Jews (*Adversus Judaeos*). Tr. Sister Marie Liguori, in Fathers of the Church, v. 27, 1955.

———— Answer to the Letters of Petilian. Tr. J. R. King, in Dods ed., v. 3, 1872. Repr. in Nicene Fathers, v. 4, 1887.

———— On Baptism, Against the Donatists. Tr. J. R. King, in Dods ed., v. 3, 1872. Repr. in Nicene Fathers, v. 4, 1887.

———— On Care for the Dead. Tr. H. Browne, in Library of the Fathers, 22, 1847. Repr. in Nicene Fathers, v. 3, 1887.

Tr. John A. Lacy, in Fathers of the Church, v. 27, 1955.

———— On Catechizing the Uninstructed (*Rudibus*). Tr. C. L. Cornish, in Library of the Fathers, v. 22, 1847.

Tr. S. D. F. Salmond, in Dods ed., v. 9, 1875. Repr. in Nicene Fathers, v. 3, 1887.

Tr. W. J. Vashon Baker, in Preaching and Teaching According to St. Augustine. London and Oxford, Mowbray, 1907. iv, 166 p.

Tr. E. Phillips Barker. London, Methuen, 1912. 88 p.

Tr. R. K. Davis and E. B. Lock. London, Bell, 1913. 56 p.

Tr. Joseph P. Christopher. Washington, Catholic Univ. of Amer. Pr., 1926. xxi, 365 p. Repr. as The First Catechetical Instruction, in Ancient Christian Writers, v. 2, 1946, 171 p.

————— The Catholic and Manichaean Way of Life (*De moribus ecclesiae Catholicae,* etc.). Tr. Donald A. and Idella J. Gallagher. Fathers of the Church, v. 56, 1966. xx, 135 p.

————— On Christian Combat (*Agone*). Tr. C. L. Cornish as On the Christian Conflict, in Library of the Fathers, v. 22, 1847.

Tr. Robert P. Russell, in Fathers of the Church, 8, 1947.

————— On Christian Doctrine. Tr. F. J. Shaw, in Dods ed., v. 9, 1875. Repr. in Nicene Fathers, v. 2, 1886; repr. in Great Books, v. 18, 1952.

Tr. D. W. Robertson, Jr. N.Y., Liberal Arts Pr., 1958. xxii, 169 p.

————— The Christian Life. Tr. Sister Mary Sarah Muldowney, in Fathers of the Church, v. 16, 1952.

————— The City of God. Tr. John Healey. London, 1610. 921 p. Repr. 1620; 1890; (Temple Classics) 1903, 3 v., repr. 1931; Edinburgh, 1909; London, 1934; 1945; EL, 1947.

Tr. Marcus Dods, in Works, v. 1, 2: 1872. Repr. Nicene Fathers, v. 1886; London, 1934; N.Y., Hafner, 1948; ML, 1950; Great Books, v. 18, 1952.

Tr. Gerald G. Walsh et al., in Fathers of the Church, v. 8, 14, 24 (1950–54). Repr. abr., Garden City, N.Y., Doubleday (Image Books), and London, Mayflower, 1958, 551 p. paper

Ed. and tr. George E. McCracken and William C. Greene, as The City of God Against the Pagans. LCL, 1957—(in process). v. 1, 1957; v. 2, 1963; v. 6, 1961.

Many part trs. since 1660, e.g., in Basic Writings, v. 2.

————— The Confessions. Tr. Sir Tobie Mathew. St. Omer, 1620. 800 p. Repr. Paris, 1638. Repr. rev. Dom Roger Hudleston, London, Burns Oates, and N.Y., Benziger, 1923, xxx, 410 p.; repr. 1948; 1954; Chicago, Regnery, 1956; abridged, Glasgow, Collins (Fontana Books), 1957.

Tr. William Watts. London, 1631. 1012 p. Repr. Boston, 1843; Andover, Mass., 1860, 1871; LCL, 1912, 2 v., repr. 1919, 1922, 1925. Repr. rev. E. B. Pusey, Library of the Fathers, v. 1, 1838; repr. 1853; 1883; 1900; EL, 1907 et seq.; Harvard Classics, v. 7, 1909; Medici Society, 1930; part repr. Basic Writings, v. 1, 1948; ML, 1949; Pocket Books, 1952; Great Books, v. 18, 1952; EL, 1957; N.Y., Collier Books, 1962.

Tr. J. G. Pilkington, in Dods ed. of Works, v. 14, 1876. Repr. in Nicene Fathers, 1, 1886; N.Y., Boni and Liveright, 1929; N.Y., Tudor, 1944; London, Chapman, 1947; Cleveland, Fine Editions Pr., 1960; Limited Editions Club, 1962; N.Y., Heritage Pr., 1963, xxx, 296 p.

Tr. F. J. Sheed. London and N.Y., Sheed and Ward, 1943. xxii, 354 p. Repr. 1951, 1959.

Tr. ed. J. M. Lelen. N.Y., Catholic Book, 1952. 384 p.

Tr. Vernon J. Bourke, in Fathers of the Church, v. 21, 1953. xxxii, 481 p.

Tr. Albert C. Outler (with the *Enchiridion*), in Library of Christian Classics, 7, 1955. 423 p.

Tr. John K. Ryan. Garden City, N.Y., Doubleday (Image Books), and London, Mayflower Pr., 1960. 429 p.

Tr. R. S. Pine-Coffin. Penguin, 1961. 346 p.

Tr. Rex Warner. N.Y., New American Library, 1963. xv, 351 p.

Many part trs.

———— Of Continence. Tr. C. L. Cornish, in Library of the Fathers, v. 22, 1847. Repr. Nicene Fathers, v. 3, 1887.

Tr. Sister Mary Francis McDonald, in Fathers of the Church, v. 16, 1952.

———— On the Correction of the Donatists. Tr. J. R. King, in Dods ed., v. 3, 1872. Repr. Nicene Fathers, v. 4, 1887.

———— On the Creed: A Sermon to Catechumens. Tr. H. Browne, in Library of the Fathers, v. 22, 1847. Repr. in Nicene Fathers, v. 3, 1887.

Tr. Sister Marie Liguori, in Fathers of the Church, v. 27, 1954.

———— On the Destruction of Rome, A Sermon. Ed. and tr. Sister Marie Vianney O'Reilly. Washington, Catholic Univ. of Amer. Pr., 1955. xvii, 95 p.

———— The Divination of Demons. Tr. Ruth W. Brown, in Fathers of the Church, v. 27, 1954.

———— Eight Questions of Dulcitius. Tr. Mary E. Deferrari, in Fathers of the Church, v. 16, 1952.

———— The *Enchiridion* to Laurentius: see Faith, Hope, and Charity.

———— Expositions on ᵗhe Book of Psalms. Tr. J. E. Tweed, et al., in Library of the Fathers, v. 24, 25, 30, 32, 37, 39: 1847–57. Repr. Nicene Fathers, v. 8, 1890.

Part tr. Joseph Rickaby as Readings on the Psalms. London, Burns Oates, 1925. xii, 259 p.

Tr. Scholastica Hebgin and Felicitas Corrigan (Psalms 1–37) in Ancient Christian Writers, v. 29, 30: 1960–61.

———— On Faith and the Creed. Tr. C. L. Cornish, in Library of the Fathers, v. 22, 1847.

Tr. Tr. S. D. F. Salmond, in Dods ed., v. 9, 1875. Repr. Nicene Fathers, v. 3, 1887.

Tr. Robert P. Russell, in Fathers of the Church, v. 27, 1954.

———— Faith, Hope, and Charity (*Enchiridion* to Laurentius). Tr. C. L. Cornish, in Library of the Fathers, v. 22, 1847. Repr. rev. H. De Romestin, in St. Augustine, 1885.

Tr. J. F. Shaw as The *Enchiridion,* in Dods ed. of Works, v. 9, 1875. Repr. Nicene Fathers, v. 3, 1887. Repr. London, Religious Tract Society, 1887, 160 p.; repr. in Basic Writings, v. 1, 1948; repr. Chicago, Regnery, 1961.

Tr. Louis A. Anand. Ancient Christian Writers, v. 3, 1947.

Tr. Bernard M. Peebles, in Fathers of the Church, v. 2, 1947.

Tr. Ernest Evans as The *Enchiridion* or Manual. London, S.P.C.K., 1953. xxviii, 146 p.

———— On Faith in the Unseen. Tr. C. L. Cornish, in Library of the Fathers, v. 22, 1847. Repr. H. De Romestin, in St. Augustine, 1885. Repr. Nicene Fathers, v. 3, 1887.

Tr. Roy E. Deferrari and Sister Mary Francis McDonald, in Fathers of the Church, v. 4, 1947.

————— On Faith and Works. Tr. C. L. Cornish, in Library of the Fathers, v. 22, 1847.

Tr. Gregory Joseph Lombardo. Washington, D.C., Catholic Univ. of Amer. Pr., 1950. lv, 160 leaves (microcards).

Tr. Sister Marie Liguori, in Fathers of the Church, v. 27, 1955.

————— On Free Will. Ed. and tr. Francis E. Tourscher, Philadelphia, Peter Reilly, 1937. vii, 442 p.

Tr. Carroll Mason Sparrow. Univ. of Virginia Studies. Richmond, Va., Dietz, 1947. xii, 149 p.

Tr. Mark Pontifex as The Problem of Free Choice, in Ancient Christian Writers, v. 22, 1955. 255 p.

Tr. Anna S. Benjamin and L. H. Hackstaff. N.Y., Bobbs-Merrill, 1964. xxxi, 162 p.

————— On the Gift of Perseverance. See On Perseverance to the End, below.

————— Of the Good of Marriage. Tr. C. L. Cornish, in Library of the Fathers, v. 22, 1847. Repr. Nicene Fathers, v. 3, 1887.

Tr. Charles T. Wilcox, in Fathers of the Church, v. 27, 1954.

————— On the Good of Widowhood. Tr. C. L. Cornish, in Library of the Fathers, v. 22, 1847. Repr. Nicene Fathers, v. 3, 1887.

Tr. Sister M. Clement Eagan as The Excellence of Widowhood, in Fathers of the Church, v. 16, 1952.

————— On the Grace of Christ and Original Sin. Tr. Peter Holmes, in Dods ed., v. 12, 1875. Repr. Nicene Fathers, v. 5, 1888. Repr. Basic Writings, v. 1.

————— On Grace and Free Will. See Against Two Letters of the Pelagians.

————— On Greatness of the Soul. Tr. John J. McMahon as The Magnitude of the Soul, in Fathers of the Church, v. 4, 1947.

Tr. Joseph M. Colleran, in Ancient Christian Writers, v. 9, 1950.

————— The Happy Life (*De beata vita*). Ed. and tr. Francis E. Tourscher as Happiness—A Study (with Immortality of the Soul). Philadelphia, Peter Reilly, 1937. vii, 95 p.

Ed. and tr. Ludwig Schopp as The Happy Life. St. Louis and London, Herder, 1939. v, 152 p. Repr. (English only) in Fathers of the Church, v. 5, 1948.

Tr. Ruth Allison Brown. Washington, D.C., Catholic Univ. of Amer. Pr., 1944. 193 p.

───────── The Harmony of the Evangelists. Tr. S. D. F. Salmond, in Dods ed., v. 8, 1875. Repr. Nicene Fathers, v. 6, 1888.

───────── On Heresies. Ed. and tr. Liguori G. Muller. Washington, D.C., Catholic Univ. of Amer. Pr., xix, 229 p.

───────── On the Immortality of the Soul. Ed. and tr. Francis E. Tourscher (with The Happy Life). Philadelphia, Peter Reilly, 1937. vii, 75 p.

Tr. George G. Leckie (with The Teacher). N.Y., Appleton-Century (Philosophy Source-Books), 1938. xxxviii, 88 p. Repr. Basic Writings, v. 1, 1948.

Tr. Ludwig G. Schopp, in Fathers of the Church, v. 4, 1947.

───────── On Lying. Tr. H. Browne, in Library of the Fathers, v. 22, 1847. Repr. in Nicene Fathers, v. 3, 1887.

Tr. Sister Mary Sarah Muldowney, in Fathers of the Church, v. 16, 1952.

───────── On Marriage and Concupiscence. Tr. Peter Holmes, in Dods ed., v. 12, 1875. Repr. in Nicene Fathers, v. 5, 1887.

───────── The Measure of the Soul (*De quantitate animae*). Ed. and tr. Francis E. Tourscher. Philadelphia, Peter Reilly, and London, Herder, 1933. xi, 230 p.

───────── On Merits and the Forgiveness of Sins. Tr. Peter Holmes, in Dods ed., v. 4, 1872. Repr. Nicene Fathers, v. 5, 1888.

───────── Of the Morals (*De moribus*) of the Catholic Church. Tr. Richard Stothert, in Dods ed., v. 5, 1873. Repr. in Nicene Fathers, v. 4, 1887. Repr. in Basic Writings, v. 1, 1948.

───────── On the Morals of the Manichaeans. Tr. Richard Stothert, in Dods ed., v. 5, 1873. Repr. in Nicene Fathers, v. 4, 1887.

───────── On Music. Tr. R. C. Taliaferro, in Fathers of the Church, v. 4, 1947.

───────── On the Nature of the Good, Against the Manichaeans. Tr. Albert B. Newman, in Nicene Fathers, v. 4, 1888. Repr. in Basic Works, v. 1, 1948.

Ed. and tr. A. Anthony Moon. Washington, D.C., Catholic Univ. of Amer. Pr., 1955. xvii, 281 p.

———————— On Nature and Grace. Tr. Peter Holmes, in Dods ed., v. 4, 1872. Repr. Nicene Fathers, v. 5, 1888. Repr. in Basic Writings, v. 1, 1948.

———————— On Order. Ed. and tr. Robert P. Russell as Divine Providence and the Problem of Evil. N.Y., Cosmopolitan Science and Art Service, 1942. 191 p. Repr. (English only) in Fathers of the Church, v. 5, 1948.

———————— On Patience. Tr. H. Browne, in Library of the Fathers, v. 22, 1847. Repr. in Nicene Fathers, v. 3, 1887.

Tr. Sister Luanne Meagher, in Fathers of the Church, v. 16, 1952.

———————— On the Perfection of Man's Righteousness. Tr. Peter Holmes, in Dods ed. v. 4, 1873. Repr. in Nicene Fathers, v. 5, 1888.

———————— Of Perseverance to the End (*De dono perseverantiae*). Tr. Nicholas Lesse (with The Predestination of the Saints). London, 1550.

Tr. John Scory, in Two bokes of . . . S. Augustine (with The Predestination of the Saints). Emden, 1556? 123 leaves.

Tr. Robert E. Wallis, in Dods ed., v. 15, 1876. Repr. Nicene Fathers, v. 5, 1888.

Ed. and tr. Sister Mary Alphonsus Lesousky. Washington, D.C., Catholic Univ. of Amer. Pr., xxii, 310 p.

———————— On Prayer. Tr. Thomas A. Hand. Westminster, Md., Newman Pr., and London, Gill, 1963. 133 p.

———————— Of the Predestination of the Saints. Tr. Nicholas Lesse, 1550, with Perseverance, see above.

Tr. John Scory, 1556? with Perseverance, see above.

Tr. Robert E. Wallis, in Dods ed., v. 15, 1876. Repr. in Nicene Fathers, v. 5, 1888; in Basic Writings, v. 1, 1948.

———————— On the Proceedings (*De gestis*) of Pelagius. Tr. Peter Holmes, in Dods ed., v. 4, 1873. Repr. in Nicene Fathers, v. 5, 1888.

———————— On Rebuke (*De correptione*) and Grace. Tr. Robert E. Wallis, in Dods ed., v. 15, 1876. Repr. in Nicene Fathers, v. 4, 1887.

———————— Reply to Faustus the Manichaean. Tr. Richard Stothert, in Dods ed., v. 5, 1873. Repr. in Nicene Fathers, v. 4, 1887.

———— The Sermon on the Mount Expounded. Tr. William Findlay, in Dods ed., v. 8, 1875. Repr. in Nicene Fathers, v. 6, 1889.

Tr. John J. Jepson as The Lord's Sermon on the Mount. Ancient Christian Writers, v. 5, 1948. vi, 227 p.

Tr. Denis J. Kavanagh, as Commentary on the Lord's Sermon on the Mount, with Seventeen Related Sermons. Fathers of the Church, v. 11, 1951. vi, 382 p. Repr. 1963.

———— The Soliloquies. King Alfred's Old English Version, Tr. into Modern English by H. L. Hargrove (Latin-English). Yale Studies in English. N.Y., Holt, 1902. lvii, 120 p. Repr. (English only), 1904, 47 p.

Tr. C. C. Starbuck, in Nicene Fathers, v. 7, 1888. Repr. in Basic Writings, v. 1, 1948.

Tr. Rose E. Cleveland. Boston, Little Brown, and London, Williams and Norgate, 1910. xlv, 180 p.

Tr. Thomas F. Gilligan. N.Y., Cosmopolitan Science and Art Service, 1943. 173 p. (parallel texts) Repr. (English only), in Fathers of the Church, v. 5, 1948.

Another work called The Soliloquies (*Soliloquia animae ad Deum*) has been ascribed to St. Augustine, and has often been tr. into English, sometimes with the also supposititious Meditations, and the Manual of Devotion. For trs. of these works, beginning in 1574, see Farrar and Evans, nos. 472–485, p. 14, above.

———— On the Soul and its Origin. Tr. Peter Holmes, in Dods ed., v. 12, 1875. Repr. in Nicene Fathers, v. 5, 1888.

———— On the Spirit and the Letter. Tr. Peter Holmes, in Dods ed., v. 4, 1873. Repr. in Nicene Fathers, v. 5, 1888; in Basic Writings, v. 1, 1948.

Tr. W. J. Sparrow Simpson. London, S.P.C.K., and N.Y., Macmillan, 1925. 127 p.

Tr. John Burnaby, in Library of Christian Classics, v. 8, 1955.

———— The Teacher. Tr. Francis E. Tourscher as The Philosophy of Teaching. Philadelphia, Peter Reilly, 1924. 99 p.

Tr. George G. Leckie as Concerning the Teacher (with The Immortality of the Soul). N.Y. and London, Appleton-Century (Philosophy

Source-Books), 1938. xxxviii, 88 p. Repr. in Basic Writings, v. 1, 1948.

Tr. Joseph M. Colleran, in Ancient Christian Writers, v. 9, 1950.

————— On the Trinity. Tr. Arthur W. Haddan, in Dods ed., v. 7, 1873. Repr. in Nicene Fathers, v. 3, 1887.

Tr. John Burnaby, in Library of Christian Classics, v. 8, 1955.

Tr. Stephen McKenna. Fathers of the Church, v. 45, 1963. 539 p.

————— Of True Religion. Tr. J. H. S. Burleigh. Chicago, Regnery, 1959. xix, 107 p.

————— On Two Souls, Against the Manichaeans. Tr. Albert B. Newman, in Nicene Fathers, v. 4, 1887.

————— On the Utility of Fasting. Ed. and tr. Sister Dominic Ruegg. Washington, D.C., Catholic Univ. of Amer. Pr., 1951. xviii, 133 p.

Tr. Sister Mary Sarah Muldowney, in Fathers of the Church, v. 16, 1952.

————— Of the Work of Monks. Tr. H. Browne, in Library of the Fathers, 22, 1847. Repr. in Nicene Fathers, v. 3, 1887.

Tr. Sister Mary Sarah Muldowney, in Fathers of the Church, v. 16, 1952.

CASSIAN (Johannes Cassianus of Marseilles, A.D. c. 360–c. 435). The Works of John Cassian. Tr. Edgar C. S. Gibson, in Nicene Fathers, ser. 2, v. 11 (1894), p. 161–641.

————— Readings from John Cassian. Tr. W. R. V. Brade, and ed. W. B. Trevelyan in A Master of the Desert. London, Faith Pr., 1927. x, 168 p.

COMMODIANUS (fl. A.D. 4th c.). The Instructions in favour of Christian Discipline. Tr. prose R. E. Wallis, in Ante-Nicene Library, v. 18 (1870), p. 434–74. Repr. Ante-Nicene Fathers, v. IV (1885), p. 199–219.

CYPRIAN, ST. (Caecilius Cyprianus, fl. A.D. c. 250). The Genuine Works. Tr. Nathaniel Marshall. London, 1717. xl, 278, 276 p.

Tr. Charles Thornton (The Treatises) in Library of Fathers, v. 3 (1839), and Henry Carey (The Epistles, etc.), *ibid.,* v. 17 (1844).

Tr. R. E. Wallis in Ante-Nicene Library, v. 8 and 13 (1868–69). Repr. in Ante-Nicene Fathers, v. V (1886).

See Farrar and Evans, nos. 1140–1141, p. 14, above, for contents of v. 8 and 13.

———— Treatises. Tr. various hands, in Fathers of the Church, v. 36 (1958). xvi, 372 p.

To Donatus; The Lapsed; To Demetrian; The Unity of the Church; The Lord's Prayer; Works and Almsgiving; Jealousy and Envy; Exhortation to Martyrdom, to Fortunatus; That Idols are not Gods. Tr. Roy J. Deferrari.

The Dress of Virgins. Tr. Sister Angela Elizabeth Keenan.

The Good of Patience. Tr. Sister George Edward Conway.

Mortality. Tr. Sister M. Hannan Mahoney.

———— On the Dress of Virgins. Ed. and tr. Sister Angela Elizabeth Keenan. Washington, D.C., Catholic Univ. of America Pr., 1932. xiii, 188 p. (parallel texts). Repr. (English only) in preceding item.

———— Epistles. Tr. W. S. Flower in Select Treatises. London, Masters, 1846. Part 4.

———— The Lapsed (*De lapsis*). Tr. Maurice Bevenot, in Ancient Christian Writers, v. 25 (1957) (with The Unity of the Church). 134 p.

———— Letters (nos. 1–81). Tr. Sister Rose Bernard Donna. Fathers of the Church, v. 51 (1965). xxvi, 358 p.

———— On the Lord's Prayer. Tr. Henry Gee. London, Bell, 1904. 41 p.

Earlier trs. Thomas Paynell, 1539; T. Herbert Bindley, S.P.C.K., 1898, repr. 1914.

———— On Mortality. Tr. Sir Thomas Elyot (with Mirandola's Rules of a Christian Lyfe). London, 1534. Repr. 1539.

Ed. and tr. Mary Louise Hannan. Washington, D.C., Catholic Univ. of Amer. Pr., 1933. xii, 103 p. Repr. in Treatises, above.

Also tr. John Scory in Certein Works, 1556; and anon. from the French, 1607.

———— On the Unity of the Church. Ed. and tr. E. H. Blakeney. London, S.P.C.K., 1928 vii, 63 p.

Tr. Maurice Bevenot (with The Lapsed), in Ancient Christian Writers, v. 25, 1957. 134 p.

Also tr. John Fell, 1681; Samuel Brewster, 1701; in Tracts for the Times, v. 2, 1836, repr. 1838.

———— On Works and Alms. Ed. and tr. Edward V. Rebenack. Washington, D.C., Catholic Univ. of Amer. Pr., 1962. 162 p. (parallel texts)

GENNADIUS OF MARSEILLES (A.D. 5th c.). Lives of Illustrious Men. Tr. E. C. Richardson, in Nicene Fathers, ser. 2, v. 3, 1892, p. 385–402.

HILARY OF POITIERS, ST. (A.D. 4th c.). Select Works. Tr. E. W. Watson, L. Pullan, et al., in Nicene Fathers, ser. 2, v. 9, 1899. vii, xcvi, 258 p.

———— The Hymns in the Codex Aretinus. Ed. and tr. Walter Neidig Myers. Univ. of Pennsylvania dissertation. Philadelphia, pr. pr., 1928. 82 p.

———— Sermon on the Life of St. Honoratus. Tr. Roy J. Deferrari, in Fathers of the Church, v. 15, 1952.

———— The Trinity. Tr. Stephen J. McKenna in Fathers of the Church, v. 25, 1954. xx, 555 p.

JEROME, ST. (Eusebius Hieronymus, A.D. c. 350–420). The Principal Works. Tr. W. H. Freemantle, in Nicene Fathers, ser. 2, v. 6, 1893. xxxv, 524 p.

———— Dogmatic and Polemical Works. Tr. John H. Hritzu in Fathers of the Church, v. 53, 1965. 410 p.

———— The Homilies. Tr. Sister Marie Liguori Ewald. V. 1 (on Psalms 1–59), in Fathers of the Church, v. 48, 1964. 430 p. V. 2 (on Psalms 60–96). Tr. the same. *Ibid.*, v. 57, 1966. x, 303 p.

———— The Letters. v. 1 (nos. 1–22). Tr. Charles Christopher Mierow in Ancient Christian Writers, v. 33, 1963. 281 p.

———— Satirical Letters. Tr. Paul Carroll. Chicago, Regnery, 1956. 198 p.

———— Select Letters. Ed. and tr. F. A. Wright. LCL, 1933. xvi, 510 p. (18 letters)

Also tr. in The Principal Works, see above. Cf. Certaine selected Epistles, tr. Henry Hawkins, St. Omer, 1630.

———————— Apology against Rufinus. Tr. W. H. Freemantle, in Nicene Fathers, ser. 2, v. 3, 1892.

———————— Lives of Illustrious Men. Tr. E. C. Richardson (with Gennadius' continuation), *ibid.*

———————— Lives of St. Paul the First Hermit, St. Hilarion, and Malchus. Tr. Sister Marie Liguori Ewald, in Fathers of the Church, v. 15, 1952.

Also tr. in The Principal Works, above, and in Certaine Selected Epistles, above.

———————— Lives of the Saints (*Vitas patrum*). Tr. William Caxton from the French as The . . . lyff of the old Auncyent holy faders hermytes. Westminster, de Worde, 1495.

See also Syriac Literature (for The Histories of the Monks), in v. V.

LACTANTIUS, L. Caecilius Firmianus (fl. A.D. c. 300). The Works of Lactantius. Tr. William Fletcher in Ante-Nicene Library, v. 21, 22: 1871. Repr. v. VII, 1886.

———————— The Divine Institutes, i–vii. Tr. Sister Mary Francis McDonald. Fathers of the Church, v. 49, 1964. xxvi, 561 p.

See Epitome of the Divine Institutes, tr. E. H. Blakeney (London, S.P.C.K., 1950, xiv, 175 p.)

————————The Minor Works. Tr. Sister Mary Francis McDonald. Fathers of the Church, v. 54, 1966. 248 p.

———————— The Phoenix. Tr. George Stephens from the Old English version as The King of Birds. London, Nichols, 1844. 69 p.

Ed. and tr. Mary Cletus Fitzpatrick. Philadelphia, Univ. of Pennsylvania Pr., 1933. 98 p. (parallel texts)

See also Minor Latin Poets, LCL, p. 650–65.

———————— A Relation of the Death of the Primitive Persecutors. Tr. Gilbert Burnet. Amsterdam, 1687. Repr. as Gods Judgments upon Tyrants, London, 1715.

Tr. Sir David Dalrymple as Of the Manner in which the Persecutors Died. Edinburgh, Murray and Cochrane, 1782. xxxvii, 236 p.

MINUCIUS FELIX, M. (fl. A.D. c. 150). Octavius, Tr. Robert E. Wallis, in Ante-Nicene Library, v. 13, 1869, p. 451–517. Repr. in v. IV.

Freely tr. Arthur A. Brodribb as Pagan and Puritan. London, Bell, 1903. xiv, 89 p.

Tr. J. H. Freese. London, S.P.C.K., and N.Y., Macmillan, 1918. xxv, 102 p.

Ed. and tr. G. H. Rendall (with Tertullian). LCL, 1931. xxviii, 476 p.

Tr. Rudolph Arbesmann (with Tertullian), in Fathers of the Church, v. 10, 1951, p. 321–402.

Earlier trs.: Richard Jones, Oxford, 1636; P. Lorrain, 1682; Edward Combe, 1703; P.B., 1708; William Reeves (with Justin Martyr and Tertullian), 1709, repr. 1716–17; Sir David Dalrymple, Edinburgh, 1781, repr. Cambridge, 1854.

NICETA OF REMESIANA (A.D. c. 335–c. 414). Writings (The Name and Titles of Our Saviour; An Instruction on Faith; The Power of the Holy Spirit; An Explanation of the Creed; The Vigils of the Saints; Liturgical Singing). Tr. Gerald G. Walsh, in Fathers of the Church, v. 7, 1949, p. 9–76.

NOVATIAN (A.D. 3rd c.). The Writings. Tr. Robert E. Wallis, in Ante-Nicene Library, v. 13, 1869, p. 293–395. Repr. in Ante-Nicene Fathers, v. V.

———— Treatise on the Trinity. Tr. Herbert Moore. London, S.P.C.K., and N.Y., Macmillan, 1919. vi, 147 p.

OPTATUS, ST., Milevitanus (Bishop of Mela, fl. A.D. c. 370). The Work Against the Donatists. Tr. C. R. Vassall-Phillips. London, Longmans, 1917. xxxv, 438 p.

PACIAN, ST., Bishop of Barcelona (A.D. 4th c.). Extant Works. Tr. C. H. Collyns in Library of the Fathers, v. 17, 1844, p. 317–84.

PAULINUS OF MILAN (fl. A.D. 375–422). Life of St. Ambrose. Ed. and tr. Sister Mary Simplicia Kaniecka. Washington, D.C., Catholic Univ. of Amer. Pr., 1928. xvi, 186 p. (parallel texts)

Tr. John A. Lacey, in Fathers of the Church, v. 15, 1952.

Tr. Frederick R. Hoare, in The Western Fathers. London, and N.Y., Sheed and Ward, 1954, p. 145–88.

PAULINUS OF NOLA, ST. (Meropius Pontius Paulinus, A.D. 353–431). Paulinus' Churches at Nola. Ed. and tr. R. C. Goldschmidt. Amsterdam, Noord-Hollandsche Uitgevers Maatschappij, 1940. 302 p. (extracts from Epistle 32, Carmen 27, 28)

PETER CHRYSOLOGUS, ST. (A.D. c. 405–c. 450). Selected Sermons. Tr. George E. Ganss (with the Homilies of Valerian), in Fathers of the Church, v. 17, 1953. viii, 454 p.

POMERIUS, JULIAN (d. A.D. c. 400). The Contemplative Life. Tr. Sister Mary Josephine Suelzer, in Ancient Christian Writers, v. 4, 1947. 220 p.

PONTIUS (A.D. 3rd c.). Life of St. Cyprian. Tr. Charles Thornton, in Fathers of the Church, v. 3, 1839.

Tr. R. E. Wallis, in Ante-Nicene Library, v. 8, 1868. Repr. in Ante-Nicene Fathers, v. V, 1886.

Tr. Sister Mary Magdeleine Mueller and Roy J. Deferrari, in Fathers of the Church, v. 15, 1952.

POSSIDIUS, ST., Bishop of Calama (fl. A.D. 370–437). The Life of St. Augustine. Ed. and tr. Herbert T. Weiskotten. Princeton, N.J., Princeton Univ. Pr., 1919. 174 p.

Tr. Edward A. Foran, in The Augustinians. London, Burns Oates, 1938. xii, 180 p.

Tr. Sister Mary Magdeleine Mueller and Roy J. Deferrari, in Fathers of the Church, v. 15, 1952.

Tr. Frederick R. Hoare, in The Western Fathers. London and N.Y., Sheed and Ward, 1954. p. 189–244.

PROSPER OF AQUITAINE, ST. (A.D. 5th c., earlier part). The Call of All Nations (De vocatione gentium). Tr. Prudentius de Letter, in Ancient Christian Writers, v. 14, 1952. 234 p.

———— *Carmen de Ingratis*. Tr. Charles T. Huegelmeyer. Washington, D.C., Catholic Univ. of America Pr., 1963. xx, 264 p.

———— The Defense of St. Augustine. Tr. Prudentius de Letter, in Ancient Christian Writers, v. 32, 1963. v, 248 p.

———— Grace and Free Will. Tr. J. Reginald O'Donnell, in Fathers of the Church, v. 7, 1949, p. 343–418.

PRUDENTIUS CLEMENS, A. (A.D. 248–c. 405). The Poems. Tr. prose R. J. Thomson. LCL. 1949–53. 2 v.

Tr. Sister M. Clement Eagan, in Fathers of the Church, v. 43, 52: 1962–65.

———— A Selection from the Works. Tr. verse F. St. John Thackeray. London, Bell, 1890. lxxiii, 231 p.

———— The Origin of Sin (*Hamartigenia*). Tr. prose G. Stam. Amsterdam, H. J. Paris, 1940. 274 p.

———— The Psychomachia. Tr. Mary Louise Porter. Raleigh, N.C., Meredith College Quarterly Bulletin, 1929. 39 p.

Also tr. anon., London, 1743.

———— The Twelve Hymns (*Cathemerinon*). Tr. Ernest Gilliat Smith as Songs from Prudentius. London and N.Y., Lane, 1898. 90 p.

Tr. verse R. Martin Pope and R. F. Davis as The Hymns. London, Dent, and N.Y., Dutton (Temple Classics), 1905. 208 p. (parallel texts)

The Hymns were separately tr. and published by G. Morison, Cambridge, 1887–88, 8 v.

RUFINUS, TYRANNIUS (A.D. c. 345–510). Life and Works, with Jerome's Apology Against Rufinus. Tr. William Henry Freemantle, in Nicene Fathers, ser. 2, v. 3, 1892, p. 405–568.

———— Commentary on the Apostles' Creed (*De fide et symbolo*). Tr. Charles A. Heurtley in On Faith and the Creed. Oxford and London, 1886, p. 78–143. Repr. ed. S. C. Gaylord, 1916.

Tr. Charles Whitaker, in A Sketch of Rufinus and his Times. Cambridge, Deighton Bell, and London, Bell, 1887. iv, 142 p.

Tr. Ernest F. Morrison. London, Methuen, 1916. 63 p.

Tr. J. N. D. Kelly, in Ancient Christian Writers, v. 20, 1955. 166 p.

Ed. and tr. Sister Mary William Miller. Washington, D.C., Catholic Univ. of Amer. Pr., 1964. xxiv, 204 p. (lithographed)

SIDONIUS APOLLINARIS, ST., Bishop of Clermont (5th c.). (The Writings). Ed. and tr. W. B. Anderson as Poems and Letters. LCL, 1936–65. 2 v.

————— The Letters. Tr. O. M. Dalton. Oxford, Clarendon Pr., 1915. 2 v.

SULPICIUS SEVERUS (fl. c. A.D. 400). The Works. Tr. Alexander Roberts, in Nicene Fathers, ser. 2, v. 11, 1895, p. 1–122. (Life of St. Martin of Tours, letters, dialogue, chronicle)

————— St. Martin of Tours (the life and some letters and dialogues). Tr. Mary Caroline Watt from the French version of Paul Monceaux. London, Sands, 1928. xix, 260 p.

————— Writings (Life of St. Martin; Letters to Eusebius, Aurelius, Bassula; Three Dialogues). Tr. Bernard M. Peebles, in Fathers of the Church, v. 7, 1949, p. 101–254.

TERTULLIAN (O. Septimius Florens Tertullianus, b. c. A.D. 160). The Writings. Tr. various hands in Ante-Nicene Library, v. 7 (Five Books Against Marcion), 11, 15, 18 (shorter treatises), 1870. Repr. in Ante-Nicene Fathers, v. III, IV (1885).

————— Apologetic and Practical Treatises. Tr. Charles Dodgson, in Library of Fathers, v. 10, 1842. viii, xix, 534 p. (v. 1 of 2 projected). Repr. 1854.

————— Apologetical Works. Tr. Rudolph Arbesmann et al. (with Minucius Felix), in Fathers of the Church, v. 10, 1951, p. 7–309.

————— Disciplinary, Moral, and Ascetical Works. Tr. Rudolph Arbesmann, Sister Emily Joseph Daly, and Edwin A. Quain, in Fathers of the Church, v. 40, 1951. 323 p.

Particular Works

————— The Address to Scapula Tertullus, Proconsul of Africa. Tr. Sir David Dalrymple. Edinburgh, Murray & Cochrane, 1790. viii, 139 p.

————— Against Praxeas. Tr. Alexander Souter. London, S.P.C.K., 1919. 125 p.

Tr. Ernest Evans. London, S.P.C.K., 1948. 368 p.

———— Apology for the Christians. Tr. T. H. Bindley (with letters of Pliny and Trajan). London, Parker, 1890. xvi, 158 p.

Ed. and tr. Alexander Souter. Cambridge Univ. Pr., 1917. xx, 496 p.

Earlier trs.: Henry Brown, 1655, repr. 1657; William Reeve (with Justin Martyr and Minucius Felix), 1708, repr. 1716, 1889 (with Marcus Aurelius).

———— Apology, and *De Spectaculis*. Ed. and tr. T. R. Glover (with Minucius Felix). LCL, 1931. xxviii, 446 p.

———— Prescription against Heretics. Tr. Joseph Betty (with St. Theophilus). Oxford, 1722. 313 p.

———— Concerning the Resurrection of the Flesh. Tr. Alexander Souter. London, S.P.C.K., and N.Y., Macmillan, 1922. xxiv, 205 p.

Ed. and tr. Ernest Evans as Treatise on the Resurrection. London, S.P.C.K., 1960. xxxvi, 361 p.

———— On The Testimony of the Soul and On the "Prescription" of Heretics. Tr. T. Herbert Bindley. London, S.P.C.K., and N.Y., Gorham, 1914. 96 p.

———— Tract on Prayer. Ed. and tr. Ernest Evans. London, S.P.C.K., 1953. xx, 69 p.

———— Treatise against Hermogenes. Tr. J. H. Waszink, in Ancient Christian Writers, v. 24, 1956. vi, 178 p.

———— Treatise on the Incarnation. Ed. and tr. Ernest Evans. London, S.P.C.K., 1956. xliii, 197 p.

———— Treatises on Marriage and Remarriage. Tr. William P. LeSaint, in Ancient Christian Writers, v. 13, 1951. 203 p.

———— Treatises on Penance (*De poenitentia, De pudicitia*). Tr. William P. LeSaint, in Ancient Christian Writers, v. 28, 1959. vi, 330 p.

———— Treatises Concerning Prayer, Concerning Baptism. Tr. Alexander Souter. London, S.P.C.K., and N.Y., Macmillan, 1919. 75 p.

VALERIAN, ST., Bishop of Cemele (d. A.D. c. 460). Homilies. Tr. George E. Ganss (with Peter Chrysologus), in Fathers of the Church, v. 17, 1953.

MEDIEVAL LATIN LITERATURE
A.D. 450-1450

Richard W. Emery

BACKGROUND

WITH ADDITIONS BY CHARLES R. DAHLBERG

CAMBRIDGE MEDIEVAL HISTORY. Cambridge Univ. Pr. and N.Y., Macmillan, 1911–36, 8 v.

DEANESLEY, MARGARET. History of the Medieval Church, 590–1500. London, Methuen, 1925. viii, 280 p. Repr. to 7th ed., 1951.

DILL, SIR SAMUEL. Roman Society in the Last Century of the Roman Empire. 2d ed. rev. London, Macmillan, 1899, and N.Y., 1906. xxviii, 459 p. Repr. N.Y., Meridian Books, 1958, and London, Mayflower, 1959.
——————— Roman Society in Gaul in the Merovingian Age. London and N.Y., Macmillan, 1926. xiii, 566 p.

GIBBON, EDWARD. The Decline and Fall of the Roman Empire. London, 1776–88. 6 v. Repr. 1783–90, 6 v. Many reprs., esp. that ed. J. B. Bury, London, 1896–1900, 7 v. et seq. in Methuen's Standard Library; also repr. WC, 1903–06, 7 v.; in EL, 1910, repr. 1954, 6 v.; in ML, and London, John Lane, 1932, 2 v.; in London, Penguin, 1937, 2 v.; in N.Y., Heritage, 1946, 3 v. Abridged by D. M. Low, London, Chatto, 1960, 924 p.; by Moses Hadas, N.Y., Putnam, 1962, xxi, 320 p.; by Jacob Sloan, N.Y., Collier Books, 1962, 2 v.; by anon., N.Y., Twayne, 1963, xxxviii, 456 p.

GILSON, ETIENNE. History of Christian Philosophy in the Middle Ages. N.Y., Random House, and London, Sheed, 1955. 829 p.

HASKINS, CHARLES H. The Renaissance of the Twelfth Century. Cambridge, Mass., Harvard Univ. Pr., 1927. Repr. N.Y., Meridian Books, 1962. 437 p.

LAISTNER, M. L. W. Thought and Letters in Western Europe A.D. 500 to 900. N.Y., Dial Pr., 1931. 354 p. Repr. Ithaca, N.Y., Cornell Univ. Pr., and London, Methuen, 1957. 416 p.

THE LEGACY OF THE MIDDLE AGES. Ed. C. G. Crump. London and N.Y., Oxford Univ. Pr., 1926. xii, 550 p. Repr. 1938.

LOT, FERDINAND. The End of the Ancient World and the Beginning of the Middle Ages. Tr. from the French by Philip and Mariette Leon. London, Routledge, and N.Y., Knopf, 1931. xxvi, 454 p. Repr. N.Y., Barnes and Noble, 1953; N.Y., Harper and Row, 1961, paper.

RAND, EDWARD K. Founders of the Middle Ages. Cambridge, Mass., Harvard Univ. Pr., and London, Oxford Univ. Pr., 1928. xi, 365 p. Repr. N.Y., Dover, and London, Mayflower, 1958, paper.

RASHDALL, HASTINGS. The Universities of Europe in the Middle Ages. 2d ed., F. M. Powicke and A. B. Emden. London and N.Y., Oxford Univ. Pr., 1936. 3 v.

SARTON, GEORGE. An Introduction to the History of Science. Baltimore, Williams and Wilkins, 1931, 2 v. Repr. with v. 3, Baltimore, the same, and London, Baillière, 1945–48.

    V. 2 and 3 cover the Middle Ages to 1400; bio-bibliographical.

TAYLOR, HENRY OSBORN. The Classical Heritage of the Middle Ages. N.Y., Columbia Univ. Pr., 1901. 400 p. Repr. N.Y., Macmillan, 1903; 1911; N.Y., Ungar, 1957, and London, Constable, 1958; N.Y., Harper, 1958, paper (as The Emergence of Christian Culture in the West); N.Y., Ungar, 1961, paper.

———— The Medieval Mind. N.Y. and London, Macmillan, 1911. 2 v. Repr. 1914; 1919; 1930; 1938. Repr. Cambridge, Mass., Harvard Univ. Pr., and London, Oxford Univ. Pr., 1959.

THORNDIKE, LYNN. A History of Magic and Experimental Science. N.Y., Macmillan, 1923. 2 v. (from the first to the 13th centuries A.D.) Repr. 1929. Vols. 3–4 (14th–15th centuries), N.Y., Columbia Univ. Pr., 1934. (Vols. 5–8 to the end of the 17th century).

BIBLIOGRAPHY

CHEVALIER, ULYSSE. Répertoire des sources historiques du moyen âge. [v. 1] Bio-Bibliographie (in 2 v.). Paris, 1883–88. Re-ed. rev., 1905–7; repr. N.Y., Kraus, 1960.

An index of authors

FABRICIUS, JOHANN ALBERT. Biblioteca latina mediae et infimae aetatis. Hamburg, 1734–46. 6 v. Re-ed. rev. Florence, 1858–59, 6 v. in 3; repr. Graz, Akademische Druck- und Verlagsanstalt, 1962, 6 v. in 3.

A biographical dictionary, still useful.

FARRAR, CLARISSA P., and EVANS, AUSTIN P. Bibliography of English Translations from Medieval Sources. N.Y., Columbia Univ. Pr., 1946. 534 p.

A comprehensive listing of works from 300 to 1500 A.D. which have been tr. into English: a large proportion is from the Latin.

HURTER, HUGO. Nomenclator literarius theologiae Catholicae theologos exhibens. 3d ed. Innsbruck, Libraria academica Wagneriana, 1909–13. 5 v. in 6.

Earlier eds. listed only modern authors since 1564. In this ed., v. 1 reaches 1109 A.D., v. 2, 1563 A.D.

McGUIRE, MARTIN R. P. Introduction to Mediaeval Latin Studies: A Syllabus and Bibliographical Guide. Washington, D.C., Catholic Univ. of America Pr., 1964. xvi, 152 p. paper.

PAETOW, LOUIS JOHN. A Guide to the Study of Medieval History. Re-ed. rev. N.Y., Crofts, 1931, 643 p.

An indispensable guide to historical materials, and therefore to a large part of the Latin literature.

See also *Tusculum-Lexikon* for medieval authors and works.

For current records of medieval scholarship, see *Speculum*, pub. 1926—
by the Mediaeval Academy of America; and for the scholarship of medieval
Latin, *The Year's Work in Foreign Language Studies,* 1930—, and *PMLA,*
1957—.

LITERARY STUDIES

With additions by Charles R. Dahlberg

ALLEN, PHILIP SCHUYLER. Medieval Latin Lyrics. Chicago, Univ. of
Chicago Pr., 1931. ix, 341 p.

——————— The Romanesque Lyric: Studies in Its Background and Development . . . 50–1050, with Renderings into English Verse by Howard
Mumford Jones. Chapel Hill, Univ. of North Carolina Pr., 1928.
xviii, 373 p.

AUERBACH, ERICH. Literary Language and Its Public in Late Latin Antiquity and in the Middle Ages. N.Y., Pantheon, and London, Routledge, 1965. 405 p.

BALDWIN, CHARLES SEARS. Medieval Rhetoric and Poetic. N.Y., Macmillan, 1928. xvii, 321 p.

BRITTAIN, FRED. The Medieval Latin and Romance Lyric to A.D. 1300.
Cambridge Univ. Pr., and N.Y., Macmillan, 1937. xiii, 273 p. Repr.
1951.

CURTIUS, ERNST. European Literature and the Latin Middle Ages. Tr.
from the German by Willard R. Trask. N.Y., Pantheon, and London,
Routledge, 1953. xviii, 662 p.

DRONKE, PETER. Medieval Latin and the Rise of the European Love-Lyric.
Oxford, Clarendon Pr., 1965–66. 2 v. v. 1, Problems and Interpre-
tations; v. 2, Texts [Latin].

DUCKETT, ELEANOR S. The Gateway to the Middle Ages. N.Y., Macmillan, 1938. xii, 620 p. Repr. Ann Arbor, Univ. of Mich. Pr., 1961, 3 v., paper.

Concerns writings of the 6th c.

——————— Latin Writers of the Fifth Century. N.Y., Holt, 1930. xviii, 271 p.

——————— Anglo-Saxon Saints and Scholars. N.Y. and London, Macmillan, 1947. x, 488 p.

HAYES, CARLTON J. H. An Introduction to the Sources Relating to the Germanic Invasions. N.Y., Columbia Univ. Pr., 1909. 229 p.

HÉLIN, MAURICE. A History of Medieval Latin Literature. Tr. from the French by Jean Chapman Snow. N.Y., Salloch, 1949. v, 130 p.

JACKSON, W. H. T. The Literature of the Middle Ages. N.Y., Columbia Univ. Pr., 1960. 432 p.

LEWIS, C. S. The Allegory of Love. Oxford, Clarendon Pr., and N.Y., Oxford Univ. Pr., 1936. ix, 376 p. Repr. 1938; 1958, paper.

MANITIUS, MAXIMILIAN. Geschichte der lateinischen Literatur des Mittelalters. Munich, Beck, 1911–31. 3 v. (to the year 1200)

MARROU, HENRI. Saint Augustine and his Influence Through the Ages. Tr. from the French by Patrick Hepburne-Scott. London, Longmans, and N.Y., Harper, 1957. 192 p.

RABY, F. J. E. A History of Christian-Latin Poetry from the Beginnings to the Close of the Middle Ages. Oxford, Clarendon Pr., and N.Y., Oxford Univ. Pr., 1927. 491 p.

——————— A History of Secular Latin Poetry in the Middle Ages. Oxford, Clarendon Pr., and N.Y., Oxford Univ. Pr., 1934. 2 v. Repr. 1957.

ROBERTSON, D. W., Jr. A Preface to Chaucer: Studies in Medieval Perspective. Princeton, N.J., Princeton Univ. Pr., 1962. 519 p.

WRIGHT, FREDERICK A., and SINCLAIR, T. A. A History of Later Latin Literature [A.D. 350–1700]. London, Routledge, and N.Y., Macmillan, 1931. 417 p.

YOUNG, KARL. The Drama of the Medieval Church. Oxford, Clarendon Pr., and N.Y., Oxford, Univ. Pr., 1933. 2 v.

COLLECTIONS

ANONYMOUS PILGRIMS I–VIII (11th and 12th c.). Tr. Aubrey Stewart. Palestine Pilgrims' Text Soc., v. 6, 1894. 86 p.

BEASTS AND SAINTS. Tr. Helen Waddell from Latin Sources (4th to 12th c.). London, Constable, and N.Y., Holt, 1934. xx, 151 p.

Tales and legends, e.g., of St. Jerome and the lion.

CATHAY AND THE WAY THITHER. Ed. and tr. Henry Yule. London, Hakluyt Soc., v. 36, 37, 1866. Re-ed. rev. Henri Cordier, Hakluyt Soc., series 2, v. 33, 37, 38, 41, 1913–16.

Reports mostly of the Franciscan missionaries to China in the 13th and 14th centuries, beginning with Odorico da Pordenone (q.v. below). See also The Mongol Missions, in Collections, below.

CHIEF PRE-SHAKESPEAREAN DRAMAS. Ed. Joseph Quincy Adams. Boston, Houghton Mifflin, 1924. 712 p.

Includes some fifteen Latin dialogues and short religious plays from the 10th c. on, with trs.

CONTEMPORARIES OF MARCO POLO. Ed. Manuel Komroff. N.Y., Boni, and London, Cape, 1928. xxiii, 358 p.

The journeys of John of Pian di Carpini (1245–47) and William of Rubruck (1253–55) to Mongolia; of Odorico da Pordenone to China (1318–1330); of Rabbi Benjamin of Tudela to the Jewish communities in Europe and the Near East (1160–1173). See the first three authors in separate entries below. (The fourth wrote in Hebrew.)

EARLY CHRISTIAN POETS FROM THE FOURTH TO THE SIXTH CENTURY. Ed. and tr. Otto J. Kuehnmunch. Chicago, Ill., Loyola Univ. Pr., 1929. 472 p.

Selections from Lactantius, Prudentius, Paulinus of Nola, Sedulius, and others.

(GOLIARD POETS.) Tr. verse John Addington Symonds as Wine, Women, and Song: Mediaeval Latin Students' Songs. London, Chatto, 1884. 183 p. Repr. Portland, Maine, Mosher, 1899; London, King's Classics, 1907, as Mediaeval Latin Students' Songs, frequent reprs. to 1928.

Tr. Helen Waddell in The Wandering Scholars. London, Constable, and Boston, Houghton Mifflin, 1927. xxviii, 291 p. Repr. to 7th ed., 1934. Repr. Penguin, 1954.

Tr. verse George F. Whicher as The Goliard Poets. Norfolk, Conn., New Directions, 1949. 303 p. Repr. 1965, paper.

Tr. Edwin H. Zeydel as Vagabond Verse: Secular Latin Poems of the Middle Ages. Detroit, Wayne State Univ. Pr., 1966. 307 p.

HISTORICAL DOCUMENTS OF MEDIEVAL EUROPE. See Farrar and Evans, nos. 1966–1984; of England, nos. 1356–1406; of Scotland, 3441–3448; of the Jews, see index, s.v. "Jews"; of university life, nos. 2735–2736a.

HYMNS OF THE WESTERN CHURCH. Ed. and tr. E. H. Blakeney. London, Scholartis Pr., 1927. 103 p.

24 hymns with trs. For other collections, see Farrar and Evans, "Hymns"; also A Dictionary of Hymnology, ed. John Julian (London, Murray, and N.Y., Scribner, 1892; repr. 1907, 1908, 1925).

LIVES OF THE SAINTS. Tr. J. F. Webb. Penguin, 1965. 206 p.

The Voyage of St. Brendan; Bede's Life of Cuthbert; Eddi's Life of Wilfrid, qq.v. below.

MEDIEVAL LATIN LYRICS. Ed. and tr. Helen Waddell. London, Constable, 1929. vii, 352 p. Reprs. to the 4th ed., 1933. Repr. Penguin, 1952, 1963.

MEDIEVAL LATIN POETS. Tr. verse Jack Lindsay. London, Elkin Matthews, 1934. 274 p.

MEDIEVAL LITERATURE IN TRANSLATION. Ed. Charles William Jones, various trs. N.Y., Longmans, 1950. 1004 p.

A wide range of shorter pieces and selections. The Latin works include the *Waltharius* (Walter of Aquitaine), a play of Hrotsvita, Abelard's *Historia,* qq.v. below.

MEDIEVAL NARRATIVE: A BOOK OF TRANSLATIONS. Ed. and tr. Margaret Schlauch. N.Y., Prentice-Hall, 1928. viii, 456 p.

The Latin works tr. are those of Dares Phrygius, Leo the Archpresbyter, and the *Golden Legend* (parts), qq.v. below.

THE MONGOL MISSION: Narratives and Letters of the Franciscan Missionaries in Mongolia and China in the 13th and 14th Centuries. Tr. a Nun of Stanbrook Abbey, ed. Christopher Dawson. London and N.Y., Sheed and Ward, 1955. xxxix, 246 p. Repr. (as Mission to Asia), N.Y., Harper, 1966, paper.

The journeys of John of Pian di Carpini, etc. (see *Contemporaries of Marco Polo*, above).

PALESTINE PILGRIMS' TEXT SOCIETY Publications. London, 1890–97. 14 v.

Some 30 accounts of travels to and descriptions of the Holy Land, tr. from Greek, Latin, Arabic, Old French, Old and Middle High German. The longer Latin ones are listed separately below. An earlier collection is Thomas Wright, *Early Travels in Palestine* (London, Bohn, 1848, xxxi, 517 p.): the Latin writings are those of the travelers Arculf, Willibald, Bernard the Wise, Saewulf (8th to 12th c.).

THE PASTORAL ELEGY: AN ANTHOLOGY. Ed. Thomas P. Harrison, Jr., trs. by Harry Joshua Leon. Austin, Univ. of Texas Pr., 1939. xi, 312 p.

Includes an eclogue from Paschasius Radbertus (d. c. 860), two eclogues by Petrarch, one by Boccaccio, three selections from Sannazaro (see Italian Literature, in v. III).

THE PENGUIN BOOK OF LATIN VERSE. Tr. prose Frederick Brittain. Penguin, 1962. lxvi, 381 p.

Classical, medieval, and modern. $C_{6} p^{211}$

THE POLITICAL SONGS OF ENGLAND, from the Reign of John to that of Edward II. Ed. and tr. Thomas Wright. Camden Society, v. 6, 1839. 408 p. Repr. rev. Edmund Goldsmid. Bibliotheca curiosa, Edinburgh, 1884, 4 v. in 1.

(SAINTS' LIVES.) Ancient Lives of Scottish Saints. Tr. W. M. Metcalfe. Paisley, A. Gardner, 1895. xxiii, 373 p.

For the most popular collection of saints' lives, *The Golden Legend*, see Jacopo de Varagine, in Italian Literature, Medieval, in v. III. See also *Vitae patrum*, below.

SELECTIONS FROM THE MEDIEVAL PHILOSOPHERS. Ed. Richard McKeon. N.Y., Scribner, 1929–30. 2 v. Repr. 1959, paper.

V. 1, from Augustine to Albertus Magnus; v. 2, from Roger Bacon to William Ockham.

VITTORINO DA FELTRE AND OTHER HUMANIST EDUCATORS: Essays and Versions. Tr. W. H. Woodward. Cambridge Univ. Pr., 1897. 256 p. Repr. 1905, 1912, 1921, 1964 (N.Y., Teachers College, paper).

The authors are Vergerio, Bruni, Aeneas Silvius, Guarini, all but the last writing before A.D. 1450.

THE WESTERN FATHERS: The Lives of SS. Martin of Tours, Ambrose, Augustine of Hippo, Honoratus of Arles, and Germanus of Auxerre. Tr. Frederick Russell Hoare. London, Sheed and Ward, 1954. xxxii, 320 p.

WESTERN LITURGIES. Ed. R. C. West. London, S.P.C.K., and N.Y., Macmillan, 1938. 105 p.

See also the separate items in Farrar and Evans, nos. 2495 to 2523.

YOUNG, KARL. The Drama of the Medieval Church. See above, Literary Studies.

Includes many Latin texts and trs.

INDIVIDUAL AUTHORS AND WORKS

EARLY MEDIEVAL PERIOD: A.D. 450 TO 1000

ADAMNAN, ST. (d. 704). The Pilgrimage of Arculfus in the Holy Land (about the year 670). Tr. James Rose Macpherson. Palestine Pilgrims' Text Society 3 (1895). 91 p.

An abridged version is in Thomas Wright, *Early Travels in Palestine* (1848).

————— Vita S. Columbae. Prophecies, Miracles, and Visions of St. Columba. Tr. J. T. Fowler. London, Oxford Univ. Pr., 1895. 140 p.

Tr. Wentworth Huyshe. [Dublin,] Educational Co. of Ireland, [1905]. lix, 255 p. Repr. New Universal Library, London, Routledge, and N.Y., Dutton, 1906; 1908; 1922.

Called the best tr.

Other trs. 1874, 1875, and in *Ancient Lives of Scottish Saints* (see Collections, above).

AETHELWEARD (10th c.). The Chronicle [to the year 975]. Ed. and tr. A. Campbell. London, Nelson, 1962. 187 p. (parallel texts)

Earlier trs. J. A. Giles in *Six Old English Chronicles,* 1848 *et seq.*; and Joseph Stevenson, *Church Historians of England,* v. II, 1854.

ALCUIN (d. 804). The Rhetoric of Alcuin and Charlemagne. Ed. and tr. Wilbur Samuel Howell. Princeton, N.J., Princeton Univ. Pr., 1941. 175 p. (parallel texts)

See Eleanor S. Duckett, *Alcuin, Friend of Charlemagne,* N.Y., Macmillan, 1951, and London, Macmillan, 1952, xii, 337 p.

ALDHELM, ST. (640?–709). The Riddles of Aldhelm. Ed. and tr. verse James Hall Pitman. New Haven, Yale Univ. Pr., 1925. (10), vii, 85 p. (parallel texts)

ALEXANDER THE GREAT, The Legend of. See Leo, Archipresbyter, below.

ANTONINUS MARTYR (6th c.). Of the Holy Places (c. A.D. 560–570). Tr. Aubrey Stewart. Palestine Pilgrims' Text Society, v. 2, 1896. 44 p.

APOLLONIUS OF TYRE (6th c.) Tr. Benjamin Thorpe from the Old English version (11th c.). London, 1834. v, 92 p. (parallel texts)

Tr. (paraphrase in verse) John Gower in the *Confessio Amantis* (1390), book VIII, lines 271–2008 (from the paraphrase in Godfrey of Viterbo, *Pantheon* (12th c.)). Ed. C. G. Macaulay, in the Works. Oxford, Clarendon Pr., 1901, v. 3, p. 393–440. Re-ed., from the 1554 ed., Geoffrey Bullough, in Narrative and Dramatic Sources of Shakespeare, London, Routledge, and N.Y., Columbia Univ. Pr., 1966, v. 6, p. 375–423, the lines numbered 251–2036.

Tr. Robert Copland from the French as Kynge Apollin of Thyre. London, de Worde, 1510. Re-ed. C. J. Ashbee, London, 1870.

Tr. Laurence Twyne as The Patterne of Painefull Adventures (from the version in the *Gesta Romanorum*). London, registered for publication 1576; ed. [1594?]; re-ed. 1607; re-ed. J. Payne Collier in Shakespeare's Library, London, 1843, v. I, p. 184–257; re-ed. Geoffrey Bullough, as cited above, p. 423–82 (a source of Shakespeare's Pericles Prince of Tyre).

Tr. Charles Swan in *Gesta Romanorum*. London, Rivington, 1824. 2 v. Several reprs., not all including the Apollonius tale (no. 153); it is repr. in the Broadway Translations ed., 1924. See *Gesta,* below.

Tr. verse Raymond L. Grismer and Elizabeth Atkins from a Spanish version (13th c.). Minneapolis, Univ. of Minnesota Pr., 1936. xx, 113 p.

Tr. Paul Turner. London, Golden Cockerel Pr., 1956. 68 p.

ASSER (d. 909?). Asser's Life of King Alfred. Tr. Albert S. Cook. Boston, Mass., Ginn, 1906. 83 p.

Tr. L. C. Jane. King's Classics, London, Chatto, 1908. lix, 163 p. Repr. Medieval Library, 1924.

BEDE, THE VENERABLE, ST. (679–735). The Historical Works. Ed., in part tr., in part rev. J. A. Giles, in The Complete Works . . . in the Original Latin. London, Whittaker, 1843–44. 12 v.

V. 1 to 4 contain the trs.: v. 1, *Letters to Albinus and Egbert;* v. 2, 3, *Ecclesiastical History;* v. 4, *Lives of Saints, On the Holy Places.* Repr. separately (English only) as *The Historical Works,* London, Bohn, 1843–45, 2 v. For other reprs. of separate works, see titles below.

Tr. Joseph Stevenson, in Church Historians of England, v. 1, part 2. London, Seeleys, 1853. xlviii, p. 305–664.

———— The Explanation of the Apocalypse. Tr. Edward Marshall. Oxford and London, Parker, 1878. v, 180 p.

———— The Gospels. Tr. by Bede from Latin into Old English, and into modern English by J. B. Phillips. N.Y., Macmillan, 1953. x, 243 p.

———— The History of the Church of England. Tr. Thomas Stapleton. Antwerp, John de Laet, 1565. 192 fols. Repr. St. Omer, 1622; 1626; ed. Philip Hereford, Oxford, Blackwell, 1930, and repr. in modern spelling, London, Burns Oates, 1935. Tr. rev. J. E. King, LCL, 1930, v. 1 of The Historical Works.

Tr. as Ecclesiastical History of the English Nation by (it is supposed) John Stevens. London, Batley, 1723. 479 p. Rev. ed. J. A. Giles, London, Lumley, 1840, repr. in The Complete Works, 1843–44, v. 2, 3, see above, and repr. in The Historical Works, 1843, v. 1, see above. Many reprs., esp. London, Bohn, 1847 *et seq.*; Temple Classics, 1903; EL, 1910 *et seq.* to 1954, with The Lives.

Tr. Leo Sherley-Price as A History of the English Church and People. Penguin, 1955. 340 p.

Other trs. William Hurst, 1814; Lawrence Gidley, 1870. See Farrar and Evans, nos. 573, 575.

——————— The Life of St. Cuthbert. Tr. Joseph Stevenson. London, Burns and Oates, and N.Y., Catholic Publication Soc., 1887. xxiv, 195 p.

Tr. Bertram Colgrave, in Two Lives of Saint Cuthbert. Cambridge Univ. Pr., 1940, p. 141–307 (parallel texts)

Tr. J. F. Webb, in Lives of the Saints, 1965, p. 71–129 (see Collections, above.)

Also tr. J. A. Giles and Joseph Stevenson respectively, in The Historical Works, above.

——————— The Lives of the Abbots [of Wearmouth and Yarrow]. Tr. Peter Wilcock. Sunderland, 1818. Repr. Sunderland, Hills and Co., 1910, iii, 115 p.

Tr. J. E. King. LCL, 1930, v. 2.

Tr. also by J. A. Giles and Joseph Stevenson respectively, in the Historical Works, above.

BEGA, ST. (7th c.). The Life and Miracles of Sancta Bega. Written by a Monkish Historian. Tr. C. C. Tomlinson. Carlisle, Jefferson, 1842. 80 p.

BENEDICT, ST. (c. 480–c. 550). The Rule of St. Benedict. Tr. Abbot [F. A., later Cardinal] Gasquet. King's Classics. London, Chatto, 1909. xxviii, 130 p. Repr. Medieval Library, 1925.

Tr. W. K. Lowther Clarke. London, S.P.C.K., 1931. 107 p.

Tr. Leonard J. Doyle as Rule for Monasteries. Collegeville, Minn., St. John's Abbey Pr., 1948. 255 p.

Tr. Abbot Justin McCann. London, Burns Oates, and Westminster, Md., Newman Pr., 1952. xxiv, 214 p.

Two Old English versions of the *Rule* are extant, and also a Middle English version; Caxton published (1491) an abstract of the *holy rule of Saynte Benet* with the *Orologium sapiencie* of Heinrich Suso, q.v., below. The first separate publication in English was tr. by Bishop Richard Foxe (1516). For later trs. before 1900, see Farrar and Evans, nos. 584–589.

BOETHIUS (d. 524). The Consolation of Philosophy. Tr. King Alfred (9th c.); repr. modern English W. J. Sedgefield. Oxford, Clarendon Pr., 1900. liv, 253 p.

Tr. Geoffrey Chaucer (1377). Pub. by Caxton, 1478, and in the eds. of Chaucer's works, and notably Chaucer Soc. Pubs. 75, 76 (1886), and EETS ES 5 (1868).

Tr. John Walton (1410). Ed. Mark Science in EETS OS 170, 1927. lxviii, 380 p.

Tr. as The Comforte of Philosophye or Wysedome, by George Coluile, alias Coldewel. London, 1556. Repr. 1561; 1897 (Tudor Library, London, Nutt, xx, 138 p.)

The tr. has been called "terse" and "vigorous."

Tr. Queen Elizabeth (1593). Ed. Caroline Pemberton in EETS OS 113, 1899. (with other trs. by the Queen)

* Tr. as Five bookes of Philosophicall Comfort by I. T. London, 1609. 144 fols. Repr. rev. H. F. Stewart, LCL, 1918 (with the Theological Tractates); repr. 1962.

Called scholarly and readable.

Farrar and Evans lists also trs. of 1664, 1674, 1695, 1730, 1768, 1785, 1789, 1792, and 1897 (nos. 706, 709–716).

* Tr. W. V. Cooper. Temple Classics. London, Dent, 1902. 175 p. Repr. 1924; 1933; ML, 1943.

Called scholarly and readable.

* Tr. Richard Green. N.Y., Bobbs-Merrill, 1963. 134 p. paper.

Excellent.

————— The Theological Tractates. Tr. H. F. Stewart and E. K. Rand. LCL, 1918 (with The Consolation). xvi, 419 p. Repr. 1962.

See Howard R. Patch, *The Tradition of Boethius. A Study of His Importance in Medieval Culture.* N.Y. and London, Oxford Univ. Pr., 1935. viii, 200 p.

BONIFACE, ST. (680–755). The Letters of St. Boniface. Tr. Ephraim Emerton. CURC. N.Y., Columbia Univ. Pr., 1940. 204 p.

BRENDAN, ST. Brendaniana. St. Brendan the Voyager in Story and Legend. Ed. Rev. Denis O'Donoghue. Dublin, Browne and Nolan, 1893. xxviii, 399 p.

Includes the Voyage (*Navigatio*, 9th c.) from the Latin, tr. only; tr. of part of a Latin life; etc.

———— The Voyage of St. Brendan. Tr. J. F. Webb, in Lives of the Saints. Penguin, 1965, p. 31–68.

The Middle English life of Saint Brendan, ed. Thomas Wright in Percy Society, v. 14, 1844, seems to have been tr. from a collection of saints' lives like *The Golden Legend*; this seems also to be true of the *Lyfe of saynt Brandon* printed by de Worde [1520?], repr. in the Wright ed, *ibid.*

CAESARIUS, ST., Bishop of Arles (c. 470–543). The Rule for Nuns. Tr. Maria Caritas McCarthy. Washington, D.C., Catholic Univ. of Amer. Pr., 1960. viii, 230 p.

———— Sermons. Tr. Sister Mary Magdelene Mueller. N.Y., Fathers of the Church v. 31, 47, 1956–64.

CASSIODORUS SENATOR (c. 487–c. 580). An Introduction to Divine and Human Readings. Tr. Leslie Webber Jones. CURC. N.Y., Columbia Univ. Pr. 1946. 233 p.

———— The Letters of Cassiodorus. A Condensed Version of the *Variae epistolae* by Thomas Hodgkin. London, Frowde, 1886. xxviii, 560 p.

CHARLEMAGNE, LIVES OF. See Einhard; Poeta Saxo; Turpin; also *Gueno's Treason.*

CIARAN, ST. (6th c.) The Latin and Irish Lives of Ciaran. Tr. R. A. Stewart Macalister. London, S.P.C.K., and N.Y., Macmillan, 1921. 190 p.

Trs. of one Irish and three Latin lives.

COLUMBA, ST. (d. c. 597). The Book of Hymns of the Ancient Church of Ireland. Ed. and tr. James Hentorn Todd. Irish Archaeological and Celtic Soc., v. 17, 23. Dublin, Univ. of Dublin Pr., 1855–69. 2 v. (parallel texts)

CUTHBERT, ST. (d. 687). Two Lives of St. Cuthbert: A Life by an Anonymous Monk of Lindisfarne, and Bede's Prose Life. Ed. and tr. Bertram
Colgrave. Cambridge Univ. Pr., 1940. xiii, 375 p. (parallel texts)

For other trs. of Bede's Life, see Bede, above.

DARES PHRYGIUS (supposed author; actually an anon. writer of the 6th
c. A.D.). The History of the Fall of Troy. Tr. Thomas Paynell as
The faythfull and true storye of the distruction of Troye. London,
1553.

Tr. Margaret Schlauch, in Medieval Narrative (see Collections, above),
p. 247–279.

Tr. R. M. Frazer, Jr., in The Trojan War: The Chronicles of Dictys of
Crete and Dares the Phrygian. Bloomington, Indiana Univ. Pr., 1966.
185 p.

A 6th c. Latin work, translating a lost Greek text of perhaps the first c. A.D.,
once ascribed to a Trojan eye-witness.

EDMUND, ST., King of East Anglia (841–870). Corolla Sancti Edmundi,
The Garland of Saint Edmund King and Martyr. Ed. and tr. Lord
Francis Hervey. London, Murray, 1907. lxiii, 672 p.

Various biographies, 11th to 15th c.

EINHARD (or EGINHARD, d. 840). The History of the Translation of
the Blessed Martyrs . . . Marcellinus and Peter. Tr. Barrett Wendell.
Cambridge, Mass., Harvard Univ. Pr., 1926. 114 p.

——————— The Letters of Einhard. Tr. Henry Preble, in Papers of the Amer.
Soc. of Church History, 2d ser., v. 1, 1913, p. 107–158.

——————— Life of the Emperor Charles the Great. Tr. William Glaister. London, Bell, 1877. vi, 100 p.

Tr. Samuel Epes Turner. N.Y., Harper, 1880. 82 p. Repr. Cincinnati,
Ohio, [189–?]; Ann Arbor, Univ. of Michigan Pr., 1960, 74 p. paper.

Tr. A. J. Grant, in Early Lives of Charlemagne by Eginhard and the
Monk of St. Gall. King's Classics. London, Moring, 1905. xxix,
179 p. Repr. 1907; repr. 1892, Medieval Library; repr. 1926, New
Medieval Library.

EKKEHARD [I] of St. Gall (fl. 910). Walter of Aquitaine (*Waltharius*). Tr. prose F. P. Magoun, Jr., and H. M. Smyser, in Walter of Aquitaine: Materials for the Study of his Legend. New London, Connecticut College Monographs 4, 1930, p. 3–37.

Part tr. verse Charles W. Jones, in Medieval Literature in Translation (see Collections, above), 1950, p. 193–208.

ENNODIUS, MAGUS FELIX, ST., Bishop of Pavia (474–521). The Life of Saint Epiphanius. Tr. Sister Genevieve Marie Cook. Washington, D.C., Catholic Univ. of Amer. Pr., 1942. xvii, 262 p. Repr. in Fathers of the Church, v. 15, 1952.

EUGIPPIUS (fl. 511). The Life of Saint Severinus. Tr. George W. Robinson. Cambridge, Mass., Harvard Univ. Pr., 1914. 141 p.

Tr. Ludwig Bieler and Ludmilla Krestan. Fathers of the Church, v. 55, 1966. 139 p.

FASTIDIUS (5th c.). The Works. Ed. and tr. R. S. T. Haslehurst. London, Society of SS. Peter and Paul, 1927. li, 317 p.

FELIX. (fl. 730) Life of Saint Guthlac. Tr. Bertram Colgrave. Cambridge, Univ. Pr., 1956. xv, 205 p.

GILDAS (6th c.). "The Works of Gildas, Surnamed the Wise." (The *De excidio Britanniae*.) In the Works of Gildas and Nennius. Tr. J. A. Giles. London, Bohn, 1841. 102 p. Repr. in J. A. Giles, Six Old English Chronicles, 1848; repr. 1872; 1891; 1900. Repr. as Old English Chronicles, London, Bell, 1906; 1908; 1910; 1912.

GREGORY, ST., THE GREAT, Pope (c. 540–604). The Book of Pastoral Rule, and Selected Epistles. Tr. Rev. James Barmby. Nicene Fathers, ser. 2, v. 12, 13, 1895–98.

Tr. of the Pastoral Care by King Alfred (9th c.), retr. modern English, ed. Henry Sweet. EETS OS 45, 50, 1871–72.

Tr. as S. Gregory on the Pastoral Charge, by Rev. H. R. Bramley. Oxford, Parker, 1874. xvi, 405 p.

Tr., as Pastoral Care, by Henry Davis. Westminster, Md., Newman Pr. 1950, and London, Longmans, 1952. 281 p.

————— The Dialogues. Tr. P.W., Paris, 1608. Repr. ed. Henry James Coleridge, London, Burns and Oates, 1874. Repr. ed. Edmund G. Gardner, London, P. L. Warner, 1911. Also partial reprs. Also partial retrs., esp. of the Life of S. Benedict, from bk. 2.

Tr. Odo J. Zimmerman. Fathers of the Church, v. 39, 1959. xvi, 287 p.

————— Morals on the Book of Job. Tr. J. Bliss. Library of the Fathers, v. 18, 21, 23, 31: 1844–50.

GREGORY VII, ST., Pope (d. 1085). The Correspondence of Pope Gregory VII. Selected Letters from the Registrum. Tr. Ephraim Emerton. CURC. N.Y., Columbia Univ. Pr., 1932. xxxi, 212 p.

GREGORY, ST., Bishop of Tours (538–94). The History of the Franks by Gregory of Tours. Tr. O. M. Dalton. Oxford, Clarendon Pr., 1927. 2 v.

Partial tr. Ernest Brehaut. CURC. N.Y., Columbia Univ. Pr., 1916. xxv, 284 p.

————— Selections from the Minor Works. Tr. William Coffman McDermott. Philadelphia, Univ. of Pennsylvania Pr., and London, Oxford Univ. Pr., 1950. xi, 109 p.

HROTSVIT OF GANDERSHEIM (10th c.). The Non-dramatic Works of Hvrosvitha. Ed. and tr. Sister M. Gonsalva Wiegand. St. Louis, Mo., Herder, 1936. xxiv, 273 p.

————— The Plays of Roswitha. Tr. Christopher St. John (pseud.) with intro. Cardinal Gasquet. Medieval Library. London, Chatto, 1923. xxxv, 160 p.

One play, *Paphnutius,* repr. Charles W. Jones, in Medieval Literature in Translation, p. 211–227 (see Collections, above).

Tr. H. J. W. Tillyard. London, Faith Pr., 1923. 123 p.

————— Abraham. Gallicanus. Tr. John Heard. In Poet Lore, 42 (1933–35), 291–328.

————— Abraham. Tr. Richard S. Lambert. Wembley Hill, Stanton Pr., 1922. 37 p.

——————— Callimachus. Tr. the same. *Ibid.*, 1923. 35 p.

——————— Dulcitius. Tr. Arthur F. McCann. Elmira, N.Y., pr. pr., 1916. 16 p.

——————— *Liber Tertius*. Ed. and tr. Sister Mary Bernadine Bergman. Covington, Ky., Sisters of St. Benedict, 1943. 178 p.

The *Gesta Ottonis* and the *Primordia coenobii gandersheimensis*.

ISIDORE, BISHOP OF SEVILLE (d. 636). An Encyclopedist of the Dark Ages, Isidore of Seville. By Ernest Brehaut. CURC. N.Y., Columbia Univ. Pr., 1912. 275 p.

Includes trs. of parts of the *Etymologiae*.

——————— History of the Kings of the Goths, Vandals, and Suevi. Tr. Guido Donini and Gordon B. Ford, Jr. Leiden, Brill, 1966. viii, 46 p. paper.

JORDANES (6th c.). Jordanes, The Origin and Deeds of the Goths. Tr. Charles C. Mierow. Princeton, N.J., Princeton Univ. Pr., 1908. 100 p. Repr. rev. 1915; N.Y., Barnes and Noble, 1962.

JUSTINIAN I, EMPEROR (483–565). "The Institutes." Tr. Robert Warden Lee in The Elements of Roman Law. London, Sweet and Maxwell, 1949. xxviii, 489 p. Repr. 3d ed. 1952.

LEO, Archpriest of Naples (fl. 950). The Legend of Alexander the Great (*Historia de preliis Alexandri*). Tr. (books 1, 3) Margaret Schlauch, in Medieval Narrative (see Collections, above), 1928, p. 285–331.

A Latin version of the Greek pseudo-Callisthenes, *The Life of Alexander of Macedon* (c. A.D. 200, see Callisthenes, in Greek Literature, Hellenistic). Middle English adaptations of Leo are the *Wars of Alexander* (15th c., alliterative verse, ed. W. W. Skeat, EETS ES 47, 1886, xxiv, 478 p.), and the prose *Lyfe of Alexander* (Thornton Ms., c. 1440, ed. J. S. Westlake, EETS OS 143, 1911, 115 p.).

LEO I, ST., THE GREAT, Pope (fl. 429–461). The Letters. Tr. Edmund Hunt. Fathers of the Church, v. 34, 1957. 312 p. Repr. 1963.

——————— The Letters and Sermons. Tr. Charles Lett Feltoe. Nicene Fathers, 2d ser., v. 12, 1895. xv, 216 p.

——————— The Tome. Ed. and tr. E. H. Blakeney. London, S.P.C.K., and N.Y., Macmillan, 1923. 46 p.

LIBER PONTIFICALIS. The Book of the Popes. I: To the Pontificate of Gregory I. Tr. Louise Ropes Loomis. CURC. N.Y., Columbia Univ. Pr., 1916. xxii, 169 p.

LITURGY AND RITUAL. See Western Liturgies, in Collections, above.

LIUDPRAND, BISHOP OF CREMONA (d. c. 972). The Works. Tr. F. A. Wright. Broadway Medieval Library. London, Routledge, 1930. 287 p.

LUXORIUS (fl. 496–534). Luxorius. A Latin Poet Among the Vandals. Ed. and tr. Morris Rosenblum. N.Y., Columbia Univ. Pr., 1961. 310 p.

NENNIUS (9th c.). The *Historia Britonum*. Ed. and tr. Rev. W. Gunn. London, J. and A. Arch, 1819. lvi, 187 p. Repr. J. A. Giles, in The Works of Gildas and Nennius, London, Bohn, 1841; and in Six Old English Chronicles, London, Bohn, 1841, and numerous reprs. to 1912.

Tr. A. W. Wade-Evans. London, S.P.C.K., 1938. 156 p.

OROSIUS, PAULUS (fl. c. 417). Seven Books of History Against the Pagans. The Apology of Paulus Orosius. Tr. Irving Woodworth Raymond. CURC. N.Y., Columbia Univ. Pr., 1936. 436 p.

Tr. Roy J. Deferrari. Fathers of the Church, v. 50, 1964. xxi, 422 p.

PATRICK, ST. (?389–461). The Writings. Tr. Rev. George Thomas Stokes and Rev. Charles H. H. Wright, London, Nisbet, and Dublin, Hodges Figgis, 1887. 72 p.

Tr. Most Rev. John Healy in The Life and Writings. Dublin, Gill, 1905. xi, 754 p.

Tr. Newport J. D. White in Writings and Life. London, S.P.C.K., and N.Y., Macmillan, 1920 v, 142 p. The Writings repr. 1932.

Other trs. in Farrar and Evans, nos. 3073–3084.

PATRICK'S PURGATORY, ST. See Later Medieval Period, below.

PAULUS DIACONUS (d. 797?). History of the Longobards by Paul the Deacon. Tr. William Dudley Foulke. N.Y., Longmans, 1907. xliii, 437 p.

POETA SAXO. The Saxon Poet's Life of Charles the Great. Tr. Mary E. McKinney. N.Y., Pageant Pr., 1956. vii, 118 p.

RATRAMNUS, monk of Corbie (d. c. 868). The Book of Ratram, the Priest and Monk of Corbie commonly called Bertram, on the Body and Blood of the Lord . . . [and] the Saxon Homily of Aelfric. Oxford, Parker, 1838. 69, 52 p. (parallel texts). Preface signed H. W. and W. C. C.

Tr. W. F. Taylor. London, Simpkin Marshall, 1880. 67 p.

Eight eds. are recorded of earlier trs. 1548 to 1686.

RIMBERT, ST. (d. 888). Anskar, the Apostle of the North, 801–865. Tr. Charles H. Robinson. London, S.P.G., 1921. 139 p.

SALVIAN (5th c.). Writings (The Governance of God; Letters; The Four Books of Timothy to the Church). Tr. Jeremiah F. O'Sullivan. Fathers of the Church, v. 3, 1947. iv, 398 p.

————— On the Government of God: A Treatise Wherein Are Shown the Ways of God toward his Creatures. Tr. Eva M. Sanford. CURC. N.Y., Columbia Univ. Pr., 1930. 241 p.

An earlier tr. by R. T., 1700.

————— *Quis dives salus*, how a rich man may be saved (*Adversus avaritiam.*) Tr. N. T. [Douai?], 1618. (16), 314, (5) p.

SEDULIUS, COELIUS (5th c.) The Easter Song: Being the First Epic of Christendom. Tr. verse George Sigerson. Dublin, 1922. 269 p.

The *Carmen Paschale*, based on the four Gospels.

SIDONIUS, C. Sollius Modestus Apollinaris (d. c. 489). The Letters of Sidonius. Tr. O. M. Dalton. Oxford, Clarendon Pr., 1915. 2 v.

————— Sidonius, Poems and Letters. Tr. W. B. Anderson. LCL, 1936. lxxv, 483 p.

SOLOMON, THE DIALOGUES OF (*Contradictio Salomonis,* 5th c., not extant). Tr. anon. into Old English (9th or 10th c.), and retr. into modern English by John Mitchell Kemble as The Dialogue of Solomon and Saturnus. London, Aelfric Soc., 1848. v, 326 p. (parallel Old English and modern English texts).

The Old English texts are fragmentary, two in verse and one in prose. Since the Latin original is lost, it is not known if the tr. was made from the 5th c. text or from later versions. For the development, which may go back to the Greek *Testament of Solomon* (? 4th c., see Byzantine Literature), see the intro. by Robert J. Menner to his ed. of the Old English: *The Poetical Dialogues of Solomon and Saturn* (N.Y., Modern Language Association, and London, Oxford Univ. Pr., 1941).

——————— The Dialogue of Solomon and Marculphus. Tr. anon. from an unidentified Latin prose version (presumably 15th c.), as The Dialogue or Communing between the wise King Solomon and Marcolfus. Antwerp, Leeu, 1492. Repr. facs. ed. E. Gordon Duff, London, Lawrence and Bullen, 1892, xxvi, [36], 46 p.

The 12th c. Latin versions of the Solomon dialogues turned toward the satirical, and invented a new interlocutor, Marcolphus. No Latin text has survived, but early French versions (12th c.) are extant. This item was tr. from a later Latin version, presumably a retr. from the French.

——————— The sayinges or prouerbes of King Salomon. Tr. anon. from a late French version (unidentified) of different content, deriving from *La Disputacyon de Marcoux et de Salamon.* London, Pynson, 1530.

SYLVESTER II, POPE (fl. 999–1003). The Letters of Gerbert, with his Papal Privileges as Sylvester II. Tr. Harriet P. Lattin. CURC. N.Y., Columbia Univ. Pr., 1961. x, 412 p.

TURPIN, ARCHBISHOP (fl. 753–800). Pseudo-author of the *Historia de Carolo magno,* now thought to have been written (anon.) c. 1150. See Charlemagne entry in next section (Later Medieval Period).

VINCENT DE LÉRINS, ST. (5th c.). The Commonitory . . . against the Profane Novelties of All Heresies. Tr. C. A. Heurtley, in Nicene Fathers, 2d ser., v. 11, 1894, p. 123–159.

Tr. T. Herbert Bindley. London, S.P.C.K., 1914. 128 p.

Tr. Rudolph E. Morris, in Fathers of the Church, v. 7, 1949.

Some ten earlier trs. of the Commonitory or Golden Book go back to 1554: see Farrar and Evans, nos. 3768–3773.

VISIGOTHS, LAWS OF. The Visigothic Code (*Forum judicum*). Ed. and tr. S. P. Scott. Boston, Boston Book Co., 1910. lxxxiv, 419 p.

VITAE PATRUM. The Desert Fathers. Tr. Helen Waddell. London, Constable, and N.Y., Holt, 1936. ix, 312 p. Repr. Ann Arbor, Univ. of Michigan Pr., 1957, 209 p. paper.

Selections tr. from the Rosweyde ed. (1628), going back to St. Jerome's lives. An earlier tr. from the French was made by William Caxton, pub. 1495.

WALAHFRID STRABO (?808–849). *Hortulus,* or The Little Garden. A Ninth Century Poem. Tr. verse Richard Stanton Lambert. [Wembley Hill,] Stanton Pr., [1924]. 38 p.

———— The Life of St. Gall. Tr. Maud Joynt. London, S.P.C.K., and N.Y., Macmillan, 1927. 168 p.

WALTER OF AQUITAINE (*Waltharius*). See Ekkehard, above.

WIDUKIND (d. c. 1004). Widukind the Monk of Corvey, Relating the Deeds of the Saxons [919–973]. Tr. Claude J. Dolan. N. P. [England], n. pr., 1957. 175 p.

WILLIBALD (8th c.). The Life of Saint Boniface. Tr. George W. Robinson. Cambridge, Mass., Harvard Univ. Pr., 1916. 114 p.

WILLIBALD, ST. (8th c.) The *Hodoeporicon*, Tr. W. R. Brownlow. London, Palestine Pilgrims' Text Society 3, 1895, x, 58 p.

The journey to Palestine 754 A.D., together with a condensed tr. of the rest of the autobiography. Another tr. of the travel narrative in *Early Travels in Palestine:* see Collections, above.

LATER MEDIEVAL PERIOD: A.D. 1000 TO 1450

ABÉLARD, PIERRE (1079–1142). Abailard's Ethics. Tr. J. Ramsey Mc-Callum. Oxford, Blackwell, and N.Y., P. Smith, 1935. x, 93 p.

———— *Historia Calamitatum*, the Story of My Misfortunes. An Autobiography. Tr. Henry Adams Bellows, intro. Ralph Adams Cram. St. Paul, Minn., T. A. Boyd, 1922. xxi, 96 p. Repr. Glencoe, Ill., Free Pr., 1958.

Tr. J. T. Muckle as The Story of Abelard's Adversities, intro. Etienne Gilson. Toronto, Pontifical Institute, 1954. 70 p.

———— The Letters of Abelard and Heloise. Tr. C. K. Scott Moncrief. London. G. Chapman, 1925. 211 p. Repr. N.Y., Knopf, 1926; 1933; 1942.

The *Historia Calamitatum* is included. Called a "beautiful translation."

ADAM (12th c. liturgical play). Tr. Edward Noble Stone. Univ. Washington Pubns. Lang. and Lit. 4, p. 159–193. Seattle, Univ. of Washington Pr., 1926. Repr. 1928.

See also Antichristus, below.

ADAM OF BREMEN (fl. 1069–1076). History of the Archbishops of Hamburg-Bremen. Tr. Francis J. Tschan. CURC. N.Y., Columbia Univ. Pr., and London, Oxford Univ. Pr., 1959. xxxiv, 253 p.

ADAM OF ST. VICTOR (d. 1192). The Liturgical Poetry. Tr. in the original metres by Digby S. Wrangham. London, Kegan Paul, 1881. 3 v.

ADAM OF USK (fl. 1400). *Chronicon Adae de Usk*, A.D. 1377–1404. Ed. and tr. Edward Maunde Thompson. London, Murray, 1876. 243 p. 2d ed., with continuation to 1421 A.D., London, Frowde, 1904.

ADELARD OF BATH (12th c.). *Quaestiones Naturales*. Tr. Hermann Gollancz. In *Dodi ve-nechdi*, The Work of Berchya Hanakden. London, Milford, 1920, pp. 85–161.

AEGIDIUS OF ASSISI (d. 1262). The Golden Sayings of the Blessed Brother Giles of Assisi. Ed. and tr. Rev. Paschal Robinson. Philadelphia, Dolphin Pr., 1907. lxiii, 141 p.

See also Italian Literature, Medieval, s.v. St. Francis, in v. III.

AEGIDIUS ROMANUS (c. 1243–1316). *Errores philosophorum.* Ed. Joseph Koch, tr. John O. Riedl. Milwaukee, Wis., Marquette Univ. Pr., 1944. lix, 67 p. (parallel texts)

———— Theorems on Existence and Essence. Tr. Michael V. Murray, S. J. Milwaukee, Marquette Univ. Pr., 1952. xiv, 112 p.

———— A tr. of the *De regimine principum* was made by John de Trevisa c. 1400: it remains in Ms in the Bodleian Library, Oxford (Ms. Digby 233).

AELRED OF RIEVAULX, ST. (1109–1166). Life of S. Ninian. Ed. and tr. Alexander Penrose Forbes. Historians of Scotland, 5. Edinburgh, Edmonston and Douglas, 1874. 9, cv, 380 p.

———— The Mirror of Charity. Tr. Geoffrey Webb and Adrian Walker. London, Mowbray, 1962. xv, 159 p.

———— The Pastoral Prayer. Tr. a Religious of C.S.M.V. Westminster, Md., Dacre Pr., 1955. 32 p.

Cf. *The Life of Ailred of Rievaulx,* by Walter Daniel. Tr. F. M. Powicke. London, Nelson, 1950. cii, 180 p. (parallel texts)

ALANUS DE INSULIS (d. 1202). The Anticlaudian of Alain de Lille. Tr. William Hafner Cornog. Univ. of Pennsylvania dissertation, Philadelphia, 1935. 192 p.

————The Complaint of Nature. Tr. Douglas M. Moffat. Yale Studies in English 36. N.Y., Holt, 1908. 95 p.

ALBERTUS MAGNUS, ST. (?1193–1280). *Libellus de Alchimia.* Tr. Sister Virginia Heines, intro. Pearl Kibre. Berkeley, Univ. of California Pr. and London, Cambridge Univ. Pr., 1958. xxii, 79 p.

———— The Paradise of the Soule. Tr. Thomas Everard, S.J. [St. Omer,] 1617. 372 p.

Tr. N. N. London, Brooks, 1682. 240 p. Repr. ed. Raymund Devas, N.Y., Kenedy, 1921.

——————— Of the Union with God. Tr. Thomas Everard, S.J., in The Paradise of the Soule. [St. Omer,] 1617.

Tr., as A Treatise of Adhering to God, by Sir Kenelme Digby. London, Herringman, 1654. 139 p.

Tr., as Of Cleaving to God, by Elisabeth Stopp. London, Mowbray, 1954. 52 p.

Three other trs. 1692, [1850?], 1911.

ALFONSO, PEDRO (1062–1110). Peter Alphonso's *Disciplina clericalis*. Tr. William Henry Hulme. Western Reserve Studies 1, no. 5. Cleveland, Ohio, Western Reserve Univ., 1919. 71 p.

ANDREAS CAPELLANUS (fl. 1170). The Art of Courtly Love. Ed. and tr. John Jay Parry. CURC. N.Y., Columbia Univ. Pr., 1941. xi, 218 p. Repr. abridged N.Y., Ungar, 1959.

ANGELA OF FOLIGNO (1248–1309). The Book of Visions and Instructions of Blessed Angela of Foligno as taken down from her own lips by Brother Arnold. Tr. by a secular priest [A. P. J. Cruikshank]. London, Thomas Richardson, 1871. xxiv, 349 p.

ANSELM, ST., of Aosta (1039–1109). *Proslogion, Monologium*, An Appendix in Behalf of the Fool by Gaunilon, and *Cur Deus homo*. Tr. Sidney Norton Deane . . . with the Opinions of Leading Philosophers . . . on the Ontological Argument. Chicago, Ill., Open Court, 1903. xxxv, 288 p. Repr. 1910; 1926; 1951; 1962 as Basic Writings, paper.

The *Cur deus homo* is in the tr. of J. G. Vose, originally pub. in *Bibliotheca Sacra*, v. XI–XII, 1854–55. Other trs. of the same work by anon., 1858; by Edward S. Prout, 1886; by R. C., 1889.

——————— Meditations and Prayers to the Holy Trinity and our Lord Jesus Christ. Tr. anon., with intro. E. B. Pusey. Oxford and London, Parker, 1856. xix, 277 p. (18 meditations, 25 prayers)

Tr. M. R., with intro. by Archbishop of Westminster. London, Burns and Oates, 1872. xvi, 294 p. (2 meditations)

———— *Proslogion,* with Gaunilon's Reply on Behalf of the Fool, and the Author's Reply. Tr. M. J. Charlesworth. Oxford, Clarendon Pr., 1965. vi, 196 p.

———— A Selection from his Letters. Tr. anon., intro. by R. C., with the *Cur deus homo.* London,, Griffith, Farran, [1889]. xxviii, 244 p. (89 letters)

ANTICHRISTUS (12th c.). Antichrist and Adam. Two Medieval Religious Dramas. Tr. Sarah F. Barrow and William H. Hulme. Cleveland, Ohio, Western Reserve Univ., 1925. 68 p.

AQUINAS, ST. THOMAS. See Thomas Aquinas.

ASIA, TRAVELERS to. See Collections (Cathay) above, and John of Pian di Carpini, Odorico of Pordenone, William of Rubruck.

AUNGERVILLE, RICHARD, known as Richard de Bury (1281–1345). *Philobiblon.* A Treatise on the Love of Books. Tr. J. B. Inglis. London, T. Rodd, 1832. 151 p. Repr. Albany, N.Y., 1861; N.Y., 1889; 1901.

Tr. and ed. Ernest C. Thomas. London, Kegan Paul, 1888, and N.Y., Lockwood, 1889. lxxxv, 259 p. Repr. King's Classics, London, Moring, 1903; repr. 1909; repr. Medieval Library, 1925.

Tr. and ed. Andrew Fleming West. N.Y., Grolier Club, 1889. 3 v. Repr. N.Y., Duschnes, 1945. 80 p.

Tr. Archer Taylor. Berkeley, Univ. of California Pr., 1948. 111 p.

BACON, ROGER (1214–94). The *Opus Majus* of Roger Bacon. Tr. Robert Belle Burke. Philadelphia, Univ. of Pennsylvania Pr., 1928. 2 v. Repr. N.Y., Russell and Russell, 1962.

For trs. of other treatises of Bacon, see Farrar and Evans, nos. 502–10.

BARTHOLOMAEUS ANGLICUS (13th c.). *De Proprietatibus Rerum.* Tr. John de Trevisa (14th c.). Westminster, 1495. Repr. 1535; 1582.

An abridged tr. ed. Robert Steele as *Medieval Lore,* London, E. Stock, 1893, 154 p. Repr. King's Classics, 1905; 1907; New Medieval Library, 1924.

BARTOLUS DE SAXOFERRATO (1314–1357). On the Conflict of Laws. Tr. Joseph Henry Beale. Cambridge, Mass., Harvard Univ. Pr., 1914. 86 p.

————— On Guelphs and Ghibellines. Tr. Ephraim Emerton in his Humanism and Tyranny, Studies in the Italian Trecento. Cambridge, Mass., Harvard Univ. Pr., 1925, p. 255–284.

————— *Tractatus de tyrannia*. Tr. the same. *Ibid.*, p. 119–154.

BEAST EPIC. See Ecbasis, below.

BERNARD OF CLAIRVAUX, ST. (1091–1153). Life and Works of St. Bernard, ed. Dom Joh. Mabillon. Tr. Samuel J. Eales. London, J. Hodges, 1889–1896. 4 v. Repr. London, Burns and Oates, n.d. 4 v.

V. 1–3 contain the Letters, 3–4 the Sermons.

————— The Letters. Tr. Bruno Scott James. Chicago, Ill., Regnery, and London, Burns, 1953. 550 p.

————— Sermons on the Canticle of Canticles. Tr. a Priest of Mount Melleray. Dublin, Browne and Nolan, [1920]. 2 v.

The same sermons were tr. in v. 4 of Life and Works, above.

————— Sermons for the Seasons and Principal Festivals of the Year. Tr. by the same. Dublin, Browne and Nolan, [1921–25]. 3 v. Repr., Westminster, Md., Carroll Pr., 1955.

Individual Works

————— St. Bernard on Consideration. Tr. George Lewis. Oxford, Clarendon Pr., 1908. 171 p.

Tr. a Priest of Mount Melleray. Dublin, Browne and Nolan, [1921]. xvi, 254 p.

————— Of Conversion, a Sermon to the Clergy. Ed. and tr. Watkin Williams. London, Burns, Oates, 1938. xiv, 102 p.

————— Life of St. Malachy of Armagh. Tr. H. J. Lawlor. London, S.P.C.K., and N.Y., Macmillan, 1920. lxvi, 183 p.

————— St. Bernard on the Love of God. Tr. Marianne Caroline and Coventry Patmore. London, Kegan Paul, 1881. 151 p. Repr. London, Burns and Oates, 1884.

Tr. as On Loving God by William Harman van Allen. Tenby, Caldey Abbey, and Milwaukee, Wisc., Morehouse, 1910. 93 p.

Ed. and tr. Edmund G. Gardner. London, Dent, and N.Y., Dutton, [1915]. 181 p.

Tr. Rev. Terence L. Connolly. London, Burns, and N.Y., Spiritual Books, 1937, xii, 259 p. Repr. Westminster, Md., Newman Pr., 1951.

Tr. a Religious of C.S.M.V. London, Mowbray, and N.Y., Morehouse-Gorham, 1950. 76 p.

Tr. as On Loving God, with Selections from Sermons on the Song of Songs, by Hugh Martin. London, S.C.M. Pr., 1959. 125 p.

———— Nativity. Tr. L. Hickey. Dublin and Chicago, Scepter, 1959. 160 p.

———— On the Song of Songs. Tr. a Religious of C.S.M.V. London, Mowbray, and N.Y., Morehouse-Gorham, 1952. 272 p.

———— Treatise Concerning Grace and Free Will. Tr. Watkin W. Williams. London, S.P.C.K., and N.Y., Macmillan, 1921. xxiii, 95 p.

———— The Twelve Degrees of Humility and Pride. Tr. Barton R. V. Mills. London, S.P.C.K., and N.Y., Macmillan, 1929. xxxv, 95 p.

Tr. as The Steps of Humility by George Bosworth Burch. Cambridge, Mass., Harvard Univ. Pr., and London, Oxford Univ. Pr., 1940. xi, 287 p. (parallel texts). Repr. Notre Dame, Ind., Univ. of Notre Dame Pr., 1963. 287 p.

Tr. as The Steps of Humility, by Geoffrey Webb and Adrian Walker. London, Mowbray, and N.Y., Morehouse-Gorham, 1957. 87 p.

———— The Story of His Life as Recorded by Certain of his Contemporaries. (*Vita Prima Bernardi*). Tr. Geoffrey Webb and Adrian Walker. London, Mowbray, and Westminster, Md., 1960. 130 p.

Many supposititious works were given early trs.: see Farrar and Evans, nos. 648–656.

BERNARD DE MORLAIX (12th c.). The Source of "Jerusalem the Golden," Together with Other Pieces. Tr. Henry Preble, intro., etc., Samuel Macauley Jackson. Chicago, Univ. of Chicago Pr., 1910. 207 p.

A prose tr. of the poem *De contemptu mundi*, of which the first part, *On the celestial country*, gave rise to the hymn; earlier trs. are listed here. The tr. first appeared in the *American Journal of Theology*, X (1906).

BESTIARIES. The Book of Beasts, from a Latin Bestiary (12th c.). Tr. T. H. White. London, Cape, 1954, and N.Y., Putnam, 1960. 296 p.

See also *Physiologus*, Byzantine, above.

BIRGITTA, ST., OF SWEDEN (c. 1302–1373, canonized 1391). The Fifteen O's. Tr. anon. Westminster, Caxton, [1491]. 22 leaves Repr. facs. ed. Stephen Ayling, London, Griffith and Farran, 1869.

Tr. anon. as The XV Oos in Englysshe with other prayers. London, Coplande, 1529.

Also tr. and pub. by English Catholics abroad, Bruges 1576 et seq.: see British Museum Catalogue.

———— The Revelations (*Revelationes Celestes*). Tr. anon. (1450–75). Ed. from Ms. William P. Cumming. EETS OS 178, 1929. xxxix, 135 p.

Tr. anon., preface by Cardinal Manning. London, T. Richardson, 1873. li, 170 p. Repr., London, Art and Book Co., 1892.

Partial tr. Dom Ernest Graf as Revelations and Prayers of St. Bridget of Sweden. London, Burns, Oates, 1928. vii, 88 p.

BOCCACCIO, GIOVANNI (1313–1375). See Italian Literature, in v. III.

BONAVENTURA, ST., CARDINAL (1221–74). A Franciscan View of the Spiritual and Religious Life, being Three Treatises from the Writings of St. Bonaventure. Tr. Dominic Devas. London, Thomas Baker, 1922. 149 p.

———— *Breviloquium*. Tr. Erwin E. Nemmers. St. Louis, Mo., Herder, 1946. xxii, 248 p.

Tr. José de Vinck. (Works, v. 2). Paterson, N.J., St. Anthony Guild, 1963. 348 p.

———— The Enkindling of Love, also called The Triple Way. Adapted by William I. Joffe. Paterson, N.J., St. Anthony Guild, 1956. 71 p.

———— On the Eternity of the World. Tr. Paul Byrne (with St. Thomas Aquinas and Siger de Brabant on the same subject). Milwaukee, Wis., Marquette Univ. Pr., 1964. xii, 117 p.

———— The Franciscan Vision. Tr. of . . . *Itinerarium mentis in Deum*, with intro. Father James [Edward O'Mahony]. London, Burns, Oates, 1937. 74 p.

Tr. as The Mind's Road to God, by George Boas. N.Y., Liberal Arts Pr., 1953. 46 p.

Ed. and tr. Philotheus Boehner. (Works, no. 2). St. Bonaventure, N.Y. St. Bonaventure Univ., 1956. 132 p.

————— Holiness of Life, Being St. Bonaventure's Treatise *De perfectione vitae ad sorores*. Tr. Laurence Costello and ed. Fr. Wilfrid. St. Louis, Mo., and London, Herder, 1923. xxxi, 103 p. Repr. 1928.

————— The Life of St. Francis. See Italian Literature, s.v. St. Francis, in v. III.

————— The Mirror of the Blessed Life of Jesus Christ (*Meditationes vitae Christi*). Tr. Nicholas Love (c. 1420). Ed. Westminster, Caxton, c. 1486, et seq. Re-ed. L. F. Powell, Oxford, 1908. Re-ed. modernized, London, Burns, Oates, 1926. xxvi, 332 p.

Tr. as Meditations on the Life of Christ, by Sister M. Emmanuel. St. Louis, Mo., and London, Herder 1934. xviii, 441 p.

Tr. (from incomplete Italian illuminated Ms. completed from the Latin) by Isa Ragusa and Rosalie B. Green. Princeton, N.J., Princeton Univ. Pr., 1961. xxxvi, 465 p.

Other trs. of this supposititious work are recorded in 1739, 1868, 1881, 1883; Farrar and Evans, nos. 732–735.

————— St. Bonaventure's *De reductione artium ad theologiam*. Ed. and tr. Sister Emma Thérèse Healy. St. Bonaventure, N.Y., St. Bonaventure College, 1939. ix, 212 p. Repr. (as Works, no. 1) 1955.

————— The Soliloquies of St. Bonaventura. And also a Bundle of Myrrh, concerning the Passion of our Savior. London, 1655. 332 p.

————— *Stimulus divini amoris*, that is, The Goade of Divine Love. Tr. B. Lewis Augustine. Douay, 1642. 591 p. Re-ed. W. A. Phillipson, London, Washbourne, 1907.

Tr. Walter Hilton (d. 1396). Ed. Clare Kirchberger. N.Y., Harper, 1953. 223 p.

Also of supposititious authorship.

————— The Virtues of a Religious Superior [*De sex alis seraphim*]: Instructions by the Seraphic Doctor. Tr. Fr. Sabinus Mollitor. St. Louis, Mo., and London, Herder, 1920. 112 p. Repr. 1921.

BRACTON, HENRY DE (d. 1268). *De legibus et consuetudinibus Angliae libri quinque*. Ed. and tr. Travers Twiss. Rolls series. London, Longmans, 1878–1883. 6 v.

BRUNI, LIONARDO, Aretino (1369–1444). See Italian Literature, in v. III.

BUONACCORSO DA MONTEMAGNO (d. 1429). The declamacion of noblesse. Tr. John Tiptoft. Westminster, Caxton, 1481. Repr. R. J. Mitchell in John Tiptoft (1427–1470). London, Longmans, 1938, p. 213–41.

From the *Controversia de nobilitate*. The dialogue was adapted in the play by Henry Medwall, *Fulgens and Lucres,* written c. 1495.

BURCHARDUS DE MONTE SION (13th c.) Burchard of Mount Sion, A.D. 1280. Tr. Aubrey Stewart. Palestine Pilgrims' Text Society 12, 1896. 136 p.

BURY, RICHARD de. See Aungerville, above.

CAESARIUS VON HEISTERBACH (c. 1180–c. 1240). The Dialogue on Miracles. Tr. H. von E. Scott and G. C. Swinton Bland, with intro. G. G. Coulton. Broadway Medieval Library. London, Routledge, 1929. 2 v.

CAPGRAVE, JOHN (1393–1464). The Book of the Illustrious Henries. Tr. Francis Charles Hingeston. London, Longmans, 1858. xxii, 285 p.

CESSOLIS, JACOBUS DE (fl. 1290). The Game and Play of the Chesse. Tr. William Caxton from a French version, pub. by Caxton, Bruges, [1475?]. Repr. Westminster, [1481?]. Repr. of 1st ed., London, Stock, 1883, lxxii, 201 p. Facs. repr. of 2d ed., London, 1855, repr. 1860.

The game moralized in political terms.

CHARLEMAGNE. History of Charles the Great and Orlando, Ascribed to Archbishop Turpin (*Historia de Carolo magno*). Tr. Thomas Rodd. London, Rodd, 1812. 2 parts in 1 v. Repr. in Ancient Spanish Ballads Relating to the Twelve Peers of France, London, 1821; repr. in Medieval Tales, ed. Henry Morley, London, Routledge, 1884, repr. 1886, 1890.

Now dated c. 1150. For the Welsh and Irish versions of the pseudo-Turpin, see Farrar and Evans, nos. 859 et seq. For the Charlemagne literature, see the Enc. Brit. article "Charlemagne Legends," by L. M. Brandin; and for translations from the French, see French Literature, in v. III.

CHRISTINA OF MARKYATE (12th c.). The Life of Christina of Markyate: A 12th Century Recluse. Ed. and tr. C. H. Talbot. Oxford, Clarendon Pr., 1959. x, 193 p.

CHRONICA BURIENSIS. The Chronicle of Bury [St. Edmunds], 1212–1301. Ed. and tr. Antonia Gransden. London, Nelson, and N.Y., Oxford Univ. Pr., 1964. 397 p. (parallel texts).

CHRONICA REGUM MANNIAE ET INSULARUM. The Chronicle of Man and the Sudreys. Tr. Dr. Goss. Manx Society, 22, 23. Douglas, Isle of Man, 1874. 2 v.

An abridgement by William Camden was tr. Richard Hakluyt and pub. in his *Principal Navigations*, v. 1, 1598.

CHRONICON ANGLO-SCOTICUM. A Scottish Chronicle known as the Chronicle of Holyrood. Ed. Marjorie Ogilvie Anderson. 3 Scottish History Society, v. 30. Edinburgh, Univ. Pr., 1938. 221 p. (parallel texts)

A.D. 1065–1187, with additions to 1356.

CHRONICON DE LANERCOST. The Chronicle of Lanercost, 1272–1345. Tr. with notes by Sir Herbert Maxwell. Glasgow, Maclehose, 1913. xxxi, 357 p. (Repr. from Scottish Historical Review, v. 6–10, 1908–13.)

CLARA OF ASSISI, ST. (d. 1253). The Life: see Thomas of Celano, below.

COLONNE, GUIDO DELLE (fl. 1270–1287). The Hystory Sege and Dystruccyon of Troye (*Historia troiana*). Tr. John Lydgate in verse paraphrase (1420). London, 1513. Re-ed. 1555. Repr. EETS ES 97, 103, 106, 126: 1906–35.

Tr. Anne Gentry Johnson. New Orleans, La., Tulane Univ. dissertation, 1964.

CRUSADES. The Crusade of Richard I, 1189–92, selected and arranged by T. A. Archer. N.Y. and London, Putnam, 1889. 395 p. Repr. 1900.

———— The First Crusade. The Accounts of Eyewitnesses and Participants, by August C. Krey. Princeton, N.J., Princeton Univ. Pr., 1921. 299 p.

For the individual authors of narratives of the crusades, see the bibliography following the article "Crusades" in Encyclopaedia Britannica; also the index of Farrar and Evans, s.v. "Crusades."

CUSA, NICHOLAS OF. See Nicholas.

DANTE ALIGHIERI (1265–1321). See Italian Literature, in v. III.

DAVID VON AUGSBURG (d. 1272). Spiritual Life and Progress, being a tr. of his *De exterioris et interioris hominis compositione*, by Dominic Devas. London, Burns, Oates, 1937. 2 v.

DIALOGUS INTER MILITEM ET CLERICUM (14th c.). Richard Fitz-Ralph's Sermon. Tr. John Trevisa (d. 1402). London, Berthelet, 1535? Repr. of this ed. and of a Ms., modernized, ed. Aaron Jenkins Perry. EETS OS 167, 1925. clvi, 116 p.

DRAMA, RELIGIOUS. Liturgical Plays Dealing with the Story of Christ. Ed. and tr. Joseph Quincy Adams, in Chief Pre-Shakespearean Dramas. Boston, Houghton Mifflin, 1924, p. 3–48. Parallel texts.

8 dramatic scenes, 9th to 12th c., including the *Herod* noted below.

———— Liturgical Plays Dealing with Miscellaneous Bible Stories and with the Legends of the Saints. Ed. and tr. ibid., p. 51–69. Parallel texts.

Anon., *Conversion of St. Paul* (13th c.); Hilarius, *The Image of St. Nicholas* (*Super Iconia Sancti Nicolai*, A.D. 1125); anon., *St. Nicholas and the Three Schoolboys* (*Tres clerici*, 12th c.); anon., *Deodatus and St. Nicholas* (*Filius Getronis*, 12th c.) all from Fleury Ms.

———— (Three Plays of St. Nicholas). Tr. verse Roger S. Loomis and Henry W. Wells, in Representative Medieval and Tudor Plays. N.Y., Sheed and Ward, 1942, p. 32–41.

St. Nicholas and the Schoolboys; *St. Nicholas and the Image,* both as in the preceding entry; also *St. Nicholas and the Virgins* (*Tres filiae,* 12th c.).

————— The Play of Daniel (the Beauvais version, c. 1150). Tr. anon., the music ed. Rembert Weakland, O.S.B., a narrator's part added by W. H. Auden. Pamphlet accompanying Decca Record DL 79402 [1958] of the performance by the N.Y. Pro Musica, director Noah Greenberg, at the Cloisters, 3 to 8 January 1958, and thereafter on television. Parallel texts.

A typescript in the New York Public Library, Theater Division, contains the English text as prepared for performance (16 p.). Credit is given in the pamphlet for help with the tr. by Jean Misrahi.

————— The Play of Herod. Ed. and tr. Joseph Quincy Adams from the 12th c. text, in Chief Pre-Shakespearean Dramas, as above, p. 32–40. Parallel texts.

Tr. W. L. Smoldon and H. C. Greene, in pamphlet accompanying Decca Record Dx SA 7187 [1964] of performance at the Cloisters by the New York Pro Musica, Noah Greenberg director. Repr. (performing ed.), N.Y. Oxford Univ. Pr., 1965, paper.

Ed. and tr. Terence Bailey as the Fleury Play of Herod. Toronto, Pontifical Institute of Medieval Studies, 1965. 72 p. Parallel texts.

See also Hrotsvit, in Early Medieval section above, for religious plays.

DUBOIS, PIERRE. The Recovery of the Holy Land. Tr. Walter I. Brandt. CURC. N.Y., Columbia Univ. Pr., 1956. 267 p.

Written 1306 to Edward I of England.

DUNS SCOTUS, JOHN (c. 1265–1308). Philosophical Writings: A Selection. Tr. Allan Wolter. London and N.Y., Nelson, 1962. xxiii, 555 p. (parallel texts). Repr. (English only), Indianapolis, Ind., Bobbs-Merrill, 1964, xxiii, 205 p.

————— A Treatise on God as First Principle (*De primo principio*). Ed. and tr. Allan B. Wolter. Chicago, Franciscan Herald Pr., 1966. xxiii, 189 p. parallel texts, paper.

DURANTIS, GULIELMUS (c. 1237–1296). The Sacred Vestments. Tr. of the third book of the *Rationale divinorum officiorum* of Durandus, with notes by Rev. T. H. Passmore. London, Sampson Low, 1899. xxix, 188 p.

———— The Symbolism of Churches and Church Ornaments. (A tr. of the first book of the *Rationale divinorum officiorum.*) Tr. John Mason Neale and Benjamin Webb. London, T. W. Green, 1843. cxxxv, 252 p. 2d ed., N.Y., Scribner, 1893; 3d ed., London, Gibbings, 1906.

EADMER (c. 1055–1124). History of Recent Events in England (*Historia novorum*). Tr. Geoffrey Bosanquet. London, Cresset Pr., 1964. 240 p.

———— Life of St. Anselm. Ed. and tr. R. W. Southern. Medieval Texts. London, Nelson, and N.Y., Oxford Univ. Pr., 1963. [388 p.]

EBBO (d. 1169). The Life of Otto, Apostle of Pomerania, 1060–1139, by Ebo and Herbordus. Tr. Charles H. Robinson. London, S.P.C.K., and N.Y., Macmillan, 1920. 193 p.

ECBASIS (c. 1046). (*Ecbasis Cuiusdam captivi per tropologiam*). The Escape of a Certain Captive Told in a Figurative Manner. Ed. and tr. Edwin H. Zeydel. Chapel Hill, Univ. of North Carolina Pr., 1964. 110 p. (parallel texts).

The earliest Latin beast-epic, anon., 11th c.

ECKHART, MEISTER (d. 1327). See German Literature, v. IV.

EDDI (fl. 669). The Life of Bishop Wilfrid by Eddius Stephanus. Ed. and tr. Bertram Colgrave. Cambridge Univ. Pr., 1927. xvii, 192 p. (parallel texts).

Tr. J. F. Webb, in Lives of the Saints, 1965, p. 133–206 (see Collections, above).

EDWARD THE CONFESSOR, King of England (d. 1066). The Life of Edward Who Rests at Westminster (*qui apud Westmonasterium requiescit*). Ed. and tr. Frank Barlow. London, Nelson, 1962. lxxxii, 81, 145 p. (parallel texts).

Ascribed to a Monk of St. Bertin. Another biography, written in Anglo-Norman c. 1163, is ed. and tr. in Rolls Series, v. 3, 1858: see French Literature, v. III.

ENGLAND, HISTORICAL DOCUMENTS CONCERNING. See Farrar and Evans, nos. 1356–1405.

FITZNEALE, RICHARD (d. 1198). The Ancient Dialogue Concerning the Exchequer. Tr. John Rayner. London, J. Worrall, 1758. 76 p.

Tr. Ernest F. Henderson, in Selected Historical Documents of the Middle Ages. London, Bell, 1892, p. 20–134. Repr. 1896.

Ed. and tr. Charles Johnson. London, Nelson, 1950, and N.Y., Oxford Univ. Pr., 1951. lxiv, 144 p.

FLORENCE OF WORCESTER (d. 1118). The Chronicle of Florence of Worcester, with the Two Continuations: . . . from the Departure of the Romans to the Reign of Edward I. Tr. Thomas Forester. London, Bohn, 1854. 512 p.

Tr. Joseph Stevenson, in The Church Historians of England, II, pt. 1. London, 1853, p. 169–404.

FORDUN, JOHN (d. 1384?). John of Fordun's Chronicle of the Scottish Nation. Tr. Felix J. H. Skene, ed. William F. Skene. Historians of Scotland, 4. Edinburgh, Edmonston and Douglas, 1872. lxxviii, 492 p.

Omits the continuation 1383–1437.

FOUCHER DE CHARTRES (?1059–1127). Chronicle of the First Crusade. Tr. Martha Evelyn McGinty. Philadelphia, Univ. of Pennsylvania Pr., 1941. 90 p.

FRANCIS OF ASSISI, ST. See Italian Literature, in v. III for his works, and the works of his followers, in both Italian and Latin.

FREDERICK II, Emperor of Germany (1194–1250). The Art of Falconry, Being the *De arte venandi cum avibus*. Ed. and tr. Casey A. Wood and F. Marjorie Fyfe. Stanford, Calif., Stanford Univ. Pr., 1943. cx, 637 p. Repr. 1961.

GALBERT DE BRUGES (fl. 1127). The Murder of Charles the Good, Count of Flanders. Tr. James B. Ross. CURC. N.Y., Columbia Univ. Pr., 1960. xiv, 352 p.

GEOFFREY OF MONMOUTH (?1110–1154). *Historia Regum Britanniae.* Tr. as The British History. Aaron Thompson. London, Bowyer, 1718. cxi, [16], 401, [53] p. Rev. ed. J. A. Giles, London, 1842; in Six Old English Chronicles, 1848, 1872, 1891, 199; in Old English Chronicles, 1960, 1908, 1912.

Tr. as History of the Kings of Britain, by Sebastian Evans. Temple Classics. London, Dent, 1904. 370 p. Repr. EL 1912 et seq., rev. Charles W. Dunn, 1958.

Tr. Lewis Thorpe. Penguin, 1966. 373 p.

——————— The Life of Merlin. Ed. and tr. John Jay Parry. Urbana, Univ. of Illinois Pr., 1925. 138 p. (parallel texts).

GERARD OF ZUTPHEN (1367–1398). The Spiritual Ascent. A Devotional Treatise, with a Life of the Author by Thomas à Kempis. Tr. J. P. Arthur [John Arthur Pott]. London, Burns and Oates, 1908. xviii, 165 p.

GERSON, JOANNES (1363–1429). "Poems by Jean Charlier de Gerson." Tr. Sebastian Evans, in The Studio: A Decade of Poems. London, 1875, p. 194–221.

——————— Practical Guide to Spiritual Prayer (*De mystica theologia practica*). Tr. Rev. H. Austin. London, Richardson, 1884. 67 p.

——————— The Snares of the Devil (*De diversis diaboli temptationibus*). Tr. by Beta. London, Richardson, 1883. 68 p.

GERTRUDE, ST., THE GREAT (1265–c. 1301). The Exercises of Saint Gertrude. Tr. anon. London, Burns and Lambert, 1863. xxx, 216 p.

——————— The Life and Revelations of Saint Gertrude, by a Religious of the Order of Poor Clares. London, Burns and Lambert, 1865. xlv, 565 p.

Includes trs. of books 2–5 of *Insinuationes divinae pietatis.*

——————— "*O Beata Trinitas.*" The Prayers of St. Gertrude and St. Mechtilde. Tr. Rev. John Gray. London, Sheed and Ward, [1927]. vii, 141 p. Repr. 1928, 1936.

GESTA FRANCORUM (c. 1100). The Deeds of the Franks and Other Pilgrims to Jerusalem. Ed. and tr. Rosalind Hill. Medieval Texts. London, Nelson, 1962. [260] p.

GESTA ROMANORUM (c. 1340). The Old English Versions of the *Gesta Romanorum*. Ed. Sir Frederic Madden. Roxburghe Club 55, 1838. xxi, 530 p. Re-ed. S. J. Herrtage. EETS ES 33, 1879.

The trs. of this story collection date from c. 1440 A.D.; they were published from c. 1510, many reprs through the 17th c.

Tr. as *Gesta Romanorum*, or Entertaining Moral Stories, by Rev. Charles Swan. London, Rivington, 1824. 2 v. Many reprs., esp. 1877 in Bohn's Antiquarian Library; 1905 in Library of Early Novelists; 1924 in Broadway Translations; 1959, N.Y., Dover Pubns.

GESTA STEPHANI, Regis Anglorum (12th c.). The Deeds of Stephen. Ed. and tr. Kenneth R. Porter. London, Nelson, and N.Y., Oxford Univ. Pr. 1955. xxxii, 159, 163 p.

GIRALDUS CAMBRENSIS (or Gerald of Barri, ?1146–?1220). The Autobiography of Giraldus Cambrensis. Tr. H. E. Butler, with intro. C. H. Williams. London, Cape, 1937. 368 p.

The narrative is put together from various writings, especially the *De rebus a se gestis* and the *De iure et statu Menevensis ecclesiae*.

————— Concerning the Instruction of Princes. Tr. Joseph Stevenson, in The Church Historians of England. London, 1858. v. 1, pt. 1, p. 131–241.

————— The Historical Works of Giraldus Cambrensis, Containing The Topography of Ireland and The History of the Conquest of Ireland. Tr. Thomas Forester. [Also] The Itinerary Through Wales, and The Description of Wales. Tr. Sir Richard Colt Hoare, rev, and ed. Thomas Wright. London, Bohn, 1863. 534 p. Repr. 1892.

For other trs. of *The Conquest*, see Farrar and Evans, nos. 1795–1796.

————— The Itinerary of Archbishop Baldwin Through Wales. Tr. Richard Colt Hoare. London, W. Miller, 1806. 2 v. Repr. EL, 1908 et seq.

Includes *The Description of Wales.*

GIRARDUS DE FRACHETO (d. 1271). Lives of the Brethren of the Order of Preachers, 1206–1259. Tr. Fr. John Placid Conway. Newcastle, Mawson, Swan, 1896. 326 p. Re-ed. Father Bede Jarrett. London, Burns, Oates, 1924.

GLANVILLE, RANULF DE (1130–90). Translation of Glanville, by John Beames. London, W. Reed, 1812. xi, 362, [17] p. Repr. with intro. J. H. Beale, Jr., Washington, D.C., 1900.

Tr. G. D. G. Hall, as The Treatise of the Laws and Customs of the Realm of England Commonly Called Glanvill. London, Nelson, for the Selden Society, 1966. 213 p. (parallel texts)

GOLDEN LEGEND. See Varagine, Jacobus de.

GOWER, JOHN (1330?–1408?). The Major Latin Works: The Voice of One Crying, The Tripartite Chronicle. Tr. Eric W. Stockton. Seattle, Univ. of Washington Pr., 1962. vii, 503 p.

GUENO'S TREASON (Carmen de proditione Guenonis, 12th c.) Tr. Arthur Livingston, Romanic Review, v. 2 (1911), p. 61–79.

A source of the Roland legend, together with Turpin, q.v.

GUIBERT DE NOGENT (1053–c. 1124). The Autobiography of Guibert Abbot of Nogent-sous-Coucy. Tr. C. C. Swinton Bland, intro. G. G. Coulton. Broadway Translations. London, Routledge, and N.Y., Dutton, 1925. 223 p.

GUIGO II, or Guigues de Chastel, General of the Carthusians (d. c. 1188). Eden's Fourfold River. An Instruction on Contemplative Life and Prayer. Ed. with intro. by a Monk of Parkminster. London, Burns and Oates, and N.Y., Benziger, 1927. xxvii, 98 p.

Much abridged from the Liber de quadripartito exercitiae cellae. Also ascribed to Adam Dryburgh (Adam the Carthusian, d. c. 1213).

————— Meditations of Guigo. Tr. John J. Jolin. Milwaukee, Wisc., Marquette Univ. Pr., 1951. 84 p.

HAROLD II, King of England (?1022–1066). *Vita Haraldi*. The Romance of the Life of Harold. Ed. from Ms. and tr. Walter de Gray Birch. London, Stock, 1885. xv, 203 p.

Written c. 1216.

HELMOLD (fl. 1168). The Chronicle of the Slavs by Helmold, Priest of Bosau. Tr. Francis Joseph Tschan. CURC. N.Y., Columbia Univ. Pr. 1935. 321 p.

HENRY OF HUNTINGDON (?1084–1155). The Chronicle of Henry of Huntingdon, to the Accession of Henry II. [also] The Acts of Stephen, King of England and Duke of Normandy. Tr. Thomas Forester. London, Bohn, 1853. xxviii, 442 p.

HENRY OF LIVONIA (Henricus Lettus, 1186–1227). The Chronicle of Henry of Livonia. Tr. James A. Brundage. Madison, Univ. of Wisconsin Pr., 1961. 262 p.

The *Origines Livoniae sacrae et civilis*.

HERBERT DE LOSINGA, Bishop of Norwich (d. 1119). The Life, Letters, and Sermons. Ed. and tr. Edward Myrick Goulburn and Henry Symonds. Oxford and London, Parker, 1878. 2 v.

HEROLT, JOHANNES (15th c.). Miracles of the Blessed Virgin Mary [by] Johannes Herolt, Called Discipulus (1435–1440). Tr. Eileen Power. Broadway Medieval Library. London, Routledge, and N.Y., Harcourt, 1928. xxv, 148 p.

HIGDEN, RANULF (d. 1364). *Polychronicon Ranulphi Higden monachi cestrensis*. Tr. John Trevisa (1387). Ed. with the original by Joseph Rawson Lumby. Rolls Series. London, Longmans, 1865–86. 9 v.

A modernized version of this tr. was printed by William Caxton 1482, with a continuation of the Chronicle to 1460: many reprs. 1495 to 1527.

HILARIUS (fl. 1125). See Drama, Religious, above.

HILDEGARDE, ST. (c. 1098–c. 1179). Life and Visions of St. Hildegarde. Tr. Francesca Maria Steele (Darley Dale), preface by Very Rev. Vincent McNabb. London, Heath, Cranton, and Ousley, 1914. 246 p.

Selected visions from her *Scivias* and her *Liber divinorum operum simplicis hominis.*

HOVEDEN, ROGER of: see Roger.

HUGH CANDIDUS (or Albus, Abbot of Peterborough, c. 1107–1156). The [Peterborough] Chronicle of Hugh Candidus. (*Coenobii Burgensis Historia.*) Tr. William Thomas Mellows (with *La Geste de Burch*). London, Oxford Univ. Pr., 1949. xxxvi, 251 p.

HUGH OF ST. VICTOR (?1097–1141). *Didascalicon.* A Medieval Guide to the Arts. Tr. Jerome Taylor. CURC. N.Y., Columbia Univ. Pr., 1961. xii, 254 p.

———— The Divine Love. (*De laude caritatis,* and *De amore sponsi ad sponsam*). Tr. A Religious of C.S.M.V. London, Mowbray, 1956. 38 p.

———— Explanation of the Rule of St. Augustine. Tr. Dom Aloysius Smith. London and Edinburgh, Sands, 1911. ix, 121 p.

An earlier tr. was published by Richard Whytford in 1525.

———— On the Sacraments of the Christian Faith. Tr. Roy J. Deferrari. Cambridge, Mass., Medieval Academy, 1951. xx, 486 p.

———— Selected Spiritual Writings. Tr. A Religious of C.S.M.V. London, Faber, and N.Y., Harper and Row, 1962. 196 p.

Noah's Ark, 1, 3; *The Soul's Three Ways* of Seeing; *Of the Nature of Love.*

———— Soliloquy on the Earnest Money of the Soul. Tr. Kevin Herbert. Milwaukee, Wis., Marquette Univ. Pr., 1956. iv, 37 p.

HUS, JAN (1371–1415). *De Ecclesia,* the Church, by John Huss. Tr. David S. Schaff. N.Y., Scribner, 1915. xlvi, 304 p.

———— Letters of John Huss Written During his Exile and Imprisonment, with Martin Luther's Preface and a General View of the Works of Huss by Emile de Bonnechose. Tr. Campbell Mackenzie. Edinburgh, William Whyte, 1846. xxiii, 220 p.

15 letters during the interdiction and exile 1410 and 1411; 50 letters at the time of the Council of Constance, with 6 written to him.

Tr. (another collection) as The Letters of John Huss, by Herbert B. Workman and R. Martin Pope. London, Hodder and Stoughton, 1904. 286 p.

> 82 letters from 1408 to 1415.

Tr. (letters and other writings) by Matthew Spinka as John Hus at the Council of Constance. CURC. N.Y., Columbia Univ. Pr. 1966. 366 p.

Includes the account by Peter Mladoňovice of Hus's trial and condemnation, with an intro. on his life and reforming activity.

THE IMITATION OF CHRIST (c. 1425, long ascribed to Thomas à Kempis). This devotional work has evoked numerous English trs., beginning with 1460 A.D., and numbering three in the 16th c., seven in the 17th c., five in the 18th c. (including John Wesley's), six in the 19th c., and thirteen in the 20th c. (six since 1949). Most of these trs. have been reprinted, so that the number of editions is large. We list only the earliest and the latest, referring the reader to the nearly complete list down to 1941 in Farrar and Evans, nos. 2108–2132.

Tr. as The Imytacion and followynge . . . of Criste, by William Atkynson (3 books) and the Lady Margaret, mother of Henry VII (book 4). London, Pynson, 1503–4. Repr. six times in the 16th c.; repr. ed. John K. Ingram, EETS ES 63, 1893. Repr. modernized EL 1910 et seq. to 1960.

Tr. as The folowynge of Cryste, by Richard Whytford. London, Wyer, [1531?]. Repr. six times in the 16th c.; modernized 1872; 1925; N.Y. and London, Harper, 1941, intro. Edward J. Klein on the 16th c. eds.; N.Y., Pocket Books, 1953; Garden City, N.Y., Image Books, also Hanover House Books, 1955 (intro. Rev. Harold C. Gardiner).

New trs. are recorded in 1568, 1580, 1633, 1639, 1657 (twice), 1698, 1722, 1735, 1737, 1749, 1763, 1851, 1860, 1874 (also in Harvard Classics, v. 7), 1881, 1889, 1896, 1900, 1907, 1908, 1910, 1927, 1940.

Tr. Edgar Daplyn. London, Latimer House, 1949, and N.Y., Sheed and Ward, 1950. 184 p. Repr. London, Sheed and Ward, 1955.

Tr. Abbot Justin McCann. London, Burns and Oates, 1952, and Westminster, Md., Newman Pr., 1953. xvi, 262 p. Repr. N.Y., New Amer. Lib., 1957, 1962, 189 p.

Tr. Lionel Digby Sherley-Price. Penguin, 1952. 214 p. Repr. 1959.

Tr. George F. Maine. London, Collins, 1957, and N.Y., Norton, 1959. 280 p.

Tr. Rev. Ronald Knox and Michael Oakley. London, Burns and Oates, 1959, and N.Y., Sheed and Ward, 1960. 217 p.

Tr. Daughters of St. Paul. [Boston,] St. Paul Eds., [1962]. 445 p.

IMPERIAL LIVES AND LETTERS of the Eleventh Century. Tr. Theodor Mommsen and K. F. Morrison. CURC. N.Y., Columbia Univ. Pr., 1962. x, 215 p.

INGULF, ABBOT OF CROYLAND (d. 1109). Ingulf's Chronicle of the Abbey of Croyland, with the Continuations by Peter of Blois and anonymous writers. Tr. Henry T. Riley. London, Bohn, 1854. 546 p. Repr. 1893.

The Chronicle is thought a forgery of the 14th c.

INNOCENT III, POPE (c. 1160–1216). "The View of Worldly Vanities." (*De contemptu mundi sive de miseria humanae conditionis*). Tr. George Gascoigne, in The Droomme of Doomes Day. London, Cawood, 1576. Repr. 1586; repr. 1910 in The Complete Works of George Gascoigne, v. 2.

Tr. as The Mirror of Mans Lyfe, by Henry Kerton. London, Bynneman, 1576. Repr. 1580, 1586.

Tr. Bernard Murchland as On the Misery of Man (with Giannozzo Manetti, q.v.). N.Y., Ungar, 1966. xxi, 103 p.

Chaucer's tr. as "the Wreched Engendring of Mankinde, As man may in pope Innocent y-finde" has not survived except for numerous echoes in the Man of Lawes Tale.

JACOBUS DE VARAGINE, ARCHBISHOP OF GENOA (d. 1298). The Golden Legend. Tr. William Caxton. Westminister, Caxton, 1483. Repr. William Morris, Kelmscott Pr., 1892, 2 v. Repr. modernized text by F. S. Ellis, Temple Classics, London, Dent, 1900, 7 v.; repr. 1914.

Tr. and adapted Granger Ryan and Helmut Ripperger. London and N.Y., Longmans, 1941. 2 v. Repr. 1948 (1 v.)

JACQUES DE VITRY, CARDINAL (d. 1240). The Exempla or Illustrative Stories from the Sermones Vulgares of Jacques de Vitry. Tr. Thomas Frederick Crane. Folk-lore Society Pub. 26. London, Nutt, 1890. cxvi, 303 p.

————— The History of Jerusalem, A.D. 1180. Tr. Aubrey Stewart. Palestine Pilgrims' Text Society 11, 1896. 128 p.

JEAN DE VENETTE (c. 1307–c. 1370). The Chronicle [1340–1368]. Tr. Jean Birdsall. CURC. N.Y., Columbia Univ. Pr., 1953, and London, Oxford Univ. Pr., 1954. 354 p.

JEANNE D'ARC (1412–1431). The Trial of Jeanne d'Arc. A Complete Translation of the Text of the Original Documents, intro. W. P. Barrett. Broadway Medieval Library. London, Routledge, 1931. 352 p. Repr. N.Y., Gotham House, 1932.

See also French Literature, in v. III.

JOCELIN DE BRAKELOND (fl. 1200). The Chronicle of Jocelin of Brakelond. A Picture of Monastic Life in the Days of Abbot Samson. Tr. Sir Ernest Clarke. King's Classics. London, Moring, 1903. xliv, 285 p.

Tr. L. C. Jane, intro. Abbot Gasquet. King's Classics. London, Chatto, 1907. xxxvi, 255 p. Repr. Medieval Library, 1922, 1925, 1931.

Tr. Harold Edgeworth Butler. London, Nelson, and N.Y., Oxford Univ. Pr., 1949. xxviii, 139, 167 p.

JOCELIN, MONK OF FURNES (12th c.). The Life and Acts of St. Patrick the Archbishop, Primate and Apostle of Ireland. Tr. Edmund L. Swift. Dublin, Hibernia Pr. Co., 1809. 266, 43 p. Repr. Philadelphia, 1823.

JOHN XXI, POPE (Peter of Spain, c. 1210–1277). The *Summulae Logicales*. Ed. and tr. Joseph P. Mullaly. Notre Dame, Indiana, Univ. of Notre Dame Pr., 1945. civ, 172 p. paper.

Tract vii, the *Logica moderna*.

————— *Tractatus Syncategorematum* and Selected Anonymous Treatises. Tr. Joseph P. Mullaly. Milwaukee, Wis., Marquette Univ. Pr., 1964. ix, 156 p.

JOHN OF GARLAND (c. 1195–c. 1272). *Morale Scolarium* of John of Garland, a Professor in the Universities of Paris and Toulouse in the Thirteenth Century. Ed. and tr. Louis John Paetow. Berkeley, Univ. of California Pr., 1927 (Memoirs of the University), p. 69–273.

JOHN OF HALIFAX (or de Sacrobosco, 13th c.) The Sphere. Ed. and tr. Lynn Thorndike, in The Sphere of Sacrobosco and its Commentators. Chicago, Univ. of Chicago Pr., 1949. 506 p.

JOHN OF HILDESHEIM (d. 1375). The Three Kings of Cologne. An Early English Translation. Ed. and tr. C. Horstmann. EETS OS 85, 1886. xxi, 312 p.

JOHN OF PIAN DE CARPINE (13th c.) The Journey of Friar John of Pian de Carpine to the Court of Kuyuk Khan, 1245–1247. Tr. William W. Rockhill, in The Journey of William of Rubruck. 2 Hakluyt Society, v. 4, 1900, p. 1–32

The *Historia Mongolorum*; the *Itinerarium* has not been tr. in full. An abridged version of these two parts of the Friar's report, from Vincent of Beauvais, *Speculum Historiale*, was ed. and tr. by Richard Hakluyt in *The Principal Navigations*, London, 1598, v. 1, p. 53–71; repr. in re-eds. of Hakluyt, and separately in *The Texts and Versions of John de Plano Carpini and William de Rubruquis by Hakluyt*, ed. C. Raymond Beazley, Hakluyt Society 1903. Repr. also in A. W. Pollard, ed., *Travels of Sir John Mandeville* (1900 et seq., including N.Y., Tudor, 1964); and in *Contemporaries of Marco Polo*, and in *The Mongol Mission*, see Collections, above.

JOHN OF SALISBURY (d. 1180). Frivolities of Courtiers and Footprints of Philosophers, being a Translation of . . . the *Policraticus* (bks. 1, 2, 3, and part of 7, 8). Tr. Joseph B. Pike. Minneapolis, Univ. of Minnesota Pr., 1938. 436 p.

Tr. as the Statesman's Book (containing the remaining books), by John Dickinson. N.Y., Knopf, 1927. xc, 410 p. Repr. N.Y., Russell, 1963.

————— Letters. V. 1, The Early Letters (1153–1161). Ed. and tr. W. J. Millor and H. E. Butler. London, Nelson, and N.Y., Oxford Univ. Pr., 1955. 595 p.

————— Memoirs of the Papal Court. Ed. and tr. Marjorie Chibnall. Medieval Texts. London, Nelson, and N.Y., Oxford Univ. Pr., 1956. 247 p.

———— The *Metalogicon*, a Twelfth-Century Defense of the Verbal and Logical Arts of the Trivium. Tr. Daniel D. McGarry. Berkeley, Univ. of California Pr., 1955. xxvii, 305 p.

JORDAN OF SAXONY (d. 1237). [Letters]. Tr. as Love Among the Saints, by Kathleen Pond. London, Bloomsbury Pub. Co., 1958. vii, 139 p.

Tr. in Gerald Vann, To Heaven with Diana. London, Collins, and N.Y., Pantheon, 1960. 160 p.

———— A New Life of St. Dominic, Founder of the Dominican Order. Tr. (via the Spanish) by Fr. Edmond Ceslas McEniry. Columbus, Ohio, Aquinas College, 1926. 168 p.

JORDANUS CATALANI (fl. 1330). *Mirabilia descripta*, the Wonders of the East, by Friar Jordanus of the Order of Preachers and Bishop of Columbum in India the Greater (c. 1330). Tr. Henry Yule. Hakluyt Society 31. London, 1862. 68 p. Repr. N.Y., Burt Franklin, 1964.

JORDANUS OF GIANO (13th c.). See Thomas of Eccleston.

LEGNANO, GIOVANNI da (d. 1383). *Tractatus de bello, de represaliis et de duello*. Tr. J. L. Brierly, and ed. Thomas Erskine Holland. Classics of International Law. Printed for the Carnegie Institution of Washington D.C. at the Oxford Univ. Pr., 1917. xxxviii, 458 p.

LEWES, THE SONG of. Ed. and tr. C. L. Kingsford. Oxford, Clarendon Pr., 1890. xxxvi, 168 p. Repr. Oxford, Univ. Faculty of Modern History, 1963.

An anonymous battle poem, 1264.

LISBON. *De expugnatione Lyxbonensi*, The Conquest of Lisbon [1147]. Ed. and tr. Charles Wendell David. CURC. N.Y., Columbia Univ. Pr., 1936. 201 p.

LOMBARD, PETER. See Peter Lombard.

LUDOLPHUS DE SAXONIA (d. 1378). The Hours of the Passion, Taken from the Life of Christ by Ludolph the Saxon. Tr. Henry J. Coleridge. London, Burns and Oates, 1887. 452 p.

LUDOLPHUS DE SUCHEM (14th c.). Description of the Holy Land and of the Way Thither, Written in the Year A.D. 1350. Tr. Aubrey Stewart. Palestine Pilgrims' Text Society 12, 1895. 142 p.

MANETTI, GIANNOZZO (1396–1459). On the Dignity of Man. Tr. (book iv) Bernard Murchland (with Innocent III, q.v.). N.Y., Ungar, 1966. xxi, 103 p.

MAP, WALTER (fl. 1200). *De nugis curialium.* Tr. Montague R. James, with historical notes by John Edward Lloyd, Ed. E. Sidney Hartland. Cymmrodorion Record Series 9. London, 1923. 283 p.

Tr. as Courtiers' Trifles, by Frederick Tupper and Marbury Bladen Ogle. London, Chatto, and N.Y., Macmillan, 1924. xxx, 363 p.

MARSIGLIO OF PADUA (1270–1342). The Defence of Peace. Tr. William Marshall. London, 1534. 140 leaves.

Tr. Alan Gewirth as The Defender of the Peace. CURC. N.Y., Columbia Univ. Pr., 1956. 450 p.

MATTHEW OF WESTMINSTER (supposititious). The Flowers of History, Especially Such as Relate to the Affairs of Britain, to the Year 1307. Tr. C. D. Yonge. London, Bohn, 1853. 2 v.

MECHTILDE OF HACKEBORN, ST. (1241–1299). *"O Beata Trinitas."* See St. Gertrude the Great, above.

———— Love of the Sacred Heart. Tr. anon. London, Oates, and N.Y., Benziger, 1922. 169 p.

———— Select Revelations of St. Mechtild, Virgin, Taken from the Five Books of Spiritual Grace. Tr. by a Secular Priest. London, Richardson, 1875. 238 p.

MIRABILIA ROMAE (12th c.). *Mirabilia urbis Romae.* The Marvels of Rome or a Picture of the Golden City. Tr. Francis Morgan Nichols. London, Ellis and Spivey, and Rome, Spithoever, 1889. xxxiii, 205 p.

NICHOLAS OF CUSA, CARDINAL (1401–1464). The Idiot, in four books. Tr. anon. London, 1650. 231 p. Repr. (typescript offset)

California State Library, Sutro Branch, Reprint Series 19, San Francisco, 1940. iii, 190 leaves.

———— Of Learned Ignorance. Tr. Fr. Germain Heron from a French version. London, Routledge, and New Haven, Yale Univ. Pr., 1954. xxviii, 174 p.

———— The sentence and mynde of . . . the donation . . . of Constantyne (*De concordantia catholica*, book 3, ch. 2). Tr. anon. in [Lorenzo Valla,] A treatyse of the donation . . . by Constantine. London, 1534.

———— Unity and Reform: Selected Writings. Tr. James B. Dolan. Notre Dame, Indiana, Univ. of Notre Dame Pr., 1962. viii, 260 p.

———— The single eye, entituled the Vision of God (*De visione Dei*). Tr. Giles Randall. London, 1646. 178 p.

Tr. Emma Gurney Salter as The Vision of God, with intro. Evelyn Underhill. London, Dent, and N.Y., Dutton, 1928. xxx, 130 p. Repr. N.Y., Ungar, 1960.

NICHOLAS OF DRESDEN (14th c.) The Old Color and the New: Selected Works Contrasting the Primitive Church and the Roman Church. Ed. and tr. Howard Kaminsky, Dean Loy Bilderbeck, Imre Boba, Patricia Rosenberg. Philadelphia, Pa., Transactions American Philosophical Society, v. 55, part 1, 1965. 93 p.

OCKHAM, WILLIAM (d. c.1349). The *De sacramento altaris*. Ed. and tr. T. Bruce Birch. Burlington, Iowa, Lutheran Literary Board, 1930. xlvii, 576 p.

———— Philosophical Writings. Tr. Philotheus Boehner. Edinburgh, Nelson, 1927. lix, 147 p. (parallel texts). Repr. (English only) Indianapolis, Ind., Bobbs-Merrill, 1964, lix, 167 p.

ODO OF DEUIL (d. c.1162). *De profectione Ludovici VII in orientem.* [On the second Crusade] Tr. Virginia G. Berry. CURC. N.Y., Columbia Univ. Pr., 1948. xliv, 154 p.

ODORICO DA PORDENONE (c. 1286–1331). The Journal of Friar Odoric (to China 1318). Ed. and tr. Richard Hakluyt in Principal Navigations, II, 1599, p. 39–67. Repr. in later eds. of Hakluyt; also in A. W. Pollard, ed., Travels of Sir John Mandeville, 1900 (Library of English Classics), repr. 1905, 1915; in EL, 1928, and N.Y., Tudor, 1964. Repr. in Contemporaries of Marco Polo, 1928, p. 211–250, see Collections, above.

Tr. Henry Yule, in Cathay and the Way Thither, 1866, v. 1, p. 1–162, see Collections, above. Repr. 1913, see *ibid.*

OLIVER OF PADERBORN, CARDINAL (1170–1227). The Capture of Damietta. [by St. Louis of France]. Tr. John J. Gavigan. Philadelphia, Univ. of Pennsylvania Pr., 1948. 112 p.

ORDERICUS VITALIS (1075–?1143). The Ecclesiastical History of England and Normandy. Tr. Thomas Forester, with intro. M. Guizot. London, Bohn, 1853–56. 4 v.

OTTO, BISHOP OF FREISING (d. 1158). The Deeds of Frederick Barbarossa. Tr. Charles Christopher Mierow and Richard Emery. CURC. N.Y., Columbia Univ. Pr., 1953. xi, 366 p.

——— The Two Cities. A Chronicle of Universal History to 1146. Tr. Charles C. Mierow, ed. Austin P. Evans and Charles Knapp. CURC. N.Y., Columbia Univ. Pr., 1928. 523 p.

PARIS, MATTHEW (1200–1259). English History from 1235 to 1273. Tr. J. A. Giles. London, Bohn, 1852–54. 3 v. Repr. 1854; 1902.

See Roger of Wendover, below, for the earlier part of the *Chronica.*

ST. PATRICK'S PURGATORY. A Record from History and Literature. Compiled by Shane Leslie. London, Burns and Oates, 1932. xlvii, 215 p.

Trs. of reports of various pilgrims to the scene in Ireland.

PECKHAM, JOHN, ARCHBISHOP (d. 1292). Philomena, a Poem. Tr. Rev. William Dobell. London, Burns and Oates, 1924. viii, 29 p.

PENITENTIALS. Medieval Handbooks of Penance. A Translation of the Principal *libri poenitentiales*, by John T. McNeill and Helena M. Gamer. CURC. N.Y., Columbia Univ. Pr., 1938. 476 p.

PETER DAMIAN, ST. (c. 1007–1072). Selected Writings on the Spiritual Life. Tr. Patricia McNulty. N.Y., Harper, 1960. 187 p.

PETER LOMBARD, BISHOP OF PARIS (12th c.). Peter Lombard and the Sacramental System, by Elizabeth Frances Rogers. CURC. N.Y., Columbia Univ. Pr., 1917. 250 p.

Includes a tr. of book IV, *distinctiones* i–xxvi, of the *Sentences*.

PETERSEN, GERLAC, of Deventer (1377–1471). The Fiery Soliloquy with God. Tr. A. P. J. Cruikshank. London, Richardson, 1872. xvi, 160 p.

PETRARCA, FRANCESCO (1304–1374). See Italian Literature, in v. III.

PHILIPPE OF NOVARA (13th c.). The Wars of Frederick II against the Ibelins in Syria and Cyprus. Tr. John L. LaMonte, with verse trs. of the poems by Merton Jerome Hubert. CURC. N.Y., Columbia Univ. Pr., 1936. 203 p.

PIUS II, POPE (Aeneas Silvius Piccolomini, 1405–1464). The Commentaries of Pius II. Tr. Florence Alden Gragg, intro. and notes by Leona C. Gabel. Smith College Studies in History, vols. 22, 25, 30, 35, 43. Northampton, Mass., Smith College, 1937–1957.

A one-volume abridgement of this tr. was ed. Leona C. Gabel as *Memoirs of a Renaissance Pope*. N.Y., Putnam, 1959, and London, Allen and Unwin, 1960. 381 p. Repr. N.Y., 1961.

————— Certain egloges of Alexander Barclay. London, de Worde, [1515?] et seq. The 1570 ed. repr. Spenser Society 39, Manchester 1885, and EETS OS 175, ed. Beatrice White, London, 1928.

The first three eclogues are a paraphrase of *De curialium miseriis*.

————— (On the education of children: *De liberorum educatione*). Tr. William H. Woodward, in his Vittorino da Feltre and Other Humanist Educators. Cambridge Univ. Pr., 1897 et seq., p. 134–58.

Tr. Brother Joel Stanislaus Nelson. Washington, D.C., Catholic Univ. of Amer. Pr., 1940. ix, 231 p.

———— Eurialus and Lucrece. Tr. anon. London, 1550? Repr. 1560; 1567; London, Roxburghe Club 96, 1873, p. 113–61.

Tr. Flora Grierson as The Tale of Two Lovers. London, Constable, 1929, xxi, 139 p. Repr. [1930], 1933.

Other early trs., 1596, 1639, 1708, 1741: see CBEL, I, 818, and II, 785.

POGGIO BRACCIOLINI (1380–1459). The Facetiae or Jocose Tales of Poggio. Tr. anon. Paris, Isidore Liseux, 1879. 2 v. (parallel texts)

Tr. Edward Storer. Broadway Trs. London, Routledge, and N.Y., Dutton, [1928]. x, 172 p.

Many of the facetiae are included in the collections of Aesop as tr. e.g. by William Caxton, 1484, and Sir Roger L'Estrange, 1692.

PRESTER JOHN, LETTER OF (c. 1165). Tr. Sir E. Denison Ross, in Travel and Travellers in the Middle Ages, ed. Arthur P. Newton. London, Kegan Paul, and N.Y., Knopf, 1930, p. 174–178.

Tr. anon. as Of Pope John and his landes (from a Dutch version, pub. 1508, of a 15th c. French expanded version of the Latin), in Of the newe landes, etc. Antwerp, Jan van Doesborch, [c. 1509]. Repr. Edward Arber in The First Three English Books on America, Westminster, Constable, 1895, p. xxxii–xxxvi.

Tr. Vsevolod Slessarev (from the same French version, pub. c. 1500), in Prester John: The Letter and the Legend. Minneapolis, Univ. of Minnesota Pr., 1959, p. 57–69 (with facs. repr. of the French).

RAYMOND OF CAPUA (de Vineis, d. 1399). The Life of St. Catherine of Siena. Tr. anon. as The lyf of saint Katherin of Senis. London, de Worde, [c. 1493]. Repr. ed. C. Horstmann, Archiv für das Studium der neueren Sprachen, v. 76, 1886, p. 33–112, 265–314, 353–400.

Tr. from the French version by the Ladies of the Sacred Heart. N.Y., Kenedy, and Philadelphia, Pa., Cunningham, 1860. 432 p.

Tr. George Lamb. N.Y., Kenedy, 1960. 384 p.

RICHARD DE BURY. See Aungerville, above.

RICHARD OF CIRENCESTER (c. 1335–1401). The Description of Britain (*De situ Britanniae*) ascribed to him, but actually an 18th c. fabrication. Tr. J. A. Giles with Richard of Devizes, q.v.

Richard's history of Britain (*Speculum historiale*) to 1066 was ed. in the Rolls Series, no. 30, but not tr.

RICHARD OF DEVIZES (fl. 1191). The Chronicle of Richard of Devizes Concerning the Deeds of Richard the First. Tr. Joseph Stevenson in The Church Historians of England. V. 5, part 1, 1858, p. 143–292.

Tr. J. A. Giles, with Richard of Cirencester's supposed Description of Britain, q.v. London, Bohn, 1841. iv, 226 p. Repr. in Chronicles of the Crusades, London, Bohn, 1848 et seq.

Ed. and tr. John T. Appleby. London and N.Y., Nelson, 1963. xxvi, 106, 106 p. (parallel texts)

RICHARD OF HEXHAM (fl. 1141). The Acts of King Stephen and the Battle of the Standard. Tr. Joseph Stevenson in The Church Historians of England. V. 4, part 1, 1856, p. 35–58.

The events of 1135 to 1139.

RICHARD, PRIOR OF HOLY TRINITY, LONDON (end 12th c.). The Itinerary of Richard I and Others to the Holy Land. Tr. anon. in Chronicles of the Crusades. London, Bohn, 1848 et seq., p. 65–339.

In this tr. the *Itinerary* is erroneously ascribed to Geoffrey of Vinsauf.

RICHARD OF ST. VICTOR (d. 1173). Selected Writings on Contemplation. Tr. Clare Kirchberger. London, Faber, 1957. 269 p.

The *Benjamin Minor, Of the Preparation of the Soul for Contemplation*, p. 78–128; the *Benjamin Major, Of the Grace of Contemplation*, p. 131–212; and short pieces.

———— Benjamin Minor. Tr. Anne Chamberlain Garrison. East Lansing, Michigan State Univ., dissertation, 1959.

Tr. S. V. Yankowski. Ansbach, pr. pr., 1960. 97 p.

An English abridged paraphrase, *A Tretyse of the Stodye of Wysdome that Men Clepen Beniamyn* (c. 1350), by the author of *The Cloud of Unknowing*, was ed. Phyllis Hodgson in EETS 231, 1955, p. 11–46.

ROBERT OF SHREWSBURY (d. 1167). The Life of Saint Winefride. Tr. William Caxton. Westminster, Caxton, 1485.

Tr. Thomas Swift (with another, anon., Life). Holywell, St. Winefride's Presbytery, 1910. x, 116 p.

ROGER OF HOVEDEN (or Howden, d. 1201?). The Annals of Roger de Hoveden, Comprising the History of England and Other Countries of Europe from A.D. 732 to A.D. 1201. Tr. Henry T. Riley. London, Bohn, 1853. 2 v.

ROGER OF WENDOVER (d. 1236). Flowers of History, Comprising the History of England . . . to A.D. 1235, Formerly Ascribed to Matthew Paris. Tr. J. A. Giles. London, Bohn, 1849. 2 v. V. 1 repr. London and N.Y., Bell, 1892.

ROLLE, RICHARD, OF HAMPOLE (1290?–1349), The Fire of Love or Melody of Love, and the Mending of Life or Rule of Living. Tr. Richard Misyn, Carmelite (1434). Ed. and modernized by Frances M. M. Comper, with intro. Evelyn Underhill. London, Methuen, 1914. lxii, 278 p. Repr. 1920.

———— The Fire of Love, Being a Translation of the *Incendium Amoris* of Richard Rolle, Hermit, by G. C. Heseltine. London, Burns and Oates, 1935. 198 p.

———— The Mending of Life. Tr. anon. about 1400, ed. and modernized Dundas Harford. London, H. R. Allenson, 1913. lv, 95 p.

Tr. Rev. H. L. Hubbard. London, J. M. Watkins, 1922. 92 p.

Tr. as The Amending of Life by Richard Misyn, Carmelite, 1434, ed. and modernized A. P. London, Burns and Oates, 1927. 55 p.

Also ed. Frances M. M. Comper with The Fire of Love, see above.

———— Some Minor Works. Tr. and ed. Geraldine E. Hodgson. London, Watkins, 1923. 225 p.

RUODLIEB (c. 1050). Ed. and tr. Edwin H. Zeydel as Ruodlieb: The Earliest Courtly Novel. Chapel Hill, Univ. of North Carolina Pr., 1959. 165 p., paper, parallel texts.

Tr. Gordon B. Ford, Jr. as The Ruodlieb: The First Medieval Epic of Chivalry from Eleventh Century Germany. Leiden, Brill, 1965. vii, 104 p.

SAEWULF (fl. 1102–1103). [Travels to the Holy Land]. Tr. W. R. Brownlow. Palestine Pilgrims' Text Society, 4. viii, 55 p.

Another tr. in Thomas Wright, Early Travels in Palestine (1848).

(SALERNO MEDICAL SCHOOL). *Regimen Sanitatis Salernitatum* (12th c.). Tr. verse as The Englishmans Doctor, or, The Schoole of Salerne by Sir John Harington. London, Helme, 1607. 22 leaves. Repr. 4 times to 1624; Oxford, 1830; re-ed. Francis R. Packard in The School of Salernum, N.Y., Hoeber, 1920, and London, Oxford Univ. Pr., 1922, 215 p.

Ed. and tr. Philemon Holland as The Schoole of Salernes . . . Directorie. London, Alsop, 1617. 208, [12] p. Repr. 1634, 1649, 1806, 1807.

Includes also a tr. of the *Commentary* by Arnaldus de Villanova (c. 1300) by Thomas Paynell, printed separately 1548, reprs. to 1634.

Tr. verse John Ordronaux. Philadelphia, Lippincott, 1870. 167 p. Repr. 1871.

SALIMBENE OF PARMA (1221–1287/8). From St. Francis to Dante. A Tr. of All that is of Primary Interest in the Chronicle of the Franciscan Salimbene, by G. G. Coulton. London, Nutt, 1906. 364 p. Repr. enl. 1907.

See also Thomas of Eccleston, below, for other selections from the *Chronicle.*

SALUTATI, COLUCCIO (1331–1406). Coluccio Salutati, *De tyranno.* Tr. Ephraim Emerton, in Humanism and Tyranny, Studies in the Italian Trecento. Cambridge, Mass., Harvard Univ. Pr., 1925, p. 70–116.

The volume also includes Salutati's letters in defence of liberal studies. Cf. the comprehensive study by Berthold L. Ullman, *The Humanism of Coluccio Salutati* (Padua, Antenore, 1963, xvi, 297 p.).

SAXO, GRAMMATICUS (fl. 1200). The First Nine Books of the Danish History of Saxo Grammaticus. Tr. Oliver Elton, with intro. Frederick York Powell. Folklore Society Pubs. 33. London, Nutt, 1894. cxxvii, 435 p. Repr. Norroena Society, London, 1905, 2 v.

Of interest especially for the history of Hamlet.

SECRETA SECRETORUM. The Governance of Kings and Princes. Tr. verse by John Lydgate, et al. London, Pynson, 1511. Repr. with intro. D. T. Starnes, Gainesville, Fla., Scholars' Facsimiles, 1957, xx, 87 p.

The Lydgate tr. (c. 1440) was also ed. from Ms by Robert Steele in EETS ES 66, 1894. xxxiv, 122 p.

Three other 15th c. prose trs. from the Latin or the French, ed. Robert Steele EETS ES 74, 1898. 293 p.

A 15th c. Scots tr. pub. Scottish Text Society 62, 1914. lii, 165 p.

Another tr. anon. pub. London, Copland, 1528.

> This work ascribed to Aristotle was written in Arabic or Syriac in perhaps the 8th c., and circulated in the west in Latin.

SEVEN SAGES (Book of Sindibad). The Seven Sages of Rome. Ed. Killis Campbell. Boston, Mass., Ginn, 1907. cxiv, 217 p.

> A middle English tr. (c. 1400) of a 12th c. Latin version of this originally Persian narrative.

Trs. from 15th c. Mss. ed. Karl Brunner. EETS 191, 1933. xxxi, 233 p.

Tr. anon. pub. as Ye VII Wyse Maysters of Rome. London, de Worde, [1515?]. Many reprs. to 1885, Villon Society.

Tr. Scots verse Johne Rolland (1578). Edinburgh, R. Smythe, 1592. 271 p. Repr. ed. David Laing, Bannatyne Club, 1837. Repr. ed. George F. Black, Scottish Text Soc., v. 43, 1932, xxxi, 400 p.

Other trs., 1674; Percy Society, 1845.

SIGER OF BRABANT (c. 1235–1281?). On the Eternity of the World. Tr. Lottie H. Kendzierski (with St. Thomas Aquinas and St. Bonaventura on the same subject). Milwaukee, Wis., Marquette Univ. Pr., 1964. xii, 117 p.

SIMEON OF DURHAM (d. c. 1129). The Historical Works. Tr. Rev. Joseph Stevenson. Church Historians of England, v. 3, part 2. London, Seeleys, 1855, p. 425–791.

SUSO, HEINRICH (d. 1366). Ye seuen poyntes of trewe loue and euerlastynge wysdom drawen out of . . . Orologium sapiencie . . . Tr.

anon., in The Book of divers ghostly matters. Westminster, Caxton, 1491, ff. 1–96.

Suso made a Latin version, *Horologium sapientiae*, of his *Büchlein der ewigen Weisheit*; the Latin was printed 1480 et seq. For trs. of the original German, and of other works by Suso, see German Literature, in v. IV.

THEOPHILUS (also called Rugerus, 11th c.) An Essay upon Various Arts . . . forming an Encyclopaedia of Christian Art of the Eleventh Century. Tr. Robert Hendrie. London, Murray, 1847. li, 447 p.

Ed. as *De diversis artibus*, and tr. C. R. Dodwell. London, Nelson, and N.Y., Oxford Univ. Pr., 1961. 319 p. (parallel texts)

Tr. John G. Hawthorne and Cyril S. Smith as On Divers Arts. Chicago, Ill., Univ. of Chicago Pr., 1963. xxxv, 216 p.

On bell founding, organ building, bone and gem carving.

THOMAS AQUINAS, ST. (1225?–1274).

Selected Works

———— Basic Writings. Ed. Anton C. Pegis. N.Y., Random House, 1945. 2 v. (1150 p., 1210 p.).

Selections from the *Summa contra gentiles* and the *Summa theologica*.

———— The Homilies for the Sundays [of the church year]. Tr. John M. Ashley. London, Church Press Co., 1866–67. 3 parts. Repr. rev. as The Homilies . . . upon the Epistles and Gospels for the Sundays of the Christian Year, London, J. T. Hayes, 1873, 6 parts.

———— Philosophical Texts. Tr. Thomas Gilby. London and N.Y., Oxford Univ. Pr., 1951. xxii, 405 p. Repr. N.Y., 1960.

———— The Pocket Aquinas: Selections. Ed. Vernon J. Bourke, et al. N.Y., Washington Square Pr., 1960. 372 p. paper.

The Political Ideas of St. Thomas Aquinas. Ed. Dino Bigongiari. N.Y., Hafner, 1953. 255 p.

Selections from the *Summa theologica* and the *De regimine principum*.

———— Selected Political Writings. Tr. J. G. Dawson, ed. A. P. D'Entrèves. Oxford, Blackwell, and N.Y., Macmillan, 1949. xxxii, 199 p.

———————— Selected Writings. EL, [1939]. xvi, 287 p.

———————— Selected Writings: The Principle of Nature, On Being and Essence, On the Virtues in General, On Free Choice. Tr. Robert P. Goodwin. N.Y., Bobbs-Merrill, 1965. xxi, 162 p.

———————— Theological Texts. Tr. Thomas Gilby. London and N.Y., Oxford Univ. Pr., 1955. xix, 423 p.

Individual Works

———————— An Apology for the Religious Orders. Tr. Very Rev. John Procter. London, Sands, 1902. 488 p.

———————— Aristotle's De Anima . . . and The Commentary of St. Thomas Aquinas. Tr. Kenelm Foster and Silvester Humphries. New Haven, Conn., Yale Univ. Pr., and London, Routledge, 1951. 504 p.

———————— Aristotle on Interpretation, Commentary by St. Thomas and Cajetan. Tr. Jean T. Oesterle. Milwaukee, Wis., Marquette Univ. Pr., 1962. 271 p.

———————— On Being and Essence (*De ente et essentia*). Tr. Clare C. Riedl. Toronto, Ont., St. Michael's College, 1934. 66 p. Rev. re-ed. London and N.Y., Sheed, 1937, 52 p.

Tr. George G. Leckie. N.Y. and London, Appleton-Century, 1937. xliv, 47 p.

Tr. Armand Augustine Maurer, Toronto, Pontifical Institute of Medieval Studies, 1949. 63 p.

Tr. Joseph Bobick. Notre Dame, Ind., Univ. of Notre Dame Pr., 1965. 285 p.

For Cajetan's *Commentary* on the work, see below Neo-Latin, s.v.

———————— Catena Aurea: Commentary on the Four Gospels, Collected out of the Works of the Fathers. Tr. J. D. Dalgairns, M. Pattison, and T. D. Ryder, preface signed J. H. N. [J. H. Newman]. Oxford, Parker, and London, Rivington, 1841–45. 4 v. in 8.

———————— On Charity (*Quaestiones disputatae de caritate*). Tr. Lottie H. Kendzierski. Milwaukee, Wis., Marquette Univ. Pr., 1960. 115 p.

———————— Commentary on Aristotle's Physics. Tr. R. J. Blackwell, R. J. Spath, and W. E. Thirlkel, intro. Vernon J. Bourke. New Haven, Yale Univ. Pr., and London, Routledge, 1963. xxxii, 599 p.

———————— Commentary on the Metaphysics of Aristotle. Tr. John P. Rowan (with the text of the Metaphysics in tr.). Chicago, Ill., Regnery, 1961. 2 v.

———————— Commentary on the Nicomachaean Ethics. Tr. C. I. Litzinger. Chicago, Ill., Regnery, 1964. 2 v.

———————— Commentary on St. Paul's Epistle to the Ephesians. Tr. Matthew L. Lamb. Albany, N.Y., Magi Books, 1966. vi, 313 p.

———————— Commentary on St. Paul's Epistle to the Galatians. Tr. F. R. Larcher. Albany, N.Y., Magi Books, 1966. x, 211 p.

———————— Compendium of Theology. Tr. Cyril Vollert, S.J. St. Louis, Mo., and London, Herder, 1952. xx, 366 p.

Part 1, tractate 2, was also tr. Ross. J. Dunn: Toronto, St. Michael's College, 1934, 194 p.

———————— On the Eternity of the World. Tr. Cyril Vollert, S.J. (with the trs. by others of Siger de Brabant and St. Bonaventura on the same subject, q.v.). Milwaukee, Wis., Marquette Univ. Pr., 1964. xii, 117 p.

———————— Exposition of the Posterior Analytics. Tr. Pierre Conway. Quebec, Librairie M. Doyon, 1956. xvi, 449 p.

———————— On the Governance of Rulers (*De regimine principum*). Tr. Gerald B. Phelan. Toronto, Ont., St. Michael's College, 1935. 143 p. Repr. rev. London and N.Y., Sheed & Ward for the (Toronto) Institute of Mediaeval Studies, 1938. Re-ed. rev. I. T. Eschmann, O.P., as On Kingship, ibid., 1949, 119 p.

———————— The Letter *De occultis operibus naturae*. Ed. and tr. Joseph Bernard McAllister. Washington, D.C., Catholic Univ. of America Pr., 1939. 209 p. (parallel texts)

———————— The Philosophy of Teaching of St. Thomas Aquinas. Tr. of *De magistro* by Mary Helen Mayer. Milwaukee, Wis., Bruce, 1929. 164 p.

———————— On the Power of God (*Quaestiones disputatae de potentia Dei*). Tr. Dominican Fathers (Fr. Lawrence Shapcote). London, Burns Oates, 1932–34. 3 v.

———————— The Religious State, the Episcopate, and the Priestly Office (*De perfectione vitae spiritualis*). Tr. Rev. John Procter. London, Sands, 1902. 166 p.

———————— The Soul. Tr. John Patrick Rowan. St. Louis, Mo., Herder, 1949. 299 p.

————— On Spiritual Creatures. Tr. Mary C. FitzPatrick and John J. Wellmuth. Milwaukee, Wis., Marquette Univ. Pr., 1949. 135 p.

————— The *Summa contra gentiles*. Tr. by the English Dominican Fathers (i.e., Fr. Lawrence Shapcote). London, Burns and Oates, and N.Y., Benziger, (1923)–1929. 4 v. in 5.

Tr. Anton C. Pegis (bks. 1, 2), Vernon J. Bourke (bk. 3), and Charles J. O'Neil (bk. 4). Garden City, N.Y., Hanover House, 1956–57, 4 v.; also ibid., Image Books, 4 v. paper.

Tr. abridged as Of God and His Creatures, by Joseph Rickaby. London, Burns and Oates, and St. Louis, Mo., Herder, [1905]. xxi, 423 p. Repr. Westminster, Md. Carroll Pr., 1950. 444 p.

————— The *Summa theologica*. Tr. by Fathers of the English Dominican Province (i.e., Fr. Lawrence Shapcote). London, Washbourne, and N.Y., Benziger, 1911–1925. 20 v. Repr. London, Burns and Oates, [1921?]–1932, 22 v. Repr. N.Y., Benziger, 1948, 3 v. Repr. Great Books, 1952, 2 v. Repr. London, Burns, Oates, 1957, 3 v.

Tr. various hands, ed. Thomas Gilby and P. K. Meagher. For the Blackfriars, London, Eyre & Spottiswoode, and N.Y., McGraw-Hill, 1964—(in progress, to be 60 v.: 17 v. to 1965).

Selections from the Summa Theologica

————— Aquinas Ethicus, or The Moral Teaching of St. Thomas. Tr. of the principal portions of part two by Joseph Rickaby. London, Burns and Oates, 1892. 2 v. Repr. 1896.

————— On Man. Tr. anon. Chicago, Regnery, 1951. 121 p.

Tr. James F. Anderson. Englewood, N.J., Prentice-Hall, 1962. xiv, 178 p.

————— On Nature and Grace. Tr. Alan M. Fairweather. London, S.C.M. Pr., and Philadelphia, Westminster Pr., 1954. 386 p.

————— On Prayer and the Contemplative Life. Tr. Very Rev. Hugh Pope, with preface by Very Rev. Vincent McNabb. London, Washbourne, 1914. 272 p.

Other Individual Works

————— Treatise on Separate Substances. Tr. Francis J. Lescoe. West Hartford, Conn., Saint Joseph College, 1959. x, 138 p. Repr. 1963, with the Latin text.

———— Truth. (*Quaestiones disputatae de veritate*). Tr. R. W. Mulligan, J. V. McGlynn, R. W. Schmidt. Chicago, Regnery, 1952–54 3 v.

In general, see Josef Pieper, *Guide to Thomas Aquinas*, tr. from German by Richard and Clara Winston (N.Y., Pantheon, 1962, and London, Faber, entitled *Introduction to Thomas Aquinas*, 1963, 181 p.).

THOMAS À BECKET, ST. (d. 1170). The Life and Letters . . . Gathered from the Contemporary Historians [and tr.] J. A. Giles. London, Whittaker, 1846. 2 v.

Tr. (of documents) W. H. Hutton as St. Thomas of Canterbury: An Account of his Life and Fame. London, Nutt, 1889. 286 p. Repr. 1899; repr. rev. as Thomas Becket, London, Pitman, 1910; repr. rev., Cambridge, Eng., 1926.

THOMAS OF CELANO, FRIAR (13th c.) The Life of St. Clare. Tr. Fr. Paschal Robinson, with The Rule of St. Clare. Philadelphia, Dolphin Pr., 1910. xliii, 169 p.

———— The Lives of St. Francis. See Italian Literature, s.v. St. Francis, in v. III.

THOMAS OF ECCLESTON (fl. 1250). The Friars and How They Came to England, Being a Tr. of . . . *De adventu FF. Minorum in Angliam*. Tr. Father Cuthbert (L. C. Hesse). London, Sands, 1903. 252 p. Repr. London and St. Louis, Mo., Herder, 1909.

Tr. E. Gurney Salter as The Coming of the Friars Minor to England and Germany, Being the Chronicles of Brother Thomas of Eccleston and Brother Jordan of Giano. London, Dent, and N.Y., Dutton, 1926. xxxvi, 198 p. (Thomas' Chronicle is p. 3–126).

Tr. Marie-Thérèse Laureilhe, in XIII Century Chronicles. Chicago, Ill., Franciscan Herald Pr., 1961. xvii, 302 p. (Thomas, Jordan, and selections from Salimbene.)

THOMAS À KEMPIS (1380–1471). The Works. London, Kegan Paul, 1903–7. 5 v.

V. 1. Prayers and Meditations on the Life of Christ. Tr. W. Duthoit. 1903. xxviii, 329 p. Repr. 1908.

V. 2. The Founders of the New Devotion, being the Lives of Gerard Groote, Florentius Radewin, and their Followers. Tr. J. P. Arthur. 1905. xlvii, 262 p.

V. 3. The Chronicle of the Canons Regular of Mount St. Agnes. Tr. J. P. Arthur. 1906. 234 p.

V. 4. A Meditation on the Incarnation of Christ. Sermons on the Life and Passion of Our Lord. Of Hearing and Speaking Good Words. Tr. Dom Vincent Scully. 1907. 255 p.

V. 5. Sermons to the Novices Regular. Tr. Dom Vincent Scully. 1907. xxvi, 255 p.

Individual Works

——————— The Imitation of Christ. (This is no longer attributed to Thomas. See the title, above.)

——————— In Praise of the Blessed Virgin Mary. Tr. Robert E. Patterson. Milwaukee, Wis., Bruce, 1956. 52 p.

——————— Meditations on the Life of Christ. Tr. Archdeacon Wright and Rev. S. Kettlewell. London and N.Y., Dutton, 1892. liii, 378 p. Repr. 1894.

——————— *Vera Sapientia*, or True Wisdom. Tr. Right Rev. [Frederick] Byrne. London, Washbourne, and N.Y., Benziger, 1904. 204 p.

For earlier trs., from 1653, see Farrar and Evans, nos. 3630–3643.

THOMAS OF MONMOUTH (12th c.). The Life and Miracles of St. William of Norwich. Ed. and tr. Augustus Jessopp and Montague Rhodes James. Cambridge, Univ. Pr., 1896. xc, 303 p.

THORNE, WILLIAM (14th c.). Chronicle of St. Augustine's Abbey, Canterbury. Tr. A. H. Davis, with pref. Professor A. Hamilton Thompson. Oxford, Blackwell, 1934. lxii, 740 p.

Covering the years A.D. 578–1397.

UPTON, NICHOLAS (1400?–1457). The Essential Portions of . . . *De studio militari* (before 1446). Tr. John Blount (c. 1500), ed. Francis Pierrepont Bernard. Oxford, Clarendon, Pr., 1931. 66 p.

VALLA, LORENZO (1406–1457). Dialogue on Free Will. Tr. C. E. Trinkaus, in The Renaissance Philosophy of Man. Chicago, Univ. of Chicago Pr., 1948, p. 155–82. Repr. 1956, paper.

———— Treatise on the Donation of Constantine. Ed. and tr. Christopher B. Coleman. New Haven, Conn., Yale Univ. Pr., 1922. 183 p.

An anon. tr. was published 1534.

VEGIUS, MAPHAEUS (Maffeo Vegio, 1407–1458). The Thirteenth Book of the Aeneid. Tr. Gavin Douglas, in his tr. of the Aeneid. London, 1553. Repr. Edinburgh, 1710; Edinburgh, 1839 (Bannatyne Club); Edinburgh, 1874 (in the Poetical Works of Douglas, v. 4); Stanford, California, 1930 (in Anna Cox Brinton, Maphaeus Vegius and his Thirteenth Book of the Aeneid).

Tr. Thomas Twine in his tr. of the Aeneid (with Thomas Phaer). London, 1583. Several 16th c. reprs; repr. in Anna Cox Brinton, *op. cit. supra.*

VERGERIO, PIETRO PAOLO (1349–c. 1444). (On the Principles of Learning and of Conduct: *De ingenuis moribus.*) Tr. William H. Woodward in Vittorino da Feltre and Other Humanist Educators. Cambridge Univ. Pr., 1897 et seq., p. 93–118.

VILLEDIEU, ALEXANDER DE (c. 1170–c. 1250). *Ecclesiale.* Ed. and tr. L. R. Lind. Lawrence, Univ. of Kansas Pr., 1958. 155 p. (A calendar computer.)

WHITERIG, JOHN (d. 1371). The Monk of Farne. The Meditations of a Fourteenth Century Monk. Tr. a Benedictine of Stanbrook, and ed. Hugh Farmer. Benedictine Studies. London, Longmans, and Baltimore, Helicon Pr., 1961. vii, 155 p. ill.

WILLIAM OF MALMESBURY (c. 1080–c. 1142). The History of the Kings of England, and The Modern History. Tr. Rev. John Sharpe. London, Longmans, 1815. 610 p. Repr. rev. J. A. Giles, London, Bohn, 1847; repr. 1904. Also repr. rev. Joseph Stevenson, in The Church Historians of England, v. 3, pt. 1, 1854.

———— The *Historia Novella.* Ed. and tr. K. R. Potter. London and N.Y., Nelson, 1955. xliii, 77, 84 p.

WILLIAM OF NEWBURGH (1136–1198?). The History of William of Newburgh. Tr. Joseph Stevenson, in The Church Historians of England, v. 4, pt. 2, 1856, p. 395–672.

From 1066 to 1197.

WILLIAM OF RUBRUCK (c. 1220–c. 1270). The Journey to the Eastern Parts of the World. Tr. William W. Rockhill. London, 2 Hakluyt Society, v. 4, 1900. lvi, 304 p.

Journey to Mongolia; included in this volume also the account of the previous journey of John of Pian de Carpini.

Earlier partial tr. by Richard Hakluyt in *The Principal Navigations*, I, 1598, et seq.; also by Samuel Purchas in *Purchas his Pilgrimes*, I, 1625, et seq. Trs. also in A. W. Pollard ed., *Travels of Sir John Mandeville* (1900 et seq., including N.Y., Tudor, 1964); and in *Contemporaries of Marco Polo*, and in *The Mongol Mission*, q.v. in Collections, above.

WILLIAM OF ST. THIERRY (?1085–?1148). The Golden Epistle to the Carthusians of Mont Dieu. Tr. Walter Shewring, and ed. Dom Justin McCann. London, Sheed and Ward, 1930. lvi, 119 p.

The epistle was long ascribed to St. Bernard of Clairvaux.

————— The Meditations. Tr. a Religious of C.S.M.V. N.Y., Harper, 1954. 108 p.

————— The Mirror of Faith. Tr. Geoffrey Webb and Adrian Walker. London, Mowbray, 1959. 74 p.

————— On the Nature and Dignity of Love. Tr. the same. London, Mowbray, 1956. 64 p.

————— St. Bernard of Clairvaux, The Story of his Life. See Bernard, St., above.

WILLIAM, ARCHBISHOP OF TYRE (c. 1130–1190). A History of Deeds Done Beyond the Sea. Tr. Emily Atwater Babcock and A. C. Krey. CURC. N.Y., Columbia Univ. Pr., 1943. 2 v.

Tr. from a French version by William Caxton as Godefroy of Bologne or the Last Siege of Jerusalem, and pub. Westminster, 1481. Repr. ed. Mary N. Colvin, EETS ES 64, 1893. xli, 348 p.

WIREKER, NIGEL (c. 1130–c. 1200). A Mirror for Fools. (*Speculum stultorum*). Tr. Graydon W. Regenos as The Book of Daun Burnel the Ass. Austin, Univ. of Texas Pr., 1959. 165 p.

    Tr. J. H. Mozley. Notre Dame, Ind., Univ. of Notre Dame Pr., 1963, xvi, 143 p.

WYCLIFFE, JOHN (c. 1320–1384). Tracts and Treatises, with Selections and Trs. from his Manuscript and Latin Works. Ed. Robert Vaughan. London, Wycliffe Society, 1845. xciv, 332 p.

The Latin works translated are some chapters of the *Trialogus*.

————— "On the Pastoral Office," "On the Eucharist." Tr. Ford Lewis Battles, in Advocates of Reform from Wyclif to Erasmus. Library of Christian Classics, v. 14, 1953, p. 32–88.

NEO-LATIN LITERATURE
FROM A.D. 1450

GEORGE B. PARKS

BIBLIOGRAPHY

CONLEY, C. H. "Translations from Mediaeval and Contemporary Authors." Cambridge Bibliography of English Literature. Cambridge, Univ. Pr., and N.Y., Macmillan, 1941. v. 1, 809–820 (for 1500–1660).

RIEDL, JOHN O., et al. A Catalogue of Renaissance Philosophers. Milwaukee, Wis., Marquette Univ. Pr., 1940. 179 p.

SMITH, F. SEYMOUR. The Classics in Translation. London and N.Y., Scribner, 1930. 307 p.

An annotated list of some of the best trs. of many Greek and Latin authors, including a number of neo-Latin.

WATERHOUSE, G. "International Literature" (Literary Relations with the Continent). Cambridge Bibliography of English Literature, as above. v. 1, 326–329 (for 1500–1660); v. 2, 31–32 (for 1660–1800).

Some periodicals listing current studies of Neo-Latin literature are *Neo-Latin News*, issued with *Seventeenth Century News* since 1954; and *PMLA Bibliography*. A catalogue of Latin books by contemporary authors published in the 16th century has been undertaken by Don Cameron Allen and Leicester Bradner, and a trial printing of entries beginning with the letter A has been done for the Renaissance Society of America.

LITERARY STUDIES

ALLEN, DON CAMERON. "Latin Literature" [of the Renaissance: a survey of scholarship]. Modern Language Quarterly, 2 (1941), 403–20.

BRADNER, LEICESTER. "The Latin Drama of the Renaissance 1314–1640". Studies of the Renaissance, 4 (1957), 31–70.

Adds a "List of Original Latin Plays Published Before 1650."

———— Musae Anglicanae: A History of Anglo-Latin Poetry, 1500–1925. N.Y., Modern Language Association, 1940. 383 p.

BURCKHARDT, JAKOB CHRISTOPH. The Civilization of the Renaissance in Italy. Tr. from the German (3d ed.) by S. G. G. Middle-
more. London, 1878. Tr. (from the 15th ed.) by the same, London,
Harrap, and N.Y., Harper, 1929. 526 p. Repr. Vienna, Phaidon Pr.
and London, Allen and Unwin, 1937, 640 p. Repr. ML, 1954. Repr.
rev. Irene Gordon, N.Y., New American Library, 1961.

Esp. Part iii, "The Revival of Antiquity," with chapters on neo-Latin
literature.

GRANT, W. LEONARD. Neo-Latin Literature and the Pastoral. Chapel
Hill, Univ. of North Carolina Pr., 1965. x, 434 p.

HALLAM, HENRY. Introduction to the Literature of Europe in the 15th,
16th, and 17th Centuries. London, Murray, 1837–39. 4 v. Many
reprs. to 1881–82.

SYMONDS, JOHN ADDINGTON. The Revival of Learning. V. 2 of The
Renaissance in Italy. London, Smith Elder, 1877. Many reprs., including ML, 1935, v. 1; London, Murray, 1937.

Esp. ch. viii, "Latin Poetry."

VAN TIEGHEM, PAUL. La littérature latine de la renaissance. Étude d'histoire littéraire européenne. Bibliothèque d'Humanisme et Renaissance,
4. Paris, Droz, 1944. 254 p.

The most comprehensive study.

WRIGHT, F. A. and SINCLAIR, T. A. A History of Later Latin Literature
from the Middle of the Fourth to the End of the Seventeenth Century.
London, Routledge, and N.Y., Macmillan, 1931. 417 p.

COLLECTIONS

LATIN POETRY IN VERSE TRANSLATION from the Beginnings to the
Renaissance. Ed. L. R. Lind, various trs. Boston, Houghton Mifflin,
1957. xxxix, 438 p.

38 poems by Renaissance authors, from Beccadelli (Panormita) to Crashaw.

THE PENGUIN BOOK OF LATIN VERSE. Ed. Frederick Brittain. Penguin, 1962. lxvi, 381 p. (parallel texts, prose trs.)

THE RENAISSANCE PHILOSOPHY OF MAN. Ed. Ernst Cassirer, Paul Oskar Kristeller, and John H. Randall, Jr. Chicago, Univ. Pr., 1948. 405 p. Repr. 1956, paper.

Contents: Petrarch, *On His Own Ignorance*, and other essays, tr. Hans Nachod, p. 34–143; Lorenzo Valla, *Dialogue on Free Will,* tr. Charles E. Trinkaus Jr., p. 155–82; Marsilio Ficino, *Five Questions Concerning the Mind* (*Epistolae*, book ii, no. 1), tr. Josephine L. Burroughs, p. 193–212;. Pico della Mirandola, *Oration* on *the Dignity of Man*, tr. Elizabeth L. Forbes, p. 223–54; Pietro Pomponazzi, *On the Immortality of the Soul,* tr. William H. Hay II, revised, p. 280–381; Juan Luis Vives, *A Fable About Man,* tr. Nancy Lenkeith, p. 387–93.

A SOURCE BOOK IN MATHEMATICS. Ed. David Eugene Smith, trs. various hands. N.Y. and London, McGraw-Hill, 1929. xvii, 701 p. Repr. N.Y., Dover, 1959, and London, Constable, 1960, 2 v. paper.

Passages or treatises important in the history of mathematics since about 1500, mostly trs. Latin authors are: 15th c., Regiomontanus; 16th c., Girolamo Cardano, Christopher Clavius, Bartholomaeus Pitiscus; 17th c., Bonaventura Cavalieri, Pierre de Fermat, Gottfried Wilhelm von Leibniz, John Napier, Isaac Newton, John Wallis; 18th c., Jacques Bernoulli, Leonhard Euler, Abraham de Moivre, Geronimo Saccheri; 19th c., Janos Bolyai, Carl Friedrich Gauss.

INDIVIDUAL AUTHORS AND WORKS

Note. Translations of Latin works of English authors are not included if the translation was published during the author's lifetime: e.g., the works of John Foxe, William Fulke, Joseph Hall.

ACONTIUS, JACOBUS (d. 1566?). Satans Stratagems, or the Devils Cabinet-Councel discovered. Tr. John Goodwin (4 books out of 8). London, 1648 [for 1647]. 136 p. Repr. 1651.

Tr. Walter T. Curtis. Published mimeographed (WPA project) as Occasional Papers, English Series, no. 5, with intro. C. D. O'Malley. San Francisco, California State Library, 1940. 2 v.

———— The True Order and Methode of Wryting and Reading Hystories, according to the precepts of Francis Patricio and Accontio Tridentino. Tr. Thomas Blundevill from the Italian. London, 1574, 32 leaves. Repr. ed. Hugh G. Dick, Huntington Library Quarterly, 3 (1940), 149–170.

Actually Blundevill combined an abridged version of Patrizi's *Della Historia Dieci Dialoghi* (p. 155–165 in the Dick repr.) with a like version of Acontius' *Delle osseruationi*, etc. (p. 165–170 *ibid.*)

ADDISON, JOSEPH (1672–1719). Latin Poems. Tr. various hands in The Works of Addison, ed H. G. Bohn. London, Bohn, 1856, v. 6. Reprs. to 1913.

ADRICHOMIUS, CHRISTIANUS (1533–1585). A brief Description of Hierusalem and of the Suburbs thereof . . . in the time of Christ. Tr. Thomas Tymme. London, 1595. 112 p. Repr. 1654, 1666.

AGRICOLA, GEORG (1490–1555). *De re metallica*. Tr. from 1st ed. 1556 by Herbert Clark Hoover and Lou Henry Hoover. London, Mining Magazine, 1912. xxxi, 640 p. Repr. N.Y., Dover, 1960, 669 p.

AGRIPPA, HENRICUS CORNELIUS VON NETTESHEIM (1494–1555). The Commendation of Matrimony (*De sacramento matrimoniali declamatio*). Tr. David Clapam. London, Berthelet, 1540. 48 p. Repr. 1545.

———— Three Books of Occult Philosophy. Tr. J. F. London, Moule, 1651. 583 p. Repr. rev. (book i only) Chicago, Hahn and Whitehead, 1898.

The Fourth Book of Occult Philosophy, a supposititious work of Agrippa's, was tr. Robert Turner, London, Harrison, 1655, 217 p.

————— A Treatise of the Nobilitie and Excellencie of Womankynde. Tr. David Clapam. London, Berthelet, 1542. 102 p.

Tr. verse Hugh Crompton as The Glory of Women, or a Looking-Glasse for ladies. London, Coles, 1652. 47 p.

Tr. Edward Fleetwood. London, Ibbitson, 1652. 32 p.

Tr. Henry Care as Female Pre-eminence. London, T. R., 1670. 83 p.

————— Of the Vanitie and Uncertaintie of Artes and Sciences (*De incertitudine et vanitate scientiarum*). Tr. James Sanford. London, Wykes, 1569. 187 leaves. Repr. 1575.

Tr. anon. London, Speed, 1676. 368 p. Repr. 1684, 1694.

ALSTED, JOHANN HEINRICH (1588–1638). For trs. of excerpts from his *Encyclopaedia* and other works, see British Museum Catalogue.

ALTHUSIUS, JOHANNES (1557–1638). Politics Methodically Set Forth (*Politica methodice digesta*). Tr. abridged Frederick S. Carney. London, Eyre and Spottiswoode, and Boston, Mass., Beacon Pr., 1964. xxxvii, 232 p.

ANDREA, JOHANN VALENTIN (1586–1654). Christianopolis: An Ideal State of the Seventeenth Century. Tr. Felix Held. London and N.Y., Oxford Univ. Pr., 1916. x, 287 p.

ANDREWES, LANCELOT (1535–1626). The Private Devotions. Tr. anon. London, Moseley, 1647. 166 p.

Tr. Peter Hall. London, Pickering, 1830. xxx, 458 p.

Tr. from the Greek by J. H. Newman, from the Latin by J. M. Neale, as The Devotions. Oxford, Parker, 1842–44. 2 v. Repr. 1867.

Tr., ed., and arranged by Henry Veale. London, Stock, 1895. Tr. F. E. Brightman as The *Preces Privatae*. London, Methuen, 1903. lxii, 392 p. Repr. N.Y., Meridian Books, 1961.

For other eds. and selections, see the British Museum Catalogue. The other Latin works, especially of the Bellarmine controversy, repr. Oxford 1851–53, have not been tr.

ANGHIERA, PIETRO MARTIRE D' (Petrus Martyr Anglerius): see
Martyr.

ARMINIUS, JACOBUS (1550–1609). The Works of James Arminius. Tr.
(v. 1, 2) James Nichols and (v. 3) William Nichols. London,
Longmans, 1825–28. 3 v. Repr. (v. 3 retr. W. R. Bagnall) Auburn
and Buffalo, N.Y., Derby, and London, Longmans, 1853; this version
repr. Grand Rapids, Mich., Baker Book House, 1956, 3 v.

———— The Just Man's Defence: Or . . . the Declaration . . . concerning
the Principal Points of Religion. Tr. Tobias Conyers. London, 1657.
156 p.

ASLACUS, CUNRADUS BERGENSIS (Kurt Aslaksen, 1564–1624). The
Description of Heaven. Or a Divine and Comfortable Discourse of the
Nature of the Eternall Heaven. Tr. Ralph Jennings. London, 1623.
85 p.

Part 3 of *De natura coeli triplicis*, entitled *De coelo perpetuo*.

AYALA, BALTASAR (1548–1584). Three Books on the Law of War
(*De jure et officiis bellicis*). Text, v. 1. ed. John Westlake; tr., v. 2,
John Pawley Bate. Classics of International Law. Washington, D.C.,
Carnegie Institution, 1912. 2 v.

BACON, FRANCIS (1561–1626). The Philosophical Works Methodized
and Made English by Peter Shaw. London, 1733. 3 v. Repr. 1737;
1802–03.

Actually the scientific works, as distinguished from the Moral Works and
the Political Works. They are: v. 1, *De Augmentis Scientiarum, De Sapientia Veterum*; v. 2, *Novum Organum Scientiarum*; v. 3, other Latin works
(*History of Winds, History of Life and Death*, etc.). The *New Organon*
was repr. separately in this tr., see below.

Tr. ed. Basil Montagu, in The Works of Lord Bacon. London and Philadelphia, 1844 et seq. 3 v.

V. 1. includes the tr. of *The Wisdom of the Ancients* by Sir Arthur Gorges,
see below; v. 3, the *Novum Organum* in the Wood tr.; *History of the
Winds*, tr. R.G.; *History of Life and Death*, tr. Walter Rawley; *Of the*

Scaling Ladder of the Intellect, and *Anticipations of the Second Philosophy,* tr. Francis Wrangham, and other shorter fragments.

This is quite another ed. than Montagu's 16–v. ed. (1825–36), which prints the Latin works in the original only, as do most of the earlier eds. of Bacon's collected works.

Ed. Joseph Devey as The Physical and Metaphysical Works. London, Bohn, 1853, et seq. vi, 567 p.

On the Dignity and Advancement of Learning, in the Peter Shaw tr.; *Novum Organum* in the Wood tr., see below.

Tr. R. L. Ellis, James Spedding, et al., in The Collected Works of Francis Bacon, ed. by the two with D. D. Heath. London, 1857–74 et seq. 14 v. (the standard ed.)

The trs. are in v. 4–6 of the English eds.; in the Boston eds., beginning 1860–64 et seq., the trs. are in v. 8–10. See individual works, below, for their place in this ed.

The trs. in this ed. have generally been accepted for repr.: e.g., in *The Philosophical Writings* (N.Y., Hurd & Houghton, 1878, 438 p.); *The Philosophical Works,* ed. J. M. Robertson (London, Routledge, and N.Y., Dutton, 1905, xx, 920 p.); and in such volumes of selections from Bacon's writings as that ed. Richard Foster Jones (Garden City, N.Y., Doubleday-Doran, 1937), and that ed. Hugh G. Dick (ML, 1955), which emphasize Bacon's scientific writings.

Individual Works

———— Of the Advancement and Proficience of Learning (*De Augmentis Scientiarum*). Tr. Gilbert Wats. Oxford, 1640. 2 parts. Repr. 1674.

Tr. Peter Shaw in The Philosophical Works, v. 1, 1733. Repr. in Joseph Devey ed., 1853.

Tr. Francis Headlam and James Spedding, in The Collected Works, v. 5–6 (American ed., v. 8–9).

———— History of Life and Death. Tr. anon. London, 1638. 323 p.

Tr. William Rawley. London, 1638. 395 [for 435] p. Repr. Sir John Sinclair, in The Code of Health, v. 4, 1806; in Montagu ed. v. 3, 1844.

Tr. James Spedding in v. 5 (American ed., v. 10), with other scientific studies.

——————— Naturall and Experimentall History of the Winds. Tr. R. G. London, 1653. 384 p. Repr. in Montagu ed., v. 3, 1844.

Tr. Francis Headlam, rev. James Spedding, in v. 5 (American ed., v. 9).

——————— The New Organon (*Novum Organum*). Tr. Peter Shaw, v. 2, 1733.

Tr. William Wood. London, Pickering, 1844. 336 p. Repr. in Montagu ed., v. 3, 1844; repr. 1850; repr. Joseph Devey in Bohn ed., 1853; repr. 1893; repr. in Great Books, 30, 1952.

Tr. G. W. Kitchin. Oxford, Univ. Pr., 1855. xxix, 338 p.

Tr. Andrew Johnson. London, Bell and Daldy, 1859. viii, 354 p.

Tr. Francis Headlam, rev. James Spedding and R. L. Ellis, in v. 4 (American ed., v. 8). Many reprs. including ed. Gail Kennedy, in The Great Instauration (with Hobbes and Locke), Garden City, N.Y., Doubleday Doran, 1937; and ed. Fulton H. Anderson, N.Y., Liberal Arts Pr., 1960, 292 p.

——————— The Wisdom of the Ancients. Tr. Sir Arthur Gorges. London, 1619. 175 p. Repr. 1619, 1622, 1658, Edinburgh, 1681; repr. in Montagu ed., v. 1, 1844.

Tr. Peter Shaw as Fables of the Ancients, 1733, v. 1.

Tr. Francis Headlam, rev. James Spedding, in Ellis-Spedding ed., v. 6 (American ed., v. 13).

Other fragments of the encyclopedia have been noted above as tr. in the Montagu ed., and most completely in the Ellis-Spedding ed. Note should be taken of the memorial volume to Bacon, the *Memoriae Sacrum*, ed. William Rawley (1626), tr. by E. K. Rand as *A Translation of Thirty-two Latin Poems in Honor of Francis Bacon* (Boston, pr. pr. 1904, 88 p., parallel texts). The help is acknowledged here of R. W. Gibson, *Bacon: A Bibliography of his Works and of Baconiana to the Year 1750* (Oxford, Clarendon Pr., 1950, xvii, 369 p.)

BALE, JOHN (1495–1563). The Pageant of Popes, Contayninge the lyues of all the Bishops of Rome to . . . 1555 (*Acta Romanorum Pontificum*). Tr. John Studley. London, 1574. 20, 198 leaves.

For Bale's own trs. from the Latin, see Stephen Gardiner and Thomas Kirchmeyer, below.

BARCLAY, JOHN (1582–1621). Argenis. Tr. Kingsmill Long and (the verses) Thomas May. London, 1625. Repr. 1626.

Tr. Sir Robert LeGrys and Thomas May. London, 1629.

Tr. John Jacob as The Adventures of Poliarchus and Argenis. Dublin, 1734. xiii, 274 p.

Tr. Clara Reeve as The Phoenix, or The History of Polyarchus and Argenis. London, 1772. 4 v.

———— Euphormio's Satyricon. Tr. Paul Turner (from the 1605 ed.). London, Golden Cockerel Pr., 1954. 158 p.

———— The Mirrour of Mindes (*Icon animorum*). Tr. Thomas May. London, 1631, 380 p. Repr. 1633.

BARCLAY, WILLIAM (1546–1608). Of the Authoritie of the Pope (*De potestate papae*). Tr. anon. London, 1611. 220 p.

Tr. George Albert Moore as The Kingdom and the Regal Power. Chevy Chase, Md., Country Dollar Pr., 1954. 724 p.

BARLETIUS, MARINUS (15th c.) The Historie of George Castriot, surnamed Scanderbeg, King of Albanie, containing his famous actes . . . against the Turkes. Tr. by Z. I. Gentleman from the French version by Jacques de Lavardin of the Latin Original [Rome, 1508]. London, Ponsonby, 1596. 14, 498 p.

BARTHOLIN, THOMAS (1616–1680). On the Burning of his Library. On Medical Travel. Tr. C. D. O'Malley. Lawrence, Univ. of Kansas Libraries, 1961. viii, 101 p.

BARTOLOTTI, GIAN GIACOMO (15th c.) On the Antiquity of Medicine. Ed. and tr. Luigi Belloni (with Giovanni Tortelli, On Medicine and Physicians). Milan, Stucchi, 1954. xliv, 226 p. (parallel texts)

BATHE, WILLIAM (1564–1614). *Janua Linguarum Latine et Hispanice.* English version added by William Welde. London, 1615. 89 p. Reprs. to 9th ed., 1645.

BAUMGARTEN, ALEXANDER GOTTLIEB (1714–1762). Reflections on Poetry. Ed. and tr. Karl Aschenbrenner and William B. Holter.

Berkeley, Univ. of California Pr., and London, Cambridge Univ. Pr. 1954. ix, 91, 40 p. (parallel texts).

BELLARMINO, ST. ROBERTO, CARDINAL (1542–1621). An Ample Declaration of the Christian Doctrine. Tr. (from the Italian original) by Richard Hadock. Douay, 1604. 320 p. Repr. 1605, Rouen, ?1610, Douai, 1611, 1617.

Ed. and tr. C. B. Fairbanks. Boston, 1853.

————— The Art of Dying Well. Tr. Edward Coffin. 2d ed. St. Omer, 1622. 416 p.

Tr. John Ball. London, 1720. Repr. 1723, 1726.

————— On the Eternall Felicity of the Saints. Tr. Thomas Everard. [St. Omer] 1638. 441 p.

Tr. Benjamin Jenks as Ouranography, or Heaven Opened. London, 1710. xix, 276 p.

Tr. T. Foxton, as The Joys of the Blessed. London, 1722.

————— Extracts on Politics and Government. Tr. George Albert Moore. Chevy Chase, Md., Country Dollar Pr., 1951. xi, 134 p.

————— A Ladder Whereby our Minds May Ascend unto God. Tr. T. B. Douai, 1616. Repr. as The Ascent of the Mind to God, with intro. James Broderick. London, Burns Oates, 1928. xxxi, 311 p.

Tr. H. Hall as Steps of Ascension to God. 2d ed. London, 1705.

Tr. J. Dalton as A Gradual Whereby to Ascend unto God. London, 1844.

Tr. Monialis, as The Mind's Ascent to God, with pref. P. N. Waggett. London, Mowbray, and Milwaukee, Wis., Morehouse, 1925. xx, 229 p.

————— De Laicis, or The Treatise on Civil Government. Tr. Kathleen E. Murphy. N.Y., Fordham Univ. Pr., 1928. 83 p.

————— The Power of the Pope in Temporal Affairs, against William Barclay. Ed. and tr. George Albert Moore. Chevy Chase, Md., Country Dollar Pr., 1950. xxi, 239 p.

————— Reply to the . . . argument . . . for the succession of Henry of Navarre to the Kingdom of France. Tr. the same, ibid., 1949. xiv, 85 p. Repr. 1950.

————— Of the Seaven Words Spoken by Christ upon the Crosse. Tr. A. B. St. Omer, 1638.

————— *Die Selbstbiographie*. Ed. and tr. into German by J. J. I. von Doellinger and F. H. Reusch. Bonn, 1887. v, 352 p.

————— Short Christian Doctrine (Catechism) . . . revised and approved. Ed. and tr. anon. Rome, P. Aurelij, 1836. 49, 49 p. (parallel Italian and English texts).

BENEDETTI, ALESSANDRO (c. 1450–1512). Diary of the Caroline War [of 1495]. Ed. and tr. Dorothy M. Schullian. N.Y., Ungar, for Renaissance Society of Amer., 1967. ix, 276 p. (parallel texts).

BENIVIENI, ANTONIO (d. 1502). The Hidden Cause of Disease. Ed. and tr. Charles Singer. Springfield, Ill., C. C. Thomas, 1954. xlvi, 217 p. (parallel texts).

BERENGARIO, JACOPO (fl. 1521). A Short Introduction to Anatomy. Tr. L. R. Lind. Chicago, Univ. of Chicago Pr., 1959. xi, 227 p.

BEZA, THEODORUS (Théodore de Bèze, 1519–1605). A briefe and pithie [sic] summe of the Christian faith. Tr. Robert Fyll from the French [version of the *Confessio Christianae fidei,* 1560]. London, Serll, [?1565]. 195 leaves. Repr. [?1566], 1572, 1589.

————— Beza's *Icones,* Contemporary Portraits of Reformers. Tr. C. G. McCrie. London, Religious Truth Society, 1906. xvi, 249 p., facs. ill.

————— Beza's Introduction to his Translation of the New Testament. Ed. and tr. anon. London, Painter, 1856. xiv, 122 p. (parallel texts).

————— The Life of John Calvin. Tr. Henry Beveridge, in John Calvin, Tracts Relating to the Reformation, v. 1. London, 1844.

————— The New Testament . . . Translated out of Greeke [into Latin] by Theodore Beza. Tr. Laurence Tomson. London, Barker, 1576. 460 leaves. Repr. 1577, 1578, 1580, 1583, 1586, 1596, 1601, 1602, 1609, 1610, 1612, 1613, 1616.

————— The Psalms of David, Truly Opened and Explaned [sic] by Paraphrasis. Tr. Anthonie Gilbie. London, 1581. Repr. 1590.

————— A Tragedy of Abraham's Sacrifice. Tr. Arthur Golding from the French original. London, 1577. Repr. ed. Malcolm W. Wallace with the French, Toronto, Univ. of Toronto Pr., 1906, lxi, 127 p.

Eleven other books by Beza were tr. in the Elizabethan period: see the British Museum Catalogue, and the *Short-Title Catalogue of English Books . . . to 1640.*

BIRCK, SIXT (Xystus Betuleius, 1500–1554). *Sapientia Salomonis.* Ed. and tr. Elizabeth Rogers Payne. Yale Studies in English. New Haven, Yale Univ. Pr., and London, Oxford Univ. Pr., 1938. ix, 167 p.

BLOSIUS, LUDOVICUS (François Louis de Blois, Abbot, O.S.B., 1506–1566). The Works. Tr. Bertrand A. Wilberforce and others. London, Burns Oates, and N.Y., Benziger, 1926, 6 v., 1930, v. 7. (The ed. collects earlier separate trs., the original dates of publication given in parenthesis.)

V. 1. Book of Spiritual Instruction (*Institutio spiritualis*). Tr. B. A. Wilberforce (1900). Repr. London, Burns, Oates, and Westminster, Md., Newman Pr., 1955. xxvi, 143 p.

V. 2. Comfort for the Faint-Hearted (*Consolatio pusillanimium*). Tr. the same (1903).

V. 3 Mirror for Monks. Tr. anon. (Paris, 1676), rev. and ed. Dom Roger Hudleston (1901).
The Paris tr. was also repr. ed. John Duke Coleridge, Baron Coleridge, London 1871; repr. 1872.

V. 4–5. Sanctuary of the Faithful Soul (*Sacellum fidelis animae*). Part 1. The Spiritual Mirror, tr. B. A. Wilberforce (1905). Part 2. A String of Spiritual Jewels, tr. anon., rev. ed. Bertrand Delany.

V. 6. Paradise of the Faithful Soul. Part 1. Rule of Spiritual Life, tr. anon. (1871) as A Manual of the Spiritual Life rev. for this ed.

V. 7. Brief Rule and Daily Exercise for the Beginner, with The Oratory of the Faithful Soul. Tr. B. A. Wilberforce (1901) and (The Oratory) Robert A. Coffin (1848).

Another tr., *Spiritual Works*, ed. John Edward Bowden (London, Washbourne, 1871, xii, 306 p.).

BODIN, JEAN (1530–1596). Method for the Easy Comprehension of History. Tr. Beatrice Reynolds. N.Y., Columbia Univ. Pr., 1945. xxix, 402 p.

———————— The Response to the Paradoxes of Malestroit, and The Paradoxes. Tr. George Albert Moore from the French. Chevy Chase, Md., Country Dollar Pr., 1946. xvii, 90 p.

———————— Six Books of a Commonweal. Tr. Richard Knolles from French and Latin. London, Bishop, 1606. 794 p. Repr. facs. ed. Kenneth Douglas McRae, Cambridge, Mass., Harvard Univ. Pr., and London, Oxford Univ. Pr., 1962. xiv, 214, v, 794 p.

Tr. abridged M. J. Tooley. Oxford, Blackwell, and N.Y., Macmillan, 1955. xlviii, 212 p.

BOEMUS, JOHANNES, AUBANUS (Johann Beham, fl. 1500–1520). The Manners, Lawes, and Customes of all Nations. Tr. Edward Aston. London, Eld, 1611. 598 p.

Earlier part trs., 1554, 1555.

BOERHAAVE, HERMANN (1668–1738). For trs. of his medical treatises, see British Museum Catalogue.

BOETHIUS, HECTOR (BOECE, ?1465–1536). The Chronicles of Scotland. Tr. Scots by John Bellenden. Edinburgh, 1535. Repr. Bannatyne Club, 1821, 2 v.; re-ed. from Ms by R. W. Chambers and Edith C. Batho, Scottish Text Society, ser. 3, v. 10, 15, 1936–41.

Tr. Scots verse by William Stewart as The Buik of the Chronicles of Scotland (c. 1535). Ed. W. B. D. Turnbull. London, Rolls Series 6, 1858. 3 v.

BONEFONIUS, JOANNES (Jean Bonnefons the elder, 1554–1614). Pancharis, Queen of Love: or Woman Unveil'd. Being the Basis of Bonefonius. Tr. several hands. London, Curll, 1721. 52 p. Repr. with Johannes Secundus, 1824, 1838, ?1850, 1853.

BOSCOVICH, RUDJER JOSIP (1711–1787). A Theory of Natural Philosophy. Ed. and tr. James Mark Child. Chicago and London, Open Court, 1922. xix, 463 p.

BOURNE, VINCENT (1695–1747). (The Latin Poems). Part tr. William Cowper, as follows.

(four poems) in Poems by William Cowper. London, 1782. Repr. in later eds. of his poems, notably in the Robert Southey ed., v. 8, 1834.

(eighteen poems) in William Hayley, Life and Posthumous Writings of William Cowper. London, 1803, v. 1. Repr. in subsequent eds. of the Poems, notably that by Robert Southey, v. 10, 1834, and in the Globe ed.

The 22 poems repr. in the *Oxford Standard Authors* ed. of Cowper.

BUCER, MARTIN (1491–1551). Instruction in Christian Love (1523). Tr. Paul Traugott Fuhrmann from the German original. Richmond, Va., John Knox Pr., 1952. 68 p.

For contemporary English versions of his religious pamphlets, see British Museum Catalogue, and also B. Q. Morgan, *German Literature in English Translation,* s.v. John Milton's tr. of extracts from book ii of Bucer's *De regno Christi* was published as *The Judgment of Martin Bucer Concerning Divorce* (London 1644, 40 p.), and repr. in eds. of Milton's prose works from that by Thomas Birch, v. 1, 1738, to the Yale ed., v. 2, 1959.

BUCHANAN, GEORGE (1506–1582). Ane Detection of the Duinges of Marie Quene of Scottes. Tr. ?Thomas Wilson. Edinburgh, 1571. Repr. St. Andrews, 1572; repr. rev. as A Detection of the Actions of Mary Queen of Scots, London 1651, repr. 1689, 1825. Repr. 1958 in The Tyrannous Reign: see The History of Scotland, below.

————— Dialogue Concerning the Rights of the Crown of Scotland. Tr. Robert Macfarlan. London, Cadell, 1799. 205 p.

Tr. C. F. Arowood as The Powers of the Crown in Scotland. Austin, Univ. of Texas Pr., 1949. xi, 150 p.

————— The Franciscan Friar, a Satire, and The Marriage Ode of Francis of Valois and Mary [Stuart]. Tr. George Provand. Glasgow, Brash and Reid, 1809. xvi, 160 p.

————— Fratres, Fraterrimi, Three Books of Epigrams, and Book of Miscellanies. Tr. Robert Monteith. Edinburgh, Anderson, 1708. 76 p.

————— The History of Scotland. Tr. anon. London, Churchill, 1690. 2 parts. Repr. 1722; (5th ed.) 1762; 1766; 1799; 1821; 1827.

Tr. James Aikman. Glasgow, Blackie, 1827. 4 v. Repr. 1829–30, 6 v.; 1851–55, 6 v.

Tr. part by W. A. Gatherer as The Tyrannous Reign of Mary Stewart: George Buchanan's Account. Edinburgh, Univ. Pr., 1958. xii, 228 p.

Books 17–19 of the *Historia*, together with *Ane Detection* (see above) and the vernacular *Ane Admonition*.

———————— The Sphere. Tr. James R. Naiden. Philadelphia, W. H. Allen, 1952. vii, 184 p.

The Plays

———————— The Jephtha and Baptist. Tr. Alexander Gibb. Edinburgh, Miller, 1870, 222 p.

Tr. separately as Jephthes, John the Baptist, by A. Gordon Mitchell. Paisley. Gardner, 1903 (130 p.)—1904 (127 p.)

Tr. Alexander Brown as The Sacred Dramas. Edinburgh, Thin, 1906. x, 162 p.

Tr. (Scots) by Robert Garioch Sutherland as Jephthah, The Baptist. Edinburgh and London, Oliver and Boyd, 1959. 99 p.

———————— Baptistes. Tr. verse anon. as Tyrannical Government Anatomized. London, 1642. 38 p. Repr. in George Neilson, George Buchanan (Glasgow Quatercentenary Studies). Glasgow, 1907.

———————— Jephthes. Tr. William Tait. Edinburgh, 1750.

Tr. C. C. Truro. London, 1853.

BUDÉ, GUILLAUME (1467–1540). On the Transition from Hellenic to Christian Studies. Ed. and tr. Daniel Frank Penham. N.Y., Columbia Univ. dissertation, 1955, typescript, the tr. on alternate p. 2–718.

BULLINGER, HEINRICH (1504–1575). Common Places of Christian Religion. Tr. John Stockwood. London, East, 1572. 252 leaves.

———————— Discourse of the Woorthynesse, Autoritie, and Sufficiencie of the Holy Scripture. Tr. John Tomkys. London, Dawson, 1579. 119 leaves.

———————— Fiftie Godlie and Learned Sermons, diuided into fiue Decades, conteyning the chiefe and principall Pointes of Christian Religion. Tr. H. I. Student of Divinite. London, Newberrie, 1577. 1142 p. Repr. 1587; repr. as The Decades of Henry Bullinger, Oxford, Parker Society, 1849–52, 4 v.

"Of the Holy Catholic Church", Decade 5, sermon 1, was tr. G. W. Bromiley in Library of Christian Classics, v. 24, 1953, p. 288–325.

———— The Tragedies of Tyrantes Exercised upon the Church of God, from the Birth of Christ unto . . . 1572. Tr. Thomas Twyne from the German. London, How, 1575. 142 leaves.

For his other tracts, sermons, and Biblical commentaries tr. in the 16th c., see British Museum Catalogue.

BURCHARD, JOHANN (d. 1506). The Diary of John Burchard of Strasburg, Pontifical Master of Ceremonies, A.D. 1483–1506. Tr. with notes by Arnold Harris Mathew. London, Francis Griffiths, 1910. V. I, A.D. 1483–92. xlii, 431 p.

Part tr. Geoffrey Parker as At the Court of the Borgia. London, Folio Society, 1963. 245 p.

Extracts ed. F. L. Glaser as *Pope Alexander VI and his Court* [1492–1503], N.Y., N.L. Brown, 1921, xxi, 191 p.

BUSBECQ, OGIER GHISELIN DE (1522–1592). Life and Letters. Tr. C. T. Forster and F. H. B. Daniell. London, Kegan Paul, 1881. 2 v.

Not all the letters are tr. in this biography.

———— Letters to the Holy Roman Emperor Maximilian II [from France, 1574–76]. Tr. Robert E. Jones and Bernard C. Weber. N.Y., Bookman Associates, 1962. 180 p.

———— The Turkish Letters. Tr. Edward S. Forster. Oxford, Clarendon Pr., 1927. xvi, 265 p.

Earlier partial trs., 1694, 1744, 1761.

BYNKERSHOEK, CORNELIS VAN (1673–1743). *De dominio maris dissertatio*. Facs ed. and tr. Ralph van Deman Magoffin. Classics of International Law. N.Y., Oxford Univ. Pr., 1923. 429 p.

———— On Questions of Public Law. Facs. ed., tr. Tenney Frank. Classics of International Law. Oxford, Clarendon Pr., 1930. 2 v.

Book i was tr. P. S. Du Ponceau as *A Treatise on the Law of War. American Law Journal,* v. 3 (1808). Repr. Philadelphia, Farrand and Nicholas, 1810, xxxiv, 218 p.

CAIUS, JOHN, M.D. (1510–1573). Of Englishe Dogges, the diuersities, the names, the natures, and the properties. Tr. Abraham Fleming. London, 1576. 44 p. Repr. in The Works of John Caius, Cambridge Univ. Pr., 1912.

CAJETAN DE VIO, THOMAS CARDINAL (1468–1534). The Analogy of Names and the Concept of Being. Tr. Edward A. Bushinski and Henry J. Koren. Pittsburgh, Duquesne Univ. Pr., 1953. x, 93 p.

———— Aristotle on Interpretation, Commentary by St. Thomas and Cajetan. Tr. Jean T. Oesterle. Milwaukee, Wis., Marquette Univ. Pr., 1962. 271 p.

———— Commentary on St. Thomas Aquinas, On Being and Essence. Tr. Lottie H. Kendzierski and Francis C. Wade, S.J. Milwaukee, Wis., Marquette Univ. Pr., 1965. 356 p.

CALVIN, JEAN (1509–1564). The Works of John Calvin. Trs. various, from Latin and French. Edinburgh, Calvin Translation Society, 1844–56. 22 v. in 51. Repr. Grand Rapids, Michigan, Eerdmans, and London and Edinburgh, Oliver and Boyd, 1948–60, as indicated; some v. retr. for the same publishers, see next entry.

1. Commentary upon the Epistle of St. Paul to the Romans. Tr. Christopher Rosdell (1583), rev. Henry Beveridge. 1844. xxxi, 437 p. Not repr.

2. Tracts Relating to the Reformation. Tr. Henry Beveridge. 1844–51. 3 v. Repr. as Tracts and Treatises, with a Short Life by Theodore Beza, ed. Thomas F. Torrance, Eerdmans, 1958, Oliver, 1960.

    V. 1, *On the Reformation of the Church*; v. 2, *On the Doctrine and Worship of the Church*; v. 3, *In Defense of the Reformed Church*.

3. Commentary upon the Acts of the Apostles. Tr. Christopher Fetherstone (1583), rev. Henry Beveridge. 1844. 2 v. Not repr.

4. The Institute of the Christian Religion. Tr. Henry Beveridge. 1845–46. 2 v. Repr. Edinburgh, J. Clarke, 1863, 1949; Eerdmans, Oliver, 1953, repr. 1957, 1959 paper.

5. Commentary on a Harmony of the Evangelists Matthew, Mark, and Luke. Tr. William Pringle. 1846–48. 3 v. Repr. Eerdmans, Oliver, 1949.

6. Commentary on the Book of Psalms. Tr. James Anderson. 1845–49. 5 v. Repr. Eerdmans, Oliver, 1949.

7. Commentaries on the Twelve Minor Prophets. Tr. John Owen. 1846–49. 5 v. Repr. Eerdmans, Oliver, 1950.

8. Commentary on the Gospel According to John. Tr. William Pringle. 1847. 2 v. Repr. Eerdmans, Oliver, 1949. Retr., 1959–60, see next entry.

9. Commentaries on Genesis. Tr. John King. 1847–50. 2 v. Repr. Eerdmans, Oliver, 1948.

10. Commentary on the Epistle to the Corinthians. Tr. John Pringle. 1848–49. 2 v. Repr. Eerdmans, Oliver, 1948. Retr. 1960, see next entry.

11. Commentaries on the First Twenty Chapters of . . . Ezekiel. Tr. Thomas Myers. 1849–50. 2 v. Repr. Eerdmans, Oliver, 1948.

12. Commentaries on the Epistle of Paul to the Romans. Tr. John Owen. 1849. 592 p. Retr. 1960–64, see next entry.

13. Commentary on . . . Isaiah. Tr. William Pringle. 1850–53. 4 v. Repr. Eerdmans, Oliver, 1948.

14. Commentaries on . . . Jeremiah. Tr. John Owen. 1850–55. 5 v. Repr. Eerdmans, Oliver, 1950.

15. Commentaries on the Epistles of Paul to the Philippians, the Colossians, and the Thessalonians. Tr. John Pringle. 1851. 490 p. Repr. Eerdmans, Oliver, 1948. Part retr. 1961.

16. Commentaries on . . . the Four Last Books of Moses. Tr. Charles W. Bingham. 1853–55. 4 v. Repr. Eerdmans, Oliver, 1950.

17. Commentaries on the Book of the Prophet Daniel. Tr. Thomas Myers. 1852–53. 2 v. Repr. 1949.

18. Commentaries on the Epistle of Paul to the Hebrews. Tr. John Owen. 1853. 448 p. Repr. 1948. Retr. 1963, see next entry.

19. Commentaries on the Epistles of Paul to the Galatians and the Ephesians. Tr. William Pringle. 1854. 383 p. (First pub. separately Edinburgh, Clarke, 1841). Repr. 1948.

20. Commentaries on the Book of Joshua. Tr. Henry Beveridge. 1854. 500 p. Repr. 1950.

21. Commentaries on the Epistles to Timothy, Titus, and Philemon. Tr. William Pringle. 1856. 398 p. Repr. 1948. Retr. 1964.

22. Commentary . . . on the Catholic Epistles. Tr. John Owen. 1855. 488 p. Repr. 1948.

———————— (Commentaries, a new series of trs. as follows.) Edinburgh and London, Oliver and Boyd, and Grand Rapids, Michigan, Eerdmans, 1959—(in progress)

On the Gospel According to John. Tr. T. H. L. Parker. 1959–61. 2 v.

On the Epistles to the Romans and to the Thessalonians. Tr. Ross Mackenzie. 1961. 433 p.

On the First Epistle to the Corinthians. Tr. John W. Fraser. 1960. 370 p.

On the Epistle to the Hebrews and on I and II Peter. Tr. W. B. Johnston. 1963. 378 p.

On II Corinthians, Timothy, Titus, Philemon. Tr. T. A. Smail. 1964. 410 p.

———————— The Commentaries. Tr. Joseph Haroutunian and Louise P. Smith. Library of Christian Classics, v. 23, 1958. 414 p. (9 commentaries)

———————— Theological Treatises. Tr. J. K. S. Reid. Library of Christian Classics, v. 22, 1954. 355 p. (16 treatises)

Individual Works

———————— The Commentary vpon . . . John. Tr. Christopher Fetherstone. London, 1584. 2 parts (with A Harmonie, see next entry but one).

———————— The Golden Booklet of the True Christian Life (*Libellus aureus*). Tr. ed. Henry J. van Andel. Grand Rapids, Michigan, Baker Book House, 1952. 98 p.

———————— A Harmonie upon the Three Euangelists. Tr. Eusebius Pagit. London, 1584. 2 parts (with the Commentary upon John, above)

———————— The Institute of the Christian Religion. Tr. Thomas Norton. London, Wolfe, 1561. 8 reprs. to 1634.

Tr. John Allen. London, Walker, 1813. 3 v. Repr. 1838, etc., to 7th American ed., Philadelphia, Westminster Pr., 1936, repr. Grand Rapids, Michigan, Eerdmans, 1949, 2 v.

Tr. Henry Beveridge, in The Works, Edinburgh ed., v. 4, 1845–46, see above.

Tr. Ford Lewis Battles, ed. John T. McNeill. Library of Christian Classics, v. 20–21, 1960.

———————— Instruction in the Faith. Ed. and tr. Paul T. Fuhrmann. Philadelphia, Westminster Pr., 1949. 96 p.

———————— The Judgment of Cardinal Cajetan against the Immaculate Conception. Tr. R. C. Jenkins. Canterbury, Ashenden, 1888.

———————— The Letters. Tr. David Constable. Edinburgh, Constable, and Philadelphia, Presbyterian Board of Education, 1855–57. 4 v.

————————The Necessity of Reforming the Church: Presented to the Imperial Diet at Spires A.D. 1544 . . . A Paternal Admonition by Pope Paul III to the Emperor Charles V, and Remarks on the Paternal Admonition by John Calvin. Tr. Henry Beveridge. London, Dalton, 1843. viii, 291 p.

———————— Reply to Sadoleto. Tr. John C. Olin in A Reformation Debate: Jacopo Sadoleto's Letter to the Genevans and Calvin's Reply. N.Y., Harper (Torch Books), 1966. 136 p. paper.

———————— Sermons upon the Book of Job. Tr. Arthur Golding from the French. London, 1574. 32, 821 p.

———————— A Treatise on Relics. Tr. Count Walerian S. Krasinski from the French original. Edinburgh, Johnstone & Hunter, 1854. x, 293 p. Repr. 1870.

For contemporary trs. and for trs. of selections, see the British Museum Catalogue.

CAMDEN, WILLIAM (1551–1623). Annales. The True and Royall History of . . . Elizabeth Queen of England. Tr. Abraham Darcie (part one, from the French version) and Thomas Browne (part two). London, 1625–29. 2 v.

Tr. Richard Norton (four parts). London, 1630. Repr. 1635, 1675, 1688, 1706 (in White Kennett, Complete History, v. II), 1719.

———————— Britain, or a Chorographicall Description of England, Scotland, and Ireland. Tr. Philemon Holland. London, 1610. Repr. 1637.

Tr. with additions by Edmund Gibson, London, 1695. Repr. 1722, 2 v.; 1753; 1772.

Tr. with additions by Richard Gough. London, 1789. 3 v. Repr. 1806, 4 v.

CAMERARIUS, PHILIPPUS (1537–1624). The Walking Librarie, or Meditations and Obseruations historical, natural, moral, political, and poetical. Tr. John Molle from the French version. London, Islip, 1621. 403 p. Repr. 1625 (adding parts of Century ii), 428 p.

The *Operae horarum subsicivarum . . . Centuria prima* (1602). Another issue of the 1621 tr. is entitled *The Living Librarie*.

CAMPANELLA, TOMMASO (1568–1639). The City of the Sun. See Italian Literature, in v. III.

———— A Discourse Touching the Spanish Monarchy: Wherein we have a political glasse, representing each particular country . . . of the world, with wayes of government by which they may be kept in obedience. Tr. Edward Chilmead [from the 3d ed. of the *De Monarchia Hispanica*]. London, Stevens, 1654. 232 p. Repr. 1659, with preface, Advice to the King of Spain. Repr. Harleian Miscellany, v. 1, 1744; repr. 1808.

CAMPION, EDMUND (1540–1581). Ten Reasons Proposed to his Adversaries for Disputation in the Name of the Faith. Ed. J. H. Pollen (Latin text) and tr. Joseph Rickaby. London, Herder, 1914. 145 p.

First tr. and pub. with Whitaker's *Answere*, q.v. below. For other trs., 1632, 1687, 1827, etc., in 47 eds., see British Museum Catalogue.

CANISIUS, PETER, ST. (Kanees or Kanys, 1521–1597). Certayne Necessarie Principles of Religion . . . A Catechisme Conteyning all the Partes of the Christian and Catholique Fayth. Tr. T. I. Douai, [?1580]. 72 leaves.

Tr. Adam King as Ane Catechisme or Short Instruction of Christian Religion. Paris, 1588. Repr. Scottish Text Society 45, 1901. p. 173–216.

Tr. Henry Garnet, as A Summe of Christian Doctrine. St. Omer, 1622. 687 p.

Tr. L. de San Martin. Douai, 1639. 475 p.

The above are trs. of successive versions of the *Catechism*.

CANTEMIR, DEMETRIUS (Prince of Moldavia, 1673–1723). The History of the Growth and Decay of the Othman Empire. Tr. Nicholas Tindal from the Latin Ms. London, 1734–35. xv, 460 p. Repr. 1756.

CARDANO, GIROLAMO (1501–1576). The Book on Games of Chance. Tr. Sydney Henry Gould. In Oystein Ore, Cardano the Gambling

Scholar, Princeton, N.J., Princeton Univ. Pr., 1953, p. 181–241. Repr. N.Y., Dover, 1965, paper.

———— The Book of My Life. Tr. Jean Stoner. N.Y., Dutton, and London, Dent, 1931. xviii, 331 p.

———— Cardanus Comforte. Tr. Thomas Bedingfield. London, 1573. Repr. 1576, 102 leaves.

Tr. anon. as Three Books of Consolation. London, 1683.

———— The First Book of Jerome Cardan's *De Subtilitate*. Tr. Myrtle Marguerite Cass. Williamsport, Pa., Bayard Pr., 1934. 191 p.

CASIMIR (Polish Poet). See Sarbiewsky, below.

CASMANN, OTTO (d. 1607). Vade mecum. Goe with mee: Deare Pietie, and rare Charitie. (*Vade Mecum, Cara Pietas et rara Caritas*). Tr. Henry Tripp. London, 1606.

CASTELLIO, SEBASTIANO (1515–1563). Concerning Heretics, Whether they are to be Persecuted. Tr. Roland H. Bainton. CURC. N.Y., Columbia Univ. Pr., 1935. xiv, 342 p.

———— Good and True. A Holy Collection made out of the Old Testament. (*Dialogi sacri*). Tr. anon. London, 1610. 496 p.

Tr. anon. as The History of the Bible Collected into 119 Dialogues (books 1–3). London, Wyatt, 1715. 292 p.

CELTIS, CONRAD (1459–1508). Selections. Tr. Leonard Foster. London, Cambridge Univ. Pr., and N.Y., Macmillan, 1948. xii, 122 p.

CHANCY, DOM MAURICE (c. 1514–1581). The History of the Sufferings of Eighteen Carthusians in England, Who . . . were Cruelly Martyred. Part tr. by a London Carthusian. London, Burns and Oates, and N.Y., Catholic Pub. Soc., 1890. xvi, 78 p.

Ed. and tr. A. F. Radcliffe from Ms. London, Church History Soc., 1935. 165 p. (parallel texts)

CHYTRAEUS, DAVID (1531–1600). On Sacrifice: A Reformation Treatise in Biblical Theology. Tr. John W. Montgomery. St. Louis, Mo., Concordia Pr., 1962. 151 p.

COLET, JOHN (1467?–1519). An Exposition of St. Paul's Epistle to the Corinthians. Ed. from Ms. and tr. J. H. Lupton. London, Bell and Daldy, 1876. iv, 274 p. (parallel texts)

———— An Exposition of St. Paul's Epistle to the Romans. Ed. from Ms. and tr. J. H. Lupton. London, Bell and Daldy, 1873. xliii, 235 p. (parallel texts).

———— *Opuscula quaedam theologica.* (Commentary on I Peter [unfinished]; On the Composition of Christ's Mystical Body the Church; Exposition of St. Paul's Epistle to the Romans; Letters to Radulphus on the Mosaic Account of the Creation). Ed. from Ms. and tr. J. H. Lupton. London, Bell, 1876. lii, 320 p. (parallel texts).

———— The Sermon made to the Convocacion at Paulis. Tr. ascribed to Thomas Lupset. London, [1530?]. Repr. J. H. Lupton, in The Life of Colet, London, 1887.

Tr. Thomas Smith as A Sermon of Conforming and Reforming: Made to the Convocation. Cambridge, Morden, 1661. 80 p. Repr. London, 1701, 1707, 1724 in Samuel Knight, Life of Dr. John Colet; 1823, *ibid.*

———— Two Treatises on the Hierarchies of Dionysius (*Super opera Dionysii*). Ed. from Ms. and tr. J. H. Lupton. London, Bell and Daldy, 1869. xlvii, 275 p. (parallel texts).

———— A Treatise on the Sacraments of the Church. Ed. and tr. from Ms. J. H. Lupton. London, Bell and Daldy, 1867. vi, 96 p. (parallel texts).

COMENIUS (Komensky, Jan Amos, 1592–1671)

Educational Works

———— The Analytical Dialectic. Tr. Vladimir Jelinek (from Ch. 10 of *Linguarum methodus novissima*). Chicago, Univ. Pr., and London, Cambridge Univ. Pr., 1953. xvii, 239 p.

———— The Gate of Tongues Unlocked and Opened (*Janua linguarum reserata et aperta*). Tr. Thomas Horn. London, 1631. 226 p. (parallel texts, Latin, French, English). Repr. 1633, 1637, 1639, 1641; rev. John Robothan, 1643, 1645, 1647; repr. rev. William Dugard, 1650, repr. 1652, 1656, 1659, 1662 (Latin, English), 1667 (the same), 1670 (Latin, Greek, English), 1670 (Latin, English).

———————— The Great Didactic. Tr. M. W. Keatinge. London, Black, and N.Y., Macmillan, 1896. 468 p. Repr. London, 1910; repr. abridged, N.Y. and London, McGraw-Hill, 1931, 255 p.

———————— Naturall Philosophie Reformed by Divine Light, or A Synopsis of Physics (*Physicae ad lumen reformatae synopsis*). Tr. anon., London, 1651.

———————— *Orbis sensualium pictus:* The Visible World. Tr. Charles Hoole. London, 1659. 309 p. (parallel texts). Repr. 1664, and many reprs. to 14th ed., 1763; also repr. Syracuse, N.Y., C. W. Hardeen, 1887, xxxi, 194 p.

———————— A Patterne of Universal Knowledge (*Pansophiae Diatyposis*). Tr. Jeremy Collier. London, 1651. Repr. 1651.

———————— A Reformation of Schools (*Pansophiae prodromus*). Tr. Samuel Hartlib. London, 1642. 94 p.

———————— The School of Infancy (*Schola-ludus*). Tr. D. Benham. London, 1858. x, 168, 75 p. Repr. rev. Will S. Monroe, Boston, Heath, 1896, xvi, 99 p.

Tr. Ernst N. Eller. Chapel Hill, Univ. of North Carolina Pr., 1956. viii, 130 p.

———————— *Vestibulum technicum,* or the last Porch. Tr. anon. London, 1647. Repr. to 4th ed., corrected S. Boncle, as An Artificial Vestibulum, Wherein the Sense of Janua linguarum is contained, London, 1701, 82 p.

———————— The Way of Light (*Via lucis*). Tr. with intro. E. T. Campagnac. Liverpool, Univ. Pr., and London, Hodder and Stoughton, 1938. xix, 26, 234 p.

Other Works

———————— The Angel of Peace. Ed. Milos Safranek in *Angeles pacis ad legatos pacis Anglos et Belgas* . . . 1667. Prague, 1926. (texts in five languages, the English tr. by W. A. Morison). Repr. (Latin and English), N.Y., Pantheon, 1944, 125 p.

———————— An Exhortation of the Churches of Bohemia to the Church of England. Tr. Joshua Tymparchus. London, 1661. 78, 54 p.

———————— A generall Table of Europe. Representing the Present and Future State Thereof. Tr. anon. London, 1670.

————— The History of the Bohemian Persecution (894–1632). Tr. anon. London, Walker, 1650. 376 p.

————— The Labyrinth of the World, and the Paradise of the Heart. Tr. Count Francis Lützow (from the 2d ed., 1663, of the Czech original). London, Swan Sonnenschein, and N.Y., Dutton, 1901. 347 p. Repr. Temple Classics, 1905; Golden Cockerel Pr., 1950.

Tr. Matthew Spinka (from the 1631 ed., with recourse to the Ms.). Chicago, National Union of Czechoslovak Protestants in America, 1942. vi, 170 p.

CONTARINI, GASPARO, CARDINAL (1483–1542). The Commonwealth and Gouernment of Venice. Tr. Lewis Lewkenor. London, 1599. 230 p.

————— The State of the Church of Rome . . . as it appears by the Advices given to Paul III and Julius III by Creatures of their Own. Tr. William Clagett. London, 1688. Repr. 1738; 1848; in Somers Tracts, v. III, 1751, repr. v. IX, 1809. (The *De emenda ecclesia,* by a committee of cardinals 1538).

COPERNICUS, NICOLAUS (1473–1543). On the Revolutions of the Heavenly Spheres. Tr. Charles Glenn Wallis, in Great Books, v. 16, 1952, p. 505–838.

Part tr. (preface and book i) John F. Dobson and Selig Brodetsky. London, Royal Astronomical Society, 1955. 32 p., plates.

————— Three Copernican Treatises: The *Commentariolus* of Copernicus, the Letter Against Werner, the *Narratio prima* of Rheticus. Tr. Edward Rosen. N.Y., Columbia Univ. Pr., 1939. x, 211 p. Repr. N.Y., Dover, 1960. x, 283 p.

CORDIER, MATHURIN (?1480–1564). Corderius Dialogues. Tr. John Brinsley. London, 1636. 306 p. Repr. 1653.

Many eds. of selections, parallel texts, as school texts published 1657 to 1834.

COWLEY, ABRAHAM (1618–1667). Six Books of Plants. Tr. J. O., C. Cleve, Nahum Tate, Aphra Behn. in The Third [part] of the Works of Cowley. London, 1689. Repr. 1700, 1708, 1711, 1721.

CRASHAW, RICHARD (1612–1649). (The Latin Poems). Tr. Clement Barksdale, A. B. Grosart, et al., in The Complete Works, ed. A. B. Grosart, v. 2. London, 1873. (parallel texts)

The Barksdale tr. was (selected) *Sacred Epigrams Englished* (London, 1682).

Tr. Sister Maris Stella Milhaupt, O.P., as The Latin Epigrams. Univ. of Michigan dissertation, 1963.

CRELLIUS, JOHANNES (Johann Crell, 1590–1633). The Expiation of a Sinner. London, 1646.

————— The Justification of a Sinner. London, 1650.

————— A Learned and Exceeding Well-Compiled Vindication of Liberty of Religion. Tr. by N. Y. (no place, no printer), 1646. 71 p.

————— The Two Books . . . Touching One God the Father. Kosmoburg [sic], 1665. 315 p. Repr. as The Unity of God, London, 1691.

CUNAEUS, PETRUS (Pierre van der Kun, 1586–1638). Of the Common-Wealth of the Hebrews. Tr. C. B. London, 1653.

CURIO or CURIONE, CELIO SECONDO (1503–1569). A Defence of the True and Old Authority of Christ's Church (*pro vera et antiqua Ecclesiae Christi autoritate in Antonium Florebellum Mutinensem Oratio*). Tr. John Philpott (d. 1555). Ed. from Ms. by Robert Eden, in Parker Society Pubs. 5, 1852, 318–432.

————— Italy and the Gospel: Letters and Discourses of Celio Curio. Tr. anon. from the Italian ed of 1552. London, Nisbet, 1848. xv, 122 p.

————— A New History of the War in Malta, 1565. Tr. Granville Pacha from an Italian version. Rome, Tipografia Leonina, 1928. 163 p.

————— Pasquine in a Traunce . . . newes out of Heauen, Pugatorie and Hell (*Pasquillus ecstaticus*). Tr. William Phiston from an Italian version. London, 1566. 112 leaves. Repr. 1584.

DEDEKIND, FRIEDRICH (1524–1598). The Schoole of Slovenrie (*Grobianus*). Tr. verse R. F. London, 1605. 136 p. Repr. in Ernst Rühl, Grobianus in England, see below.

Tr. (paraphrase) Roger Bull as Grobianus or the Compleat Booby. London, 1739. xiii, 276 p.

Cf. Ernst Rühl, *Grobianus in England,* Palaestra, 38 (Berlin, 1904, lxxxii, 191 p.).

DESCARTES, RENÉ (1596–1650). The Essential Works. Tr. Lowell Bair, from Latin and French. N.Y., Bantam, 1961. 233 p.

————— Philosophical Essays. Tr. Laurence J. Lafleur. Indianapolis, Ind., Bobbs-Merrill, 1964. xxiv, 236 p.

Discourse on Method. Meditations. Rules for the Guidance of our Native Powers. The first two essays were pub. separately 1950, 1951; repr. 1956, 1961.

————— The Philosophical Works. Tr. Elizabeth S. Haldane and G. R. T. Ross. Cambridge, Univ. Pr., 1911–12. 2 v. Repr. 1931–34; repr. (with the Geometry, and with Spinoza's Ethics) in Great Books, v. 31, 1952, 463 p.; repr. N.Y., Dover, 1955.

Rules for the Guidance of our Native Powers. Discourse on Method. Meditations. Objections and Replies. Search after Truth. Passions of the Soul.

————— Philosophical Writings. Tr. Norman Kemp Smith. London, Macmillan, 1952. Repr. ML, 1958. xvii, 300 p.

Rules for the Guidance, etc. *Discourse on Method. Meditations. Letters on the Mind Body Problem and Replies. Passions of the Soul.*

Individual Works

————— A Discourse on Method. Tr. anon. from the French. London, 1649. 127 p.

Tr. John Veitch. Edinburgh and London, Simpkin Marshall, 1850. xli, 150 p. Repr. (with Meditations, and Principles), see below.

————— The Discourse on Method, and Other Writings. Tr. Arthur Wollaston. Penguin, 1960. 192 p.

————— The Discourse on Method, Optics, Geometry, Meteorology. Tr. Paul Olscamp. Indianapolis, Ind., Bobbs-Merrill, 1965. xxxvi, 361 p.

————— Excellent Compendium of Musick. Tr. Viscount Brouncker. London, 1653. 16, 94 p.

Tr. Walter Robert as Compendium of Music. [Rome?], American Institute of Musicology, 1961. 53 p.

————— The Geometry. Tr. David Eugene Smith and Marcia L. Latham. Chicago and London, Open Court, 1925. xiii, 246 p. Repr. in Great Books, v. 31, 1952; repr. N.Y., Dover, 1954.

————— The Meditations, and Selections from the Principles of Philosophy. Tr. John Veitch from the Latin, and collated with the French. Edinburgh, Sutherland and Knox, and London, Simpkin Marshall, 1853, et seq. xiv, 212 p. Repr. Chicago, Ill., Open Court, 1901, repr. 1913, 1948, 1959. Repr. (with A Discourse on Method) EL, 1912, et seq. Repr. in The World's Great Thinkers, N.Y., Random House, 1947, v. 4; in The Rationalists (with Spinoza and Leibnitz), N.Y., Doubleday, 1962.

Tr. (The Meditations) Richard Lowndes from the Latin. In René Descartes, His Life and Meditations. London, Norgate, 1878. 8, 297 p.

————— The Passions of the Soule. Tr. anon. London, 1650. 173 p.

EPISTOLAE OBSCURORUM VIRORUM (uncertain authorship, 1516). Ed. and tr. F. Griffin Stokes as Letters of Obscure Men. London, Chatto, 1909. lxiii, 559 p. (parallel texts). Repr. (English only) as On the Eve of the Reformation, N.Y., Harper (paper), and Gloucester, Mass., Peter Smith, 1964, xiv, 262 p.

ERASMUS, DESIDERIUS (1466?–1536). The Essential Erasmus. Tr. John P. Dolan. N.Y., New Amer. Lib., 1964. 397 p.

Handbook of the Militant Christian. Praise of Folly. Complaint of Peace. Inquiry Concerning Faith. The Eating of Fish. The Immense Mercy of God. On Mending the Peace of the Church.

————— Selected Writings. Ed. John C. Olin as Christian Humanism and the Reformation. N.Y., Harper, 1965. 201 p. paper.

Compendium vitae. Paraclesis. 6 Letters. Axiomata.

Individual Works

————— The Adages. Tr. Richard Taverner (in part) as Proverbes or Adagies . . . gathered . . . out of Erasmus. London, 1539. Repr. 1545, 1552, 1569; facs. repr. of the last ed., Gainesville, Fla., Scholars' Facsimiles, 1956, 71 leaves.

Tr. anon. as Erasmus Adagia in Latine and English contayning fyue hundreth proverbes. Aberdeen, 1622.

Tr. R. Bland as Proverbs, Chiefly Taken from the Adagia of Erasmus. London, 1814. 2 v.

Some trs. by Margaret Mann Phillips in *The Adages, A Study*. London and N.Y., Cambridge Univ. Pr., 1965. xvi, 418 p.

——————— Apophthegmes. Tr. Nicholas Udall. London, 1542. Repr. 1564; repr. ed. Edwin Johnson, Boston, Roberts, 1877, 38, xxviii, 488 p.

——————— *Ciceronianus,* or A Dialogue on the Best Style of Speaking. Tr. Izora Scott. N.Y., Teachers College, Columbia Univ., 1900. 130 p.

——————— The Colloquies. Tr. H. M. London, 1671. 555 p.

Part tr. Sir Roger L'Estrange as Twenty Select Colloquies. London, 1680. Reprs., esp. rev. in Abbey Classics, London, Chapman and Dodd, 1923, xv, 256 p.

Tr. Nathan Bailey. London, 1725, et seq., to repr. N.Y. Scribner, 1905, 2 v.

Tr. Craig R. Thompson. Chicago, Univ. of Chicago Pr., 1965. 664 p.

Cf. the latter's partial tr. as *Ten Colloquies,* N.Y., Liberal Arts Pr., 1957, xxx, 174 p.—For many trs. of one or more dialogues, see the *Short-Title Catalogue of English Books . . . to 1640.*

——————— The Complaint of Peace. Tr. Thomas Paynell. London, 1559. Reprs., esp. Chicago and London, Open Court, 1917. Repr. rev. W. J. Hirten, N.Y., Scholars' Facsimiles, 1946, 184 p.

——————— Concerning the Aim and Method of Education. Extracts tr. W. H. Woodward. Cambridge, Univ. Pr., 1904. 244 p. Repr. N.Y., Teachers College, 1964, paper.

——————— On Copia of Words and Ideas *(De copia).* Tr. Donald B. King and H. David Rix. Milwaukee, Wis., Marquette Univ. Pr., 1963. 111 p.

——————— Discourse on Free Will. Tr. Ernst F. Winter. N.Y., Ungar, 1961. xiv, 138 p. (with extracts from Martin Luther, The Bondage of the Will).

——————— Education of a Christian Prince. Tr. Lester K. Born. N.Y., Columbia Univ. Pr., 1936. 277 p. Repr. N.Y., Octagon Books, 1965.

——————— The Enchiridion. Tr. ascribed to William Tyndale as The Manuell of the Christen Knight. London, de Worde, 1533. Many reprs., to London, Methuen, 1905, 287 p.

Tr. John Spier as The Christian's Manual. London, Ware, 1752. xvi, 274 p.

Tr. Ford Lewis Battles, in Library of Christian Classics, v. 14, 1953, p. 295–379.

Tr. John P. Dolan as Handbook of the Militant Christian. Notre Dame, Ind., Fides, 1962. 159 p. Repr. in The Essential Erasmus, see above.

Tr. Raymond Himelick as The Enchiridion. Bloomington, Indiana Univ. Pr., 1963. 222 p.

——————— The Epistles of Erasmus . . . to his 51st Year [1516]. Tr. Francis Morgan Nichols. London and N.Y., Longmans, 1901–18. 3 v. Repr. N.Y., Russell and Russell, 1962, 3 v.

Selected. Cf. *Erasmus and Cambridge: The Cambridge Letters*, tr. D. F. S. Thomson, intro. H. C. Porter (Toronto, Univ. of Toronto Pr., 1963, 233 p.).

——————— (Julius Exclusus). Tr. anon. 1534 as The dyalogue bytwene Jullius the Seconde Genius and Saynt Peter. London, Byddell, 1535. (Short-Title Catalogue 14482, under Julius II)

Tr. anon. as The Pope shut out of Heaven Gates. London, Vaughan, 1673. 48 p.

Tr. anon. London, Warner, 1719. viii, 88 p.

Tr. J. A. Froude, in his Life and Letters of Erasmus, London, Longmans, 1894. Repr. 1916, p. 156–74.

——————— The Paraphrase upon the newe testament. Tr. Nicholas Udall, Myles Coverdale, John Dee. London, 1548–49. 2 v.

——————— The Praise of Folly. Tr. Sir Thomas Chaloner. London, 1549. Repr. 1560?, 1569, 1577, and (ed. J. E. Ashbee), London, Arnold, 1901; repr. EETS ES 257, 1965, li, 225 p.

Tr. John Wilson. London, 1668. Repr. (ed. Mrs. P. S. Allen), 1913; repr. Ann Arbor, Univ. of Michigan Pr., 1958, 150 p.

Tr. White Kennett. London, 1683. Repr. 1709, 1725?, 1726, 1735, 1740, 1870, 1887.

Tr. James Copner. London, 1878.

Tr. Hoyt H. Hudson. Princeton, N.J., Princeton Univ. Pr., 1941. xl, 166 p. Repr. ML, 1962.

Accurate, rather formal style of tr.

Tr. Leonard F. Dean. Chicago, Packard, 1946. viii, 273 p.

> Facile, familiar style of tr.

For other earlier trs. of the shorter works of Erasmus, see British Museum Catalogue.

FABRICIUS, HIERONYMUS (c. 1533–1619). The Embryological Treatises: The Formation of the Egg and of the Chick; The Formed Fetus. Facs. ed. and tr. Howard B. Adelmann. Ithaca, N.Y., Cornell Univ. Pr., 1942. xxiii, 883 p.

———— *De venarum ostiolis* 1603. Facs. ed. and tr. K. J. Franklin. Springfield, Ill., and Baltimore, Md., C. C. Thomas, 1933. 98 p.

FAERNO, GABRIELLO (fl. 1549–1561). Fables in English and French Verse. Tr. anon. from the Latin (with the Fables of Perrault in French). London, 1741.

FICINO, MARSILIO (1439–1499). Commentary on Plato's Symposium. Tr. Sears R. Jayne. Columbia, Mo., Univ. of Missouri Pr., 1944. 247 p.

———— Five Questions Concerning the Mind (*Epistolae,* book ii, no. 1). Tr. Josephine L. Burroughs, in The Renaissance Philosophy of Man. p. 193–212: see Collections, Neo-Latin Literature, above.

Cf. Paul Oskar Kristeller, *The Philosophy of Marsilio Ficino,* tr. from German by Virgina Conant (N.Y., Columbia Univ. Pr., 1943, xiv, 441 p. Repr. Gloucester, Mass., Peter Smith, 1964).

FIERA, BATTISTA (1469–1538). *De iusticia pingenda.* On the Painting of Justice: A Dialogue between Mantegna and Momus. Tr. James Wardrop, Royal College of Art. London, Lion and Unicorn Pr., 1957. 54 p. (parallel texts)

FISHER, JOHN CARDINAL, ST. (?1469–1535). The Defence of the Priesthood against Luther. Tr. P. E. Hallett. London, Burns Oates, 1935. x, 150 p.

FLAMINIO, MARCO ANTONIO (1498–1550). The Scholar's Vade Mecum . . . being a translation by John Norton. London, 1674.

Prose versions of 3 prayers, 17 hymns, a poem to Marguerite of Navarre.

Tr. Thomas Morell (6 poems) in Poems on Divine Subjects. London, 1732, p. 239–68.

Tr. H. D. Skrine as The Sacred Songs. (parallel texts). London, pr. pr., 18—. 71 p.

An apparent tr., E. W. Barnard, *Fifty Selected Poems* (Chester, England, pr. pr. 1829), is in fact a series of imitations.

FORTESCUE, SIR JOHN (?1394–?1476). A Learned Commendation of the Politique Lawes of Englande. Tr. Robert Mulcaster (parallel texts). London, Tottell, 1567. 132 leaves. Repr. 1573, 1575, 1578, 1609, and (with notes by John Selden) 1616, 1660, 1672.

Tr. Francis Gregor as *De laudibus legum Angliae*, With the Selden Notes. London, 1737. lxiv, 130 etc. p. Repr. 1741, 1775, 1825, 1869 (in v. 1 of the Works of Fortescue, ed. Thomas Lord Clermont), 1874, 1917 (without notes).

Ed. and tr. S. B. Chrimes (parallel texts). Cambridge Studies in Legal History. Cambridge Univ. Pr., 1942. cxiv, 235 p.

FRACASTORO, GIROLAMO (1483–1553). *De Contagione et contagiosis morbis.* Ed. and tr. with notes by Wilmer Cave Wright. N.Y., Putnam, 1930. lvii, 356 p. (parallel texts).

————— The Maiden's Blush, or Joseph. Tr. Joshua Sylvester. London, 1620. Repr. 1621.

————— *Naugerius, sive de poeta dialogus.* Ed. and tr. Ruth Kelso, intro. Murray W. Bundy. Urbana, Univ. of Illinois Pr., 1924. 88 p.

————— Syphilis. Tr. Nahum Tate. London, 1686. 84 p. Repr. 1686; 1692 (in John Dryden, Miscellany 2).

Tr. prose Solomon Claiborne Martin. St. Louis, Mo. Philmar Co., 1911. 58 p. Repr., with life of Mario Truffi tr. Philip Frank, St. Louis, Mo., Urologic and Cutaneous Pr., 1931, 104 p.

Tr. William Van Wyck as The Sinister Shepherd. Los Angeles, Primavera Pr., 1934. xxii, 85 p.

Tr. Heneage Wynne-Finch. London, Heinemann, 1934. vii, 253 p.

GAEOMEMPHION CANTALIENSIS (World-scorner of Cantal, pseud. of anon.). Satyricon (n. p., 1628). Ed. and tr. Robert E. Pike as The Strangest Book in the World. Eatontown, N.J., H. H. Press, 1963. xv, 253 p. (parallel texts)

GAGER, WILLIAM (fl. 1580–1609). Pyramis. Ed. and tr. C. F. Tucker Brooke. Connecticut Academy of Arts and Science, 32 (1936), 247–349. (parallel texts).

GANSFORT, JOHAN WESSEL (?1420–1489). Principal Works. Tr. Jared W. Scudder, in Edward W. Miller, Wessel Gansfort: Life and Writings. N.Y., American Society of Church History, 1917. 2 v. Also N.Y. and London, Putnam, 1917.

GARDINER, STEPHEN (?1483–1555). Obedience in Church and State: Three Political Tracts (On Fisher's Execution. Oration of True Obedience. Answer to Bucer). Ed. and tr. Pierre Janelle. Cambridge Univ. Pr., 1930. lxx, 221 p. (parallel texts).

The tr. of the *Oration of True Obedience* (*De vera obedientia*) is the anon. one of 1553, ascribed to John Bale.

GASSENDI, PIERRE (1592–1655). The Mirrour of True Nobility and Gentility. Being the Life of Nicolaus Claudius Fabricius, Lord of Peiresk. Tr. William Rand. London, 1657. 216, 296 p.

——————— Three Discourses of Happiness, Virtue and Liberty. Tr. anon. from the French. London, 1699. 452 p.

——————— The Vanity of Judiciary Astrology. Tr. by a Person of Quality. London, Moseley, 1659. vi, 162 p.

The philosophical works of Gassendi have not been tr.

GAUSS, KARL FRIEDRICH (1777–1855). General Investigations of Curved Surfaces. Tr. J. C. Morehead and A. M. Hiltebeitel. Princeton, N.J., Princeton Univ. Library, 1902. v, 126 p.

——————— Inaugural Lecture on Astronomy and Papers on the Foundations of Mathematics. Tr. G. Waldo Dunnington. Baton Rouge, Louisiana State Univ. Pr., 1937. xi, 91 p.

———— Theory of the Heavenly Bodies Moving About the Sun in Conic Sections. Tr. Charles Henry Davis. Boston, Little Brown, 1857. xvii, 326 p.

GENTILI, ALBERICO (1552–1608). *De jure belli libri tres.* Facs. ed. and tr. John C. Rolfe. Classics of International Law. Oxford, Clarendon Pr., 1933. 2 v.

———— *De legationibus.* Facs of 1594 ed. and tr. Gordon J. Laing. Classics of International Law. N.Y., Oxford Univ. Pr., 1924. 2 v.

———— *Hispanicae advocationis libri duo.* Facs. of 1661 ed., tr. Frank Frost Abbott. Classics of International Law. N.Y., Oxford Univ. Pr., 1921. 2 v.

GERARD, JOHN, S. J. (1564–1617). Autobiography. Tr. G. R. Kingdon, London, Burns and Oates, 1872. xvi, 270 p.

Tr. Philip Caraman as An Autobiography of an Elizabethan. London, Longmans, 1951. xxiv, 287 p.

GESNER, KONRAD (1516–1565). On the Admiration of Mountains. A Description of Mount Pilatus. Tr. H. B. D. Soulé, in J. M. Thorington, On Conrad Gesner and the Mountaineering of Theuerdank. San Francisco, Calif., Grabhorn Pr., 1937. 54 p.

———— The History of Four-footed Beastes and Serpents Collected Out of All the Volumes [i.e., v. 1, 5] of Conrad Gesner. By Edward Topsell. London, 1607. Repr. 1658 (as v. 2 of Moffett, Theatre of Insects, q.v. below), 1130 p.

Not a tr., but based on v. 1 and 5 of the *Historia animalium.*

———— The Treasure of Euonymus: Conteyninge the Hid Secretes of Nature (*Euonymus sive de remediis secretis,* part 1). Tr. Peter Morwyng. London, Day, 1559. Repr. 1565.

Tr. (part 2) George Baker as The newe Jewell of Health . . . secretes of Phisicke. London, 1576. 258 leaves. Repr. 1599 as The Practice of the New and Old Phisicke, 256 leaves.

GILBERT, WILLIAM (1540–1603). On the Lodestone and Magnetic Bodies, and on the Great Magnet the Earth. Tr. P. Fleury Mottelay. London, Quaritch, and N.Y., Wiley, 1893. liv, 368 p. Repr. Great

Books, v. 28, 1952. Repr. London, Constable, 1958, and N.Y., Dover, 1959, paper.

Tr. Silvanus P. Thompson as On the Magnet. Magnetick Bodies also, and on the Great Magnet the Earth. London, Gilbert Club and Chiswick Pr., 1900. viii, 246 p. Repr. N.Y., Basic Books, 1958.

GILLES, PIERRE (Gyllius, 1490–1555). The Antiquities of Constantinople: In Four Books. Tr. enlarged by John Ball. London, 1729. 2 parts.

GIOVIO, PAOLO (Jovius, 1483–1552). The Historie . . . of the Legation or Ambassade of . . . Moscovia to Pope Clement the VII. Tr. Richard Eden in [Peter Martyr Anglerius], The Decades of the newe world. London, 1555, p. 277–289. Repr. 1577; repr. in Edward Arber, The First Three English Books on America (Westminster, 1895, p. 308–317); repr. in Hakluyt Society Pubs., 12, 1852, p. 228–256.

———— An Italian Portrait Gallery: Being the Elogia of Paolo Giovio. Tr. Florence Alden Gragg. Boston, Chapman and Grimes, 1935. 187 p.

GNAPHEUS, GULIELMUS (or Fullonius: William de Volder, 1493–1568). The Comedye of Acolastus [of the Prodigal Son]. Tr. John Palsgrave. London, 1540. (parallel texts) Repr. ed. P. L. Carver, EETS ES 202, 1937, civ, 312 p.

Tr. and ed. W. E. D. Atkinson. London, Univ. of Western Ontaria, 1964. 234 p. (parallel texts)

GÓIS, DAMIÃO (1502–1574). The Faith, Religion, and Manners of the Aethiopians. Tr. Edward Aston, in Joannes Boemus: The Manners, Lawes, and Customs of All Nations. London, 1611. (See Boemus, above).

———— The legacye or embassate of prester John vnto Emanuell, Kynge of Portyngale. Tr. John More. London, 1533.

GOSLICIUS, LAURENTIUS GRIMALIUS (Wawrzyniec Goslicki, 1533?–1607). The Counsellor (*De optimo senatore*). Tr. anon. London, 1598. 155 p.

Tr. anon. as A Commonwealth of good counsaile. London, 1607.

Tr. William Oldisworth as The Accomplished Senator. London, 1733. xxxii, 330 p.

GOTT, SAMUEL (1614–1671). Nova Solyma, the Ideal City: or Jerusalem Regained. Tr. William Begley. London, Murray, 1902. 2 v.

GOUVEA, ANTONIO DE (1505–1556). The Latin Letters. Ed. and tr. Martha Katharine Zeeb. Philadelphia, 1932. 92 p.

GRAY, THOMAS (1716–1771). (The Latin poems tr. in:) The Complete Poems. Ed. H. W. Starr and J. R. Hendrickson. Oxford, Clarendon Pr., 1966. xv, 284 p.

Part trs.: The Latin Odes [four poems], tr. verse Edward B. Greene, 1775; (three poems), tr. Thomas Warton, ed. Leicester Bradner in Modern Philology 25 (1927), 124–127.

GRIMALD, NICHOLAS (1519?–1562?). The Archprophet, A Tragedy [of John the Baptist]. Tr. L. R. Merrill, in The Life and Poems of Nicholas Grimald. New Haven, Yale Univ. Pr., 1925, p. 228–357, parallel texts.

———— The Resurrection of Christ: A New Sacred Tragi-comedy (*Christus redivivus*). Tr. L. R. Merrill, *ibid.*, p. 90–215, parallel texts.

GROTIUS, HUGO (1583–1645)

Historical Works

———— *De rebus Belgicis,* or the Annals and History of the Low-Country Wars. Tr. Thomas Manley. London, 1665. 8, 974 p.

———— The Opinions of Grotius, as Contained in the *Hollandsche Consultatien en Advijsen*. Tr. Daniel P. de Bruyn. London, Stevens and Haynes, 1894. xlviii, 668 p.

———— On the Origin of the Native Races of America. Tr. Samuel Goldsmid. Bibliotheca Curiosa. Edinburgh, Goldsmid, 1884. 63 p.

Tr. Herbert F. Wright, in Some Less Known Works (of Grotius). Leyden, Brill, 1928.

———— Politick Maxims and Observations. Tr. H. C. F. B. London, Moseley, 1654. 142 p.

──────── A Treatise of the Antiquity of the Commonwealth of the Battavers. Tr. Thomas Woods. London, 1649.

Legal Works

──────── Commentary on the Law of Prize and Booty. Classics of International Law. Ed. facs. of Ms (in v. 2) and tr. from Ms by Gwladys L. Williams. Oxford, Clarendon Pr., and London, Oxford Univ. Pr., 1950. 2 v.

──────── The Freedom of the Seas. Ed. and tr. Ralph van Deman Magoffin. Classics of International Law. Washington, Carnegie Peace Endowment, and N.Y., Oxford Univ. Pr., 1916. xii, 79, 83 p. (parallel texts).

──────── The Introduction to Dutch Jurisprudence. Tr. Charles Herbert. London, van Voorst, 1845. xix, 548 p.

Tr. Sir A. F. S. Maasdorp. Capetown, J. C. Juta, 1878. xix, 557 p.

Tr. R. W. Lee as The Jurisprudence of Holland. Oxford, Clarendon Pr., 1926–36. 2 v.

──────── Of the Law of Warre and Peace. Tr. Clement Barksdale. London, 1654.

Tr. William Evats as The Rights of War and Peace. London, 1682.

Tr. J. Morrice. London, 1715.

Tr. A. C. Campbell. London, 1814. Repr. 1905.

Tr William Whewell. Cambridge, 1853. 3 v.

Ed. facs. (*De Jure belli ac pacis*)and tr. Francis W. Kelsey et al. Classics of International Law. Washington, D.C., Carnegie Institution, 1913–27. 4 v. Rc-cd. (English only), Indianapolis, Ind., Bobbs-Merrill, 1962, xlvi, 946 p.

Plays

──────── *Adamus Exsul*; or the Prototype of Paradise Lost. Tr. Frederic Barham. 2d ed. London, 1839. 51 p. Repr. 1847.

──────── Christ's Passion. Tr. George Sandys. London, 1640. (12), 123 p. Repr. 1687, 1885.

──────── Sophompaneas, or Joseph. Tr. Francis Goldsmith. London, 1652. 102 p.

Religious Works

——————— Anti-Dodwellisme, being two . . . tracts [on the Eucharist]. Tr. William Baxter. London, 1683.

——————— Of the Authority of the Highest Powers about Sacred Things. Tr. Clement Barksdale. London, 1651.

——————— Catechism. Tr. Francis Goldsmith. London, 1668. 26 p.

——————— A Defense of the Christian Faith . . . against Faustus Socinus. Tr. W. H. London, 1692.

Tr. Frank H. Foster. Andover, Mass., Draper, 1889. lvii, 314 p.

——————— Of the Government and Rites of the Ancient Church. Tr. Clement Barksdale. London, 1675. 4, 48 p.

——————— The Truth of the Christian Religion. Tr. Symon Patrick. London, Royston, 1680. 298 p. Repr. 1683, 1689, 1694, 1707, rev. 1711, 1719, 1729, 1743, 1754, 1767, 1779, 1786, 1793, 1809, 1829.

Tr. verse William Atwood. London, J. Robinson, 1686. 168 p.

Tr. Spencer Madan. London, 1782. Repr. 1797, 1814.

Tr. T. Sedger. 2d ed. London, 1859.

For Grotius generally, cf. Jacob ter Meulen, *Concise Bibliography* (Leyden, Sitjthoff, 1925, 88 p.)

GUARINO, BATTISTA (1434–1513). Concerning the Order and the Method . . . in Teaching and in Reading the Classical Authors (*De ordine docendi et studiendi*). Tr. William H. Woodward in Vittorino da Feltre, etc., p. 159–78 (see Collections, Medieval Latin Literature, above).

GUARNA, ANDREAS (fl. 1511). *Bellum Grammaticale*: A Discourse of Great War and Dissention betwene . . . the noune and the verbe. Tr. William Hayward. London, Bynneman, 1569. Repr. 1576; repr. Somers Tracts, I, 1750, repr. 1809.

HADDON, WALTER (1516–1572). Against Jerome Osorius . . . and against his Slaunderous Invectives . . . by M. W. Haddon . . . continued by M. J. Foxe. Tr. John Bell. London, Day, 1581. 510 p. Repr. Legh Richmond, Fathers of the English Church, v, 8, 1807.

——————— The Poetry. Ed. and tr. Charles J. Lees. Columbus, Ohio State Univ. dissertation, 1961. 2 v.

——————— A Sight of the Portugall Pearle, that is the Aunswere of D. Haddon [to Osorio's Letter to Queen Elizabeth]. Tr. Abraham Hartwell [from the *Pro Reformatione Anglica Epistola Apologetica*]. London, 1565.

Cf. Lawrence V. Ryan, "The Haddon-Osorio Controversy 1563–1583", in *Church History*, v. 22 (1953), p. 3–15.

HALLER, ALBRECHT VON (1708–1777). Dr. Albert Haller's Physiology. Tr. Samuel Mihlis. London, 1754. 2 v. Repr. 1772.

Tr. anon. as First Lines of Physiology. Edinburgh, 1779. Repr. 1807; repr. Troy, N.Y., 1808, 498 p.

Haller's other scientific writings were not tr. For trs. of his writings in German, see German Literature, in v. IV.

HARVEY, GABRIEL (1545–1630). *Ciceronianus*. Ed. and tr. H. S. Wilson and C. A. Foster. Lincoln, Univ. of Nebraska Pr., 1945. vii, 149 p. (parallel texts).

HARVEY, WILLIAM (1578–1657). The Works. Tr. Robert Willis. London, Sydenham Society, 1847. xcvi, 624 p. Repr. Great Books, v. 28, 1952, p. 267–496. Repr. N.Y., Johnson Reprint Corporation, 1965, xcvi, 624 p.

——————— The Circulation of the Blood, and Other Writings. Tr. Kenneth J. Franklin. N.Y., Dutton, 1963. xvii, 236 p.

——————— The Generation of Living Creatures (*De generatione animalium*). Tr. anon. London, 1653.

Tr. Robert Willis, in The Works, above.

——————— The Motion of the Heart and Blood in Animals. Tr. anon. London, 1653. Repr. 1673; repr. ed. Geoffrey Keynes, 1928.

Tr. Robert Willis, in The Works, above. Repr. separately, 1889; 1907; 1908 EL, et seq.; Harvard Classics, v. 38; Chicago, Regnery, 1962.

Tr. Chauncey D. Leake. Springfield, Ill., C. C. Thomas, and London, Baillière, 1928. xvii, 150 p. Repr. 1930, 1941.

Ed. and tr. Gweneth Whitteridge. London, Cambridge Univ. Pr., 1959. 162 p.

Also tr. M. Ryan, London, 1832; Geoffrey Moreton, Canterbury, 1874.

HAUSTED, PETER (d. 1644). *Senile Odium* (1633). Ed. and tr. Laurens J. Mills. Bloomington, Indiana Univ. Pr., 1949. 202 p. (parallel texts).

The editor disclaims Hausted as author of the play.

————— *Senilis Amor.* Ed. and tr. Laurens J. Mills. *Ibid.,* 1952. 167 p. (parallel texts).

HELMONT, JEAN BAPTISTE VAN (1577–1644). *Deliramenta Catarrhi:* or the Incongruities . . . couched under the vulgar opinion of defluxions. Paraphrase by Walter Charleton. London, 1650. 75 p.

————— One Hundred fifty three Chymical Aphorisms. To which are added some other phylosophick Canons. Tr. Charles Packe. London, 1688. Repr. 1690 with the Latin.

————— Oriatrike, or Physick Refined, the common errors therein refuted . . . a new rise and progress of philosophy and medicine. Part (of *Opuscula medica inaudita*) tr. John Chandler. London, 1662. 2 parts. Repr. 1664 as Van Helmont's Workes, containing his . . . Philosophy, Physick, Chirurgery, Anatomy.

————— *De tempore,* and Biological Time. Part (of *De tempore*) tr. Walter Pagel. Osiris, v. 8 (1948), p. 346–417.

————— A Ternary of Paradoxes of the Magnetic Cure of Wounds, [the] nativity of tartar in wine, [and the] image of God in Man. Tr. and ampliated [*sic*] by Walter Charleton. London, 1650.

HENRY VIII, KING (1491–1547). *Assertio Septem Sacramentorum* Against Martin Luther. Tr. Thomas Webster. London, 1687. 133 p.

Tr. and ed. Rev. Louis O'Donovan. N.Y., Benziger, 1908. 478 p. (parallel texts).

Tr. in the following item.

————— The Miscellaneous Writings. Ed. Francis McNamara. Waltham St. Lawrence, Golden Cockerel Pr., 1924. 218 p.

For the king's public letters, see British Museum Catalogue.

HERBERSTEIN, SIGISMUND VON (1486–1566). Notes upon Russia. *Rerum Moscoviticarum Commentarii.* Tr. R. H. Major. London, Hakluyt Society Pubs. 10, 12, 1851–52. 2 v. Repr. N.Y., Burt Franklin, 1963.

HERBERT OF CHERBURY, EDWARD, LORD (1583–1648). The Ancient Religion of the Gentiles, and Causes of their Errors Considered. Tr. William Lewis. London, 1705.

———— *De Religione Laici*. Ed. and tr. Harold R. Hutchinson. New Haven, Yale Univ. Pr., 1944. x, 199 p. (parallel texts).

———— *De Veritate*. Tr. Meyrick H. Carré. Univ. of Bristol Studies. Bristol, Arrowsmith, 1937. 334 p.

HERBERT, GEORGE (1593–1633). The Latin Poetry. Ed. and tr. Mark McCloskey and Paul R. Murphy. Athens, Ohio, Ohio University Pr., 1965. 181 p. (parallel texts).

HOBBES, THOMAS (1588–1679). *De mirabilibus Pecci*: Being the Wonders of the Peak in Darby-shire. Tr. anon., with the Latin. London, 1678.

———— A True Ecclesiastical History, from Moses to the Time of Martin Luther, in verse. Tr. anon. London, Curll, 1722.

The mathematical works written in Latin remain untranslated.

HOENEN, PETRUS, S.J. (1880—). The Philosophical Nature of Physical Bodies. Tr. David J. Hassel. West Baden Springs, Indiana, West Baden College, 1955. vi, 75 p.

Book 4, parts 1 and 2, of the *Cosmologia*.

HOFFMANN, FRIEDRICH, of Halle (1660–1742). A System of the Practice of Medicine (*Medicina rationalis systematica*). Tr. W. Lewis and Alexander Duncan. London, Murray, 1783. 2 v.

For trs. of his pamphlets, see British Museum Catalogue.

HOLBERG, LUDVIG, BARON (1684–1754). An Introduction to Universal History (*Synopsis historiae universalis*). Tr. Gregory Sharpe. London, 1755. Repr. 1758; repr. rev. William Radcliffe, 1787, xxv, 354 p.

———— A Journey to the World Under-Ground by Nicholas Klimius. Tr. anon. London, 1742. 324 p. Repr. 1828.

Tr. from the Danish version by John Gierlow. Boston and N.Y., 1845. xix, 190 p.

————— Memoirs of Lewis Holberg. Tr. anon. London, Hunt and Clarke, 1827. vii, 289 p. (three autobiographical epistles)

For trs. of his other works, especially the plays, see Danish Literature, in v. IV.

HOSIUS, STANISLAUS CARDINAL (1504–1579). Of the Expresse Word of God. Tr. Thomas Stapleton. Louvain, 1567. 113 leaves.

HOTMAN, FRANÇOIS (1525–1590). The Ambassador. Tr. James Shawe. London, 1603. 154 p.

————— Franco-Gallia: or An Account of the Ancient Free State of France and of most Other Parts of Europe before the Loss of their Liberties. Tr. Robert Viscount Molesworth. London, 1711. (28), 144 p.

————— A Patterne of Popish Peace (*Historia tragica de furoribus Gallicis*). Tr. anon. London, 1644.

HUET, PIERRE DANIEL, Bishop of Avranches (1630–1721). Memoirs of the Life . . . written by himself (*Commentarius de rebus ad eum perti-nentibus*). Tr. John Aikin. London, Longmans, 1810. 2 v.

For his historical and literary writings, see French Literature, in v. III.

HUMPHREY, LAURENCE (?1527–1590). The Life of John Jewell. Tr. abridged Daniel Featley, in The Works of John Jewell. London, 1609, sigs. ¶¶ 1–6.

HUTTEN, ULRICH VON (1488–1523). *De Morbo Gallico*. Tr. Thomas Paynell. London, 1533. Repr. 1536 as Of the Wood Called Guaiacum; 1540; 1730.

————— Preface to A Treatyse of the donation . . . vnto Sylvester pope of Rhome, by Constantyne. London, 1534. See Lorenzo Valla, in Medieval Latin Literature, above.

See also *Epistolae Obscurorum Virorum*, above, in which Hutten may have had a hand.

HUYGHENS, CHRISTIAAN (1629–1695). The Celestial Worlds Discovered. Tr. John Clarke. London, 1698. 160 p. Repr. rev. 1722; Glasgow, 1757 (as *Cosmotheoros*).

————— Of the Laws of Chance. Largely a tr. by Dr. John Arbuthnot. London, 1692. 93 p. Repr. 1714. (*De ratiociniis in ludo aleae*).

————— Treatise on Light. Tr. Sylvanus P. Thomson. London, Macmillan, 1912. xii, 128 p. Repr. Chicago, Univ. Pr., 1946; Great Books, v. 34, 1952, p. 551–619.

JOÃO DE SANTO TOMAZ, O. P. (1589–1644). The Gifts of the Holy Ghost. Tr. Dominic Hughes. London and N.Y., Sheed & Ward, 1950, 1951. ix, 292 p. (one of the disputations from the *Cursus theologicus*, v. 5)

————— The Material Logic of John of St. Thomas: Basic Treatises. Tr. Yves R. Simon, John Glanville, and G. Donald Hollenhort, with pref. by Jacques Maritain. Chicago, Univ. Pr., and London, Cambridge Univ. Pr., 1955. xxxiv, 638 p.

Extracts from the *Ars logica* were tr. by Francis C. Wade as *Outlines of Formal Logic* (Milwaukee, Wis. Marquette Univ. Pr., 1955, 136 p.)

KECKERMANN, BARTHOLOMÄUS (1571–1608). A Manuduction to Theologie (*Systema S. S. Theologiae*). Tr. Thomas Vicars. London, 1622. Repr. 1626.

KEPLER, JOHANN (1571–1630). Conversation with Galileo's Sidereal Messenger. Tr. Edward Rosen. N.Y. and London, Johnson Reprint Corporation, 1965. xix, 164 p.

————— Epitome of Copernican Astronomy, books iv, v. The Harmonies of the World, book v. Tr. Charles Glenn Wallis. Annapolis, Md., St. John's College Bookstore, 1939 (mimeographed). Repr. Great Books, v. 16, 1952, p. 505–838.

————— Kepler's Dream (*Somnium, sive astronomia lunaris*). Tr. Patricia Frueh Kirkwood, with intro. John Lear. Berkeley, Univ. of California Pr., 1965. 182 p.

For trs. of shorter pieces, see bibliography in the tr. (from the German) by C. Doris Hellman of Max Casper, *Kepler* (N.Y. and London, Abelard-Schuman, 1959, p. 393–94).

KIRCHMEYER, THOMAS (or Naogeorgos, 1511–1563). The Popish
    Kingdome, or reigne of Antichrist (*Regnum papisticum*). Tr. verse
    Barnabe Googe. London, 1570. 88 leaves. Repr. ed. R. C. Hope,
    London, Satchell, 1880, xviii, 74 p.

Kirchmeyer's play *Pammachius* was tr. by John Bale in 1545: the tr. is
not extant.

KRÄMER, HEINRICH (Institoris, 15th c.) See *Malleus Maleficarum*, below.

LANGUET, HUBERT (1518–1581). The Correspondence of Sir Philip
    Sidney and Hubert Languet. Tr. Steuart A. Pears. London, Pickering,
    1845. lxxxii, 240 p. Repr. ed. William Aspenwall Bradley, Humanist's
    Library, 5: Boston, Merrymount Pr., 1912, xxxi, 229 p.

See below, *Vindiciae contra Tyrannos*, often ascribed to Languet.

LANSPERGIUS, JOHANN JUSTUS, called (1490–1539, Carthusian). An
    Epistle in the Person of Christ to the Faithfull Soule. Tr. [Philip
    Howard, Earl of Arundel]. (with A Dialogue betwixt a Christian and
    Christ Hanging on the Cross written in Latine by Marcus Marulus,
    and tr.). Antwerp, 1595. 301 p. Repr. St. Omer, 1610; London, 1867;
    London, Burns Oates, 1926, xliv, 236 p.

LEEUWENHOEK, ANTHONY VAN (1632–1723). The Select Works . . .
    Containing his Microscopicall Discoveries. Tr. Samuel Hoole from
    Dutch and Latin. London, 1798–1807. 2 v.

———————— The Leeuwenhoek Letter . . . 1676 (to the Royal Society). Tr.
    Barnett Cohen. Baltimore, Society of American Bacteriologists, 1937.
    46 p.

———————— The Selected Letters. Ed. by a committee of Dutch scientists.
    Amsterdam, Swets and Zeitlinger, 1939–65. 4 v. (to 1684) (parallel
    texts Dutch-English).

Selections from Leeuwenhoek's books and mss. were collected and tr. by
Clifford Dobell as *Anthony van Leeuwenhoek and His "Little Animals"*
(London, Bale, and N.Y., Harcourt, 1932, vii, 435 p.; repr. N.Y., Russell
and Russell, 1958; N.Y., Dover, 1960).

LEGGE, THOMAS (1535–1607). *Richardus Tertius*. Ed. and tr. Robert J. Lordi. Urbana, Univ. of Illinois dissertation, 1958.

LEIBNITZ, GOTTFRIED VON (1646–1716). Discourse on Metaphysics, Correspondence with Arnauld, an1 Monadology. Tr. George R. Montgomery, intro. Pierre Janet. Chicago, Open Court, 1902. xxi, 272 p. Repr. of the first and third of these treatises (with Descartes and Spinoza), Garden City, N.Y., Doubleday, 1962.

————— The Monadology and Other Philosophical Writings. Tr. Robert Latta. Oxford, Clarendon Pr., 1898. x, 437 p. Repr. London, Oxford Univ. Pr., 1925.

————— Philosophical Papers and Letters. Tr. Leroy E. Loemker. Chicago, Univ. of Chicago Pr., 1956. 2 v.

————— Philosophical Works. Tr. George Martin Duncan from Latin and French. New Haven, Conn., Tuttle, 1890. (8,) 392 p. Repr. 1908.

————— Philosophical Writings. Tr. Mary Morris. EL, 1934. xxxiii, 284 p.

————— Selections. Ed. Philip P. Wiener. Modern Students' Library. N.Y., Scribner, 1951. li, 606 p.

Individual Works

————— A Collection of Papers [i.e., letters] . . . between the Late Learned Mr. Leibnitz, and Dr [Samuel] Clarke . . . 1715 and 1716 Relating to the Principles of Natural Philosophy and Religion [with discourses by other persons]. Tr. anon. (French and English). London, Knapton, 1717. 416 p.

————— Discourse on Metaphysics. Tr. Peter G. Lucas and Leslie Grant. Manchester, Univ. Pr., 1953. xxix, 63 p.

————— The Early Mathematical Manuscripts. Tr. J. M. Child. Chicago, and London, Open Court, 1920. iv, 238 p.

————— The Monadology. Tr. H. Wildon Carr (from the French original). London, Favil Pr., 1930. ix, 213 p.

————— New Essays Concerning Human Understanding. Tr. Alfred G. Langley from the French original, in Journal of Speculative Philosophy (St. Louis, Missouri), v. 19, 21, 22 (1879–82). Repr. N.Y. and London, Macmillan, 1896, xix, 861 p. Repr. Chicago and London, Open Court, 1916.

——————— The Preface to Leibniz' *Novissima sinica*. Tr. Donald F. Lach. Honolulu, Univ. of Hawaii Pr., 1957. 104 p.

——————— A Refutation of Spinoza. Tr. Octavius Freire Owen. Edinburgh, Constable, and London, Hamilton Adams, 1855. xix, 155 p.

——————— A Summary Account of Leibnitz' Memoir, Addressed to Lewis the Fourteenth, Recommending the Conquest of Egypt (*Consilium ægyptiacum*). Ed. Granville Penn. London, 1803. xiii, 89 p.

——————— A System of Theology. Tr. C. W. Russell. London, Burns and Lambert, 1850. cliv, 232 p. Repr. 1855.

——————— Theodicy. Essays on the Goodness of God, the Freedom of Man, and the Origin of Evil. Tr. E. M. Huggard from the French original, with intro. Austin Farrer. London, Routledge, 1951. 448 p.

For several brief trs. in the *Journal of Speculative Philosophy*, St. Louis, 1871 et seq., see B. Q. Morgan, *German Literature in Translation*, s.v. Leibniz.

LESLIE, JOHN, Bishop of Ross (1527–1596). The Historie of Scotland. Tr. Father James Dalrymple, ed. E. G. Cody. Scottish Text Society, 1888–95. 2 v.

LESSIUS, LEONARDUS (Léonard Leys, S.J., 1554–1623). A Consultation what Faith and Religion is Best to be Embraced. Tr. William Wright. St. Omer, 1618.

——————— A Controversy whether Every Man may be Saved in his own Religion. Tr. anon. St. Omer, 1614.

——————— *Hygiasticon:* or the Right Course of Preserving Life and Health unto Extream Old Age. Tr. [Nicholas Ferrar?], (with Lodovico Cornaro, A Treatise of Temperance and Sobrietie, tr. George Herbert from Italian). Cambridge, 1634. 210, 70 p. Repr. 1634, 1636, 1678 as The Temperate Man.

Tr. Thomas Smith as A Treatise of Health and Long Life (with Cornaro), London, 1767.

——————— The Names of God and Meditative Summaries of the Divine Perfections. Tr. T. J. Campbell, S.J., N.Y., America Pr., 1912. xxi, 230 p.

——————— Rawleigh his Ghost. Or, a Feigned Apparition . . . to a Friend . . . for the Translating . . . *De providentia Numinis, & Animi immortalitate*. Tr. A. B. St. Omer, 1631. 457 p.

——————— The Treasure of Vowed Chastity in Secular Persons. Also the Widdowes Glasse. Tr. J. W. P. St. Omer, 1621. 348 p.

——————— The Virtues Awakened, from the Treatise on Perfect Happiness. Tr. Henry Churchill Semple, S.J. (from book 4, *De summo bono*). St. Louis and London, Herder, 1924. 50 p.

LINNAEUS (Carl von Linné, 1707–1778). The Animal Kingdom, or Zoological System. Tr. R. Kerr. London, 1792. v. 1.

——————— The *"Critica Botanica"*. Tr. Sir Arthur Hort, rev. M. L. Green. London, Ray Society, 1938. xxvii, 239 p.

——————— A Dissertation on the Sexes of Plants. Tr. James Edward Smith. London, 1786. xv, 62 p.

——————— The Elements of Botany (*Philosophia botanica*). Tr. H. Rose. London, 1775.

Many trs. were published of parts of this work.

——————— The Families of Plants. Tr. Erasmus Darwin. Lichfield, Botanical Society, 1787. 2 v.

A tr. of the *Genera plantarum*, the *Mantissae plantarum*, and the *Supplementum*. A part of the *Genera* was tr. by C. Milne as *The Institute of Botany*, London, Griffin, 1771, 302 p.

——————— *Fundamenta Entomologiae*: or An Introduction to the Knowledge of Insects. Tr. William Curtis. London, 1772. viii, 90 p.

——————— A General System of Nature, Through the Three Grand Kingdoms of Animals, Vegetables, and Minerals. Tr. William Turton. London, Leckington, 1806. 7 v.

——————— A Generic and Specific Description of British Plants. Tr. James Jenkinson. Kendal, 1775. xxviii, 258 p.

——————— A Genuine and Universal System of Natural History. Tr. anon. in Ebenezer Sibley, An Universal System of Natural History. London, 1794–1807. 14 v.

V. 1–7 are by Linnaeus; 8–14 are additions by J. F. Gmelin (1788–1793).

——————— Lachesis Lapponica, or A Tour in Lapland. Tr. James Edward Smith from Ms. London, 1811. 2 v.

———— Miscellaneous Tracts Relating to Natural History, Husbandry and Physick. Tr. Benjamin Stillingfleet. London, 1759. Repr. enlarged 1762, xxi, 391 p.

———— A Selection of the Correspondence of Linnaeus and Other Naturalists. Tr. Sir J. E. Smith. London, 1821. 2 v.

———— A System of Vegetables. Tr. anon. Lichfield, Botanical Society, 1783. 2 v.

For numerous smaller works in tr., see British Museum Catalogue.

LIPSIUS, JUSTUS (547–1646). A Brief Outline of the History of Libraries. Tr. John Cotton Dana. Chicago, McClurg, 1907. 121 p.

———— A Direction for Travailers. Tr. adapted by Sir John Stradling. London, 1592. 14 leaves.

———— The Life of Seneca. Tr. Thomas Lodge. London, 1614. Repr. Temple Classics, 1899.

———— Miracles of the Blessed Virgin [of Halle]. Tr. anon. London, 1688.

———— Six Bookes of Politickes or Civil Doctrine. Tr. William Jones. London, 1594.

———— Two Books of Constancie. Tr. Sir John Stradling. London, 1595. Repr. rev. ed. Rudolf Kirk, New Brunswick, N.J., Rutgers Univ. Pr., 1939, ix, 223 p.

Tr. R. G. London, 1654.

Tr. Nathaniel Wanley as War and Peace Reconciled: or a Discourse of Constancy. London, 1672. 288 p.

LOYOLA, ST. IGNATIUS OF (Iñigo López de Recalde, 1491–1556). Letters. Selected and tr. William J. Young, S.J., Chicago, Loyola Univ. Pr., 1959. xiv, 450 p. (228 letters)

———— Letters and Instructions. Tr. D. F. O'Leary, ed. Alban Goodier, S.J. St. Louis, Mo. Herder, and London, Manresa Pr., 1914. v. 1 only.

———— Letters to Women. Tr. Kathleen Pond and S. A. H. Weetman from a collection in German tr. N.Y., Herder, 1960. xxiii, 564 p.

———— The Spiritual Exercises. Tr. C. Seager from Latin. London, 1847.

Tr. Joseph Rickaby (Spanish and English). London, Burns and Oates, 1915. xii, 234 p.

Tr. John Norris and others from the original Spanish as The Text of the Spiritual Exercises. London, Burns and Oates, 1880. xii, 125 p. Several reprs. to 1952 (5th ed.).

Tr. Thomas Corbishley from the Latin. London, Burns and Oates, and N.Y., Kenedy, 1963. 124 p.

Tr. Anthony Mottola. Garden City, N.Y., Image Books, 1964. 200 p.

——————— The Testament: Being "Sundry Actes . . . taken down from the Saint's Own Lips." Tr. E. M. Rix. London, Sands, 1900. vii, 230 p.

LUTHER, MARTIN (1483–1546)

Collected Editions

——————— The Precious and Sacred Writings. Ed. John Nicholas Lenker. Minneapolis, Minn., Lutherans in All Lands Co. (later the Luther Press), 1903——.

16 vols. published, the edition incomplete.

V. 1. Commentary on the First Twenty-two Psalms, 1. Tr. Henry Cole, rev. J. N. Lenker. 1903. 462 p.

V. 2. On the Creation . . . Commentary on Genesis, 1. Tr. Henry Cole, rev. J. N. Lenker. 1903. 448 p.

V. 3. Epistles of St. Peter and St Jude. Tr. J. N. Lenker. 1904. 383 p.

V. 7, 8, 9. Epistles Sermons (Advent to Advent). Tr. J. N. Lenker. 1908. 3 v.

V. 10–14. Church Postil Gospels: Sermons (Advent to Advent). Tr. J. N. Lenker. 1904–10. 4 v.

V. 24. Luther's Catechetical Writings: God's Call to Repentance, Faith, and Prayer. The Bible Plan of Salvation, 1. Tr. J. N. Lenker, et al. 1908. 377 p.

——————— The Works. Philadelphia Edition, ed. Henry Eyster Jacobs, trs. various. Philadelphia, A. J. Holman Co., 1915–32. 6 v. Repr. *ibid.*, Muhlenberg Pr., 1930–43, 6 v.

V. 1–5, Treatises, 1517–1539; v. 6, Liturgical Writings, and Prefaces to Books of the Bible.

——————— The Works. American Edition. Ed. Jaroslav Pelikan, The Commentaries, v. 1–30, St. Louis, Concordia Publishing House, with a Companion Volume unnumbered, and ed. Helmut T. Lehman, v. 31–55, Other Works, Philadelphia, Muhlenberg Pr., later Fortress Pr., 1955— (in progress).

So far published:

V. 1–4. Lectures on Genesis. Tr. George V. Schick, 1958, 1960, 1961, 1964.

V. 7, 8. Lectures on Genesis. Tr. P. D. Pahl. 1964, 1966.

V. 9. Lectures on Deuteronomy. Tr. Richard R. Caemmerer. 1960. x, 334 p.

V. 12–14. On Selected Psalms. Tr. Lewis W. Spitz et al. 1955–58.

V. 21. Sermons on the Sermon on the Mount, and on the Magnificat. Tr. J. Pelikan and A. T. W. Steinhaeuser. 1956. xxi, 383 p.

V. 22–24. Sermons on the Gospel of St. John. Tr. Martin H. Bertram. 1957, 1958, 1964.

V. 26–27. Lectures on Galatians. Tr. Richard Jungkuntz. 1926–63. Companion Volume: Jaroslav Pelikan, Luther the Expositor: Introduction to the Exegetical Writings. 1959. xiii, 286 p.

V. 30. The Catholic Epistles. Tr. Martin H. Bertram. 1967. xi, 347 p.

V. 31. The Career of the Reformer, 1 (1517–20). Ed. Harold J. Grimm, et al. 1957. (the treatises, etc.)

V. 32. The Career of the Reformer, 2. Ed. George W. Forell. 1959.

V. 34. The Career of the Reformer, 4. Ed. Lewis W. Spitz. 1960.

V. 35–37. Word and Sacrament. Ed. E. Theodore Buchman, 1960; A. R. Wentz, 1959; R. H. Fischer, 1959.

V. 40, 41. Church and Ministry, 2. Ed. Conrad Bergendorff, 1958. 3. Ed Eric W. Gritsch, 1966.

V. 44, 45. The Christian in Society, 1. Tr. James Atkinson, 1966. 2. Tr. Walther I. Brandt, 1962.

V. 48. Letters, 1. Ed. and tr. Gottfried G. Krodel. 1963. (119 letters) xxi, 426 p.

V. 51. Sermons, 1. Tr. John W. Doberstein from German. 1959. xxi, 405 p.

V. 53. Liturgy and Hymns. Tr. Paul Zeller Strodach, rev. and ed. Ulrich S. Leupold. 1964. xx, 356 p.

————— Early Theological Works. Ed. and tr. James Atkinson. Library of Christian Classics, v. 16, 1962. 380 p.

————— The First Principles of the Reformation: The 95 Theses and the Three Primary Works. Tr. with intro. Henry Wace and C. A. Buchheim. London, Murray, 1883. lxxxviii, 245 p. Repr. as Luther's Primary Works, Londoon, Hodder and Stoughton, 1896, xvi, 492 p.; repr. Harvard Classics, v. 36.

The Address to the Nobility; *On Christian Liberty*; *On the Babylonian Captivity*. The same works tr. C. M. Jacobs et al. as *Three Treatises* (Philadelphia, Muhlenberg Pr., 1947, 290 p.; repr. Fortress Pr., 1960, 316 p.).

————— Reformation Writings. Tr. Bertram Lee Woolf. London, Lutterworth Pr., 1952–56, and N.Y., Philosophical Library, 1955–56. 2 v.

————— Selections. Ed. John Dillenberger. Garden City, N.Y., (Anchor Books) Doubleday, and Chicago, Quadrangle Books, 1961. xxxiii, 526 p.

————— What Luther Says: An Anthology Compiled Alphabetically by Subject, by Ewald M. Plass. St. Louis, Concordia Pub. House, 1959. 3 v.

Individual Works

————— The Autobiography. Compiled and tr. J. P. Lawson. London, Smith Elder, and Edinburgh, 1836. 8, 392 p.

Tr. William Hazlitt from the French of Jules Michelet (*Mémoires de Luther*). London, Bogue, 1846. xv, 471 p. Repr. London, Bell, 1882.

————— On the Bondage of the Will (*de servo arbitrio*). Tr. Edward Thomas Vaughan. London, pr. pr., 1823. lxxxviii, 470 p.

Tr. Henry Cole. London, Simpkin, 1823. viii, 402 p. Repr. rev. Henry Atherton. Grand Rapids, Michigan, Eerdmans, and London, Sovereign Grace Union, 1931, 419 p.

Tr. J. I. Packer and O. R. Johnston. London, J. Clarke, and Westwood, N.J., Revell, 1957. 323 p.

Tr. (extracts) Ernst F. Winter (with Erasmus, The Free Will). N.Y., Ungar, 1961. p. 95–138.

————— The Book of Vagabonds and Beggars, with a Vocabulary of Their Language (*Liber vagatorum*). Tr. John Camden Hotton. London, J. C. Hotten, 1860. xxxvii, 64 p.

————— A Commentary on St. Paul's Epistle to the Galatians. Tr. Erasmus Middleton. London, 1807. lxxxviii, 416 p. Reprs., repr. ed. J. P. Fallowes, London, Harrison Trust, 1939, xviii, 388 p.; repr. rev. and completed, London, J. Clarke, 1953, vi, 567 p.

Tr. S. S. Schmucker. Philadelphia, Pa., Quaker City Pub. House, 1872. 632 p.

Tr. abridged Theodore Graebner. Grand Rapids, Zondervan, 1939. 282 p. Reprs. to 4th ed., 1962.

————— Commentary on the Epistle to the Romans. Tr. abridged J. Theodore Mueller. Grand Rapids, Mich., Zondervan, 1954. 207 p.

————— Commentary on Genesis. Tr. J. Theodore Mueller. Grand Rapids, Mich., Zondervan, 1958. 2 v.

————— Correspondence and Other Contemporary Letters. Tr. Preserved Smith and Charles M. Jacobs. Philadelphia, Pa., Lutheran Pub. Soc., 1913–18. 2 v.

Another tr. Margaret A. Currie as *The Letters* (London, Macmillan, 1908, xxxv, 482 p.) The German ed. of the lettters occupies 15 v. (1884– 1932).

————— An Exposition of Ecclesiastes. Tr. anon. London, 1573. 187 leaves.

————— Lectures on Romans. Tr. Wilhelm Pauck. Library of Christian Classics, v. 18, 1961. lxvi, 444 p.

————— Letters of Spiritual Counsel. Tr. Theodore G. Tappert. Library of Christian Classics, v. 18, 1955. 367 p.

————— Reply to King Henry VIII. Tr. E. S. Buchanan. N.Y., no pub., 1928. 57 p.

————— Sermons on the Passion of Christ. Tr. E. Smid and I. T. Isensee from the German. Rock Island, Ill., Augustana Pr., and Philadelphia, Pa., Fortress Pr., 1956. vii, 233 p.

————— Table Talk (*Colloquia mensalia*). Tr. Henrie Bell as Divine Discourses at his Table. London, 1652. 541 p. Repr. 1791, 1818, 1848 (rev. William Hazlitt), 1857, 1875, 1886, 1902, 1952 (rev. Thomas S. Kepler: N.Y., World Pub. Co., xxiii, 345 p.).

Part tr. Preserved Smith and H. P. Gallinger as Conversations. Boston and N.Y., Pilgrim Pr., 1915. xxvii, 260 p.

For other trs. of selections, hymns, etc., see B. Q. Morgan, *German Literature in English Translation*, p. 316–319. For trs, before 1660, see *CBEL*, I, 815, and *Short-Title Catalogue of English Books . . . to 1640*.

MAGNUS, OLAUS, Archbishop of Upsala (1490–1558). A Compendious History of the Goths, Swedes, and Vandals, and Other Northern Nations (*Historia de gentibus septentrionalibus*). Tr. John Streater. London, 1658.

MAJOR, JOHN (1470–1550). A History of Greater Britain. Tr. Archibald Constable. Edinburgh, Scottish Text Society, 1892. cxxxv, 476 p.

MALDONATUS, JOANNES (Juan Maldonat, S.J., 1534–1583). A Commentary on the Holy Gospels. Tr. G. J. Davie. London, 1888–89. 2 v.

The tr. covers only the first of the four Gospels.

MALLEUS MALEFICARUM. The Hammer of Witches. Tr. Montague Summers. London, Rodker, 1928. xlv, 277 p.

A book of rules for dealing with witches, compiled by Heinrich Krämer and Jakob Sprenger, published 1489.

MALPIGHI, MARCELLO (1628–1694). On the Formation of the Chick in the Egg.—Repeated . . . Observations on the Incubated Egg. Tr. Howard B. Adelmann, in Marcello Malpighi and the Evolution of Embryology. Ithaca, N.Y., Cornell Univ. Pr., 1966. 5 v.

The two treatises (1672) are ed. and tr. in v. 2, p. 932–1013 (parallel texts). In this work are also ed. and tr. (parallel texts also) passages from Latin treatises in embryology by Anton Everard (1671); Pierre Gassendi (1658); William Harvey (1651); Albrecht von Haller (1744); and Honoré Fabri (1666). These are all in v. 2. In the "Excursuses" which make up v. 3–5, that is commentaries on matters discussed in the treatises, numerous passages are quoted and tr. from many scientific works, usually in Latin.

MANASSEH BEN JOSEPH BEN ISRAEL (1604–1657). The Bible Conciliator, or Rabbi Manasseh ben Israel: A Reconcilement of the

Apparent Contradictions in Holy Scripture. Tr. E. H. Lindo. London, 1842. 2 v. Repr. Glasgow, Oppenheim, 1902.

First pub. in Spanish (1632), then in Latin (1633).

——————— The Hope of Israel . . . The Relation of Antonio Montezinus . . . of what Befell him as he Travelled over the Mountaines Cordillaere. Tr. anon. London, 1650. Repr. 1652, 62 p. Repr. in Manasseh Ben Israel's Mission to Oliver Cromwell, ed. Lucien Wolf, London, Jewish Historical Soc., 1901, lxxxviii, 191 p., with the pamphlets in English pub. to urge the re-admission of the Jews to England.

——————— *De termino vitae*; or, the Term of Life. Tr. Thomas Pocock. London, 1699. Repr. 1700, 1709.

MANCINI, DOMENICO (later 15th c.). The Mirrour of Good Manners (*De quatuor virtutibus*). Tr. verse Alexander Barclay. London, Pynson, c. 1523. Repr. 1570; repr. Spenser Soc., v. 38, Manchester, 1885, 83 p.

Tr. anon. prose. London, 1520?

Tr. verse George Turbervile. London, Bynneman, 1568.

——————— The Usurpation of Richard the Third. Ed. and tr. C. A. J. Armstrong from Ms. London, Oxford Univ. Pr., 1936. xv, 172 p.

MANTUANUS, BAPTISTA (Spagnuoli, 1448–1516). The Eglogs. Tr. verse George Turbervile (nine of the ten eclogues). London, 1567. Repr. ed. Douglas Bush, N.Y., Scholars' Facsimiles, 1937, vii p., (4), 93 leaves.

Tr. Thomas Harvey. London, Moseley, 1656. 104 p.

MANUALE SCHOLARIUM (1481). The *Manuale Scholarium*: An Original Account of Life in the Medieval University. Tr. Robert Francis Seybolt. Cambridge, Mass., Harvard Univ. Pr., 1921. 122 p.

MARIANA, JUAN DE, S.J. (1536–1624). The General History of Spain . . . to which are added Two Supplements, the first by F. Ferdinand Camargo y Salcedo, the other by F. Basil Varen de Soto, Bringing it down to the Present Reign. Tr. John Stevens. London, 1699. 563, 95 p.

Tr. from the author's Spanish version of his *Historia de rebus Hispaniae*.

———— The King and the Education of the King (*De rege et regis institutione*). Tr. George Albert Moore. Chevy Chase, Md., Country Dollar Pr., 1948. 466 p.

MARLIANUS, JOANNES BARTHOLOMAEUS (d. c. 1560). The Topographie of Rome in Ancient Time. Tr. Philemon Holland, in The Romane Historie (of Livy). London, 1600, p. 1347–1403. Repr. 1659.

A tr. of the *Epitome* (1552) of Marlianus' *Antiquae Romae Topographia* (1534).

MARTYR, PETER, ANGLERIUS (of Anghiera, d. 1526). History of the West Indies (*De novo orbe*). Tr. Michael Lok. London, 1612. Repr. in Richard Hakluyt, Collection of Early Voyages, 1809 ed., v. 5.

Tr. Francis A. McNutt as *De orbe novo*: The Eight Decades. N.Y. and London, Putnam, 1912. 2 v.

Three of the eight *Decades* were tr. Richard Eden as *The Decades of the newe worlde*, London, 1555; repr. 1577; repr. ed. Edward Arber, in *The First Three English Books on America* (Westminister, 1895, p. 61–185).

For Peter Martyr the theologian, see Vermigli, below.

MARULUS, MARCUS, SPALATENSIS (Marko Marulić, 1450–1524). A Dialogue betwixt a Christian and Christ Hanging on the Cross. Tr. Philip Howard, Earl of Arundel (with An Epistle in the Person of Christ to the Faithfull Soule, by Johann Justus Lanspergius, 1595, q.v. above).

MARVELL, ANDREW (1621–1678). Marvell's Latin Poetry. Ed. and tr. William A. McQueen and Kiffen A. Rockwell. Chapel Hill, Univ. of North Carolina Pr., 1964. 89 p. (parallel texts).

MAYOW, JOHN (1640–1679). Medico-Physical Works (*Tractatus quinque medico-physici*). Tr. A. C. B. and L. D. Edinburgh, Alembic Club, 1907. xxiii, 331 p. Repr. Oxford, Ashmolean Reprs. 5, 1926.

MELANCHTHON, PHILIP (1497–1560). Selected Writings. Tr. Charles
Leander Hill, ed. E. E. Flack and L. J. Satre. Minneapolis, Minn.,
Augsburg Pub. House, 1962. xiv, 190 p.

Includes with shorter pieces: *Paul and the Scholastics* (1520), p. 30–56;
Luther and the Paris Theologians (1521), p. 68–87; *Summary of Doctrine*
(1524), p. 92–101; *Against the Anabaptists* (1528), p. 102–22; *The
Church and the Authority of the Word* (1539), p. 130–86.

———————— (The Augsburg Confession). Tr. Richard Taverner as The Confession of the Fayth of the Germaynes in the Councell. London, 1536.
2 eds.

Tr. Charles P. Krauth (from the Latin, but incorporating the important
additions from the German text). Philadelphia, Lutheran Bookstore,
1868. p. 1 [50], 91.

Other trs., notably in the Lutheran prayer-book.

———————— (*Epitome philosophiae moralis*). Tr. John Goodale as A civile
Nosegay wherein is Contayned not onlye the Offyce and Dewty of all
Magistrates and Judges but of all Subjectes. London, 1550.

———————— The Hystory [of] the lyfe & actes of Martine Luther, John Oeco-
lampadius, and Huldericke Zuinglius. The declaration of Martin
Luthers Faythe before the Emperoure . . . with an Oration of hys
Death. Tr. Henry Bennet. London, 1561. 2 parts.

Part 1 is by Melanchthon; part 2, on the other reformers, is by Wolfgang
Capito, Simon Grynaeus, and Oswald Mykonius.

———————— The *Loci Communes*. Tr. Charles Leander Hill from the first ed.,
1521. Boston, Meador, 1944. 274 p.

Tr. Clyde L. Manschreck as On Christian Doctrine: *Loci Communes*, 1555.
London and N.Y., Oxford Univ. Pr., 1965. lvii, 356 p.

The other major works have not been tr. For trs. of pamphlets published
in England during his lifetime, see *CBEL*, I, 327, 816; *Short-Title Catalogue
to 1640*; and B. Q. Morgan, *German Literature in English Translation*
(1938 ed.), p. 328.

MENSA PHILOSOPHICA (c. 1470). The Schoolemaster or Teacher of
Table Phylosophie. Part tr. anon. London, 1583. 64 leaves.

Tr. W. B. as The Philosophers Banquet. London, 1603. 526 p. Repr.
1614, 1633.

Part tr. Arthur S. Way as The Science of Dining. London, Macmillan, 1936. viii, 174 p.

Cf. Thomas F. Dunn, *The Facetiae of the Mensa Philosophica* (St. Louis, Mo., Washington Univ. Studies, 1934, 55 p.).

MILTON, JOHN (1608–1674). (The Latin Poems) Tr. Thomas Warton in his ed. of Milton's Poems upon Several Occasions.. London, 1785. xxviii, 620 p. Repr. 1791.

Tr. verse William Cowper. Ed. William Hayley, in Latin and Italian Poems of Milton Translated. London, 1808. xxiv, 328 p. Repr. in Life and Poetical Works of Milton, ed. William Hayley, Chichester, 1810, v. 3. Repr. in Robert Southey, ed. of Works of William Cowper, v. 10, 1837, and generally in later eds. of Cowper's Poems: also in J. H. Hanford ed., Poems of John Milton, N.Y., Ronald Pr., 1953 (the Elegies, not the *Sylvae*).

Tr. verse Jacob George Strutt as The Latin and Italian Poems. London, 1814. viii, 144 p.

Tr. Andrew J. George in The Shorter Poems of Milton. N.Y., Macmillan, 1898. xxvi, 299 p.

Tr. prose William Vaughn Moody, in The Poems of Milton. Cambridge ed., Boston, Houghton-Mifflin, 1899, p. 323 77. Tr. rev. E. K. Rand in new ed., 1924, 1941.

Ed. and tr. prose Walter MacKellar, in The Latin Poems. (Cornell Studies in English) New Haven, Yale Univ. Pr., and London, Milford, 1930. xli, 382 p. (parallel texts).

Tr. prose Nelson G. McCrea in F. A. Patterson ed., The Student's Milton. N.Y., Crofts, 1930 et seq., p. 83–109, Latin text p. 111–151.

Tr. prose Charles Knapp in Columbia ed. of The Works of Milton. N.Y., Columbia Univ. Pr., 1931, v. 1, p. 154–329 (parallel texts). Repr. in Oxford Standard Authors, ed. of Milton, 1938 et seq.

Tr. verse Walter Skeat as Milton's Lament for Damon and his Other Latin Poems (*Elegiae, Sylvae*). London, Oxford Univ. Pr., 1935. vii, 109 p. Repr., with tr. by A. Vesselo of the Epigrams, in E. H. Visiak ed. of Milton's Complete Poetry and Selected Prose, London, Nonesuch Pr., and N.Y., Random House, 1938, p. 755–819.

Tr. prose Merritt Y. Hughes in his ed. of Complete Poems and Major Prose. N.Y., Odyssey Pr., 1957, p. 6–61 (*Elegiae* only).

Tr. prose Douglas Bush in Cambridge ed. of The Complete Poetical Works, Boston, Houghton Mifflin, 1965, p. 8–157.

The Prose Works

Trs. of the Latin prose works are usually printed or reprinted in the collected eds. of the prose writings, beginning with John Toland, 1698, 2 v., and Thomas Birch, 1738, 2 v., repr. enlarged 1753. (Earlier and some later eds. print the Latin works in the original.) Later eds. including trs.: Charles Symmons, 1806, 7 v.; George Burnett, 1809, 2 v.; Robert Fletcher, 1833; Rufus W. Griswold, N.Y. and Philadelphia, 1845, 2 v.; J. A. St. John, Bohn ed., 1848–53, et seq., 5 v. John Mitford, v. 3–8 of *The Works in Verse and Prose*, 1851; F. A. Patterson et al., Columbia Univ. ed., v. 3–18, 1931–38 (parallel texts); Don M. Wolfe, Yale Univ. Pr. ed., 1953— (in progress, v. 2, 1959; v. 3, 1963; v. 4, parts 1, 2, 1966).

————— The Art of Logic. Ed. and tr. Allan H. Gilbert. Columbia ed., v. 11, 1935. xiii, 537 p. (parallel texts)

————— The Commonplace Book. Tr. Nelson G. McCrea. *Ibid.*, v. 18, 1938. p. 128–227 (parallel texts).

Tr. Ruth Mohl in Yale ed., v. 1, 1953, p. 344–513.

————— The Correspondence of Milton and Mylius. Tr. T. O. Mabbott and Nelson G. McCrea, in Columbia ed., v. 12, 1936, p. 338–382.

Retr. in Private Correspondence, Yale ed., see below.

————— The Defence of Himself. Tr. George Burnett, v. 2, p. 449–587. Repr. rev. Moses Hadas in Columbia ed., v. 9, 1833. 308 p.

Tr. Paul W. Blackford, in Yale ed., v. 4, p. 697–825.

————— A Defence of the People of England. Tr. Joseph Washington. Amsterdam?, 1692. xxii, 246 p. Repr. Toland, v. 2, p. 557–658; Birch, v. 1; Symmons, v. 3; Burnett, v. 2, p. 3–259; Fletcher, p. 338–411; Griswold, v. 2, p. 5–126; St. John, v. 1, p. 1–213; Mitford, v. 8, 1–252.

Ed. and tr. Samuel Lee Wolff, in Columbia ed., v. 7, 1932. 582 p.

Tr. Paul W. Blackford. Northwestern Univ. dissertation, 1951.

Tr. Donald Mackenzie, in Yale ed., v. 4, 296–527.

————— Familiar Epistles. Tr. Robert Fellowes, in Symmons, v. 1, p. i–xliii (31 letters). Repr. in Fletcher, p. 950–963; in Griswold, v. 2, p. 527–550; in St. John, v. 3, p. 487–522.

Tr. John Hall (with the Prolusions). Philadelphia, Littell, 1829. vi, 120 p.

Tr. David Masson, in The Life of Milton. London, 1870–80, 6 v. (the letters scattered through the volumes). Repr. in Columbia ed., v. 12, 1936, p. 1–115.

Tr. Phyllis B. Tillyard as Private Correspondence (with Prolusions). Cambridge, Eng., Univ. Pr., 1932. xxxix, 143 p.

Tr. W. Arthur Turner and Alberta B. Turner in Yale ed., v. 1, p. 307–343; v. 2, p. 759–775; v. 4, p. 828–874.

——————— Letters of State (*Literae Pseudo-Senatus Anglicani*). Tr. anon. as Milton's Republican Letters. London, 1682.

Tr. Edward Phillips. London, 1694. Repr. in Toland, v. 2, p. 659–740; Birch, v. 2, p. 153–234; in Symmons, v. 4, 5; in Fletcher, p. 587–646; in Griswold, v. 2, p. 380–477; in St. John, v. 2, p. 200–333; in Mitford, v. 8, p. 252–430; ed. H. Fernow, Hamburg 1903, 51 p.; in Columbia ed., with additions from Mss., v. 13, 1937, p. 4–433.

——————— Prolusions. Tr. Bromley Smith (with Familiar Letters, tr. John Hall). Philadelphia, 1829. Repr. in Columbia ed., v. 12, 1936, p. 118–291.

Tr. Phyllis B. Tillyard in Private Correspondence and Academic Exercises. Cambridge, England, Univ. Pr., 1932. xxxix, 143 p. Prolusions repr. in Yale ed., v. 1, 1953, p. 211–306.

——————— A Second Defence of the English People. Tr. Robert Fellowes, in Symmons, v. 6, p. 361–477. Repr. Fletcher, p. 919–49; Griswold, v. 2, p. 477–527; St. John, v. 1, p. 214–300.

Tr. George Burnett, in v. 2, p. 328–448. Repr. rev. Moses Hadas, in Columbia ed., v. 8, 1933, 266 p.

Tr. Francis Wrangham. London, 1816. 199 p. Repr. in Sermons, London, 1816, v. 3.

Tr. Helen North, in Yale ed., v. 4, p. 547–686.

——————— A Treatise on Christian Doctrine. Tr. Charles R. Sumner. Cambridge, England, Univ. Pr., 1825. xlii, 711 p. Repr. Boston, 1825, 2 v.; repr. in St. John ed., v. 4, 5; in Columbia ed., v. 14–17, 1933–34 (parallel texts)

For Milton's tr. from Bucer, The Judgment Concerning Divorce, see Bucer, above.

MOFFET, THOMAS (1553–1604). *Nobilis*: or A View of the Life and Death of Sidney, and A Sorrowful Lamentation (*Lessus lugubris*). Ed. from Ms. and tr. Virgil B. Heltzel and Hoyt H. Hudson. San Marino, Calif., Huntington Library, 1940, p. 69–108.

———————— The Theater of Insects. Tr. Dr. John Rowland, in Edward Topsell, History of Four-footed Beasts and Serpents, 1658 ed. (as book 3).

MORE, HENRY (1614–1687). An account of Virtue: or Dr. More's Abridgement of Morals. Tr. Edward Southwell. London, Tooke, 1690. (16,) 268 p. Repr. as *Enchiridion Ethicum*, N.Y., Facsimile Text Society, 1930.

———————— *Enchiridion Metaphysicum*: Selections, in Philosophical Writings of Henry More, ed. Flora Isabel MacKinnon. N.Y., and London, Oxford Univ. Pr., 1925.

———————— The Theological Works of Henry More, According to the Author's Improvements in his Latin Edition [*Opera Omnia,* v. 1, 1675]. London, 1708.

MORE, SIR THOMAS, ST. (1478–1535). History of the Passion. Tr. by his granddaughter Mary Bassett as An exposicion of a parte of the passion, in The [English] Workes of Sir Thomas More. London, Rastell, 1557, p. 1350–1404. Repr. ed. and modernized Monsignor P. E. Hallet. London, Burns Oates, 1941. xxii, 133 p.

———————— The Latin Epigrams. Ed. and tr. Leicester Bradner and C. A. Lynch. Chicago, Univ. Pr., and London, Cambridge Univ. Pr., 1953. xliv, 255 p.

———————— Selected Letters. Tr. Elizabeth F. Rogers. Yale Ed., Selected Works, 1. New Haven, Conn., Yale Univ. Pr., 1962. xxiii, 271 p.

———————— A Translation of . . . *Responsio ad Lutherum*. Tr. Gertrude Joseph Donnelly. Washington, D.C. Catholic Univ. of America Pr., 1962. 295 p.

———————— Utopia. Tr. Raphe Robinson. London, 1551. Repr. 1556 and many later eds., esp. with the Latin ed. J. H. Lupton, Oxford, Clarendon Pr., 1895; Harvard Classics, v. 36; EL 1910 et seq., rev. 1951; ed. George Sampson, London, Bell, 1910, xxv, 442 p. (parallel texts); many later reprs., modernized text, especially in More's Utopia and its Critics, ed. Ligeia Gallagher, Chicago, Scott Foresman, 1964, 182 p.

Tr. Gilbert Burnet. London, 1684. Repr. ed. Sir Sidney Lee (with the Poems), London, Methuen, 1906, xv, 104 p.

Tr. Sir Arthur Cayley, in Memoirs of Sir Thomas More. London, Cadell, 1808, v. 2, p. 1–145.

Tr. Valerian Paget as More's Millennium. London, Rivers, 1909. xxiii, 258 p.

Tr. G. C. Richards. Oxford, Blackwell, 1923. xxi, 137 p. Repr. rev. Edward Surtz in Yale Ed., Selected Works, v. 2, 1964, xxxiv, 158 p.; also in Complete Works, v. 4, 1965, 629 p. (parallel texts).

Tr. H. S. V. Ogden. Crofts Classics. N.Y., Appleton-Century-Crofts, 1949. x, 84 p. paper.

Tr. Peter K. Marshall. N.Y., Washington Square Pr., 1965. xxxii, 127 p.

Tr. Paul Turner. Penguin, 1965. 154 p.

MORGAGNI, GIOVANNI BAPTISTA (1682–1771). The Seats and Causes of Diseases Investigated by Anatomy (*De sedibus et causis morborum*). Tr. Benjamin Alexander. London, 1769. 3 v. Repr. abr. 1822; Boston, 1824; selections repr. in Emerson C. Kelly, Medical Classics, v. 4, no. 70: Baltimore, Williams and Wilkins, 1940, p. 629–839.

MOSELLANUS, PETRUS (1493?–1524). Renaissance Student Life: The *Paedologia*. Tr. Robert F. Seyboldt. Urbana, Univ. of Illinois Pr., 1927. 100 p.

MOSHEIM, JOHANN LORENZ (1694?–1755). Commentaries on the Affairs of the Christians Before . . . Constantine the Great. Tr. Robert S. Vidal. London, Cadell, 1813–35. 3 v. Repr. N.Y., 1851.

———— An Ecclesiastical History, Ancient and Modern . . . to the Present Century. Tr. Archibald Maclaine. 2d ed. London, Cadell, 1782. 6 v. Repr. 1802–03; N.Y., 1821; Glasgow, 1838; Cincinnati, 1857, 1858.

———— Institutes of Ecclesiastical History. Tr. James Murdock. New Haven, Conn., Maltby, 1832. 3 v. Repr. N.Y., 1839, 1841, 1854 (5th ed.), 1867; London, ed. William Stubbs, 1863; Boston, ed. H. L. Hastings, 1892.

MUSCULUS, WOLFGANG (1497–1563). Commonplaces of Christian Religion . . . two other treatises, one of Othes, and an other of Usurye. Tr. John Man. London, 1563. 587 leaves. Repr. 1578, 1340 p.

For contemporary trs. of his pamphlets, see B. Q. Morgan, *German Literature in English Translation*.

NAOGEORGUS (see Thomas Kirchmeyer, above).

NAUSEA, FRIEDRICH, Bishop of Vienna (d. 1552). Of all Blasing Starrs in generall, as well Supernaturall and naturall. Tr. Abraham Fleming. London, 1577. Repr. 1618 as A Treatise of Blazing Starres.

————— A Bright Burning Beacon . . . Conteining a generall Doctrine of Sundrie Signes and Wonders, specially Earthquakes . . . And a praier for the Appeasing of Gods Wrath. Tr. Abraham Fleming. London, 1580.

————— A Sermon of the Sacrament of the Aulter. Tr. John More. London, 1533.

NEWTON, SIR ISAAC (1642–1727). The Mathematical Principles of Natural Philosophy. Tr. Andrew Motte, London, 1729. 2 v. Repr. (with Newton's System of the World) London, 1803, 3 v.; repr. 1819; N.Y., 1848; repr. annotated by Florian Cajori, Berkeley, Univ. of California Pr., 1934, xxxv, 680 p.; repr. in Great Books, 1952, v. 34, p. 1–372; repr. Berkeley, as before, 1962, 2 v. paper.

————— The Method of Fluxions and Infinite Series. Tr. J. Colson. London, 1736. Repr. 1737; repr. facs. in Mathematical Works, ed. Derek T. Whiteside, v. 1, N.Y., Johnson Reprint Corp., 1964.

————— Two Treatises of the Quadrature of Curves, and Analysis by Equations of an Infinite Number of Terms. Tr. John Stewart. London, 1745. xxxii, 479 p. Repr. facs. in Mathematical Works, v. 1, with the preceding item.

————— Universal Arithmetick: or A Treatise of Arithmetical Composition and Resolution. Tr. John Ralphson, rev. Samuel Conn. 2d ed., London, 1728. (8), 271 p. Repr. 1769.

————— Unpublished Scientific Papers: A Selection from the Portsmouth Collection in the University Library, Cambridge. Ed. and tr. A. Rupert Hall and Marie Boas Hall. Cambridge, Univ. Pr., 1962. xx, 415 p.

Cf. also *The Philosophy of Nature: Selections*, ed. H. S. Thayer (N.Y., Hafner, 1953, xvi, 207 p.).

NIDER, JOHANNES (fl. 1468). On the Contracts of Merchants. Tr. Charles H. Reeves, ed. Ronald B. Shuman. Norman, Univ. of Oklahoma Pr., 1966. xiii, 77 p.

OSORIO, JERONIMO, DA FONSECA (1506–1580). An Epistle . . . to Elizabeth . . . Queene of England. Tr. Richard Shacklock. Antwerp, John de Laet, 1565. 78 leaves.

For Haddon's answer, see Walter Haddon, above.

——————— The Five Books . . . contayninge a discourse of Civill and Christian Nobilitie (*De nobilitate civili*; *De nobilitate christiana*). Tr. William Blandie. London, 1576.

——————— The History of the Portuguese during the Reign of Emmanuel [II]. Tr. James Gibbs. London, 1752. 2 v.

——————— A Learned Treatise . . . wherein he confuteth the Aunswere made by M. W. Haddon . . . Tr. John Fen. Louvain, Fouler, 1568. 283 leaves.

For the rebuttal, see again Haddon, above.

OWEN, JOHN (?1564–1622). Epigrams of that Most Wittie and Worthie Epigrammist. Tr. John Vicars. London, 1619.

Tr. Thomas Pecke, in *Parnassi Puerperium*. London, 1659 (with epigrams of Martial, More, Pecke).

Tr. Thomas Harvey as Latine Epigrams. London, 1677. (8,) 208 p.

PACE, RICHARD (1483–1536). The Benefit of a Liberal Education (*De fructu qui ex doctrina percipitur*). Ed. and tr. Frank Manley and Richard S. Sylvester. N.Y., Ungar, for the Renaissance Soc. of Amer., 1967. xxvi, 190 p. (parallel texts).

PALINGENIUS, MARCELLUS (Petro Angelo Manzolli, 1501?–1543?). The Zodiake of Life. Tr. verse Barnabe Googe. London, 1560 (three books); 1561 (six books); 1565 (all twelve books); repr. rev., 1576, (12,) 242, (22) p.; repr. 1588. Repr. with intro. Rosemund Tuve, N.Y., Scholars' Facsimiles, 1947, 360 p.

PARACELSUS (Theophrastus Bombast von Hohenheim, 1493–1541). Selected Writings. Tr. Norbert Guterman from a German collection. London, Routledge, and N.Y., Pantheon, 1951. 346 p. Repr. 1958.

——————— Four Treatises. Tr. Henry E. Sigerist et al. from the German version. Baltimore, Johns Hopkins Univ. Pr., 1941. xii, 256 p.

Seven Defensiones. Miner's Sickness. Diseases (of insanity). *Nymphs and Spirits.*

——————— The Hermetic and Alchemical Writings. Tr. Arthur Edward Waite. London, J. Elliot, 1894. 2 v. Repr. Chicago, De Laurence, Scott, 1910, 2 v.; repr., New Hyde Park, N.Y., Univ. Books, 1967, 2 v.

——————— Of the Supreme Mysteries of Nature. Of the Spirits of the Planets. Of Occult Philosophy. (The . . . Cure of Wounds and Diseases. The Signs of the Zodiack). Tr. Robert Turner. London, 1656. (20), 158 p.

For other 17th c. trs., see British Museum Catalogue.

PARKER, SAMUEL, Bishop of Oxford (1640–1688). History of his Own Time (*De rebus sui temporis commentarii*). Tr. Thomas Newlin. London, 1727. 424 p. Repr. 1728.

His doctrinal writings in Latin have not been tr.

PATRIZI, FRANCESCO (1413–1492). A Moral Methode of Civil Policie . . . the Institution, State, and Government of a Common Weale. Abridged out of the Commentaries (*De regno deque institutione reipublicae*). Tr. Ralph Robinson. London, 1576.

——————— (Of reading and writing history). Part tr. and abridged by Thomas Blundeville, The True Order and Methode of wryting and reading Hystories. London, 1574. 32 leaves. Repr. Hugh G. Dick, Huntington Library Quarterly, 3 (1940), 149–170.

Blundeville combined an abridgment of Acontius, q.v. above, with the last five of the ten dialogues of Patrizi.

PERERIUS, BENEDICTUS, VALENTINUS (Bento Pereira, S.J., 1535–1610). The Astrologer Anatomized, or the Vanity of the Star-gazing Art. Tr. Philip Enderbie. London, 1661.

The first ed. of the original (1591) was entitled *Adversus fallaces et superstitiosas artes;* the 1598 ed., *De Magia,* etc.

PICO DELLA MIRANDOLA, GIOVANNI (1463–1494). See Italian Literature, in v. III. Also *ibid.* for his nephew Gianfrancesco.

PLATINA (Bartolommeo de' Sacchi di Piadena, 1421–1481). The Lives of the Popes from the Time of . . . Christ to the Reign of Sixtus IV. Tr.

Paul Rycaut (with a continuation to date). London, 1685. 416, 394 p. Repr. 1688; 1888, in William Benham, Ancient and Modern History of Theological Literature, v. 11, 17.

POLE, REGINALD CARDINAL (1500–1558). The Defense of the Unity of the Church. Tr. Joseph G. Dwyer. Westminster, Md., Newman Pr., 1965. xii, 342 p.

Part tr. Fabyane Withers as The Seditious and Blasphemous Oration . . . the defence of the ecclesiastical unitye. London, 1560.

———— The Reform of England by the Decrees of Cardinal Pole (*Reformatio Angliae*). Tr. Henry Raikes. Chester, 1839.

POMPONAZZI, PIETRO (1462–1525). On the Immortality of the Soul. Tr. William H. Hay II, in The Renaissance Philosophy of Man, p. 280–381: see Collections, above.

PONTANO, GIOVANNI (1426–1503). The Eclogues. Ed. and tr. Elaine Jeannette Harper. Bloomington, Indiana Univ. dissertation, 1958.

PORTA, GIOVANNI BAPTISTA DELLA: see Italian Literature in v. III, s.v. Della Porta.

PUFENDORF, SAMUEL VON (1632–1694). The Compleat History of Sweden. Tr. Charles Brockwell from the German version. London, 1707. 624 p.

———— The Divine Feudal Law, or Covenants with Mankind. Tr. Thomas Dorrington. London, 1703. 365 p. Repr. 1714 as A View of the Principles of the Lutheran Churches.

———— Elements of Universal Jurisprudence. Facs. ed., tr. W. A. Oldfather. Classics of International Law. London, Oxford Univ. Pr., 1931. 2 v.

———— The History of Popedom: Containing the Rise, Progress, and Decay Thereof. Tr. John Chamberlayne from German. London, 1691.

———— An Introduction to the History of the Principal Kingdoms and States of Europe. Tr. John Crull from the German original. London, 1695. Repr. 1697, 1699, 1700, 1702, 1706, 1719 (8th ed.)

Tr. Joseph Sayer from French. London, 1748. 2v. Repr. 1764.

————— Of the Law of Nature and Nations. Tr. Basil Kennett and William Percivale. Oxford, 1703. 400, 262 p. Reprs. to 1749, 5th ed.

Tr. abridged John Spavan. London, 1716. 2 v.

Ed. and tr. C. H. and W. A. Oldfather. Classics of International Law. Oxford, Clarendon Pr., 1934. 2 v. (parallel texts).

————— Of the Nature and Qualification of Religion, in Reference to Civil Society. Tr. John Crull from the German version. London, 1698. 182 p.

Tr. anon. as Of the Relation between Church and State. London, 1719.

————— The Present State of Germany (*De statu imperii germanici*). Tr. and continued by Edmund Bohun. London, 1696. xiv, 223 p.

————— The Whole Duty of Man According to the Law of Nature (*De officio hominis et civis*). Tr. Andrew Tooke. London, 1691. Repr. 1698, 336 p.; repr. 1705, 1716, 1735.

Ed. facs. and tr. Frank Gardner Moore as The Two Books on the Duty of Man and Citizen According to the Natural Law. Classics of International Law. N.Y., Oxford Univ. Pr., 1927. 2 v.

QUILLET, CLAUDE (1602–1661). *Callipaediae*; or, an Art how to Have Handsome Children . . . [with] *Paedotrophiae*, or, the Art of Nursing and Breeding Up Children . . . by M. St. Marthe [Scévole de Sainte-Marthe]. Tr. verse anon. 1710. Repr. 1718, 163 p.

Tr. verse William Oldisworth, et al. London, 1710. 72 p. Repr. (3d ed.) 1729; 1776.

Tr. verse Nicholas Rowe, et al. London, 1712. Repr. 1720; 1733; in Miscellaneous Works of Nicholas Rowe, 1733, 144 p.; 1761; Dublin, 1771; re-ed. abridged Mary R. Mahl, Los Angeles, Calif., pr. pr., 1963, 111 p.

RACHEL, SAMUEL (1628–1691). Dissertations on the Law of Nature and of Nations. Ed. facs., and tr. John Pawley Bate. Classics of International Law. Washington, D.C., Carnegie Institution, 1916. 2 v.

RAINOLDS, JOHN (1549–1607). An Oration in Praise of the Art of Poetry. Tr. Walter Allen, Jr., with intro. William Ringler. Princeton, N.J., Princeton Univ. Pr., 1940, 93 p. (parallel texts).

RAMUS, PETRUS (Pierre de la Ramée, 1515–1572). The Art of Arithmeticke. Tr. William Kempe. London,1592. 83 p.

———— The Elements of Geometry. Tr. Thomas Hood. London, 1590. 4, 24 leaves.

Tr. and enlarged by William Bedwell as *Via regia ad geometriam*. London, 1636. 22, 299 p.

———— The Latine Grammar. Tr. anon. London, 1585. 148 p. Repr. Cambridge, 1585.

———— The Rudiments of Latin Grammar. Tr. anon. London, 1585. 60 p.

———— The Logike (*Dialectica*). Tr. Roland M'Kilwein. London, 1574. 102 p. Repr. 1581.

Tr. Dudley Fenner, in The Artes of Logike and Rethorike. Middelburg, 1584. 72 unnumbered p. Repr. 1584, 1588.

Free tr. Abraham Fraunce as The Lawiers Logike, exemplifying the Praecepts of Logike by the Practice of the Common Lawe. London, 1588. 10, 151 leaves. Repr. 1588 (2).

Translating the text of Ramus' principles, but providing his own illustrations from the law. Cf. Fraunce's Ms adaptation as *The Sheapheardes Logike* (c. 1580), likewise supplying the illustrative examples from classical and contemporary literature.

Free tr. Thomas Granger as *Syntagma Logicum,* or The Divine Logike. London, 1620. (8), 387 p.

Tr. Samuel Wotton as The Art of Logike. London, 1626. 8, 2, 189 p.

Tr. Thomas Spencer. London, 1628. 8,311 p. Repr. 1656 as Logick Unfolded.

Tr. Robert Fage as *Dialectica* . . . digested into questions and answers. London, 1632. 20, 127 p. Repr. 1635; 1636; 1651 (with Fenner's tr. of the Rhetoric), 12, 323 p.; 1658 (ed. Edward Phillips, in Mysteries of Love and Eloquence); 1685 (ed. the same); 1699 (ed. the same, in The Beau's Academy).

Latin ed. adapted by John Milton as *Artis logicae plenior institutio,* published 1672, et seq. in the works of Milton. Tr. Allan H. Gilbert, in Columbia Milton, v. 11 (1935).

———— (The Rhetoric: *Rhetorica,* usually published as by Omar Talon). Tr. Dudley Fenner, in The Artes of Logike and Rethorike. Middelburg 1584. Repr. 1584, 1588, London, 1651 (with the Fage tr. of the Logic), 1681 (the tr. wrongly ascribed to Thomas Hobbes), 1840 (in The English Works of Thomas Hobbes, v. 6).

Free tr. Abraham Fraunce as The Arcadian Rhetorike (supplying illustrations from literature). London, 1588. 152 p. Repr. ed. Ethel Seaton, Oxford, Blackwell, 1950, iv, 136 p.

Tr. John Barton as The Art of Rhetorick . . . Exemplified out of Holy Writ. London, 1634. 16, 50 p. Reprs. to 1739.

We are indebted for the Ramus items to the exhaustive *Ramus and Talon Inventory,* by Walter J. Ong, S.J. (Harvard Univ. Pr., 1958, 558 p.). We follow the *Inventory* in counting as translations many much altered adaptations, and in considering as the work of Ramus his adaptations of the works of Omer Talon (c. 1510–1562).

RUGGLE, GEORGE (1575–1622). *Ignoramus* [A comedy]. Tr. Robert Codrington. London. 1662.

Tr. freely by Edward Ravenscroft as Ignoramus, or the English Lawyer. London, 1678. Repr. 1736, 1737.

SADOLETO, JACOPO CARDINAL (1477–1547). Letter to the Genevans. Tr. John C. Olin in A Reformation Debate: Sadoleto's Letter to the Genevans and Calvin's Reply. N.Y., Harper (Torch Books), 1966. 136 p.

———— Sadoleto on Education (*De pueris recte instituendis*). Tr. E. T. Campagnac and K. Forbes. London and N.Y., Oxford Univ. Pr., 1916. xlviii, 141 p.

SAINTE-MARTHE, SCÉVOLE DE (1536–1623). *Paedotrophia,* or the Art of Bringing Up Children (*Paedotrophia, sive de puerorum educatione*). Tr. anon. London, 1710 (with Claude Quillet, *Callipaedia*).

Tr. H. W. Tytler as *Paedotrophia*, or the Art of Nursing and Rearing Children: A Poem in Three Books. London, 1797.

SANDER, NICHOLAS (?1530–1581). The Rise and Growth of the Anglican Schism. Tr. David Lewis. London, Burns and Oates, 1877.

SANNAZARO, JACOPO (1458–1530). Arcadia and Piscatorial Eclogues. Tr. Ralph Nash. Detroit, Mich., Wayne State Univ. Pr., 1966. 220 p. (The Arcadia tr. from Italian; the Eclogues from Latin).

SARBIEWSKI, MACIEJ KAZIMIERZ (Casimir, 1595–1640). The Odes of Casmire. Tr. G. Hils. London, 1646. 141 p. (parallel texts). Repr. facs. and intro. Maren-Sofie Roestvig, Los Angeles, William Andrews Clark Library, Augustan Repr. Soc., 1953. (35 poems).

SAVONAROLA, GIROLAMO (1452–1498). An exposicyon . . . upon the li [51st] Psalme . . . a meditacyon . . . upon the [31st] Psalme. Paris, 1538. 50 leaves. (parallel texts). Repr. London, [1540?], [1543?], [1558?], and rev. Abraham Fleming, 1578.

Ed. and tr. E. H. Parsons as Meditations on Psalm li and part of Psalm xxxi. London, C. J. Clay, 1900. xiv, 227 p.

———— [Psalm 51] An exposition of the Psalm *Miserere mei Deus*. Tr. Rev. F. C. Cowper. Milwaukee, Wis., Young Churchman Co., 1889. 77 p.

Tr. Rev. Bertrand Wilberforce. London, Catholic Truth Society, 1900. 72 p.

———— [Psalm 31] Sorrow and Hope: A Meditation on the Thirty-first Psalm. Tr. unnamed. London, S.P.C.K., 1894. 84 p.

———— Spiritual and Ascetic Letters. Tr. Watkin Williams, ed. B. W. Randolph, with foreword by Henry Scott Holland. London, Mowbray, 1907. xxii, 115 p.

———— The Triumph of the Cross. Tr. O'Dell Travers Hill from the Latin. London, Hodder and Stoughton, 1868. xlviii, 258 p.

Tr. Very Rev. John Procter from the Italian. London, Sands, and Dublin, Gill, 1901. xxxi, 213 p.

The Italian sermons are not known to have been tr.

SCALIGER, JOSEPH JUSTUS (1540–1609). Autobiography, with Autobiographical Selections from his Letters, his Testament, and the Funeral Orations by Heinsius and Baudius. Tr. George W. Robinson. Cambridge, Mass., Harvard Univer. Pr., 1927. 128 p.

SCALIGER, JULIUS CAESAR (1484–1558). Select Translations from Scaliger's Poetics by Frederick M. Padelford. Yale Studies in English. N.Y., Holt, 1905. xviii, 96 p.

SECUNDUS, JOHANNES (Jan Everaerts, 1511–1536). *Basia* . . . or the Kisses. Tr. Thomas Stanley, in Anacreon, etc. London, 1647. Repr. London, Nonesuch Pr., 1923, 20 p.

Tr. George Ogle. London, 1731. Repr. 1788.

Tr. John Nott. London, 1775. 223 p. (parallel texts). Many reprs.

Tr. with the *Pancharis* of Jean Bonnefons (see above, Bonefonius). London, 1824. Repr. 1838, 1850?, 1853.

Tr. prose W. K. Kelly, in Propertius, etc. BCL, 1854.

Ed. and tr. F. A. Wright as The Love Poems. London, Routledge, and N.Y., Dutton, 1930. 253 p. (parallel texts of the *Basia, Amores, Odae*).

SELDEN, JOHN (1584–1654). The Dissertation Fleta. Tr. Robert Kelham. London, 1771. xii, 276 p.

Ed. (from 1647 ed.) and tr. David Ogg. Cambridge, Univ. Pr., and N.Y., Macmillan, 1925. lxvi, 204 p.

———— Of the Dominion, or Ownership of the Sea. Tr. Marchamont Needham. London, 1652. 500 p. Repr. rev. by James Howell as *Mare Clausum*: The Right and Dominion of the Sea. London, 1663.

———— The Fabulous Gods Denounced in the Bible (*De diis Syris*). Tr. W. A. Hauser. Philadelphia, Lippincott, 1880. 178 p.

———— The Reverse or Back-face of the English Janus. Tr. Redman Westcot (Adam Littleton). London, 1682. 131 p. Repr. as *Jani Anglorum Facies altera,* in Tracts Written by John Selden, London, 1683.

SERVETUS, MICHAEL (1509?–1553). Geographical, Medical, and Astrological Writings. Tr. Charles Donald O'Malley. Philadelphia, Memoirs of American Philosophical Society, v. 34, 1953. 208 p.

The prefaces to the 1535 and the 1541 eds. of Ptolemy's *Geography; Apology against Fuchs,* 1536; *The Syrups,* 1537; *Discourse in Favor of Astrology,* 1538; *The Description of the Lesser Circulation,* from *Christianismi Restitutio,* 1553.

———— The Two Treatises of Servetus on the Trinity. On the Errors of the Trinity: seven books, 1531. On the Righteousness of Christ's

Kingdom: four chapters, 1532. Tr. Earl Morse Wilbur. Harvard Theological Studies, 16. Cambridge, Mass., Harvard Univ. Pr., and London, Milford, 1932. xxxviii, 264 p.

SLEIDANUS, JOANNES (Johann Philippson, 1506–1556). A briefe Chronicle of the foure principall Empyres. Tr. Stephen Wythers. London, 1563. 105 leaves.

Tr. Abraham Darcie as The Key of Historie. London, 1627. 377 p. Repr. 1631, 1635, 1661.

Tr. anon. 1695.

————— Sleidanes Commentaries concerning the State of Religion and Common wealth, during the raigne of Charles the fifth. Tr. John Daus. London, Day, 1560. 470 leaves.

Tr. Edmund Bohun as The General History of the Reformation of the Church. London, 1689.

SOAREZ, CYPRIAN, S.J. (d. 1593). *De Arte Rhetorica* (1568). Tr. Lawrence J. Flynn. Gainesville, Univ. of Florida disseration, 1956.

SOCINUS, FAUSTUS (1539–1604). An Argument for the Authority of Holy Scripture. Tr. Edward Combe. London, 1731. Repr. as a Demonstration of the Truth of the Christian Religion. London, 1732.

————— The Racovian Catechism. Tr. Thomas Rees. London, 1815.

SOCINUS, LAELIUS (1525–1562). Confession of Faith. Tr. Edward M. Hulme, in Persecution and Liberty (G. L. Burr Essays). N.Y., 1931, p. 216–18.

SPAGNUOLI, BATTISTA: see Mantuanus, above.

SPINOZA, BENEDICT (1632–1677). The Chief Works. Tr. R. H. M. Elwes. Bohn's Philological Library. London, Bell, 1883–84. 2 v. Repr. Gloucester, Mass., Peter Smith, 1962.

————— The Correspondence. Ed. and tr. A. Wolf. London, Allen and Unwin, 1928. 502 p.

———— Earlier Philosophical Writings: The Cartesian Principles, and Thoughts on Metaphysics. Tr. Frank A. Hayes. Indianapolis, Ind., Bobbs-Merrill, 1963. xxxvi, 161 p.

———— Ethics, and *De intellectus emendatione*. Tr. A. Boyle, with intro- George Santayana. EL, 1910, et seq. xlviii, 263 p.

———— Ethics. Tr. D. D. S. N.Y., 1876.

Tr. Henry Smith, in Spinoza and his Environment. Cincinnati, 1886.

Tr. William Hale White. London, English and Foreign Philosophical Library, 1883. xxxviii, 297 p. Repr. rev., London, Unwin, 1894; London, Duckworth, 1899; rev. A. H. Stirling, London, Oxford Univ. Pr., 1910; repr. *ibid.*, 1927; repr. Great Books, v. 31, 1952, p. 355– 463.

Tr. R. H. M. Elwes (in The Works, above), repr. Garden City, N.Y., Doubleday, 1962 (with Descartes and Leibnitz).

———— *De intellectus emendatione*. Tr. William Hale White. London, Unwin, 1895. xxx, 62 p. Repr. 1899.

Tr. and expounded Harry Waton (with the *Cogitata metaphysica*), in The Philosophy of Spinoza. N.Y., Spinoza Institute, 1932. 270 p.

Tr. Joseph Katz as Spinoza on the Improvement of the Understanding. N.Y., Liberal Arts Pr., 1958. xx, 40 p.

———— Short Treatise on God, Man, and Human Welfare (*De deo et homine*). Tr. Lydia Gillingham Robinson. Chicago, Open Court, 1909. xxiv, 178 p.

Tr. A. Wolf as God, Man, & his Well-being. London, Black, 1910. cxxviii, 246 p. Repr. N.Y., Russell, 1963.

———— A Treatise Partly Theological and Partly Political (*Theologico- Politicus*). Tr. anon. London, 1689.

Tr. Robert Willis. London, 1862.

———— A Treatise on Politics. Tr. W. Maccall. London, 1854.

Cf. *Spinoza on Freedom of Thought: Selections* (from the two preceding works). Tr. T. E. Jessop (Montreal, Casalini, 1962, xxxvi, 132 p.). Cf. generally *The Spinoza Dictionary,* ed. Dagobert D. Runes (N.Y., Philo- sophical Library, 1951, 308 p.); *Spinoza Selections,* ed. John Wild (Mod- ern Student's Library, N.Y., Scribner, 1930, lxi, 479 p.); *The Living Thoughts of Spinoza,* Presented by Arnold Zweig (London, Cassell, 1939, 103 p.).

STAPHYLUS, FREDERICUS (d. 1564). The Apologie. Intreating of the True and Right Understanding of the Holy Scripture. Of the Translation of the Bible . . . Of Disagreement in Doctrine Among the Protestants. Tr. Thomas Stapleton. Antwerp, de Laet, 1565. 254 leaves.

STAPLETON, THOMAS (1535–1598). The Life and Illustrious Martyrdom of Sir Thomas More (part 3 of *Tres Thomae*). Tr. Philip E. Hallett. London, Burns Oates, and N.Y., Benziger, 1928. xvi, 235 p.

STRADA, FAMIANUS (1572–1647). *De Bello Belgico*. The History of the Low-Countrey Warres. Tr. Sir Robert Stapleton. London, Moseley, 1650. 360 p. Repr. 1667. (Decade 1 only in this tr.)

———— The Siege of Antwerp. Tr. Thomas Lancaster. London, 1656. (from Decade 2).

STURM, JOHANN (1507–1589). A ritch Storehouse of Treasure for Nobilitye and Gentlemen (*Nobilitas literata*). Tr. Thomas Browne. London, 1570.

SUAREZ, FRANCISCO, S.J. (1548–1617). Extracts: Politics and Government, from Defense of the Faith, Laws and God the Lawgiver. Tr. George Albert Moore. Chevy Chase, Md., Country Dollar Pr., 1950. xiii, 138 p.

———— Selections from Three Works: *De legibus, ac Deo legislatore,* 1612; *Defensio fidei catholicae et apostolicae adversus anglicanae sectae errores,* 1613; *De triplici virtute theologicae fide, spe et caritate,* 1621. Facs. ed., tr. Gwladys L. Williams, Ammi Brown, and John Waldron. Classics of International Law. Oxford, Clarendon Pr., 1944. 2 v. (trs. in v. 2)

———— The Dignity and Virginity of the Mother of God. Disputations 1, 5, 6 from The Mysteries of the Life of Christ. Tr. Richard J. O'Brien. West Baden Springs, Ind., West Baden College, 1954. xi, 116 p.

———— On Formal and Universal Unity. Tr. J. F. Ross. Milwaukee, Wis., Marquette Univ. Pr., 1964. 123 p.

———— On the Various Kinds of Distinctions (*Disputationes Metaphysicae,* VII). Tr. Cyril Vollert. Milwaukee, Wis., Marquette Univ. Pr., 1947. 67 p.

SUSENBROTUS, JOHANNES (d. 1543). The *Epitome Troporum et Schematum*. Ed. and tr. Joseph X. Brennan. Urbana, Univ. of Illinois dissertation, 1954 (parallel texts).

SWEDENBORG, EMANUEL (1688–1772).†

There is no collected edition of all the works of this most prolific of neo-Latin writers, and first translations continue to appear of his hitherto untranslated works. His religious works continue moreover to be reprinted, revised, and retranslated in the interest of the New Church (the first founded in London in 1787). Three publishing houses are now devoted to his writings: the (London) Swedenborg Society, founded 1810; the (New York) Swedenborg Foundation, established 1850; and the Swedenborg Scientific Association, founded in 1898 in Bryn Athyn, Pennsylvania. In addition, the New Church Press in New York and in Boston and elsewhere publishes works of greater or less dimension.

A massive bibliography of the works of Swedenborg in all languages was published by James Hyde (London, Swedenborg Society, 1906, xvi, 742 p.), listing the appearance of each work in its various editions and translations in the chronological order of first publication; it does not however note collective editions as such. The (London) *Swedenborg Society Library Catalogue* (London, Swedenborg House, 1958–65, 2 v. mimeographed: v. 1, Books, xviii, 330 p.; v. 2, Archives [including Mss of the works], 201 p.) has many later items, but the collection is far from complete. The (New York) Swedenborg Foundation expects to publish *Swedenborg Reference for Libraries: . . . Catalogue for the Writings . . . in the Library of the New Church Theological School,* Cambridge and Newton, Massachusetts. Though the collection itself is smaller than that in London, the catalogue will have the merit of listing all the successive translators and revisers of the English versions of the individual works, whereas many current editions do not bear the name of a translator or even the date of first publication or of reprint.

The Swedenborg writings are commonly divided into two classes, the scientific and philosophical (to 1745), and the major works called theological (from 1749), with an intervening category of works called preparatory. The most succinct, though not complete, list of the writings is to be

†We gratefully acknowledge the help given us in this compilation by officers of the Swedenborg Foundation, Mr. Tomas Spiers and Mrs. Virginia Branston, and by the treasurer of The Swedenborg Scientific Association, Mr. E. Boyd Asplundh.

found in the *Everyman's Library* editions of four of them, listed below. Like the bibliographies above, it is chronological by date of ms. The chronogical order will be followed below in the sections listing individual works.

Scientific and Philosophical Works

COLLECTIONS

——————— The Mechanical Inventions. Tr. and ed. Alfred Acton. Philadelphia, Swedenborg Scientific Association, 1939. 51 p.

——————— Psychologica. Tr. Alfred Acton. Philadelphia, Swedenborg Scientific Association, 1923. 232, 232 p. (parallel texts)

——————— Psychological Transactions. Tr. Alfred Acton. Ibid., 1920. 282 p. Repr. 1955.

——————— Scientific and Philosophical Treatises. Ed. Alfred H. Stroh. Ibid., part 1, 1908, 125 p. (Chemistry, Geology, Physics, Cosmology). part 2, 1905, 60 p. (Anatomy, Physiology, Psychology, Philosophy).

——————— A Series of Posthumous Philosophical Tracts. Tr. J. J. G. Wilkinson. London and Boston, 1847. 149 p. Repr. Boston, 1848, 1852.

INDIVIDUAL WORKS (CHRONOLOGICALLY, BY DATE OF MS.)

1722. Miscellaneous Observations Connected with the Physical Sciences. Tr. Charles Edward Strutt. London, Newbery, and Boston, Clapp, 1847. xvi, 159 p.

1734. The *Principia,* or the First Principles of Natural Things. (v. 1 of *Opera Philosophica et Mineralia*). Tr. Augustus Clissold. London, Newbery, and Boston, Clapp, 1845–46. 2 v.

Tr. James R. Rendell and Isaiah Tansley, adding the posthumous *Minor Principia,* and the Summary of the *Principia.* London, Swedenborg Society, 1912. 2 v.

——————— The Subterranean or Mineral Kingdom: Concerning Copper and Copper Ore (v. 3 of the *Opera Philosophica et Mineralia*). Tr. Arthur II. Scarle (in 1901). London, Swedenborg Society, 1938. 3 v. mimeographed.

V. 2 on Iron has not been translated.

1734. *Prodromus* or the Forerunner of a Reasoning Philosophy Concerning the Infinite and the Final Cause of Creation . . . Designed . . . as an

Introduction to the Economy of the Animal Kingdom. Tr. John Roberts, and Samuel and Henry Osbaldiston. Manchester, William Cowherd, 1795. ix, 189 p.

Tr. J. J. G. Wilkinson as Outlines of a Philosophical Argument on the Infinite. London, Swedenborg Association, and Boston, Clapp, 1847. xxx, 160 p. Repr. Boston, 1848. Repr. as The Infinite and the Final Cause of Creation, London, Swedenborg Society, 1902, lxvii, 235 p., repr. 1908, 1915.

1740. The Economy of the Animal Kingdom Considered Anatomically, Physically, and Philosophically. Tr. Augustus Clissold. London, Newbery, and Boston, Clapp, 1845–46. 2 v. (v. 1, The Blood; v. 2, The Brain). Repr. Boston, 1868; N.Y., New Church Board of Pub., 1903, repr. 1919; repr. Philadelphia, Swedenborg Scientific Association, 1955.

——————— The Fibre and Diseases of the Fibre (part 3, posthumous). Tr. Alfred Acton. Philadelphia, Swedenborg Scientific Association, 1918, 348 p.

1740–44 (Ms., pub. 1869). The Brain Considered Anatomically, Physically, and Philosophically. Tr. in part R. L. Tafel. London, James Speirs, 1882–87. 2 v. (v. 1, The Cerebrum and its Parts; v. 2, The Pituitary Gland, etc.) Repr. 1934, 649 p.

Tr. Alfred Acton as Three Transactions on the Cerebrum. Philadelphia, Swedenborg Scientific Association, 1938–40. 3 v.

1742 (Ms., pub. 1849). The Soul, or Rational Psychology. Tr. Frank Sewall. N.Y., New Church Board of Pub., 1887. xxvi, 338 p. Repr., ibid., and London, Spiers, 1900; repr. N.Y., 1914.

Tr. Norbert H. Rogers and Alfred Acton as Rational Psychology. Philadelphia, Swedenborg Scientific Association, 1950. 343 p.

1744–45. The Animal Kingdom Considered Anatomically, Physically, and Philosophically. (Part 1, The Viscera of the Body; part 2, The Upper Organs). Tr. J. J. G. Wilkinson. London, Newbery, and Boston, Clapp, 1843–44. 2 v. Repr. St. Clairsville, Ohio, 1850; Cincinnati and Boston, 1858; Philadelphia, Swedenborg Scientific Association, 1960.

——————— The Five Senses. (Part 3, Ms 1744, pub. 1848). Tr. Enoch S. Price. Philadelphia, Swedenborg Scientific Association, 1914. 338 p.

————— The Generative Organs. (Parts 4, 5, Ms 1743, pub. 1849). Tr. J. J. G. Wilkinson. London, Newbery, for Swedenborg Association, 1852. x, 327 p. Repr. Philadelphia, Swedenborg Scientific Association, 1960, with parts 1 and 2.

Tr. Alfred Acton as The Organs of Generation, the Breasts, the Periosteum. Philadelphia, Boericke, 1912. 389 p. Repr. Bryn Athyn, Pa., Academy of the New Church, 1928; Swedenborg Scientific Association, 1955.

Preparatory Works

INDIVIDUAL WORKS (CHRONOLOGICALLY, BY DATE OF MS.)

1745. On the Worship and Love of God. Tr. Robert Hindmarsh. London, Aurora Pr., 1801. 251 p. Repr. N.Y., 1812.

Tr. John Clowes as On the Worship and Love of God: Treating of the Birth of the Earth; of the Marriage of the First-begotten. Manchester and London, Society for the Printing of the Works of Swedenborg, 1816. xxv, 291 p. Repr. London, 1828, Boston, 1832, 1864, London, 1885.

Tr. Alfred H. Stroh and Frank Sewall, adding the first tr. of part 3. Boston, Rotch Trustees, Massachusetts New Church Union, 1914. 292 p.

1745, Ms. Concerning the Messiah About to Come. Tr. from Ms. Alfred Acton. Bryn Athyn, Pa., Academy of the New Church, 1948. 112 p.

1746–48, Ms. (pub. 1842–54, 6 v.) The Word of the Old Testament Explained. Tr. Alfred Acton. Bryn Athyn, Swedenborg Scientific Association, 1928–48. 8 v.

1746–65, Ms. The Memorabilia, or Spiritual Diary. Tr. John H. Smithson and George Bush. London and Boston, 1846–72. 3 v. Repr., adding v. 4, tr. George Bush and J. F. Buss, and v. 5, tr. J. F. Buss, London, Swedenborg Society, 1883–1902, 5 v.

Tr. W. H. and A. W. Acton as The Spiritual Diary. London, Swedenborg Society, 1962. v. 1— (in progress).

Theological Works

The major religious writings of Swedenborg which formulate the doctrines of the New Church have been systematically translated almost from the time of his death. Editions, not numbered however, may be dated back to 1774, when A Society of Gentlemen undertook to publish in London and

Manchester the translations made by the Rev. John Clowes. (Most of the translators have been clergymen.) As we cannot give here the full list of revisions and retranslations and reprints, we note only the significant British-American editions of about 1850; the individualist translation by George Harrison in the 1850s; the (American) Rotch edition from 1875, reprinted in numbered volumes in 1907; the current New York Swedenborg Foundation edition, first known as the Library edition, now as the Standard edition; and the London Swedenborg Society editions and recent retranslations. We give first the collective editions so designated; then the first translations of the individual works and, omitting the many revisions and reprints in the earlier nineteenth century, for which see the Hyde bibliography, the more recent translations in the three series: Rotch, London, New York.

COLLECTIVE EDITIONS

———— A New Translation of Some Parts of Swedenborg's Theological Works. Tr. George Harrison. London, 1857–60. 12 v.

———— The Theological Works, Rotch ed. (A new translation, supported by the Lydia Rotch fund, was begun in Philadelphia, with Lippincott as publisher, in 1875; it was then undertaken by the New Church Board of Publication in New York from 1892, and then by the Massachusetts New-Church Union in Boston. Completed in 1907, the Rotch ed. was reprinted in 32 numbered volumes by Houghton Mifflin, Boston and New York, 1907. The contents of the volumes in this edition follow.)

V. 1–20. The Heavenly Arcana (*Arcana Coelestia*).

V. 21. Heaven and Hell (*De coelo et inferno*).

V. 22. Miscellaneous Works: The Final Judgment. The White Horse. The Earths in the Universe. The Summary Exposition of the Doctrine of the New Church.

V. 23. The Four Doctrines. The New Jerusalem and its Heavenly Doctrines.

V. 24. Divine Love and Wisdom. Intercourse between the Soul and the Body.

V. 25. Divine Providence.

V. 26–28. The Apocalypse Revealed.

V. 29. Marriage Love.

V. 30–32. The True Christian Religion.

added v. 33–38. The Apocalypse Explained.

———————— Everyman's Library eds. as follows:

Divine Love and Wisdom. Tr. rev. F. Bayley. EL, 1912. xxiii, 216 p.

Divine Providence. Tr. rev. the same. EL, 1912. 319 p.

Heaven and its Wonders, and Hell. Tr. rev. the same. EL, 1909. xviii, 340 p.

The True Christian Religion. Tr. rev. the same. EL, 1933. xxxii, 928 p.

INDIVIDUAL WORKS (CHRONOLOGICALLY, BY DATE OF COMPOSITION)

1749–56. *Arcana Coelestia* or Heavenly Mysteries Contained in the Sacred Scriptures. Tr. John Clowes. London and Manchester, A Society of Gentlemen, 1774–1788. 12 v. For reprs., see Hyde.

Tr. rev. John Faulkner Potts. N.Y., Swedenborg Printing and Publishing Society, 1853–57. 12 v. Repr. Swedenborg Foundation, Standard ed., to 1965.

Tr. rev. John Worcester. Rotch ed., N.Y., and Boston, New-Church, 1892–1902. 14 v. Repr., 1907, v. 1–20.

Tr. A. H. Searle, rev. various hands. London, Swedenborg Society, 1915–49. 12 v.

1756. Index to the *Arcana Coelestia*. Tr. J. A. Tulk. London, 1810 et seq., 459 p. Repr. Rotch ed., 1907, v. 20.

Tr. James Hyde. London, Swedenborg Society, 1909.

1758. Of the Earths in our Solar System (*De telluribus*). Tr. John Clowes. London, 1787, et seq. 212 p. Repr. N.Y., American Swedenborg Printing and Publishing Society, in Miscellaneous Theological Works, 1857 et seq., repr. rev. John C. Ager, ibid., 1908 et seq.; repr. rev. J. Bayley, London, Swedenborg Society, 1875 et seq.; repr. rev. John Worcester, Rotch ed., N.Y., 1892, repr. 1907, v. 22.

1758. A Treatise Concerning Heaven and Hell (*De coelo et inferno*). Tr. William Cookworthy and Thomas Hartley. London, 1778. liii, 603 p. Many reprs.

Tr. John Clowes as A Treatise Concerning Heaven and its Wonders, and Hell. London, Society for Printing Swedenborg, etc., 1817. li, 525 p.

Many reprs., esp. rev. by Speranza (Lady Wilde) as The Future Life, Belfast, etc., 1853, viii, 603 p., many reprs.

Tr. B. F. Barrett. Philadelphia, Lippincott, 1867 et seq. 453 p. Repr. rev. John Worcester, Rotch ed., 1892, repr. 1907, v. 21.

Tr. J. R. Rendell. London, Swedenborg Society, 1899. ix, 396 p. Reprs., esp. Penguin Books, 1938.

Tr. J. C. Ager. N.Y., for Swedenborg Foundation, 1900, 449 p. Repr. Library ed., 1908; Standard ed., 1915 to 1964; N.Y., Popular Library, 1960, 335 p. paper; N.Y., Citadel Pr., 1965, 496 p. paper.

Tr. rev. F. Bayley. EL, 1911, et seq. (see above)

Tr. Doris H. Harley. London, Swedenborg Society, 1958. 398 p.

1758. A Treatise Concerning the Last Judgment (*De ultimo judicio*). Tr. Robert Hindmarsh. London, 1788. xvi, 154 p. Repr. 1810 et seq. Repr. rev. J. J. G. Wilkinson, London, 1839 et seq. and in Miscellaneous Theological Works, v. 1, 1857. Repr. rev. John Worcester, in Rotch ed., 1899, repr. 1907, v. 22.

Tr. John Whitehead, in Posthumous Theological Works. N.Y., for Swedenborg Foundation, 1914, v. 1. Reprs. to 1962, see below.

Tr. P. H. Johnson. London, Swedenborg Society, 1951. xviii, 110 p.

Tr. Doris H. Harley as The Last Judgment and Babylon Destroyed. London, Swedenborg Soc., 1961. 144 p.

1758. The Heavenly Doctrine of the New Jerusalem. Tr. Peter Provo and Robert Hindmarsh. London, 1780 et seq. viii, 347 p. Many revisions: London, 1811, 1873, 1892, 1896, rev. E. C. Mongredien, 1938; also N.Y., in Miscellaneous Theological Works, 1857 et seq.

Tr. T. B. Hayward. Boston and Chicago, 1867. iv, 104 p. Repr. Rotch ed., 1896, repr. 1907, v. 23.

1758. Concerning the White Horse, Mentioned in the Revelation, ch. xix. Tr. Robert Hindmarsh. London, 1788. 98 p. Repr. esp. in Four Leading Doctrines, 1826; in Miscellaneous Theological Writings, N.Y., 1857 et seq.; in Rotch ed., 1899, repr. 1907, v. 22.

1759. (Ms., 9 v., ed. London, 1785-89, 4 v.) The Apocalypse Explained. Tr. William Hill, rev. John Clowes. London, 1811-14. 5 v. Reprs. and revisions.

Ed. and tr. J. C. Ager. N.Y., for the Swedenborg Foundation, 1889–97. 12 v. (parallel texts). The tr. repr., Rotch ed., 1907, added v. 33–38; repr. N.Y., Standard ed., 1928, et seq., 6 v.

Tr. Isaiah Tansley. London, Swedenborg Society, 1896–1901. 6 v.

Tr. R. L. Tafel, rev. John Whithead. N.Y., for Swedenborg Foundation, 1915. 6 v.

1761 Ms. (ed. London, 1784, 103 p.). A Summary Exposition of the Internal Sense of the Prophets and the Psalms. Tr. C. W. Leadbeater. London, etc., 1799. 182, cvi p.

Tr. Robert Hindmarsh. London, 1800. 245 p. Many reprs.

Tr. R. L. Tafel. London, Swedenborg Society, 1887. Repr. 1896, 163 p.

Tr. E. J. E. Schreck. N.Y., for Swedenborg Foundation, 1900. 312 p.

1763. Angelic Wisdom Concerning Divine Love and Divine Wisdom. Tr. N. Tucker as The Wisdom of Angels Concerning etc. London, 1788, et seq. xxii, 461 p.

Tr. John C. Ager. N.Y., for Swedenborg Foundation, 1885. viii, 246 p. Many reprs. to Standard ed., 1946, 1960; Citadel Pr., 1965, paper.

Tr. rev. John Worcester. N.Y., Rotch ed., 1892. 269 p. Repr. 1907, v. 24.

Tr. Isaiah Tansley. London, Swedenborg Society, 1901. 190 p.

Tr. rev. F. Bayley. EL, 1912 et seq. xxiii, 216 p.

Tr. H. Goyder Smith. London, Swedenborg Society, 1937. 321 p.

1763. The Wisdom of Angels Concerning the Divine Providence. Tr. N. Tucker. London, 1790. xl, 600 p. Many reprs. and revisions, as Angelic Wisdom Concerning etc., esp. rev. T. B. Hayward, Boston 1840 etc. Rev. Isaiah Tansley. London and N.Y., Warne, 1906. Rev. F. Bayley, EL, 1912, 319 p. Rev. William F. Wunsch, N.Y., for Swedenborg Foundation, 1961 et seq. 376 p. Repr. N.Y., Citadel Pr., 1964, 419 p. paper.

Tr. Norman Foster. Rotch ed., Philadelphia, Lippincott, 1877. 328 p. Repr. N.Y., 1892; repr. 1907, v. 25.

Tr. John C. Ager. N.Y., for Swedenborg Foundation, 1889. xv, 386 p. Repr. Library ed., 1908; Standard ed., 1941 et seq.

Tr. William C. Dick and E. J. Pulsford. London, Swedenborg Society, 1949. 359 p.

1763. Doctrine of the New Jerusalem Concerning the Lord. Tr. Peter Provo. London, etc., 1799. 182, cvi p.

Tr. William Hill. London, 1815. Many reprs., combined in The Four Doctrines, Boston, 1826 et seq., and in Four Leading Doctrines, London, 1826 et seq., see below.

Tr. John F. Potts. N.Y., for Swedenborg Foundation, 1904. et seq. xvii, 203 p.

———— Doctrine of the New Jerusalem Concerning Holy Scripture. Tr. Peter Provo. London, 1786. Repr. rev. J. A. Tulk and Samuel Noble, in Four Leading Doctrines, London, 1826, et seq.

Tr. Samuel M. Warren. London, 1862. Rev. repr. in The Four Doctrines, 1880, see below.

———— Doctrine of the New Jerusalem Concerning Faith. Tr. William Cowherd. Manchester, 1792, et seq. xxviii, 80 p. Combined in Four Leading Doctrines, from 1826.

———— The Doctrine of Life for the New Jerusalem. Tr. William Cookworthy. Plymouth, 1772. vi, 52 p.

Tr. John Clowes. London, 1786. xx, 147 p. Revisions.

Tr. Samuel M. Warren. London, Swedenborg Society, 1864. 46, 10 p. Repr. in The Four Doctrines, 1880 et seq.

The *Four Doctrines* were combined in one volume from 1826. The Warren trs. were rev. John Worcester for the Rotch ed., Philadelphia, Lippincott, 1880, iv, 103 p.; repr. 1907, v. 23.

Tr. rev. A. H. Searle as The Four Leading Doctrines. London, Swedenborg Society, 1897. 4 parts. Repr. 1920.

Tr. John F. Potts. N.Y, for Swedenborg Foundation, 1904. 4 parts. (Library ed.), Repr. in Standard ed., 1915 to 1961, 491 p.

Tr. William C. Dick. London, Swedenborg Society, 1954. 424 p.

1766. The Apocalypse Revealed. Tr. N. Tucker. Manchester and London, 1791. 2 v. Many reprs.

Tr. T. B. Hayward, rev. John Worcester. Rotch ed., Philadelphia, Lippincott, 1875. 2 v. Reprs. to 1907, v. 26–28.

Rev. W. Bruce. London, Swedenborg Society, 1876. 913 p.

Tr. John Whitehead. N.Y., Swedenborg Foundation, 1909 et seq. 2 v. Reprs. to 1962.

1768. The Delights of Wisdom Pertaining to Conjugial Love. Tr. John Clowes. London, 1794. xliv, 523 p. Reprs.

Tr. A. H. Searle. London, Swedenborg Society, 1891. xvii, 544 p. Reprs. to 1934.

Tr. Samuel M. Warren as The Delights of Wisdom Pertaining to Marriage Love. Rotch ed., Boston, New-Church Union, 1903. 598 p. Repr. rev. Louis H. Tafel, N.Y., for Swedenborg Foundation, Library ed., 1910, xxiii, 612 p.; repr. Standard ed. of 1915 to 1954. Rev. W. H. Alden, Bryn Athyn, Academy of the New Church, 1915, 596 p.

Tr. William F. Wunsch as Marital Love, Its Wise Delights. N.Y., Swedenborg Foundation, 1938. 760 p. Rev. W. McGeorge Jr. and H. L. Cornell. Los Angeles, Cornell Pub. Co., 1938. 442 p.

Tr. Alfred Acton. London, Swedenborg Society, 1953. xxxix, 484 p.

1769. A Theosophic Lucubration of the Nature of Influx (De commercio animae et corporis). Tr. Thomas Hartley. London, 1770 et seq. xxiv, 48 p. Rev. John Worcester, as Intercourse Between Soul and Body, Rotch ed., 1892, p. 5–42, repr. 1907, v. 24.

Tr. M. Sibly as On the Intercourse between the Soul and the Body. London, 1812. Rev. J. Bayley and H. Butter, London, 1870, repr. in Miscellaneous Theological Works, N.Y., 1871 et seq., see below.

Tr. T. M. Gorman as Christian Psychology: The Soul and the Body. London, Longmans, 1875. 113 p.

1769. A Brief Exposition of the Doctrine of the New Church. Tr. J. Marchant. London, 1769. 159 p.

Tr. Robert Hindmarsh. London, 1789. 183 p. Reprs. to Miscellaneous Theological Works, 1871; to Rotch ed., to 1907, v. 22.

1771. The True Christian Religion. Tr. John Clowes. London, 1781 et seq. 472 p. Repr. London, Newbery, 1847, 986 p.; repr. N.Y., Swedenborg Foundation, 1855, 982 p.

Tr. R. Norman Foster. Philadelphia, Lippincott, 1869, 2 v. Repr. Rotch ed., 1878 et seq., to 1907, v. 30–32.

Tr. J. C. Ager. N.Y., for Swedenborg Foundation, 1906. 2 v. (Library ed.) Reprs. to 1964.

Tr. Isaiah Tansley. London, Swedenborg Society, 1908. xx, 858 p.

Tr. rev. F. Bayley. EL, 1933. xxxii, 928 p.

Tr. W. C. Dick. London, Swedenborg Society, 1950. xxiii, 972 p.

Other Collections

———————— Letters and Memorials (1709–1772). Tr. Alfred Acton. Bryn Athyn, Pa., Swedenborg Scientific Association, 1948–55. 2 v.

———————— Miscellaneous Theological Works. Trs. various. N.Y., for Swedenborg Foundation, 1857 et seq., now 634 p. in Standard ed. (The New Jerusalem and its Heavenly Doctrine; Brief Exposition; Intercourse of the Soul and Body; The White Horse; The Earths in the Universe; The Last Judgment).

The Rotch ed. contains four of these works in v. 22, and one each in v. 23 and v. 24 with other works. See above for this ed.

———————— Posthumous Theological Works. Trs. various, ed. John Whitehead. N.Y., for Swedenborg Foundation, 1914. 2 v. Standard ed., reprs. to 1962.

Contains sixteen shorter items, not listed above. V. 1: Autobiographical Letters; Coronis; Consummation of the Age; Invitation to the New Church; Additions to the True Christian Religion; Canons; Doctrine of Charity; Sketch of Ecclesiastical History of the New Church; Word of the Lord from Experience; The Last Judgment (posthumous); Theological Extracts from Swedenborg's Correspondence; Gad and Asher.

V. 2. Prophets and Psalms; Scripture Confirmations; Precepts of the Decalogue; Marriage (posthumous); Indexes on Marriage; Brief Bibliography of Swedenborg's Works [listing only].

TALAEUS (Omer Talon, c. 1510–1562). See Ramus, above.

TEXTOR, JOHANN WOLFGANG (1638–1701). Synopsis of the Law of Nations. Ed., Ludwig van Bar, tr. John Pawley Bate. Classics of International Law. Washington, D.C., Carnegie Institution, 1916. 2 v. (parallel texts)

THUANUS, JACOBUS (Jacques-Auguste de Thou, 1553–1617). History of his Own Time. Part tr. Benjamin Wilson (books 1–6). London, 1729–30. 2 v.

For trs. of briefer extracts, see British Museum Catalogue. The complete work (138 books) was tr. into French as *Histoire universelle de Jacques-*

Auguste de Thou (London, 1734, 16 v.), repr. The Hague (1740, 11 v.) and Basel (1742, 11 v.)

TINCTORIS, JEAN (1434–1520). Dictionary of Musical Terms. Ed. and tr. Carl Parrish. N.Y., Free Press of Glencoe, 1963. xi, 108 p. (parallel texts)

TOLAND, JOHN (1670–1722). Pantheisticon, or the Form of Celebrating the Socratic-Society. Tr. anon. London, 1751.

TORTELLI, GIOVANNI (c. 1400–1466). On Medicine and Physicians. Ed. and tr. Dorothy M. Schullian (with Gian Giacomo Bartolotti, On the Antiquity of Medicine). Milan, Stucchi, 1954. xliv, 226 p. (parallel texts).

TURRETINUS, FRANCISCUS (François Turretini, 1623–1687). The Tyranny of the Church of Rome . . . With a Preliminary Discourse Showing that the Principles and Spirit of Popery are the same now as at the Reformation. Tr. Thomas Rankin (from *De necessaria secessione nostra ab ecclesia Romana*). London, 1820.

VERGIL, POLYDORE (?1470–1555). An Abridgement of . . . the deuisers and fyrst fynders out . . .(*De rerum inventoribus*). Tr. Thomas Langley. London, 1546. vii, 156 leaves. Reprs. to 1663 as The Original of All Arts, Sciences, Mysteries; repr. from the 1603 ed., N.Y., Agathynian Club, 1868, xvi, 242, xvii p.

The tr. is said to give about one-third of the original.

———— The English History (*Anglica historia*). Part tr. anon. (16th c.), ed. Sir Henry Ellis as The First Eight Books [to 1066]. Camden Soc., v. 36, 1846. xv, 324 p.

Part tr. anon. (16th c.), ed. Sir Henry Ellis as Three Books of English History [1421–1485]. Camden Soc., v. 29, 1844. xxix, 244 p.

Part ed. and tr. Denys Hay as The *Anglica Historia*, 1485–1537. 3 Camden Soc., v. 74, 1950. xiii, 373 p. (parallel texts).

An ed. with tr. of the 1513 Ms. draft, plus the changes and additions of the Latin eds. of 1537, 1546, and 1555.

VERMIGLI, PETER MARTYR (1500–1562). The Common Places of . . . Peter Martyr. Tr. Anthony Martin. London, 1583. 640 p.

————— Most Fruitfull and Learned Commentaries [on the Book of Judges]. Tr. anon. London, Day, 1564. 288 leaves.

For 16th c. trs. of Vermigli's short tracts and letters, see British Museum Catalogue.

VERNULAEUS, NICOLAUS (Nicolas de Vernulz, 1583–1649). Henry VIII: A Neo-Latin Drama. Ed. and tr. Louis Anthony Schuster, S.M. Austin, Univ. of Texas Pr., 1964. xii, 331 p. (parallel texts)

VESALIUS, ANDREAS (1514–1564). The Bloodletting Letter of 1539. Tr. J. B. de C. M. Saunder and C. D. O'Malley. London, Heinemann, 1948. 94 p.

————— The Epitome (*de humani corporis fabrica*). Facs. ed. and tr. L. R. Lind, with anatomical notes by C. W. Asling, etc. Yale Medical Library. N.Y., Macmillan, 1949. xxxvi, 103 p.

This ed. does not include the legends or captions accompanying the illustrations. These legends were tr. from the original Vesalius in Nicholas Udall's apparent English version of the *Epitome* (1553, repr. 1559), which includes the plates and their captions, but is otherwise a mostly English text by Thomas Vicary (1548). The Udall work was facs. repr. with intro. by C. D. O'Malley (London, Dawson's, 1959: 39, 117 p., 40 pl.)†

————— Vesalius on the Human Brain. Tr. Charles Singer. London, Oxford Univ. Pr., 1952. xxvi, 151 p.

A tr. of book vii of the *Fabrica,* but using now the 1543 ed., now the variant 1555 ed.

VIDA, MARCO GIROLAMO, Bishop of Alba (d. 1566). The Art of Poetry. Tr. Christopher Pitt, in The Poetical Treatises of Horace, Vida, and Boileau. London, Betterworth, 1725. 118 p. Repr. Dublin, 1726; London, 1742; in Chalmer's English Poets, v. 19, 1810; in Albert S. Cook, ed., The Art of Poetry, Boston, Ginn, 1892.

Tr. J. Hampson as The Poetics of M. H. Vida. Sunderland, 1793. 397 p. (parallel texts)

†Thanks are expressed to Professor O'Malley for information on this entry.

————— The Christiad. Ed. and tr. J. Granwell. Cambridge, 1768.

Tr. E. Granan. London, 1771.

————— *Ludus Scacchiae.* Tr. verse G. B. as Chess Play. London, 1597. 30 p.

Tr. William Erskine as The Game of Chess (with the three pastoral eclogues). London, 1736. 219 p.

Ed. and tr. Samuel Pullein. Dublin, 1750. vi, 95 p. (parallel texts)

Tr. Thomas Morell. Eton, 1769. 71 p.

Tr. Arthur Murphy, in Works, v. 7, 1786, 68–147 (parallel texts). Repr. Amsterdam, 1876.

Ed. and tr. Richard Stanton Lambert. Wembley Hill, Stanton Pr., 1921. 61 p.

Also tr. G. Jeffreys, 1736; anon., Oxford, 1778; Philip Williams, Winchester, 1844.

————— Poems on Divine Subjects, Original and Translated from the Latin of M. Hieron. Vida [by] Thomas Morell. London, 1732. 288 p.

————— The Silkworm (*Bombyx*). Tr. John Rooke, in Select Trs. London, 1726. 80 p. (separate pagination)

Ed. and tr. verse Samuel Pullein. Dublin, 1750. ii, 141 p. (parallel texts)

Also tr. anon., 1723.

VINDICIAE CONTRA TYRANNOS: A Defence of Liberty against Tyrants (1579). Tr. anon. 1622.

Tr. William Walker. London, 1648. 148 p. Repr. 1660; 1689; 1689 ed. repr. with intro. Harold J. Laski, London, Bell, and N.Y., Harcourt, 1924, 229 p.

VITORIA, FRANCISCO DE (?1486–1546). *De Indis et de jure belli relectiones.* Ed. Ernest Nys and tr. John Pawley Bate. Classics of International Law. Washington, D.C., Carnegie Institution, 1917. 475 p.

————— *Relectiones undecim de potestate ecclesiae.* Tr. of parts in James B. Scott, The Spanish Origins of International Law, v. 1, Francisco de Vitoria and his Law of Nations. Oxford, Clarendon Pr., 1933, and N.Y., Oxford Univ. Pr., 1934. 288, clviii p.

VITRINGA, CAMPEGIUS (1659–1722). The Synagogue and the Church. Tr. condensed J. L. Bernard. London, 1842.

VIVES, JUAN LUIS (1492–1540). Commentary on St Augustine, The City of God. Tr. in John Healey, The Citie of God, with the Learned Comments of Io. Lod. Vives. London, 1610. Repr. 1620.

———— A Fable About Man. Tr. Nancy Lenkeith, in The Renaissance Philosophy of Man (see Collections, above), p. 387–93.

———— The Instruction of a Christian Woman. Tr. Richard Hyrde. London, 1540. Repr. 1540, 1541, 1557; extracts repr. in Foster Watson. Vives and the Renascence Education of Women, London, Arnold, 1912, 259 p.

———— An Introduction to Wysedome. Tr. Richard Moryson. London, 1540?. Repr. 1540, 1544, 1875.

———— The Office and Duetie of an Husband. Tr. Thomas Paynell. London, 1553?

———— Tudor Schoolboy Life: The Dialogues (*Linguae latinae exercitatio*). Tr. Foster Waton. London, Dent, 1908. li, 247 p.

———— Vives on Education (*De tradendis disciplinis*). Tr. Foster Watson. Cambridge Univ. Pr., 1913. cvlii, 328 p.

WARE, SIR JAMES (1594–1666). The Writers of Ireland. Tr. Walter Harris. Dublin, 1764. 2 v.

WATSON, THOMAS (1513–1584). Absalom. Tr. John Hazel Smith. Urbana, Univ. of Illinois Pr., 1964. 293 p. (parallel texts)

WATSON, THOMAS (1557–1592). The Lamentations of Amyntas for the Death of Phyllis (*Amynta*). Tr. in hexameters by Abraham Fraunce. London, 1587. Repr. in The Countess of Pembroke's Yvychurch, London, 1591; repr. separately, London, 1596. Repr. ed. W. F. Staton, Jr., and F. M. Dickey. Chicago, Univ. of Chicago Pr., 1967 (parallel texts)

———— An Ould Fashioned Love (*Amyntae gaudia*). Tr. J. T. London, 1594.

WHITAKER, WILLIAM, Archbishop of Canterbury (1548–1595). An Answere to the Ten Reasons of Edmud Campion. Tr. Richard Stocke (with the Ten Reasons: see Campion, above). London, 1606. 326 p.

———— A Disputation on Holy Scripture against the Papists, especially Bellarmine and Stapelton. Tr. William Fitzgerald. Parker Soc., v. 45, 1849. 718 p.

WILLES (or WILLS), RICHARD (fl. 1558–1578). *De Re Poetica.* Ed. and tr. A. D. S. Fowler. Oxford, Blackwell, 1958. ix, 146 p. (parallel texts)

WILLIS, THOMAS (1621–1675). The London Practice of Physick: or the Whole Practical Part of Physick Contained in the Works of Dr. Willis. Tr. Eugenius Philiatros. London, 1685. 672 p.

———— *Pharmaceutice rationalis,* or the Operations of Medicines in Human Bodies. Tr. anon. London, 1679. 2 parts. Repr. 1684.

———— The Remaining Medical Works [eight treatises]. Tr. Samuel Pordage. London, 1681. 3 parts.

———— Two Discourses Concerning the Soul of Brutes (*De anima brutorum*). Tr. Samuel Pordage. London, 1683. 234 p.

WILLUGHBY, FRANCIS (1635–1672). The Ornithology. Tr. and enl. John Ray. London, 1678.

WOLFF, CHRISTIAN FRIEDRICH VON (1679–1754). The Law of Nations Treated According to a Scientific Method. Ed., with tr. Joseph H. Drake. Classics of International Law. Oxford, Clarendon Pr., 1934. 2 v.

———— Logic: or Rational Thoughts on the Powers of the Human Understanding. Tr. anon. from the German original. London, 1770.

———— Preliminary Discourse on Philosophy in General. Tr. Richard J. Blackwell. Indianapolis, Ind., Bobbs-Merrill, 1963. xviii, 122 p.

———— The Real Happiness of a People . . . from the Undoubted Experience of the Chinese (*Oratio de Sinarum philosophia practica*). Tr. anon. London, 1750. vii, 96 p.

ZWINGLI, HULDRICH (1484–1531) The Latin Works and the Correspondence, together with Selections from the German Works. Ed. Samuel A. Jackson, tr. Henry Preble, Walter Lichtenstein, and Lawrence A. McLouth, N.Y., Putnam (v. 1, 1510–1522), and Philadelphia, Heidelberg Pr., (v. 2, 3), 1912–29.

———— Selected works. The German Works tr. Lawrence A. McLouth, the Latin by Henry Preble and George W. Gilmore. Ed. Samuel M. Jackson. Philadelphia, Univ. of Pennsylvania, 1901. 258 p.

———— (Four Essays and a Sermon). Tr. G. W. Bromiley from Latin or German, in Library of Christian Classics, v. 24, 1953, p. 58–279.

Sermon on the Clarity and Certainty of the Word of God. Of the Education of Youth. Of Baptism. Of the Lord's Supper. An Exposition of the Faith.

For tracts tr. in the 16th c., see British Museum Catalogue.

ADDENDA

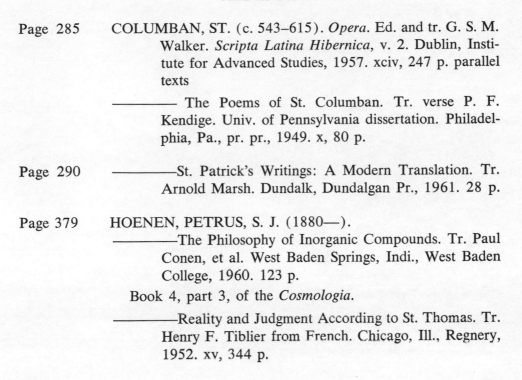

Page 285 COLUMBAN, ST. (c. 543–615). *Opera*. Ed. and tr. G. S. M. Walker. *Scripta Latina Hibernica*, v. 2. Dublin, Institute for Advanced Studies, 1957. xciv, 247 p. parallel texts

———— The Poems of St. Columban. Tr. verse P. F. Kendige. Univ. of Pennsylvania dissertation. Philadelphia, Pa., pr. pr., 1949. x, 80 p.

Page 290 ————St. Patrick's Writings: A Modern Translation. Tr. Arnold Marsh. Dundalk, Dundalgan Pr., 1961. 28 p.

Page 379 HOENEN, PETRUS, S. J. (1880—).
————The Philosophy of Inorganic Compounds. Tr. Paul Conen, et al. West Baden Springs, Indi., West Baden College, 1960. 123 p.

Book 4, part 3, of the *Cosmologia*.

————Reality and Judgment According to St. Thomas. Tr. Henry F. Tiblier from French. Chicago, Ill., Regnery, 1952. xv, 344 p.

INDEX